EAST ANGLIAN ARCHAEOLOGY

Frontispiece Part of the Love's Farm site (the area of Settlement 7) from the air, looking north

Dedicated to Terry Mortlock

Conquering the Claylands: Excavations at Love's Farm, St Neots, Cambridgeshire

by Mark Hinman and
John Zant

with contributions from
Ian Baxter, Barry Bishop, Paul Blinkhorn,
Steve Boreham, Brendan Chester-Kadwell,
Steve Critchley, Nina Crummy, Natasha Dodwell,
Taleyna Fletcher, Rachel Fosberry, Val Fryer,
F.M.L. Green, Sarah Henley, Alice Lyons,
Gwladys Monteil, Quita Mould, Liz Muldowney,
Sarah Percival, Tom Phillips, Alexandra
Pickstone, Ruth Shaffrey, David Starley, Emma
Tetlow, Stephen Wadeson and Heather Wallis

illustrations by
Gillian Greer, Daniel Bashford and Jon Cane

reconstructions by
Peter Lorimer

edited by Elizabeth Popescu

East Anglian Archaeology
Report No. 165, 2018

Oxford Archaeology East

EAST ANGLIAN ARCHAEOLOGY
REPORT NO. 165

Published by
Oxford Archaeology East
15 Trafalgar Way
Bar Hill
Cambridge
CB23 8SQ

in conjunction with
ALGAO East
http://www.algao.org.uk/england

Editor: Andy Thomas
EAA Managing Editor: Jenny Glazebrook

Editorial Board:
James Albone, Historic Environment, Norfolk County Council
Abby Antrobus, Historic Environment, Suffolk County Council
Brian Ayers, University of East Anglia
Stewart Bryant, Archaeological Consultant
Will Fletcher, Historic England
Kasia Gdaniec, Historic Environment, Cambridgeshire County Council
Maria Medlycott, Historic Environment, Essex County Council
Zoe Outram, Historic England Science Adviser
Debbie Priddy, Historic England
Isobel Thompson, Historic Environment, Hertfordshire County Council
Adrian Tindall, Archaeological Consultant

Set in Times Roman by Sue Anderson using ™Corel Ventura Publisher
Printed by Henry Ling Ltd, The Dorset Press

© OXFORD ARCHAEOLOGY EAST
ISBN 978 1 907588 11 2

East Anglian Archaeology was established in 1975 by the Scole Committee for Archaeology in East Anglia. The scope of the series expanded to include all six eastern counties and responsibility for publication rests with the editorial board in partnership with the Association of Local Government Archaeological Officers, East of England (ALGAO East).

For details of *East Anglian Archaeology*, see last page

Cover illustrations:
Front cover: (Top) Reconstruction of an Iron Age settlement (© Oxford Archaeology, by Peter Lorimer); part of Coin Hoard 1; (Bottom) Selected finds from the Love's Farm site, comprising (left to right): prehistoric greenstone axe, Trumpet-headed brooch (2nd century AD), late Roman imitation samian, wax spatula handle in the form of Minerva (2nd to early 3rd century AD), early Saxon saucer brooch (6th century AD)
Back cover: (Top) Reconstruction of an Iron Age cremation burial (© Oxford Archaeology, by Peter Lorimer); (Bottom) late Roman worked bone plaque

Contents

List of Plates	vi
List of Figures	vii
List of Tables	ix
Contributors	x
Acknowledgements	xi
Abbreviations	xii
Summary/Résumé/Zusammenfassung	xii

Chapter 1. Introduction, by John Zant and Mark Hinman, with Brendan Chester-Kadwell and Tom Phillips

I.	Project background	1
II.	Location, geology and topography	3
III.	Archaeological background	5
IV.	Project methodology	11
V.	Research objectives	13

Chapter 2. Neolithic and early Bronze Age (Periods 1 and 2), by John Zant and Mark Hinman

I.	Introduction	15
II.	Period 1: Neolithic (c.4000–2500 BC)	15
III.	Period 2: Bronze Age (c.2500–800 BC)	15
IV.	Discussion: origins	18

Chapter 3. Middle to late Iron Age (Period 3), by John Zant and Mark Hinman, with Taleyna Fletcher, Sarah Henley, Liz Muldowney, Tom Phillips and Alexandra Pickstone

I.	Introduction	21
II.	Periods 3.1–3.2: middle Iron Age (c.400–100 BC)	21
III.	Period 3.3: late Iron Age (c.100 BC to early 1st century AD)	33
IV.	Period 3.4: late pre-Roman Iron Age (first half of the 1st century AD)	52
V.	Period 3.5: transitional (mid to late 1st century AD)	63
VI.	Discussion: the Iron Age	77

Chapter 4. Romano-British (Period 4), by John Zant and Mark Hinman, with Taleyna Fletcher, Sarah Henley, Liz Muldowney, Tom Phillips and Alexandra Pickstone

I.	Introduction	87
II.	Period 4.1: early Romano-British (late 1st to early 2nd century AD)	87
III.	Period 4.2: middle Romano-British (2nd century AD)	95
IV.	Period 4.3: middle Romano-British (3rd century AD)	103
V.	Period 4.4: late Romano-British (4th century AD)	110
VI.	Period 4.5: late Romano-British (late 4th to early 5th century AD)	121
VII.	Discussion: Romano-British settlement	127

Chapter 5. Post-Roman (Periods 5–7), by John Zant and Mark Hinman

I.	Introduction	133
II.	Period 5: early Anglo-Saxon (late 5th to 6th century)	133
III.	Periods 6 and 7: medieval and post-medieval field systems (c.1066–1800)	134
IV.	Discussion: Anglo-Saxon	136

Chapter 6. The finds

I.	Worked flint, by Barry Bishop	138
II.	Coins and jetons, by Nina Crummy	140
III.	Metalwork, by Nina Crummy	146
IV.	Metalworking debris, by David Starley	177
V.	Glass and amber objects, by Stephen Wadeson	181
VI.	Stone, shale, ceramic and fired clay objects, by Sarah Percival, Ruth Shaffrey, Nina Crummy and Alice Lyons	182
VII.	Architectural stonework, by Ruth Shaffrey	188
VIII.	Ceramic building material and fired clay, by Alice Lyons with Heather Wallis	189
IX.	Bone and antler objects, by Nina Crummy	192
X.	Leather shoes, by Quita Mould	197

Chapter 7. The pottery

I.	Introduction, by Alice Lyons	200
II.	Earlier prehistoric pottery, by Sarah Percival	202
III.	Iron Age and Iron Age/Romano-British transitional pottery, by Sarah Percival and Alice Lyons	203
IV.	Romano-British pottery, by Alice Lyons	219
V.	Mortaria, by Alice Lyons	234
VI.	Samian, by Stephen Wadeson and Gwladys Monteil	235
VII.	Discussion of the late pre-Roman Iron Age and Romano-British pottery, by Alice Lyons and Sarah Percival	239
VIII.	Post-Roman pottery, by Paul Blinkhorn	243

Chapter 8. Zooarchaeological and botanical evidence

I.	Human skeletal remains, by Natasha Dodwell	248
II.	Radiocarbon dating	250
III.	Animal bone, by Ian Baxter	250
IV.	Plant remains, by Val Fryer	274
V.	Mollusca, by Val Fryer and Rachel Fosberry	281
VI.	Insects, by Emma Tetlow	282
VII.	Pollen, by F.M.L. Green and Steve Boreham	287

Chapter 9. Discussion and conclusions, by John Zant

I.	Revisiting the research objectives	292
II.	Origins	293
III.	The local and regional context	295
IV.	Iron Age and Romano-British settlement	298
V.	The agricultural economy	303
VI.	Craft and 'industry', by John Zant, with Nina Crummy	308

VII.	Trade, exchange and status	311	Appendix 1: Geological survey, by Steve Critchley	325
VIII.	Burial practices	315	Appendix 2: Catalogue of Roman coins, by Nina Crummy	328
IX.	Ritual and votive practices	316		
X.	The Anglo-Saxon period	321	Appendix 3: Romano-British pottery fabrics and forms, by Alice Lyons	341
XI.	Medieval and beyond	323		
XII.	Conclusions	324	Bibliography	347
			Index, by Sue Vaughan	368

List of Plates

Frontispiece Part of the Love's Farm site (the area of Settlement 7) from the air, looking north

Plate 1.1 Aerial photograph of St Neots, showing the site prior to the excavations 1

Plate 1.2 Working shot of excavations in progress 12

Plate 3.1 Aerial view of Enclosure 8 and Boundary 10, looking north-west (Period 3.2) 25

Plate 3.2 Section through ditch *2332*, part of the primary perimeter ditch of Enclosure 8, looking east (Period 3.2), showing later recut *2221* (Period 3.3) 25

Plate 3.3 Section through pit *2364*, one of the internal features within Enclosure 8, looking south-east (Period 3.2) 26

Plate 3.4 Roundhouse 9, Settlement 3, looking east (Period 3.2) 31

Plate 3.5 Roundhouse 11, Settlement 3, looking south (Period 3.3) 43

Plate 3.6 Four-post structure (Structure 3), Settlement 3, looking east (Period 3.3) 44

Plate 3.7 Waterhole 4, Settlement 3, looking south-west (Period 3.3) 45

Plate 3.8 Enclosure 1, Settlement 6: southern terminal (*10747*) of perimeter ditch, looking north (Period 3.3) 46

Plate 3.9 Detail of animal bones at the base of ditch *10747*, southern terminal of perimeter ditch for Enclosure 1, Settlement 6, looking west (Period 3.3) 46

Plate 3.10 Excavation of iron 'trident' (SF 3106) in ditch *10747*, southern terminal of perimeter ditch Enclosure 1, Settlement 6, looking north-west (Period 3.3) 47

Plate 3.11 Detail of iron 'trident' (SF 3106) in ditch *10747*, southern terminal of perimeter ditch for Enclosure 1, Settlement 6, looking east (Period 3.3) 47

Plate 3.12 Roundhouse 12, Settlement 4, viewed from the south-west (Period 3.3) 51

Plate 3.13 Roundhouse 8, Settlement 4, from the air, looking north-east (Period 3.3) 51

Plate 3.14 Stone-lined hearth pits associated with Settlement 4 (Period 3.3) 51

Plate 3.15 Enclosure 158, Settlement 2, looking south (Period 3.4) 58

Plate 3.16 Cemetery 2, Settlement 7, looking north-east, showing graves *5810*, *5813* and *5816* (Period 3.5) 70

Plate 3.17 Southern terminal of ditch *8804*, looking north-west, showing cattle skull in foreground. Enclosure 163, Settlement 6 (Period 3.5) 74

Plate 3.18 Routeway 9, Settlement 4, looking south-west (Period 3.5) 77

Plate 4.1 Coin hoard (Hoard 1) *in situ*, Settlement 6 (Period 4.2) 100

Plate 4.2 Metalwork from 'votive' deposit *6752*, Settlement 6 (Period 4.2) 100

Plate 4.3 Corn drier *6727*, Pit Group 5, Settlement 6, looking east (Period 4.2) 101

Plate 4.4 Pottery and other finds in pit *6531*, Pit Group 3, Settlement 6, looking west (Period 4.2) 102

Plate 4.5 Burnt deposit *11805*, oven *11803* in perimeter ditch of Enclosure 109, Settlement 6, looking east (Period 4.2) 102

Plate 4.6 A. Near-complete pottery vessel in ditch *11411*, Settlement 6 (Period 4.2). B. Complete pottery vessel in ditch *11411*, Settlement 6 (Period 4.2) 103

Plate 4.7 Remains of hobnnailed shoe in pit *10589*, Enclosure 104 (Period 4.3) 109

Plate 4.8 Cobbled surface *5507*, Enclosure 133, Settlement 7 (Phase 2), looking south-west (Period 4.4) 116

Plate 4.9 Southern terminal (*14077*) of eastern entrance Enclosure 113, Settlement 6, looking south-west and showing iron anvil (SF 3760) *in situ* (Period 4.4) 121

Plate 5.1 Enclosure 139, Settlement 7: perimeter ditch 5592 under excavation, showing deliberately placed red deer antlers (SFs 2601–3) 134

Plate 5.2 Detail of red deer antlers (SFs 2601–3) placed in the perimeter ditch (*5592*) of Enclosure 139, Settlement 7 134

List of Figures

Fig. 1.1	Site location showing the excavation areas and local HER sites	xiv
Fig. 1.2	Geology of the local area	2
Fig. 1.3	Key sites mentioned in the text, showing the local Roman road network	4
Fig. 1.4	The western claylands: sites and cropmarks in the vicinity of Love's Farm	6
Fig. 1.5	The Love's Farm site in its local context, showing adjacent sites at Wintringham Park and Tithe Farm	7
Fig. 1.6	All feature plan, showing evaluation trenches and constraints on excavation areas	10
Fig. 2.1	Period 1: Neolithic and Bronze Age features and deposits	16
Fig. 2.2	Periods 1 and 2: Neolithic activity in natural hollow, showing early Bronze Age well/waterhole 1	17
Fig. 2.3	Period 1: Neolithic activity in natural hollow	19
Fig. 3.1	Period 3.1: Field system 1 and associated routes	22
Fig. 3.2	Period 3.2: Field system 1 and contemporary activity	23
Fig. 3.3	Period 3.2: Enclosure 8	26
Fig. 3.4	Period 3.2: Settlement 1	27
Fig. 3.5	Period 3.2: Boundary 1, selected sections	28
Fig. 3.6	Period 3.2: Settlement 3	29
Fig. 3.7	Period 3.2: Settlements 4 and 6	30
Fig. 3.8	Period 3.2: Settlement 6, grave *8100*	32
Fig. 3.9	Period 3.3: Late Iron Age phase plan	34
Fig. 3.10	Period 3.3: Enclosure 8 and Boundary 10	36
Fig. 3.11	Period 3.3: Settlement 1	37
Fig. 3.12	Period 3.3: Settlement 2, showing the extent of Enclosure 10	38
Fig. 3.13	Period 3.3: Settlement 2, showing detail of Cemetery 1	40
Fig. 3.14	Period 3.3: Settlement 3. Scale 1:1000	41
Fig. 3.15	Period 3.3: Settlements 4, 5 and 6	42
Fig. 3.16	Period 3.3: Settlement 5, grave 11729 (sk. 11730)	48
Fig. 3.17	Period 3.3: Settlement 4	50
Fig. 3.18	Period 3.4: Late pre-Roman Iron Age phase plan	53
Fig. 3.19	Period 3.4: Enclosure 8 and Boundary 10	54
Fig. 3.20	Period 3.4: Settlement 1	56
Fig. 3.21	Period 3.4: Settlement 2	57
Fig. 3.22	Period 3.4: Settlement 3	59
Fig. 3.23	Period 3.4: Settlement 6	60
Fig. 3.24	Period 3.4: Settlement 4	61
Fig. 3.25	Period 3.5: Transitional phase plan	62
Fig. 3.26	Period 3.5: Enclosure 22	64
Fig. 3.27	Period 3.5: Enclosure 22, showing its relationship to adjacent boundary features and settlements	66
Fig. 3.28	Period 3.5: Settlement 2	68
Fig. 3.29	Period 3.5: Settlement 7	69
Fig. 3.30	Period 3.5: Settlement 7, Cemetery 2	71
Fig. 3.31	Period 3.5: Settlement 8	72
Fig. 3.32	Period 3.5: Settlement 6	73
Fig. 3.33	Period 3.5: Settlement 6, grave *7593*	75
Fig. 3.34	Period 3.5: Cemeteries 3 and 4	76
Fig. 3.35	Period 3.5: Settlement 4	77
Fig. 4.1	Period 4.1: Early Roman phase plan	88
Fig. 4.2	Period 4.1: Settlement 7, showing detail of possible hayrick (Structure 110)	89
Fig. 4.3	Period 4.1: Settlement 6	90
Fig. 4.4	Period 4.1: Settlement 6, horse burial *10611/11210*	92
Fig. 4.5	Period 4.2: 2nd century AD phase plan	94
Fig. 4.6	Period 4.2: Settlement 7	96
Fig. 4.7	Period 4.2: Settlement 6	98
Fig. 4.8	Period 4.2: Settlement 6, Structure 103	99
Fig. 4.9	Period 4.3: 3rd century AD phase plan	104
Fig. 4.10	Period 4.3: Settlement 7	105
Fig. 4.11	Period 4.3: Settlement 6	106
Fig. 4.12	Period 4.3: Settlement 6, Structure 105	108
Fig. 4.13	Period 4.3: Settlement 6, Structure 107	108
Fig. 4.14	Period 4.4: 4th century AD phase plan	111
Fig. 4.15	Period 4.4: Settlement 7 (Phase 1)	112
Fig. 4.16	Period 4.4: Settlement 7, Structure 114	114
Fig. 4.17	Period 4.4: Settlement 7 (Phase 2)	115
Fig. 4.18	Period 4.4: Settlement 6	117
Fig. 4.19	Period 4.4: Settlement 6, dog burial *8959/8960*	118
Fig. 4.20	Period 4.4: Settlement 6, Structure 108	120
Fig. 4.21	Period 4.5: Late 4th to early 5th century AD phase plan	122
Fig. 4.22	Period 4.5: Settlement 7	123
Fig. 4.23	Period 4.5: Settlement 7, well *5387*	124
Fig. 4.24	Period 4.5: Settlement 7: Structures 115 and 117	126
Fig. 5.1	Period 5.1. Early Saxon phase plan	132
Fig. 5.2	Ridge and furrow	135
Fig. 6.1	Greenstone axe	139
Fig. 6.2	Love's Farm, Haddon and Bob's Wood, Hinchingbrooke coins, by Coin Period set against the British mean	141
Fig. 6.3	Love's Farm, Haddon and Bob's Wood coins by Coin Period	142
Fig. 6.4	Love's Farm coins with and without the coin hoards	143
Fig. 6.5	Percentages of coins by Coin Period from Settlements 6 and 7	144
Fig. 6.6	Love's Farm small finds assemblage by function, shown as percentages	147
Fig. 6.7	Objects from 'votive' layer *6572* by type	148
Fig. 6.8	Small finds from Settlements 6 and 7 by broad functional groups	149
Fig. 6.9	Copper alloy brooches, Colchester type	152
Fig. 6.10	Copper alloy brooches, Hod Hill type	153
Fig. 6.11	Copper alloy brooches, Nauheim derivative type	153
Fig. 6.12	Copper alloy brooch, Colchester BB derivative type	153
Fig. 6.13	Copper alloy brooches, Polden Hill/Rearhook hybrid type	154

Fig. 6.14	Copper alloy brooches, Headstud, Trumpet and T-shaped type	155
Fig. 6.15	Copper alloy brooches, 'Plate' type	155
Fig. 6.16	Penannular copper alloy brooches	156
Fig. 6.17	Copper alloy hairpins	157
Fig. 6.18	Copper alloy armlets	158
Fig. 6.19	Copper alloy armlets	158
Fig. 6.20	Copper alloy finger rings	161
Fig. 6.21	Iron cleats	161
Fig. 6.22	Copper alloy nail cleaners	162
Fig. 6.23	Copper and lead alloy possible cups	163
Fig. 6.24	Silver and copper alloy spoons	163
Fig. 6.25	Copper alloy box fittings	164
Fig. 6.26	Lead weights and iron dividers	165
Fig. 6.27	Iron stylii, copper alloy spatula handle	166
Fig. 6.28	Copper alloy lunula	167
Fig. 6.29	Iron knives	167
Fig. 6.30	Copper alloy fittings and studs	168
Fig. 6.31	Iron fittings	169
Fig. 6.32	Iron and lead fittings	170
Fig. 6.33	Iron agricultural equipment	170
Fig. 6.34	Copper alloy *armilla* and military mount	172
Fig. 6.35	Copper alloy bell and rings	173
Fig. 6.36	Iron block anvil	174
Fig. 6.37	Iron punches	175
Fig. 6.38	Iron bar fragments	175
Fig. 6.39	Miscellaneous copper alloy objects	176
Fig. 6.40	Miscellaneous metalwork	176
Fig. 6.41	Iron object	177
Fig. 6.42	Early Anglo-Saxon metalwork	178
Fig. 6.43	Metalworking debris through time	180
Fig. 6.44	Quern and millstone	185
Fig. 6.45	Hones	186
Fig. 6.46	Fired clay loomweight	186
Fig. 6.47	Fired clay ?bobbin	187
Fig. 6.48	Stone and chalk spindlewhorls	188
Fig. 6.49	Kiln furniture	192
Fig. 6.50	Worked bone dress accessories	194
Fig. 6.51	Worked antler toilet instruments	195
Fig. 6.52	Worked bone plaque	196
Fig. 6.53	Worked bone and antler tools	197
Fig. 6.54	Boneworking debris	198
Fig. 6.55	Leather shoe fragments	198
Fig. 7.1	Model of the currency of later Iron Age potting tradition in southern Cambs	201
Fig. 7.2	Early prehistoric pottery	203
Fig. 7.3	Weight of Iron Age pottery sherds by fabric type and ceramic period	205
Fig. 7.4	Number of Iron Age vessels from the entire site, by type	208
Fig. 7.5	Iron Age pottery (Nos 1–7)	210
Fig. 7.6	Iron Age pottery (Nos 8–13)	211
Fig. 7.7	Iron Age pottery (Nos 14–15)	212
Fig. 7.8	Iron Age pottery (Nos 16–22)	213
Fig. 7.9	Iron Age pottery (Nos 23–29)	214
Fig. 7.10	Late pre-Roman Iron Age to Romano-British transitional pottery (Periods 3.4–3.5) (Nos 1–8)	218
Fig. 7.11	Early to Middle Romano-British pottery (Periods 4.1–4.2) (Nos 9–30)	222
Fig. 7.12	Middle Romano-British pottery (Period 4.3) (Nos 31–39)	229
Fig. 7.13	Late Romano-British pottery (Period 4.4) (Nos 40–60)	231
Fig. 7.14	Late Romano-British pottery (Period 4.5) (Nos 61–68)	232
Fig. 7.15	Romano-British pottery: samian	238
Fig. 7.16	Romano-British pottery: samian stamps	239
Fig. 7.17	Changes in pottery supply through time from the late pre-Roman Iron Age to the Romano-British period (by sub-period) using weight (%) as a ceramic measure	240
Fig. 7.18	Post-Roman pottery	246
Fig. 8.1	Frequency by NISP of the main domestic mammals by period	253
Fig. 8.2	Frequency of the main domestic mammals compared with other Iron Age sites in Cambridgeshire	253
Fig. 8.3	Frequency of the main domestic mammals compared with other Romano-British sites in Cambridgeshire	254
Fig. 8.4	Cattle skulls from Structure 106 (Settlement 6, Period 4.4)	255
Fig. 8.5	Distribution of cattle and sheep/goat mandibles by age stage	256
Fig. 8.6	Pathologies to horse skeleton *10610*, Period 4.1	258
Fig. 8.7	Horse burial *4317*, ditch *4318*, Settlement 6, Period 4.1	259
Fig. 8.8	Pathologies to horse skeleton *4882*, Period 4.2	260
Fig. 8.9	Isolated dog burial *4395/4394*, Period 3	261
Fig. 8.10	Dog and cattle skulls from Enclosure 113, Settlement 6, Period 4.3	262
Fig. 8.11	Dog burial *8960*, ditch *8959*, Settlement 6, Period 4.4	263
Fig. 8.12	Antler offcuts and craft waste from ditch *5075* (fill *5074*), Enclosure 131, Settlement 7, Period 4.4	264
Fig. 8.13	Location of samples taken from Enclosure 22, Period 3.5	266
Fig. 8.14	Enclosure 22 (*2466*), Period 3.5. Relative frequency of taxa compared with bones derived from owl pellets at Drayton II villa, Leics	266
Fig. 8.15	The faunal assemblage from well *5387*, Period 4.5	268
Fig. 8.16	Cattle skulls from fill *5890*, well *5387*, Period 4.5	269
Fig. 8.17	Well *5387*. Size and shape of cattle horncores compared with other Iron Age and Romano-British sites in Cambs	270
Fig. 8.18	Well *5387*. Length of the molar row in the cattle crania, compared with those from Springhead, Kent	271
Fig. 8.19	Well *5387*. Percentage of fused epiphyses for cattle and sheep	272
Fig. 9.1	Late Iron Age tribal boundaries in eastern England, showing location of St Neots	297
Fig. 9.2	Reconstruction of an Iron Age settlement similar to those at Love's Farm, showing four-post structure in foreground	302
Fig. 9.3	Reconstruction of a late Iron Age/early Romano-British rural settlement similar to those found at Love's Farm, showing a cremation in progress	317
Fig. A1.1	Site areas, showing related field numbers	326

List of Tables

Table 1.1	Summary of site phasing	13
Table 6.1	Composition of the flint assemblage	138
Table 6.2	Coins from Love's Farm, Bob's Wood and Haddon by number and percentage	142
Table 6.3	Coins from Settlements 6 and 7, their adjacent fields, and as combined southern and northern assemblages by number and percentage	144
Table 6.4	Summary composition of Hoard 1	145
Table 6.5	Summary composition of Hoard 2	146
Table 6.6	Metalwork by function, excluding hobnails and structural nails	147
Table 6.7	Distribution of dress accessories by location and period, excluding hobnails	150
Table 6.8	Percentages of hairpins from Love's Farm compared to other dress accessories, and percentages of bone and metal hairpins within the complete hairpin assemblage, from sites in the eastern region and East Midlands	151
Table 6.9	Iron nails from the northern and southern settlements by period	168
Table 6.10	Summary of metallurgical debris	178
Table 6.11	Smithing hearth bottom dimensions, all phases	179
Table 6.12	Metalworking debris from Iron Age and Roman deposits	180
Table 6.13	Smithing hearth bottoms by phase	180
Table 6.14	Querns and millstones, by site period	183
Table 6.15	Non-diagnostic structural stonework, all from Settlement 7 (Period 4.4)	189
Table 6.16	Ceramic building material quantities	189
Table 6.17	Ceramic building material by period (% weight)	189
Table 6.18	Ceramic building material (% weight) by feature type	190
Table 6.19	Ceramic building material fabric quantities	190
Table 6.20	Tile types	190
Table 6.21	Daub quantified by fabric type	191
Table 6.22	Daub from pit *4626*, Quarry 7, Settlement 7, Period 4.2	192
Table 6.23	Bone and antler objects by general location and functional category	193
Table 7.1	The ceramic assemblage by site period	200
Table 7.2	Quantity and weight of earlier Neolithic pottery by fabric	202
Table 7.3	Iron Age to transitional pottery (Period 3) quantified by site period	204
Table 7.4	Quantity and weight of Iron Age pottery from the entire site, by ceramic period	204
Table 7.5	Quantity and weight of Iron Age pottery from the entire site, by fabric group	204
Table 7.6	Quantity and weight of Iron Age pottery from the entire site, by fabric	207
Table 7.7	Number of Iron Age vessels from the entire site, by vessel form	207
Table 7.8	Percentages of Iron Age pottery recovered from ditches and pits by ceramic period	207
Table 7.9	Quantity and weight of Iron Age pottery from the entire site, by feature type	209
Table 7.10	Pottery from features assigned to the LPRIA (Period 3.4)	216
Table 7.11	Pottery recovered from transitional deposits (Period 3.5), in descending order of weight	217
Table 7.12	Romano-British pottery (Period 4) quantified by sub-period	220
Table 7.13	Pottery from features assigned to the Early Roman period (Period 4.1)	220
Table 7.14	Pottery from features assigned to the Romano-British period (Period 4.2)	227
Table 7.15	Pottery from features assigned to the Romano-British period (Period 4.3))	228
Table 7.16	Pottery from features assigned to the Romano-British period (Period 4.4)	230
Table 7.17	Pottery from features assigned to the Romano-British period (Period 4.5)	233
Table 7.18	The mortaria assemblage	234
Table 7.19	Samian quantified by fabric source	236
Table 7.20	List of comparative sites, their main ceramic characteristics and publication	240
Table 7.21	The amphora fabrics	241
Table 7.22	Romano-British vessel forms found in this assemblage and their Estimated Vessel Equivalent (EVE)	241
Table 7.23	Anglo-Saxon pottery by fabric type	244
Table 8.1	Inhumation burials (by period, cemetery and settlement)	249
Table 8.2	Period 3.5 cremations (by cemetery and settlement)	249
Table 8.3	Results of radiocarbon dating	250
Table 8.4	Number of hand-collected mammal, bird and amphibian bones (NISP)	251
Table 8.5	Number of mammal, bird, amphibian and fish bones (NISP) in sieved assemblage	252
Table 8.6	Frequencies of the three major domesticates by number of identified specimens (NISP) and by minimum number of individuals (MNI)	255
Table 8.7	Number of hand-collected mammal bones (NISP) from well *5387* (Settlement 7, Period 4.5)	267
Table 8.8	Number of mammal and amphibian bones in sieved assemblage (NISP) from well *5387* (Settlement 7, Period 4.5)	267
Table 8.9	Morphology, age and sex of the cattle crania from well *5387*	267
Table 8.10	Body parts of the main domestic mammals from well *5387*, by number of fragments (NISP) and minimum number of individuals (MNI)	272
Table 8.11	Plant macrofossils and other remains from Enclosure 22 (Period 3.5)	276
Table 8.12	Plant macrofossils and other remains from well *5387* (Settlement 7)	281
Table 8.13	Insects from Iron Age Quarry 5 (Settlement 2) and the Late Roman well (*5387*, Settlement 7)	285

Table 8.14	Pollen recorded at assessment stage	288		Table A2.4	Hoard 2, pit *7476*, Settlement 7, Period 4.4	334
Table 8.15	Pollen recorded at analysis (percentage data)	289		Table A2.5	Coins from Settlement 6 and adjacent fields	339
Table A2.1	Roman coins from the Iron Age settlements	328		Table A2.6	Unstratified Roman coins (context *99999*)	341
Table A2.2	Hoard 1, pit fill *260*, Settlement 6, Period 4.2	329		Table A3.1	Quantification of the samian assemblage	343
Table A2.3	Coins from Settlement 7 and adjacent fields	334				

Contributors

Daniel Bashford
Formerly Illustrator, Oxford Archaeology East

Ian Baxter
Freelance faunal remains specialist

Barry Bishop
Freelance lithics specialist

Paul Blinkhorn
Freelance pottery specialist

Steve Boreham
Pollen specialist

Jon Cane
Formerly Illustrator, Oxford Archaeology East

Brendan Chester-Kadwell
Freelance landscape historian

Steve Critchley
Freelance geology specialist

Nina Crummy
Freelance finds specialist

Natasha Dodwell
Freelance human remains specialist

Taleyna Fletcher
Project Officer, Oxford Archaeology East

Rachel Fosberry
Project Officer: Archaeobotanist, Oxford Archaeology East

Val Fryer
Freelance environmental specialist

F.M.L. Green
Freelance pollen specialist

Gillian Greer
Illustrator, Oxford Archaeology East

Sarah Henley
Formerly Supervisor, Oxford Archaeology East

Mark Hinman
Formerly Senior Project Manager, Oxford Archaeology East

Peter Lorimer
Freelance archaeological illustrator

Alice Lyons
Project Officer, Oxford Archaeology East

Gwladys Monteil
Freelance samian specialist

Quita Mould
Freelance leather specialist

Liz Muldowney
Formerly Project Officer, Oxford Archaeology East

Sarah Percival
Pottery specialist, Oxford Archaeology East

Tom Phillips
Project Officer, Oxford Archaeology East

Alexandra Pickstone
Formerly Project Officer, Oxford Archaeology East

Ruth Shaffrey
Finds Specialist, Oxford Archaeology South

David Starley
Metalworking specialist

Emma Tetlow
Insect specialist

Stephen Wadeson
Finds Supervisor/Specialist, Oxford Archaeology East

Heather Wallis
Freelance

John Zant
Project Manager, Oxford Archaeology North

Acknowledgements

The authors would like to thank all those whose hard work, dedication and support have helped to reveal the hidden past of Love's Farm. Particular thanks are extended to the client, Gallagher Estates and their representatives Darren Mace and Mukesh Ladwa. The project was monitored on behalf of Cambridgeshire County Council by Andy Thomas, who is thanked for his continued interest and support.

The fieldwork stage was managed by Mark Hinman, ably assisted by Project Officers Liz Muldowney and Taleyna Fletcher, as well as Supervisors Sarah Henley, Alexandra Pickstone and Tom Phillips. Machine stripping was organised by Mick Murfitt and led by Nick Richardson. The digging team, who kept going whatever the weather, were: Tristan Adfield, David Andrews, Abby Antrobus, Joanne Archer, Glenn Bailey, Celine Beauchamp, Jon Bolderson, Ben Brogan, David Brown, Imogen de Burgh, Louise Bush, Mikiel Cerbing, Spencer Cooper, Andy Corrigan, Thomas Eley, Chris Faine, James Fairbairn, Helen Fowler, Liz Gatti, Clionadh McGarry, Nick Gilmour, John Grant, Kathryn Grant, Ian Hogg, Mo Jones, Ross Lilley, Adam Lodoen, Tom Lyons, Laura Maccalman, Tikshna Mandal, Vera Manning, Claire Martin, Emma Nordstrom, Dennis Payne, Hannah Pethen, Will Punchard, Gareth Rees, Shelley Rodwell, Helen Stocks, David Strachan, Chris Thatcher, Gemma Tully, Eleanor Vincent, Rob Wardill, Sam Whitehead and Andrew Wyer. The metal detector survey was conducted by Steve Critchley with support from Nick Richardson.

Volunteers and outreach events were co-ordinated by David Crawford-White. The team of volunteers who helped with the digging and finds processing were: Nicola Babbs, Tamsin Barker, Hannah Bosworth, Louis Budworth, Elizabeth Button, Julie Clarke, Vaughan Clements, Rikki Collier, Jean Crysell, Jeannie De Rycke, Amelia Downs, Edmund Dunger, Terry Dymot, Sarah Evans, Neil Farrer, Sue and Gerry Feakes, Claire Finn, Ben Greene, Richard Halliday, Nicola Herson, Anna-Lisa Hill, Heather and Peter Hinman, Jack Hiscock, Michael Horgan, Debbie Hudson, Catherine Hunter, Anne Jarzabek, John Jarzabek, Bonnie Knapp, Claudia Loffredo, Iona McLean, Zoe Miller, Jenny Mohr, Charlie Moore, Terry Mortlock, Matthew O'Connell, Charlotte O'Connor, Sheena Palmer, Jane Paynter, Rhiannon Philp, Cyril Pritchett, David Roberts, Rodney Scarle, Nick Sennett, Neil Smith, Pam Sneath, Susan Stratton, Ian Taylor, Bernice Thornton, Stephanie Wagg, James Walker, Andrew Webb, Carol Webster, Peter Weston, David Whiter, Victoria Wisbeach and Matthew Wood.

OA East's Operations Team of Nicola Gifford-Cowan, Jason Graham, Joe Worth and Karl Bishop are thanked for keeping us supplied with everything and making sure the bills got paid on time. Thanks are also due to Sarah Poppy, Sally Thompson and Hazel White of the Cambridgeshire Historic Environment Team for answering many queries and providing relevant data.

The survey team who helped to put us on the map were Crane Begg (GPS survey, digitisation, illustration and GIS applications) and Taleyna Fletcher (site survey and GPS training). The illustrators who produced the excellent published drawings and photographs are warmly thanked (and, in particular, Gillian Greer), as is Andrew Corrigan for booklet design and technical support in the later stages of the project.

Processing of the substantial assemblages of finds and environmental remains was co-ordinated by Stephen Wadeson, Carole Fletcher and Rachel Fosberry, each of whom is thanked for their perseverance. Chris Montague is also thanked for his patience in sample processing all year round. Each of the contributing specialists to this volume is warmly thanked for their reports and for the expert advice offered throughout the project, along with Rog Palmer for aerial photographs. Alice Lyons would like to thank David Williams (Southampton University) for his assistance, while Stephen Wadeson would also like to thank Edward Biddulph (OA South) and Geoff Dannell for their time.

The initial stages of post-excavation analysis were undertaken by Liz Muldowney and Taleyna Fletcher, followed by Sarah Henley and Alexandra Pickstone; between them they phased the site and produced the draft text and illustrations that form the basis for the stratigraphic narrative included here. The project was managed by Mark Hinman, who finalised the phasing and drafted the initial version of the publication text. Following his departure from OA East, the publication was completed by John Zant at OA North. The finds and environmental chapters were collated by Elizabeth Popescu, who also revised, edited and prepared the volume for publication.

Abbreviations

General
EVE	Estimated vessel equivalent
ERB	Early Romano-British
IA	Iron Age
LPRIA	Late pre-Roman Iron Age
MSW	Mean sherd weight
MVC	Minimum vessel count
RB	Romano-British
RH	Roundhouse
SF	Small find
Wt	Weight

Prehistoric and Iron Age pottery fabric codes
See Tables 7.2 and 7.6

Romano-British pottery fabric codes
See Appendix 3

Abbreviated references
CK	Carson and Kent (1972)
HK	Hill and Kent (1972)
K19	Knorr 1919
K52	Knorr 1952
ORL	*Der Obergermanisch-Raetischen Limes des Römerreichs*
Os	Oswald (1936–37)
RIB	Collingwood and Wright (1965)
RIC	Mattingly *et al.* (1923–94)
S&S	Stanfield and Simpson (1958); S&S 90 (1990)

Summary

Love's Farm, St Neots, lies on the claylands near the western boundary of Cambridgeshire. Fieldwork was conducted here by Cambridgeshire County Council's Archaeological Field Unit, CAM ARC (now Oxford Archaeology East) between 2005 and 2008 over a 60ha area, following on from geophysical survey, fieldwalking and evaluation. This extensive project permitted a detailed archaeological examination of a later prehistoric and Roman agricultural landscape on a previously unprecedented scale within the county.

Evidence was revealed for the exploitation of the area in early prehistory, with field systems present from the middle Iron Age, if not before. By the late Iron Age, several farmsteads were set within what may have been three 'landholdings', bounded to the south by a major routeway previously identified as a possible Roman road (Margary 1973, Road 231). Dominant features were a large square enclosure and a subsequent sub-circular monument, positioned on a ridge overlooking the settlements. Given its location close to major routes, the site was ideally situated to provide evidence for the impact of the Roman conquest and the influence of Romanisation on the countryside. Although little trace of the disruption of everyday life was noted, metalwork with military associations was found. Many of the finds show a distinct bias towards votive offerings, providing new insights into local religious observance. At around the time of the conquest, the minor farmsteads fell from use and activities eventually coalesced into two settlements: one which developed from an Iron Age farm and the other effectively a 'new' foundation that burgeoned in the 4th century. The older of the two settlements was abandoned in the late 4th century, while the other apparently remained in use into the early Anglo-Saxon period. The site eventually became medieval fields, although some of the ancient hedgerow boundaries survived.

This publication seeks to illustrate the site's character and to examine its social, economic and morphological development in its wider context. The archaeological remains unearthed at the site link to a wide range of issues that have the potential to enhance current understanding of social organisation and the evolution of the countryside. The results shed significant new light on the past of this previously little-known part of the Cambridgeshire landscape, that was once thought to be cold, wet and uninviting.

Résumé

Love's Farm se trouve à St Neots sur des terres argileuses près de la limite ouest du Cambridgeshire. Entre 2005 et 2008, le Cambridgeshire County Council's Archaeological Field Unit, CAM ARC (actuellement l'Oxford Archaeology East) a conduit un travail sur le terrain couvrant une superficie de 60 hectares. Ce travail a commencé par une étude géophysique, une exploration du terrain et une évaluation des résultats obtenus. Le projet a permis un examen archéologique détaillé d'un paysage agricole datant de l'époque romaine et de la période préhistorique tardive à une échelle inédite jusqu'à présent dans le comté.

Les fouilles ont permis de mettre à jour des vestiges de l'exploitation de la zone au début de la préhistoire, avec des systèmes de champs présents depuis l'âge du fer moyen et peut-être même avant. À la fin de l'âge du fer, plusieurs fermes furent établies dans trois 'propriétés foncières', limitées vers le sud par une importante voie de communication orientée est-ouest. Cette dernière avait été auparavant identifiée comme étant peut-être une route romaine (Margary 1973, Road 231). Les principales caractéristiques du lieu se résument à une grande enceinte carrée et à un monument sous-circulaire ultérieur, placé sur une crête surplombant les implantations. Étant donné son emplacement à proximité des principales voies de communication, le site était idéalement situé pour contenir des vestiges de l'impact de la conquête romaine et de l'influence de la romanisation sur le territoire. On a trouvé des traces du travail des métaux associé à des activités militaires, alors même qu'il existe peu de marques de perturbation de la vie quotidienne. Beaucoup des découvertes correspondent clairement à des offrandes votives, ce qui apporte des éclaircissements sur l'observance des faits religieux locaux. Dans la période avoisinant la conquête, les petites fermes furent abandonnées et les activités finirent par se concentrer dans deux implantations. L'une se développa à partir d'une ferme de l'âge du fer, alors que l'autre représentait en réalité une 'nouvelle' fondation qui s'est épanouie au 4ème siècle. La plus ancienne des deux implantations fut abandonnée à la fin du 4ème siècle, tandis que l'autre est apparemment restée active jusqu'au début de la période anglo-saxonne. Au Moyen Âge, le site a finalement pris la forme de champs, même si d'anciennes haies ont continué à servir de limites.

Cette publication vise à illustrer les caractéristiques du site et à examiner son développement social, économique et morphologique dans un contexte plus large. Les vestiges archéologiques mis à jour sur le site ont permis de soulever un grand nombre de questions susceptibles d'approfondir la compréhension de l'organisation sociale et de l'évolution de la campagne environnante. Les résultats obtenus apportent des éclaircissements significatifs sur le passé de cette partie peu connue de la campagne du Cambridgeshire, qui, à une certaine époque, eut la réputation d'être froide, humide et inhospitalière.

(Traduction: Didier Don)

Zusammenfassung

Die Love's Farm in St Neots liegt auf einer Tonschicht unweit des Westrands von Cambridgeshire. Die Archaeological Field Unit des Cambridgeshire County Council, CAM ARC (heute Oxford Archaeology East), führte hier zwischen 2005 und 2008 auf einer Fläche von 60 Hektar Feldforschungen durch, gefolgt von einer geophysikalischen Untersuchung, Begehung und Evaluierung. Das umfangreiche Projekt ermöglichte die detaillierte archäologische Untersuchung einer Kulturlandschaft aus der jüngeren Urgeschichte und der Römerzeit von bis dahin in der Grafschaft ungekanntem Ausmaß.

Es fanden sich Belege für die Nutzung des Gebiets in der älteren Urgeschichte, wobei spätestens ab der mittleren Eisenzeit Feldfluren vorhanden waren. In der jüngeren Eisenzeit gab es mehrere Gehöfte auf vermutlich drei Besitztümern, die im Süden von einer wichtigen, von Ost nach West verlaufenden Route gesäumt waren, die zuvor als mögliche Römerstraße ausgemacht worden war (Margary 1973, Road 231). Besonders auffällig waren eine große Viereckschanze und ein späteres kreisförmiges Monument auf einer Kammlinie oberhalb der Siedlungsplätze. Angesichts seiner Lage in der Nähe wichtiger Routen war dieser Ort perfekt, um Aufschlüsse über die Auswirkungen der römischen Eroberung und den Einfluss der Romanisierung auf die Landschaft zu geben. Auch wenn es kaum Belege für eine Störung des normalen Alltagslebens gab, deuteten Metallobjekte auf militärische Aktivitäten hin. Viele Funde ließen sich mit hoher Wahrscheinlichkeit als Votivgaben einordnen, die neue Einblicke in die religiösen Bräuche vor Ort liefern. Etwa um die Zeit der römischen Eroberung wurden die kleineren Gehöfte aufgegeben, so dass die Aktivitäten letztlich auf zwei Siedlungsplätze konzentriert waren: Der erste entstand aus einem eisenzeitlichen Gehöft, während der zweite als Neugründung anzusehen ist, die im 4. Jahrhundert aufblühte. Die ältere der beiden Siedlungen wurde Ende des 4. Jahrhunderts verlassen, die zweite blieb jedoch offenbar bis in die angelsächsische Frühzeit bestehen. An der Stätte wurden letzthin mittelalterliche Fluren angelegt, auch wenn einige der alten Heckenraine weiterbestanden. In dieser Veröffentlichung wird der Charakter der Stätte illustriert und ihre soziale, wirtschaftliche und morphologische Entwicklung im größeren Kontext untersucht. Die archäologischen Befunde der Stätte weisen eine Verbindung zu zahlreichen Themen auf, die möglicherweise geeignet sind, das derzeitige Verständnis der sozialen Organisation und der landschaftlichen Entwicklung zu verbessern. Die Ergebnisse werfen ein neues Licht auf die Vergangenheit dieses zuvor wenig bekannten Landschaftsteils von Cambridgeshire, der einst als kalt, feucht und wenig einladend galt.

(Übersetzung: Gerlinde Krug)

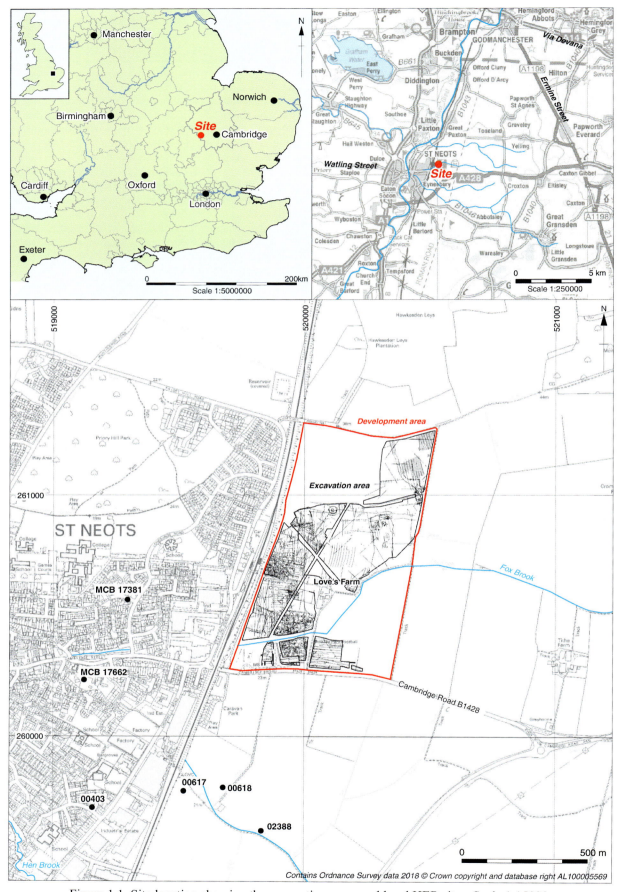

Figure 1.1 Site location showing the excavation areas and local HER sites. Scale 1:15000

1. Introduction

by John Zant and Mark Hinman, with Brendan Chester-Kadwell and Tom Phillips

I. Project background
(Fig. 1.1; Pl. 1.1)

Between 2005 and 2008, a major programme of archaeological excavations, covering approximately 30ha of a 60ha development area, was undertaken by Cambridgeshire County Council's Archaeological Field Unit, CAM ARC (now Oxford Archaeology East, OAE), at Love's Farm, St Neots, Cambridgeshire. The project, which represented the culmination of several years of archaeological assessment and evaluation, was carried out in advance of development of the site by Gallagher Estates for housing, a primary school and a football ground. In the present-day landscape, the site lies on the north-eastern periphery of St Neots (NGR TL 201 607), immediately east of the London to Peterborough railway line (Fig. 1.1), which effectively formed the eastern limit of the modern built-up area prior to the commencement of the excavations (Pl. 1.1). The development area was bounded to the south by the B1428 road, to the west by the railway line, to the north by Priory Hill Road (leading from St Neots to the medieval manor of Monks Hardwick), and to the east by modern field boundaries. Love's Farm itself (a post-enclosure farm first established in the 1770s) was located towards the centre of this area, but was swept away by the new development. Most of the site lay in open farmland at the time of the excavations.

St Neots was founded in the 12th century by the monks of St Neots Priory at a crossing point on the River Great Ouse, which formed the boundary between the historic counties of Bedfordshire and Huntingdonshire. Prior to the English Settlement this area was in the tribal lands of the Catuvellauni, and its significance lay in the fact that it was on the route between Cambridge (*Duroliponte*) and those territories west of the Great Ouse, near the point

Plate 1.1 Aerial photograph of St Neots, showing the Love's Farm site prior to the excavations (by Rog Palmer)

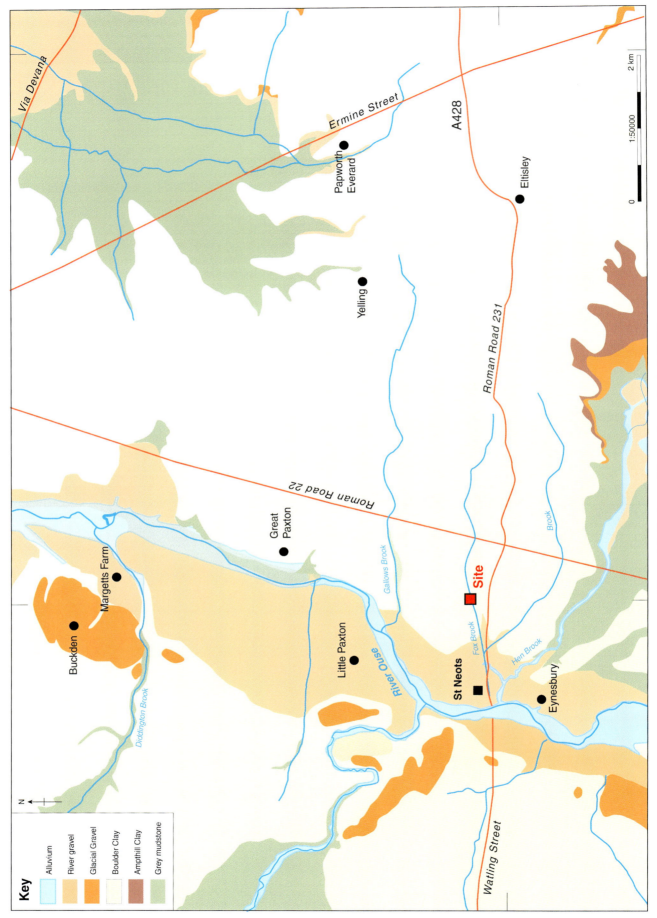

Figure 1.2 Geology of the local area. Scale 1:50000

where the river crossed the way between Sandy and Godmanchester (*Durovigutum*).

II. Location, geology and topography

Geology and topography
(Fig. 1.2)

St Neots lies within the valley of the River Great Ouse, the dominant local landscape feature, which winds through the area from south to north, *c.*2km west of Love's Farm. The river, with its sources in the Cotswolds and Chiltern hills, is one of the largest in England, both in terms of its length (*c.*210 km), and its catchment area, which covers approximately 7,800 sq km (*c.*3,000 sq miles) (Summers 1973, 13; Green 2000, 5). In its lower reaches, the river has undergone significant changes in its course (and its potential navigability) since prehistoric times. At St Neots, the flat valley floor lies at *c.*14m OD, and is approximately 1,500m wide; on both sides of the valley, the land rises gradually to *c.*40m OD. Love's Farm lay on rising ground east of the river, on the western edge of a plateau of higher ground extending from St Neots eastwards to Cambridge. Over much of this area, the underlying drift geology, largely comprising a thick layer of boulder clay, resulted in the formation of heavy clay soils, contrasting with the generally lighter soils that formed over the alluvial gravels and silts in the river valleys. The development site was situated on heavy clay soils on the east side of the valley.

This higher ground above the course of the river is broken by a number of shallow, broadly east to west aligned valleys, formed by minor tributaries of the Great Ouse; in the vicinity of Love's Farm these include Hen Brook, Gallows Brook and Fox Brook. The latter is a seasonal stream or winterbourne (*i.e.* a stream that is dry during the summer months) that now flows from north-east to south-west through the southern part of the development area. On the southern part of the Love's Farm site, a palaeochannel infilled with coarse silty sands and gravels runs adjacent to, and immediately south of, the modern course of Fox Brook, which today occupies a semi-artificial channel created as part of a managed agricultural landscape. This palaeochannel, the fills of which are typical of those observed within the Devensian Stage Ouse Terrace gravels, forms a part of a former fluvial system of palaeochannels occupying the current valley of the Fox Brook. The present watercourse has contributed a series of finer flood silts and sands that overlie the older gravels within the palaeochannel. The ancient course of the stream was one of the determining factors in the development of settlement at Love's Farm, and similar settlements are now known to have existed in the immediate vicinity. Roads and trackways leading eastwards from St Neots across this undulating terrain generally follow the low ridges of higher ground located between the stream valleys.

The southern limit of the site was located on roughly level ground at *c.*20m OD, adjacent to Fox Brook. To the north, the ground rose gently through the central portion of the development area to a level plateau at *c.*40m OD on the northern part of the site, forming part of the ridge of higher ground between Fox Brook, to the south, and Gallows Brook to the north. The natural topography of the site provided a relatively sheltered, well-drained, south-facing location.

A detailed report on the surface geologies of the site, based on on-site observations, is presented elsewhere in this volume (Critchley, Appendix 1); this includes important and previously unpublished information on the origin of the local natural resources that were exploited by the early inhabitants of the area, as well as the formation processes behind the natural hollows evident in various parts of the site. The local solid geology comprises mudstones of the Oxford Clay Formation, assignable to the Callovian and Oxfordian Stages of the Middle and Upper Jurassic (British Geological Survey 1987). These are overlain by a substantial thickness of glacial chalky till (or chalky boulder clay) of the Hanslope Association, deposited during the Quaternary System mid-Pleistocene Anglian Glaciation, which reached its peak around 500,000 years ago. This masks the solid geology almost everywhere within the Great Ouse basin, and may vary in thickness from a few metres to as much as 70m. The south-western portion of the site also contains a limited exposure of fluvial sands and gravels, a distal part of the River Ouse Second Terrace. Field observations indicate that the latter deposits extend further to the east than the geological map would suggest. A number of subsequent, climate-controlled glacial and interglacial periods extensively modified the till deposits throughout the late Pleistocene and Holocene, producing a complex of periglacial, near-surface 'permafrost active zone' structures and associated sedimentation.

Local road networks
(Figs 1.3–1.4)

Love's Farm lay little more than 1km west of a Roman road (Margary 1973, Road 22, Fig. 1.3) running south-west from Godmanchester (*Durovigutum*), *c.*7km north-east of the site (Green 1977; Jones 2003), to the settlement at Sandy, Bedfordshire (Edgeworth and Steadman 2003), *c.*10km to the south of the development area, and onwards to Braughing, in Hertfordshire. To the north, Road 22 was linked to Ermine Street, the great north to south aligned road from London to Lincoln and beyond, which was constructed by the Roman army soon after the conquest of AD 43 (Frere 1987, 55). Ermine Street itself (Margary 1973, Road 2b) ran north-west to south-east, *c.*10km due east of Love's Farm, on the line of the modern A1198.

Of greater significance to the Love's Farm site is a lesser, east to west aligned Roman road, running approximately on the line of the modern A428 (and the B1428), that connected the Roman town at Cambridge (*Duroliponte*), to the east, with Ermine Street, to the west (Margary 1973, Road 231; Fig. 1.3). This road, which is thought to have roughly followed the line of a prehistoric ridgeway (Abrams and Ingham 2008, 37), is also believed to have extended further west, as part of a linking route connecting Ermine Street with Roman Watling Street (Spoerry 2000, 146). The precise line of this road in the vicinity of Love's Farm is uncertain, but it is held to follow the old St Neots to Cambridge road (now the B1428), which formed the southern boundary of the Love's Farm development area: this route is postulated to have crossed the River Great Ouse a few hundred metres north of the medieval bridge at St Neots, in the vicinity of Islands Common (Spoerry 2000, 146). If this is correct, Love's Farm would have been located at a significant Roman road junction, in reasonably close proximity to the river crossing.

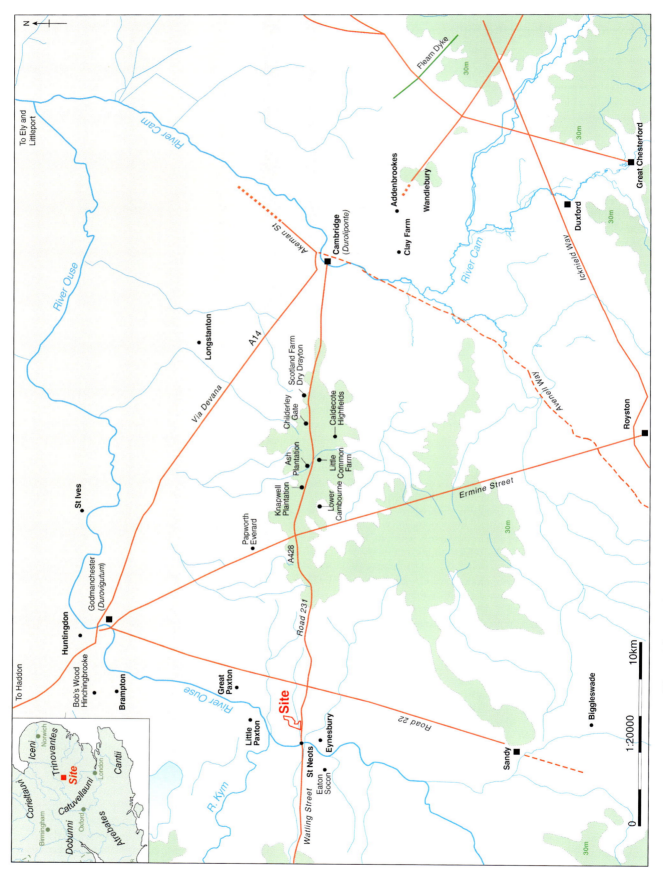

Figure 1.3 Key sites mentioned in the text, showing the local Roman road network. Scale 1:20000

There is also a 'Romanised' trackway, the Mear Way (also called Hail's Lane, Fig. 1.4), which crosses the modern parish in a north-north-easterly direction, parallel to, and about 4km east of, the Ouse. Although its exact antiquity is unknown, there is evidence that parts of this route at least were modified by the Romans, albeit that it does not have the precision of a Roman military road. It is along the alignment of this ancient trackway, often at some distance from it on either side, that many settlement features are to be found in the parishes of Eynesbury, St Neots and Abbotsley. Indeed, settlement evidence is so widespread in this part of the Ouse Valley (perhaps measuring up to 500m across), that it has been suggested that St Neots, and specifically Eynesbury, on the southern side of the modern town, may have been the focus of a major Romano-Celtic estate centre, or possibly even a small town (Spoerry 2000, 148).

III. Archaeological background

Overview
(Figs 1.3–1.5)
Prior to the commencement of the excavations, little archaeological work had been undertaken on the claylands of west Cambridgeshire. This was due partly to a lack of development, including mineral extraction, in the area, which limited opportunities for investigation, but also resulted from the fact that many archaeologists held to the view that prehistoric (and, indeed, Romano-British) settlement in the region was focused on the lighter, more easily-worked, soils in the river valleys, the south-eastern fen-edge and the chalklands of south Cambridgeshire, with the 'heavy claylands' west and north of Cambridge (and elsewhere in East Anglia and the Midlands; Cunliffe 2005, 260) remaining largely uninhabited (*e.g.* Malim 2000, 11). This view, which led to the potential of these areas being frequently dismissed until very recently (Mills and Palmer 2007, 91–4; Evans *et al.* 2008, 185), had been arrived at through a long history of research and fieldwork. At the beginning of the 20th century, Haverfield included the Ouse Valley amongst his sparsely inhabited 'thin spots' of Roman Britain, where 'great woodlands' and 'damp and chilly clay', together with a lack of mineral resources, resulted in a 'less richly developed civilization' than elsewhere in the Midlands and East Anglia (Haverfield 1900, 22; 1902, 165–6). In the 1920s, Sir Cyril Fox echoed Haverfield's view in his seminal and highly influential work, *The Archaeology of the Cambridge Region* (Fox 1923). Fox noted that the distribution of Bronze Age finds and metalwork hoards was largely confined to the southern fen edge and the Cam Valley, with few finds in the Ouse Valley. He also noted the scarcity of known Bronze Age settlement sites on the 'cold claylands' adjacent to the Ouse, as opposed to the comparative wealth of settlement evidence on the chalk. His view that areas of heavy clay were unsuitable for early settlement was further expounded in *The Personality of Britain* (Fox 1932), with the Midlands claylands being portrayed as thickly wooded throughout prehistory (Clay 2002, 1). Furthermore, the perceived 'low status' of those few sites that were known in these areas evidently made them unattractive to earlier researchers (Abrams and Ingham 2008, 37).

Since Fox's time, a large number of excavations in the Middle and Lower Ouse Valley, many of them development-led projects undertaken in the past 20–30 years, have transformed understanding of the archaeology of the river valley itself (*e.g.* Dawson 2000a; Ellis 2004), with sites of all periods from the early Neolithic to the Anglo-Saxon period being discovered. Extensive programmes of research undertaken as part of the Fenland Project have also been carried out in the Lower Ouse Valley (Hall and Coles 1994; Fincham 2002). On the clay uplands of west and north Cambridgeshire, however, excavation remained extremely limited until very recently, for reasons already noted, with the result that research into the origins and development of human settlement in these areas lagged behind work on claylands in other regions, such as those in the East Midlands and the adjacent Nene Valley, which research programmes such as the Raunds Area Project (Parry 2006) demonstrated to have been densely occupied at certain periods.

The situation began to change in the 1990s, due in part to increased aerial coverage (although several recently-excavated clayland sites had not been identified by aerial survey; Abrams and Ingham 2008, 19), but mainly to an upsurge in development-led archaeological fieldwork, which continued throughout the first decade of the 21st century (Mills and Palmer 2007, 8–11). In the immediate environs of Love's Farm itself, further archaeological works, thus far limited to evaluation and/or aerial photography, have been conducted to the south at Wintringham Park (Hinman and Phillips 2008) and to the east at Tithe Farm (Figs 1.4–1.5). At Wintringham Park, remains dating from the Neolithic period, the later Iron Age and the Romano-British period were found, although no activity of the Bronze Age or earlier Iron Age was noted. Traces of later medieval ridge and furrow systems were present across much of the site, which was crossed by the Hen Brook and a second (un-named) brook to the north. The evaluation and related aerial photography and geophysics provided evidence for fifteen individual Iron Age farmsteads, similar to those found at Love's Farm, that developed throughout the Romano-British period.

Other major programmes of excavation have also now been undertaken on the clay plateau between Cambridge and St Neots (Fig. 1.3), including numerous sites associated with the upgrading of the A428 (Abrams and Ingham 2008), and the Cambourne New Settlement development (Wright *et al.* 2009). In the same area, a significant excavation was carried out at Caldecote Highfields, just south of the A428 (Kenney 2007; Kenney and Lyons 2011), and another small excavation was undertaken at Scotland Farm, Dry Drayton (Ingham 2008), adjacent to one of the A428 sites. These sites again yielded evidence for intensive activity in the Iron Age and/or the Romano-British period, principally in the form of enclosed farmsteads, with associated field systems, trackways, and other rural landscape features. More limited evidence for earlier prehistoric activity, early Anglo-Saxon occupation, and medieval cultivation, was also recorded at many sites.

Other 'clayland' projects in the county include those at Haddon, near Peterborough (French 1994; Hinman 2003), Longstanton, north-west of Cambridge (Evans *et al.* 2008, 174) and Papworth Everard (Hounsell 2007; Gilmour *et al.* 2010). From these and many other sites, both in Cambridgeshire and the wider region, it is now clear that – whilst settlement may not always have been as widespread or as intensive as in the adjacent river valleys, or on the

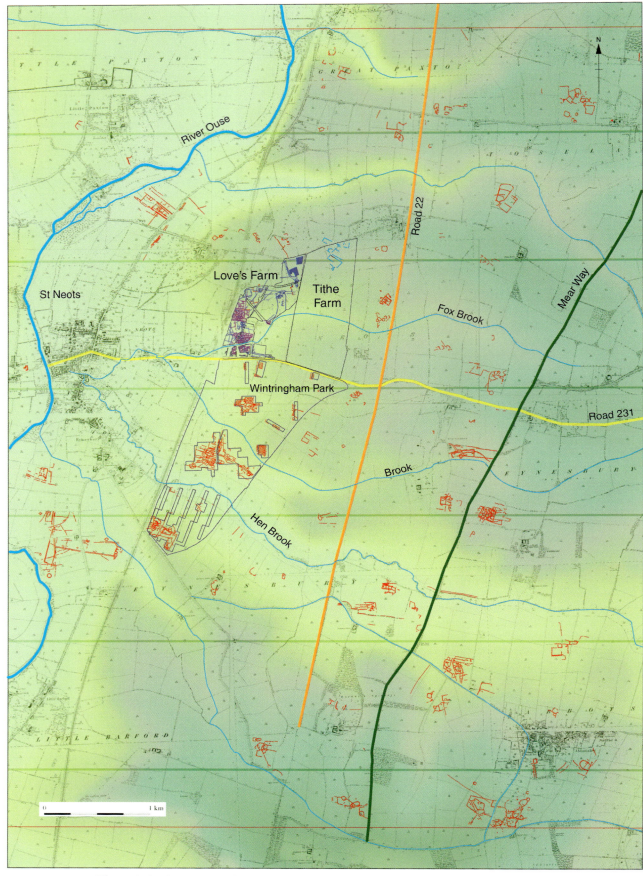

Figure 1.4 The western claylands: sites and cropmarks in the vicinity of Love's Farm

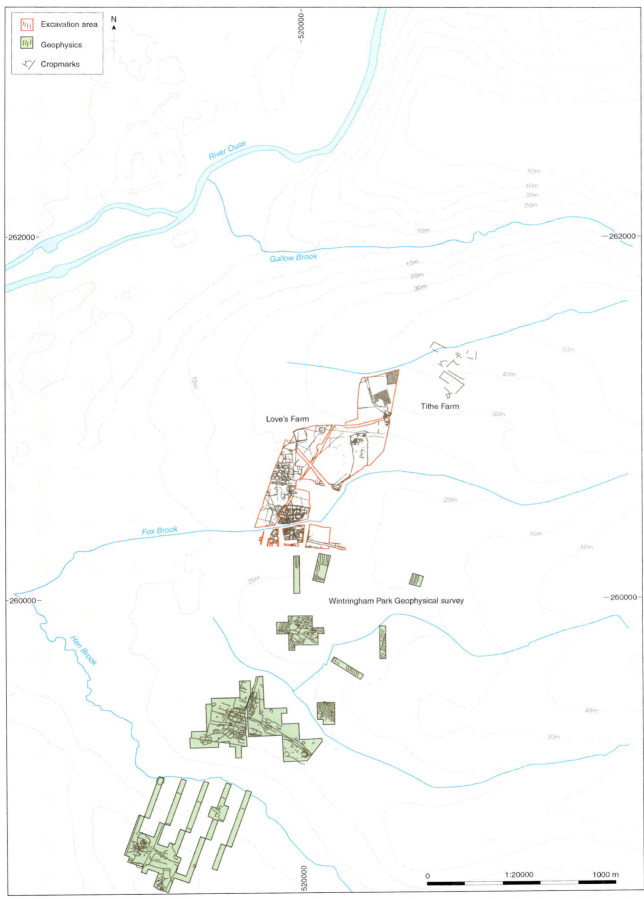

Figure 1.5 The Love's Farm site in its local context, showing adjacent sites at Wintringham Park and Tithe Farm

lighter soils of the chalklands – the clay uplands of eastern England were widely exploited by ancient communities, particularly in the Iron Age and Roman periods (see further discussion in Chapter 9).

Previous work
(Figs 1.1 and 1.3–1.5)

Early prehistoric
Extensive remains of prehistoric activity have now been recorded in the vicinity of Love's Farm, including ritual and settlement activity ranging in date from the Mesolithic to the Iron Age. In the majority of cases however, this evidence has been recovered from sites on the alluviated flood plain of the Ouse Valley and until very recently sites on the heavier clay uplands of western Cambridgeshire, which have a greater relevance to the current project, have been notably absent. The role of the Ouse corridor in the development of trade and continental contact was noted by Malim (1998) with surviving evidence of Neolithic occupation, mainly in the form of a developing ritual landscape. An increase in finds along the Ouse corridor datable to this period suggests the development of riverside activity. It has also been suggested that an early fording point just north-west of the study site at Little Paxton was in use at this time (Alexander 1992). This would have supported both communication and movement of goods along the valley corridor, as well as facilitating east to west trade from the Midlands and East Anglia.

Excavations in advance of the construction of the St Neots bypass in 1983–4 approximately 4km to the south-west of the Love's Farm site, close to the river, revealed remains of Mesolithic and Neolithic flint-working sites as well as a ritual site in the form of a Bronze Age ring ditch and associated features (Herne 1984; CHER 10198, 10198a). Directly to the north of this, Wessex Archaeology excavated a 12ha area in Eynesbury and uncovered a prehistoric ritual complex (Ellis 2004; CHER 00381, 11671, MCB17676). Neolithic remains included two cursus enclosures, a hengiform ring-ditch, a long barrow, a double enclosure believed to represent another ritual or funerary monument and discrete pits containing placed deposits. Later funerary activity included an Early Bronze Age urned cremation burial, a small number of unurned cremation burials and a large enclosure made up of c.440 pits of late Bronze Age/early Iron Age date (CHER MCB17704), which may also have been of ritual significance. This important site is seen as an integral part of the ritual landscape of the Neolithic and Bronze Age along the Ouse Valley (Malim 2000).

A number of ritual complexes were located on the light sandy soils of the Ouse Valley including examples found at the Buckden/Diddington complex (Jones and Ferris 1994; Jones 1995, 1998; Evans 1997), and at Brampton, where the complex included ceremonial monuments such as mortuary enclosures, cursus, hengiform monuments and ring ditches spanning several hundred years (White 1969; Malim 1990; Malim and Mitchell 1993). Slightly further afield at Biddenham Loop, significant concentrations of Neolithic and Bronze Age burial monuments and settlement-related activity were examined in some detail (Luke 2008). Activity has also been noted at Huntingdon Racecourse where boundary ditches and a Bronze Age co-axial field system were found (Macaulay 1994). More recently at Bob's Wood, Hinchingbrooke occasional flints, a Neolithic pit and several Bronze Age features were excavated (Oxford Archaeology East, in prep.), while at Haddenham the remains of a Neolithic long barrow and causewayed enclosure were noted (Evans and Hodder 2006).

Although early prehistoric finds are rare on the heavier clay soils, a number of Bronze Age finds in the surrounding area have revealed evidence for settlement occupation at Cambourne (Wessex Archaeology 2003). Closer to the study area, excavation in and around Papworth has revealed evidence of Bronze Age to Iron Age settlement (Casa Hatton 2002; Hatton and Kemp 2002; Kenney 2000; HER 13049). At Papworth Everard a Bronze Age cremation cemetery with a population of 41 identifiable individuals is amongst the largest of its type known in the region (Gilmour *et al.* 2010). This evidence, combined with emergent traces of widespread early field systems, also serves to indicate that previous estimates of population densities in this area should be revised and may imply that competition for land and other resources was more intensive than could have been anticipated previously.

Iron Age
Many of the earlier prehistoric sites along the Ouse Valley continued to be used in the Iron Age period and include a late Iron Age settlement enclosure in Miller Way, Brampton (White 1969) and another adjacent settlement enclosure (Malim and Mitchell 1993). At Eynesbury (Kemp 1996; Wessex Archaeology 2002) and Brampton (Malim and Mitchell 1993) this continuity of activity developed from a ritual/ceremonial use of the landscape into what is currently interpreted as a more agricultural one. At Papworth Everard (Kenny 2000; Hatton and Kemp 2002) there was evidence for Bronze Age/early Iron Age activity on the marginal heavy clay soils with an organised landscape of field boundaries incorporating possible mortuary enclosures and stockades. North of Love's Farm is the middle to late Iron Age settlement site at Bob's Wood, Hinchingbrooke (Oxford Archaeology East, in prep.) which was established on a hilltop on the heavier soils overlooking Alconbury Brook, a tributary of the Ouse.

This apparent trend of movement onto the heavier soils is observed elsewhere in Britain, and may point to increased pressure on land from the later Neolithic period onwards. With the use of land for agriculture increasing it is not surprising that the heavy soils show increasing evidence for multi-phase use, with many Iron Age farmstead complexes continuing well into the Romano-British period, as found east of Love's Farm at Caldecote (Kenny 2001; Kenny and Lyons 2011), Cambourne (Wessex Archaeology 2003), the A428 Improvement Scheme (Abrams and Ingham 2008), Scotland Farm (Ingham 2008) and the Papworth Everard Bypass (Hounsell 2007). At Cambourne, earlier settlement and field systems seem to have been part of an organised landscape of economically specialised settlements. These were located at regular intervals of c.400m, along possible trackways, on the south-east facing slope of a plateau.

Recent archaeological work including the Wintringham Park evaluation (Hinman and Phillips 2008) and Tithe Farm adjacent to Love's Farm has further demonstrated that the local landscape appears to have been fairly densely settled in the later prehistoric and Roman periods, contradicting published syntheses (Malim 2000; Taylor 2007) which indicated that the Cambridgeshire Claylands were largely uninhabited at this time. In particular, the heavy clay soils which the Love's Farm site lies on, have been shown to have supported numerous farmsteads and rural settlements (see above).

Romano-British
Although use of the Ouse corridor continued during the Roman period with the development of road and river communications, so too did the development and land re-organisation on the heavier soils where there was also a degree of continuity of settlement from the late Iron Age into the Roman period. Excavations along the Ouse Valley have recorded many Iron Age and Roman occupation sites stretching from Huntingdon (Malim 1990; Hinman 1997, 2000) and Brampton (Malim and Mitchell 1993), to Paxton (Greenfield 1968; Alexander 1992) and Eynesbury (Alexander 1993; Kemp 1993, 1997; Ellis 2004). Branches of the Icknield Way, an ancient drove route, continued to be used and crossed the south of the county on a south-west to north-east axis (Taylor 1997); while Ermine Street (now the A1198), constructed by the Roman army soon after the conquest of AD 43 (Frere 1987, 55), ran south to north to the east of the site. In the early Roman period towns such as Great Chesterford (Draper 1986), Sandy (Edgeworth and Steadman 2003) and Godmanchester (*Durovigutum*) (Green 1977; Jones 2003) were beginning to thrive, stimulated by troop movements and trade. Godmanchester was the nearest town and probable market for Love's Farm, located only *c.*7km to the north-north-east, although Sandy, 10km to the south, would probably also have been an important centre in terms of trade and religious matters.

Evidence from sites to the east of the Ouse such as the multi-period site at Bob's Wood, Hinchingbrooke (Oxford Archaeology East, in prep.) suggests that a mixed agricultural system was now operating in the area. The presence of stock enclosures adjacent to Ermine Street, for cattle and possibly sheep, suggests that livestock were an important part of the agricultural system and that a service industry based on this had developed, perhaps to support *Durovigutum*. On the Boulder Clay at Cambourne (Wessex Archaeology 2003) it was only in the later part of the Roman period that re-organisation brought about a change in the landscape, with a cellular arrangement of field systems and enclosures being replaced by a rectilinear one. Excavations at Caldecote (Abrams 2000; Kenney 2001) also produced evidence for a multi-phase Iron Age farmstead complex, which continued in use into the Roman period. These remains again seem to have been part of an organised landscape of economically specialised settlements.

The site of the earlier prehistoric complex at Eynesbury was also occupied in the Roman period, at which time it was part of an agricultural landscape, as evidenced by field boundaries, enclosures and droveways (Ellis 2004; CHER MCB17705). A Roman settlement consisting of pits, ditches and possible hut sites was uncovered 1.5km to the south-west of Love's Farm during building work in the 1960s (CHER 00403). A further 0.5km to the west of this, test-pitting revealed Roman pits, ditches and wall footings (Alexander 1993; CHER 10898). Limited evidence of a villa was found close to the river in 1967. A large room with a hypocaust was uncovered (CHER 00396a), along with 3rd- and 4th-century pottery, while close by Roman pottery, tiles and tesserae were collected (CHER 00684). Some 1.5km to the south-west of the site at Longsands College, an evaluation found evidence of early Roman agricultural enclosures (Thatcher 2006; CHER MCB17381).

In the vicinity of Wintringham Park, to the south of Love's Farm, evidence of a Roman metalled trackway and fragments of pottery were discovered during a small excavation (CHER 02388). A further metalled trackway, along with a coin of Claudius and a shallow pit, were found during the digging of ditches on a field boundary adjacent to the east coast railway line (CHER 00618). The corner of a rectangular earthwork is recorded as having been observed somewhere close by (CHER 00617). The record, from 1967, stated that it measured 215ft by 390ft and the northern arm had been ploughed away, while the western arm now lies under the railway embankment.

Anglo-Saxon to Norman
The early and middle Saxon period saw a gradual shift of settlement from the higher claylands to lower areas closer to the river. At Eynesbury (to the south-west) seven sunken-featured buildings and associated features were recorded (Ellis 2004; CHER MCB17706). Within St Neots town itself, evidence of middle Saxon occupation comes from the site of the later priory. Under the southern end of the kitchen range a ditch was discovered orientated east to west. A few sherds of black micaceous pottery along with a 7th-century sceatta were retrieved from an undisturbed section of the ditch (Tebbutt 1966; CHER 00548b). This location is strategically important, lying just to the north of the modern bridge which forms a major crossing point of the River Great Ouse in St Neots.

Although finds of Anglo-Saxon date in the vicinity are not extensive there is every reason to believe that the light soils of the Ouse Valley were still exploited. A similar assertion for the use of the heavier clay soils during this period is more difficult to support, with little evidence from excavations at Papworth Everard (Alexander 1998; Kenney 2000; Casa Hatton 2002; Hatton and Kemp 2002), Caldecote (Abrams 2000; Kenney 2001) and Cambourne (Wessex Archaeology 2003). At Caldecote, it would appear that the area was abandoned during this period and reverted to open field systems during medieval times. Limited agricultural activity at this time is tentatively suggested by the presence of stratigraphically late but currently undated features recorded during the recent excavations at Bob's Wood, Hinchingbrooke (Oxford Archaeology East, in prep.). The relative paucity of Anglo-Saxon artefacts at that site again serves to highlight the difficulties in recovering conclusive proof of activity during the early part of the Anglo-Saxon period.

The late Saxon settlement precursor of St Neots is believed to lie in the area to the east of Church Street, bounded by the Hen Brook to the south (Addyman 1973), approximately 1km to the west of Wintringham Park (Fig. 1.4). Two excavations have taken place in this area. The first was identified between 1929 and 1932 at Hall Place (Lethbridge and Tebbutt 1933; CHER MCB17662, Fig. 1.1). Several sunken-featured buildings and a wide array of domestic debris dating to the late Saxon period were found. Excavations approximately 100m to the south in

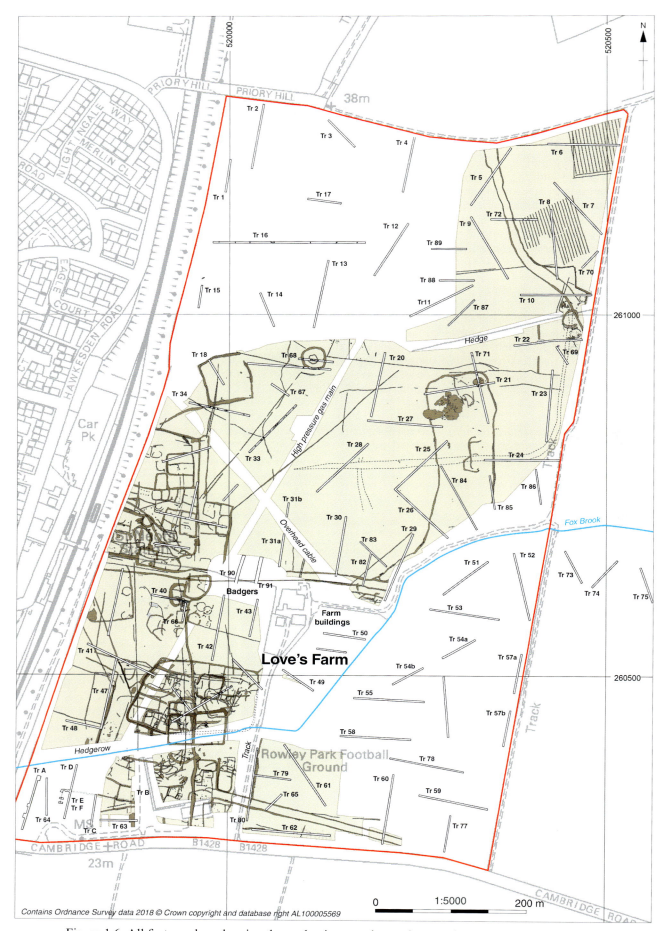

Figure 1.6 All feature plan, showing the evaluation trenches and constraints on the excavation areas

1961–2 revealed at least one large late Saxon timber building of some complexity and there were traces of perhaps five or six more, together with ditches, postholes and pits.

On the west bank of the Ouse, to the south-west at Eaton Socon, a late Saxon timber building was found adjacent to the 12th-century castle (Addyman 1965). The name 'Eaton' is Saxon, meaning 'tun' or 'farm by the river', suggesting an early date for the settlement. The fact that a castle was built there in c.AD 1140 hints at the importance of the location; presumably the castle was built to control a river crossing. At the time of Domesday the area that now comprises the town of St Neots was within two large Saxon parochiae – Eaton Socon west of the river and Eynesbury to the east. The priory (CHER 00548) was first established in the 10th century and the town received its charter in AD 1113. Manor houses established at Eynesbury and Eaton Socon are mentioned in Domesday Book.

Medieval
During the medieval period most of the land in the Love's Farm area was open fields subdivided into furlongs. Ridge and furrow still survives as discrete earthwork remains and cropmarks visible on aerial photographs. The site and the surrounding landscape preserved evidence of an extensive ridge and furrow system which had dominated the medieval landscape. In common with many of the ridge and furrow systems of the East Midlands, the furrows ran with the slope and helped to drain the clay soils.

IV. Project methodology

Desk-based assessment
In 1998, a desk-based survey was undertaken to assess the archaeological and historical background of the development site (CPM 1998); this was later substantially revised and updated. The study identified numerous sites and find spots of potential significance dating from the prehistoric to post-medieval periods; however, none was identified within the development area itself.

Geophysical survey
A geophysical (fluxgate gradiometer) survey was conducted by the West Yorkshire Archaeological Service (WYAS) in 2002. The survey comprised magnetic scanning of the whole development site, followed by a more detailed sample survey covering approximately 8ha. Two different archaeological sites were tentatively identified within the western half of the development area (corresponding to Iron Age/Romano-British Settlements 6 and 7 as recorded during excavation; see Chapters 3 and 4). Evidence for ridge and furrow activity was identified in other parts of the site.

Fieldwalking
A programme of fieldwalking, supported by a metal detector survey, was carried out in 2002. The site was initially divided into units of 1ha, each numbered individually and defined with reference to the Ordnance Survey grid. It was then further sub-divided into 20m transects aligned north to south and numbered 1–5 from west to east within each hectare. The walking of the entire site at 20m transect intervals identified finds and sites dating from the prehistoric to the post-medieval periods. Evidence for Romano-British settlement was concentrated principally within the south-western quadrant of the development area, reflecting the results of the geophysical survey (Whitehead 2003).

Evaluation (trial trenching)
(Fig. 1.6)
In 2003–4, 89 trial trenches, with a total length of 6570m, were excavated over an area of 50.4ha within the site. Positioning of the trenches was designed to provide a uniform level of cover across the development area and to test, where relevant, the validity of the geophysical survey results. Constraints on the placement of trenches included underground pipes (water and gas), overhead cables, and badger-runs identified as part of the initial desk-based survey (CPM 1998). Targeted excavation of exposed features and deposits was conducted in order to characterise and date the surviving archaeological remains. Relative artefact densities across the area were examined through controlled scanning of the spoil heaps generated by mechanical removal of the topsoil within each trench.

The evaluation revealed both a greater intensity and more extensive survival of archaeological remains than had been suggested by the results of the geophysical survey and the fieldwalking programme. Evidence was found for human activity in most periods from the Neolithic (c.4000–2300 BC) to modern times, although the most intensive occupation seemingly occurred during the Iron Age (c.800 BC–AD 43) and the Romano-British period (c.AD 43–410).

Excavation
(Fig. 1.6; Pl. 1.2)
The archaeological excavation that forms the basis of this report was undertaken in two stages, with the bulk of the work completed between February 2005 and March 2006; a second stage of excavation took place at the southern end of the site in July and August 2008, following demolition of the old football ground. All work was undertaken in accordance with an archaeological brief prepared by the Cambridgeshire Archaeology, Planning and Countryside Advice team (CAPCA).

Excavation in certain areas of the site was prohibited or constrained, for a variety of reasons. A 3m-wide exclusion zone was maintained adjacent to a high pressure gas main, which crossed the entire site from north-east to south-west, although limited excavation within this zone was undertaken in accordance with instruction and guidance provided by representatives of Transco. A high voltage overhead cable also crossed the site, from south-east to north-west. Movements of all on-site machinery were subject to a 15m exclusion zone either side of the line of the cables: limited excavation within this zone was undertaken in accordance with instruction and guidance provided by EDF Energy. In order to minimise environmental disturbance, a zone at least 2m wide was established around all retained hedgerows to prevent any impact on the root systems. All mature trees were fenced off to reduce impact to the root system through compaction.

The excavation area numbers are not used in the publication, but are illustrated in Fig. App. 1.1. All excavation areas were cleaned as necessary to facilitate the identification of archaeological features (Pl. 1.2). A Leica GPS1200 system was used to locate site planning grids, excavated features and small finds. All features were mapped onto a base plan by hand (1:50). All significant features were located on the Ordnance Survey National Grid. Site plans were digitised using AutoCAD.

The site was recorded using CAM ARC's standard single context recording system, resulting in a total archive from works undertaken during 2003–2008 of 8,698 contexts, which was expanded during post-excavation to a total of 11,000 contexts. A metal detector was used extensively on the site, being initially used to scan the subsoil after the topsoil had been removed by the 360° excavator. After this material was removed, the archaeological features were scanned to aid the identification of potential find spots. The spoil from features was also scanned to aid the recovery of artefacts. A minimum 50% of each discrete feature was excavated unless it was unsafe to do so. Linear features were excavated sufficiently to provide evidence for an informed interpretation of their date and function. Environmental and bulk samples were taken in consultation with the English Heritage Regional Scientific Advisors (Peter Murphy and Jen Heathcote).

The on-site photographic archive was supplemented by a series of air reconnaissance surveys undertaken by Rog Palmer at opportune moments during machine stripping. The overhead photographic record was reviewed on site during excavation as an aid to identifying additional remains not visible at ground level, to gain an overview of development in individual areas and a greater appreciation of the landscape context.

Plate 1.2 Working shot of excavations in progress

Outreach

A comprehensive and inclusive approach was taken to community and public involvement during the fieldwork, and also the initial post-excavation processing phase of the project. Large numbers of local people and students from Britain and abroad were able to participate in the project, through a range of events and activities: attendance at public open days funded by the developer, visiting a display of finds and photographs at St Neots Museum, the involvement of A-level archaeology students and members of the Young Archaeologists Club in field trips, or by direct participation in the fieldwork programme. Aspects of the project's findings were also incorporated into the design of the Roundhouse School, which was built on the site following completion of the excavations, and contact with the new community on the site was retained through involvement with the community liaison officer. A popular publication was produced at the request of the developer and distributed to local inhabitants and schools (Hinman 2011).

Post-excavation analysis, phasing and publication

Post-excavation analysis of the results of the project began whilst excavation was still underway, resulting in the production of a post-excavation assessment report (Hinman 2008). The archaeological sequence was divided into eight broad chronological periods (Periods 1–8; Hinman 2008, table 11), each representing a major episode of activity in the history of the site. For the Iron Age and Romano-British periods (Periods 3 and 4 respectively), it proved possible to refine these broad chronological divisions further, with reference to stratigraphic, morphological and spatial data, allied with dating evidence provided by the associated assemblage of pottery and (to a lesser degree) other datable artefacts. For the Iron Age, it was possible to identify five sub-phases of activity, broadly corresponding to the early Iron Age (Period 3.1), middle Iron Age (Period 3.2), late Iron Age (Period 3.3), late pre-Roman Iron Age (Period 3.4) and the period of the late pre-Roman Iron Age/early Romano-British transition (Period 3.5). Subsequently, however, it became apparent that there was no good reason to attribute any of the features on the site to the early Iron Age, and that those elements previously believed to date to this period were almost certainly of middle Iron Age origin: for this reason, the middle Iron Age phase is represented here by Periods 3.1–3.2. The Romano-British occupation sequence could be sub-divided, again on stratigraphic, spatial, and artefactual evidence, into five sub-phases, broadly corresponding to the following chronological periods: the late 1st to early 2nd century AD (Period 4.1); the 2nd century AD (Period 4.2); the 3rd century AD (Period 4.3); the 4th century AD (Period 4.4) and the late 4th to early 5th century AD (Period 4.5). Table 1.1 summarises this sequence.

This publication presents the archaeological sequence in three period chapters (Chapters 2–4), each of which includes a brief discussion of the development of the particular period, with more extensive and overarching discussion linking to the project's research objectives in the concluding chapter (Chapter 9). The substantial assemblages of finds appear in two chapters, with all finds other than pottery being dealt with in Chapter 6. Given the scale of the ceramic assemblage, it is presented in a separate chapter (Chapter 7). Zooarchaeological and botanical evidence appears in Chapter 8.

Period	Chronological period	Sub-period	Sub-period date
1	Neolithic: c.4000–2500 BC	-	
2	Bronze Age: c.2500–800 BC	-	
3	Iron Age: c.800 BC–AD 43		
		3.1/2	Middle Iron Age (c.400–100 BC)
		3.3	Late Iron Age (c.100 BC–early 1st century AD)
		3.4	Late Pre-Roman Iron Age (c. first half 1st century AD)
		3.5	Transitional (c. mid-late 1st century AD)
4	Roman: AD 43–c.410 AD		
		4.1	Early Romano-British (c. late 1st–early 2nd century AD)
		4.2	Middle Romano-British (c.2nd century AD)
		4.3	Middle Romano-British (c.3rd century AD)
		4.4	Late Romano-British (c.4th century AD)
		4.5	Late Romano-British (c. late 4th–early 5th century AD)
5	Early Saxon: late 5th–6th century AD	-	
6	Medieval: 1066–1550	-	
7	Post-medieval: 1550–1800	-	
8	Modern: 1800–present	-	

Table 1.1 Summary of site phasing

The original post-excavation numbering for some interpretative entities has been retained (*e.g.* Roundhouse 3, Enclosure 150 *etc.*), meaning that they do not appear in numerical order in the text. Some elements, however, were renumbered for publication (*e.g.* the cemeteries, routeways, waterholes). A concordance table of these changes is held in the project archive.

V. Research objectives

Introduction
The original research objectives for the project, as set out in the specification for the work prepared by CAM ARC, were revised during the excavation and post-excavation assessment to take account of the results of the fieldwork. The updated research aims (Hinman 2008, 35–7) took cognisance of national and regional research priorities; at the national level, general themes have been defined by English Heritage (English Heritage 1997; 1998), whilst regional priorities are presented in the research framework for the eastern counties (Glazebrook 1997; Brown and Glazebrook 2000), and in the revised research framework (Medlycott 2011).

The updated research design presented in the assessment report (Hinman 2008, 35–7) identified five principal research aims, to be considered during the analytical phase of the post-excavation programme. It was envisaged that analysis of the excavated data had the potential to advance archaeological knowledge in the following areas of research:

1. the nature and development of the landscape, and patterns of land-use, over time;
2. the character and relative economic status of the site in the Iron Age and the Romano-British period;
3. the precise nature of specific activities undertaken on the site in all chronological periods;
4. the character and date of any ceremonial or ritual activities conducted on the site;
5. the changing role of the site within its landscape setting over time.

National research priorities
The following national research priorities, based on the themes identified by English Heritage (1997) have particular relevance to the Love's Farm project.

Processes of change:
communal monuments into settlement and field landscapes (c.2000–300 BC): evidence to advance understanding of the gradual change from the monument-dominated landscape of the Neolithic and early Bronze Age to the settlement-dominated landscape of later prehistory (English Heritage 1997, 44);
Briton into Roman (c.300 BC–AD 200): evidence for the extent to which the indigenous population of the area embraced (or rejected) the opportunities presented by the arrival of the Roman army and, subsequently, the development of a 'Romanised' civil infrastructure, including transport networks and market centres (English Heritage 1997, 44);
Empire into kingdom (c.AD 200–700): evidence for the nature of society in the area during the 3rd–7th centuries AD (English Heritage 1997, 44).

Chronological priorities:
late Bronze and Iron Age landscapes: evidence for changes in landscapes in later prehistory, and the causes of such changes (English Heritage 1997, 47–8).

Themes:
settlement hierarchies and interaction: evidence to advance understanding of the complexities of past societies (English Heritage 1997, 51);
rural settlement: evidence to advance knowledge of rural settlement patterns, which are key to understanding the economic, social and political structures of rural England in all chronological periods (English Heritage 1997, 52–3);
patterns of craftsmanship and industry (including agriculture): evidence for industry and craftsmanship, particularly ancient agricultural practices, which appear to have been largely overlooked in this context in the past (English Heritage 1997, 53–4).

Landscapes:
cognitive landscapes: the exploration of all aspects of temporal landscapes from different perspectives, to aid in the development of more sophisticated models of social interaction (English Heritage 1997, 55);
improving regional chronologies: evidence to refine and develop regional chronologies, in order to assist in understanding temporal landscapes (English Heritage 1997, 55).

Regional research priorities
In the original and revised regional research agendas (Brown and Glazebrook 2000; Medlycott 2011), the elements of particular importance for the Love's Farm project were those dealing with the Iron Age (Bryant 2000; Medlycott 2011, 21–32) and the Romano-British period (Going and Plouviez 2000; Medlycott 2011, 33–48). To a lesser extent, the research agendas for the Neolithic/Bronze Age (Brown and Murphy 2000; Medlycott 2011, 9–21) and the Anglo-Saxon period (Wade 2000; Medlycott 2011, 49–59) were also of some relevance, albeit that the data recovered for these periods were extremely limited and consequently proved to be of comparatively little value in addressing current research priorities.

For the Iron Age, the Love's Farm project had the potential to address the following research topics identified by the original and revised research agendas (Bryant 2000, 16; Medlycott 2011, 30–31):

chronology, with particular reference to the investigation of datable pottery assemblages;

development and nature of the agrarian economy;

settlement chronology and dynamics;

finds studies, including artefact production, distribution, and associations;

processes of economic and social change and development during the late Iron Age and Iron Age/Roman transition.

For the Romano-British period, the following research topics (Going and Plouviez 2000, 21–2; Medlycott 2011, 46–48) were considered to be of potential significance:

food consumption and production, with particular reference to the agricultural regimes and other activities practiced on Romano-British rural sites;

rural settlements and landscapes, and, in particular, the chronology of the extensive systems of fields and other relict landscape features across the region;

Romano-British rural settlement, including evidence for occupation during the late Roman/early post-Roman transitional period;

the character and development of 'Romanisation' within the region.

The original research agenda also set out some areas of research which cut across chronological boundaries. Paramount amongst these, from the perspective of the Love's Farm project, was the need for further research into the origins, character and development of settlement on the region's claylands (Brown *et al.* 2000, 45–6), which remained poorly understood at the time the research agenda was compiled. Other research topics of relevance to the Love's Farm project can be summarised as follows:

agricultural developments during the Iron Age;

the origins and development of field systems; their change and continuity;

production and exchange in the Iron Age, Roman and Anglo-Saxon periods;

analysis of prehistoric human remains.

Local research priorities
Local research objectives that have been highlighted recently and which are relevant to this project include investigation of the use of handmade versus wheelmade pottery on prehistoric sites in the region. Project-specific research objectives identified during the excavation and post-excavation assessment included the need to determine the physical character and morphology of the ritual elements of the site; and to examine how and why they developed and declined. It was also hoped to analyse the social structure of the communities in as far as they were visible within the archaeological remains and to improve understanding of the environment and economy of the site through artefactual, environmental and stratigraphic analysis, related to contemporary sites in the region.

Chapter 2. Neolithic and Early Bronze Age (Periods 1 and 2)

by John Zant and Mark Hinman

I. Introduction
(Fig. 2.1)

Whilst a relatively substantial assemblage of Neolithic pottery and broadly contemporary flint artefacts was recovered from the site, direct archaeological evidence for activity during this period was largely restricted to a few truncated pits and localised soil deposits. Most of the remains were concentrated in two areas, one situated towards the northern end of the site, the other a little over 600m to the south-west. Both locations were naturally sheltered parts of the site that also attracted later prehistoric settlement. Small amounts of residual pottery and flints recovered from later deposits across the site also suggests the possibility of more widespread, but dispersed, activity over much of the investigated area. The artefact assemblages indicate that most of the activity occurred during the earlier Neolithic, but limited evidence for late Neolithic occupation was also found.

Evidence for Bronze Age occupation was restricted to a small assemblage of early Bronze Age pottery, well over half of which came a single well or waterhole in the north-eastern part of the site. No trace of middle to late Bronze Age activity was evident, and it would appear that intensive use of the Love's Farm site did not begin until the middle Iron Age.

II. Period 1: Neolithic (*c.* 4000–2500 BC)
(Figs 2.2–2.3)

Neolithic activity in the northern part of the site (Fig. 2.2) was focused on a sheltered natural hollow located near the crest of the hill, where a pit (*661*: not illustrated) containing three early Neolithic sherds was recorded when the site was evaluated. This feature was not relocated during the excavation, but it probably formed part of a larger, irregular natural hollow containing two layers of pale brown silty clay (*11115* below *11114*). This hollow was roughly sub-rectangular in plan, measuring *c.*10m long, east to west, 2.3–2.6m wide, and up to 0.21m deep. Deposits *11114* and *11115* yielded 92 sherds of earlier Neolithic pottery and a small assemblage of worked flint. Layer *11114* was subsequently cut by a small, sub-circular pit (*11117*), *c.*1 x 1.1m and 0.3m deep, which contained four sherds of early Neolithic pottery and two fragments of worked flint.

In addition to these features and deposits, a few shallow, irregular features of probable natural origin were recorded in the same area (*e.g. 11119* and *11120*). All were undated, but several contained small fragments and flecks of charcoal and burnt clay, suggestive of human activity nearby. Several Neolithic flint artefacts also occurred residually in later deposits on this part of the site, including a finely made plano-convex knife.

Over 600m to the south-west, further evidence for Neolithic activity was recorded within another sheltered natural hollow (Fig. 2.3). Here, a layer of dark soil (*7357*), *c.*4.5 x 1.8m and 0.15m thick, containing eight sherds of early Neolithic pottery, was cut by a small, roughly circular pit (*7444*), 0.6–0.7m in diameter and 0.38m deep containing numerous cobbles/stones at its base. This feature produced an assemblage of 182 sherds of early Neolithic pottery, primarily from plain bowls, as well as a serrated flint knife (SF 3373). Immediately north of the pit was a short, north to south-aligned gully or sub-rectangular pit (*7393*), *c.*0.8 x 0.3m and 0.25m deep, which also cut layer *7357*. Approximately 5m to the east were two further small pits or short gullies (*7144*, *7146*), situated less than 1m apart. Both measured *c.*0.8–1 x 0.3–0.4m and were 0.2–0.3m deep, with wide, U-shaped profiles and mid-grey-brown/yellow-orange silty clay fills. Pit *7144* contained thirteen early Neolithic pottery sherds, similar in character to those from the adjacent features and deposits. However, feature *7146* yielded nineteen sherds of Peterborough ware, indicating a late Neolithic date for its infilling.

III. Period 2: Bronze Age (*c.* 2500–800 BC)
(Fig. 2.2)

Evidence for Bronze Age occupation was extremely slight: although forty sherds of early Bronze Age pottery were found, more than half of these came from a single feature, a probable well or waterhole (*11136*; Waterhole 1) located in the north-eastern part of the site, only 12m south-west of the northernmost focus of Neolithic activity represented by deposits *11114/11115* and the features that cut them. The well/waterhole was sub-circular, 1.7m in diameter, and at least 1.5m deep (it could not be bottomed), with near-vertical sides. The lower excavated fills were largely sterile silty clays, and it was the uppermost fill (*11113*) which yielded all the pottery.

Elsewhere, evidence for possible early Bronze Age activity was confined to a single sherd of Beaker pottery from the sheltered natural hollow in the southern part of the site that also provided evidence for Neolithic activity (*7357*). The rim of a large Collared Urn with cord-impressed decoration was recovered during trial-trenching in the same area. The Beaker fragment came from a thin (0.04m) layer of dark soil (*7356*; not illustrated), covering an area of approximately 7.5 x 3m, that overlay some of the Neolithic features and deposits in this area (soil layer *7357*, pit *7444*, and pit/gully *7393*).

While there was no evidence for middle Bronze Age activity, evidence for the late Bronze Age was limited to a few worked flints that may date to this period (see Bishop, Chapter 6.I).

Figure 2.1 Period 1: Neolithic and Bronze Age features and deposits. Scale 1:5000

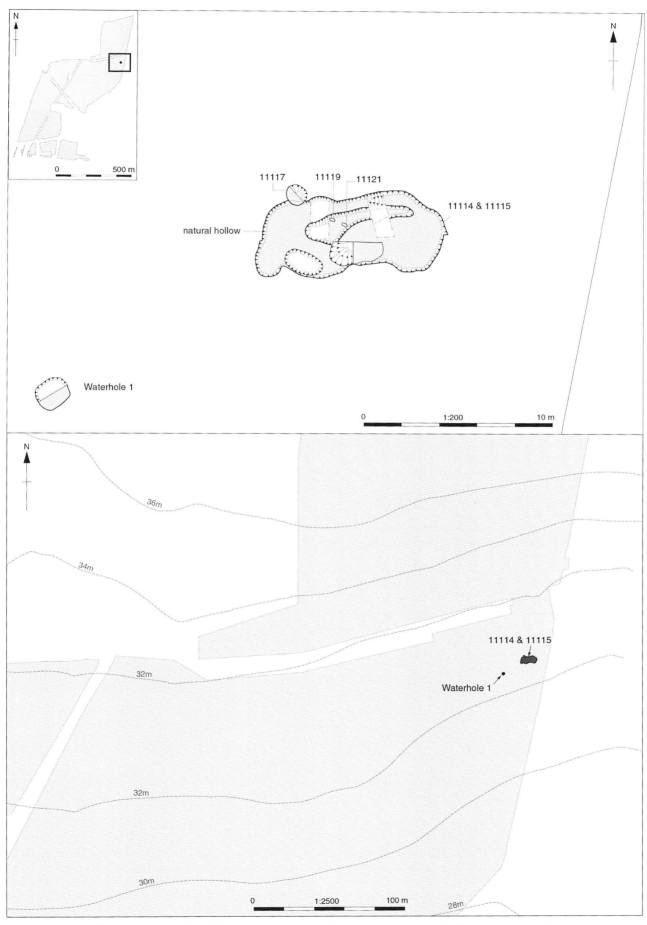

Figure 2.2 Periods 1 and 2: Neolithic activity in natural hollow, showing early Bronze Age well/waterhole 1.
Scale 1:200 and 1:2500

IV. Discussion: origins

Early activity

The earliest evidence for human activity at Love's Farm comprises a single micro-burin, of a type usually associated with the manufacture or repair of Mesolithic microlithic equipment (Bishop, Chapter 6.I), which came from an Iron Age ditch. Whilst this was the only unequivocal Mesolithic artefact recovered, the occurrence of a high proportion of prismatic blades within the flint assemblage possibly indicates a more extensive presence during this period, although this material (which was also residual or unstratified) might equally be of early Neolithic date. An overview of the local landscape and wider context at this time appears in Chapter 9.II.

Activity during the early Neolithic was focused on two parts of the site; one to the north, within a sheltered, south-facing hollow later occupied by an Iron Age settlement (Settlement 1), the other in a similarly sheltered location to the south, occupied during the Iron Age by Settlement 3. In addition, a number of tree-throw hollows were recorded across the site. Most of these contained no finds and could, therefore, belong to any chronological period, but a few yielded early Neolithic pottery and flints, suggesting that they were cleared at this time. The two activity foci comprised clusters of small pits and/or hollows filled with layers of brownish silty clay. Almost three-quarters of the early Neolithic pottery recovered from the site came from three features/deposits associated with these foci (layers *11114* and *11115* to the north, and the fills of pit *7444* to the south), with smaller quantities deriving from most of the other features and deposits in these areas. Small amounts of flintwork were also recovered from both areas, mostly comprising a few simple cutting tools (principally flakes) and some knapping waste (Bishop, Chapter 6.I). The early Neolithic ceramic assemblage (391 sherds in total) mostly consists of plain, flint-tempered bowls, with simple rounded, rolled, or folded rims (Percival, Chapter 7.II), although a sherd of somewhat later Mildenhall ware also came from deposit *11114*. The collection is similar in character, and probably also in date, to early Neolithic assemblages from sites in the Ouse Valley such as Eynesbury (Mepham 2004), where early Neolithic ritual monuments and other features were scientifically dated to the period from the 5th to mid-4th millennium BC (Allen *et al.* 2004, 66). The dominant flint-tempered fabric found at Love's Farm is also characteristic of Neolithic ceramic assemblages from East Anglia as a whole (Percival, Chapter 7.II).

With the exception of the pits, which are of unknown purpose, no other occupation features, such as hearths, were found, and no trace of any structures was recorded. The paucity of 'structural' evidence may, however, be the result of truncation, since the character of the flint assemblage is strongly suggestive of a 'domestic' or 'settlement' context, indicating that the two sites should probably be regarded as more than temporary encampments (Bishop, Chapter 6.I); the relatively large pottery assemblages recovered from both areas would be consistent with this view. The flintwork includes a large proportion of retouched pieces, especially edge-trimmed flakes and scrapers, which form the largest category of retouched implements at many early settlement sites in the area, including several in the adjacent stretch of the Ouse Valley. A variety of forms is also represented, indicating that implements suitable for a wide range of activities were being manufactured and repaired on the site. Furthermore, raw materials included flint obtained from alluvial gravels, suggesting that resources were transported to the site from the adjacent river valleys. The diversity of the assemblage is accentuated by the tip of a leaf-shaped arrowhead and two axes. One of the latter is probably a product of the Great Langdale industry in Cumbria, and had clearly been traded over a considerable distance before reaching the site. The axes are notable for being found in what was seemingly a 'domestic' context, since regionally they are more commonly associated with ceremonial or 'ritual' sites, although some were presumably used for – and lost or discarded during – 'day-to-day' activities, such as forest clearance (Clay 2002, 30). Unfortunately, both of the Love's Farm specimens were residual, meaning that the circumstances of their original deposition at the site cannot be established. The putative Langdale axe had, however, been heavily used prior to deposition, having been worked down from a larger implement, perhaps on more than one occasion, and re-polished (Bishop, Chapter 6.I), which attests both to its longevity and value.

Despite the slight nature of the Neolithic remains and their restricted extent (those to the north were confined to an area of no more than *c.*10 x 5m, whilst the southern activity focus measured up to *c.*9 x 3m), occupation may have extended over a considerable period of time, since both areas also yielded evidence for activity during the later Neolithic and early Bronze Age. To the north, the evidence comprised the discovery, within the general area, of a late Neolithic/early Bronze Age plano-convex knife, which occurred residually in a later deposit (Bishop, Chapter 6.I), and a single well or waterhole (Waterhole 1), located close to the northern occupation focus, which yielded parts of two Collared Urns from its upper fill. In view of its steep, near-vertical profile and relatively small size (*c.*1.7m diameter), this feature was probably unsuitable for watering livestock, and may, therefore, have had a domestic purpose, although no other evidence for Bronze Age settlement was noted in the vicinity. To the south, a small pit or short gully (*7146*) containing late Neolithic Peterborough ware was located on the eastern periphery of the occupation area. Evidence for early Bronze Age activity here was restricted to the recovery of two pottery sherds, another Collared Urn fragment and a Beaker sherd, from a thin layer of dark soil overlying some of the early Neolithic features. Two arrowheads, an oblique example of late Neolithic date and an early Bronze Age barbed and tanged arrowhead, also occurred residually within later features.

The possibility that some of the early strip fields (Field System 1) were Bronze Age in origin is considered in Chapter 3.

Conclusions

Evidence for early prehistoric activity at Love's Farm represents a useful addition to the body of data pertaining to the earliest settlement of the area. Finds of late Mesolithic flints suggest opportunistic visits by hunter-gatherer groups, whilst Neolithic/early Bronze Age settlement was seemingly characterised by periodic visitations to two sites over an extended period. The latter is consistent with the view that settlement in the region remained semi-permanent well after the introduction of farming in the early Neolithic. The implications of the new findings in terms of their wider context are discussed in Chapter 9.II.

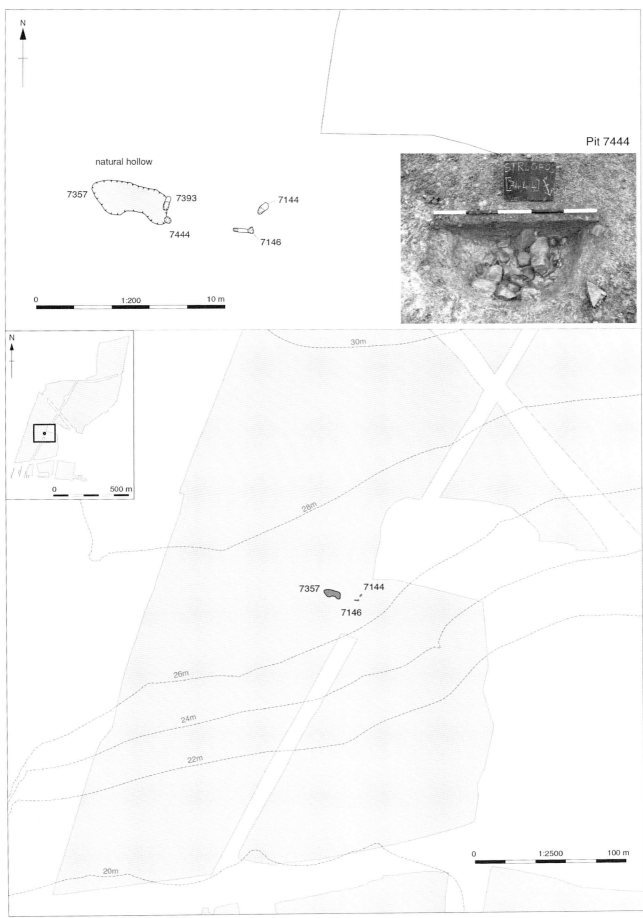

Figure 2.3 Period 1: Neolithic activity in natural hollow. Scale 1:200 and 1:2500

Chapter 3. Middle to Late Iron Age (Period 3)

by John Zant and Mark Hinman,
with Taleyna Fletcher, Sarah Henley, Liz Muldowney, Tom Phillips and Alexandra Pickstone

I. Introduction

Following limited activity during the Neolithic and early Bronze Age, the evidence recovered from Love's Farm strongly suggests that occupation of the site did not commence in earnest until the middle Iron Age, some time after *c.*400 BC. From this date, settlement of the site appears to have been continuous through the late Iron Age and the Romano-British period and perhaps beyond, with its focus gradually shifting southwards. In the middle and later Iron Age, settlement was largely dispersed, with a clear tendency for nucleation during the late Iron Age that was to intensify in the Romano-British period. Within the Iron Age occupation sequence, three principal sub-divisions could be identified, broadly corresponding to the middle Iron Age (Periods 3.1–3.2), the late Iron Age (Periods 3.3–3.4), and the transitional period between late Iron Age and early Romano-British (Period 3.5).

The preferred locations for the earliest settlers, clustered into eight identified settlements or farmsteads, were shallow natural depressions on south-facing slopes, ideally those with an easterly aspect. Twenty-four roundhouses were found, some set within ditched enclosures, others seemingly unenclosed. These structures were associated with a wide variety of other features, lying within a developing framework of fields, tracks, paddocks and agricultural enclosures. In order to bring the clay pastures into a suitable condition for arable farming and habitation it was necessary to control drainage, primarily through ditch digging. Such activity also served to reinforce and gradually redefine boundaries and began the process of enclosure. The water-retaining properties of the clay meant easy access to fresh water, and waterholes were dug periodically to collect and store surface water, presumably at those times when the adjacent seasonal stream (the Fox Brook) was not flowing.

The physical remains of the Iron Age inhabitants of the site took the form of twenty-one burials (thirteen inhumations and eight cremations). These were scattered across the site, either in isolation or in small cemeteries, the largest of which comprised only six inhumations. A single middle Iron Age inhumation, dated to the 4th–2nd centuries BC, was recorded, the remainder of the graves being of late Iron Age or late Iron Age/early Romano-British date. The placement of possibly 'votive' items or deposits within other features such as ditch terminals was noted, although evidence for 'ritual' behaviour was generally scarce at this time, and is for the most part likely to represent what might be regarded as everyday practice or superstition on the part of individuals or the wider community.

II. Periods 3.1–3.2: middle Iron Age (*c.*400–100 BC)

Introduction
(Figs 3.1–3.2)

Fragmentary remnants of a possible system of strip fields were found across the site (Period 3.1–3.2; Field System 1), the origins of which may lie in the Bronze Age or early Iron Age, but the lack of dating evidence from them and the general absence of finds of this date from the site has been taken to indicate a middle Iron Age origin. These fields were associated with three parallel tracks or droveways, which themselves linked the fields to the surrounding area and were to form the framework for the development of the site throughout its history. Two large enclosures of unusual form were found on the crest of the hill in the northern part of the site and may have performed agricultural or perhaps ceremonial functions.

On the extreme north-western edge of the site, a sub-square ditched enclosure (Enclosure 8, Period 3.2), was laid out adjacent to Routeway 1, its southern boundary ditch respecting the position of the track. To the north-east lay a small, nucleated settlement (Settlement 1) which consisted, in its original form, of a cluster of at least four roundhouses (Roundhouses 1, 2, 4 and 5) associated with (but lying outside) a small, C-shaped enclosure (Enclosure 150). The north-western limit of the settlement may have been defined by a double-ditched boundary (Boundary 6), but this did not fully enclose the settled area. The excavated remains covered approximately 0.27ha, but the full extent of the occupied area is unknown, since it clearly extended east of the excavation area. The settlement was placed on a sheltered, south- facing and relatively level part of the hillside, which had already attracted activity in the Neolithic, and continued to be developed and occupied into the late Iron Age (Periods 3.3 and 3.4). No further evidence for middle Iron Age activity was found in the northern part of the site, north of Routeway 2.

To the south, considerably more remains of middle Iron Age settlement were recorded. One of the most notable features in this area was a major north to south aligned boundary ditch (Boundary 1), which was traced across much of the southern part of the site.

South of Routeway 2, two roundhouses (Roundhouses 9 and 10) provided the principal focus for middle Iron Age activity within Settlement 3. Surrounding both structures was a poorly preserved and extremely fragmentary system of ditched enclosures (Enclosures 4, 151–155). Roundhouse 9 was sited directly over one of the north to south aligned field boundary ditches of Field System 1 (Field Line 3). However, no element of the settlement had any direct relationship with Boundary 1, which appears to have terminated (presumably deliberately) to the north

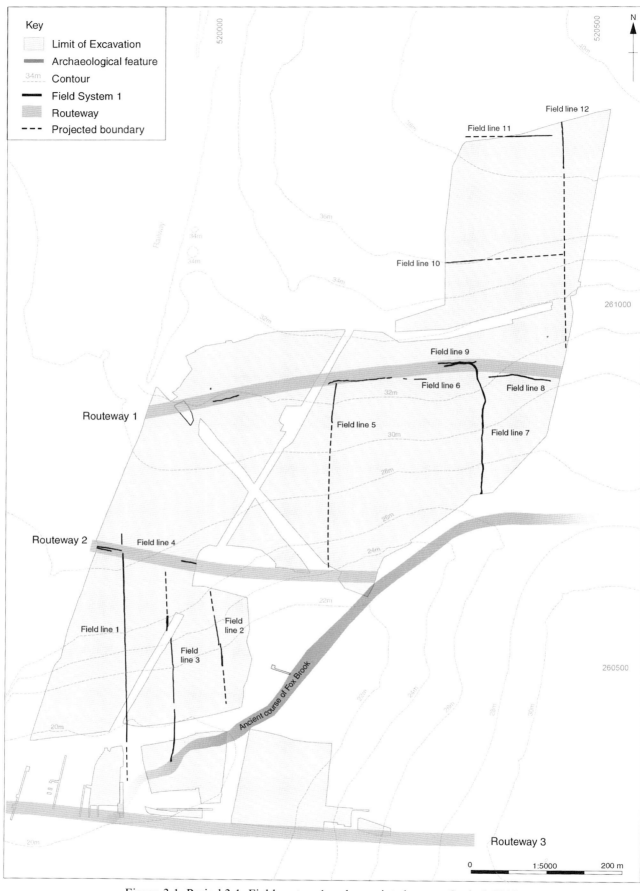

Figure 3.1 Period 3.1: Field system 1 and associated routes. Scale 1:5000

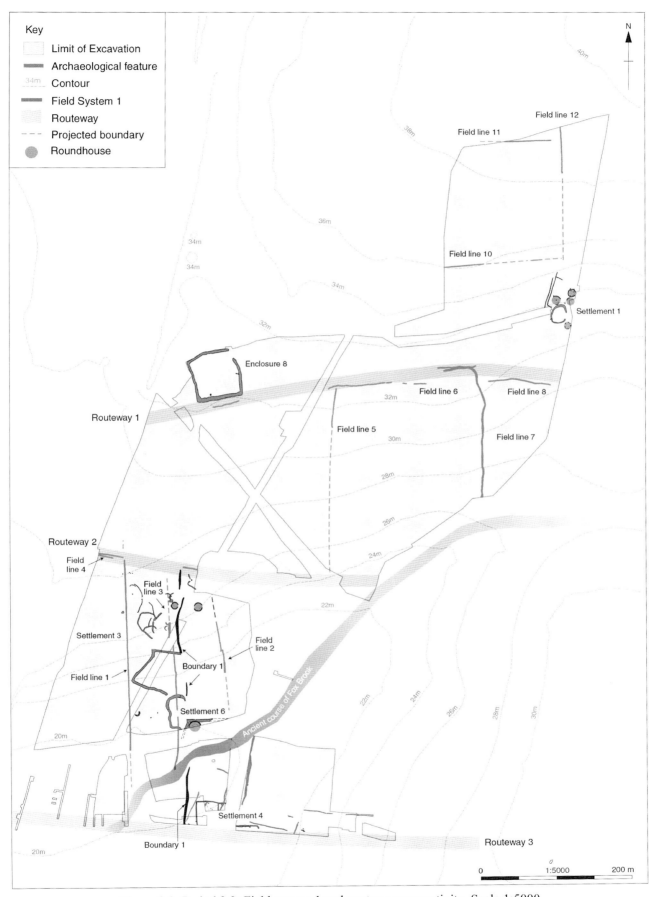

Figure 3.2 Period 3.2: Field system 1 and contemporary activity. Scale 1:5000

and south of the main focus of the settlement. To the south, the boundary ditch was dug on the line of Field Line 3, but north of the settlement it followed a new line, several metres east of the old field boundary. The fact that Boundary 1 does not appear to have extended through Settlement 3, but terminated either side of it, suggests that the settlement was already in existence when the ditch was dug, unless its absence in this sector was due to truncation. With the exception of a large waterhole (Waterhole 2), located immediately north-west of Roundhouse 9, few other features of certain or possible middle Iron Age date were recorded, although the site remained a focus for settlement into the late Iron Age.

Another roundhouse, and further fragmentary ditched enclosures, were recorded less than 100m to the south on a slight south-facing slope above the north bank of Fox Brook (Settlement 6). It seems likely that these two 'settlements' actually represented related foci for activity within a dispersed pattern of settlement extending over much of the south-eastern part of the site, including a few possibly contemporary features located south of Fox Brook (Settlement 4). Initially, Settlement 6 appears to have contained only a single roundhouse (Roundhouse 14), located within the north-western corner of a ditched enclosure (Enclosure 2), the greater part of which lay outside the investigated area, or had been destroyed, although its western arm appears to have referenced the position of Boundary 1, the major north to south aligned boundary ditch that extended across much of the southern part of the site. The roundhouse remained in use, and was rebuilt or repaired on no less than five separate occasions before the end of the Iron Age.

Immediately west of Enclosure 2 were the remains of an irregular, possibly oval, enclosure (Enclosure 1), which also seems to have referenced the position of Boundary 1, and to the north-west of this was a rectilinear enclosure (Enclosure 156), the north-western corner of which lay in close proximity to Enclosures 4 and 153 within Settlement 3. A short stretch of curving ditch located south of Enclosure 156 and west of Enclosure 1 may have been all that remained of another small, curvilinear enclosure (Enclosure 5). Approximately mid-way between Enclosures 1 and 5, an inhumation burial was also found, radiocarbon dated to the middle Iron Age (see below).

Field System 1 and Routeways 1–3
(Fig. 3.1)
The ditches constituting Field System 1 were generally poorly preserved, having been destroyed by later features over much of the site: they survived best towards the south-west corner of the area investigated, and to the north and east (Fig. 3.1). These fields appear to have been long and narrow, aligned north to south, and were traced across most of the site, although the surviving remains were extremely fragmentary. Morphologically, such strip fields might be considered to be Bronze Age, but with the exception of a small assemblage of possible late Bronze Age flint (all of which was either residual or unstratified; Bishop, Chapter 6.I), no pottery or other finds of the later Bronze Age or early Iron Age were found and the early ditches themselves were entirely undated, other than the fact that some were cut across by middle Iron Age features.

The individual ditches (Field Lines 1–12) were up to 1.2m wide and 0.75m deep, but were frequently considerably narrower and shallower as they survived; none yielded any finds. On the south-western part of the site, the putative fields may have been approximately 60–70m wide, and were at least 270m long, although so few of the boundary ditches were seen (only parts of three north–south-aligned features, Field Lines 1–3, and a single, fragmentary, east–west-aligned feature (Field Line 4)) that it is difficult to be certain. To the north, the remains were so fragmentary that no estimate of the width of the fields could be made, although it may be significant that the four ditches running east to west recorded in this area (Field Lines 8 and 10–11) were seemingly spaced at intervals of $c.$160m.

The field system appears to have been laid out between a series of east–west-aligned tracks or droveways (Routeways 1–3), positioned to take advantage of natural changes in the slope of the hillside. Each was approximately 10m wide. Two of these (Routeways 1 and 2) were spaced $c.$250–270m apart, whilst the third (Routeway 3) is presumed to have lain approximately 350m south beneath the modern road (the Cambridge Road, B1428) which formed the southern boundary of the investigated area and perhaps itself lay on the line of a Roman road (Margary Road 231). Confirmation of an early origin for these routes was provided by two of the east–west-aligned ditches of Field System 1 (Field Lines 4 and 8), which respected their positions.

Enclosure 8 (Phase 1)
(Figs 3.2–3.3; Pls 3.1–3.3)
Mirroring the northern edge of Routeway 1 on the crest of the hill was a large, sub-square ditched enclosure (Enclosure 8). This was the largest enclosure of any period recorded on the site, measuring $c.$55–60m internally in each dimension, and enclosing an area of approximately 2880m^2 (Fig. 3.3, Pl. 3.1). Where best preserved, the broadly U-profiled enclosure ditches were up to 3m wide and 1.15m deep (Fig. 3.3; Pl. 3.2), although truncation and other disturbances had reduced their size and depth in many areas. Fills were predominantly mid-yellowish brown silty clays, similar in nature to the local natural clay. The position of an entrance was marked by a gap at the north-east corner of the enclosure ditch, the eastern arm of which terminated some 12m short of the northern ditch, which also ended in a rounded terminal. A second entrance may have existed in the south-eastern corner, but any evidence for its presence was obscured by later recuts (see Phase 2 below). The weathered appearance of the upper parts of the ditches suggests that they had remained open for some time, silting up gradually, largely through weathering and other natural processes. The enclosure seemingly remained in use into the late Iron Age, when its boundary ditches were redefined (Periods 3.3 and 3.4).

Only a few small features were found within the interior of Enclosure 8. One of the most substantial was a large, sub-rectangular pit (*2451*), 2.7 x 1.7m and 0.78m deep, located in the eastern part of the enclosure. Only traces of the original fill (*2373*) had survived around the edges, as the feature was subsequently re-cut (as *2364*; Pl. 3.3). This recut contained nine fills, the first seven of which appeared to represent discrete dumps. The upper fill (*2363*) was probably a post-use deposit that had accumulated in the hollow above the disused pit. The fourteen sherds of Iron Age pottery recovered from this feature were of similar character and date to those from the

Plate 3.1 Aerial view of Enclosure 8 and Boundary 10, looking north-west (Period 3.2)

Plate 3.2 Section through ditch *2332*, part of the primary perimeter ditch of Enclosure 8, looking east (Period 3.2), showing later recut *2221* (Period 3.3)

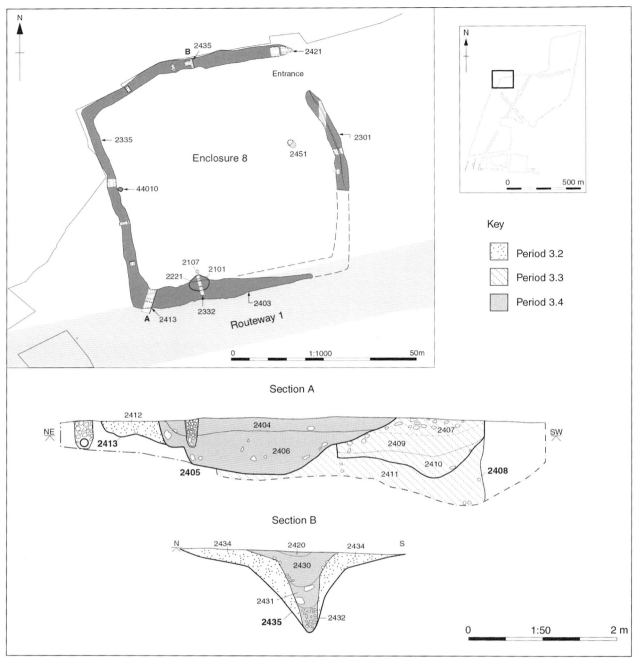

Figure 3.3 Period 3.2: Enclosure 8. Plan scale 1:1000; section scale 1:50

Plate 3.3 Section through pit *2364*, one of the internal features within Enclosure 8, looking south-east (Period 3.2)

enclosure ditch itself. On the western edge of the enclosure was a pit (*44010*) with a possibly conical profile, 2 x 1.6m and 0.9m deep. The eastern side of the pit had an eroded upper edge perhaps indicating a point of access, whilst its profile suggests that it may have been dug to catch and store rainwater. To the south, another pit (*2107*), 1.23m in diameter and 0.8m deep, yielded several sherds of middle Iron Age pottery, and a third pit (*2101*), located adjacent to pit *2107*, had been truncated when the enclosure ditch was redefined in the later Iron Age. Despite the presence of these pits, the overall paucity of internal features, together with a lack of charcoal and other anthropogenic material within the enclosing ditches, suggests that Enclosure 8 was not a focus for domestic occupation. Its precise function therefore remains uncertain and it may have been associated with stock enclosure or with some form of ceremonial use (see further discussion below and in Chapter 9.IX).

Settlement 1
(Fig. 3.4)

Enclosure 150
The C-shaped enclosure (Enclosure 150), measuring up to 21m north to south by 18m east to west internally (Fig. 3.4), was defined by a flat-bottomed, V-profiled boundary ditch 0.8–1.4m wide and 0.55–0.77m deep. An entrance into the enclosure from the east was marked by a gap in the ditch *c.*8.25m wide, on both sides of which the ditch ended in rounded terminals. In the southern part of the enclosure ditch, a saddle quern (Percival and Shaffrey, Chapter 6.VI; SF 2718) had been placed, perhaps deliberately, with its worked side face down against the base of the cut. Although this enclosure remained in use into the late Iron Age (Period 3.3), very little evidence for activity within it was found, and the ditch yielded relatively few finds. An agricultural function therefore seems likely, although precisely what this may have been is not clear.

Boundary 6
A pair of parallel ditches, set 2m apart, was traced north-east to south-west for a distance of approximately 50m (Fig. 3.4). These features were 0.5–0.8m wide and 0.25–0.32m deep, with roughly U-shaped profiles. In the south, the boundary appears to have terminated adjacent to Enclosure 150, with the innermost (eastern) ditch turning inwards (*i.e.* south-eastwards) through almost 90°, to terminate *c.*2.75m short of the outer lip of the enclosure ditch. Some 40m north of this, a short length of ditch, *c.*10m long, also branched off to the south-east from the inner ditch. However, this terminated abruptly, and there is no evidence that it ever fully enclosed the northern side of the settlement. It is possible that the upcast from the double ditches may have been used to create an internal hedge-bank, thereby providing a more substantial boundary, but no trace of this had survived.

Roundhouse 1
A roundhouse (Roundhouse 1) was located approximately 5m south-west of Enclosure 150, just south of the enclosure's eastern entrance (Fig. 3.4). It is possible, although in the absence of dating evidence it cannot be proven, that this building represents the earliest Iron Age structure on the site, since its post-built construction was quite different to that of all the other excavated roundhouses, the structural remains of which invariably comprised what were either foundation trenches or eaves-drip gullies, in some cases associated with a few internal postholes. Alternatively, the distinctive construction technique employed in Roundhouse 1 may reflect a function distinct from the remainder of the contemporary buildings on the site, although there is no hint of this from the surviving evidence. Whatever the case, the recovery of a few sherds of middle Iron Age sand- and quartz-tempered pottery from some of its postholes indicates that the building did not significantly pre-date any of the other Period 3.1–3.2 activity on the site. An additional 79 sherds of very similar pottery were also recovered from a pit (*11053*) located to the south-west of the roundhouse.

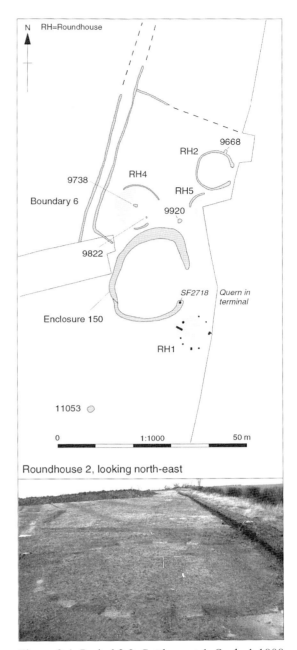

Figure 3.4 Period 3.2: Settlement 1. Scale 1:1000

The structure was 8–9m in diameter, its walls marked by a series of roughly circular postholes, each 0.2–0.4m in diameter and 0.06–0.28m deep. The fact that additional postholes or stakeholes were located immediately adjacent to at least three of these features suggests that some wall-posts may have needed replacing, or perhaps bracing, during the lifetime of the building. A rectangular pit, 2m x 0.53m and 0.19m deep, was located on the projected wall line on the western side of the structure. The function of this feature is unclear, but it was filled with cobbles, which might have served as packing around a vanished upright or may indicate a function as a drain/soakaway. No internal features or deposits were recorded, and no definite evidence for an entrance (or entrances) was found, although spacing of the wall-posts suggested that the most likely location for a doorway was on the south-east.

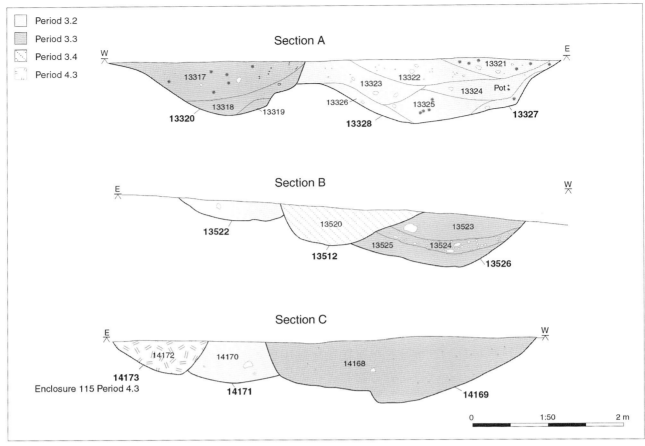

Figure 3.5 Period 3.2: Boundary 1, selected sections (located on Figure 3.7). Scale 1:50

Roundhouse 2
A second building (Roundhouse 2), which lay 35m north of Roundhouse 1 and *c.*14m north-east of Enclosure 150, had an internal diameter of 9.8m, its walls being defined by a continuous foundation trench or eaves-drip gully, up to 0.7m wide and 0.22m deep (Fig. 3.4). A break in the trench, marked by rounded terminals, demonstrated that a single entrance, *c.*0.6m wide, had existed on the eastern side of the building, but this had been largely destroyed by a later enclosure ditch (Period 3.3, Enclosure 6). There was evidence of maintenance in the form of re-cutting in two places along the gully/trench. Internally, no floor or occupation deposits had survived, but a pit (*9668*) cut the outer lip of the eaves-drip or foundation trench on its northern side. This oval feature, which could well have been dug up against the outer face of the wall, measured *c.*1 x 0.7m and 0.17m deep, and also contained a small amount of Iron Age pottery.

Roundhouse 4
Another structure (Roundhouse 4) was located 11m south-east of Roundhouse 2, but little more than a metre north of Enclosure 150. It had been severely damaged by later Iron Age features (Fig. 3.4), but enough remained to demonstrate that it was 11.6m in diameter internally, with a foundation trench or eaves-drip gully surviving to 0.5m wide and 0.1m deep. Although only two fragments of the gully/trench survived, the eastern end of the southern fragment was clearly a rounded terminal, indicating that the entrance lay on the south-east side of the building. Two possible internal features were found, although these were undated and it is possible that they were unrelated to the roundhouse. They comprised a roughly circular clay hearth base (*9822*), 0.25m in diameter and 0.08m deep, located near the entrance, and a possible cooking pit (*9738*) situated towards the centre of the structure. The pit contained many heat-affected sandstone cobbles.

Roundhouse 5
Nestled between Roundhouse 2 and Enclosure 150, a short fragment of a curvilinear gully or trench, 5m in length, represented the only surviving remains of Roundhouse 5 (Fig. 3.4). This feature, which lay on the north-western side of the building, was 0.45–0.8m wide and 0.3–0.37m deep; its curve, when projected, suggests that Roundhouse 5 was approximately 10m in diameter. No internal features or deposits were recorded.

An isolated, sub-circular pit (*9920*), 1.1m in diameter and 0.3m deep, was located between Roundhouses 4 and 5, and could conceivably have been associated with one of these structures. Its lower fill, a mid-grey/green silty clay with occasional charcoal flecks, was overlain by an upper fill of dark brownish-grey silty clay containing moderate charcoal lumps and flecks and frequent large cobbles. An assemblage of 44 sherds of middle Iron Age pottery was recovered from this latter deposit.

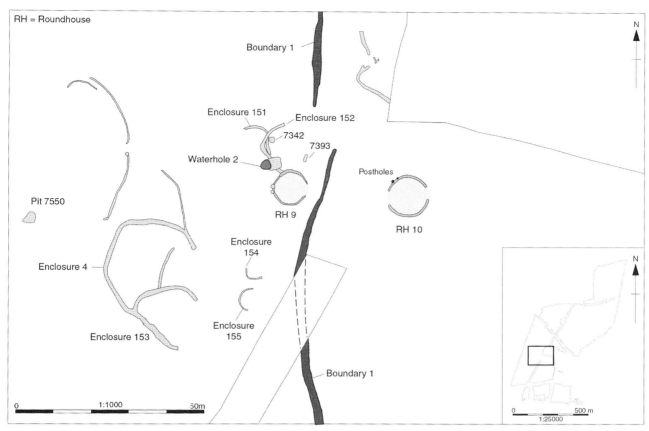

Figure 3.6 Period 3.2: Settlement 3. Scale 1:1000

Boundary 1
(Figs 3.2 and 3.5–3.7)
Extending north to south across much of the south-eastern part of the site was a substantial ditch (Boundary 1). This feature appears to have originated in the middle Iron Age, but had been so extensively re-cut and re-defined in later periods that very little trace of its original form had survived. In places, it was dug on the line of one of the north to south aligned boundary ditches that formed part of Field System 1, but for the most part it followed a new line, several metres east of the old field boundary. Where best preserved, at the extreme southern end of the site, the primary ditch was up to 1.2m wide and 0.9m deep, with a variable profile (*13328, 13327, 13522, 14171*, Fig. 3.5; *11365*, Fig. 3.7).

Settlement 3
(Fig. 3.6; Pl. 3.4)

Enclosures 151 and 152
Pre-dating Roundhouse 9 were the fragmentary remains of two possible small ditched enclosures (Fig. 3.6). The earliest (Enclosure 151) was represented by a curvilinear ditch, which ran from south-west to north-east for approximately 15m before curving westwards to run for a further 7m. The ditch was 0.85–1.75m wide and up to 0.75m deep, with a flat-bottomed, V-shaped profile. Finds included middle Iron Age jars/bowls (see Chapter 7, Fig. 7.5, Nos 1 and 2).

Enclosure 151 was cut by an L-shaped ditch, possibly the north-west corner of a curvilinear or rectilinear enclosure (Enclosure 152) that had been otherwise largely destroyed. This ran from south-east to north-west for *c*.10m before turning north-east through almost 90° to run for a further 8m. Its ditch was of similar size and appearance to that associated with Enclosure 151. A circular pit (*7342*) was located immediately inside the boundary ditch of Enclosure 152, but it is not known whether it was associated with either of the enclosures in this area, or with Roundhouse 9 immediately to the south.

Enclosures 4, 153, 154 and 155
Some 30m south-west of Enclosures 151 and 152 lay another enclosure (Enclosure 4) that was seemingly attached to the northern side of another enclosure (Enclosure 153; Fig. 3.6). It appears to have been roughly semi-circular in plan, *c*.20–23m in diameter, and was defined by a curving boundary ditch, 0.85–1.75m wide and between 0.3–0.75m deep. Adjacent Enclosure 153 may have been sub-circular or D-shaped, and was *c*.15m long in each dimension internally, although its southern side had not survived. Its boundary ditch was of similar size and character to that of Enclosure 4. The latter appears to have been entered from the south-east, through a 10m-wide gap in the boundary ditch. Later, this entrance may have been narrowed to 5m or less by the digging of a ditch, which also cut across the northern boundary ditch of Enclosure 153 and ran into Enclosure 4 for several metres. It is presumed that Enclosure 153 itself was accessed from the south or east, where its boundary ditch had been destroyed, as no gaps in the ditch were evident to the north or west.

North of Enclosure 4, a few narrow, curving ditches were recorded, at least one of which seems to have run

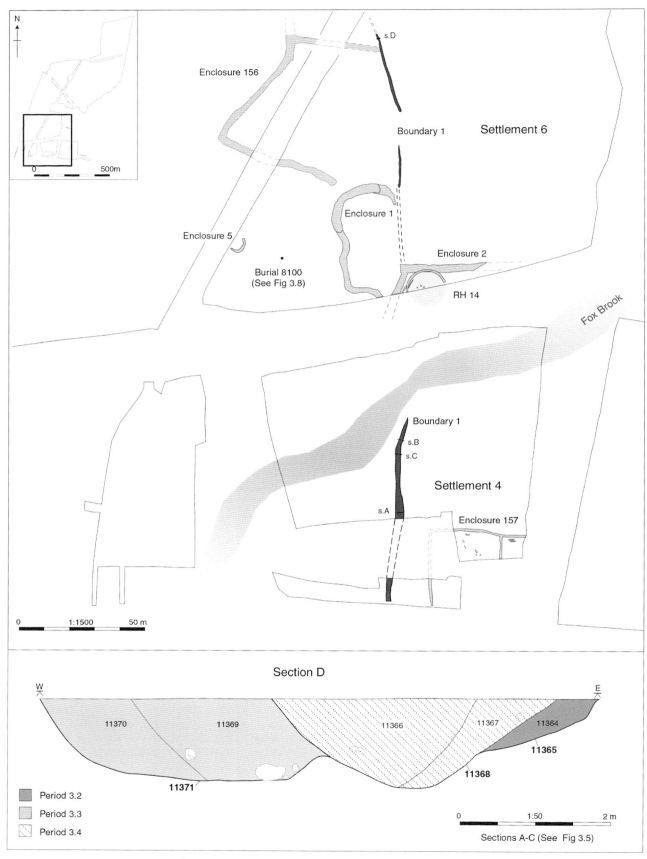

Figure 3.7 Period 3.2: Settlements 4 and 6. Scale 1:1500

Plate 3.4 Roundhouse 9, Settlement 3, looking east (Period 3.2)

north-west from the north-eastern corner of Enclosure 4 itself, if it was not an earlier feature. The significance of these ditches is not clear, but it is possible that they represented the fragmentary remains of subsidiary enclosures of broadly contemporary date. Additionally, fragments of two curvilinear ditches, interpreted as the possible remains of small livestock pens (Enclosures 154 and 155), were located c.10–15m east of Enclosures 4 and 153. One of these, of which less than half survived, appears to have been no more than 5m in diameter, whilst the other, even more poorly preserved, may have been smaller still. West of Enclosure 4 was an isolated pit (7550), which also yielded middle Iron Age pottery.

Roundhouse 9
Another building (Roundhouse 9) had been constructed over the southern ends of the fragmentary boundary ditches for Enclosures 151 and 152 (Fig. 3.6). Its walls were marked by a curving gully or trench, enclosing an internal area 8.7m in diameter (Pl. 3.4). A segment of the trench on the northern side of the structure had been re-cut once, indicating that maintenance had occurred during the building's lifetime. An east-facing entrance, 3m wide, was marked by a gap in the gully/trench on that side of the building. No internal features or deposits were recorded, but middle Iron Age pottery was retrieved from both the fill of the gully/trench itself and from two small pits which cut this feature on its western side.

Roundhouse 10
A little over 20m east of Roundhouse 9 lay another circular building (Roundhouse 10), defined by a foundation trench or eaves-drip gully enclosing an area 10.3m in diameter (Fig. 3.6). No internal deposits were recorded, but three small postholes located inside the north-western part of the building may have been all that remained of an internal setting of roof supports. Unlike Roundhouse 9, which appears to have had a single entrance on the east, Roundhouse 10 seemingly had a pair of opposed entrances on the east and west, 2m and 4m wide respectively. The single fill of the foundation trench or eaves-drip gully yielded a range of middle Iron Age pottery types consisting predominantly of sandy- and quartz-based fabrics.

Waterhole 2
A waterhole lay adjacent to Roundhouse 9, cutting across the boundary ditch of Enclosure 152, and had been re-cut twice. In its final form it was sub-circular, c.4.5m in diameter and 0.8m deep (Fig. 3.6). Its fills yielded a total of 139 sherds of middle Iron Age pottery, including some scored sherds. A nearby oval pit (7393), 1.23 x 0.8m and 0.38m deep, also contained fifteen sherds of middle Iron Age pottery.

Settlement 6
(Fig. 3.7)

Enclosure 2
Only the extreme north-western corner of this ditched enclosure was available for excavation, the rest either lying outside the investigated area or having been destroyed (Fig. 3.7). The surviving fragment of the enclosure ditch was up to 2.86m wide and 1.34m deep; it was traced east to west for c.35m, then turned southwards to run for a further 10m before extending beyond the limit of the excavation. This western arm of the ditch appears to have been aligned on Boundary 1. The ditch fills were

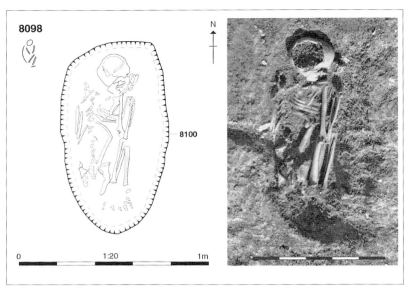

Figure 3.8 Period 3.2: Settlement 6, grave *8100*. Scale 1:20

greenish in colour, suggesting that they may have incorporated organic occupation material derived, perhaps, from the adjacent roundhouse (Roundhouse 14). An assemblage of 47 sherds of middle Iron Age pottery was recovered from the ditch fills.

Roundhouse 14
Located in the extreme north-west corner of Enclosure 2 was a building (Roundhouse 14) which lay immediately adjacent to the inner lip of the enclosure ditch (Fig. 3.7). The remains of its earliest phase had been heavily disturbed by later modifications, and only the northern half of the structure lay within the excavated area. In its earliest form, it was defined by a curving foundation trench or eaves-drip gully, suggesting a structure 9.4m in diameter. The gully was U-profiled, 0.45m wide and 9.2m deep, with steep sides and a flattish base. Its single fill yielded a sherd of quartz-tempered middle Iron Age pottery, an upper rotary quern fragment (SF 3527) and small quantities of charcoal.

Enclosures 1, 5 and 156
Immediately west of Enclosure 2 was a large curvilinear enclosure (Enclosure 1), which was oriented broadly north to south (Fig. 3.7). It measured *c.*40 x 23m internally at its greatest extent, but its eastern side was largely undefined, perhaps being indicated by the position of Boundary 1; this major boundary ditch did not survive immediately adjacent to the enclosure, but traces were found to the north, and it was considerably better preserved to the south, beyond Fox Brook. Projected south and north from these points, the line of the ditch would have passed directly down the eastern side of the enclosure.

Where best preserved, the ditches forming Enclosure 1 were large and steep-sided, measuring 2.3–3.8m wide and 1.1–1.6m deep. The northern and southern ditches cut across Field Line 3, one of the north to south aligned field boundary ditches of Field System 1, which had clearly silted-up and gone out of use before the enclosure was constructed.

A little over 35m west of Enclosure 1 was a short fragment of a curvilinear ditch, 0.8–0.92m wide and 0.3–0.54m deep, possibly all that remained of a small, curvilinear enclosure (Enclosure 5), or possibly even a roundhouse, *c.*7m in diameter.

North-west of Enclosure 1, and some 35m north of Enclosure 5, were the remains of a much larger, rectilinear enclosure (Enclosure 156), aligned roughly north-west to south-east. Only the south and west sides of the enclosure ditch could be traced, together with a short fragment of the western end of the northern arm, meaning that its full dimensions are not known; it measured *c.*50m north-east to south-west internally, and at least 45m north-west to south-east. If it had originally extended east to link up with the north side of Enclosure 1, which seems possible, it may have been approximately 50m square. The ditches were of similar size and form to those of Enclosure 1.

No internal features were found within any of these enclosures, and their precise function is unknown. They are, however, likely to have had some agricultural purpose, most probably serving as livestock pens or even, in the case of the larger examples, small fields.

Burial 8100
(Fig. 3.8)
Approximately mid-way between Enclosure 1, to the east, and Enclosure 5, to the west, lay a single inhumation grave. The burial (grave *8100*) was that of a mature woman (skeleton *8098*) of over 45 years of age, who had been interred in a tightly crouched position, lying on her left side with her head to the north. The skeleton showed evidence for osteoarthritis, and the woman had suffered from dental caries and abscesses (Dodwell, Chapter 8.I). Radiocarbon dating of the bone yielded a determination of 360–110 cal BC, placing the grave firmly in the middle Iron Age (Chapter 8.II, Table 8.3, SUERC-21982 (GU-17895)).

Settlement 4
(Figs 3.5 and 3.7)
South of Fox Brook, Boundary 1 was traced across much of the excavated area, and a rectilinear ditched enclosure

(Enclosure 157) was located a few metres to the east. This was undated, but may have been of the middle Iron Age, since it was cut across by a late Iron Age enclosure on a different alignment (Period 3.3, Enclosure 26). Enclosure 157 lay on the extreme southern edge of the site and was clearly rectilinear, but could only be partly investigated, since it extended south and east of the excavated area. Internally, it seems to have been partitioned into two by a north to south aligned ditch. The western part of the enclosure was rectangular, measuring at least 32m north to south (it extended south of the excavated area) and 28m east to west. Only the extreme north-western corner of the eastern part of the enclosure was exposed, measuring approximately 9 x 9m. The boundary ditches were 0.92–1.1m wide, and 0.35–0.56m deep. Several undated postholes lay within the western part of the enclosure, but these were arranged in no obviously coherent pattern, and two undated pits were also found – one to the west, one to the east – both located towards the north side of the enclosure.

III. Period 3.3: late Iron Age (*c*.100 BC to early 1st century AD)

Introduction
(Fig. 3.9)
Over most of the site, settlement activity seems, broadly speaking, to have intensified during the course of the late Iron Age, although this was not the case everywhere. Activity within Settlement 1, for example, on the northern part of the site, seems to have gradually dwindled, and what had been quite a significant focus for settlement in the middle Iron Age appears to have been abandoned altogether before the beginning of the Romano-British period.

Before this period, most of the significant alignments recorded on the site, including the boundaries of Field System 1, the lines of Routeways 1–3, and of major boundary features such as Boundary 1, on the southern part of the site, had tended to be broadly north to south and east to west. However, from Period 3.3 onwards, although many of these features were maintained on their original alignments into the Romano-British period, and some new enclosures, boundaries and other features continued to be laid out with reference to them, the beginnings of a change are evident, with an increasing number of features being laid out north-west/south-east and north-east/ south-west, including a new field system (Field System 2). This was particularly noticeable in the southern part of the site, where occupation clearly intensified through the course of the late Iron Age, as opposed to the north, where activity petered out during this period.

During Period 3.3 (Fig. 3.9), the perimeter ditch of Enclosure 8, which occupied the crest of the hill immediately north of Routeway 1, was re-cut, albeit possibly in a piecemeal fashion over a prolonged period, and the north-east entrance was slightly modified. As in Period 3.2, the internal area was largely devoid of features, providing little clue as to the purpose of the enclosure. Outside Enclosure 8, a substantial ditch (Boundary 10) was dug south-westwards from its south- west corner; this ran along the northern edge of Routeway 1, westwards from the enclosure to the edge of the excavation, and continued to be maintained into Period 3.4.

On the north-eastern part of the site, Settlement 1 remained in use into the late Iron Age, but there was little or no evidence for activity thereafter. The central, C-shaped enclosure (Enclosure 150) appears to have continued in use initially, since its ditches were re-cut, its southern ditch being dug on a different line, but there was little or no evidence for contemporary activity within it. Of the four excavated middle Iron Age roundhouses, Roundhouse 1 was replaced on the same site by a new building (Roundhouse 3), but the three other structures (Roundhouses 2, 4, and 5) went out of use and were not replaced, their remains being cut (in the case of Roundhouse 2), by the ditch for a new enclosure (Enclosure 6) and (in the case of Roundhouses 4 and 5) by the flanking ditches of a new track or road (Routeway 4), which crossed the north-eastern end of the site on a north-west to south-east alignment. This road also cut across the earlier double-ditch (Boundary 6) on the north-western side of the settlement, but seems, initially at least, to have respected the position of Enclosure 150. On the southern side of the road, a short distance north of Enclosure 150, lay a group of small, intercutting quarry pits (Quarry 1), and a scatter of other late Iron Age features, mostly small pits and possible postholes, was recorded across the site.

Further south, a new focus for settlement (Settlement 2) developed at the northern end of a long, rectilinear ditched enclosure (Enclosure 10) that appears to have extended north to south between Routeways 1 and 2. Occupation was clearly focused at the northern end of the enclosure, in an area measuring no more than 50m, north to south, the rest of the enclosure being apparently devoid of any traces of occupation. In Period 3.3, the main focus for activity was a single roundhouse (Roundhouse 6), located on the eastern side of the enclosure. This was associated with two linear ditches of uncertain purpose to the north and west, whilst further west was a concentration of small, scattered quarry pits (Quarry 2). At the extreme northern end of the enclosure, a cluster of three human burials (Cemetery 1) was also recorded, together with a nearby dog burial.

To the south, activity in Settlement 3 appears to have intensified considerably during the late Iron Age, with the construction of several new ditched enclosures or paddocks (Enclosures 7, 17, 14, 15, 16, 31, 159, 160), the replacement of one of the earlier roundhouses with a new building (Roundhouse 11), and the construction of four rectilinear structures, including a comparatively large, rectangular building (Structure 2), which was erected on practically the same site as the other middle Iron Age roundhouse, and two or three smaller four-post structures (Structures 3, 4 and possibly 6). A large waterhole (Waterhole 3) was located just outside Roundhouse 11, and a similar feature (Waterhole 4) was found to the south-west, between two of the new enclosures.

Boundary 1 continued to be maintained and was incorporated into the new system of enclosures. The northern ditch of the northernmost enclosure within the settlement (Enclosure 17) effectively formed the southern edge of Routeway 2 during this period, and a major boundary ditch (Boundary 8) ran westwards from it, defining the southern edge of Routeway 2 across the full width of the site. As was the case in the middle Iron Age, Settlement 3 was located no great distance north of Settlement 6, and it seems highly likely that the two were

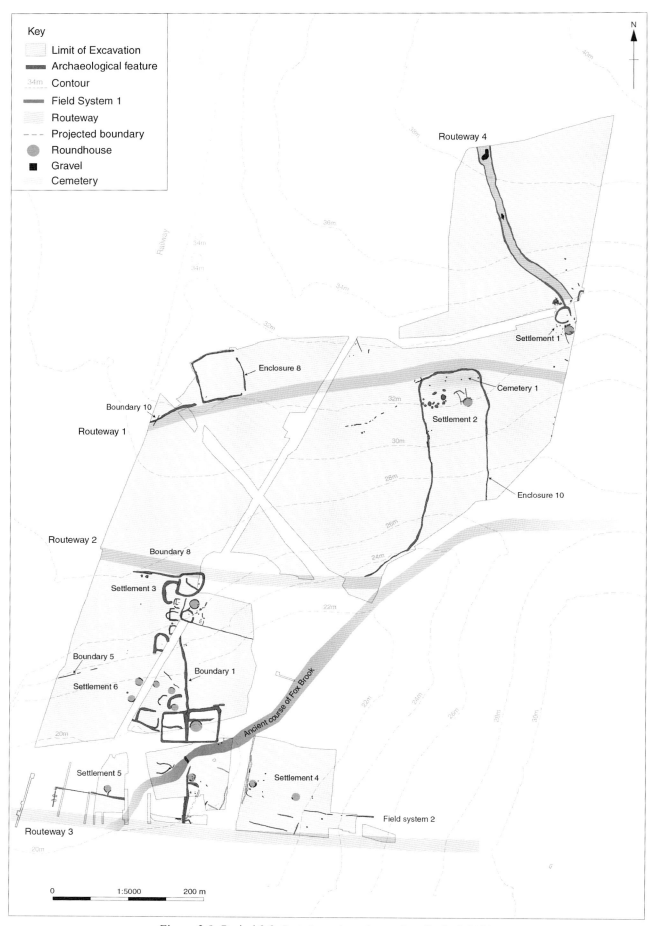

Figure 3.9 Period 3.3: Late Iron Age phase plan. Scale 1:5000

merely foci of activity within a more dispersed pattern of middle to late Iron Age settlement extending over much of the southern and eastern parts of the site.

The settlement focus on the north side of Fox Brook, which originated in the middle Iron Age, saw a marked intensification of activity during the late Iron Age. Where it passed through the settlement, Boundary 1 was redefined at this time, and a pair of opposing, sub-square enclosures or paddocks (Enclosures 11 and 13) were constructed on either side of this major boundary, immediately adjacent to the north bank of the stream. The easternmost (Enclosure 11) contained a roundhouse (Roundhouse 14) – a middle Iron Age feature that was rebuilt at this time. The western enclosure (Enclosure 13) was subdivided internally into two smaller paddocks, but contained no buildings or other features. To the northwest, five new roundhouses (Roundhouses 15–19) were built. Four of these were unenclosed, but one (Roundhouse 18) was set within a curvilinear enclosure, formed by re-cutting the north-western part of the perimeter ditch of Enclosure 1, a pre-existing feature of the middle Iron Age. Thus redefined, Enclosure 1 lay on the northern side of Enclosure 13, in the angle formed by the northern arm of that enclosure and Boundary 1. Immediately west of Enclosure 13 was a detached, rectangular enclosure (Enclosure 12), and the remains of a small, curvilinear enclosure (Enclosure 161) were recorded west of Enclosure 1. A waterhole (Waterhole 5) was located a short distance to the north-west of Roundhouse 19, and a segmented ditch of uncertain significance (Boundary 5) was recorded further north-west still, beyond the core area of settlement.

South and south-east of the main settlement focus, but still on the northern side of Fox Brook, very little evidence for Iron Age activity was found next to the stream. The best evidence came from the area to the south-west, where a single roundhouse (Roundhouse 13) lay north of a possible rectilinear enclosure (Enclosure 165). Some 4m west of the roundhouse, and conceivably associated with it, was a single inhumation burial. Following the disuse of Roundhouse 13 and Enclosure 165, this area does not appear to have been occupied again until the Romano-British period. Settlement activity also seems to have intensified south of Fox Brook in the late Iron Age (see Settlement 4), although not to the same degree as further north.

The south-western part of the site, south of Fox Brook, yielded little evidence for activity during the middle Iron Age. However, during the late Iron Age, this area saw a significant increase in occupation, mirroring the situation in Settlement 6, to the north of the stream, and appears to have become a significant occupation focus in its own right, at least for a time (Fig. 3.17). Doubtless, this activity was closely associated with Settlement 6.

Three roundhouses (Roundhouses 8, 12, and 22) were recorded in this area, all east of Boundary 1, which appears to have formed the settlement's western boundary. A second north–south-aligned boundary ditch (Boundary 3) was located east of Boundary 1, and aligned broadly parallel to it. East of this, slight traces of a rectilinear field system (Field System 2) were recorded, although very little of this had survived. Roundhouse 8 was located in close proximity to the eastern edge of Boundary 3, and Roundhouse 12 was similarly located in relation to Boundary 1. Both Roundhouses 8 and 22 appear to have been unenclosed, but Roundhouse 12 may have been situated within a rectilinear enclosure (Enclosure 26) that was added, together with a possible second, triangular, enclosure (Enclosure 164) to the eastern side of Boundary 1. It is possible that the gap between Enclosure 26 and Boundary 3 contained a track/droveway.

Enclosure 8 (Phase 2)
(Fig. 3.10)
In the northern part of the site, the perimeter ditch of Enclosure 8 was re-cut along its entire length during the late Iron Age (Fig. 3.10), although it is possible that the work was carried out in piecemeal fashion, with sections of the ditch being redefined as and when needed as part of a prolonged period of general maintenance, rather than as a single event. The northern, western and southern arms were continuous, while the eastern arm was a separate entity, due to the presence of entrances into the enclosure. The creation of an in-turned terminal (*2279*) at the eastern end of the southern arm provides good evidence for the location of a second entrance on the eastern side of similar proportions to the narrowed north-eastern entrance. At the north-east corner of the enclosure, the original entrance was narrowed slightly (from 12m to 10m), by extending the ditch terminals. That to the north (*i.e.* at the eastern end of the northern boundary ditch) was steep-sided and square, unlike the original rounded terminal. Where best-preserved, the new ditch was up to 2.98m wide and 1.85m deep, but truncation had reduced the depth to as little as 1m in places, and some segments were only 0.6m wide, as they survived. In profile, the ditch was steep-sided with a slightly rounded base (Fig. 3.10, Sections C and D), and its upper edges showed less evidence of erosion than the primary ditch, suggesting that it may have filled more rapidly. The main fills recorded in all excavated segments were relatively clean clays and, as was the case in the primary phase, suggest that the enclosure did not represent a focus for domestic activity in the late Iron Age.

Boundary 10
A substantial north-east to south-west aligned ditch (*2398=2066*) now formed the northern boundary of Routeway 1 immediately west of Enclosure 8 (Fig. 3.10). Whether it merely served to define the edge of the routeway, or formed part of a ditched enclosure attached to the western side of Enclosure 8, is not known, since very little of the area west of Enclosure 8 was available for investigation. It is possible that a gap, 8m wide, between the north-eastern end of the ditch and the south-western corner of Enclosure 8 marked the position of a causeway across the ditch, an hypothesis supported by the fact that a cobbled surface was laid within the gap in a later phase (Period 3.4). Where best-preserved, the ditch was up to 2.3m wide and 1.26m deep, with steep sides and a slightly rounded base (Fig. 3.10, Sections A and B). It was traced for 65m, but extended beyond the boundary of the site to the south-west. The primary fills clearly derived from rapid weathering of the natural clays through which the ditch had been cut, but the upper fills suggested a more stable period of gradual deposition. The lack of humic material and finds within these deposits suggests a lack of domestic activity in the vicinity.

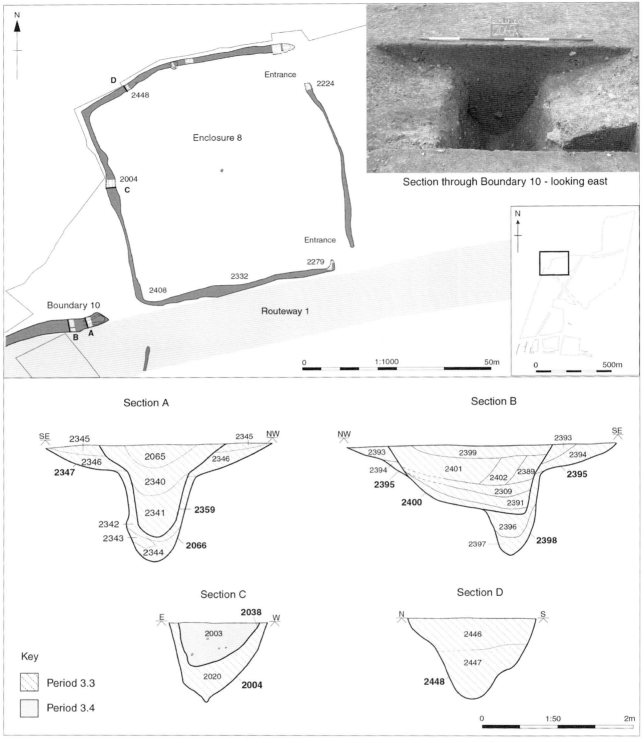

Figure 3.10 Period 3.3: Enclosure 8 and Boundary 10. Plan scale 1:1000, section scale 1:50

Subsequently, the ditch was re-defined as a wide (3m) but shallow (0.18–0.3m) feature with a U-shaped profile (*2400*). Various fills were recorded, some of which suggested gradual silting, although they were slightly darker than the fills of the primary ditch, suggesting the possibility of a higher humic content.

Settlement 1
(Fig. 3.11)

Routeway 4
A road or track (Routeway 4) was laid out on a north-west to south-east alignment, and was traced across the north-east corner of the site over a distance of approximately 275m, but extended beyond the limits of the excavation to the north-west and south-east (Fig. 3.11). Within the area of Settlement 1, it cut across the

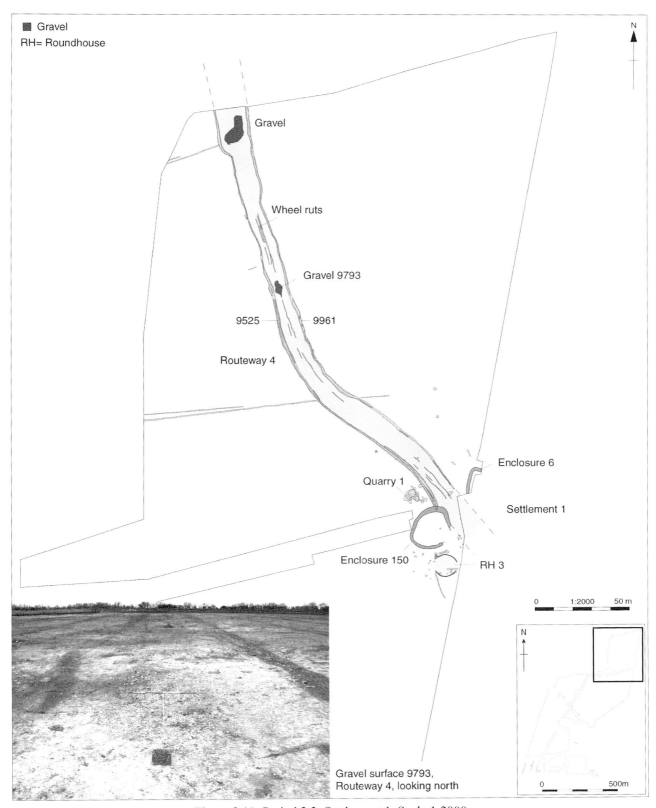

Figure 3.11 Period 3.3: Settlement 1. Scale 1:2000

sites of middle Iron Age Roundhouses 4 and 5, but appeared to respect the position of Enclosure 150, which was seemingly now attached to its southern side. For the most part, the road was *c*.10m wide, although its width varied from 9m to as much as 15m in places. The flanking ditches (*9525* to the west, *9961* to the east) were fairly narrow (0.3–1m) and quite shallow (0.07–0.4m), and meandered considerably in places, suggesting that they may have been maintained as hedgerows. Evidence for a gravel road surface survived in two places, one near the northern limit of excavation and another approximately 80m to the south (*9793*). The gravel used was a distinctive

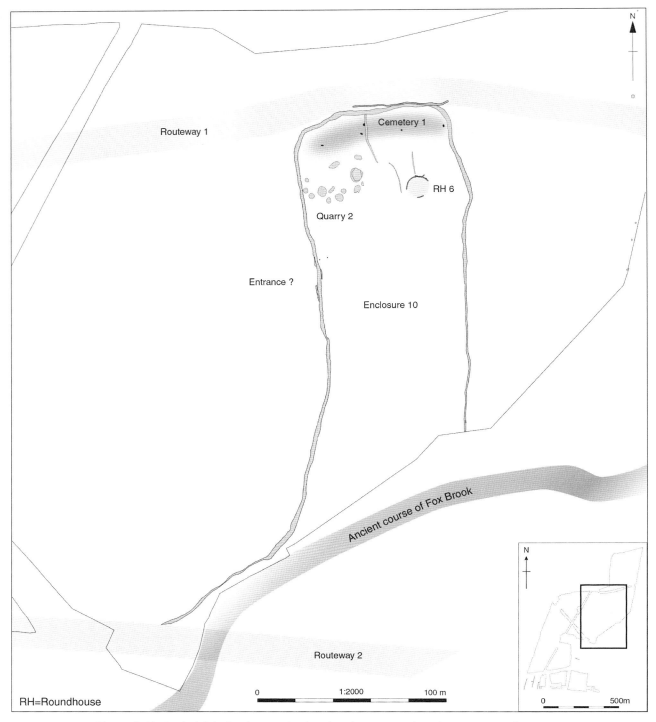

Figure 3.12 Period 3.3: Settlement 2, showing the extent of Enclosure 10. Scale 1:2000

pale colour, and may have originated from a series of late Iron Age quarry-pits located *c*.175m south-west of Settlement 1, within the area of Settlement 2 (Quarry 2). Wheel ruts were evident along much of the excavated section of the road, aligned parallel to the flanking ditches. These were generally 0.22–0.24m wide and 0.05–0.07m deep, and many contained traces of the pale gravel road metalling. In places two roughly parallel ruts were visible, whilst in others three lines of impressions had survived. Typically, when two wheel ruts were evident, the distance between them was approximately 3m. Dating evidence was scarce, but a few small sherds of late Iron Age pottery were recovered from the south-western ditch.

Enclosure 6
Immediately north-east of the road, the extreme north-west corner of a new ditched enclosure (Enclosure 6) was found (Fig. 3.11). Too little was seen for the morphology of the enclosure to be determined, and no internal features were present within the very small area available for investigation. A short stretch of the western enclosure ditch, *c*.15m long, was exposed; on the north, this turned

east through 90°, to run for a further 3m before extending beyond the excavated area. The western ditch cut across a middle Iron Age building (Roundhouse 2), demonstrating that this structure had been demolished by this time.

Enclosure 150

The perimeter ditch of Enclosure 150 was re-defined during the late Iron Age (Fig. 3.11). For the most part, the re-cut followed precisely the line of the original ditch, but to the south, the ditch was dug on a new line, 2m north of its original position. This increased the width of the eastern entrance by about a metre, to $c.9.25$m. No evidence for contemporary activity was, however, found within the enclosure, and it is presumed that, as was the case in the middle Iron Age, it had not been used for domestic occupation but had served some agricultural purpose, probably as a stock enclosure. The northern side of the enclosure was initially abutted by the south-western ditch of Routeway 4, indicating that the enclosure continued in use, but subsequently, the roadside ditch was taken across the north-east side of the enclosure. Finds from the ditch fills included an unfinished spindlewhorl (Fig. 6.48, SF 2742) and a socketed bone tool (Fig. 6.53, SF 2723).

Roundhouse 3

Lying to the south of Enclosure 150 was a building (Roundhouse 3) that was 12.2m in diameter, and was defined by an eaves-drip gully or foundation trench, 0.22–0.43m wide and up to 0.28m deep (Fig. 3.11). To the west, the gully had been truncated, but a gap 5m wide marked the position of an entrance in the usual position on the eastern side of the building. No internal floors or occupation deposits had survived, but a cluster of four postholes and stakeholes located just inside the southern terminal of the eastern entrance could have been associated with the structure. Immediately north of these, extending east to west from the interior of the building through the south side of the entrance, was a short, U-profiled ditch or long trench, 6m long, 0.6–0.83m wide and 0.2–0.33m deep. The purpose of this feature is not known, nor is it certain that it was associated with the roundhouse, since it had no stratigraphic relationship with the building's gully/foundation trench.

Externally, a number of features were recorded that may, from their spatial relationship with the structure's encircling gully/foundation, have been contemporary with it. On the south, a shallow ditch ran south-east for 15m from the south-western part of the roundhouse gully. The purpose of this is not known, but it may possibly have been a drainage feature designed to carry away water from the vicinity of the building. The position of several pits and possible postholes on the western side of the building, which appeared to respect the curve of the roundhouse gully, also suggests that these features may have been dug when the building was in use.

Quarry 1

Lying to the north-west of Enclosure 150 and less than 4m south-west of the southern ditch of Routeway 4, was a cluster of 11 small, intercutting quarry pits (Quarry 1) (Fig. 3.11). These measured up to $c.9 \times 7.5$m at their greatest combined extent, and were presumably dug for extraction of the natural clay, either for building works or some other purpose.

Settlement 2
(Figs 3.12–3.13)

Enclosure 10

Approximately 125m south-west of Settlement 1 was a long, rectangular ditched enclosure (Enclosure 10), that was established during the late Iron Age. The irregular curve of the enclosure's plan may reflect the local contours and the position of the Fox Brook, just to the south-east. The northern end of the enclosure extended over the former line of Routeway 1, its northern ditch seemingly following, at least approximately, the line of an east to west aligned ditch (Field Line 9) on the northern side of the routeway, that had formed part of Field System 1 (Period 3.1; Fig. 3.1). Routeway 1 was evidently redefined to run slightly north of its original position at this time, skirting round the northern limit of the enclosure. The western and eastern perimeter ditches of Enclosure 10 were also seemingly dug approximately on the lines of two north to south aligned field aligned ditches (Field Lines 6 and 7) within Field System 1, indicating that these features remained visible into the late Iron Age. To the south, the enclosure extended beyond the excavated area, but it apparently respected the line of Routeway 2. It therefore appears to have measured approximately 295m, north to south, and was $c.72$–84m wide.

Evidence for the earliest phase of the enclosure ditch was sparse, presumably since it had been largely destroyed by later recuts on the same line. However, three short stretches of the western perimeter ditch survived, and these seemingly marked the position of an entrance into the enclosure on this side. The terminal ends of the northern and southern ditch segments were set 10m apart, but access was restricted by the central ditch segment which effectively created two narrower gaps, each $c.3$m wide. This central ditch was also set back $c.2$m east (*i.e.* inside of) the line of the other two segments, presumably as a further measure to control access. Two postholes located immediately inside the northernmost ditch segment could conceivably have been associated with the entrance.

Roundhouse 6

In the north-eastern part of the enclosure lay a roundhouse (Roundhouse 6) which was 11.1m in diameter, and survived as a fragmentary eaves-drip gully or foundation trench, 0.22–0.4m wide and 0.06–0.13m deep (Fig. 3.13), of which only four segments had survived. No internal features or deposits were recorded, and no convincing evidence for an entrance was noted, but it is likely that this was located on the eastern side of the building, as was the case in all the other excavated roundhouses where the evidence had survived. A mixed assemblage of middle to late Iron Age pottery was recovered from the fills of the gully/trench.

Two NNW to SSE oriented ditches lay immediately north and west of the roundhouse and may have been contemporary with the building since, like Roundhouse 6, they were subsequently cut by the perimeter ditch of a small enclosure (Period 3.4, Enclosure 158). The easternmost example measured 12.5m in length and the westernmost 17.5m: both were narrow and shallow features, the fills of which contained fragments of fired clay but no datable artefacts. Three shallow pits (*6143, 6147, 6191*), ranging between 0.12–0.35m deep, were

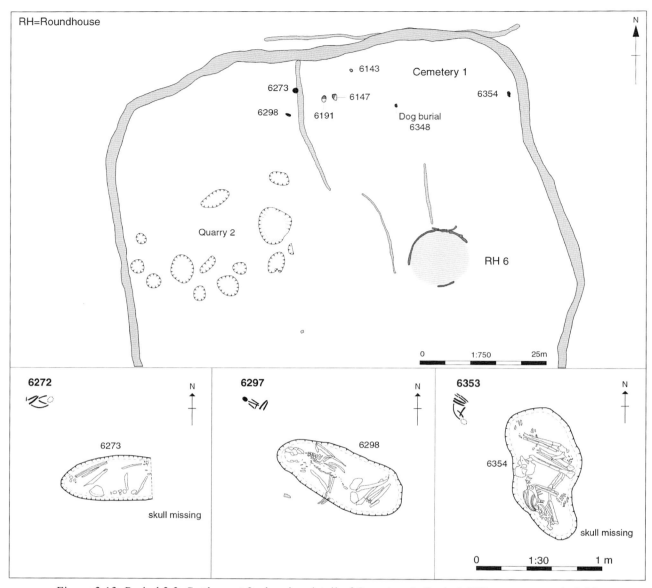

Figure 3.13 Period 3.3: Settlement 2, showing detail of Cemetery 1. Scale 1:750, graves at scale 1:30

located north of the roundhouse. Each contained a layer of burnt or fire-cracked cobbles and a large amount of charcoal, suggesting that they were either cooking pits or rubbish pits that contained debris from nearby hearths.

Quarry 2

Approximately 25m west of Roundhouse 6 was a group of thirteen small quarry pits (Fig. 3.13), that had clearly been dug for the extraction of a distinctive white gravel. The area of quarrying in this phase covered an area measuring approximately 40m^2, and none of the individual pits intercut, although extraction intensified markedly later (Period 3.4). The pits were predominantly located within the limits of the outcrop of glacial gravels, with several discrete pits on the periphery of the area and a greater concentration towards the centre of the outcrop. There was some variation in the form of the quarry pits; most were circular or sub-circular and fairly narrow and shallow, although three examples were larger and deeper, measuring up to c.7.5 x 5.5m and 0.72m deep. The homogeneous appearance of the fills suggests that the pits were quickly backfilled with topsoil. The pottery assemblage from these features includes middle Iron Age and late Iron Age material, with a small amount of intrusive mid-2nd century AD material also present.

Cemetery 1

Three inhumation burials formed a small cemetery (Fig. 3.13): two adjacent graves (*6273, 6298*), located c.35m north-west of Roundhouse 6, a few metres inside the northern boundary of Enclosure 10, and a third (*6354*) situated towards the north-east corner of the enclosure, just over 40m east of the other burials and c.30m north-east of the roundhouse. A dog burial (*6348*) was also located in this area. The graves were all sub-rectangular, 1.04–1.07m long and 0.36–0.53m wide. They were uniformly shallow, only 0.04–0.1m in depth, having been badly truncated by later ploughing. Orientation and burial position varied. Burial *6298*, aligned north-west to south-east, was that of a young adult of unknown sex, who had been buried in a semi-flexed position, with the head to the north-west. Grave *6273* contained a poorly-preserved

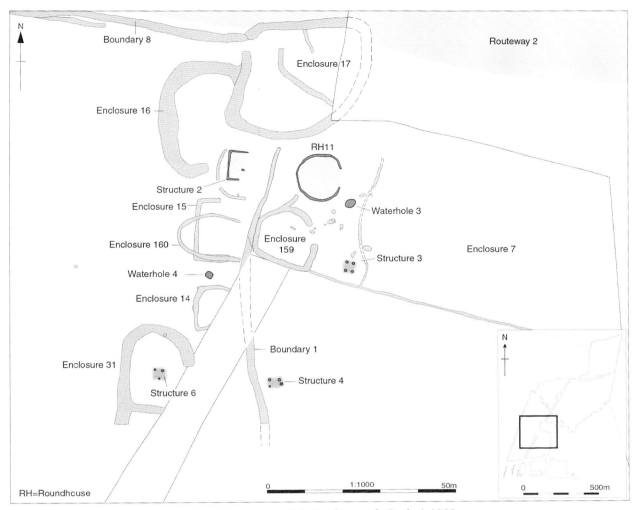

Figure 3.14 Period 3.3: Settlement 3. Scale 1:1000

young adult of indeterminate sex, buried in a crouched position on its right-hand side and on an east–west alignment, although the eastern end of the grave had been removed by a later ditch. Burial *6354* contained a semi-flexed adult female, lying on her right-hand side and orientated south to north. The dog burial (*6348*) had been set in a pit 0.55m in diameter, which survived to a depth of 0.08m. It had been heavily disturbed by a post-medieval field drain, and only a few vertebrae and long bones survived.

Boundary 1
(Figs 3.5, 3.7, 3.9 and 3.14–3.15)
Established in the middle Iron Age, this major north to south aligned boundary ditch was maintained throughout the late Iron Age (Fig. 3.5, *13320, 13526, 14169*; Fig. 3.7, *11371*). Extending from the southern side of Routeway 2, the ditch ran southwards through Settlements 3 and 6, before continuing south beyond the limits of the excavation (Fig. 3.9). In the late Iron Age, the ditch appears to have become an integral part of the layout of Settlement 3. To the south, it was extended northwards to the edge of a new enclosure (Enclosure 17), and itself served as the western boundary of another enclosure (Enclosure 7), which seems to have been the focus for the most intensive activity at this time (Fig. 3.14).

Further south, within the area of Settlement 6 (Fig. 3.15), the original, middle Iron Age, form of Boundary 1 was re-cut as a substantial ditch in the late Iron Age. In this phase, it ran north to south across the whole of the settled area, and enclosures or paddocks were laid out on either side of it. Some of these contained roundhouses, and further unenclosed roundhouses were also located west of the boundary. On the southern side of the settlement, the ditch was reworked to create an entrance, 2.7m wide, across Boundary 1. The rounded ditch terminals on either side of this entrance were 2.3m wide and 0.33m deep (northern) and 1.9m wide and 0.53m deep (southern). The boundary ditch was also re-cut on the extreme southern edge of the site, in the area of Settlement 4. There it was up to 3.6m wide and 0.92m deep.

Settlement 3
(Fig. 3.14; Pls 3.5–3.7)

Enclosure 7
A large enclosure formed the eastern element of Settlement 3 at this time, although its full extent is unknown, since it extended north and east of the site (Fig. 3.14). It was probably rectangular, measuring in excess of 100m north-west to south-east, and at least 47m wide. Within the excavated area, its western edge was defined by

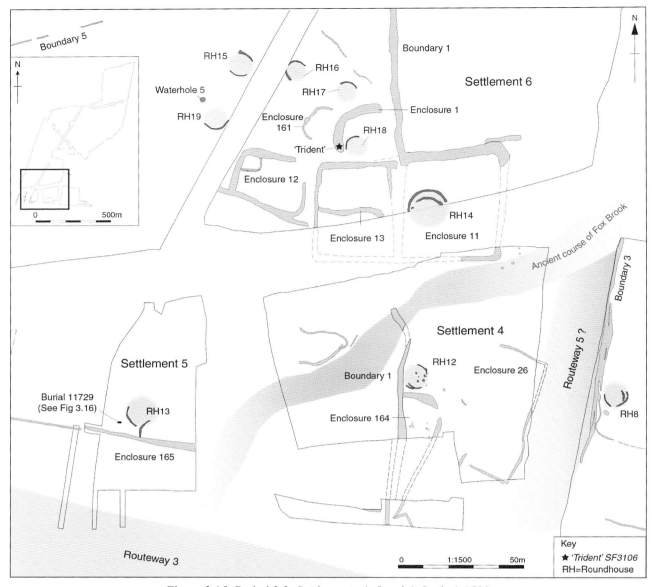

Figure 3.15 Period 3.3: Settlements 4, 5 and 6. Scale 1:1500

Boundary 1, and its north-west corner was formed by the south-western part of the perimeter ditch for Enclosure 17. A probable entrance, c.3m wide, was located at the north-west corner, marked by a gap between the northern end of Boundary 1 and the perimeter ditch of Enclosure 17. The southern boundary of Enclosure 7 was marked by a fairly insubstantial ditch, 0.5–0.8m wide and 0.17–0.37m deep.

Internally, the north-western end of Enclosure 7 appears to have been separated from the rest of the enclosure by a segmented ditch, 0.5–0.7m wide and 0.29–0.48m deep, which ran north-east to south-west, broadly parallel to the enclosure's western perimeter (marked by Boundary 1). Three ditch segments, each approximately 6m long, lay within the site, separated by gaps 4–5m wide. This area, which measured only 25–30m wide internally, was clearly a focus for intensive activity during the late Iron Age, since it contained all the occupation features recorded within Enclosure 7. The eastern part of the enclosure measured c.70 x 47m within the limits of the excavation and may have served as a paddock or small field. Occupying the south-west corner of Enclosure 7 was a small, sub-circular enclosure (Enclosure 159), to the north of which lay Roundhouse 11 and Waterhole 3, together with a seemingly random scatter of pits. South-east of Enclosure 159 lay one of the four-post structures erected during this phase (Structure 3).

Enclosure 159
Set in the south-western corner of Enclosure 7 (Fig. 3.14), this small, sub-circular enclosure encompassed an area of approximately 166m^2, measuring c.14 x 13m internally, and was accessed from the north-east via an entrance, 5m wide. The perimeter ditch was 1.5–2.07m wide and 0.66–0.95m deep; unsurprisingly, given the close proximity of Roundhouse 11, the presence of bone and charcoal within the ditch fills indicates nearby domestic activity. The assemblage of predominantly middle to late Iron Age pottery recovered from the ditch comprises over 100 sherds, including at least two semi-complete vessels, from the southern entrance terminal; another fairly large

Plate 3.5 Roundhouse 11, Settlement 3, looking south (Period 3.3)

assemblage, that contains a near-complete storage vessel, was also recovered from the northern terminal. Examples of the Iron Age forms appear in Fig. 7.7–7.8, Nos 14 and 19–22.

With the exception of a shallow pit of uncertain significance, and two shallow features located within the entrance (which need not necessarily have been contemporary with the use of the enclosure), no internal features or occupation deposits were recorded.

Roundhouse 11
Approximately 5m north-east of Enclosure 159 lay Roundhouse 11, and a direct association between the two was suggested by the fact that a short ditch spur, c.4m long, ran off the northern side of the enclosure ditch, terminating little more than 1m short of the roundhouse (Fig. 3.14). The building may have been a direct replacement for Roundhouse 10 (Period 3.2), since it partly overlay the remains of that middle Iron Age structure. It was 12.2m in diameter, and was defined by a curvilinear eaves-drip gully or wall foundation trench, 0.3–0.45m wide and 0.05–0.18m deep (Pl. 3.5). An entrance, 5m wide, lay on the east side of the building, through which a roughly cobbled surface had been laid. Traces of this had only survived where it had settled over part of the infilled gully/foundation trench for Roundhouse 10; elsewhere, it had been completely removed by later truncation, together with any other occupation deposits that may have accumulated within the building.

Waterhole 3
This feature, located c.3m south-east of Roundhouse 11 (Fig. 3.14), was a sub-circular, V-profiled pit, with steep sides (eroded towards the surface) and a flat base. It measured c.2.8m in diameter and was 1.6m deep. The two lower fills consisted of silty clays, while the upper fill had a higher humic content.

Structure 3
Structure 3 was one of two, or possibly three, four-post structures erected in Settlement 3 during this period, the others being Structure 4 and (possibly) Structure 6, both of which were located outside Enclosure 7, to the south and south-west (Fig. 3.14). Structure 3 was situated c.8m south-east of Enclosure 159 (c.18m south-east of Roundhouse 11), and measured approximately 2.2m square (Pl. 3.6). The four postholes were roughly circular, 0.55–0.75m in diameter and 0.42–0.51m deep. The western pair were sloped to the east, indicating that the uprights they had contained were inclined to the east, whilst those on the east sloped to the west. If this was not a product of the removal of the posts when the structure was dismantled, it suggests that the superstructure was pitched. Whilst some carbonised grain was recovered from some of the postholes, it has been suggested, from the presence of a wide range of carbonised weed seeds, that the excavated four-post structures on the site may have served as hay ricks rather than grain storage silos (Fryer, Chapter 8.IV).

Plate 3.6 Four-post structure (Structure 3), Settlement 3, looking east (Period 3.3)

Enclosures 17 and 16
The northern limit of Settlement 3 was defined by two substantial, conjoined enclosures (Fig. 3.14). The largest (Enclosure 17) was roughly D-shaped, *c.*30 x 28m at its widest points, with an entrance, *c.*3.5m wide, at its north-western corner. Its perimeter ditch was substantial, at 2m wide and 0.9m deep. Internally, it was sub-divided into two roughly equal parts (one to the south-west, the other to the north-east), by a north-west to south-east-aligned ditch. This ran into the enclosure from the south-east, but turned to run almost due north towards its northern end. However, it terminated approximately 5m short of the northern perimeter ditch, thus allowing access from the main enclosure entrance into both of the subsidiary enclosures. With the exception of a few short ditch segments of uncertain significance, no features were recorded within either part of the enclosure. Finds from the fills of the Enclosure 17 ditches included a middle Iron Age jar/bowl (see Chapter 7, Fig. 7.4, No. 8).

A C-shaped enclosure (Enclosure 16) was linked to the south-western corner of Enclosure 12. It measured approximately 25 x 15m internally, at its widest points, and was surrounded by a substantial ditch of similar size and form to the perimeter ditch of Enclosure 17. The south-eastern corner of the enclosure appears to have remained open, forming a broad entrance, *c.*12m wide, but this was partly obstructed by the enclosure surrounding a rectangular structure (Structure 2), leaving a gap only 5m wide. This, however, assumes that the structure was contemporary with the use of the enclosure, which is not certain.

Boundary 8
Running westwards from the north-western corner of Enclosure 17 was a large, east to west aligned ditch, up to 2.7m wide and 0.8m deep, which had been dug during the late Iron Age along the southern edge of Routeway 2, thereby redefining this side of the trackway (Fig. 3.14). This feature was traced across the full width of the site, but extended beyond the limits of the investigation to the east and west. The ditch, much modified, appears to have remained as a significant boundary feature into the Romano-British period, when it continued to define the southern edge of Routeway 2. Indeed, a boundary approximately on this line was maintained into modern times, surviving as a hedgerow until the commencement of the archaeological excavations in 2005, when the hedge was finally removed.

Structure 2
The wide gap at the south-east corner of Enclosure 16 was partly closed by a rectangular structure (Fig. 3.14), defined by a U-profiled gully or slot, 0.33–0.55m wide and 0.06–0.1m deep. This was traced around three sides of the structure but was absent on the east; it is not clear, however, whether this was because the structure was open on this side, or was the result of truncation, The building measured approximately 7m north to south, was 5m wide internally, and had been built on virtually the same site as Roundhouse 10, perhaps as a direct replacement for that middle Iron Age structure. Finds included a spatulate fragment of copper alloy (see Chapter 6, Fig. 6.39, SF 3446).

The structure appears to have been set within a small, curvilinear enclosure, defined by a ditch, 0.7–0.84m wide and 0.3–0.32m deep, which survived only on the southern and western sides of the building. A gap in the ditch suggests the position of a possible entrance, 2.5m wide, towards the south-west corner of the enclosure; this would have allowed access between Enclosure 16 to the north and Enclosure 15 to the south. The ditch contained concentrations of fired clay and daub which might, perhaps, have derived from the superstructure of Structure 2, together with pottery of middle to late Iron Age date.

Enclosures 15 and 160
Immediately south of the putative enclosure surrounding Structure 2 was a sub-square enclosure (Enclosure 15, Fig. 3.14), which appears to have utilised Boundary 1 as its eastern side. This enclosure measured *c.*14 x 13m, and was defined by a ditch, 1.3–1.55m wide and 0.56–0.7m deep, the north-eastern part of which had been destroyed by later ploughing. No internal features were noted within either of the enclosures.

Enclosure 15 was subsequently replaced by an elongated C-shaped enclosure (Enclosure 160), which also appears to have been appended to the western side of Boundary 1, the latter thus forming its eastern side. The enclosure measured *c.*17 x 10m at its longest and widest points and was surrounded by a ditch 0.95–1.3m wide and 0.28–0.43m deep, the fills of which contained middle to late Iron Age pottery. A gap at the north-eastern corner, adjacent to Boundary 1, may have marked the position of an entrance, *c.*3m wide.

Enclosure 14
Approximately 7m south of Enclosures 15 and 160 was another enclosure (Enclosure 14) that may also have been added to the western edge of Boundary 1 (Fig. 3.14), although this area lay outside the boundaries of the archaeological site. As it survived, Enclosure 14 measured 10m, north to south, and in excess of 7m east to west, internally, but would have been *c.*12m wide, had it extended up to Boundary 1. The enclosure ditch was 0.8–1.2m wide and 0.4–0.5m deep, with a flat-bottomed, V-shaped profile; it yielded a notable pottery assemblage, with a particular concentration evident at the north-western corner of the enclosure, including middle Iron Age jars/bowls (see Chapter 7, Fig. 7.5, Nos 5–7).

Plate 3.7 Waterhole 4, Settlement 3, looking south-west (Period 3.3)

Waterhole 4
Approximately equidistant between Enclosure 14 (to the south) and Enclosures 15 and 160 (to the north; Fig. 3.14), was another waterhole, measuring 2m in diameter and 1.2m deep (Pl. 3.7). Ceramic evidence suggests that the waterhole went out of use during the late Iron Age, a cremation burial later being inserted into the top of the feature (*6910*, Period 3.5).

Enclosure 31 and Structure 6
The southernmost element of Settlement 3 in this phase was a D-shaped enclosure (Enclosure 31), measuring *c.*20m north to south by 14m east to west internally (Fig. 3.14). No trace of an entrance was recorded, but the south-eastern corner of the enclosure lay outside the investigated area, making it likely that an entrance was located there. The only internal feature recorded was a small structure (Structure 6). Although only three postholes survived, this may have been the remains of a four-post structure *c.*3m square, located at the very centre of the enclosure. The surviving postholes were all approximately 0.3m in diameter and 0.15m deep.

Structure 4
Another four-post structure (Structure 4) was located *c.*28m east of Structure 6 (Fig. 3.14), on the eastern side of Boundary 1. This structure, which did not appear to have been situated within an enclosure and was not obviously associated with any other surviving features in the vicinity, was approximately 2.6m square. Its four postholes were *c.*0.3–0.5m in diameter and 0.2–0.4m deep, and two retained evidence of stone post-packing in the form of burnt cobbles. No datable finds were recovered from the structure, although environmental samples yielded similar results to those from Structure 3.

Settlement 6
(Fig. 3.15; Pls 3.8–3.11)

Enclosure 11
A new enclosure (Enclosure 11) was located on the eastern side of Boundary 1 (Fig. 3.15), directly opposite Enclosure 13. Internally, Roundhouse 14 (a structure of middle Iron Age origin) was rebuilt during Period 3.3. The new enclosure was sub-square in plan, measuring 42m, north to south, by 37m, east to west. The perimeter ditch was up to 2.82m wide and 1–1.1m deep, with a steep-sided, U-shaped profile and a rounded base. The three slots excavated across the ditch revealed from three to ten fills, several of which were greenish in colour, perhaps indicating the presence of organic occupation (faecal?) material, although pottery, bone, charcoal and other inclusions were relatively infrequent. With the exception of Roundhouse 14 itself, no internal occupation features or deposits were recorded. No evidence for an entrance was found, but the greater part of the enclosure ditch lay outside the excavated area.

Roundhouse 14
As rebuilt in Period 3.3, Roundhouse 14 was of considerable size, with a projected internal diameter of approximately 15m (Fig. 3.15). It was defined by a curvilinear, U-profiled eaves-drip gully or foundation trench, up to 0.9m wide and 0.4m deep, of which only the northern half survived. No trace of an entrance survived, but the building was reconstructed on two occasions (Phases 2 and 3), when the entrance was located on the

Plate 3.8 Enclosure 1, Settlement 6: southern terminal (*10747*) of perimeter ditch, looking north (Period 3.3)

north-east side of the structure. In these phases, its position was marked both by one surviving gully/trench terminal, and by a layer of stones, which had been laid over the soft fills of the earlier ring gullies. The ring gullies marking both reconstructions were of similar size and form to the earlier gully, and on both occasions the roundhouse appears to have been rebuilt on the same site, and to the same dimensions, as previously. The Phase 2 gully yielded 61 sherds of pottery, including grog-tempered wares of diagnostically late Iron Age date. Some bone, charcoal and fired clay was also present, and two large burnt stones were noted in the entrance terminal.

Enclosure 13
A rectangular enclosure (Enclosure 13), measuring 36 x 30m internally (Fig. 3.15), was attached to the western side of Boundary 1, directly opposing Enclosure 11. The perimeter ditch was up to 3m wide and 1m deep, but was considerably less well preserved over much of its excavated length, being generally narrower and shallower. Internally, the enclosure was sub-divided into two roughly equal halves by an east to west aligned ditch; a gap, *c*.4m wide, between the eastern end of this ditch and Boundary 1, may have marked the position of an entrance, giving access between the northern and southern parts of the enclosure. With the exception of this ditch, no internal features attributable to this phase were recorded. Finds recovered from ditch fills included fragments of middle Iron Age jars/bowls and an incised vessel, together with a later Iron Age storage jar (see Chapter 7, Fig. 7.6, Nos 9–12 and Fig. 7.8, No. 18).

Enclosure 1
This sub-circular enclosure was located on the north side of Enclosure 13 (Fig. 3.15), in the angle formed by the northern arm of that enclosure to the south and Boundary 1 to the east. It had originated in the middle Iron Age as a larger but irregular enclosure, the north-western part of which was now redefined through a re-cutting of the original perimeter ditch on the same line. This semi-circular recut now formed the north and west sides of Enclosure 1, its southern and eastern sides being defined by the northernmost ditch of Enclosure 13 and Boundary 1 respectively. The re-cut ditch terminated short of both Boundary 1 and the northern arm of Enclosure 13, seemingly creating two entrances into Enclosure 1 – one (12m wide) at its south-west corner, the other (6m wide) at its north-east corner. However, much of the south-western entrance would have been obstructed by Roundhouse 18, which was located immediately inside it.

Where best preserved, the re-cut ditch was 3m wide and 1.5m deep, with a steep-sided, V-shaped profile.

Plate 3.9 Detail of animal bones at the base of ditch *10747*, the southern terminal of the perimeter ditch for Enclosure 1, Settlement 6, looking west (Period 3.3)

46

Plate 3.10 Excavation of iron 'trident' (SF 3106) in ditch *10747*, the southern terminal of the perimeter ditch for Enclosure 1, Settlement 6, looking north-west (Period 3.3)

Plate 3.11 Detail of iron 'trident' (SF 3106) in ditch *10747*, the southern terminal of the perimeter ditch for Enclosure 1, Settlement 6, looking east (Period 3.3)

Between three and eleven fills were recorded in the excavated slots, with the character of some of the lower fills suggesting that they had been deposited in standing water. The upper fills were consistently darker in colour and contained moderate quantities of charcoal. Generally, the perimeter ditch yielded large assemblages of animal bone, pottery and other items, suggesting that it had been used as a rubbish tip for domestic refuse generated by nearby occupation areas. This is perhaps unsurprising, given the close proximity of Roundhouse 18 within the enclosure, and four other roundhouses (Roundhouses 15–19) located no great distance to the west. The deep southern terminal of the re-cut semi-circular ditch (*10747*; Pl. 3.8) contained an unusually diverse range of finds within several of its numerous fills. The animal bone assemblage (Baxter, Chapter 8.III) included two cattle skulls, a horse skull, and pig and sheep mandibles (Pl. 3.9), whilst other finds included a spindlewhorl (see Chapter 6, Fig. 6.48, SF 3107), a socketed bone tool made from a polished sheep tibia (Fig. 6.53, SF 3108), a triangular loomweight (Fig. 6.46, SF 3109), a ceramic object (SF 3136) and a trident-like, three-pronged iron object (Pls 3.10 and 3.11; Fig. 6.41, SF 3106). This 'trident' appeared to have been deliberately placed on the base of the ditch terminal; its precise function remains uncertain, although possible interpretations include a tool used in association with fire-dogs, or perhaps a totem (Crummy, Chapter 6.III). Pottery included an incised middle Iron age jar/bowl and a later Iron Age storage jar (see Chapter 7, Fig. 7.8, No. 16 and Fig. 7.7, No. 15).

Roundhouse 18
Set at the south-west corner of Enclosure 1, was a small building (Roundhouse 18), with a projected diameter of only 6m (Fig. 3.15). The ring gully, which survived only on the north-western side of the building, was 0.31–0.34m wide and 0.1–0.2m deep. The eastern side of the roundhouse was entirely truncated by medieval plough furrows. The relatively small size of the building may suggest that this was an ancillary structure, rather than a dwelling.

Roundhouses 15, 16, 17 and 19
These four roundhouses were located west and north-west of Enclosures 1 and 13 (Fig. 3.15), and were not themselves enclosed. Roundhouse 15 was the most north-westerly of the group, lying *c.*40m north-west of Enclosure 18. Its neighbour, Roundhouse 16, was located *c.*13m to the east, with Roundhouse 17 being situated 12–13m further south-east still, little more than 3m outside the perimeter ditch of Enclosure 1. Roundhouse 19, the most westerly of the group, was located 15m south of Roundhouse 15, and approximately 40m west of Enclosure 1.

Roundhouse 15 had been heavily truncated by a later Iron Age ditch, but is estimated to have been *c.*8.9m in diameter. Two segments of its ring gully survived, each up to 0.4m wide and 0.15m deep. They yielded a total of 75 sherds of predominantly grog-tempered late Iron Age pottery.

Roundhouse 16 had been heavily disturbed on its eastern side, but had a projected diameter of 7.95m. The ring gully was 0.31–0.48m wide and 0.13–0.21m deep, and contained three sherds of grog-tempered late Iron Age pottery.

Roundhouse 17 had two structural phases: of the primary building, only a fragment of the ring gully had survived, located on the north side of the building. This was 0.23–0.40m wide and up to 0.1m deep, and enough survived to suggest that the building had an internal diameter of *c.*9.8m. The surviving gully fragment was deepest at its western end, where it may have formed a terminal marking the northern side of an entrance facing north-west, towards Roundhouse 16. In its second phase, the roundhouse was approximately 11m in diameter, internally, with a ring gully 0.4m in width and up to 0.14m deep. This feature contained 47 sherds of predominantly grog-tempered late Iron Age pottery.

Only the southern half of the ring gully for Roundhouse 19 remained, the rest having been heavily truncated by a later Iron Age ditch, but the surviving remains demonstrate that the building was 10–11m in diameter. The gully was up to 0.45m wide and 0.15m

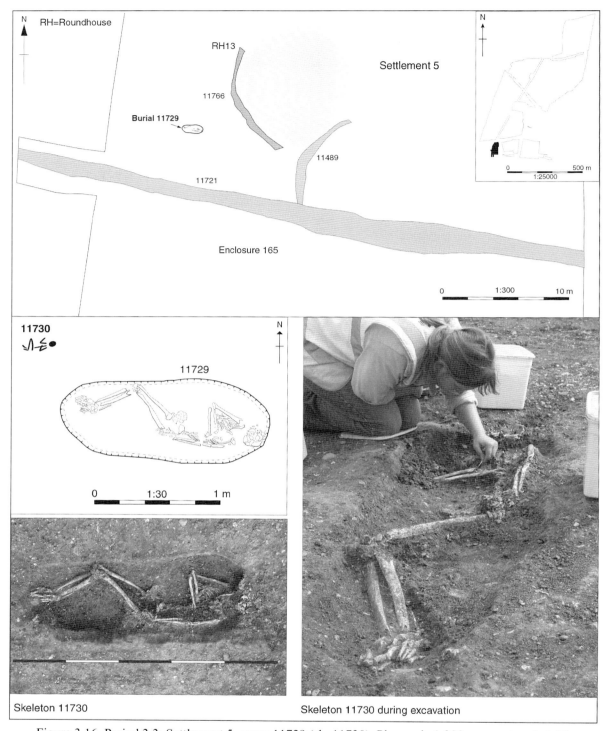

Figure 3.16 Period 3.3: Settlement 5, grave 11729 (sk. 11730). Plan scale 1:300, grave at scale 1:30

deep, and yielded a single sherd of late Iron Age pottery. No internal features or occupation deposits were recorded in any of these roundhouses, since all had been heavily truncated by later activities, particularly medieval and later ploughing.

Enclosure 12

A small, rectangular enclosure (Enclosure 12) lay immediately west of Enclosure 13, and to the south of the cluster of roundhouses (Fig. 3.15). It was aligned north-west to south-east, measuring *c*.30 x 18m internally, with a broad entrance, 9m wide, at its north-east corner. The perimeter ditch was up to 2.2m wide and 1.1m deep, and had been re-cut, in places at least, up to four times. There was a general tendency for each re-cut to occur slightly inside the line of the previous cut, with the result that the internal area of the enclosure was gradually reduced over time, although not to any very significant degree. The north-western corner of the enclosure was 'partitioned-off' by a small ditch or gully, 0.29m wide and 0.12m deep, to create a small, sub-square pen, measuring 7.3 x 6.5m. Finds from the enclosure ditches included a later Iron Age storage jar (see Chapter 7, Fig. 7.8, No. 17) and bone-working debris (see Chapter 6, Fig. 6.54, SF 3529).

Enclosure 161
A minor enclosure (Enclosure 161) was located a few metres west of Enclosure 1 but was poorly preserved, surviving only as a shallow, C-shaped ditch, which is presumed to have formed the north-western half of the enclosure (Fig. 3.15). It is possible, although evidence was lacking, that the enclosure originally extended up to the perimeter ditch of Enclosure 1; if so, it would have been roughly semi-circular, measuring *c*.13 x 10m internally. The surviving ditch segment was up to 1.22m wide and 0.29m deep.

Waterhole 5
Located 3m to the west of Roundhouse 19 (Fig. 3.15), this roughly circular feature was 2m in diameter and 0.6m deep. It yielded no artefacts, but was sealed in the Romano-British period by an accumulation of water-lain silt (Period 4.2, Chapter 4), suggesting that the area was, or subsequently became, susceptible to flooding or at least to the accumulation of standing water during wet periods.

Boundary 5
Some distance to the west of the main settled area, over 50m west of Roundhouse 15, was a narrow and shallow ditch, 0.64m wide and 0.19–0.22m deep (Boundary 5). This feature was aligned north-east to south-west (Fig. 3.15), and survived in three separate segments due to later truncation. Its direct association with Settlement 3 remains uncertain, and its significance is unclear, although it could conceivably have marked the position of hedge or other field boundary.

Settlement 5
(Figs 3.15–3.16)

Roundhouse 13
This seemingly unenclosed roundhouse was located *c*.90m south-west of Enclosure 13, and *c*.25m north-west of Fox Brook (Figs 3.15–3.16). The surviving remnants took the form of a curvilinear ring gully, which was traced for 8.3m; this appears to have formed part of the south-western side of a building *c*.10m in diameter. A short gully segment (*11489*) located south-east of this, and seemingly cutting across its line, suggested that the roundhouse may have been rebuilt subsequently. However, this feature had been heavily truncated and its precise significance could not be determined.

Enclosure 165
Approximately 6m south of Roundhouse 13 was a north-west to south-east aligned ditch (*11721=11778*; Figs 3.15–3.16). Two segments of this feature were recorded, one, 25m long, immediately south of the roundhouse, the other, 5m long, on the eastern edge of this area. Its western end was also observed during trenching to the west, where a segment 12m long was recorded. There, the ditch was seen to turn south through 90°, and was traced south for a further 18m (Fig. 3.9). It would seem, therefore, that these ditches formed the north side and north-west corner of a rectilinear enclosure (or possibly a field), measuring at least 97m north-west to south-east, and over 18m wide. This was located well to the south-west of the main focus of activity within Settlement 6, but north-west of Fox Brook, and extended beyond the investigated areas to the south and east. Finds from the enclosure ditch fills included a later Iron Age jar (see Chapter 7, Fig. 7.9, No. 25).

Grave 11729
An inhumation burial was located 4m west of Roundhouse 13 (Fig. 3.16). The east to west aligned grave cut (*11729*), 1.65m long, 0.68m wide and 0.2m deep, contained the skeleton (*11730*) of an adult male aligned with the head to the east. The body had been interred on its right side, knees slightly flexed and arms bent at the elbows, with the right hand drawn up towards the face and the left arm straight. Fragments of a copper alloy ring (SF 3305) of indeterminate function were recovered from the grave fill, but no other artefacts were found in association with the burial meaning that its precise date remains uncertain.

Settlement 4 and Field System 2
(Fig. 3.17; Pl. 3.12–3.14)

Enclosures 26 and 164
Immediately east of Boundary 1 were two enclosures (Fig. 3.17), a small, seemingly triangular example (Enclosure 164) appended to the eastern edge of Boundary 1 itself, and a larger, rectilinear, enclosure (Enclosure 26) to the east. Both followed the north-west/south-east and north-east/south-west alignment that became prevalent on the southern part of the site in the later Iron Age, in contrast to the north to south line of Boundary 1, which followed an earlier, middle Iron Age, alignment.

Enclosure 164 was defined to the north and east by ditches, and to the west by Boundary 1 itself. At its widest point, at the northern end of the enclosure, it was *c*.16m wide, internally, but it tapered gradually to nothing to the south, as a result of the oblique alignment of its eastern ditch relative to Boundary 1. Only the eastern side of Enclosure 26, and the eastern ends of its northern and southern sides, had survived, but it measured *c*.50m internally north-east to south-west, and at least 21m north-west to south-east. If it had originally extended up to abut Enclosure 164 (to the south) and Boundary 1 (to the north), it would have been *c*.55m wide at its northern end and *c*.33m wide at its southern end. It was defined by a ditch, up to 1.8m wide and 0.35m deep.

Roundhouse 12
Roundhouse 12 was located immediately north of Enclosure 164, adjacent to the eastern side of Boundary 1 (Fig. 3.17). It is presumed to have lain on the western side of Enclosure 26, tight up against the boundary marker. It was also situated little more than 20m south of Fox Brook. The roundhouse (Pl. 3.12) had been heavily truncated on its eastern and western sides by later features and the ring gully survived in three segments, one on the north-east side of the structure, and two fragments on the south side that appeared to relate to two distinct construction phases. The internal diameter of the roundhouse was 9.82m, as measured from the outermost gully on the south side (9.58m from the inner gully). The ring gully was up to 0.36m wide and 0.18m deep, with a steep-sided, U-shaped profile; its single fill yielded a total of 125 sherds of later Iron Age pottery, while the outer gully to the south also

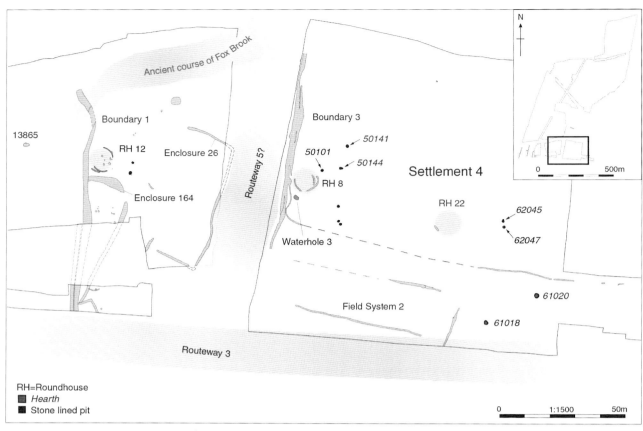

Figure 3.17 Period 3.3: Settlement 4. Scale 1:1500

contained small lumps of daub. Various stone-lined pits lay nearby.

Boundary 3 and ?Routeway 5
The section of Boundary 1 lying on the western periphery of Settlement 4 was re-cut in a slightly different form during Period 3.3, when a new ditch (Boundary 3) was also cut, 77m to the east (Fig. 3.17). The northern end of this lay adjacent to the south bank of Fox Brook, from where it was traced south for *c.*80m, but it petered out short of the southern boundary of the site. The ditch was excavated in five segments, in which three episodes of re-cutting and maintenance attributable to Period 3.3 were recorded. To its west, a possible track or droveway (?Routeway 5) may have led between Routeway 3 and the stream. At the time of the excavation, this route formed a modern track (Fig. 1.6).

Roundhouses 8 and 22
Two further roundhouses were located east of Boundary 3 and were seemingly unenclosed (Fig. 3.17). Roundhouse 8 was located adjacent to the eastern edge of Boundary 3, *c.*75m east of Roundhouse 12, and had been heavily truncated by post-medieval ploughing on its northern and southern sides. A ring gully, up to 0.5m wide and 0.27m deep, survived in three fragments, one to the west and two to the east; the latter clearly related to two separate construction phases, indicating that the structure had been repaired or rebuilt at least once (Pl. 3.13). In its primary phase, the building had an estimated internal diameter of 9.4m, but this may have been reduced to *c.*7.8m when the building was repaired or rebuilt. No gully terminals, indicative of the position of an entrance, had survived.

Associated with Roundhouse 8 was a waterhole (Waterhole 3), located 2.8m south of the building. This was sub-circular in plan, 2.3m in diameter and 1.6m deep. North and east of the building were various pits (Fig 3.17), which appeared to have functioned as hearths. Five of the pits (Pl. 3.14) formed a roughly north to south oriented line, 32m long, running approximately parallel to Boundary 3. The features (including *50141* and *50144*) were all sub-circular, varying in size from 0.55–0.75m in diameter and 0.1–0.38m deep, and all contained large quantities of fire-cracked stones. In one example, these were sealed by a soil deposit containing much orange-red burnt clay and some charcoal fragments.

Roundhouse 22, located 46m south-east of Roundhouse 8, survived only as a very short segment of a ring gully, seemingly located on the south-western side of the putative structure. The surviving gully fragment was too short for any estimate of the building's diameter to be attempted. No internal features or deposits were recorded, but two pits containing fire-cracked stones were located nearby (*62045* and *62047*). Further to the south-east was a well-preserved hearth (*61018*; Pl. 3.14), which yielded 27 sherds of Iron Age pottery; close by were three heavily truncated pits, again containing many fire-cracked stones, and another feature of this type (*61020*) was recorded some distance further east.

Field System 2
South of Roundhouses 8 and 22, the very fragmentary remains of what appears to have been a system of

Plate 3.12 Roundhouse 12, Settlement 4, viewed from the south-west (Period 3.3)

Plate 3.13 Roundhouse 8, Settlement 4, from the air, looking north-east (Period 3.3)

Plate 3.14 Stone-lined hearth pits associated with Settlement 4 (Period 3.3)

rectilinear fields, aligned WNW to ESE and defined by a series of boundary ditches, was recorded (Fig. 3.17). Only four fragmentary ditches lay within the excavated area, three parallel features aligned WNW to ESE, and another aligned at right angles to these. The system extended south and east of the investigated area, measuring in excess of c.110m, north-west to south-east, and over 35m wide. It may have been bounded on the west by Boundary 3, but this is not certain, since that feature was truncated on the extreme southern part of the site.

IV. Period 3.4: late pre-Roman Iron Age (first half of the 1st century AD)

Introduction
(Fig. 3.18)

Limited change in the pattern of settlement occurred in Period 3.4 (Fig. 3.18) – most of the earlier structures and enclosures remained in use with little or no substantial modification. In the northern part of the site, the ditch of Enclosure 8 was again re-cut at this time, but thereafter the enclosure appears to have fallen out of use. By Period 3.4, Settlement 1 seems to have been wholly or largely abandoned (although it extended eastwards beyond the area of investigation), but its accompanying track (Routeway 4) continued in use, and two small fields (Field System 3) were laid out immediately to the north.

In Settlement 2, the primary roundhouse of Period 3.3 (Roundhouse 6) went out of use, and a small, curvilinear enclosure (Enclosure 158), was constructed, the perimeter ditch for which cut through the remains of the roundhouse. Further west, the gravel extraction which commenced in Period 3.3 (Quarry 2) intensified considerably, with an expansion in the area subjected to quarrying (Quarry 3). Well preserved waterlogged plant, molluscan and insect remains were recovered from the lower fills of one of these new quarry pits. Previously, occupation had been restricted to the northern end of Enclosure 10. Now, however, activity spread further south, towards the central part of the enclosure, where a roundhouse (Roundhouse 7) was erected, seemingly within the south-western corner of a small, possibly rectangular, enclosure (Enclosure 18).

On either side of Boundary 1, Enclosures 11 and 13 remained in use, and Roundhouse 14, within Enclosure 11, was rebuilt once more. However, the other five Period 3.3 roundhouses (Roundhouses 15–19) in Settlement 6 all went out of use, as did Enclosure 1, within which Roundhouse 18 had been situated. A single, unenclosed roundhouse (Roundhouse 20) was now located west of Boundary 1, well to the north of Enclosure 13. Enclosure 12 also remained in use, its perimeter ditches being redefined and modified at this time. On the western periphery of the settlement, the extremely fragmentary remains of at least two interconnected enclosures (Enclosures 20 and 162) were located. Further west still were traces of a probable rectilinear field system (Field System 4). It is noteworthy that most of the new enclosures and boundaries followed the north-west to south-east and north-east to south-west alignment that was becoming increasingly prevalent over the southern part of the site during the late Iron Age, and which continued to develop subsequently. On the southern side of Fox Brook, the pre-existing layout was largely maintained into Period 3.4, but only the westernmost roundhouse in Settlement 4 was retained, the two eastern structures seemingly being demolished.

Enclosure 8 (Phase 3)
(Fig. 3.19)

The boundary ditches of Enclosure 8 were redefined on one more occasion before the enclosure went out of use, sometime during the late Iron Age. The re-cut ditches were slightly irregular in plan, but largely followed the line of the earlier ditches, and the north-eastern entrance into the enclosure remained essentially unchanged. Changes in this phase included the creation of a small gap

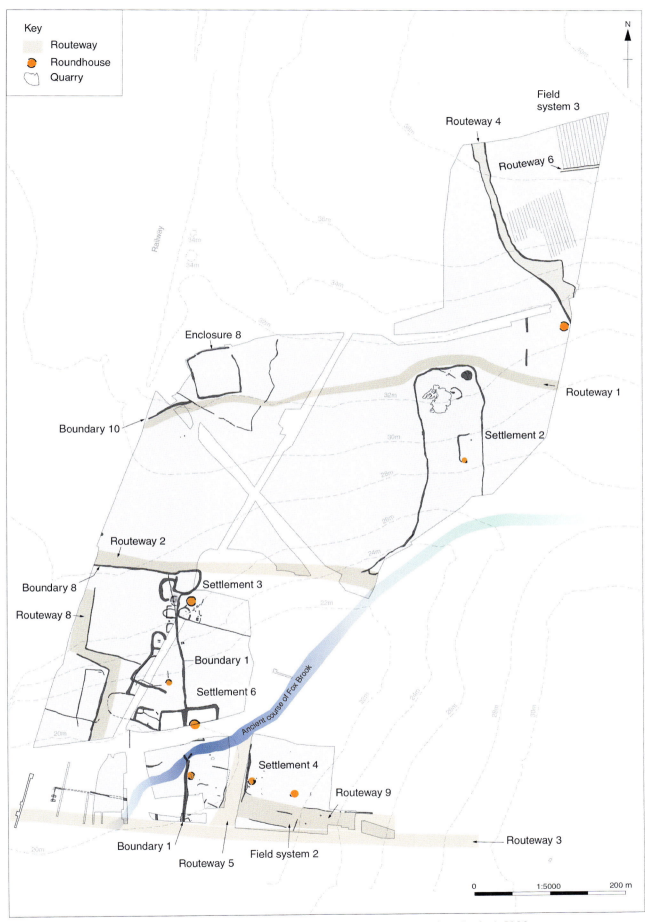

Figure 3.18 Period 3.4: Late pre-Roman Iron Age phase plan. Scale 1:5000

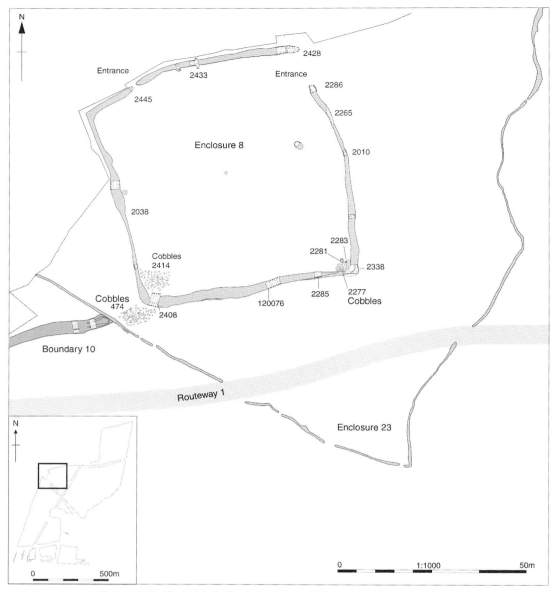

Figure 3.19 Period 3.4: Enclosure 8 and Boundary 10. Scale 1:1000

(1.40m wide, between recuts *2445* and *2433*) in the northern arm, and the closing of the south-east entranceway. In the eastern part of the enclosure, the new ditches exhibited a mostly steep, V-shaped profile, but those to the west were more U-shaped – the reason for this apparent difference is not known. All showed some evidence for weathering and erosion of the upper parts of their sides. Where best-preserved, they were up to 3.18m wide and 1m deep, but truncation had reduced some sections to as little as 0.73m wide and 0.55m deep. The sequence of filling was similar in most of the excavated ditch segments, with the lower, bluish-grey fills probably being water-lain and the dark grey-brown upper fills comprising a mixture of humic soils and redeposited natural clay.

Internally, very few features or deposits were recorded, as was the case in earlier periods. Two areas of metalling – one (*2277*) located at the south-eastern corner of the enclosure, the other (*2414*) in the south-western corner – appear to have been contemporary with the final phase of the enclosure ditch. The purpose of these cobbled surfaces is not clear, but the natural clay on the inside edge of the enclosure ditch had been eroded at both locations. It is possible that this was the result of trampling by livestock, which perhaps used the corners of perimeter ditch (on the downslope side of the enclosure) as watering holes – the cobbles may have been laid to prevent this erosion.

The only other internal features recorded were two small pits (*2281*, *2283*), which had been cut through metalled surface *2277*, in the south-eastern corner of the enclosure. Neither yielded any finds, and their significance is uncertain. A layer of silt (*2278*; not illustrated) eventually accumulated above metalling *2277*, sealing these features. This deposit was similar to (and merged with) the upper fill of the adjacent enclosure ditch, suggesting that the two deposits may have formed at the same time.

Boundary 10
This boundary ditch, which extended westwards from the south-western corner of Enclosure 8, was re-cut for the last time during Period 3.4 (Fig. 3.19, Fig. 3.5, *13512*, and Fig. 3.7, *11368*), possibly at the same time as Enclosure 8 was redefined. The new ditch, which closely followed the line of the original feature, was 1.66–2.2m wide and 0.45–1.28m deep, with a variable profile, ranging from steep-sided with a slightly rounded base close to the eastern terminal of the ditch, to a broad, shallow, U-shaped appearance only a short distance to the west. The reason for this marked change in character over so short a distance is not known. In the gap between the eastern terminal of Boundary 10, and the south-western corner of Enclosure 8, a cobbled surface (*474*) was laid, possibly at around the same time as the ditch was re-cut. The discovery of this deposit strengthens the hypothesis that this 8m-wide gap was not the result of truncation, but was a deliberate feature, marking the position of a wide causeway across Boundary 10, albeit within Enclosure 23.

Enclosure 23
Surrounding Enclosure 8 was an irregular system of heavily truncated ditches (Fig. 3.19), that appeared to form a large, roughly rectilinear enclosure (at least to the south and east) that may have been intended to guide animals towards Enclosure 8, or to provide a sheltered infield area. The south-western arm, which extended into the site from the west, on a north-west to south-east alignment, was 110m long, whilst the somewhat sinuous eastern arm, aligned north-east to south-west, was 138m long but extended beyond the limit of the investigation to the north. Whether Enclosure 8 was similarly enclosed on the north and west is not known, since these areas lay beyond the boundaries of the excavation.

Both of the excavated ditches were segmented, comprising ditch segments varying in length from 4m to as much as 63m, separated by gaps 0.2–0.8m wide: these gaps may have been intended to facilitate the passage of Routeway 1, now diverted to run through the enclosure. The ditches were relatively insubstantial and this, together with the sinuous character of the eastern ditch, might suggest that they marked the position of hedged boundaries, for which no other evidence remained. A small assemblage of pottery, including some later Iron Age material and a few intrusive sherds of the 2nd century AD, was recovered from these features. That Enclosure 23 was relatively short-lived is indicated by the fact that it was cut across by a trackway during the 1st century AD (Period 3.5, Routeway 7).

Settlement 1
(Fig. 3.20)

Routeway 4 and enclosures/ditches
A new ditch (*9816*) on the northern side of Routeway 4 ran on either side of the route, extending to the east of it for approximately 40m, before turning south through 90° to run for a further 28m (Fig. 3.20). It then turned south-east (*9818*) to extend for an additional 22m, beyond which it extended outside the excavated area. It appears to have formed the perimeter of an irregularly-shaped enclosure, in excess of 80m long, north-west to south-east (it extended south-east beyond the site), and 25m wide at its widest point, that was added to the north side of the road.

At the apex of the 'dog-leg' formed by its northern and eastern arms, was a gap in the ditch, 3m wide, marking the position of an entrance (perhaps gated) giving access from the enclosure to a field system (Field System 3) further north. The ditch was redefined on two subsequent occasions, each re-cut being similar in size and profile to the original feature, and closely following its line.

Approximately 50m south-west of Routeway 4, lying to the west of Roundhouse 3, was a north to south-aligned ditch (*11104=11109*) that was traced northwards for *c.*65m from the north side of Routeway 1 before it was truncated by later disturbances. The ditch, 1.5–2.25m wide and up to 0.5m deep, was recorded in two segments, separated by a gap, 23m wide; this seems too wide to have been a deliberate causeway, and it is therefore possible that the ditch had been completely removed in this area by later ploughing. The ditch was perhaps associated with retained Roundhouse 3, just to the east.

Field System 3 and Routeway 6
Evidence for two new fields laid out on the north-eastern side of Routeway 4 comprised a series of shallow, parallel trenches, recorded in two sharply-defined square plots, one located immediately adjacent to the road, the other *c.*25m further to the north-east, *c.*100m east of the road (Fig. 3.20). No equivalent remains were noted during evaluation on the western side of the road, and consequently this area was not stripped during the excavation. The southern field appears to have measured *c.*90 x 80m (*c.*0.72ha); that to the north extended north and east, beyond the limits of the excavation, but covered an area in excess of 0.45ha. The fields were situated on a slight, south-facing slope, and in both, the cultivation trenches were aligned north-west to south-east, although they were aligned more nearly north to south in the northern field than to the south.

It seems probable that an agricultural regime resembling a form of lazy bed cultivation was being practiced within these fields, the raised beds being formed by upcast from the trenches on either side, although it was initially thought that the trenches may have been used for viticulture. Consequently, a careful search was made for evidence of stakeholes or root activity at the base of the trenches, but, with the exception of some slight traces of root action, nothing was found, and extensive sampling for pollen and plant macrofossils failed to shed any light on the types of crops being grown.

Twenty trenches, 0.3–0.77m wide and 0.05–0.25m deep, lay in the southern field. These defined nineteen beds, each approximately 3.5m wide. The ten eastern trenches ran the entire length of the field (*c.*80m), but those on the west were 30–43m long, since they did not extend into the south-western corner of the field. The reason for this is not known; it is possible that one or more structures had been located there, but if so, no trace of these had survived, or this part of the field may simply have been used for some other purpose. In the northern field, parts of sixteen parallel trenches lay within the site, spaced at intervals of *c.*3.7–4m. Each had a squarish profile, and measured *c.*0.65–0.88m wide and 0.12–0.29m deep. In both fields, the fills of the trenches were uniform throughout, comprising either an orange-brown or mid-grey-brown silty clay.

A ditched trackway, 3m wide (Routeway 6), ran along the southern edge of the northern field. The flanking

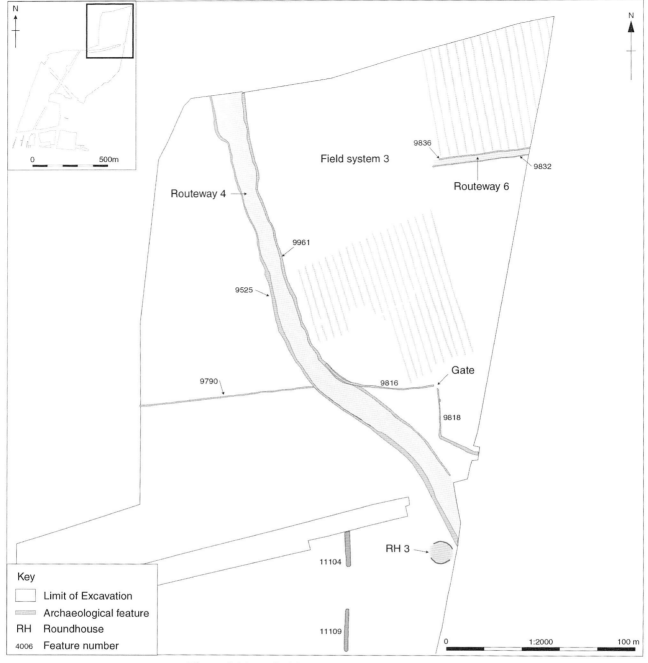

Figure 3.20 Period 3.4: Settlement 1. Scale 1:2000

ditches were relatively narrow (0.43–0.73m wide) and shallow (0.08–0.21m), with U-shaped profiles. Late Iron Age pottery was recovered from the southern ditch, but otherwise, dating evidence was extremely scarce within Field System 3. Only five sherds of abraded late Iron Age pottery and one small fragment of an early Roman samian vessel were recovered, but a blue glass bead of late Iron Age type (SF 156; Wadeson, Chapter 6.V) also came from one of the cultivation trenches (cut *890*).

Settlement 2
(Fig. 3.21; Pl. 3.15)

Enclosure 10
The main perimeter ditch of Enclosure 10 was redefined during the late pre-Roman Iron Age, to enclose an area of 14885m^2. The new ditches were up to 3m wide and 1.23m deep, but were considerably narrower and shallower over much of their length, due to later truncation; generally they survived to a greater width and depth on the western side than to the east. Both the western and eastern ditches had slight kinks in their alignments, dictated by subtle changes in the topography, which would have better controlled the progress of the water draining down slope to Fox Brook, to the south of the enclosure. A varied

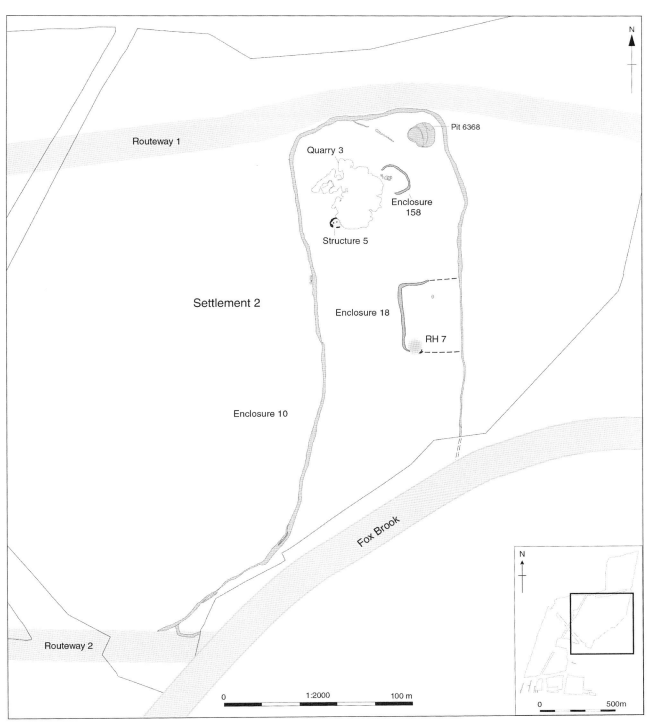

Figure 3.21 Period 3.4: Settlement 2. Scale 1:2000

ceramic assemblage was recovered from the ditch fills, consisting of 507 sherds of middle to late Iron Age pottery. The western ditch cut across four sub-circular pits, measuring from 1.02m to 2.49m in diameter and 0.3–0.56m deep. These yielded later Iron Age pottery and also some sherds datable to the 2nd century AD, which, together with a modern mustard jar, were clearly intrusive.

Enclosure 158
This small, probably C-shaped enclosure (Fig. 3.21) was defined by a ditch which cut through the north-western corner of Period 3.3 Roundhouse 6. As it survived, the enclosure measured c.14m north to south and c.10m east to west, internally (Pl. 3.15).

Quarry 3 and isolated pit
In this period the area of gravel extraction at the north-western corner of Enclosure 10, marked in Period 3.3 by a group of mostly small, scattered quarry pits (Quarry 2) was expanded, ultimately covering an area of approximately 860m^2 (Fig. 3.21). A group of intercutting extraction pits (*6368 etc.*), covering approximately 154m^2, was also dug in the north-eastern corner of the enclosure. During the excavation, the intercutting pits

Plate 3.15 Enclosure 158, Settlement 2, looking south (Period 3.4)

forming Quarry 3 were machine-dug to a depth of more than 2m, but began to fill rapidly with water from a depth of 0.8m. A similar situation is likely to have pertained during the Iron Age, in the course of the gravel extraction, since well-preserved waterlogged plant and insect remains were recovered from the lower fill (*6365*) of one of the pits (*6368*) at the north-eastern corner of the enclosure (Fryer, Chapter 8.IV; Tetlow, Chapter 8.VI). Pollen recovered from this deposit showed that it probably accumulated in wet conditions where there was limited runoff from the adjacent land surface (Green and Boreham, Chapter 8.VII). This was supported by the presence of rare soil fungal bodies (*Glomus*), which indicate limited inwash of bioactive soils. Limited erosion of surrounding soils suggests that the surface was stabilised, perhaps by grassland; indeed, the presence of grassland in the immediate vicinity was indicated by the pollen assemblage from *6365*, which was dominated by grasses. Furthermore, fungal spores associated with animal dung were also moderately abundant in this deposit (Green and Boreham, Chapter 8.VII), suggesting the existence of pasture grazed by sheep or cattle. Potentially the most interesting aspect of the pollen assemblage, however, was the identification of a significant amount of *Reseda lutea*-type pollen, which includes weld (dyers' rocket), wild mignonette and corn mignonette. All these plants grow on disturbed ground and arable land, and weld was used specifically to produce a yellow dye.

Pottery ranging in date from the middle Iron Age to the 1st century AD was found throughout the backfill of the extraction pits in both areas of quarrying. However, a particularly substantial assemblage, comprising 724 sherds of late pre-Roman Iron Age pottery, with a total weight of 3.5kg, was recovered from the uppermost fill (*6358*) of quarry pit *6368*. This group contained many grog-tempered sherds, all of which were produced in the late Iron Age tradition (Lyons, Chapter 7.III). Sandy reduced wares were the most common fabric present, although a small amount of shell-tempered ware was also found. The pottery did not appear to have accumulated gradually through piecemeal rubbish disposal, but had evidently been deliberately scattered over the top of the feature, perhaps to mark the end of its use. A coin of Cunobelin dating to the very early 1st century AD (SF 2711) was also recovered from the upper fill (Crummy, Chapter 6.II).

West of the north-eastern quarry area, a narrow ditch was traced for 19.4m, running into Enclosure 10 from the northern perimeter ditch on a north-west to south-east alignment. The ditch survived in two segments, separated by a gap 4m wide; it is not clear if this was a causeway, or was the result of truncation of a section of the ditch, although at its south-eastern end the ditch had certainly been destroyed by later disturbance.

Structure 5
Immediately adjacent to the south-western corner of Quarry 3 was a sub-circular structure (Structure 5), 5.78m in diameter (Fig. 3.21). This survived only as two fragments of a narrow, shallow, curvilinear ring ditch and two possibly associated postholes. The pottery recovered from the ditch comprised a mixture of Iron Age and late pre-Roman Iron Age wares. With the possible exception of the postholes, no internal features or deposits had survived, and the function of the structure is not known, although its proximity to Quarry 3 may suggest an association.

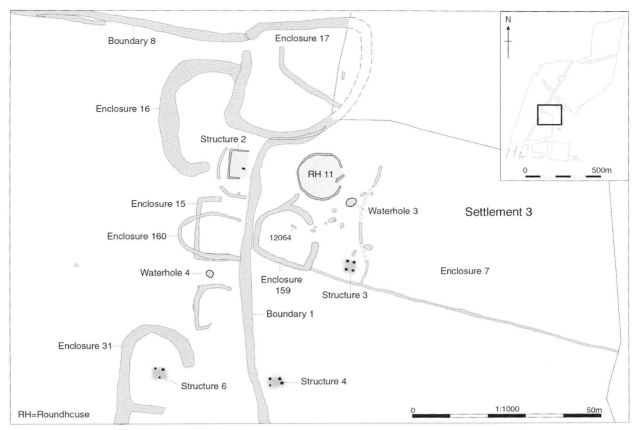

Figure 3.22 Period 3.4: Settlement 3. Scale 1:1000

Enclosure 18
In the central part of Enclosure 10, approximately 40m south-east of Quarry 3 and c.50m south of Enclosure 158, were the remains of what had probably been a sub-rectangular enclosure (Enclosure 18). Only the western perimeter ditch and parts of the northern and southern ditches had survived (Fig. 3.21), but it is possible that the eastern boundary of the enclosure was formed by the main eastern perimeter ditch of Enclosure 10. If this was the case, Enclosure 18 would have measured approximately 38m, north to south and c.30m east to west, internally. The enclosure ditch was 0.9–1.36m wide and 0.25–0.62m deep, and yielded an assemblage of late Iron Age pottery.

Roundhouse 7
Roundhouse 7 was located in the extreme south-western corner of Enclosure 18 (Fig. 3.21). It survived only as a very short segment of a curvilinear eaves-drip gully of foundation trench, 2.1m long, 0.34m wide, and 0.13m deep. The building appears to have been approximately 10m in diameter, but its orientation could not be determined and no internal features or deposits had survived. The single fill of the gully/trench yielded no datable artefacts.

Settlement 3
(Fig. 3.22)
Within Settlement 3, only a few minor changes attributable to Period 3.4 were noted. Boundary 8, the east to west aligned ditch defining the southern edge of Routeway 2, was redefined, the recut being of similar form and following the same line as the primary ditch. The northern end of Boundary 1 was also extended slightly to the north, to link up with the southern perimeter ditch of Enclosure 17, thereby closing the narrow entrance that had formerly existed at the north-western corner of Enclosure 7. The boundary ditch of Enclosure 159, which occupied the south-western corner of Enclosure 7, was also recut at this time, and was again of similar form to the primary enclosure ditch. Ceramic evidence indicates that, with the exception of Boundaries 1 and 8, which continued to be maintained, this part of the site was effectively abandoned, either during the early 1st century AD or before. Various burials were, however, later placed across the area, which were probably associated with Settlement 6 (see Period 3.5, below).

Settlement 6
(Fig. 3.23)

Roundhouse 14
Roundhouse 14 was re-built for the fourth time during Period 3.4 (Fig. 3.23), the evidence surviving as a 6m-long segment of the northern half of its curvilinear ring gully, which cut the ring gully associated with the previous phase of the building. This feature was steep-sided, 0.4–0.47m wide and 0.16–0.19m deep, with a flat or slightly rounded base. No internal features or deposits survived, but the projected curve of the surviving ring gully fragment suggests that the building was approximately 9m in diameter, internally.

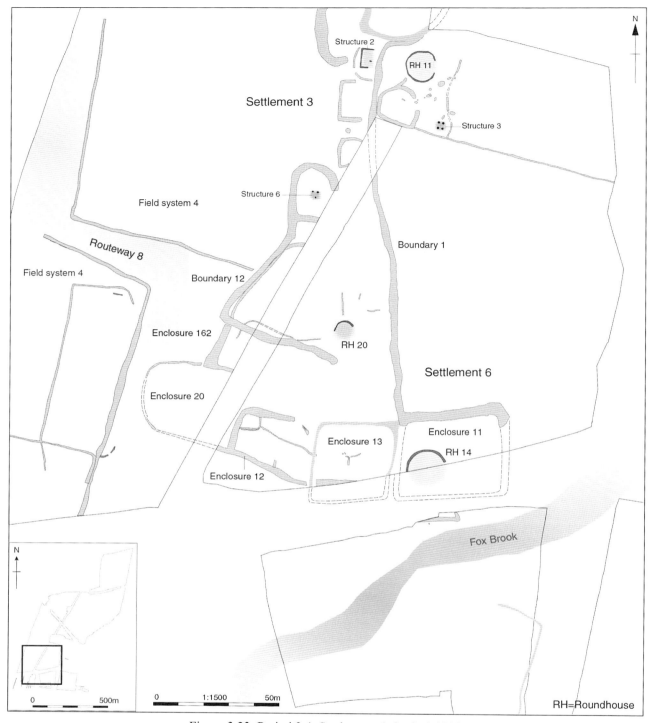

Figure 3.23 Period 3.4: Settlement 6. Scale 1:1500

Roundhouse 20
Just under 40m north-west of Roundhouse 14, and c.15m west of Boundary 1, was a small, unenclosed roundhouse (Roundhouse 20; Fig. 3.23). This lay immediately north of Period 3.3 Roundhouse 17 and might, therefore, have been a direct replacement for the earlier structure. Two surviving ring gully segments, up to 0.67m wide and 0.2–0.28m deep, suggest that the structure was c.8m in diameter internally, with an east-facing entrance. Three sherds of late Iron Age pottery were recovered from the gully fills.

Enclosures 12, 20 and 162
Enclosure 12 of Period 3.3 appears to have remained in use into Period 3.4 (Fig. 3.23), since part of its perimeter ditch was redefined, and the southern ditch was extended eastwards slightly, so that the enclosure now effectively abutted Enclosure 13. Consequently, the enclosure's eastern ditch seemingly went out of use. A gap, c.9.5m wide, at the north-eastern corner of the enclosure, indicates that an earlier entrance at this location continued to be maintained. However, a short ditch segment, c.3m long, located towards the centre of the gap, suggests that in

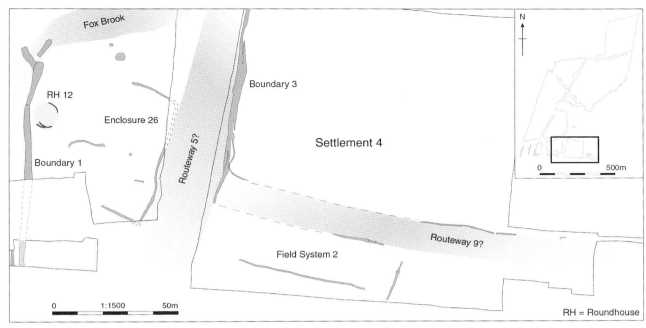

Figure 3.24 Period 3.4: Settlement 4. Scale 1:1500

this phase, access may have been restricted to a pair of narrower entrances, rather than a single, broad entrance.

Immediately west of Enclosure 12 were the fragmentary remains of a new, possibly D-shaped, enclosure (Enclosure 20), of which only part of the northern ditch, and a fragment of ditch at the south-west corner, up to 0.7m wide and 0.3m deep, had survived. This enclosure may have been appended to the western side of Enclosure 12, in which case it would have measured approximately 39m, north-west to south-east, and c.28m wide, but extremely poor survival of archaeological remains in this area means that this remains uncertain. However, Enclosure 20 does seem to have been integral with another, possibly sub-rectangular, enclosure (Enclosure 162), to the north. Only the west side of this, and a fragment of its south side, remained, but it appears to have measured c.57m, north-east to south-west, internally, and in excess of 10m wide. Its south-western corner was defined by a broad, L-shaped ditch (up to 2.5m wide and 0.45m deep), which also formed part of the northern side of Enclosure 20. The remainder of Enclosure 162 was, however, enclosed by a somewhat less substantial ditch (up to 1.3m wide and 0.4m deep). At the junction of these two perimeter ditches, another narrow ditch ran off to the south-east, seemingly partitioning off the southern 18m or so of the enclosure from the rest of the area. With the exception of a curving ditch or gully or uncertain significance, which cut across the putative internal partition, no other internal features or deposits were recorded in Enclosure 162, nor, indeed, within Enclosures 12 and 20.

Field System 4
To the west and north-west of the main habitation focus, what appear to have been two large, rectangular fields were laid out (Field System 4), with their long axes oriented north-east to south-west (Fig. 3.23). Only two sides (the south and west) of the northernmost field lay within the site, although the eastern side is presumed to have been defined by the northern elements of Settlement 6 and the southern part of Settlement 3. It therefore measured c.80–90m, north-west to south-east, and in excess of 90m long. The southernmost enclosure measured over 100 x 60m, but extended beyond the excavated areas to the south and west, with traces of internal subdivisions. The fields were defined by boundary ditches, 0.42–0.65m wide and 0.11–0.22m deep. Only a few fragments of Roman pottery were recovered from the ditch fills, but elements of the boundary ditches stratigraphically pre-dated a trackway, which can be confidently attributed to the late Iron Age/early Roman transitional period (Routeway 8, Period 3.5), but which may have existed in a slightly different form in Period 3.4, running between two fields. It seems likely, therefore, that the pottery found its way into the ditches after the field system went out of use.

Settlement 4
(Fig. 3.24)
In this phase, the section of Boundary 1 that lay within Settlement 4 was again reworked, but the small, triangular enclosure (Enclosure 164) that had been added to the east side of the boundary in Period 3.3 appears to have been abandoned. Both Enclosure 26 and Roundhouse 12 within it remained in use, but there was little evidence for activity within the enclosure at this time. To the east, Boundary 3 and Field System 2 also seem to have remained in use, but Roundhouses 8 and 22 did not. It is possible that ?Routeway 5 remained in use, while Routeway 9 may have been added at this date (or later, in Period 3.5).

In Fox Brook, which defined the northern edge of the settlement, a short, north-east to south-west aligned ditch or trench (measuring at least 8m long, 1.92m wide and 0.42m deep) lay within the former stream channel, running off the northern end of Boundary 1. Although little of this feature could be excavated, it may have been dug in an attempt to canalise that part of the stream in closest proximity to the settlement, thereby improving the flow of water and reducing the risk of flooding.

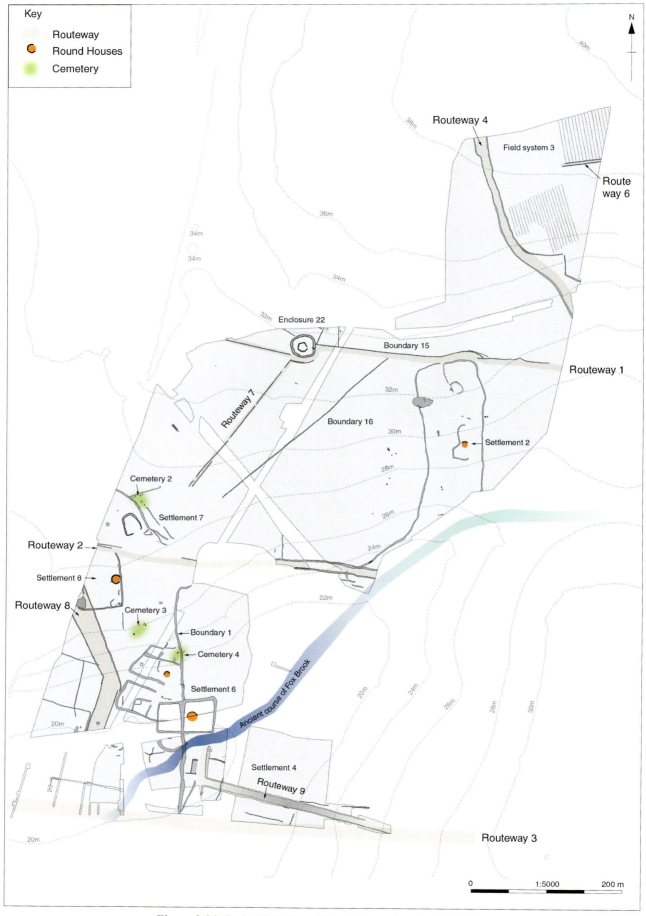

Figure 3.25 Period 3.5: Transitional phase plan. Scale 1:5000

V. Period 3.5: transitional (mid to late 1st century AD)

Introduction
(Fig. 3.25)
On some parts of the site, the decades on either side of the Roman conquest saw a considerable degree of continuity from the late Iron Age, but in other areas, quite marked changes in the local landscape occurred (Fig. 3.25). This was particularly true in the northern part of the site, where a new, roughly circular enclosure (Enclosure 22) of quite different form (and probably also purpose) to the agricultural and 'domestic' enclosures previously seen, was constructed in a prominent location on the crest of the hill. This monument was located on the north side of Routeway 1, in reasonably close proximity to Enclosure 8, the substantial square enclosure that originated in the middle Iron Age (Period 3.2), but which had gone out of use by Period 3.5. It is therefore possible that Enclosure 22 represented a direct replacement for the earlier feature. Enclosure 22 seems to have been at the hub of a network of long, ditched boundaries, and at least one track, that either radiated from the vicinity of the monument, or converged upon it. Whilst the construction of these features appeared to mark a radical break with earlier systems of spatial organisation, cutting, as they did, across pre-existing boundaries on new and very different alignments, none was retained within the subsequent pattern of Romano-British settlement.

Elsewhere on the northern part of the site, Routeway 4 continued in use, although Settlement 1, through which the road passed, had probably been abandoned in the late Iron Age (Period 3.4), unless elements of the settlement located east of the excavated area remained in use. Further south, occupation continued within Enclosure 10 (Settlement 2), although little substantial change seems to have occurred. The late Iron Age roundhouse and the subsidiary enclosure in the central part of Enclosure 10 were modified, and gravel extraction continued in the north-western corner of the enclosure, although perhaps at a somewhat reduced level. Immediately north of Routeway 2, the western part of the site had seen little or no activity during the middle to late Iron Age. Here, occupation appears to have commenced in the late Iron Age/early Romano-British transitional period, although the earliest activity was restricted to the construction of two small, ditched enclosures (Settlement 7). A small inhumation cemetery (Cemetery 2) was also established further to the north-east, separated from Enclosure 21 by a large, north-west to south-east aligned ditch (Boundary 109). A second ditch (Boundary 9) ran east from this, enclosing the north side of the cemetery, and a small, sub-oval enclosure (Enclosure 28) was located towards the southern end of Boundary 109. No roundhouses, structures, or other occupation features were recorded in this area, either within the enclosures or elsewhere. Activity on this part of the site seemingly continued throughout the Romano-British period and perhaps beyond, but the evidence suggests that it remained at a relatively low level until the late Roman period, when occupation intensified considerably (Period 4.4).

In the area immediately south of Routeway 2, the western edge of the site had seen little activity in either the middle or late Iron Age. However, this changed at around the time of the conquest (Period 3.5) with the construction of a rectilinear enclosure (Settlement 8; Enclosure 29), the northern side of which appeared to encroach somewhat on the line of the routeway. With the exception of a roundhouse, located immediately inside the eastern perimeter ditch, and a small subsidiary enclosure at its south-eastern corner, few features of note were recorded within Enclosure 29.

Adjacent to Settlement 8, Settlement 3 appears to have been abandoned by Period 3.5, although Boundary 1 continued to be maintained throughout. A dispersed group of eight cremation burials was found (Cemeteries 3 and 4), widely scattered across the area of the former settlement. Dating evidence suggests that these should be attributed to Period 3.5, and it therefore seems likely that they related to Settlement 6, located only a short distance to the south, which continued to be occupied at this time. An isolated inhumation burial was also recorded on the south-western periphery of Settlement 6. The latter settlement continued to develop in Period 3.5, the major change from earlier phases being the amalgamation of several of the fragmentary enclosures on the north-west side of the settlement into one large, roughly D-shaped, enclosure (Enclosure 163), defined by a substantial perimeter ditch and sub-divided internally into several subsidiary enclosures and occupation areas. West of the settlement, the course of an existing track or droveway (Routeway 8) was altered. At the south-eastern corner of the site, Period 3.5 saw the construction of another ditched trackway (Routeway 9) within Settlement 4, which may have followed the line of an earlier track (see Period 3.4). The surviving late Iron Age roundhouse in this area, located adjacent to Boundary 1, was also replaced at this time by a rectangular building.

Enclosure 22
(Fig. 3.26)
For the most part, the numerous Iron Age ditched enclosures investigated during the course of the Love's Farm excavations appear to have had either an agricultural purpose, as paddocks, stock enclosures and fields, or were 'domestic' in character, serving to define the boundaries of small settlements and farmsteads. Enclosure 22, however, was very different, being morphologically quite unlike any of the other enclosures recorded on the site, and containing no evidence either for agricultural or 'domestic' activities.

The enclosure was roughly circular in plan (Fig. 3.26), comprising two concentric ring ditches, and occupied a prominent position in the landscape, on the crest of a hill, with the ground falling away to the south Fig. 3.25). Although seemingly short-lived, it appears to have been an important focus for activity on the northern and central parts of the site in the late Iron Age/early Roman transitional period, with several linear features, including ditches and trackways, either radiating out from the monument, or converging upon it.

Whilst it was not possible to demonstrate conclusively that the inner and outer enclosures were constructed at the same time, there is equally no reason to suppose that they were not. Pottery from both ring ditches was predominantly of the late Iron Age/early Romano-British transitional period (c.1st century AD), but some residual Iron Age material was also present. Three principal sub-phases of activity were noted: construction and primary use (Phase 1); a possible phase of disuse or 'closure' of the

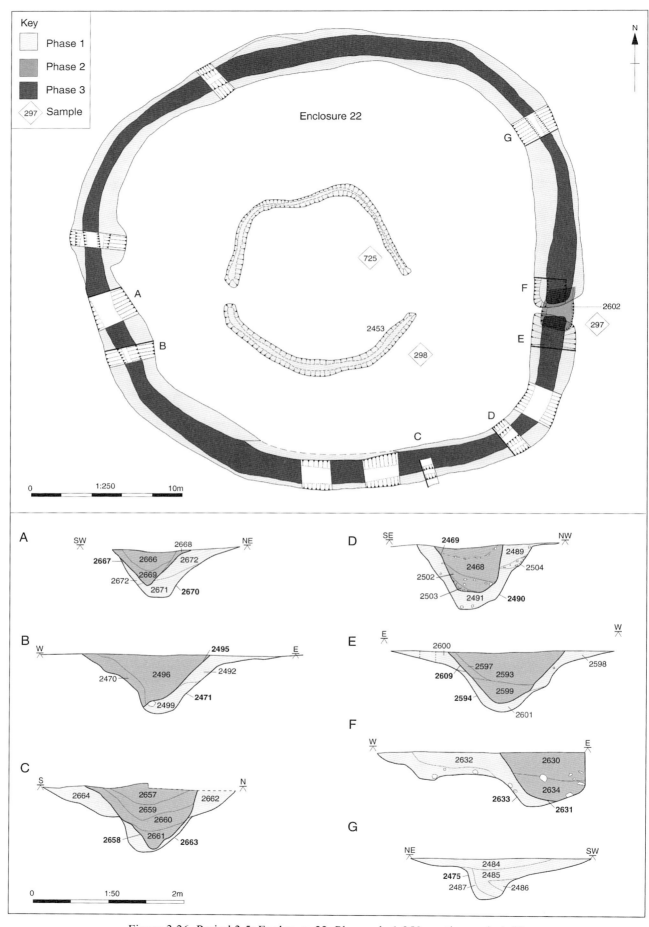

Figure 3.26 Period 3.5: Enclosure 22. Plan scale 1:250, section scale 1:50

monument (Phase 2); and a redefinition of the outer enclosure (Phase 3), marked by a re-cutting of the outer ring ditch.

Phase 1
The outer enclosure was sub-circular, measuring *c*.30m east to west and 28m north to south, internally. In its original form (*2670/2471/2663/2490/2594/2633/2475*), the perimeter ditch was U-profiled, up to 2.4m wide and 0.84m deep, with steep sides and a rounded base, although the upper edges were less steep due to erosion. The ditch was broken by a single, very narrow entrance, 0.6m wide, located on the eastern side of the enclosure. It seems likely this was deliberately constructed to control and restrict access into the interior of the enclosure, which would have been possible only for individuals walking in single file.

The basal fills of the enclosure ditch appeared to have been laid down in wet conditions, an hypothesis supported by the presence of water snails in some of these deposits (Fryer and Fosberry, Chapter 8.V). In contrast, the upper fills, the bulk of which were removed when the ditch was re-cut (Phase 2), seemed to have derived from the natural orange-brown clay through which the ditch had been dug, either as a result of erosion, or through deliberate infilling. No evidence for an associated bank was found, although it is perhaps likely that a bank did once exist, formed from the ditch upcast. Fills appear to have entered the ditch from both the interior and exterior of the enclosure.

The inner enclosure (*2453*) was also sub-circular, *c*.11.5 x 11.25m, internally, defined by a U-profiled ditch, up to 1.16m wide and 0.46m deep. A pair of opposed entrances were marked by gaps on the eastern and western sides of the enclosure ditch (elements of which were recorded during the evaluation in Trench 68); these were 2.5m and 1m wide respectively, and were flanked by rounded ditch terminals. For most of its length, the ditch contained only a single, grey-brown silty clay fill. This yielded moderate quantities of rounded flint and sandstone cobbles, the stones being markedly more numerous than in all the other excavated enclosure ditches on the site. The significance of this is unclear, however, since there is no evidence that any stones had been deliberately placed within the ditch. Unlike the outer ditch, which was subsequently re-defined, there was no evidence that the inner ditch had been re-cut or otherwise maintained.

The inner ditch contained an unusual faunal assemblage, that included the remains of several weasels or stoats, small songbirds and a high percentage of sheep mandibles and tooth fragments; elements of the assemblage suggest the presence of owl pellets rather than the result of deliberate species deposition (Baxter, Chapter 8.III). Pig bones were also present in small quantities, but cattle bones were absent, which sets this group apart from the assemblages recovered from other enclosure ditches and boundary ditches on the site. Additionally, a small fragment of copper alloy sheet (SF 2095) was recovered from one of the eastern entrance terminals and five curved fragments of an iron sheet (SF 2088) came from the southern part of the ditch.

Phase 2
At some stage, effectively closing the access point, a shallow sub-rectangular pit (*2602*) was cut across the narrow entrance on the eastern side of the outer enclosure. The fact that the pit cut into the fills of the ditch terminals flanking the entrance demonstrates that this event occurred some time after the enclosure ditch was first dug. The pit measured 3.5 x 1.72m and was 0.28m deep, with steep sides and a flat base. The primary fill (*2516*) was a very dark grey-brown silty clay, notable for a high concentration of charcoal, ash, and small fragments of burnt animal bone. This deposit was markedly different to the principal fills of both the outer and inner ring ditches, but was very similar to deposits of burnt material that were found in the ditch terminals flanking the eastern entrance of the inner enclosure. This may suggest that these deposits were contemporary. The upper pit fill (*2515*) was less well defined, and had been heavily truncated by a re-cutting of the outer enclosure ditch (Phase 3).

As already noted, the ditch terminals flanking the eastern entrance of the inner enclosure (*2453* and *2467* respectively) were ultimately filled with deposits of burnt material, containing much charcoal, ash and many small fragments of burnt animal bone. These deposits extended from each terminal, westwards along the length of the inner ditch for approximately 3m before petering out. The burnt animal bone fragments were too small to be identified to species, but these deposits also yielded charred plant remains, the only such material recovered from anywhere within the inner ring ditch (Fryer, Chapter 8.IV; samples 298 and 725, Table 8.11). Both deposits contained a moderate to high density of cereal grains, together with the seeds of various grassland plants, the latter possibly being indicative of the use of dried plant material for kindling.

Phase 3
During the 1st century AD, the entire perimeter of the outer enclosure was redefined by a re-cutting of the outer ditch, which closely followed (but was narrower than) the line of the original feature. The new ditch (*2667/2495/2658/2469/2609/2631*) was up to 2.5m wide and 0.7m deep. The new ditch cut across the earlier pit (2602) that had closed the entrance in Phase 2. The new ditch reinstated a narrow entrance (c.0.80m wide) in the original position. For the most part, the pottery recovered from the ditch fills was of late Iron Age/early Roman date, but some material datable to the mid–late 2nd century AD was also present in the upper fills, suggesting that the ditch was allowed to silt up over a prolonged period. Finds included a copper alloy hairpin, perhaps deliberately converted into a spear shape (see Crummy, Chapter 6.III, Fig. 6.17, SF 2094).

Features associated with Enclosure 22
(Fig. 3.27)

Routeway 7
A new, relatively narrow trackway (Routeway 7) was defined by a pair of roughly parallel ditches, set 3.2m apart, which were traced, in whole or in part, for up to 280m, running south-westwards from Enclosure 22 (Fig. 3.27). The ditches were both U-profiled, up to 0.67m wide and 0.29m deep, with single fills comprising pale grey-brown silty clays. The north-western ditch was visible for virtually the whole of this distance, although it survived in four separate segments, but the south-eastern ditch survived only in a comparatively short stretch, *c*.45m long, at the southern end of the track, as a consequence of

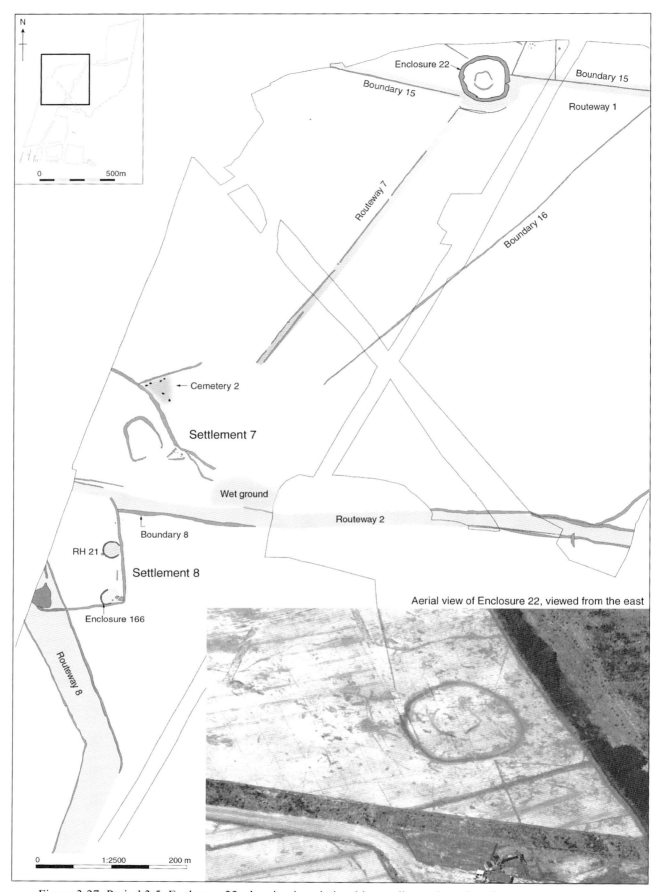

Figure 3.27 Period 3.5: Enclosure 22, showing its relationship to adjacent boundary features and settlements. Scale 1:2500

later truncation. On the north, the north-western ditch turned east through almost 90° to run, on a curving alignment, around the southern edge of Enclosure 22, 8m outside the outer enclosure ditch and roughly mirroring it. This arm of the ditch was traced east for 17m before petering out. Its relationship here with Routeway 1 and its related ditches is uncertain: some form of junction is implied.

Boundary 15
A boundary ditch (Boundary 15) extended east to west across the crest of the hill, and comprised two arms, one running east from Enclosure 22, the other extending west from that monument (Figs 3.25 and 3.27), although both in fact terminated just short of the outer enclosure ditch (4m in the case of the western arm, and 1m in the case of the eastern arm). Both elements of the boundary shared a similar alignment, but the line of the western arm lay c.12m south of that to the east, so that it ran off the southern edge of the enclosure, whereas the eastern arm extended from a point close to the centre of the enclosure's east side, just north of the narrow entrance through the outer enclosure ditch.

The boundary was marked by a U-profiled ditch, up to 1.2m wide and 0.29m deep, as it survived. On the east, it was traced for 220m, and appeared to terminate adjacent to the now diverted northern edge of Routeway 1, which presumably continued to be a significant feature in the landscape at this time. The eastern end of the ditch also seems to have kinked slightly to avoid the north-east corner of Enclosure 10 in Settlement 2, which remained in use into Period 3.5. The western arm was traced for 88m before it extended west beyond the excavated area. It appeared to reference the north-east corner of Enclosure 8, although that feature had seemingly gone out of use some time before (Period 3.4). A small assemblage of late pre-Roman Iron Age/early Roman pottery was recovered from the excavated fills of the ditch as a whole.

Boundary 16
A north-east to south-west aligned ditch was traced for nearly 300m from a point c.10m south of Boundary 15, leading south-westwards towards Settlements 7 and 8 (Fig. 3.27).

Other boundary features
In addition to Routeway 7 and Boundaries 15 and 16, three other boundary features were recorded that appeared to be contemporary with Enclosure 22 (Fig. 3.27). Indeed, one of these clearly respected the position of the outer enclosure ditch, whilst the other two extended north from Boundary 15, one immediately east of Enclosure 22, the other a short distance further to the east. The first ditch entered the site from the north-west, and was traced on a WNW to ESE alignment for 19m, before it terminated c.2m short of the outer ring ditch of Enclosure 22. It was 0.47m wide and 0.14m deep, with a U-shaped profile, and yielded a single sherd of Iron Age pottery. The second feature extended north-eastwards from the northern side of Boundary 15, at a point c.2m east of the outer ring ditch of Enclosure 22. This feature was traced north for 25m before extending beyond the excavated area. The third ditch was aligned north-west to south-east, and ran northwards from Boundary 15, c.30m east of Enclosure 22. It was also U-profiled, 0.67m wide and 0.14m deep, and was traced for approximately 27m, but again extended north of the excavated area.

Settlement 1
Routeway 4, established in Period 3.4, was apparently the only late Iron Age element on this part of the site to have remained in use into this period (Fig. 3.25), although it is possible that Field System 3, to the north also continued to be maintained at this time. Otherwise, it would seem that Settlement 1 (or, at least, that part of it available for investigation) was abandoned before the beginning of the 1st century AD.

Settlement 2
(Fig. 3.28)

Enclosure 10
During the period of transition from the late pre-Roman Iron Age to the Romano-British period, the northern ditch of Enclosure 10 was modified to create a 5m-wide entrance, located towards the centre of the enclosure's northern side, leading out onto Routeway 1. The western and eastern ditches of the enclosure were also both redefined, measuring up to 1.8m wide and 0.52m deep in this phase. As previously, the western ditch proved to be slightly wider and deeper than the eastern ditch. Pottery was rarely recovered from these ditches, but some material ranging in date from the later Iron Age to the mid 2nd century AD was found.

Internally, the northern end of the enclosure was subdivided by the digging of a new ditch, which ran south, approximately at right angles to the northern perimeter ditch, from the eastern terminal of the new entrance. As it survived, it comprised two segments, both quite narrow and shallow, running roughly north-west to south-east. The northern segment ran over a distance of 27m, cutting across one of the Period 3.3 inhumations (*6272*) within Cemetery 1, truncating its eastern end. A gap of 1.4m, possibly a causeway, separated this from the southern segment, which was traced for a further 12m. The purpose of this feature is not clear, but it may be significant that it extended between Enclosure 158 to the east, which was redefined during this period, and the area of quarrying, represented in Period 3.5 by Quarry 4, to the west. The presence of a single cremation attests to the continued use of part of the settlement for burial.

To the south, in the central part of Enclosure 10, the south-west corner of Enclosure 18 was enlarged. It is not clear whether Roundhouse 7 of Period 3.4 continued in use, but a new building (Roundhouse 23) was constructed to the north, again within Enclosure 18.

Enclosure 158
The perimeter ditch of Enclosure 158 was redefined during Period 3.5, but as previously, no internal features were recorded (Fig. 3.28), suggesting that the enclosure probably served some agricultural purpose, such as a stock pen. The new ditch yielded 259 sherds of middle Iron Age to late pre-Roman Iron Age pottery, the earlier material presumably being residual. Two groups of pits, dug across the western edge of the enclosure, may have been associated with the area of gravel extraction immediately to the west.

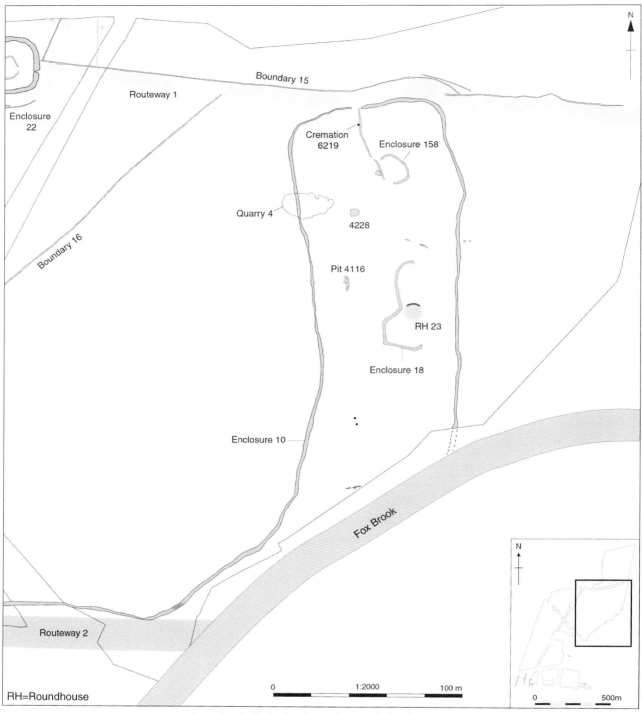

Figure 3.28 Period 3.5: Settlement 2. Scale 1:2000

Quarry 4
The final phase of quarrying in the north-western part of Enclosure 10 was represented by a very large, sub-oval extraction pit (*120062*), measuring *c*.30m east to west by 15m, and 2.45m deep, and a smaller pit (*4228*), 7m in diameter, located 15m to the east (Fig. 3.28). The larger pit contained seven fills, the earliest of which were waterlogged. One of these early fills (*120188*) contained particularly well-preserved plant and insect remains (Fryer, Chapter 8.IV; Tetlow, Chapter 8.VI). The latter includes species of beetles which favour open, sparsely vegetated, sand and gravel substrates; the type of conditions that would have existed around the quarry head during and directly after gravel extraction. In contrast, there were few aquatic and semi-aquatic fauna, suggesting that the quarry was only seasonally wet and that any standing water disappeared rapidly, leaving patches of muddier ground. As the quarry fell into disuse, the plant and insect remains record its re-colonisation by weeds and other ruderal species, which accords well with the results of the pollen analysis (Green and Boreham, Chapter 8.VII). The majority of the taxa present indicate dry, open pasture with hedgerows or an area of wooded pasture close by, and areas of disturbed ground that were

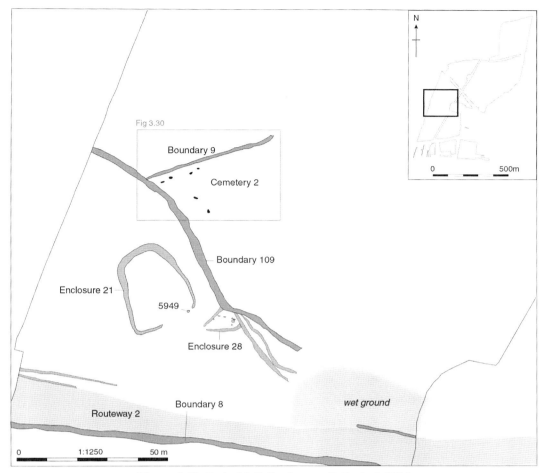

Figure 3.29 Period 3.5: Settlement 7. Scale 1:1250

colonised by weeds and ruderal species. The species found, such as plantains and mallows, are ready colonisers of bare, nutrient-poor, disturbed ground. Evidence of later stages of the plant growth took the form of nettles and vetches. Finds included a Nauheim derivative brooch (see Chapter 6, Fig. 6.11, SF 2707), a type introduced at the conquest. That the quarry remained partly visible in the landscape over a long period was indicated by the recovery of Anglo-Saxon pottery and artefacts from its upper fills (Chapter 5).

Cremation

A small inhumation cemetery (Cemetery 1), comprising two adjacent graves and a third located some distance to the east, had been established at the northern end of Enclosure 10 during Period 3.3. Within this earlier burial ground, a single cremation was seemingly added in Period 3.5 (Fig. 3.28), the burial being placed between two earlier inhumations. It comprised the poorly-fired remains of an adult male (*6218*) placed, without any obvious evidence for a container, within a shallow pit (*6219*). Although undated, the burial has been phased here on the basis of its relationship with Enclosure 158.

Enclosure 18

In the central part of Enclosure 10, the western boundary of Enclosure 18 was redefined, largely on a new line, by the digging of a new ditch, up to 1.6m wide and 0.77m deep (Fig. 3.28). The enclosure now measured c.45m, north to south, and at least 20m east to west. As previously, no trace of its eastern side was found, but if it had extended east up to the eastern perimeter ditch of Enclosure 10 (which is far from certain), it would have been up to 40m wide. The new boundary ditch contained pottery of the late Iron Age to the 1st century AD.

Roundhouse 23

Just inside the western boundary ditch of Enclosure 18 was a new building (Roundhouse 23). This was located c.8m north of Roundhouse 7 (Period 3.4), and could conceivably have replaced that structure (Fig. 3.28). The new building survived as a 7m-long curvilinear gully or trench, 0.48m wide and 0.1–0.2m deep, which formed part of the northern side of the building. The structure may have been 9–10m in diameter, but too little survived for its orientation to be determined and no internal features or deposits were recorded, the area having been severely truncated by later plough furrows. Like its predecessor, limited preservation means that it is not possible to estimate the overall dimensions of the roundhouse, nor the position of its entrance.

Settlement 7
(Figs 3.29–3.30; Pl. 3.16)

Enclosure 21
This was a sub-rectangular, or roughly horseshoe-shaped, enclosure (Fig. 3.29), measuring 25m, north-west to

south-east, by 19m, with an entrance, 10.4m wide, on its south side. The enclosure ditch was up to 1.56m wide and 0.5m deep, being wider and deeper towards the rear (north) of the enclosure, and shallower and narrower at the entrance terminals. A posthole (*5949*) located immediately inside the eastern entrance terminal may have formed part of a gate or other entrance structure. No structures, pits, or other occupation features were recorded within the enclosure, which is presumed to have served as a paddock or stock-pen. Very little dating evidence was recovered from the early ditch fills; some early Roman material was present in the upper fills, but this was considered to be intrusive, and did not, in any case, provide a date for the initial construction of the enclosure.

Boundaries 9 and 109
Broadly continuing the north-westwards curve of Boundary 1 (Fig. 3.25), Boundary 109 comprised a substantial ditch, up to 2.8m wide and 1.05m deep, which entered the site from the north-west, *c.*37m north-west of Enclosure 21 (Fig. 3.29). It was traced south-east for approximately 85m, passing within 6m of the north-eastern side of Enclosure 21, but petered out to the south. The ditch seems to have had a long life, being redefined in the early Roman period, and appears to have served an important drainage function, channelling surface runoff downslope, around the sheltered but flood-prone hollow in which Enclosure 21 was situated. Its south-eastern end braided out into smaller channels, near to the point where they drained into an area of wet ground, located on the north side of Routeway 2 – this area remained prone to flooding even during the course of the excavations. Running east, approximately at right angles to Boundary 109, was another ditch (Boundary 9). This was traced north-east for 42m, seemingly petering out on the north, and was 0.8–1.09m wide and 0.34–0.48m deep.

Enclosure 28
A small irregular ditched enclosure (measuring up to *c.*12 x 9m) was located little more than 6m south-east of the southern entrance into Enclosure 21, and seemed to be appended to the western side of Boundary 109 (Fig. 3.29). The enclosure ditch was 0.6–1.28m wide and 0.11–0.51m deep, becoming narrower and shallower towards the entrance, which was 1.2m wide and located at the narrower western end of the enclosure. Within the enclosure were eight small postholes forming no coherent pattern, but perhaps the remains of some kind of structure.

Cemetery 2
A small cemetery of six inhumation burials (graves *5809, 5812, 5815, 5900, 5903* and *5939*; sks *5810, 5813, 5816, 5901, 5904, 5940*) lay within the angle formed by the junction of Boundary 9 and Boundary 109, *c.*20–25m north-east of Enclosure 21 (Fig. 3.30, Pl. 3.16). Four of the graves were located *c.*0.5–1m inside (*i.e.* south of) Boundary 9, and were aligned north-east to south-west, parallel to that feature. They were seemingly arranged in a row, and possibly in two pairs (*5809* and *5812* on the west; *5815* and *5903* on the east) within this row, although it is possible these spatial arrangements were purely fortuitous. Most of the individuals had been buried on their left-hand sides. Graves *5809* (sk *5810*) and *5812* (sk *5813*) each contained the remains of an adult female,

Plate 3.16 Cemetery 2, Settlement 7, looking north-east, showing graves *5810*, *5813* and *5816* (Period 3.5)

whilst *5815* (sk *5816*) and *5903* (sk *5904*) held, respectively, an adult male and an adult of indeterminate sex (Dodwell, Chapter 8.I). All of these individuals were buried in crouched, flexed or semi-flexed positions, facing south (see Table 8.1). Burials *5900* and *5939* were located south of the other graves, and were aligned north-west to south-east, parallel to Boundary 109. Grave *5900* contained an adult female laid supine, whilst burial *5939* was that of another adult of indeterminate sex that was buried crouched and facing east. All the graves had been very heavily truncated by later ploughing, and no grave goods or other datable artefacts were recovered. However, radiocarbon dating of the male skeleton (*5815*) in grave *5816* yielded a date of 50 cal BC–cal AD 90 (SUERC-21978, 1965±30 BP).

Settlement 8
(Fig. 3.31)

Quarry 5
Quarry 5 was a large, irregularly-shaped gravel extraction pit which measured roughly 10 x 8m and 1.9m deep (Fig. 3.31). It was investigated in two machine-cut slots, which revealed a sequence of fourteen silty clay fills. These yielded 43 sherds of pottery datable to the 1st century AD.

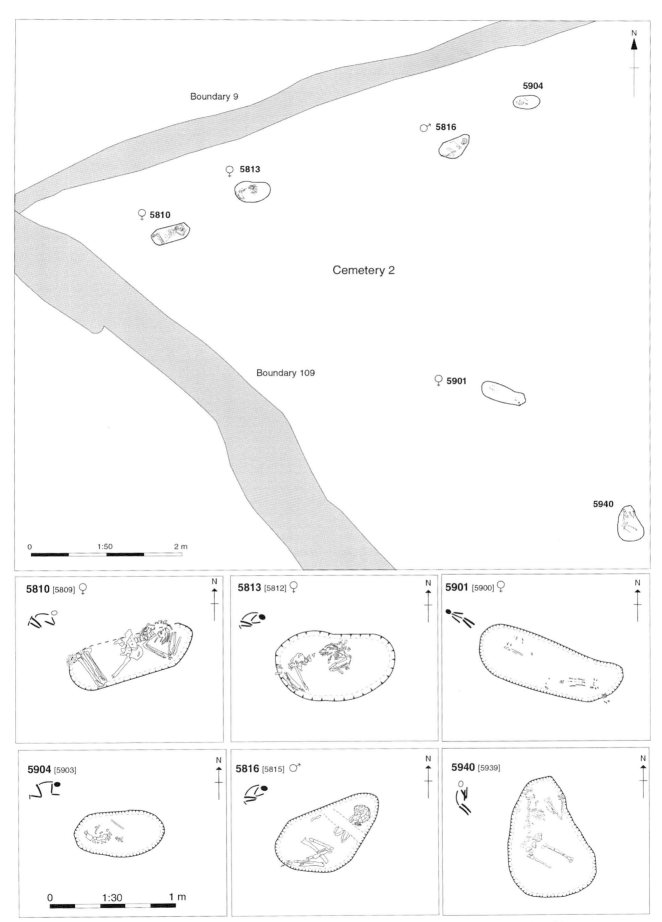

Figure 3.30 Period 3.5: Settlement 7, Cemetery 2. Plan scale 1:50, graves at scale 1:30

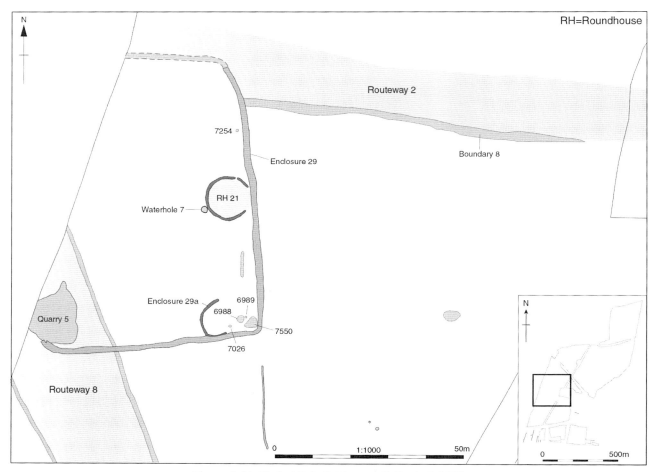

Figure 3.31 Period 3.5: Settlement 8. Scale 1:1000

Enclosure 29
Lying between Routeway 2 and Routeway 8 was a rectilinear enclosure (Enclosure 29, Fig. 3.31). Its southern perimeter ditch appeared to be beginning to turn northwards at its western end, suggesting that the south-west corner lay just inside the excavated area. Similarly, the eastern ditch seemed to be turning west at the point where it was truncated, suggesting the location of the enclosure's north-east corner. If these observations are correct, Enclosure 29 would have been rectangular in plan, measuring $c.68$m, north to south, and 56m wide, internally. The northern end of the eastern ditch cut across Boundary 8, which had defined the southern edge of Routeway 2 since Period 3.3, suggesting that the route was diverted slightly to the north at this point. The western end of the southern ditch ended in a rounded terminal, suggesting the existence of an entrance, in excess of 10m wide, at the south-west corner of the enclosure (Quarry 5 lay at this point).

Pottery from the ditch was only broadly dated to the early Roman period (1st–3rd centuries AD), but a coin of Claudius I (SF 1268), datable to AD 41–54, was found adjacent to the south-eastern corner of the enclosure (Crummy, Chapter 6.II). Such coins are thought to have fallen out of circulation by the early Flavian period (early AD 70s) at the latest.

Roundhouse 21
Enclosure 29 appears to have contained a single roundhouse (Roundhouse 21), which was located immediately inside the eastern perimeter ditch (Fig. 3.31). This survived as a fragmentary penannular gully, up to 0.6m wide and 0.35m deep, with an internal diameter of 11.29m. An entrance, 6.25m wide, was located on the eastern side of the building, which suggests that there must have been some sort of causeway or 'bridge' across the adjacent enclosure ditch, since access to the entrance would have been impossible otherwise; no trace of this was recorded, however. No internal features or deposits had survived, but pottery from the ring gully included late Iron Age/early Romano-British forms.

External features
A large circular pit or waterhole (Waterhole 7) lay immediately adjacent to the south-western side of Roundhouse 21 (Fig. 3.31). This was 1.7m in diameter and 1m deep, and yielded a few sherds of Iron Age pottery. Some 15m north of the building, a stone-lined pit (*7254*), possibly used for cooking, was also recorded. This circular feature, 0.8m in diameter and 0.4m deep, yielded pottery of similar date to that from the roundhouse gully.

Enclosure 29a
A small curvilinear enclosure, measuring approximately 14m east to west and $c.9$m north to south internally, was located at the south-east corner of Enclosure 29 (Fig.

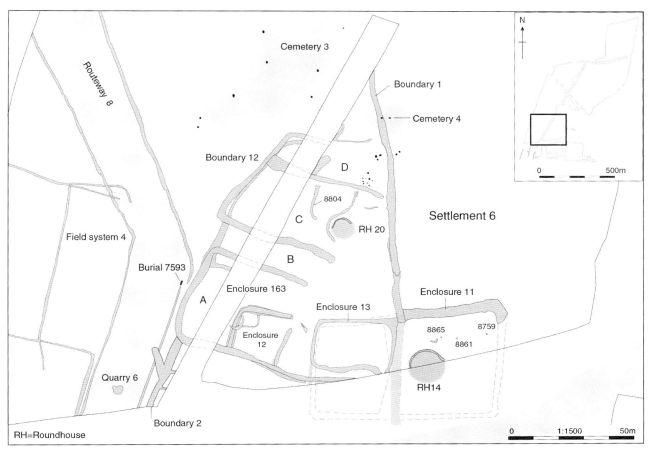

Figure 3.32 Period 3.5: Settlement 6. Scale 1:1500

3.31). Its southern and eastern sides were formed by the perimeter ditch of Enclosure 29 itself, whilst its western and north-western sides were defined by a curving ditch. On the north-east, this terminated *c*.10m short of the east ditch of Enclosure 29, suggesting the existence of a broad entrance at the north-east corner. The enclosure contained four pits (*6988, 6989, 7026, 7550*), two of which (*6988, 7026*) yielded Iron Age pottery. Pit *6988* also contained burnt animal bone.

Settlement 6
(Fig. 3.32; Pl. 3.17)

Roundhouse 14
As rebuilt for the fifth (and final) time, Roundhouse 14 measured approximately 13m in diameter, internally, with an east-facing entrance (Fig. 3.32). Two fragments of a U-profiled ring gully (*8500*), located on the northern and southern sides of the structure, had survived; these were up to 0.82m wide and 0.39m deep. The surviving gully terminal at the entrance yielded 161 sherds of pottery and a fragment of upper rotary quern (Percival and Shaffrey, Chapter 6.VI; SF 3537). The pottery assemblage (Percival and Lyons, Chapter 7.III), which represented 12%, by weight, of the total ceramic assemblage from Period 3.5, consisted mostly of handmade shell-tempered fabrics, although significant amounts of grog-tempered material were also found. This was combined with Romanised pottery fabrics including wheel-made proto-Sandy greyware sherds, and a Verulamium mortarium: the pottery may have been deliberately deposited upon the final abandonment of the roundhouse in the early post-conquest period. The later Iron Age pottery is illustrated in Chapter 7, Fig. 7.9, Nos 26–28.

A group of three pits (*8759, 8861, 8865*), located to the north-east of Roundhouse 14, were probably associated with the final phase of occupation within the building. All were 0.4–0.6m in diameter and 0.1–0.23m deep, with broad, U-shaped profiles. Pit *8759* had been lined with clay, perhaps suggesting a storage function, and was filled with two deposits of silty clay. Pit *8861* yielded a large quantity of early Roman pottery from its primary fill. The upper fill of the pit also contained charcoal and burnt stones.

A juvenile dog, aged 5–9 months (*10571*), was deposited in the upper part of the perimeter ditch of Enclosure 11, adjacent to Roundhouse 14.

Enclosure 163
This large, roughly D-shaped enclosure (Fig. 3.32) was formed through the 'joining up' of parts of three pre-existing enclosures (Enclosures 12, 20 and 162), by means of a new outer perimeter ditch (Boundary 12). This ditch was formed, in places, by re-definition of existing enclosure ditches (for example, the western ditch of Enclosure 162 and the southern ditch of Enclosure 12), but some sections appeared to have been freshly dug, unless they had completely removed all trace of earlier ditch lines. The enclosure was aligned north-east to south-west, measuring *c*.92m long, internally, and from 52m wide at its southern end (where it abutted Enclosure 13) to *c*.65m

Plate 3.17 Southern terminal of ditch *8804*, looking north-west, showing cattle skull in foreground. Enclosure 163, Settlement 6 (Period 3.5)

wide further north, where it respected the line of Boundary 1.

Internally, the enclosure was divided into at least four main subsidiary enclosures by a series of parallel, north-west to south-east-aligned ditches, which ran off the main perimeter ditch. The southernmost example (A) was *c.*35m wide and incorporated Enclosure 12 into its south-east corner. This pre-existing enclosure was seemingly also sub-divided at this time by the cutting of a new ditch, which ran north-east into the enclosure from Boundary 2, on the south. This created a roughly square paddock, *c.*17m square, at the north-western end of Enclosure 12 and closely linked to retained Enclosure 13 to the east. The recovery of a sherd of Campanian wine amphora from the contemporary infill of the terminal of Boundary 12 is notable as the only example of this form from the site.

To the north was a narrow, rectangular area (B), approximately 10m wide, which may have formed a point of access and north of this again was a larger enclosure (C), *c.*27m wide. Roundhouse 20 occupied the eastern part of this area, which seems to have been partitioned off from its surroundings by a north-east to south-west aligned ditch (*8804*), of which only a segment, 13m long, remained. A cattle skull had been placed in the southern terminal of this feature (Pl. 3.17), and the pottery assemblage included one vessel of which the base had been deliberately pierced prior to deposition. Immediately west of Roundhouse 20, a curvilinear ditch, up to 1.08m wide and 0.38m deep, clearly respected the position of the roundhouse, since it curved around the west side of the structure, between the building and ditch *8804*.

North of Roundhouse 20 was a fourth subsidiary enclosure (D), *c.*15m wide, which lay at the northern end of Enclosure 163. The western end of this was partitioned from the rest by a ditch, creating a roughly square paddock, measuring *c.*15m across, at the extreme north-west corner of Enclosure 163.

Routeway 8 and Quarry 6
To the west of Enclosure 163, a track or droveway (Routeway 8) was redefined, which probably linked to Routeways 2 and 3 at either end (Figs 3.25 and 3.32). This was a substantial feature, defined by a pair of parallel ditches set 18–27m apart. The track entered the site from the north-west, and ran north-west to south-east for *c.*125m before turning to the south-west, on which alignment it was traced for a further 75m before running beyond the limit of the investigation. In this section of the track, its western ditch appeared to respect the position of the eastern boundary ditch of the southern field in Field System 4 (Period 3.4), but it clearly cut across the boundary ditches at the north-eastern corner of this field.

That this incarnation of Routeway 8 may have been short-lived is suggested by the fact that its north-western excavated end was cut by the perimeter ditch of an enclosure that is also attributable to Period 3.5 (see Settlement 8, Enclosure 29), and by a gravel extraction pit of similar date (Settlement 8, Quarry 5). Its southern excavated end was also cut by a smaller extraction pit (Quarry 6, Fig. 3.32), which lay *c.*30m beyond the south-western corner of Enclosure 163, and by a human burial (grave *7593*). Quarry 6 comprised three intercutting pits, together measuring approximately 4 x 4m, with a maximum depth of only 0.4m.

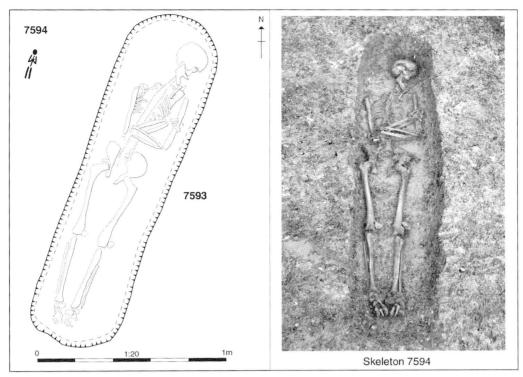

Figure 3.33 Period 3.5: Settlement 6, grave *7593*. Scale 1:20

Burials
(Figs 3.33–3.34)
Just to the west of Settlement 6, a single inhumation burial was recorded (Figs 3.32 and 3.33). In addition to this isolated grave, several other late Iron Age/early Romano-British burials were found, widely dispersed, within and around the area of former Settlement 3 (Fig. 3.34), which lay little more than 100m to the north. However, since Settlement 3 was no longer inhabited during Period 3.5, it is assumed that the graves were associated with Settlement 6. Some of these burials were placed within partially filled Iron Age settlement features, such as ditches or (in one case), the top of a waterhole, whilst others had been dug directly into the natural subsoil. The graves in this area comprised a scattered group of six cremations (Cemetery 3) and an inhumation, with two further cremations located *c*.30m to the south (Cemetery 4).

Isolated grave
The grave cut (*7593*) for the isolated burial contained the skeleton (*7594*) of a mature adult male who had been buried in a supine position with the arms crossed over the chest (Fig. 3.33). The grave was oriented north-east to south-west, measuring 2 x 0.5m and 0.25m deep. It was positioned just inside the eastern ditch of Routeway 8, offset from the northern end of the ditch. No dating evidence was recovered from the grave itself, but several sherds of early Roman Verulamium ware came from deposits associated with the trackway, into which the grave had been dug.

Cemetery 3
Six unurned cremations (*6675, 6778, 6804, 6838, 6910, 7007*) were recorded within the area of Settlement 3, scattered widely over the site of the former settlement (Fig. 3.34). Two (*6778, 6804*) had been placed in the top of the south-western perimeter ditch of Enclosure 153, a middle Iron Age feature, and another (*7007*) was dug into the northern perimeter ditch of Enclosure 31, of late Iron Age date. A fourth (*6910*) was set in the top of a disused waterhole (Waterhole 4, Period 3.3). Graves *6775* and *6838* had been dug directly into the natural clay; the former *c*.33m west of Enclosure 31, the latter within Enclosure 4, a long disused middle Iron Age feature.

Amongst the group, grave *7007* contained the remains of an adult (*7008*) of indeterminate sex. The grave fill also yielded a bone disc (SF 3374), a copper alloy pin (SF 3399) and a fragmentary copper alloy brooch (SF 3368, SF 3399, SF 3433). Burial *6910* was also that of an adult, the remains being interred with a beaker datable to the late 1st century AD or later (SF 3430). Burial *6838* contained another fragmentary brooch (SF 3397) and some iron nails and small pieces of iron sheet (SF 3398, SF 3429, SF 3410). The two brooches had almost certainly been worn, or at least placed, on the funeral pyres, whilst the nails and iron sheet probably derived from the timber used to build the pyre, or from wooden funerary deposits burnt upon it. Only pin and spring fragments remained of the brooches, meaning that their form could not be determined. Cremation *6804* yielded part of a Nauheim derivative brooch (SF 3365), indicating a date at the time of the conquest for this burial. Finds from the graves are detailed by Crummy in Chapter 6.III.

An extremely poorly-preserved inhumation burial comprised a shallow, north to south aligned grave cut (*6907*), 0.9 x 0.4m and 0.15m deep, containing the highly fragmentary remains of a crouched adult skeleton (*6906*) of indeterminate sex (Fig. 3.34). The grave was located to the south-west of the core area of occupation in Settlement 3 and yielded no dating evidence.

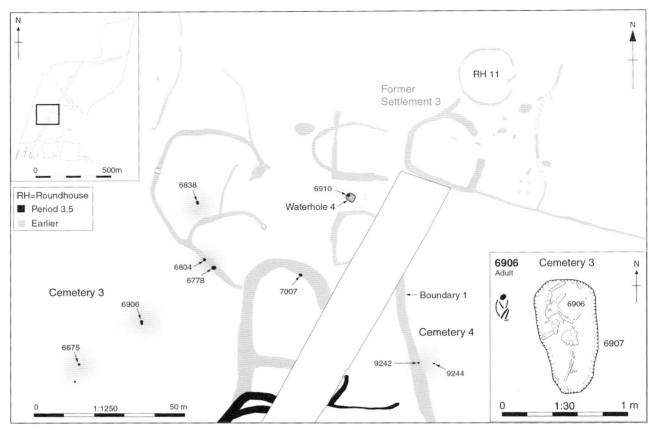

Figure 3.34 Period 3.5: Cemeteries 3 and 4. Scale 1:500

Cemetery 4

Two further unurned burials, set 3.4m apart, lay *c*.30m south-east of Cemetery 3, beyond the southern edge of Settlement 3 but north of Settlement 6 (Figs 3.32 and 3.34). One (*9242*) had been set into the top of an infilled part of Boundary 1, the major north to south boundary ditch running through Settlements 3 and 6, whilst the other (*9244*) had been dug into the natural subsoil on the eastern side of the boundary. Cremation *9242* had been placed in a circular pit, 0.38 in diameter and 0.13m deep, with steep sides and a rounded base. The burial (*9243*) was that of a young adult, and fragments of a Pompeian redware vessel, datable to the 1st century AD, were also recovered. The burial had seemingly been deliberately capped with a single large sherd of this pottery. Burial *9244* contained the cremated remains of a 5–6 year old child (*9245*), and had been capped with a flat stone.

Settlement 4
(Fig. 3.35; Pl. 3.18)

Routeway 9

Routeway 9 was 9m wide, and was bounded by two parallel ditches (Fig. 3.35; Pl. 3.18). The northern ditch was up to 0.8m wide and 0.28m deep, but that to the south was better preserved, being up to 1.3m wide and 1.3m deep. The track ran into the site from the south-east, and extended north-westwards for *c*.190m before terminating, *c*.25m short of Boundary 1. At this point, its flanking ditches turned north and south through almost 90°, to run parallel with Boundary 1. The southwards return of the southern ditch was traced for only 12m before it extended south beyond the site, but that to the north (Boundary 13), ran north as far as the south bank of Fox Brook, a distance of *c*.45m. Boundary 13 was a substantial feature, up to 3.5m wide and 1.2–1.3m deep, with steep sides and a flat base; a step was also recorded in some places along its eastern edge.

Structure 8

In the area between Boundary 1 and Boundary 13, a possible structure was erected (Fig. 3.35), immediately adjacent to the eastern side of former Roundhouse 12. Although the roundhouse had gone by this time, it is tempting to view Structure 8 as a direct replacement for the earlier building. The new structure was rectangular, aligned with its long axis north to south, 19m long and *c*.6.5m wide. On the north, south and west it was defined by square-sectioned slots or foundation trenches, measuring up to 0.6m wide and 0.27m deep; a posthole was also located at the north-eastern corner. Apart from a short segment at the extreme south-eastern corner of the structure, no trace of the east wall was recorded, although it is not clear if this was due to poor preservation or to the fact that the structure was largely open on this side. At the northern end of the structure was a slot, set 1.5m inside the north wall and aligned parallel to it. This presumably marked the position of an internal partition, perhaps indicating the existence of a narrow, corridor-like room on the northern side of the building, aligned east to west. Six evenly-spaced postholes, each *c*.0.12–0.23m in diameter and 0.03–0.08m deep, were recorded at the base of this feature, but were not present in any of the other slots. An east to west aligned slot also extended westwards for 6.4m

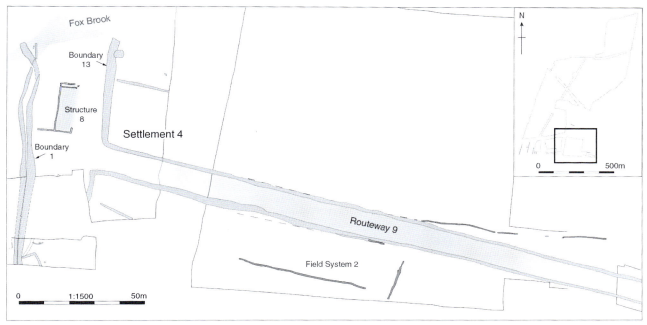

Figure 3.35 Period 3.5: Settlement 4. Scale 1:1500

Plate 3.18 Routeway 9, Settlement 4, looking south-west (Period 3.5)

from the south-western corner of the building, terminating just short of Boundary 1. This is presumed to have been an external feature, as there was no evidence that the structure itself had extended westwards towards the boundary ditch. It was undated.

VI. Discussion: the Iron Age
by John Zant

Settlement morphology

Middle Iron Age (c.400–100 BC)
(Figs 3.1–3.2)

Fields and tracks/droveways
By the Iron Age, two tracks or droveways (Routeways 1 and 2) crossed the site from east to west. In their earliest form, their positions are suggested by ditches associated with the original field system (Period 3.1, Field System 1), which was laid out between the routes (Fig. 3.1). A third parallel track (Routeway 3) is postulated to have existed just beyond the southern boundary of the site, roughly on the line of the present B1428 road, its suggested presence being based in part on the hypothesis that a prehistoric route which became a minor Roman road (Margary Road 231; Spoerry 2000, 146), once formed part of a ridgeway running west from the Ouse Valley to Cambridge (Abrams and Ingham 2008, 37).

The stratigraphically early coaxial field system associated with the tracks at Love's Farm was initially thought to be of late Bronze Age/early Iron Age date (Hinman and Phillips 2008), since field systems of this kind are a feature of the later Bronze Age in many parts of central and southern England (*e.g.* Lambrick and Robinson 2009, 73–80). On the west Cambridgeshire clay uplands, however, settlement remains of any kind pre-dating the middle Iron Age are rare, although new evidence is emerging. At Papworth Everard, for example, possible traces of late Bronze Age field systems were recorded on the clay and others have recently been found at Clay Farm near Cambridge (Phillips 2012). On present evidence, however, it appears that significant exploitation of most clayland sites in the region began in the middle Iron Age and that coaxial fields continued to be laid out, both in East Anglia and elsewhere in southern England, well into the Iron Age (Medlycott 2011, 22; Lambrick and Robinson 2009, 80–4). In the absence of any substantial evidence to the contrary (including diagnostic finds), it is therefore considered most likely that the earliest fields at Love's Farm were established during the middle Iron Age, although the possibility of an earlier origin is acknowledged. This suggested date tallies with findings at other local sites, including the A428 upgrade (Abrams and Ingham 2008) and the Cambourne New Settlement project (Wright *et al.* 2009).

Settlement
No unequivocal evidence for settlement directly contemporary with the early field system was recorded, although at a later point in the middle Iron Age (Period 3.2, Fig. 3.2), three discrete farmsteads were established, one to the north of Routeway 1 (Settlement 1) and the other two between Routeways 2 and 3 (Settlements 3 and 6), the intervening space apparently remaining in use as fields. The preferred locations for the earliest settlers, as in the preceding periods, were sheltered hollows on south-facing slopes, ideally those with an easterly aspect. The clusters of roundhouses would have appeared huddled in these sheltered dips in the landscape, perhaps masking their presence from a distance. On the northern side of Routeway 1, some distance to the west of Settlement 1, lay a substantial square enclosure (Enclosure 8) of uncertain purpose (see below).

Settlement 1 appeared more intensively occupied during the middle Iron Age than its contemporaries further south, since four closely-spaced roundhouses were revealed. The buildings may not all have been in use at the same time, however, meaning that the seemingly nucleated character of the settlement may be more apparent than real. The buildings clustered around a small, C-shaped ditched enclosure of uncertain purpose but which was probably a stock pen, the interior of which contained no archaeological features. One of the roundhouses (Roundhouse 1) was notable for being post-built rather than marked by a ring gully (see Buildings, below). It is uncertain whether Settlement 1 was enclosed, although this possibility is suggested by the presence of a double-ditched boundary to the west, which probably formed a hedge bank, and possibly also by a narrow ditch to the north. Similar evidence for hedge banks comes from Bronze Age and later sites elsewhere in southern England, including, for example, the Thames Valley (Lambrick and Robinson 2009, 57–8). At Scotland Farm, Dry Drayton the character of some of the fills in the middle Iron Age enclosure ditches suggested the possible existence of internal or external banks in various locations (Abrams and Ingham 2008, 22, 25, 31). Since many of the ditched enclosures at Love's Farm, and elsewhere, are likely to have served as paddocks and stock pens, it is likely that their associated banks were topped by stockproof hedges or fences. Environmental evidence for possible hedges, in the form of blackthorn and hawthorn-type plant remains, have been recorded at several sites in the region (Wright *et al.* 2009, 72), although these taxa are also likely to have grown wild in close proximity to many settlements.

To the south, Settlements 3 and 6 overlay elements of the initial field system; in this phase at least they may have been part of a single dispersed farmstead – both appear to have been unenclosed at this stage. Settlement 3 may have been established first, since a major Iron Age boundary ditch (Boundary 1) that extended north to south across the southern part of the site seemingly respected its position, indicating that the farmstead was already in existence when the ditch was first dug. In this initial phase, the settlement consisted of two unenclosed roundhouses on either side of Boundary 1, surrounded by minor curvilinear enclosures to the north and west. None of the latter contained structures or other features and, as in Settlement 1, they are therefore presumed to have served an agricultural purpose, perhaps as stock pens (*e.g.* Jones 2001, 25).

On the northern bank of Fox Brook lay traces of another farmstead (Settlement 6) which, as already noted, may have been part of Settlement 3 at this date. It appears to have been laid out with reference to Boundary 1 and consisted of a single roundhouse (Roundhouse 14), surrounded by ditched enclosures attached to either side of the main boundary ditch. In some respects, occupation on this part of the site resembles the middle Iron Age settlement pattern at Latton Lands, in Wiltshire, where scattered groups of roundhouses, pens and enclosures were strung out along a major linear boundary, represented in the archaeological record by a ditch (Lambrick and Robinson 2009, 110–11). Middle Iron Age settlement adjacent to a major ditched boundary is also attested at Stansted, Essex (Cooke *et al.* 2008, 82).

An inhumation burial of a woman of over 45 years of age was found in the vicinity of Settlement 6, at some distance from the ditched enclosures. Isolated inhumations of this type are not infrequently found on Iron Age settlement sites in the region; at Lower Cambourne, a similar middle to late Iron Age grave, containing the remains of a woman aged 35–50, had been cut into the fill of an enclosure ditch (Wright *et al.* 2009, 19). That the Love's Farm burial dates to the middle Iron Age was established by radiocarbon dating of the bones, which yielded a determination of 360–110 cal BC (SUERC-21982; 2165±30 BP).

To the south of Fox Brook, on the eastern side of Boundary 1, lay the corner of a large rectilinear enclosure which may represent part of another settlement (Settlement 4), the remainder of which lay outside the excavated area.

Enclosure 8
Forming a major part of the middle Iron Age landscape was a substantial enclosure (Enclosure 8) on the northern side of Routeway 1, the function of which remains uncertain. At *c.*55–60m square, it was one of the largest Iron Age enclosures found and had a substantial perimeter ditch, at up to 3m wide and 1.15m deep. The ditch was probably augmented by an internal bank, formed by upcast from the large ditch. Although the interior was entirely exposed during the excavation, only a few scattered pits were present and few artefacts were recovered. Two of the larger pits perhaps served as livestock watering holes.

A sub-rectangular enclosure of similar size (*c.*80 x 60m), albeit of late Iron Age date, was excavated at Scotland Farm, Dry Drayton (Ingham 2008, 31–3); this too was bounded by a substantial ditch, up to 4.2m wide and 1.6m deep. However, the enclosure contained at least one roundhouse (interpreted as having a possible agricultural purpose), together with pits and a few other features, and probably housed a small farmstead. A paucity of internal features, similar to Enclosure 8, was noted in a sub-rectangular ditched enclosure of middle Iron Age date at Eaton Socon (Stansbie 2008, 43). There, the excavated interior (measuring *c.*42.8m by over 28.2m), contained a single pit, but it is possible that other features lay outside the area of investigation, as only around half of the enclosure was exposed. Also in the Ouse Valley, at Little Paxton Quarry, an irregular, roughly pentagonal, ditched enclosure of early/middle Iron Age date was completely excavated. Although measuring *c.*40 x 30m at its widest points, no features were found within the interior, which was defined by a perimeter ditch up to 1.6m wide and 1m deep (Jones 2000, 134). Here, the complex treatment of the entrance into one of the middle Iron Age ditched enclosures was suggestive of a possible association with stock (Jones 2001, 24), in marked contrast to the apparently single entrance into Enclosure 8 at Love's Farm which consisted of a simple gap in the perimeter ditch. In the absence of any evidence of domestic occupation, it appears likely that Enclosure 8 either served an agricultural purpose, related presumably to livestock management, or was perhaps used in a ceremonial manner. Although no evidence for a funerary association was found, a broadly comparable example found adjacent to a braid of the Icknield Way at Hinxton was apparently used as a mortuary enclosure, since it was associated with various burials (Lyons in prep. a).

It is notable that, whilst all the other middle Iron Age enclosures on the Love's Farm site went out of use and were replaced during the late Iron Age, this enclosure continued to be maintained, its ditches being redefined on several occasions, suggesting that it was considered to be of particular importance. Furthermore, when Enclosure 8 did finally fall from use, in the late Iron Age/early Roman transitional period, another distinctive enclosure (Enclosure 22, see below) was constructed little more than 50m to the east. Although morphologically very different to Enclosure 8, this new enclosure was also dissimilar to all the other Iron Age enclosures on the site, and may have had a ceremonial purpose. Be that as it may, it is tempting to suggest a possible link between Enclosures 8 and 22, both functionally and in terms of the morphological development of the site, with the latter representing, perhaps, a direct replacement for the earlier feature.

Late Iron Age (c.100 BC to early 1st century AD)
(Fig. 3.9)

Settlement
The earliest evidence for enclosed settlement at Love's Farm dates to the earlier part of the late Iron Age (Period 3.3). An apparent progression from unenclosed to enclosed settlement in the Iron Age has been noted elsewhere in the region, for example at Lower Cambourne, where a single, seemingly unenclosed, middle to late Iron Age roundhouse pre-dated the establishment of an enclosed settlement (Wright *et al.* 2009, 14–16, fig. 6). A simplistic developmental model from unenclosed to enclosed settlement is, however, clearly inappropriate in the case of Love's Farm (as it is, no doubt, more widely). The pitfalls inherent in an over-simplistic view of enclosed and unenclosed settlement types has already been noted, since archaeological evidence suggests that many seemingly 'enclosed' settlements would, at one time or another, have become wholly or partially 'unenclosed', as enclosure ditches silted-up, or were deliberately filled (Rees 2008b, 74).

Settlement 1, in the northern part of the investigated area at Love's Farm, appears to have contracted in size in the later Iron Age, since at least three of the four earlier roundhouses fell from use, although it is possible that others lay outside the area of investigation. The principal new development in this part of the site was the construction of a ditched trackway or drove road (Routeway 4) which would have run diagonally off one of the pre-existing tracks (Routeway 1). The new route extended north-west from Settlement 1 for over 275m, but continued beyond the excavated area in that direction (as indicated by cropmarks; see Fig. 1.4) and may, therefore, have been considerably more extensive. Within Settlement 1, the track appeared to be linked to the surviving C-shaped enclosure (Enclosure 150). A new enclosure (Enclosure 6) was constructed on the northern side of the road. The association of the new route with Enclosure 150 suggests that livestock may have been driven to and from the enclosure via the drove road. However, it is clear that the road was also used by wheeled traffic, witnessed by the discovery of wheel ruts, and there was also evidence that it had once been surfaced with gravel. A cluster of intercutting pits for clay extraction (Quarry 1) lay adjacent to the track.

It was during this phase that the initial evidence for settlement between Routeways 1 and 2 was traced, in the form of a new farmstead (Settlement 2) set within a linear enclosure that reused part of the middle Iron Age field system (Field System 1; Enclosure 10). Much of this enclosure seemingly remained unoccupied throughout the late Iron Age. This farmstead seems never to have contained more than a single roundhouse, which was rebuilt on a different site at least twice. A small cemetery of three inhumation graves (Cemetery 1) lay within the enclosure to the north of the roundhouse and a dog had also been buried in a separate grave in the same area. Later, perhaps in the late Iron Age/early Roman transitional period, a single un-urned cremation was interred in the same cemetery.

In the southern part of the site, settlement expanded during the late Iron Age. Settlement 3 continued in use, whilst Settlement 6, which in the middle Iron Age may merely have comprised a few agricultural enclosures associated with Settlement 3, developed into a major settlement focus in its own right. South of the Fox Brook, Settlement 4 developed and a new settlement (Settlement 5) including a single inhumation burial now lay opposite it to the west: these may have been part of a dispersed pattern of settlement associated with Settlement 6, rather than independent farmsteads in their own right. A pre-existing, north to south aligned boundary ditch (Boundary 1), established during the middle Iron Age, was referenced by several of the enclosures within these settlements, suggesting that it remained a significant feature in the landscape into the late Iron Age. A new field system was evident adjacent to Settlement 4.

It is possible that these somewhat dispersed foci represent individual family groups within a larger community (Lambrick and Robinson 2009, 112), although it is equally possible that not all were occupied at the same time, in which case the distribution of roundhouses and other features could be the result of successive changes in location during the late Iron Age

(Bradley 2007, 259–60). Most of the late Iron Age settlements on the site conformed to what has been described as the 'house, pen and paddock' type (Lambrick and Robinson 2009, 115), known from many areas of central and southern England. These vary considerably in form and size, although most comprise a number of irregular, curvilinear, and/or rectilinear ditched enclosures, many often conjoined, some of which contain roundhouses, whilst others were probably stock pens or small fields. Evidence from many sites suggests that settlement space was segregated in diverse ways, and that it is consequently impossible to categorise such settlements purely on morphological grounds (Lambrick and Robinson 2009, 130–1).

During this period, the principal focus of occupation in Settlement 3 seems to have been at the western end of a probable field (Enclosure 7, Fig. 3.14). This part of the enclosure, perhaps defined by another shallow ditch, contained a substantial roundhouse (Roundhouse 11), a four-post structure, a waterhole, a D-shaped enclosure and a scatter of pits. Various other minor enclosures, some of which were clearly of different phases of activity, lay ranged along the line of Boundary 1, including conjoined D-shaped examples. One enclosure contained a rectilinear timber building (Structure 2), the three-sided appearance of which is paralleled elsewhere in the region in late Iron Age contexts (see Buildings, below). Another substantial D-shaped enclosure (Enclosure 31) held a second four-post structure (Structure 6), while a similar structure (Structure 4) lay in a seemingly isolated position on the southern edge of the settlement. The likely significance of Iron Age four-post structures is discussed below, but most probably had an agricultural purpose, serving either as grain stores or as fodder or drying racks. It is notable that four-post structures were only found associated with Settlement 3.

D-shaped enclosures of similar types to those found at Love's Farm are a common feature of Iron Age settlements in the region, and seem to have been used for a variety of purposes. At Lower Cambourne, a pair of conjoined enclosures containing roundhouses formed the main focus of a late Iron Age to early Romano-British farmstead (Wright *et al.* 2009, 17, fig 8), and a pair of similar enclosures, also containing roundhouses and other features, formed the core of a late Iron Age/early Romano-British settlement at Stansted, Essex (Cooke *et al.* 2008, 98). However, a broadly contemporary enclosure of this kind at Jeavons Lane, east of Lower Cambourne, seemingly contained no structures and very few other features (Wright *et al.* 2009, 44, fig. 17).

Enclosures associated with Settlement 6, to the south, included a pair of rectilinear examples laid out on either side of Boundary 1 (Fig. 3.15). The easternmost of these (Enclosure 11) contained a long-lived roundhouse (Roundhouse 14), whilst the western enclosure was sub-divided internally into three small paddocks. Set within a retained curvilinear middle Iron Age enclosure (Enclosure 1) was a second roundhouse (Roundhouse 18), to the west of which were four unenclosed buildings (Roundhouses 15–17 and 19).

Of note within Settlement 4 was the presence of numerous hearths and stone-lined pits – some located in reasonably close proximity to the excavated roundhouses, others seemingly isolated – which were scattered across the settled area. The precise function of none of these features could be determined, but they attest to quite intensive activity over a wide area.

Enclosures 8 and 22
On the northern part of the site, Enclosure 8 clearly continued in use throughout the late Iron Age (Periods 3.3 and 3.4), since the entire length of its perimeter ditch was re-cut twice during this period and new entrances were added. No reduction in the size of the ditch occurred (it was up to *c.*3m wide and 1.85m deep in Period 3.3, and 3.18m wide and 1m deep in Period 3.4), and, as in the middle Iron Age, very few internal features were located. This, together with a continuing paucity of 'domestic' refuse in the perimeter ditch, suggests that the enclosure continued to serve the purpose for which it had originally been constructed in the middle Iron Age, whether this was agricultural or ceremonial in nature, or was something else entirely. The possible creation of a second enclosure, attached to the western side of Enclosure 8, was suggested by the construction of Boundary 10, which ran south-westwards from the corner of the primary enclosure. Whilst this could simply have been a field boundary, its substantial size (2.3m wide and 1.26m deep) suggests that it may have served some other purpose.

Late pre-Roman Iron Age (first half of the 1st century AD) (Fig. 3.18)

Settlement
In the late pre-Roman Iron Age (Period 3.4), Settlement 1 was apparently in decline or had vanished and two new fields (Field System 3) were laid out to the east of Routeway 4, linking to it by a minor track (Routeway 6) and via a ?gated entrance further south. These distinctive fields contained a series of shallow, parallel trenches (nineteen in the southern field, and at least sixteen in the northernmost, which was not fully investigated), set approximately 3.5m apart. Their form closely resembles a system of fourteen parallel ditches found in association with a Romano-British farmstead at Caldecote Highfields, which were tentatively interpreted as the remains of a vineyard (Kenney 2007, 127–8). In view of their late Iron Age date, however, it is more likely that the Love's Farm fields were used for some kind of 'lazy bed' cultivation, as has also been suggested for a similar Iron Age system at Milton, north-east of Cambridge (Connor 1999).

Quarrying activity within Settlement 2, which continued in use, seemingly reached a peak at this time, since a substantial quarry pit (Quarry 3) was created. A similar instance of localised exploitation of a useful, and readily available, natural resource was recorded at Scotland Farm, where, during the middle to late Iron Age, a cluster of fifteen quarry pits, mostly located within one of the settlement's ditched enclosures, was dug into an outcrop of degraded chalk marl: this material was possibly used for liming the fields, but could also have been used for cob walling (Abrams and Ingham 2008, 26, 32).

Few major changes occurred in Settlements 3 and 6 at Love's Farm at this time, although a few additional enclosures were established on the periphery of Settlement 6. None contained roundhouses or other structures, and very few other internal features were recorded. Settlement 3 had evidently fallen from use in the 1st century AD, while Settlement 6 was to flourish and develop in the transitional period and beyond (see Chapter 4).

New ditched tracks or droveways were established to the west and south-east of the settlement (Routeways 8 and 9 respectively). Such droveways are extremely common features of Iron Age and Romano-British rural landscapes in many parts of Britain, and have been frequently recorded in association with late Iron Age and Romano-British farmsteads in the vicinity of Love's Farm, including clayland sites such as Lower Cambourne (Wright *et al.* 2009, 20, fig. 9), Poplar Plantation (Wright *et al.* 2009, 32, fig 13), and Ash Plantation (Abrams and Ingham 2008, 41–3, fig. 3.4).

Enclosure 8

As noted above, the substantial enclosure in the northern part of the site was recut during this period, and cobbled surfaces were added to its interior. In addition, a new rectilinear system of associated ditches (Enclosure 23) was created around the enclosure, with gaps permitting Routeway 1 to pass through the southern corner of the enclosure and additional access associated with Boundary 10 to the west. Depending on the function of Enclosure 8, this addition may relate to the management of livestock.

Transitional (mid to late 1st century AD)
(Fig. 3.25)

Settlement

In the years immediately following the conquest (Period 3.5), there is no direct evidence that settlement existed in the northern part of the site, although the pre-existing fields (Field System 3) may have remained in use and other settlement perhaps lay outside the excavated area. A substantial new circular enclosure was added to the north of the track (Enclosure 22, see below). Further south, Settlement 2 remained in use, and does not appear to have changed greatly in its essentials. Quarrying continued at a lower level than previously, associated with a roundhouse, minor enclosures, pits and a cremation burial.

On the western part of the site, which appears to have been unoccupied in the middle Iron Age, two small farmsteads (Settlements 7 and 8) were established on either side of Routeway 2. That to the north (Settlement 7) was represented only by minor enclosures adjacent or appended to a large boundary ditch, which braided out close to an area of wet ground. No trace of roundhouses or other buildings was found within the area of investigation, and the enclosures themselves contained few other features. However, the discovery of a small cemetery containing six inhumation burials (Cemetery 2), suggests that domestic dwellings were probably located nearby.

South of Routeway 2, Settlement 8 comprised a single roundhouse (Roundhouse 21) situated within a rectilinear ditched enclosure (Enclosure 29) that overlay part of the droveway (Routeway 8) running between Routeways 1 and 2. A superficially similar late Iron Age farmstead was excavated at Scotland Farm, Dry Drayton, on the clay uplands east of Love's Farm (Ingham 2008). There, a somewhat larger, rectangular enclosure, measuring *c.*80 x 60m, contained at least one roundhouse and a sparse scatter of other occupation features. Only a few pits, a minor enclosure and a quarry were found within the Love's Farm enclosure. This settlement proved to be short-lived, and had been abandoned by the early Romano-British period.

In Settlement 6, the transitional period saw a move towards more nucleated settlement, when an integrated complex of enclosures (Enclosure 163), surrounded by a substantial ditch, was added to the north-west corner of the farmstead. This complex was aligned north-east to south-west, at an angle to the mainly north to south orientation of the earlier enclosures and boundaries in this area, a change of alignment that would endure into the Romano-British period. A single inhumation burial lay at the end of one of the ditches associated with Routeway 8. Within the main enclosure, the existing system of interconnecting enclosures on the western side of the settlement, was developed further (although the size of the settlement remained largely unchanged, at *c.*1.5ha), creating a network of rectilinear paddocks, fields and tracks. This was in marked contrast to the situation in Settlement 3, which appears to have been abandoned in terms of settlement, but which was now used for burial (Cemeteries 3 and 4, below).

Further south, activity in Settlement 4 seems to have dwindled, although a rectilinear timber structure replaced a late Iron Age roundhouse on the western edge of the site, suggesting continuity across this period. This new building lay at the end of the track (Routeway 9) leading off Routeway 3. No other structures were recorded, however, and very little other occupation evidence was found within the excavated area. Settlement 5 seems also to have been abandoned at this time.

Enclosures 8 and 22

The precise date at which Enclosure 8 went out of use is not known, although it was seemingly abandoned by, or during, the 1st century AD. It is tempting to suggest that Enclosure 8 was replaced in the late Iron Age/early Roman transitional period by Enclosure 22, located only a short distance to the east. The new enclosure had a highly distinctive ground plan that was quite different to any of the other Iron Age (and, indeed, Romano-British) enclosures on the site. As it survived, Enclosure 22 comprised two concentric ring ditches, the outermost *c.*31–33m in diameter externally, the inner with a diameter of *c.*12m. A single entrance was positioned centrally on the eastern side of the outermost ditch, but the inner ditch was pierced by two opposed entrances, one on the east (directly opposite the entrance in the outer ditch), and one on the west. The fact that the inner ditch contained owl pellets indicates a perch for the bird during regurgitation: potentially, this might have been a centrally placed tree or totem.

As with Enclosure 8, the purpose of Enclosure 22 is unclear; at first sight (unlike Enclosure 8) an agricultural function appears unlikely on morphological grounds, principally because the entrance in the primary outer ditch was extremely narrow (only 0.6m wide), and was seemingly blocked altogether subsequently. Clearly, this would not have facilitated the easy access and egress of livestock, although it is possible that extremely tight control of such movement was required for some reason, perhaps to enable individual animals to be checked or recorded. Alternatively, it is conceivable that the size of the entrance was deliberately intended to restrict human access to single file, which, together with the monument's elevated position, and the fact that several long, ditched boundaries appeared to converge on the enclosure, could strengthen the idea that it had some kind of ceremonial purpose, an hypothesis that is considered in more detail in Chapter 9.IX. Alternatively, restricted access and a hilltop location could be indicative of a defensive function. This interpretation seems unlikely, however, since the outer ditch, whilst of reasonable size (2.4m wide and 0.84m deep, in its original form), was not particularly substantial (at least as it survived), whilst the inner ditch was no more than 1.16m wide and 0.46m deep. Furthermore, the inner enclosure was so small that it is difficult to determine what defensive purpose it could have served, except as a refuge of last resort.

The enclosure had a notable association with local routes, two of which (Routeways 1 and 7) converged upon it. This might reflect practical use as droveways leading animals towards the enclosure, or might conceivably indicate 'processional' routes.

Buildings

Roundhouses
Across the site as a whole, the number of roundhouses increased from six during the middle Iron Age (Period 3.2) to a possible maximum of thirteen during the earlier part of the late Iron Age (Period 3.3), before declining to six again in Period 3.4 and only four in Period 3.5 (although at least one roundhouse was directly replaced by a rectangular structure in Period 3.5). It is not, however, possible to determine how many of the roundhouses in each phase were actually in use at the same time. The most long-lived structure appears to have been Roundhouse 14 in Settlement 6, which was in use between the middle Iron Age and the transitional period, being rebuilt five times over this period. Its longevity, large size and position within a separate enclosure may indicate that it housed the head of the settlement.

One of the buildings in Settlement 1 is notable, in that it was the only post-built roundhouse found on the site: such buildings are generally earlier than Iron Age structures utilising ring gullies (*e.g.* Wright *et al.* 2009, 65), albeit that several of the postholes of Roundhouse 1 contained middle Iron Age pottery.

Most of the roundhouse ring gullies found at Love's Farm were of broadly similar size (*c.*9–12m in diameter), although the final phase of Roundhouse 14 in Settlement 6 (Period 3.5) was 15m in diameter. If, as seems probable, the gullies defining the structures were 'eaves-drips', rather than construction trenches, the actual buildings are likely to have been rather smaller than the above dimensions. However, at Stansted, in Essex, the lack of evidence for internal postholes or other supports suggested to the excavators that the ring gullies may indeed have been foundation slots, not eaves-drips (Havis and Brooks 2004a, 525), and indeed very few internal features were recorded within any of the Love's Farm buildings. Another possible interpretation, also postulated at Stansted, is that the roundhouses had mass walls with a timber framework, which would have supported the roof without the need for deep postholes: here, it was also suggested that, in view of the heavy clay soils at the site, the ring gullies may have served a drainage function (Cooke *et al.* 2008, 89).

At Love's Farm, an unusually small structure (Roundhouse 18 in Settlement 6, Period 3.3), was only 6m in diameter, the same size as a middle Iron Age structure recorded at Scotland Farm (Abrams and Ingham 2008, 24), but larger than the 4m-diameter ring gullies, also of middle Iron Age date, found at Little Paxton Quarry (Jones 2001, 20). Such structures might have been used for purposes other than accommodation, and the Love's Farm example was associated with several larger roundhouses located nearby. The average size of the Love's Farm roundhouses is comparable to the dimensions of many similar structures excavated at contemporary sites nearby, such as the clayland sites associated with the A428 upgrading (Abrams and Ingham 2008) and the Cambourne New Settlement development (Wright *et al.* 2009), and conforms to the average size range for roundhouses elsewhere in Britain (*e.g.* Cunliffe 2005, 318–20; Lambrick and Robinson 2009, 134, fig. 5.1). However, examples of larger structures, similar in size, or larger, than the final phase of Roundhouse 14, were rather more numerous than was the case at Love's Farm, with two middle to late Iron Age examples of 14–15m diameter being recorded at Lower Cambourne and another of 14m from a probable early Romano-British phase at the same site (Wright *et al.* 2009, 18, 21). An even larger structure, 15.7m in diameter, was attributed to a late Iron Age–early Romano-British phase at Poplar Plantation (Wright *et al.* 2009, 31), and structures in the 13–15m range are not uncommon elsewhere in the region, as at Caldecote Highfields, where two late Iron Age roundhouses, one 13m diameter, the other 15m, were located within a 'banjo' enclosure (Kenney 2007, 125–6; Kenney and Lyons 2011).

Wider discussion on the roundhouses appears in Chapter 9.IV: Buildings.

Four-post structures
Three late Iron Age four-post structures (Structures 3, 4 and 6), measuring 2.2m, 2.6m and 3m square, respectively, were associated with Settlement 3 (Period 3.3). No similar structures were recorded elsewhere on the site, or in other phases, and their presence within Settlement 3 is therefore noteworthy as potential evidence for the agricultural economy of this particular settlement in the late Iron Age. Such four-post structures, which are found widely in Iron Age contexts over much of Britain, are conventionally interpreted as granaries or storehouses (Cunliffe 2005, 412). However, in the case of scattered or isolated examples, other interpretations, such as fodder racks for livestock, or even platforms for the excarnation of the dead, are conceivable (Cunliffe 1995, 92). Local parallels are noted in Chapter 9.IV.

Rectilinear buildings
The earliest rectilinear building found at the site (Structure 2) was located within Settlement 3 and was attributed to the earlier part of the late Iron Age (Period 3.3). This building, which appears to have been enclosed, on the south and west at least, by a curving enclosure ditch, was 7m long and 5m wide, internally. It walls were marked by a shallow, U-profiled gully or construction trench, but no trace of the east wall was found, suggesting that the structure was open-sided. With the exception of a single possible posthole, no internal features or deposits were recorded.

A much larger building (Structure 8) lay within Settlement 4, to the south of Fox Brook. This rectangular structure, which was of apparent transitional date (Period 3.5), measured 19m by 6.5m. Its walls were marked by square-sectioned slots or construction trenches, except on the east. Like Structure 2, therefore, it is possible that this building was open-sided on the east. The only internal feature recorded was a post-trench, containing six evenly-spaced postholes, which seemingly partitioned off the northern end of the structure, creating a corridor-like space, 1.5m wide. A slot, extending west for over 6m from the south-west corner of the building, was thought to be external, since there was no other evidence that the building had extended westwards. The fact that Structures 2 and 8 both directly replaced earlier roundhouses (Roundhouses 10 and 12 respectively) might suggest that these structures were used for accommodation, assuming, of course, that the roundhouses themselves were dwellings. No other evidence for the possible function of either building was recovered. In view of the predominantly east-facing aspect of most of the round-house entrances (at least in those cases where the evidence had survived), the fact that the east walls of these buildings were treated differently to the rest might also be significant. However, whether the absence of slots/ construction trenches on the east means that these structures were completely open on that side, or merely indicates that the east walls were constructed differently, perhaps with structural timbers resting directly on the ground, is unclear.

Evidence for late Iron Age rectangular structures is generally sparse, although rectangular buildings are known from pre-Roman levels at Silchester, Hampshire (Fulford and Timby 2000), and a possible example defined by foundation trenches was recorded at Bierton, near Aylesbury in Buckinghamshire (Allen 1986). Possible square or rectangular structures of the conquest period, with wall-lines marked by rectilinear gully settings, were noted at Addenbrooke's Hospital, in Cambridge (Evans *et al.* 2008, 138–9). Here, the possibility that these may have been shrines was considered, although the lack of any reliable evidence for ritual associations led to the conclusion that they were probably domestic in character.

Cemeteries and isolated burials
Twenty-two human burials were recorded at Love's Farm, all of which have been assigned to the Iron Age. The earliest was middle Iron Age (Period 3.2; associated with Settlement 6), and four were dated to the earlier part of the late Iron Age (Period 3.3; three associated with Settlement 2 and one with Settlement 5). The great majority (17) were, however, attributable to the late Iron Age/early Roman transitional period (Period 3.5; one in Settlement 2, six in Settlement 7, and ten certainly or probably associated with Settlement 6). All the recorded burials were formal, in the sense that the bodies or cremated remains had been interred in discrete, individual grave cuts. There were no multiple burials, and no disarticulated, or partly articulated, bones were recovered, although disarticulated human remains, particularly skulls and limb bones, are frequent finds at Iron Age settlement sites across southern and central England (Whimster 1981; Hill 1995; Madgwick 2008). Some of the graves were stratigraphically isolated, since they did not intercut with any other features, but many of the later burials had been placed, either deliberately or fortuitously, in the tops of earlier features (mainly enclosure ditches).

The single middle Iron Age burial was attributed to this period on the basis of radiocarbon dating, which yielded a determination of 360–110 cal BC (SUERC-21982; 2165±30 BP). The grave itself contained the unfurnished remains of a woman of over 45 years of age, buried in a tightly crouched position. Isolated middle Iron Age burials of broadly similar type are known from several settlement sites in the general area, and, indeed, across southern England. At Bob's Wood, Hinching-brooke, a young/middle adult male, radiocarbon dated to the period 380–200 cal BC (SUERC-21983; 2215±30BP) had been buried in a prone position with the legs drawn up tightly under the chest, as if kneeling and slumped forwards. At Lower Cambourne, a middle to late Iron Age crouched inhumation, of a female aged 35–50, was cut into the fill of an enclosure ditch (Wright *et al.* 2009, 19). A few small inhumation cemeteries associated with middle Iron Age settlements have also been excavated elsewhere in the south, and it is possible that burial grounds of this kind were quite widespread (Cunliffe 2005, 552; Lambrick and Robinson 2009, 303), although none are yet known from the area around Love's Farm.

Of the four late Iron Age graves at Love's Farm – all inhumations and all attributed to *c*.100 BC to early 1st century AD (Period 3.3) – three were associated with Settlement 2, in the northern part of the site (Cemetery 1), whilst the fourth was an isolated burial located close to Roundhouse 13 in Settlement 5, some distance to the south-west. Two of the three burials in Cemetery 1 lay close together; both were of young adults of indeterminate sex – one crouched, the other semi-flexed. The third grave, located *c*.40m east of the other two, contained an adult female in a semi-flexed position. Two of the bodies had been placed on their right sides. None of the burials was accompanied by grave goods, although all had been badly truncated by ploughing, making it conceivable that some artefacts accompanying the graves had been lost. Almost equidistant between the two young adult graves, on the west, and the female grave on the east, was the burial of a small dog. The grave located in Settlement 5 lay close to Roundhouse 13 and might, therefore, have been associated with that structure. It contained the remains of an adult male, buried in a semi-flexed position on the right side, with the head to the east. Fragments of a copper alloy ring were recovered from the grave fill, but no other grave goods were present.

The seventeen burials attributed to Period 3.5 comprised eight inhumations and nine cremations. Six of the inhumations formed a small burial ground (Cemetery 2) contemporary with the earliest phase of activity in Settlement 7. All the individuals were adults and, of the three that could be confidently identified, all were female. A fourth may have been male, whilst the other two were of uncertain gender. Apart from the youngest individual, a young woman buried in a crouched position, all the bodies were flexed or semi-flexed, and all but one (an adult of indeterminate sex) were certainly or possibly laid on the left side; the exception may have been laid on the right side, but the grave was so badly truncated that this could not be certainly established. Three were aligned north-east to south-west, one north to south, and one east to west; the orientation of the sixth could not be determined. None of the burials was accompanied by any grave goods. The other two inhumations were isolated graves loosely associated with Settlement 6, and probably formed part of the same dispersed burial ground as Cemeteries 3 and 4 (below). Both were aligned north to south and contained adults, a mature male, in the case of grave *7593*, buried in a supine, extended position with the arms crossed over the chest, and an unsexed individual in the case of grave *6907*, possibly buried in a crouched position on the left side.

All but one of the cremations may have related to Settlement 6; they were mostly scattered across the area formerly occupied by Settlement 3, immediately to the north (Cemeteries 3 and 4), but the fact that this settlement appears to have been abandoned by Period 3.5 suggests that the graves relate to the inhabitants of the adjacent Settlement 6, which was clearly occupied at this time. These nine burials probably related to a single dispersed cremation burial ground (Lambrick and Robinson 2009, 306–7). They comprised a broad demographic range, including a child, five to six years of age, an infant/juvenile, at least two sub-adults/younger adults, and several adults. None of the individuals could be sexed with certainty, although one grave may have contained the remains of an adult female.

A further cremation was found in association with Settlement 2, and had been placed close to two of the late Iron Age inhumations, suggesting that knowledge of this area as a burial ground persisted. It was that of a mature or older adult, possibly a male.

The weight of cremated material present within the cremation pits varied considerably, from 42g to 646g, with most graves containing *c*.50–150g of material. Considering that an average of 1600g of bone would be expected from a single adult cremation (McKinley 1993), it is evident that only a proportion (and frequently a very small proportion) of the cremated material was being collected for formal burial, even allowing for the fact that many of the graves were probably truncated by ploughing, or otherwise disturbed. This phenomenon was also apparent in a small mid-late 1st century AD cemetery at Addenbrooke's Hospital (Dodwell *et al.* 2008, 49–52), where three cremations were found, and was recorded in a large, late Iron Age cremation cemetery at Westhampnett, West Sussex (Fitzpatrick 1997a). It is also commonly attested in Romano-British cremations of all dates elsewhere in Britain. Presumably, collection of all the human remains was considered unimportant, if the appropriate rites had been performed.

Unlike most of the inhumation burials, the majority of the cremations were accompanied by grave goods, mostly items of personal ornament, a feature characteristic of the Aylesford(-Swarling) (Gallo-Belgic) type burials of the late pre-Roman Iron Age in the east and south-east of England (Whimster 1981, 147–59; Fitzpatrick 1997a), in areas under Catuvellaunian influence. The burials probably relate to the final, Lexden, phase of the Aylesford(-Swarling) culture defined by Stead (1976, 401) and the third level of Late Iron Age burials defined by Haselgrove (1984) which probably dates to the period after 15–10 BC (Sealey 1997, 27–31) and continued until *c*.AD 50–55 (Atkins *et al.* 2014, 233). Such graves normally contain only pottery vessels and/or some personalia, usually dress accessories. The character of the grave goods suggests that the community at Love's Farm was of comparatively low status, as is also suggested by the lack of continental imports (Haselgrove 1982, 82–3).

The range, quantity and quality of material is meagre by comparison with that which has been found at other Cambridgeshire sites, where many such burials contained numerous complete vessels and a wide range of other items such as glass vessels, brooches and food offerings (relevant sites include Duxford (Lyons 2011), Rectory Farm, Godmanchester (Lyons in prep. b) and Hinxton (Hill *et al.* 1999)) and those further afield at Broughton, near Milton Keynes (Atkins *et al.* 2014)). Further comments on the spread of Gallo-Belgic influence, which it now appears reached at least as far as the eastern side of the Ouse Valley, appear in Chapter 7.VI and Chapter 9.VII.

Of the Love's Farm burials, one associated with Settlement 2 and two associated with Settlement 6 yielded no grave goods. However, one of the latter, containing the remains of a 5–6 year old child, had a flat stone laid over the grave as a capping. Another, the burial of a sub-adult or young adult, had also seemingly been capped, in this instance with a Pompeian red ware dish or platter. Copper alloy brooches had been placed in three other burials – those of an infant/juvenile, a sub-adult and an adult – and the remains of two other adults had been interred in pottery vessels. The adult burial containing the brooch also yielded a bone disc, and one of the urned cremations was accompanied by burnt animal bone, fragments of which were also recovered from an otherwise unfurnished, un-urned grave in the same cemetery. This is perhaps evidence for the placement of food offerings on the funeral pyre, although feasting associated with the burial rites is also a possibility (Evans *et al.* 2008, 137). The brooch types found with the Love's Farm burials are all common forms, which were also recovered from the settlements (see below and Crummy, Chapter 6.III).

As noted above, the burials in Cemetery 2 formed a discrete group, and clearly represented a formal, if small, cemetery. The lack of evidence for structures or domestic occupation within the excavated area of Settlement 7 in Period 3.5 suggests that the burial ground lay on the periphery of the settlement, as was the case at middle to late Iron Age settlement sites elsewhere in southern England (Cunliffe 2005, 552), including Stansted, in Essex, where a small cemetery of seven burials was found to the north of a late Iron Age/early Romano-British settlement enclosure (Cooke *et al.* 2008, 111–12), and at a settlement of the mid–late 1st century AD excavated at Addenbrooke's Hospital, Cambridge (Evans *et al.* 2008, 47–57). The graves loosely associated with Settlement 6, on the other hand, formed a quite dispersed pattern, mostly scattered across the area previously occupied by Settlement 3, but with some located further south, in closer proximity to the settlement.

At Addenbrooke's Hospital, the mid–late 1st-century AD cemetery comprised three urned cremations, sixteen inhumations and a single dog burial, located immediately outside a contemporary settlement. Additionally, six isolated inhumations, presumed to be of broadly similar date, were located elsewhere on the site (Evans *et al.* 2008, 55), recalling the dispersed burial pattern evident to the north of Settlement 6 at Love's Farm. These twenty-five graves (twenty-two inhumations and three urned cremations) were broadly contemporary with the seventeen burials attributed to Period 3.5 at Love's Farm. At Addenbrooke's, most of the inhumation graves were aligned broadly north-east to south-west or south-east to north-west, and a preference for this orientation has also been noted at contemporary cemeteries elsewhere (Evans *et al.* 2008, 57). At Love's Farm, three of the burials in Cemetery 2 were aligned north-east to south-west, with all but one of the other contemporary inhumations orientated north to south (the exception, grave *5939* in Cemetery 2, being aligned west to east). As at Love's Farm, the Addenbrookes' inhumation burials were all poorly furnished, with definite grave goods being found in only two of the graves in the 'formal' cemetery, a near-complete pot in one and part of a copper alloy bracelet and several copper alloy rings in another, although a pot found near one of the isolated bodies, which had been placed in a ditch terminal, may have been buried with it (Evans *et al.* 2008, 48, 55). Another of the isolated graves was also located within a ditch, but, unlike the first example, had been laid in a well-defined grave cut dug beneath the level of the base of the ditch.

At Love's Farm, none of the excavated inhumation burials had been placed within or cut into earlier features. However, the six graves in Cemetery 2 (Period 3.5), clearly referenced the adjacent boundary ditches in Settlement 7, and an isolated grave (*11729*) of the same date was laid out just beyond the northern end of (and clearly aligned on) a ditch forming the southern edge of Routeway 8, to the east of Settlement 6. Five of the nine cremation burials loosely associated with Settlement 6 cut into earlier features, principally middle to late Iron Age enclosure ditches associated with Settlement 3, which had seemingly been abandoned by the time the burials were placed, although burial *6911*, an urned adult cremation, had been placed in the top of a disused waterhole. The possible ritual or symbolic significance of burials within ditches is well attested in the Iron Age (*e.g.* Whimster 1981, 25–9, 241–8; Hill 1995), and examples are known from several sites in the area. At Lower Cambourne, for example, an Iron Age crouched inhumation had been dug into the fill of an enclosure ditch (Wright *et al.* 2009, 19), whilst at Addenbrooke's Hospital, most of the six isolated inhumation graves were associated with boundary ditches (Evans *et al.* 2008, 57). The location of burial *6911*, within what could be described as a 'watery' feature, is also suggestive; however, in view of the fact that Settlement 3 was apparently unoccupied when the cremations were deposited, a more prosaic explanation for their positioning might be appropriate, since partially filled ditches and other features would have formed convenient hollows in the ground into which it might have seemed natural to place burials.

Most of the Period 3.5 inhumations could not be dated with any precision, and might, therefore, either pre-date the Roman conquest or be contemporary with the early years of Roman occupation. Firm dating is, however, provided by one burial within Cemetery 2 (possibly a mature adult male), which yielded a radiocarbon determination of 50 cal BC–cal AD 90 (SUERC-21978; 1965±30BP). It is presumed that the other five burials in this cemetery are of broadly similar date. Of the cremations, one was interred in a greyware vessel of late 1st- to early 2nd-century date. As noted above, another grave had been capped with a Pompeian red ware dish or platter, datable to the period *c.*AD 40–80, whilst another had been furnished with a Nauheim derivative brooch, a form introduced at the conquest but continuing in use into the Flavian period. The two other brooches were too fragmentary to be certainly identified, but may have been Colchester types, attributable to the period *c.*AD 10–50 (Crummy, Chapter 6.III).

Further discussion of the wider context of the Love's Farm burials appears in Chapter 9.VIII.

'Ritual' deposition

Clear evidence for 'placed' deposits – a common feature of sites of the period – included examples possibly associated with foundation ceremonies, and others perhaps related to rituals of closure. The earliest recorded foundation deposit, attributed to the middle Iron Age (Period 3.2), comprised a saddle quern (SF 2718; Chapter 6.VI), found within the southern ditch terminal of Enclosure 150 in Settlement 1, which had been placed with its worked side face down on the base of the ditch cut.

In the earlier part of the late Iron Age (Period 3.3), an unusual, three-pronged iron object (Fig. 6.41, SF 3106) appears to have been deliberately placed on the base of a ditch terminal associated with Enclosure 1 in Settlement 6 (see further comments in Chapter 9.IX). The same ditch terminal also contained an unusually diverse range of finds within some of its fills. The animal bone included two cattle skulls, a horse skull, pig and sheep mandibles and other bones, and more than 200 sherds of predominantly middle Iron Age pottery. Other finds from the ditch terminal included a spindlewhorl (Fig. 6.48, SF 3107), a socketed bone tool made from a polished sheep tibia (SF 3108; Fig. 6.53) and a triangular clay loomweight (Fig. 6.46, SF 3109).

In Settlement 2, closure of the substantial complex of late Iron Age quarry pits (Quarry 3, Period 3.4) may have been marked by the deposition of a substantial assemblage (over 700 sherds) of late Iron Age pottery in the uppermost fill (*6358*). This pottery did not appear to have accumulated gradually as rubbish, but had apparently been deliberately scattered over the top of the feature. A coin of Cunobelin (SF 2711) was also recovered from the same fill. In Settlement 3, which was seemingly abandoned in the late Iron Age (Period 3.4), a fairly large late Iron Age pottery assemblage, comprising over 100 sherds and including at least two semi-complete vessels, was recovered from the upper fills of the southern entrance terminal of Enclosure 159, and another relatively large assemblage, including a near-complete storage vessel, came from the northern terminal. It is conceivable that both deposits were linked to the abandonment of the settlement.

In the late Iron Age/early Romano-British transitional period (Period 3.5), a relatively large assemblage (161 sherds) of pottery and a burnt rotary quern fragment (SF 3537), the latter evidently an import from Yorkshire, was recovered from the eastern entrance terminal of Roundhouse 14 in Settlement 6, possibly having been deposited at the time the roundhouse was abandoned. The quern fragment was broken, perhaps intentionally, since deliberate damage to querns has been noted on several sites in Cambridgeshire (Percival 2004a), and elsewhere in southern England (Hill 1995). A pit (*8861*), located immediately adjacent to Roundhouse 14, also contained a large quantity of early Roman pottery and a complete, but broken, rotary quern (SF 3003). Elsewhere in Settlement 6, the southern terminal of ditch *8804*, located to the rear of Roundhouse 20, yielded a cattle skull and the base of a pottery vessel that had been deliberately pierced.

There was no clear indication that either of the two Iron Age dog burials found at Love's Farm had any overtly ritual significance, although the earliest example (*6348*), attributed to the earlier part of the late Iron Age (Period 3.3), appears to have been loosely associated with Cemetery 1, within Settlement 2. It had been interred in a discrete grave cut, located almost equidistant between two human burials, on the west, and a third grave to the east. In the late Iron Age/early Roman transitional period (Period 3.5), a juvenile dog was buried in the ditch of Enclosure 11, that enclosed Roundhouse 14.

Conclusions

Intensive and sustained settlement commenced at Love's Farm in the middle Iron Age, as is now known to have been the case in many of the clay upland areas of the region. The excavated remains provide highly significant information pertaining to the origins and development of agricultural settlement within this landscape, and shed important light on the everyday lives of its ancient inhabitants. The finds and environmental evidence point to the home production of basic necessities at 'craft' level, to supply the community's everyday needs, along with a mixed farming economy (see Chapters 6–8). Evidence was sought for ritual or ceremonial activities, but – as elsewhere in the region – conclusive proof remained elusive. The most common form was the incidence of 'special' or 'structured' deposits, possibly representing propitiary offerings related to fertility and the agricultural cycle. Towards the end of the Iron Age, the appearance of traded finewares at the site was consistent with the widespread adoption of Gallo-Belgic cultural influences across the south-east in the immediate pre-Roman period, a development further reflected by several cremation burials of the Aylesford(-Swarling) type. More general discussion of the findings appears in Chapter 9.

Chapter 4. Romano-British (Period 4)

by John Zant and Mark Hinman,
with Taleyna Fletcher, Sarah Henley, Liz Muldowney, Tom Phillips and Alexandra Pickstone

I. Introduction

Whilst the 1st century AD was evidently a time of change at Love's Farm, it was often unclear in archaeological terms whether certain developments on the site occurred before the arrival of the Romans in southern England in AD 43, or during the early decades of the Roman occupation. Consequently, some overlap in the phasing of the site was required during this transitional period (Period 3.5). By the end of the 1st century AD, however, the settlement pattern within the investigated area was clearly quite different to that which pertained at the start of the century, but whether this was a direct result of the Roman occupation is more doubtful, since the most visible demographic changes, particularly the emergence of an increasingly nucleated settlement pattern, and the abandonment of settlement on the northern half of the site, had already begun prior to the Roman conquest.

The pattern of settlement during the Romano-British period was relatively simple at the broadest level. Two distinct, nucleated settlements developed on the site, one immediately north of one of the prehistoric tracks that crossed the site from east to west and the other to the south, adjacent to Fox Brook. Both farmsteads developed directly out of pre-existing Iron Age settlements (Settlement 7 to the north; Settlement 6 to the south), where occupation was clearly continuous and uninterrupted from the late Iron Age into the Roman period. Settlement 7 had only been established in Period 3.5, the period of late Iron Age/early Romano-British transition, and activity was initially very restricted, a situation that continued well into the Roman period. In contrast, Settlement 6 had been in existence far longer, its origins lying in the middle Iron Age (Period 3.2), and was consequently considerably more developed by the late 1st century AD. In the Romano-British period, Settlement 6 grew to encompass the area of pre-Roman settlement lying to the south of Fox Brook (Settlement 4), although in fact the two 'settlements' had probably always been closely linked, representing separate farmsteads (together with Settlement 3) within a larger, dispersed Iron Age settlement.

Both Romano-British settlements were sited in close proximity to pre-existing tracks or routeways that were now linked by a crossing drove- or trackway (Routeway 8), and certain significant boundaries from earlier periods were incorporated into their layouts, a pattern that was also noted in the wider landscape on the southern part of the site. Another common characteristic of both sites was the relative lack of direct evidence for the homes of the Romano-British farmers, contrasting with the generally plentiful evidence for Iron Age roundhouses on the site. Evidence for other structures was also generally scarce, being limited, for the most part, to occasional concentrations of heavily truncated postholes and post pads, which, in most cases, formed no coherent plan. The only significant exceptions were two large, rectilinear buildings, one associated with each settlement. Both buildings were of similar size and character, and were constructed during the 3rd/4th century AD; it is possible that both served as farmhouses, although they might equally have been multi-functional. With these possible exceptions, the absence of the recognisable remains of dwellings meant that the main evidence for domestic habitation was provided by localised concentrations of artefacts or rubbish, especially pottery and animal bones.

Within the Romano-British occupation sequence, four principal stratigraphic and chronological sub-divisions could be identified, broadly corresponding to activity in the late 1st–early 2nd century AD (Period 4.1), the mid–late 2nd century AD (Period 4.2), the 3rd century AD (Period 4.3), and the 4th century AD (Period 4.4). Additionally, a phase of very late Roman/early post-Roman occupation (Period 4.5) was identified in Settlement 7, but virtually no evidence for contemporary activity was noted in Settlement 6.

II. Period 4.1: early Romano-British (late 1st to early 2nd century AD)

Introduction
(Fig. 4.1)
On the northern part of the site, Settlement 7 saw very limited development during the early Roman period (Fig. 4.1). The Iron Age route (Routeway 2) that defined the southern side of the settlement continued in use throughout the Romano-British period, being redefined in the early Roman period as a trackway flanked by ditches. Several key features of the Iron Age/Romano-British transitional period (Period 3.5) were also retained, with the addition of a new enclosure and other agricultural features.

In Settlement 6 to the south, development seems to have been more rapid, perhaps because the settlement had been existence since the middle Iron Age, and was already well established by the beginning of the Romano-British period. In Period 4.1, the core area of the settlement was fully enclosed by a boundary ditch (Boundary 100), within which were several subsidiary enclosures, some newly created, others retained from Period 3.5, and incorporated into the new layout. For the most part, evidence for occupation within these enclosures was extremely limited, suggesting that most may have been used for agricultural purposes, perhaps as livestock paddocks. The exception was Enclosure 100, a feature retained from Period 3.5 (Enclosure 163 Area C), which contained all four of the timber structures that were

Figure 4.1 Period 4.1: Early Roman phase plan. Scale 1:5000

erected within this settlement during this phase (Structures 100, 101, 102 and 109).

Only limited evidence for activity outside the enclosed area was found, although Routeways 8 and 9, established in Period 3.5, both seem to have been retained; indeed, the latter appears to have continued in use into the 3rd–4th centuries AD. The highly fragmentary remains of possible ditched field systems (Field Systems 5 and 6) and a few other features, notably including a horse burial, were recorded south of the enclosed settlement on the north bank of Fox Brook.

Settlement 7
(Fig. 4.2)

Summary
Occupation within Settlement 7 in the western part of the site continued, seemingly without interruption, into the early Romano-British period (Fig. 4.2), although activity remained at a low level until the 4th century AD (Period 4.4). Routeway 2 itself continued to be maintained, its line being redefined in the early Roman period by flanking ditches to create a comparatively narrow trackway. Key features of the preceding phase, including Enclosures 21 and 28, and the major north-west to south-east aligned drainage ditch (Boundary 109) also appear to have been retained, but only a few new features were added. These included a circular structure (Structure 110) located to the west of Enclosure 21, and a small, C-shaped enclosure (Enclosure 125) to the east, separated from Boundary 109 by a new ditch (*5262*). With the exception of Structure 110, the function of which is unclear, no buildings were recorded, as was also the case in Period 3.5. Well to the north of the settlement, the discovery of a small group of plough marks containing pottery of the late 1st–2nd century AD suggests the existence of one or more arable fields, although no trace of contemporary field boundaries or other features had survived in this area.

Routeway 2
Adjacent to Settlement 7, the large ditch (Boundary 8) that had defined the southern edge of Routeway 2 since Period 3.3 had evidently been largely infilled by the beginning of the Roman period (and had been cut across in Period 3.5 by the enclosure for Settlement 8). Despite this, the feature was re-cut in Period 4.1 as part of a redefinition of Routeway 2. Evidence for this event survived best on the extreme eastern part of the site, where the route was redefined as a trackway, up to 12m wide, by the digging of a pair of parallel flanking ditches (Fig. 4.1). The re-cut of Boundary 8 formed part of the southern ditch, but no trace of the northern ditch was found within the western part of

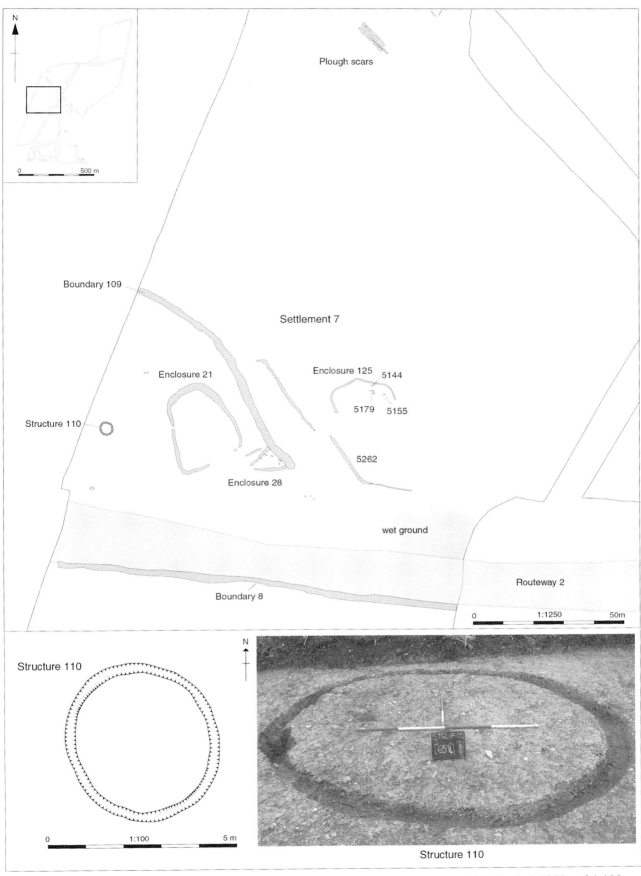

Figure 4.2 Period 4.1: Settlement 7, showing detail of possible hayrick (Structure 110). Scale 1:1250 and 1:100

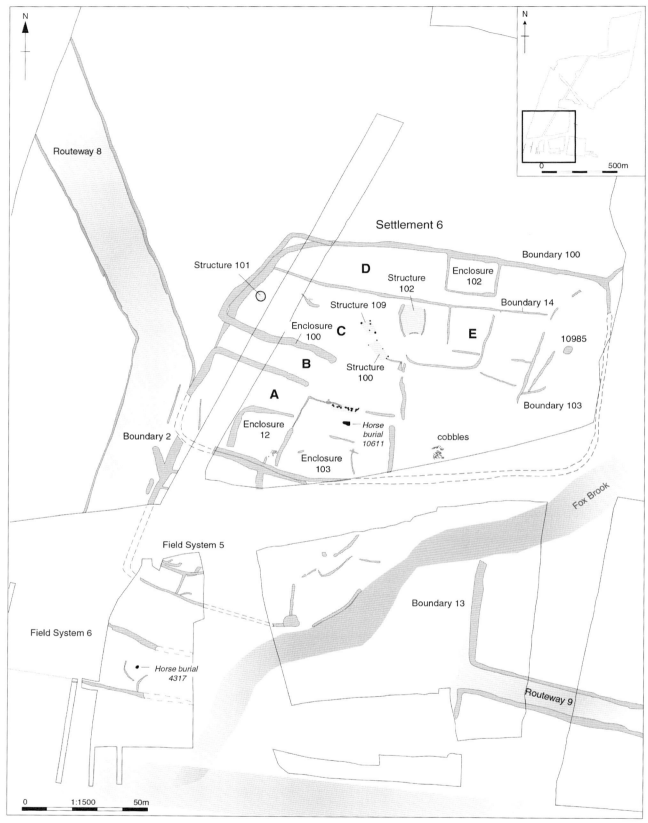

Figure 4.3 Period 4.1: Settlement 6. Scale 1:1500

the site. The new ditches, including the re-cut section of Boundary 8, were up to 1.1m wide and 0.59m deep, with steep-sided, U-shaped profiles.

Enclosures 21 and 28
The south-western side of Enclosure 21 was remodelled with the creation of a narrow entrance, 1.4m wide, across the south-western perimeter ditch (Fig. 4.2), which was re-cut. The new ditch was narrower and shallower than its predecessor, measuring 0.56–0.74m wide and 0.12–0.3m deep. A near-complete narrow-mouthed jar of late 1st- to early 2nd-century date and a stamped samian vessel (Chapter 7, Fig. 7.17, SF 3271) dating to AD 140–160 were recovered from the ditch fill.

The southernmost ditch of Enclosure 28, located immediately south-east of Enclosure 21, was also re-cut at this time. Its fills yielded a notable ceramic assemblage, comprising 202 sherds of late pre-Roman Iron Age and early Roman pottery (Lyons, Chapter 7.IV). Most of the assemblage consists of reduced ware, including the remains of two wheel-made narrow-mouthed jars, one of which was nearly complete. Vessels of this type were common in pre- and post-conquest deposits, sometimes associated with burial. Also found were the remains of a plain South Gaulish samian platter (Dr 18) dated to *c*.AD 50–100, and a Gaulish fine greyware globular beaker. Some of the pottery had been modified. These vessels include a fragmentary Gaulish Terra Rubra conical cup with post-firing holes on the vessel wall, and a flat vessel base that had evidence for at least five post-firing drilled holes. This assemblage is also remarkable in that a range of almost complete late Iron Age, imported late pre-Roman Iron Age and proto-early Roman vessels of high quality were deposited into the enclosure ditch: it is possible that the pottery, in particular reduced ware urns and the samian platter, were deposited intentionally, or represent the remains of a disturbed cremation cemetery dating to the 1st century AD.

Structure 110
Lying 18m to the west of Enclosure 21 was a small, circular structure (Fig. 4.2), 2.6m in diameter, represented by a ring ditch, 0.66m wide and 0.14m deep. The precise function of this structure is unclear, although traces of disturbance, possibly the result of burrowing by small animals, were noted within the interior, and one possible interpretation is that the structure was a hayrick, the ring-gully serving to aid drainage. A similar structure, seemingly broadly contemporary, was also found to the south, within Settlement 6 (Structure 101).

Boundary 109
The eastern side of Enclosure 28 was truncated by a re-cut of the large north-west to south-east aligned ditch (Boundary 109) to which it was appended (Fig. 4.2). As redefined, this feature was up to 2.85m wide and 1.14m deep. It drained from north-west to south-east, towards an area of wet ground on the north side of Routeway 2, which remained prone to flooding during the course of the excavations. East of Boundary 109, and aligned broadly parallel to it, was a much smaller ditch (*5262*), up to 1m wide and 0.38m deep, which was traced in two surviving segments of up to 58m. Pottery included a sandy greyware jar with a reverse S-profile (Fig. 7.11, No. 9).

Enclosure 125
Approximately 9m east of ditch *5262* were the poorly preserved remains of a small, curvilinear, ditched enclosure (Enclosure 125). Only the northern half of this enclosure, measuring *c*.18m east to west and in excess of 8m north to south, had survived (Fig. 4.2), whilst its perimeter ditch was up to 0.74m wide and 0.1m deep. Three irregularly-shaped and heavily truncated pits (*5144, 5155, 5179*) dating to the late 1st–2nd centuries AD were found in the north-eastern part of the enclosure. These were all roughly *c*.1 x 0.7m in size and 0.08–0.19m deep, and contained a few sherds of early Roman pottery and a little charcoal.

Settlement 6
(Figs 4.3–4.4)

Summary
Settlement 6 had a long history prior to the Roman conquest, having been established in the middle Iron Age (Period 3.1–3.2) and continuing in use, without interruption, throughout the late Iron Age (Periods 3.3–3.4) and the early to mid 1st century AD (Period 3.5). Occupation appears to have intensified gradually throughout this period, and a more formalised pattern of interconnected enclosures (defined by Enclosure 163 and its internal subsidiary enclosures) had begun to develop on the western part of the site, west of Boundary 1 (itself of middle Iron Age origin), by the early Roman period, a process that continued subsequently. In Period 4.1 (Fig. 4.3), the boundary ditches of Enclosure 163, which had been confined to the area west of the now disused Boundary 1, were incorporated into a new boundary (Boundary 100), which fully enclosed the core area of settlement, both east and west of the former line of Boundary 1. This effectively created a large, sub-rectangular settlement enclosure, within which were several smaller enclosures, some being newly-established (Enclosures 102, 103) and others (Enclosures 12, 100) continuing in use from Period 3.5, although Enclosure 100 at least seems to have been modified and extended. Three new rectilinear timber structures (Structures 100, 102, and 109) and a small circular structure (Structure 101) were also erected in Enclosure 100 during this period, but no contemporary buildings were found elsewhere.

Outside the settlement, the trackway on its western side (Routeway 8; established in Period 3.5), seems to have remained in use, as did the contemporary track (Routeway 9) to the south-east. A substantial ditch (Boundary 2) extended southwards from the south-western corner of Boundary 100, but its precise significance is unclear, as most of this area lay outside the site. Further south still, the highly fragmentary remains of possible ditched field systems (Field Systems 5 and 6) and a few other features, including a horse burial, were also recorded on the north bank of Fox Brook. South of the stream, virtually no contemporary features were recorded; however, spatial evidence from subsequent phases (*e.g.* Period 4.2), suggests that Routeway 9 and Boundary 13 of Period 3.5 may have continued in use well into the Romano-British period.

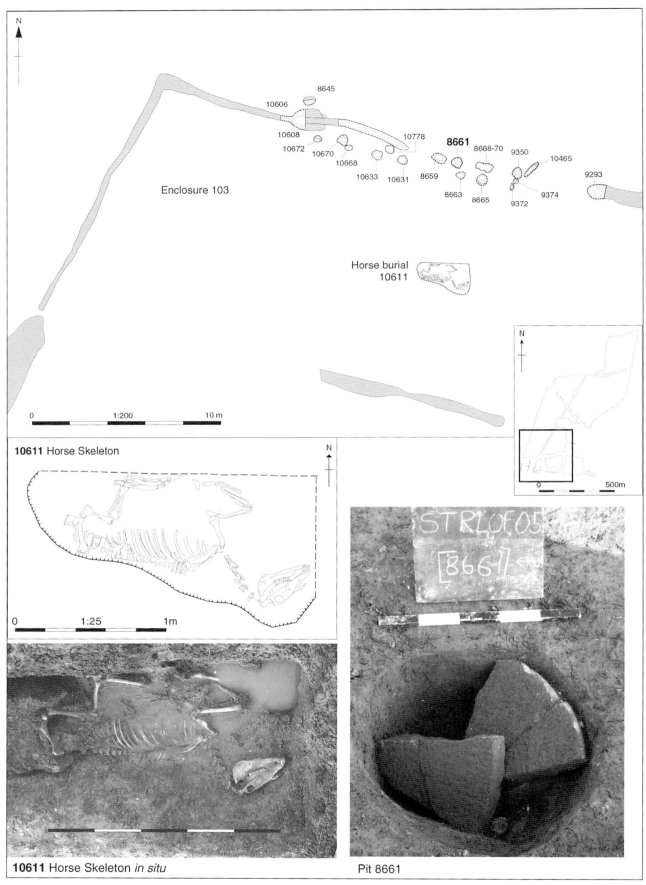

Figure 4.4 Period 4.1: Settlement 6, horse burial 10611/11210. Scales 1:200 and 1:25

The enclosed settlement

Boundary 100
As already noted, the core area of the settlement was fully enclosed, from Period 4.1, by a boundary ditch (Boundary 100), measuring 1.4m wide and 0.23m deep. This was traced around most of the settlement's perimeter (Fig. 4.3), excepting only the south-east corner and most of the east side, which lay outside the investigated area. The area enclosed was sub-rectangular, measuring *c*.140m east to west by *c*.80m, north to south, at its widest points. To the north, the ditch cut across the infilled remains of Boundary 1, which had remained in use from the middle Iron Age to the 1st century AD, but which had clearly been abandoned by this time (it was also cut across by other, internal, ditches).

Enclosure 102
This new, rectangular enclosure, measuring *c*.19.5 x 13m internally, was located immediately inside (*i.e.* to the south of) the northern arm of Boundary 100 (Fig. 4.3), utilising that ditch as its northern boundary. No internal features were recorded, and artefactual material was very limited, perhaps indicating that this area was reserved for livestock.

Enclosure 100
Enclosure 100 developed from Enclosure C located within Enclosure 163 of Period 3.5. It was bounded to the west by the western arm of Boundary 100, and to the south by a ditch that had originally been dug in Period 3.5 (Fig. 4.3). This ditch was not recut in Period 4.1, unlike the enclosure's northern ditch, which was also extended considerably to the east, across the former line of Boundary 1. This new ditch (Boundary 14) was up to 1.2m wide and 0.5m deep, and was traced eastwards from Boundary 100 for *c*.110m. It seemingly terminated adjacent to a north-east to south-west aligned ditch (Boundary 103), up to 1.1m wide and 0.5m deep, that may, therefore, have formed the eastern boundary of Enclosure 100. If this is correct, Enclosure 100 would have measured *c*.110m east to west, and *c*.25m wide, its eastern end terminating *c*.30m short of the eastern boundary of the settlement. Internally, the north-eastern corner of the enclosure may have been sub-divided by the digging of ditches of similar size and character to Boundary 14, to create a rectangular enclosure (E), measuring up to 37m east to west, by 20m north to south.

Structures 100–102 and 109
That Enclosure 100 formed the principal focus of activity during Period 4.1 is suggested by the fact that it contained all four of the structures erected within the settlement in this phase (Fig. 4.3). The westernmost example (Structure 101), lying just inside the western settlement boundary, was represented by an annular gully, 0.2–0.3m wide and 0.1–0.15m deep, with an internal diameter of 3.82m. The precise function of this structure is unclear, but a possible interpretation is that it was a hayrick, the ring-gully serving to aid drainage. A similar structure, also attributed to Period 4.1, was found to the north, within Settlement 7 (Structure 110).

Structure 100, located *c*.45m south-east of Structure 101, was rectilinear and post-built, being oriented north-west to south-east. It measured 8.2m by 4.1m and its remains consisted of five postholes, three corner posts (the south-western corner post was not found), a posthole located close to the centre of the east wall, and another located on the south wall, close to the south-east corner post. Its neighbour, Structure 109, located *c*.3m to the north, was also rectangular, and shared the north-west to south-east alignment of Structure 100. It measured *c*.7 x 4.5m and, like Structure 100, its remains comprised five postholes, three corner posts (the position of the south-west post was again not located) and two within the interior. With these exceptions, no internal features or deposits were found within either structure, and their purpose is therefore unknown.

The easternmost of the structures (Structure 102), located *c*.9m east of Structures 100 and 109, appears to have been more substantial, at least in terms of its surviving remains. It was seemingly aligned north to south, with its east and west boundaries defined by gullies or foundation trenches, up to 0.95m wide and 0.55m deep. These were noticeably curved, rather than straight, indicating that the walls of the structure (assuming these were foundation trenches, rather than external gullies) would have had a bowed appearance. No trace of a northern boundary or wall was found, whilst the possible line of the southern boundary/wall was marked by a much less substantial gully, 0.2m wide but only 0.06m deep. Within the surviving gullies, the structure was approximately 12m long, north to south, and *c*.8.8m wide, at its widest point. The presence of large quantities of charcoal and fired clay in the eastern gully, and hearth slag from the western feature (including a smithing hearth bottom (SF 3054) from the southern terminal), suggests that iron smithing may have been undertaken within the structure, or in the near vicinity.

Enclosure 12
Towards the south-western corner of the settlement, Enclosure 12 was also retained from Period 3.5 (Fig. 4.3). However, the enclosure's perimeter ditches were re-cut, now being up to 2.2m wide and 1.1m deep, and the original entrance at the north-east corner of the enclosure was retained. Despite the lack of direct evidence for domestic occupation, a notable concentration of pottery was recovered from the new enclosure ditches. With the exception of a cluster of four seemingly randomly-distributed pits or postholes, 0.27–0.66m in diameter and 0.1–0.19m deep, located at the south-east corner of the enclosure, no trace of contemporary occupation was found within it.

Enclosure 103
This new enclosure was appended to the eastern side of Enclosure 12 (Fig. 4.3), its western boundary being the eastern ditch of Enclosure 12 and its southern boundary being the southern arm of Boundary 100. The eastern side was marked by a ditch dug roughly on the line of former Boundary 1, whilst its north side was represented by a short ditch segment, to the west of which were two rows of postholes, thought to be part of a fence line (Fig. 4.4). This line of postholes or postpits ran along the northern boundary of the enclosure, effectively closing or reducing the width of the former entrance. Included amongst them was a pit (*8661*) containing a millstone (SF 3003), which appeared to have been broken *in situ* before the pit was filled. It is possible this had some votive significance. Just

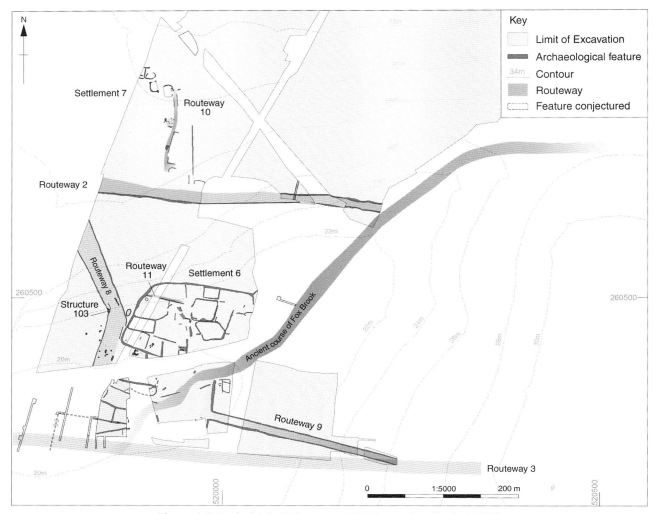

Figure 4.5 Period 4.2: 2nd century AD phase plan. Scale 1:5000

to the south, a horse (sk. *10610*) had been buried in a large pit (*10611*), *c*.2 x 1m at its widest points and 0.4m deep, which was dug into the upper fills of the northern ditch of Enclosure 13, a late Iron Age enclosure that had remained in use until Period 3.5, but which had been abandoned by Period 4.1. This stallion or gelding was approximately 9 to 10 years old at death, with some evidence for bit wear on its upper teeth, and a possibly lame front left foot (see Baxter, Chapter 8.III and Fig. 8.6). To the east of Enclosure 103, a cobbled surface was laid over the site of Roundhouse 14, a long-lived dwelling that had been abandoned some time previously.

Boundary 1
The only significant concentration of painted plaster from the site was recovered from fills of late 1st- to 2nd-century date (*10987*, *10988*) that had been deposited in the top of the largely infilled remains of Boundary 1, close to the intersection of that feature with the perimeter ditch of Enclosure 1, a middle to late Iron Age feature that had gone out of use well before the beginning of the Romano-British period. The plaster, which was mainly white, with some fragments bearing traces of red paint, also occurred residually in the fills of two large, Romano-British pits or post-pits (see Structure 107, below) that had been dug into the earlier ditch fills.

Peripheral areas
Running south-westwards from the south-western corner of Boundary 100 was a substantial ditch (Boundary 2), 2.2m wide and 1.10m deep (Fig. 4.3). This appears to have formed part of the eastern boundary ditch of Routeway 8, which was redefined at this time, but may also have formed the western perimeter of a subsidiary enclosure on the south side of the main settlement, although the relevant area lay almost wholly outside the investigated areas.

Further to the south, a series of fragmentary ditches, mostly aligned parallel to the southern arm of Boundary 100, were interpreted as the possible remains of one or more field systems (Field Systems 5 and 6). Also in this area, the scattered remains of another horse (*4317*) were buried in a pit (*4318*) measuring 1.2 x 1m and 1.14m deep (Fig. 4.3). This animal was of indeterminate sex and was approximately 12 years old (Baxter, Chapter 8.III and Fig. 8.7).

Further east, several short ditches were also found that were aligned broadly parallel to Fox Brook. These possible drainage features, which were located *c*.20–30m south of the main settlement area, varied considerably in size, from no more than 0.5m wide and 0.24m deep, to as much as 3.7m wide and 1.16m deep. One of these features yielded significant quantities of cereal chaff, especially spelt wheat glumes, as well as burnt clay and charcoal, which had clearly been dumped along the line of the ditch.

III. Period 4.2: Middle Romano-British (2nd century AD)

Introduction
(Fig. 4.5)
Occupation within Settlement 7 remained at a relatively low level during the 2nd century AD, certainly by comparison with Settlement 6, to the south (Fig. 4.5). Most pre-existing features fell out of use, and the focus of activity shifted to the vicinity of a north to south aligned track (Routeway 10), adjacent to which several small enclosures developed. A timber structure (Structure 111) was also built next to the track, and the fill of a nearby extraction pit (Quarry 7) yielded evidence for on-site pottery production.

Settlement 6 was remodelled during the 2nd century, with the creation of new enclosures and the abandonment of others. At the north-western corner, a new entrance was created from which a track (Routeway 11) ran into the interior. Some of the Period 4.1 timber structures could conceivably have remained in use, but at least one (Structure 102) had certainly gone. A single, rectangular timber building (Structure 116) was erected on the southern periphery of the enclosed settlement at this time.

Further west, Routeway 8 was cut by two groups of pits, and had, therefore, presumably narrowed or gone out of use temporarily, although a small timber structure (Structure 103) was also built on its western edge. East of the track, a small coin hoard (Hoard 1) was deposited in a pottery vessel, quite close to a spot where water-lain silts had accumulated in a damp area. The uppermost silt layer yielded a remarkable collection of mainly metal artefacts, including coins and dress accessories, which may have been votive offerings deposited in a watery place. The bulk of the datable artefacts are 2nd century, but at least one is of Claudio-Neronian date, and two of the coins are issues of the late 3rd–4th centuries. Further south, two enclosures (Enclosures 108, 109) were constructed in the areas occupied previously by Field Systems 5 and 6, on the north bank of Fox Brook. Another small enclosure (Enclosure 110) was also built further east, on the southern side of the stream. Although there is no direct evidence, it seems probable that Routeway 9, which approached the settlement from the south-east, was retained, since spatial evidence indicates that it continued in use into subsequent periods.

Settlement 7
(Fig. 4.6)

Summary
Activity on this part of the site intensified somewhat during the 2nd century AD (Fig. 4.6), although use of the area was still relatively light, compared to Settlement 6, which clearly developed rapidly in the early Roman period. Most of the earlier features in this area, including Enclosures 21 and 28 and Boundary 109 (Period 4.1) went out of use at this time, and the focus of activity appears to have shifted slightly east and north. The principal feature of this phase was a roughly north to south aligned track (Routeway 10), in the vicinity of which several new ditched enclosures (Enclosures 27, 30, 124, 129 and 166) developed, one of which (Enclosure 129) post-dated a burial pit containing a complete horse. A rectilinear timber structure (Structure 111) was also erected close to the track, on its western edge. Further south, the western edge of the track was cut by a probable clay extraction pit (Quarry 7), the fill of which yielded evidence of on-site pottery manufacture. East of the track, a north to south aligned ditch (Boundary 110) was dug, south of which, the fragmentary remains of another possible enclosure (Enclosure 140) were recorded.

Routeway 10
Routeway 10 ran roughly north to south, although on a slightly sinuous line, and was traced for approximately 95m (Fig. 4.6). It was defined by a pair of shallow, parallel ditches, set *c.*5m apart. These U-profiled features, each measuring *c.*1–1.8m wide and up to 0.55m deep, were extremely fragmentary as they survived. It would be logical to assume that the track extended south a further 25m, to link up with Routeway 2, running east to west along the southern edge of the settlement, but no direct evidence for this was found.

Enclosures 27, 30 and 129
At the northern surviving end of Routeway 10 was a complex of three small, ditched enclosures (Fig. 4.6), all of uncertain purpose. The northernmost (Enclosure 129) was roughly D-shaped, *c.*14.5m x 12m, surrounded by a ditch up to 1.2m wide and 0.3m deep. The only surviving internal feature was a short segment of a curvilinear ditch, up to 0.5m wide and 0.2m deep, located at its south-eastern corner, that yielded a collection of daub fragments. Short, poorly-preserved ditch segments extending westwards from the enclosure beyond the limit of the investigation suggested the possible existence of an 'annexe' to the west.

The southern part of the enclosure ditch cut across a large pit (*4880*), 2.41 x 1m and 0.35m deep, that had once contained the complete skeleton of a horse (*4882*), although the ditch had removed the animal's cranium. The horse, which had been lain on its left side with the head to the west, was a mare, approximately 10 years of age, with a withers height of 142cm (14 hands): it had probably suffered from arthritis in both the left and right hock joints (Baxter, Chapter 8.III, Fig. 8.8).

Approximately 5m south of Enclosure 129 was a sub-rectangular enclosure (Enclosure 27), 12.8m north to south by 9.4m east to west (internally), defined by a shallow ditch measuring 0.7–1m wide and 0.1–0.2m deep. The ditch post-dated four pits or large postholes, located approximately at the four corners of the enclosure, that could conceivably have defined an earlier phase of the enclosure. Enclosure 30 (located *c.*6m east of Enclosure 27, adjacent to the northern surviving end of Routeway 10) was sub-square, measuring *c.*12 x 10m, with a possible entrance at its south-eastern corner. It was defined by a ditch, 1–1.5m wide and 0.2–0.35m deep.

Structure 111
Structure 111 was located adjacent to the western part of Routeway 10 (Fig. 4.6). It was sub-rectangular in plan, measuring 5m x 3m, and survived as a setting of five postholes, with one placed at each corner of the building. These were all sub-circular or oval, 0.32–0.85m wide and 0.08–0.25m deep. Three pits were located next to the

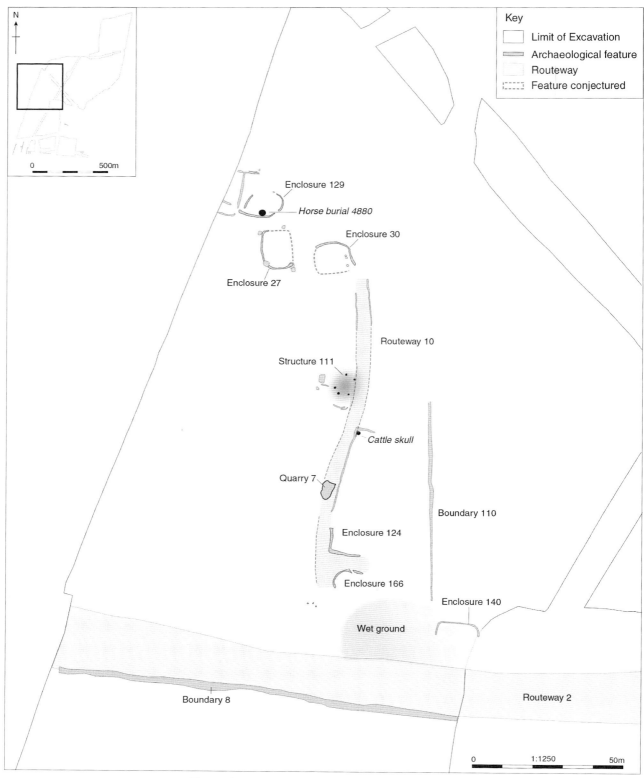

Figure 4.6 Period 4.2: Settlement 7. Scale 1:1250

structure, two were small and irregularly shaped, but the third was a square, steep-sided rubbish pit, measuring 2.5 x 1.85m and 0.26m deep. Its fill contained oyster shell, charcoal, animal bones and marine molluscs, a combination that would indicate domestic habitation. Just to the south of Structure 111 were two short fragments of a curvilinear ditch of unknown function, pottery from which dated to the late 2nd century AD.

Quarry 7
Approximately 30m south of Structure 111, the western edge of Routeway 10 was cut by a large, sub-rectangular pit, 4.1 x 2.2m and 0.40m deep (Fig. 4.6). Its fill yielded a

large pottery assemblage, together with misfired wasters of sandy greyware vessels, including spouted jugs, as well as fragments of kiln lining and kiln furniture, including a prop or spacer (SF 3836). It seems clear that a pottery kiln existed somewhere on the site in the 2nd century AD, presumably in close proximity to the pit, although no trace of this was found. The pit itself was interpreted as a possible clay extraction pit, with the clay being used for pottery manufacture.

Enclosures 124 and 166 and Boundary 110
On the eastern side of Routeway 10 was a large, rectilinear enclosure (Enclosure 124), only the western part of which survived (Fig. 4.6). The western side of the enclosure was defined by the easternmost ditch of the track, whilst its northern and southern sides were represented by short ditch segments running off from this; these were up to 1.8m wide and 0.54m deep. The eastern side of the enclosure was not recorded; a north to south aligned ditch (Boundary 110), up to 0.94m wide and 0.3m deep, was traced for 71m some 28m to the east, but this was on a different alignment to the rest of the enclosure ditches, and is therefore presumed to have been unrelated. The enclosure measured 40.65m north to south, and in excess of 12m east to west. No internal features or deposits were recorded. A cattle skull had been buried at the base of the perimeter ditch, close to the north-western corner of the enclosure.

Approximately 5m south of Enclosure 124 was a curvilinear ditch segment, that may have formed the north-western corner of a small enclosure (Enclosure 166) on the eastern side of Routeway 10. The ditch itself was up to 0.6m wide and 0.85m deep, enclosing an area in excess of *c.*9 x 6m, but had been destroyed to the south and east by later disturbances, meaning that the full extent of the putative enclosure is not known.

Enclosure 140
Approximately 8m south of the southern end of Boundary 110 was the northern side of what may have been a small, rectilinear enclosure (Fig. 4.6), measuring 10.5m east to west and over 5m north to south. To the south it had been destroyed by later truncation. The enclosure ditch was also heavily truncated, but survived up to 0.36m wide and 0.2m deep; its fills contained pottery datable to the late 2nd century AD.

Settlement 6
(Figs 4.7–4.8; Pls 4.1–4.6)

Summary
The basic layout of Settlement 6 remained essentially unchanged into Period 4.2 (Fig. 4.7), with the core area still enclosed by Boundary 100, which does not appear to have been redefined at this time. Internally, however, some of the pre-existing enclosures (notably Enclosures 12, 100 and 103), either went out of use, or were remodelled, and several new enclosures (Enclosures 101, 104, 105, 106, 107, 175 and 176) were established. Four of these were strung out along the western edge of the settlement, immediately inside the western arm of Boundary 100. Enclosures 104 and 105 were located within the interior, adjacent to each other and immediately south of pre-existing Enclosure 102. The latter, which was established in Period 4.1, appears to have remained in use, although no evidence for contemporary activity within it was recorded. At the north-western corner of the settlement, a new entrance was created across Boundary 100, from which a track (Routeway 11), located between Enclosures 101 and 175, ran into the interior. Of the Period 4.1 timber structures, there is no stratigraphic reason why Structures 100, 101 and 109 could not have remained in use, but Structure 102 had certainly gone, since it was cut by the boundary ditch for one of the new enclosures (Enclosure 104). A single, rectangular timber building (Structure 116) was erected on the southern periphery of the enclosed settlement, adjacent to Enclosure 107, and this enclosure also contained a cluster of pits (Pit Group 1).

West of Boundary 100, Routeway 8 appears to have gone out of use temporarily, since its line was cut by two groups of pits (Pit Groups 3 and 4); a timber structure (Structure 103) was also built on its western edge. To the south, a cluster of pits (Pit Group 2) lay just outside Boundary 100, and further south still, two new enclosures (Enclosures 108 and 109) were constructed in the area occupied by Field Systems 5 and 6, adjacent to the north bank of Fox Brook. Another small enclosure (Enclosure 110) was also built further east, on the southern side of the stream, north of Routeway 9 and adjacent to Boundary 13 (running north from the trackway) that appears to have remained in use from Period 3.5.

The enclosed settlement

Enclosures 101, 106, 175, 176, and Routeway 11
This north to south row of enclosures occupied the whole of the western side of the settlement, within Boundary 100, to which they were appended (Fig. 4.7). No internal features or occupation deposits were recorded in any of these enclosures, suggesting that they had not been used for habitation, unless all trace of this had been removed by later disturbances and plough truncation. The northernmost example (Enclosure 175) was roughly triangular in shape, measuring *c.*42m, east to west and *c.*20m wide, at its widest point. The southern ditch varied considerably in size, from as much as 3.5m wide and 0.7m deep at its western end, to *c.*0.8m wide and 0.3m deep to the east, whilst the eastern ditch was comparatively insubstantial along its entire length, being *c.*0.7–1m wide and 0.2–0.4m deep.

Running along the south side of Enclosure 175 was Routeway 11. It was 6–7m wide, between the flanking enclosure ditches, and was traced into the settlement from the west for *c.*50m. It provided access into the settlement from an entrance, *c.*6m wide, at the north-western corner of Boundary 100, where the boundary ditch had presumably been infilled to create a causeway.

Enclosure 101 was bounded to the north by Routeway 11 and to the south by Enclosure 106, which had clearly been constructed before Enclosure 101, as the latter's eastern boundary ditch abutted its north-eastern corner. Enclosure 101 was sub-rectangular, *c.*36 x 29m at its widest points, and was bounded to the north and east by comparatively insubstantial ditches, *c.*1.2–1.5m wide and 0.26–0.42m deep. Its western and southern sides were defined, respectively, by Boundary 100 and the northern ditch of Enclosure 106. Enclosure 106 itself was rectangular in plan with rounded corners, measuring 30.6m by 16.4m internally. Its perimeter ditch varied in

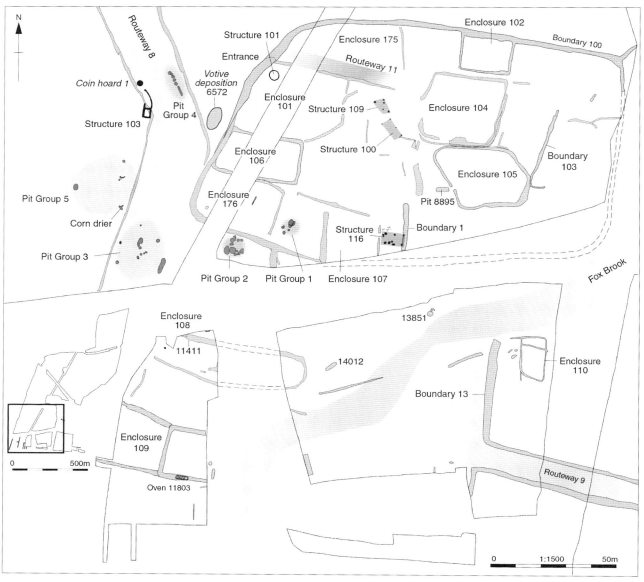

Figure 4.7 Period 4.2: Settlement 6. Scale 1:1500

profile from U- to V-shaped, but was predominantly steep-sided, with a concave base. It was up to 1.75m wide and 0.25–0.6m deep. In the south-western corner of the settlement, Enclosure 176 was defined by Boundary 100 to the west and south and, for the most part, by the southern ditch of Enclosure 106 to the north. Its eastern side, and its north-east corner, were, however, marked by an L-shaped ditch, 1–1.5m wide and 0.25–0.4m deep. This ran north-eastwards from Boundary 100 before turning through nearly 90° to run north-west to abut the southern side of Enclosure 106.

Enclosure 107

This new enclosure was sub-rectangular, c.40m east to west and c.22m wide, and was located on the southern side of the core area of settlement (Fig. 4.7), occupying much of the area of what had previously been Enclosure 103 (Period 4.1), and the eastern part of Enclosure 12. It was bounded to the south by Boundary 100, and abutted Enclosure 176 to the west. Its northern and eastern sides were defined by two ditches, 0.48–1m wide and 0.15–0.54m deep, with a possible internal partition marked by a north to south aligned ditch, c.1.3–1.7m wide and 0.5m deep, dividing the area into two sub-square 'paddocks' or minor enclosures of roughly equal size. Within the westernmost of these, towards the south-west corner, was a cluster of sixteen intercutting pits (Pit Group 1). These yielded a large ceramic assemblage, including a range of fine wares and tablewares, suggestive of domestic occupation in the near vicinity, although the closest contemporary building for which any evidence survived (Structure 116) lay c.35m to the east, just outside Enclosure 107.

Structure 116

The only evidence for new building within the main settlement enclosure during the period was a series of five stone-packed post pads (Structure 116) grouped adjacent to and extending into the southern limit of excavation (Fig. 4.7). No obvious ground plan was apparent, the surviving remnants being located between Enclosure 107 to the west and Boundary 1 to the east. Environmental samples from the structure revealed traces of barley, grain, seeds of grasses, grassland herbs, charcoal, charred wood, pea and bean seeds – all derived from domestic hearth and culinary waste.

Enclosures 104 and 105

Two further enclosures were located side by side within the settlement's interior (Fig. 4.7). The northernmost (Enclosure 104) was sub-square, measuring 31m east to west by 26m north to south, and lay immediately south of Enclosure 102, which had been retained from Period 4.1. In its original form, the enclosure had an entrance, 13m wide, to the west, and a second, *c.*5m wide, to the south, close to the south-eastern corner. The latter entrance may have gone out of use when the enclosure ditch was re-cut subsequently on its southern and eastern sides. In both phases, the ditch was 2.44–2.84m wide and 0.34–0.46m deep, with a flat bottomed, U-shaped profile. Enclosure 105 was located directly to the south of Enclosure 104, but the two had been provided with separate (although virtually abutting) boundary ditches. Enclosure 105 measured *c.*30 x 24m at its widest points, with a very narrow entrance, only 1.5m wide, on the western side. The perimeter ditch was 0.84–1.05m wide and 0.4–0.51m deep. The south-eastern corner of the enclosure respected the line of Boundary 103 of Period 4.1, which was also partially recut at this time.

Immediately outside the western entrance into Enclosure 105, a large sub-rectangular pit (*8895*) had been cut into the top of an earlier enclosure ditch. This measured 5.25m, east to west, by 1.8m wide and 0.6m deep, with a flat-based, U-shaped profile. Pottery datable to the 2nd century AD was recovered from its fills, together with a large assemblage of mussel shell, much of which appeared burnt.

Peripheral areas

Structure 103

Apart from Structure 116, which was located within the area of enclosed settlement defined by Boundary 100, the only other timber structure erected on the site during Period 4.2 was located on the western periphery of the settlement, *c.*30m west of Boundary 100 (Fig. 4.7). This building (Structure 103) was defined by continuous construction trenches (*6820*, *6856* and *6824*, Fig. 4.8), measuring up to 0.38m and up to 0.40m deep. It appears to have formed a simple, rectangular building, with a room or cell (of *c.*4 x 3.3m externally), to the south and what was either another room, or (more likely) a partly enclosed external area, to the north. This was marked by a short construction trench (*6820*) extending northwards for *c.*1.6m from the north-western corner of the southern room, and a curving gully or slot (*6791*), 0.2–0.3m wide, which extended north-westwards for *c.*6m from the north-eastern corner of the room, seemingly terminating in a small, circular posthole (*6818*). If the projecting construction trench to the north is included (excluding the length of the curving ditch), the structure appears to have measured at least 5.5m long, north to south, and was *c.*3.3m wide, externally. Finds recovered from the construction trench included a mortarium stamped with a maker's mark (SF 3426), a saw blade fragment (SF 3427) and iron nails; their findspots are located on Fig. 4.8.

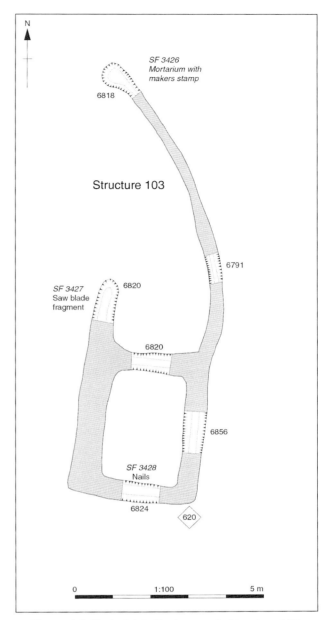

Figure 4.8 Period 4.2: Settlement 6, Structure 103. Scale 1:100

Some 10m north-west of Structure 103, a small coin hoard (Hoard 1; Crummy, Chapter 6.II), comprising 23 copper alloy coins of late 1st- to mid-2nd century date, had been buried in a pot placed within a small pit (Pl. 4.1). The hoard closed with an issue of Antoninus Pius (AD 138–61), but as all the coins are heavily worn, it is possible that it was deposited as late as the first half of the 3rd century.

Possible votive deposition

Approximately 25m south-east of the find spot of Hoard 1 (Fig. 4.7), adjacent to the eastern edge of former Routeway 8, was an area measuring up to *c.*8 x 5.5m that appears to have been damp and prone to flooding in the Romano-British period. The evidence for this comprised a build-up of water-lain silts that sealed a late Iron Age waterhole (Period 3.3, Waterhole 5). These deposits consisted of a layer of silty gravel (*7623/7489*; not

Plate 4.1 Coin hoard (Hoard 1) *in situ*, Settlement 6 (Period 4.2)

Plate 4.2 Metalwork from 'votive' deposit *6752*, Settlement 6 (Period 4.2)

Plate 4.3 Corn drier *6727*, Pit Group 5, Settlement 6, looking east (Period 4.2)

illustrated), 0.25m thick, which was sealed by 0.3m of fine, grey silty clay (*6572*). At this location (which was situated *c.*14m west of Boundary 100 and *c.*16m east of Structure 103), a notable collection of artefacts was recovered, all of which came from deposit *6572* (Crummy, Chapter 6.III). The group is illustrated in Plate 4.2 and comprises a silver artefact (SF 2801), a samian cup, and 32 copper alloy objects: a lunula (SF 2787); an *armilla* (SF 2803) (a military decoration given to soldiers below the rank of centurion); two armlets (SF 1221, SF 2792); two hairpins (SF 1209, SF 1219); four brooches (SF 2772, SF 2769, SF 2791, SF 2815); eight coins (SF 2770, SF 2789, SF 2790, SF 2794, SF 2796, SF 2798, SF 2813, SF 2817); eight rings (SF 1218, SF 1220, SF 2771, SF 2788, SF 2793, SF 2797, SF 2800, SF 2802); three fragments of sheet (SF 1197, SF 1222, SF 2799); a shank (SF 2816); a bar fragment (SF 2773) and a fragment with a transverse moulding (SF 2774).

The great majority of the datable artefacts in this group are attributable to the late 1st–2nd century AD, with most probably being of 2nd-century date. However, the *armilla* is certainly considerably earlier, being a Claudio-Neronian type, whilst the coins include a possible issue of Septimius Severus (AD 193–211), an illegible late 3rd- to 4th-century specimen, and another (also illegible) of 4th-century date. Whether the date range of the artefacts indicates that deposition occurred over a long period, potentially from the mid 1st century AD to the 4th century, is, however, debatable. Taken at face value, the objects do suggest this, but, as the bulk of the assemblage is clearly 2nd century in date, it is perhaps more likely that the peak of deposition occurred during this period, with the putative Severan coin representing the tail end of this phenomenon. In the absence of any other diagnostically 3rd- to 4th-century artefacts, it is conceivable that the two considerably later coins found their way into the silt purely by chance, since late Roman coins were common as stray finds across the site as a whole (Crummy, Chapter 6.II), whilst the 1st-century *armilla* might have been a curated heirloom that was deposited long after its period of manufacture. The significance of this collection of items is unclear, but a ritual or votive element to their deposition, seemingly in a 'watery place', cannot be ruled out (see also Chapter 9.IX), particularly when the proximity of Hoard 1 is also considered.

Pit Groups 2–5

Immediately south of Boundary 100, just outside the south-western corner of the enclosed area of settlement (Fig. 4.7), was a cluster of intercutting pits (Pit Group 2) containing a range of domestic debris. They varied considerably in size, from as little as 0.35m in diameter and 0.1m in depth, to the largest example, which measured 3 x 1.55m, although it too was shallow, at only 0.35m deep.

On the western part of the site and lying outside the settled area, Routeway 8, which had been established in Period 3.5, may have been narrowed or temporarily gone out of use, since its line was cut by large pit groups (Pit Groups 3 and 4); another, more dispersed, collection of pits (Pit Group 5), was also located on the western edge of the trackway, but did not impinge upon its line. The northernmost group (Pit Group 4) was located some 22m west of Boundary 100, and *c.*9m north-east of Structure 103. It comprised a short trench-like feature, 1.2m long, and five roughly circular pits that had been deliberately arranged in a north-west to south-east aligned row, *c.*12m long. Pit Group 5, located *c.*40–50m to the south-west,

Plate 4.4 Pottery and other finds in pit *6531*, Pit Group 3, Settlement 6, looking west (Period 4.2)

Plate 4.5 Burnt deposit *11805*, oven *11803* in perimeter ditch of Enclosure 109, Settlement 6, looking east (Period 4.2)

Plate 4.6 Top: Near-complete pottery vessel in ditch *11411*, Settlement 6 (Period 4.2). Bottom: Complete pottery vessel in ditch 11411, Settlement 6 (Period 4.2)

comprised eight features, including a large sub-circular pit (*6566*), five smaller, sub-rectangular pits and one small, circular pit and a roughly T-shaped feature, possibly a corn drier (*6727*, Pl. 4.3). The latter yielded a fragment of slag and a fragment of samian ware base datable to *c*.AD 160–90 (Wadeson, Chapter 7.V; SF 2794). The southernmost pit group in this area (Pit Group 3) was located *c*.25m south-west of the enclosed area of settlement, and comprised eleven pits, together with a possible oven (*6531*, Pl. 4.4). This was roughly circular, 1m in diameter and 0.19m deep, and appears to have been lined with pottery sherds before being infilled with stones.

Enclosures 108 and 109
South of the enclosed settlement, in the area occupied in Period 4.1 by putative Field Systems 5 and 6, two ditched enclosures were constructed (Fig. 4.7). The northernmost (Enclosure 108), lying within Field System 5, was seemingly an elongated oval, at least 50m, east to west (its western end was not located), and *c*.15m wide, internally. It was defined by a ditch, 0.66–1.1m wide and 0.24–0.45m deep. The only internal features recorded were two postholes, set 5m apart in the centre of the enclosure.

Enclosure 109 was seemingly set within Field System 6, since its northern and southern sides were formed by recutting parts of two earlier field boundary ditches. It was either square or rectangular, measuring 18m north to south and at least 15.5m east to west (it ran east of the excavated area); if it had extended east up to the edge of Fox Brook, it may have been *c*.24m long. The enclosure ditch was 0.94m wide and 0.54m deep. Its fills were very dark in colour, and the southern ditch contained dumps of burnt clay, ash and charcoal (*11800, 11802, 11803, 11805*, Pl. 4.5) that may indicate the remnants of an oven, whilst the western ditch yielded evidence for crop-processing. Fill *11803* contained a plain copper alloy ring (Chapter 6, Fig. 6.35, SF 3306).

In addition to the enclosures themselves, a number of pits and short ditch segments were also recorded in this general area, south of the enclosed settlement and north of Fox Brook. Several of these yielded evidence for crop processing, in the form of charred cereal grains and chaff, the latter largely comprising spelt wheat glumes, which, together with similar material from the ditches of Enclosure 109 itself, represented the greatest concentration of crop processing waste recorded anywhere on the site, and in any chronological period. These features included pit *11445*, pit *13851* (2.35m in diameter and 0.56m deep) and pit/trench *14012* (5.3m long, 1.6m wide and 0.65m deep). One short section of ditch (*11411*) contained two near-complete vessels dating to the early to mid 2nd century (Pl. 4.6).

Enclosure 110
This small, sub-rectangular enclosure, extending 16.6m north to south and 9.5m wide internally, was located on the south bank of Fox Brook, adjacent to Boundary 13 (Fig. 4.7). Its northern end was separated from the rest of the enclosure by an east to west aligned ditch, located *c*.3–4m inside the northern arm of the enclosure ditch. All the enclosure ditches were 0.45–0.93m wide and 0.18–0.27m deep, with fills that were very dark in places, although the results of environmental sampling were disappointing. A notable concentration of ceramics was recorded in this area, which may be indicative of domestic activity either within the enclosure or nearby. However, with the exception of a group of shallow pits situated immediately west of the enclosure, no other occupation-related evidence was found.

IV. Period 4.3: middle Romano-British (3rd century AD)

Introduction
(Fig. 4.9)
As previously, Settlement 7 saw relatively little activity during Period 4.3 (Figs 4.9 and 4.10), although some of the earlier enclosures, and possibly also the axial track (Routeway 10) continued in use. The main evidence for 3rd-century occupation comprised a series of fragmentary ditches, mostly east to west aligned, the precise significance of which is unclear.

In contrast, Settlement 6 saw considerable 3rd-century activity, although its basic layout changed little from the previous phase (Fig. 4.11). Within the enclosed settlement some of the pre-existing enclosures were remodelled, whilst others were replaced. A large timber building (Structure 105) was located within one of the enclosures and another structure of uncertain form and function (Structure 107) was situated further to the south-east. There was no evidence for contemporary activity west of the enclosed settlement, but occupation seemingly intensified to the south (particularly south of Fox Brook), where several new enclosures were constructed, and other features, including pits, waterholes, a possible corn drier and a timber structure (Structure 106) were found. Spatial evidence indicates that Routeway 9, which approached the

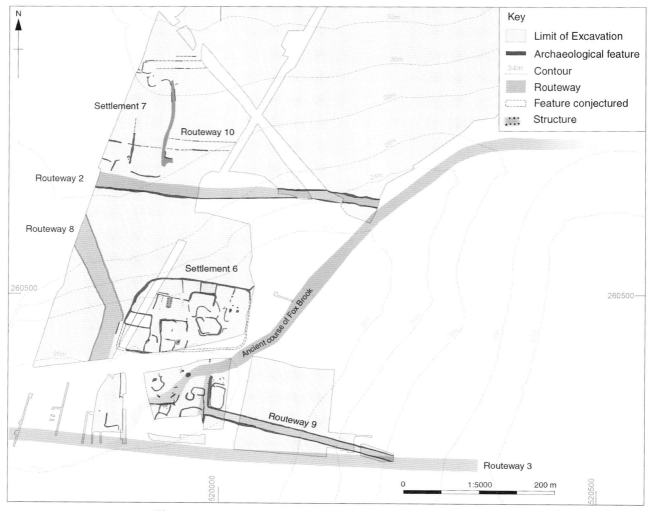

Figure 4.9 Period 4.3: 3rd century AD phase plan. Scale 1:5000

settlement from the south-east, also remained in use at this time.

Settlement 7
(Fig. 4.10)
The 3rd century probably saw some of the earlier enclosures (*e.g.* Enclosures 27, 30 and 129; Period 4.2), and perhaps also Routeway 10, continue in use (Fig. 4.10), although they were not obviously modified in any way; all other earlier features seemingly went out of use. The main evidence for continued occupation at this time was provided by a highly fragmentary series of (largely) east to west aligned ditches and a single north to south aligned ditch, that were recorded across the area. The significance of these is unclear, but some aligned with boundary ditches of the subsequent occupation phase (Period 4.4) and, as such, appear to presage the marked intensification of activity that occurred in the later Roman period.

On the northern periphery of the settlement, three parallel ditch lines were represented by five short ditch segments, all aligned east to west. The ditches, which were all poorly preserved, were 0.5–0.9m wide and up to 0.41m deep. The northernmost line (which survived as a single ditch segment, 5m long), lay *c.*6m north of the central ditch, which itself survived as two segments (*c.*11m and 10m long). The southern ditch was also represented by two segments (*c.*12m and 5m long) which lay *c.*9.5m south of the central ditch line.

Further south, three approximately west to east ditch alignments were noted, aligned roughly parallel with Routeway 2. The southernmost (Boundary 115) survived as two ditch segments, separated by a gap of *c.*40m; it was located only a few metres north of Routeway 2, and some 25–35m south of the central ditch (Boundary 118). The eastern ditch segment was 38m long, whilst that to the west was at least 13m long, but extended westwards beyond the site. Boundary 118 was traced for a total of 131m, extending beyond the limit of the excavation to the west, but survived only in six separate segments on either side of Routeway 10. It was located *c.*12m south of the northern ditch, which survived as only two short segments (*c.*6m and 9m long). All three ditches were 0.5–1.6m wide and 0.17–0.44m deep, as they survived, with steep-sided, rounded profiles. In all cases, the segmental survival of the ditches was the result of later disturbance.

Cutting across Boundary 118 on a roughly perpendicular, north-north-east to south-south-west, alignment was Boundary 111 (42m long, 1.8–3.2m wide and 0.6–0.9m deep), which does not appear to have been completely filled until the second half of the 4th century AD. A group of seven pits (Pit Group 6) was located west of the ditch's southern terminal; the fill of one of these

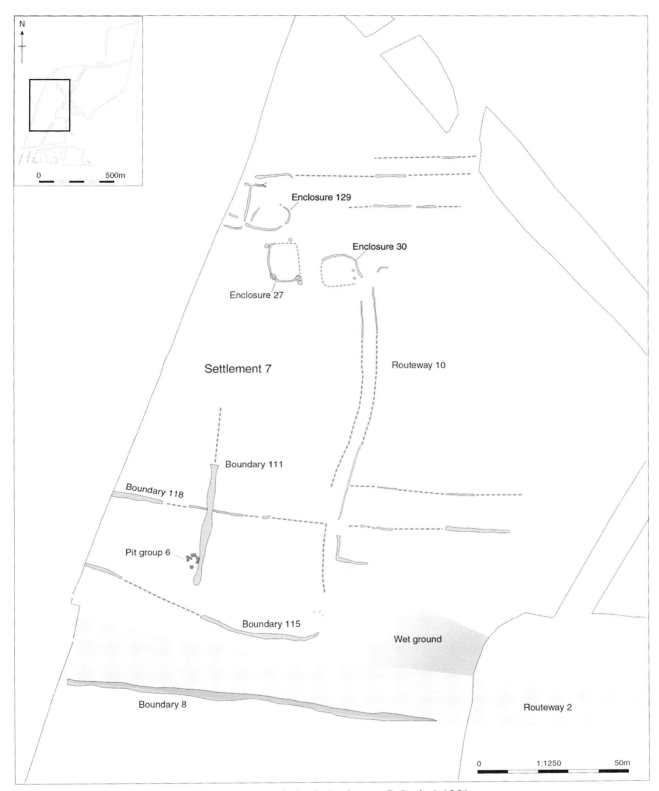

Figure 4.10 Period 4.3: Settlement 7. Scale 1:1250

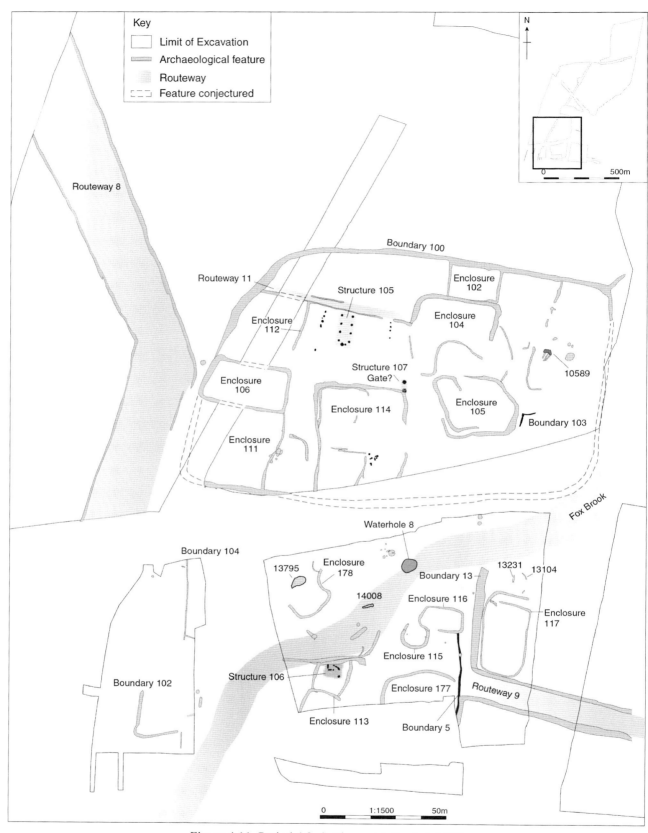

Figure 4.11 Period 4.3: Settlement 6. Scale 1:1500

features (*10196*) yielded cereal chaff, especially spelt wheat glumes, suggestive of secondary grain processing on the site.

Settlement 6
(Figs 4.11–4.13; Pl. 4.7)

Summary
During the 3rd century, Settlement 6 was the focus of considerable activity, although its basic layout changed little from Period 4.2. Within the core area of settlement, enclosed by Boundary 100 (which does not itself seem to have been redefined at this time), the north to south aligned row of four enclosures on the western edge of the settlement was retained, although two of the enclosures created in Period 4.2 (Enclosures 101 and 176) were remodelled (as Enclosures 112 and 111 respectively). Enclosure 106 was retained, seemingly unchanged from Period 4.2, but Enclosure 175, at the north-western corner of the enclosed settlement, appears to have gone out of use. Routeway 11, now located to the north of Enclosure 112, may also have been retained, although in a considerably narrower form. A large, rectangular timber building (Structure 105) was located within Enclosure 112, and an enigmatic structure (Structure 107) – possibly a gate – was also situated in its extreme south-east corner, adjacent to the north-east corner of Enclosure 114.

In the southern part of the enclosed settlement, Enclosure 107 of Period 4.2 was replaced by Enclosure 114. To the north, and in the central part of the settlement, Enclosures 102, 104 and 105 continued in use from Period 4.2, albeit with some modification.

In contrast to Period 4.2, there was no evidence for contemporary occupation west of Boundary 100, in the area formerly occupied by Routeway 8 (this route may have been retained in some form, since it was clearly in use again in later phases). To the south, Enclosures 108 and 109 of Period 4.2 seemingly went out of use; Enclosure 108 was cut across by a north to south ditch (Boundary 104), and an L-shaped ditch (Boundary 102) was dug adjacent to the south-west corner of Enclosure 109. These features may have been the remnants of later, poorly preserved, enclosures, or might have served as field boundaries. To the north-east, several pits and ditches of uncertain significance were found between the main settlement enclosure to the north, and Fox Brook to the south, including a large waterhole (Waterhole 8) on the northern edge of the seasonal stream channel, which presumably provided a water source when the stream was not active.

South of the stream, there was a clear increase in activity, with the creation of five small, mostly curvilinear, enclosures in this area (Enclosures 113, 115–117 and 177). Enclosure 113 contained a possible timber structure (Structure 106) of uncertain form and purpose. The discovery of a corn drier, together with environmental remains recovered from several pits, demonstrates the continuation of crop processing in this area. Spatial evidence suggests that Routeway 9, which approached the settlement from the south-east, remained in use. However, a ditch (Boundary 5) was cut across its western end, linking the track with Enclosure 116 to the north, and seemingly directing traffic/livestock northwards to pass between Enclosures 116 and 117.

The enclosed settlement

Enclosures 106, 111, 112, 175 and Routeway 11
Along the western edge of the enclosed settlement, immediately inside the western arm of Boundary 100, Enclosure 106 appears to have been retained without change from Period 4.2, although no contemporary occupation features or deposits were found within it (Fig. 4.11). Enclosure 101 went out of use, and its eastern side was overlain by a new, rectilinear enclosure (Enclosure 112), which was no longer attached to Boundary 100 to the west. The northern and western sides of this were defined by ditches, up to 1.07m wide and 0.63m deep (but generally narrower and shallower as they survived). The northern ditch, which was traced for 48m, bounded the southern edge of Routeway 11, which remained in use, whilst the western ditch, 21m long, terminated, on the south, *c*.8m short of the north-east corner of Enclosure 106, suggesting the existence of an entrance at the south-western corner. To the east, the enclosure seemingly abutted Enclosure 104, whilst its southern side was defined, for the most part, by the northern ditch of Enclosure 114. A 5m-wide gap in the latter ditch, close to its junction with the perimeter ditch of Enclosure 104, indicates that a second entrance may have existed at the north-eastern corner of the enclosure. A denarius of AD 206–10 (Crummy, Chapter 6.II; SF 3040) was recovered from the western terminal of this entrance (*9117*). Enclosure 112 contained both of the surviving timber structures erected in Period 4.3 within the enclosed area of settlement (Structures 105 and 107).

Approximately 2.3m north of the northern ditch of Enclosure 112, and aligned parallel with it, was another ditch, 0.52m wide and 0.13m deep, which was traced east to west for 13.5m. This probably represented the northern edge of Routeway 11, reduced from 6–7m wide in Period 4.2 to only 2.3m wide in Period 4.3, running along the northern side of Enclosure 112.

Enclosure 111 was essentially a modification of Enclosure 176, which was located at the south-western corner of the enclosed settlement. Like Enclosure 176, its southern side was defined by Boundary 100 (which itself was recut to the south of its original position) and its northern side by the southernmost ditch of Enclosure 106. Its eastern boundary was now marked by a new ditch, which ran northwards from the southern arm of Boundary 100 to abut the south-east corner of Enclosure 106, cutting across former Pit Group 1. This ditch was 25m long, 0.53–1.05m wide and 0.1–0.32m deep. No contemporary features or occupation deposits were recorded within its interior.

Structure 105: Dwelling?
Immediately adjacent to Routeway 11, with the gable end fronting onto it, was a rectangular timber building, constructed on a north to south alignment (Structure 105, Figs 4.11 and 4.12). The long sides of the building were defined by two parallel rows of four postholes set 4.3m apart, with the posts in each row spaced at 3.5m intervals. This arrangement would indicate that the structure would have been at least 11m long and 5m wide. The sub-circular postholes were 0.4–0.8m in diameter and 0.08–0.41m deep. Two shallow pits (*8630/9069* and *9058*) and a slot (*9108*) were also located at the southern end, probably just outside the structure. No internal features or deposits had

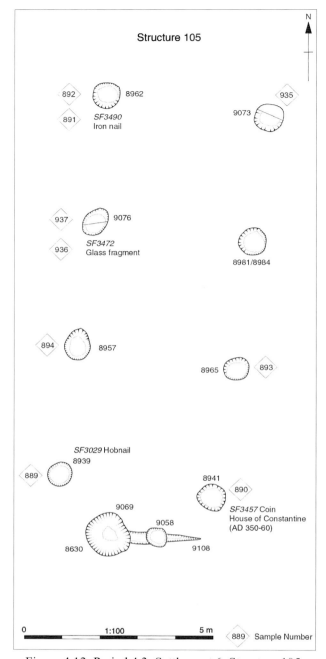

Figure 4.12 Period 4.3: Settlement 6, Structure 105. Scale 1:100

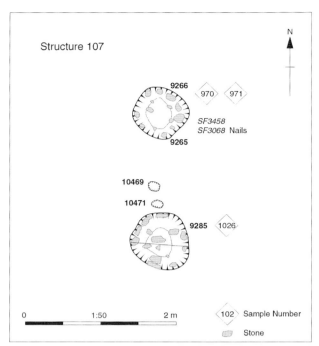

Figure 4.13 Period 4.3: Settlement 6, Structure 107. Scale 1:50

and consisted of two large, stone-filled pits (*9266, 9285*), with two small stake holes (*10469, 10471*) in between. The pits were circular, 1.5m in diameter and 0.8m deep, and were set 3.5m apart. Both were packed with cobbles and limestone fragments, suggestive of post-packing, although no evidence for post-pipes was recorded, and it is possible that the features served as large post-pads. Fragments of painted wall plaster were also present in their fills, although these were certainly residual, since identical material came from earlier ditch fills through which the pits had been dug (Period 4.1). They also contained iron nails (SF 3458 and 3068). The significance and purpose of Structure 107 is unclear; it does not seem to represent the remains of a timber building, but could have been the remains of a substantial, free-standing timber structure, such as a gate relating to the enclosure around the primary building (Structure 105).

Enclosure 114
This enclosure overlay the eastern half of Period 4.2 Enclosure 107, and, like its predecessor, may have abutted Boundary 100, the main boundary ditch of the settlement, to the south (Fig. 4.11). The new enclosure was sub-rectangular, measuring 40m, north to south, by 34m, encompassing an area of over 1400m². Its eastern side ran along the line of relict Boundary 1, which, although it had fallen out of use by the beginning of the Romano-British period, presumably remained partly visible as an earthwork. The western ditch followed the same line as the west side of Enclosure 107, but extended well to the north of the earlier feature, whilst the northern ditch was newly cut, and did not follow an earlier boundary. The perimeter ditch was up to 3.15m wide (although was generally considerably narrower as it survived), and 0.2–0.45m deep, and had been redefined at least once. A broad entrance in the eastern side of the enclosure was marked by a gap in the ditch, 10m wide. Amongst the finds

survived. Finds from the postholes include an intrusive coin of the House of Constantine dating to AD 350–60 (SF 3457), a glass fragment, and nails (including a hobnail); their findspots are shown on Fig. 4.12.

Some 8m west of the building, and aligned roughly parallel with its long axis, was a fence line, represented by a row of six postholes, 18.1m in length (Fig. 4.11). A similar posthole row, 6.7m long and comprising four individual postholes, was also recorded 15m to the east. Fragments of painted plaster were recovered from the southernmost posthole (*8851*) of the western fence line.

Structure 107: Gate?
An enigmatic structure (Structure 107) was located in the south-east corner of Enclosure 112 (Figs 4.11 and 4.13),

recovered from the ditch was a set of copper alloy Baldock-type tweezers (Crummy, Chapter 6.III; Fig. 6.22, SF 3007).

Internally, the south-western corner of the enclosure may have been divided from the rest by two ditches, forming the northern and eastern sides of a rectangular paddock, c.20m long, north to south. These ditches were, however, insubstantial, at least as they survived, being only 0.42–0.55 wide and 0.03–0.16m deep. With the exception of a cluster of ten seemingly randomly-distributed postholes, which were located in an area of c.5 x 3m towards the south-eastern corner of the enclosure, (immediately outside the north-east corner of the internal paddock), no other internal features of note were recorded within Enclosure 114.

Enclosures 102, 104 and 105
In Period 4.3, the perimeter ditch of Enclosure 104 was re-cut, although apparently only around the northern half of the enclosure (Fig. 4.11), the new ditch measuring 0.9–2.2m wide and 0.2–0.58m wide. To the north, it largely removed the southern ditch of Enclosure 102, which nonetheless seemingly remained in use at this time, now joined to Enclosure 104, although no evidence for contemporary activity was found within it. Internally, the south-eastern corner was partitioned off by a curvilinear ditch, 1m wide and 0.2–0.3m deep, to create a sub-enclosure or paddock measuring 18 x 13m, at its greatest extent. Approximately 25m east of Enclosure 104, a segmented ditch was dug on a north-east to south-west alignment. The new ditch was up to 0.9m wide and 0.23m deep, and ran into the settlement from Boundary 100, on the north. It was traced for c.46m, and turned east a short distance north-west of Enclosure 105, but terminated a short distance beyond this point. Immediately to the east of the ditch was a cluster of pits of varying sizes, one of which (*10589*) yielded a hobnailed shoe (Crummy, Chapter 6.III; SF 3098, Pl. 4.7).

The perimeter ditch of Enclosure 105 was also redefined at this time. For the most part the new ditch followed the line of the original feature, but to the west it was cut on a new line, c.3m inside (*i.e.* east of) the primary ditch, and parallel to it. This reduced the size of the enclosure to c.27 x 24m at its widest points. An entrance, c.3m wide, was provided to the north, the western side of this being marked by an inward (*i.e.* southwards) turn of the western ditch terminal, for a distance of c.5m. A possible second entrance at the south-western corner of the enclosure was suggested by the way in which the southern and western arms of the perimeter ditch overlapped at this point (the former cut on the line of the original ditch, the latter on a new line further east). This overlap created a narrow, curving passage, c.1.5–2m wide and c.16m long, between the two ditches, providing restricted access into the interior of the enclosure.

Peripheral areas

Enclosure 178 and Boundaries 102 and 104
Beyond the south-western corner of the enclosed settlement, Enclosures 108 and 109 of Period 4.2 went out of use. On the north bank of Fox Brook, the eastern side of the perimeter ditch of former Enclosure 108 was cut by the western end of a curvilinear ditch, that may have defined a small, roughly C-shaped enclosure (Enclosure 178),

Plate 4.7 Remains of hobnnailed shoe in pit *10589*, Enclosure 104 (Period 4.3)

located close to the northern edge of the stream (Fig. 4.11). This putative enclosure measured c.14m, north-east to south-west, and 7m, north-west to south-east, but was seemingly open to the north. Its perimeter ditch was c.0.8m wide and up to 0.35m deep. Immediately to the north was a large, sub-oval pit (*13795*), 4.5m long, 3.2m wide and 0.52m deep, with steep sides and a flat base. Its fills yielded significant quantities of charred cereal grains, chaff, and the seeds of arable weeds (Fryer, Chapter 8.IV), together with egg shells and fish scales.

Approximately 40m west of Enclosure 178, a narrow, north to south aligned ditch (Boundary 104), 0.8–0.9m wide and up to 0.3m deep, cut across Enclosure 108, and was traced for c.31m. To the north, it extended beyond the excavated area; a possible eastern return was noted at the southern end of this feature, but this was traced east for only 4m before it ran beyond the limit of the excavation. Further south, an L-shaped ditch (Boundary 102) was dug close to the south-western corner of former Enclosure 109.

Waterhole 8
East of Enclosure 178, a few scattered pits were, for the most part, the only features recorded on the north bank of Fox Brook. A few pits and short trenches were also found in the bed of the stream channel; these had been dug, perhaps, during dry spells in an attempt to provide a water supply. Of these features the most clearly defined and substantial was Waterhole 8, situated roughly 25m south of the enclosed settlement (Fig. 4.11). This feature measured 6 x 5.5m, and was 0.6m deep, with steep sides and a flat base. Two fills were recorded; the primary deposit (*14167*), a dump of black organic waste, was sealed by a dark grey-brown silty clay (*14166*). Environmental analysis of layer *14167* (Fryer, Chapter 8.IV) revealed evidence for wheat chaff, rushes and a variety of insects. To the south-west lay a lozenge-shaped pit (*13265=14008*) with a shallow, U-shaped profile, measuring 0.8 x 0.6m and 0.15m deep. Its fills yielded grains of sprouted spelt wheat, rye, oats, and barley, together with roughly milled wheat that had been malted. A quantity of burnt clay and fuel waste, possibly derived from an oven, had also been dumped into the feature.

Routeway 9 and Boundary 5
To the south of Fox Brook, Routeway 9, which approached Settlement 6 from the south-east, and which

was initially established in the early/mid 1st century AD, appears to have continued in use into Period 4.3, since a contemporary enclosure (Enclosure 117) respected its position and that of Boundary 13, which ran northwards from its western end (Fig. 4.11). However, the western end of the track was seemingly all but blocked at this time by the digging of a north to south ditch (Boundary 5), which ran for 36m from the south side of the track, northwards to the south-east corner of Enclosure 116. The new ditch was up to 1m wide and 0.64m deep, and was aligned roughly parallel to Boundary 13, which lay *c*.5–6m to the east. The purpose of the ditch seems to have been effectively to create a northwards extension of Routeway 9, defined by Boundary 5 to the west and Boundary 13 to the east, thereby channelling traffic and livestock northwards, between Enclosures 116 and 117, and preventing direct access from the track into several new enclosures.

Enclosures 113, 115–117 and 177
In addition to Enclosures 116 and 117, three other small enclosures (Enclosures 113, 115 and 177) were created on the southern side of the stream (Fig. 4.11), in an area that had seen little activity earlier in the Romano-British period. The westernmost of these (Enclosure 113) was possibly sub-rectangular, although it extended south of the excavated area. It measured in excess of 27m, north-east to south-west, and was up to 12m wide, internally, and appears to have been formed of two smaller, connected enclosures, the northernmost being attached to (or abutting) that on the south. The northern paddock, *c*.12m square, was defined by a ditch (*13892*), 1–1.5m wide and 0.32–0.42m deep, and was seemingly appended to the southern part of the enclosure, which was defined within the excavated area by a curving, L-shaped ditch of similar size to the others. With the exception of a possible timber structure in the northern paddock (Structure 106, below), no internal features or deposits were recorded. A partial sheep skeleton, comprising the skull and long bones, had been deposited at the north-western corner of the southern enclosure ditch (in fill *13968*).

North-east of Enclosure 113 was a pair of small, conjoined enclosures (Enclosures 115 and 116), comprising a sub-rectangular example (Enclosure 116) to the north, with a smaller, sub-circular enclosure (Enclosure 115) at its south-west corner. Enclosure 116 measured *c*.16m east to west and 8m wide, internally, whilst Enclosure 115 had an internal diameter of *c*.9m. Both were defined by ditches, up to 0.9–1.15m wide and 0.4–0.7m deep. Enclosure 116 was accessed by means of an entrance, 3.5m wide, on its southern side, adjacent to the junction of its perimeter ditch with that of Enclosure 115. Enclosure 115 itself had an entrance, *c*.4m wide, on its northern side, and its ditch fills yielded a wide range of charred palaeobotanical remains (Fryer, Chapter 8.IV), including barley and wheat grains, seeds of grasses and grassland herbs, and evidence for peas and beans, as well as charcoal and metalworking debris.

Approximately 9m south of Enclosure 115, the northern side of a larger, curvilinear enclosure (Enclosure 177) was recorded, the greater part of which probably lay south of the excavated area. The northern and western sides of the enclosure were defined by a curving ditch, whilst the eastern side may have been formed by Boundary 5. The area available for investigation, measuring 28.3m east to west and in excess of 10.7 north to south, contained no features or occupation deposits. What may have been a narrow entrance, 1.35m wide, was located in the north-east corner, between Boundary 5 to the east, and the enclosure ditch to the west.

Enclosure 117, to the east of Boundary 13, was sub-rectangular in plan with rounded corners, measuring *c*.33m, north to south and up to 18m wide, internally. It was defined by a narrow perimeter ditch, 0.58–1m wide and 0.25–0.3m deep, and had an entrance, *c*.4.5m wide, at its north-west corner. The extreme northern end of the enclosure, comprising a narrow strip only 3.5m wide, was divided from the rest by an east to west aligned ditch of similar size to the perimeter ditch. This was probably connected with the enclosure's main entrance, which lay at the eastern end of the strip, perhaps serving to control or restrict access into the enclosure. The internal ditch was itself crossed by a narrow causeway, *c*.2m wide, towards its western end; anyone wishing to reach this from the enclosure's north-eastern entrance would have had to traverse the length of the narrow northern strip, in order to access the main part of the enclosure.

Structure 106
Within the northern element of Enclosure 113, a collection of postholes and trench-like features adjacent to the northern perimeter ditch (Fig. 4.11) were interpreted as the possible remains of a timber structure (Structure 106), although the form and character of this were extremely difficult to reconstruct from the surviving remains. The postholes were sub-circular and oval in plan, varying in size from *c*.0.25 x 0.5m to *c*.0.5 x 1m, and were 0.1–0.2m deep. The two short trenches, which were aligned at right angles to each other, were 1.4–1.7m long, 0.2–0.4m wide and 0.1m deep. Overall, the features covered an area measuring *c*.6 x 5m; there was a suggestion, from the position of the postholes, that the structure's putative east wall may have been curved, with the shallow trenches on the west perhaps forming part of an internal sub-division.

Other external features
Two long, sub-rectangular pits (*13231*, *13104*), located a few metres north of Enclosure 117 (Fig. 4.11), were interpreted as the possible remains of corn driers. Feature *13231* was 2.04m long, 0.58m wide and 0.12m deep, with a flat-based, U-shaped profile. The upper fill (*13227*) comprised a highly fired red clay, possibly the collapsed remains of a clay superstructure; it yielded twenty-four sherds of 2nd- to mid 3rd-century pottery and a whetstone (SF 3641, not illustrated). Pit *13104*, located 4.9m to the east, was 1.5m long, 0.25m wide and 0.35m deep. The natural clay at the base of the cut was reddish-brown and discoloured, suggesting that it had been affected by heat, although no fired clay was present in the fills of this feature.

V. Period 4.4: late Romano-British (4th century AD)

Introduction
(Fig. 4.14)
Following a prolonged period of relatively light occupation during the 1st–3rd centuries AD, Settlement 7 expanded considerably during the 4th century (Fig. 4.14). This was marked principally by increasing formalisation

Figure 4.14 Period 4.4: 4th century AD phase plan. Scale 1:5000

of the settlement's layout, with a fairly well-ordered series of enclosures and paddocks surrounded by substantial boundary ditches, echoing the layout of Settlement 6, to the south, which had reached a similar stage of development much earlier. Settlement 6 itself does not seem to have changed greatly during the 4th century, with most of the pre-existing enclosures within the enclosed area of settlement being certainly or possibly retained, some with modification; a few new enclosures were also established in the eastern part of the settlement. Beyond the enclosed area, a new enclosure was established to the west, whilst to the south, pre-existing enclosures south of Fox Brook were either modified or replaced at this time. The spatial relationship between some of the enclosures and Routeway 9 suggests that this track also remained in use.

Settlement 7
(Figs 4.15–4.17; Pl. 4.8)

Summary
The early 4th century saw the start of an intensification of occupation within Settlement 7, and a considerable increase in the size and complexity of the settlement. The southern edge of the settlement was essentially bounded by Routeway 2. The northern and eastern sides of the settlement were defined by a series of substantial ditches (Boundaries 110 and 112), and it is likely that the western side of the settlement was similarly defined, although it lay outside the excavated area. That the settlement's layout became more formalised at this time is clear, both from the relatively ordered layout of enclosures and other features, and the fact that no settlement-related features were recorded outside the boundary ditches. The settlement now extended for 180m to the north of Routeway 2, and measured over 155m east to west, at its widest point, covering an area in excess of 0.27ha. Two principal sub-phases of occupation (Phases 1 and 2), associated with Period 4.4 could be identified.

Phase 1

Settlement boundaries and Enclosure 172
Routeway 2, which had been in use since at least the middle Iron Age, continued to form the southern boundary of Settlement 7 at this time (Fig. 4.15). However, it is possible that the pre-existing ditch defining the southern edge of the track (Boundary 8) formed the actual southern boundary, with the western excavated end of Routeway 2 being incorporated within the settlement boundaries. If this was the case, access was presumably via an entrance at the south-east corner of the settlement enclosure, but

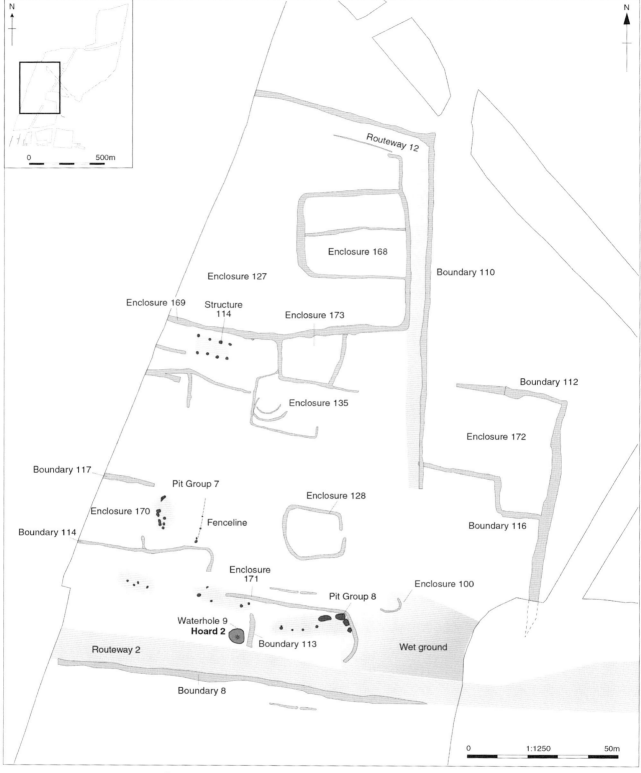

Figure 4.15 Period 4.4: Settlement 7 (Phase 1). Scale 1:1250

this could not be conclusively proven, since this area lay outside the excavated area.

Boundary 110 defined the north-eastern corner of the settlement; its northern (east to west aligned) arm was at least 59m long, but extended west of the site, whilst its eastern (north to south) arm was 158m in length. Some 80m south of the north-eastern corner, the northern arm of Boundary 112 ran eastwards, at right angles to Boundary 110, for c.43m, before turning south through 90° to run for a further 70m towards Routeway 2 (its southern end lay outside the investigated area). Boundary 112, therefore, effectively defined a projecting 'annexe' or extension at the south-eastern corner of Settlement 7, extending over 40m beyond the line of Boundary 110. This 'annexe' was further sub-divided by a dog-legged ditch (Boundary 116) running eastwards from the southern end of Boundary 110 to link up with the eastern arm of Boundary 112. The northern paddock thus defined (Enclosure 172) was roughly L-shaped, measuring c.41 x 38m internally at its widest point, with a probable entrance, c.8–9m wide, at its north-west corner. No internal features or deposits were recorded.

Despite defining the settlement boundaries, these ditches were relatively insubstantial, at least as they survived, compared to many of the boundary ditches recorded in Iron Age and Romano-British contexts elsewhere on the site, varying between 1.3–1.75m wide and 0.44m–0.7m deep, with steep-sided, U- or V-shaped profiles.

Enclosure 127
The northern end of the settlement was dominated by a large, rectangular enclosure (Enclosure 127), formed by cutting a roughly east to west aligned ditch across the interior of the settlement (Fig. 4.15), c.67m south of the northern boundary (*i.e.* the northern arm of Boundary 110). This ditch turned north, c.5m short of the eastern settlement boundary (the eastern arm of Boundary 110), to run roughly parallel with the eastern boundary. This seems to have created a track, c.5m wide, running up the eastern side of the enclosure (Routeway 12), giving access to this area from the southern part of the settlement. The track may also have extended around the northern side of Enclosure 127, immediately inside the northern boundary of the settlement.

Enclosure 127 measured in excess of 77.5m east to west (it extended west of the excavated area) and c.57–60m north to south, internally. Inside, attached to its eastern boundary ditch, was a subsidiary enclosure (Enclosure 168), c.34 x 29m, which was itself sub-divided into two rectangular spaces (the southern slightly larger, at c.487m^2, than that to the north, which covered an area of c.378m^2) by an east to west aligned ditch. No other internal features were recorded, either in Enclosure 168 itself, or more widely within Enclosure 127, and no evidence for an entrance into Enclosure 168 was noted.

Enclosures 135, 169 and 173
Attached to the southern side of Enclosure 127 was a group of three small, possibly interconnected enclosures (Fig. 4.15). Enclosures 135 and 173 were sub-square in plan, c.21.5 x 18m and c.20 x 18m respectively, at their widest points. Enclosure 173 contained no internal features, but two roughly concentric, semi-circular ditches were recorded at the south-western corner of Enclosure 135, the significance of which remains unclear. Enclosure 169 extended westwards beyond the excavated area but was clearly rectangular, measuring at least 43m, east to west, and up to 19m wide, internally.

Structure 114
Within Enclosure 169, a rectangular timber building (Structure 114, Fig. 4.16) was erected, close to the northern boundary of the enclosure. This structure measured approximately 12 x 6m, and was aligned east to west. Its north and south walls were marked by two rows of four sub-circular postholes, each c.0.5–0.7m in diameter and up to 0.4m deep, spaced at intervals of c.3–3.5m (centre to centre). Several nails and hobnails were recovered from the postholes, along with a Nene Valley colour-coated globular beaker (SF 2208, Fig. 7.13, No. 42): their findspots are shown on Fig. 4.16. Within the building, no features or deposits had survived but externally, an east to west aligned ditch ran west from close to the south-western corner of the building, extending westwards beyond the excavated area.

Enclosures 128, 170 and 171
Many of the archaeological features recorded within the southern part of the settlement had been severely truncated, meaning that the surviving evidence was generally quite fragmentary (Fig. 4.15). Extending into the site from the west was a possible rectangular enclosure (Enclosure 170), defined to the north by a re-cut (Boundary 117) of a Period 4.3 ditch (Boundary 118; above), to the south by a second ditch (Boundary 114), and to the east by a fence line, defined by a north to south aligned row of six postholes that had been constructed on the line of another Period 4.3 ditch (Boundary 111; above). The postholes were 0.3–0.8m in diameter and up to 0.2m deep. The putative enclosure thus defined measured in excess of 37m, east to west, and was up to 22m wide, internally. The only internal features recorded were numerous pits (Pit Group 7), which formed a seemingly random cluster located towards the eastern end of the enclosure. These features were sub-circular or oval in plan, varying in size from c.0.46m in diameter to c.1.2 x 1.5m, and 0.15m–0.50m in depth.

Approximately 27m east of Enclosure 170 was a small, sub-square enclosure (Enclosure 128), c.18 x 16m internally, with an east-facing entrance, c.3m wide. It was surrounded by a ditch, up to 1.2m wide and 0.3m deep; no internal features were recorded. Enclosure 171 was located c.16m to the south of this, but only its northern and eastern sides had survived, marked by two flat-bottomed ditches, up to 1.3m wide and 0.35m deep. Environmental samples taken from the fills of Boundary 113 yielded charred cereal grains and chaff, in particular spelt wheat glumes (from fill *5341*; Fryer, Chapter 8.IV). A possible internal division was represented by a short segment of a north to south aligned ditch (Boundary 113), located c.27m from the eastern end of the enclosure. On the western side of this was a large waterhole (Waterhole 9, pit *7476*), approximately 5m in diameter and in excess of 1.4m deep. The seven fills of this feature contained 280 sherds of 3rd- to 4th-century pottery, many of which came from kitchen and table wares (Lyons, Chapter 7.IV). Additionally, the upper fill yielded a small coin hoard (Hoard 2; Crummy, Chapter 6.II), comprising twelve debased *antoniniani*, terminating in the reign of Carausius (AD 287–93). Eight of the coins had corroded together, suggesting that they may have been deposited in a leather purse or wrapped in cloth. With the exception of Waterhole 9, the enclosed area contained only a seemingly random scatter of postholes and pits, including a group of four particularly large pits (Pit Group 8), at the north-east corner of the enclosure. One of these (*5342*) yielded charred cereal grains and spelt wheat glumes, the latter suggestive of secondary grain processing.

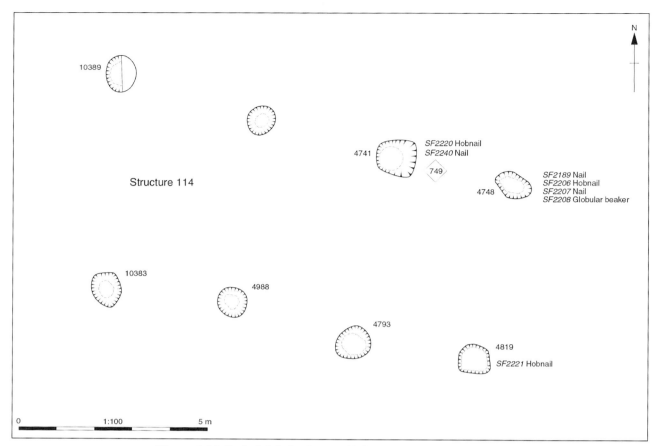

Figure 4.16 Period 4.4: Settlement 7, Structure 114. Scale 1:100

Phase 2

Settlement boundaries
During the secondary phase, Boundary 110 continued to define the core area of settlement to the north and east, and was extended southwards, towards Routeway 2 (Fig. 4.17). Towards its southern end, an entrance, *c.*5m wide, was marked by a break in the ditch, a cobbled area and – immediately inside the northern entrance terminal – a segment of an east to west aligned ditch, *c.*8.5m long, 1.5m wide, and 0.55m deep. The projecting 'annexe' at the south-eastern corner of the settlement, defined in Phase 1 by Boundary 112, went out of use, although its northern end (Phase 1, Enclosure 172) continued to be occupied by a group of small, relatively insubstantial enclosures (Enclosures 134, 138 and 174; below). To the south, a major new boundary ditch (Boundary 20) was dug along the northern edge of Routeway 2, narrowing the route considerably in places, to as little as 6m between the new ditch to the north and Boundary 8 to the south. For most of its excavated length, this ditch was *c.*1.3–2.5m wide and 0.3–0.5m deep, but in a stretch *c.*38m long (between the limit of the excavation to the west and Enclosure 126 to the east; see below), it was up to 4.4m wide and 0.7m deep.

Enclosures 127, 131 and 132
Whilst the major enclosure in the northern part of the settlement (Enclosure 127) seems to have fallen from use (its southern boundary ditch being infilled and cut by other features), elements of its eastern boundary ditch, and of subsidiary Enclosure 168 within it, appear to have been redefined and retained (Figs 4.15 and 4.17). What had been the eastern side of this latter enclosure was now provided with a narrow entrance, *c.*2m wide, flanked by rounded ditch terminals. The southern terminal (*5718*) yielded charred cereal grains, spelt wheat chaff and wild oats, together with possible evidence for malting, in the form of partly germinated cereal grains. The line of the former southern boundary ditch was straddled by a small, sub-rectangular enclosure (Enclosure 132), measuring 35m north to south, internally, and up to 21m wide, with a probable entrance, *c.*3.5m wide, on its west side. The southern end of this enclosure also overlay elements of Phase 1 Enclosures 135, 169 and 173, demonstrating that these had gone out of use. However, Structure 114, which lay within Enclosure 169, was not affected by the construction of Enclosure 132 and appears to have continued in use, positioned just outside the enclosure's western entrance.

East of Enclosure 132, Enclosure 131 was attached to the eastern boundary of the settlement (Boundary 110), whilst its northern side was formed by re-cutting a short segment of the southern boundary ditch of Enclosure 127. This sub-rectangular enclosure measured up to 25m, north to south, by 20m, east to west, at its widest points; its ditch was up to 2.1m wide and 0.78m deep. It was sub-divided into two, roughly equally, by an east to west aligned ditch, up to 0.45m wide and 0.2m deep, broken by an entrance, *c.*5m wide, giving access between the two areas. No other internal features or deposits were recorded. The eastern part of the internal ditch contained offcuts and waste fragments derived from the working of

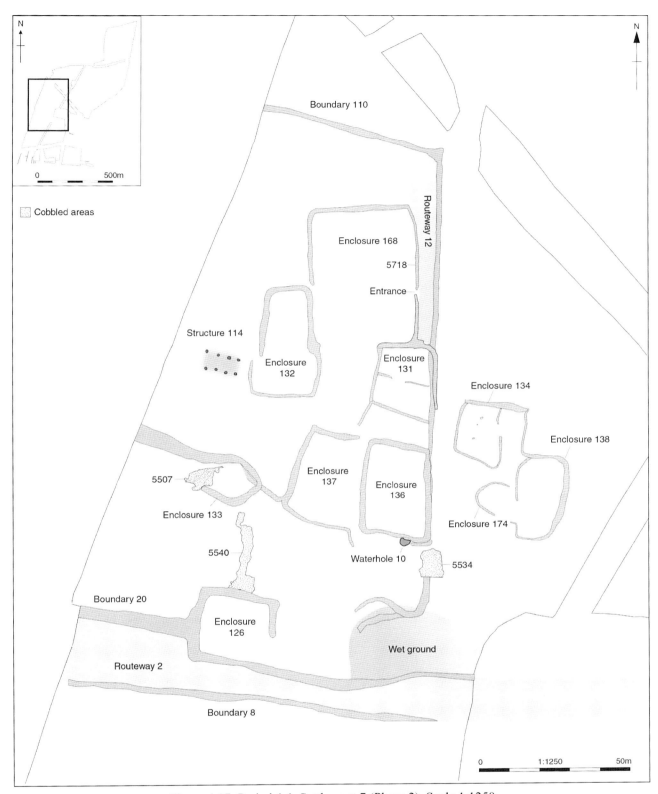

Figure 4.17 Period 4.4: Settlement 7 (Phase 2). Scale 1:1250

red deer antler, in addition to a chalk spindlewhorl and an iron bar fragment (Chapter 6, Fig. 6.48, SF 2120 and Fig. 6.38, SF 2269), all of which suggest that craft-related activities were undertaken in this area.

Enclosures 133, 136, and 137

In the central southern part of the settlement, Enclosures 128 and 170 of Phase 1 were replaced, slightly further to the north, by an east to west aligned row of three enclosures, a sub-circular example (Enclosure 133) to the west, and two rectangular enclosures (Enclosures 136 and 137) to the east (Fig. 4.17). Enclosure 133 was

Plate 4.8 Cobbled surface *5507*, Enclosure 133, Settlement 7 (Phase 2), looking south-west (Period 4.4)

Waterhole 10

Immediately outside the southern ditch of Enclosure 136, adjacent to the entrance into the settlement from the east (through Boundary 110; see above) was a steep-sided waterhole (Waterhole 10), approximately 2.7m in diameter and 0.9m deep (Fig. 4.17). Its fills yielded an assemblage of 4th-century pottery and a coin (SF 2126) datable to AD 364–78.

Enclosure 126

Attached to Boundary 20, the southern boundary ditch of the settlement, was a square enclosure (Enclosure 126), defined by a ditch, up to 2.5m wide and 0.62m deep, with an entrance, 9.5m wide, at the south-eastern corner (Fig. 4.17). One of the ditch fills (*5860*) yielded a 3rd-century gilded copper alloy brooch (Chapter 6, Fig. 6.15, SF 2194), whilst another fill (*5600*), located towards the north-western corner of the enclosure, contained a near-complete upper stone from a beehive quern (Fig. 6.44, SF 2539) and an iron cleat from a late Roman shoe or boot (SF 2699). A cobbled surface (*5540*), perhaps all that remained of a more extensive yard area, was recorded to the north of Enclosure 126. This extended northwards from the enclosure's northern perimeter ditch for over 25m, surviving in a linear strip no more than 8m wide.

Enclosures 134, 138 and 174

The projecting 'annexe' that had existed at the south-eastern corner of the settlement in Phase 1, defined by Boundary 112, went out of use, but its northern end, represented in Phase 1 by Enclosure 172, was superseded by a group of three small, relatively insubstantial, enclosures, all of which were probably interconnected (Fig. 4.17). The northernmost (Enclosure 134) was sub-rectangular, *c.*20 x 13.5m at its widest, and was enclosed to the south, west, and east by a narrow ditch, up to 0.8m wide and 0.3m deep. An east-facing entrance was marked by a gap, 4.2m wide, in the eastern ditch. The northern side of the enclosure was defined by a re-cutting of part of Boundary 112; this was more substantial, being up to 1.7m wide and 0.4m deep. This enclosure was linked to Enclosure 138 to the south-east by a shallow L-shaped ditch or gully. Enclosure 138 was also sub-rectangular, measuring *c.*29m north to south by 15m east to west, with an entrance, *c.*7m wide, towards its south-western corner. Immediately outside the entrance was a C-shaped enclosure (Enclosure 174), which was probably once attached to Enclosure 138, although truncation had removed the relevant junctions between the enclosure ditches. As it survived, Enclosure 174 was semi-circular, measuring 10m north-east to south-west, and at least 7m wide, and was defined by a ditch up to 0.9m wide and 0.35m deep. With the exception of three postholes within Enclosure 134, no internal features were recorded in any of these enclosures. However, the western ditch of Enclosure 138, and the southern terminal of the perimeter ditch for Enclosure 174, both yielded spelt wheat chaff, suggestive of on-site crop processing, and a high density of cereal grains with detached cereal sprouts, indicative of malting (Fryer, Chapter 8.IV), also came from the terminal of the ditch surrounding Enclosure 174.

approximately 12–13m in diameter internally, defined by a broad ditch which continued westwards from the north-western corner of the enclosure to form a substantial boundary ditch, up to 4.34m wide in places, and 1.4m deep. This was traced westwards for *c.*25m, but continued beyond the limit of the excavation. The western side of Enclosure 133 was essentially open, creating an entrance, 8m wide, through which a cobbled surface had been laid (*5507*, Pl. 4.8). This yielded a range of 'domestic' finds, including hobnails and coins, while a bone pin came from the enclosure ditch (Crummy, Chapter 6, *passim*).

Approximately 8m east of Enclosure 133 was a pair of rectangular enclosures (Enclosures 136 and 137), aligned north to south. The westernmost (Enclosure 137) was linked to Enclosure 133 by a short ditch, running north-westwards from its south-western corner. On the east, it had clearly been added onto the western side of Enclosure 136, although its northern and southern perimeter ditches did not quite link up with the western ditch of Enclosure 136, thus forming entrances, 3.2–3.3m wide at its north-eastern and south-eastern corners; no entrances were evident in the perimeter of Enclosure 136. Both enclosures were of similar size, measuring *c.*28–30m, north to south and *c.*16–18m wide, internally, with perimeter ditches *c.*1.1–2m wide and up to 0.75m deep. A large quantity of oyster shells was recovered from the western ditch of Enclosure 137.

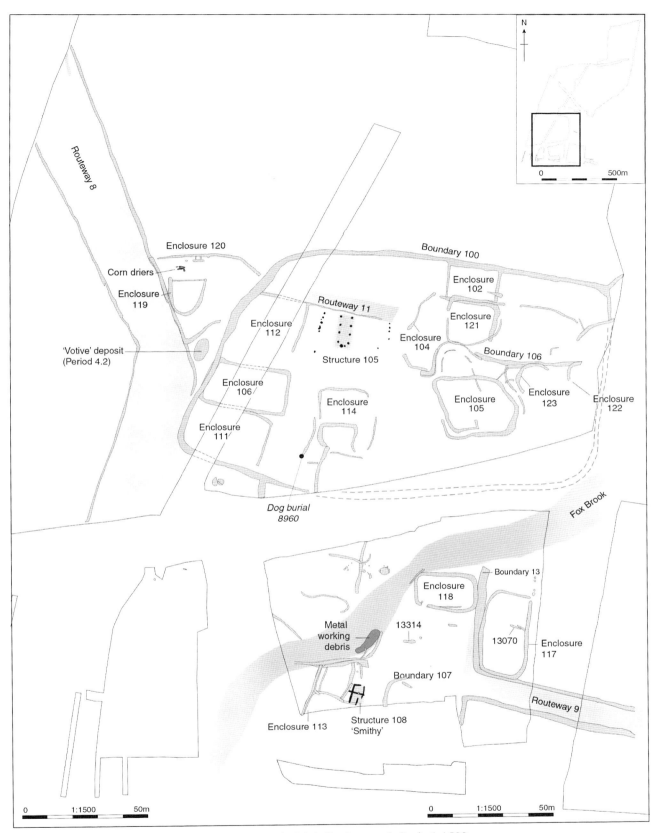

Figure 4.18 Period 4.4: Settlement 6. Scale 1:1500

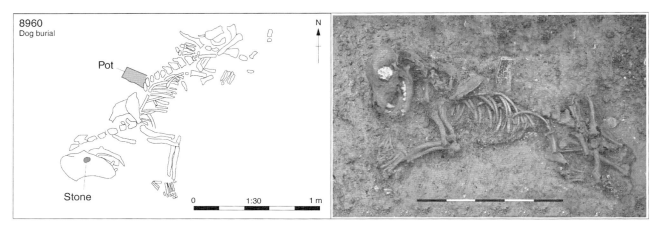

Figure 4.19 Period 4.4: Settlement 6, dog burial *8959/8960*. Scale 1:30

Settlement 6
(Figs 4.18–4.20; Pl. 4.9)

Summary

Within the enclosed area of settlement defined by Boundary 100, Enclosures 104, 105 and 114 clearly remained in use from Period 4.3, since all were modified at this time (Fig. 4.18). The other pre-existing enclosures (Enclosures 102, 106, 111 and 112) were not obviously modified, and no evidence for 4th-century activity was recorded within them. The possibility that they were retained cannot, however, be discounted, and this was also true of both Routeway 11 (which may, however, now have been blocked to the west by Enclosure 120) and Structure 105. Subsequently, the north-eastern corner of Enclosure 104 was overlain by a smaller enclosure (Enclosure 121), and its eastern perimeter ditch was cut by a substantial east to west aligned ditch (Boundary 106). The latter was itself cut by two curvilinear ditches, all that remained of two small, possibly C-shaped or sub-circular, enclosures (Enclosures 122 and 123).

Outside the north-western corner of the enclosed settlement, a roughly triangular enclosure (Enclosure 120) was appended to Boundary 100. This contained a subsidiary enclosure (Enclosure 119) and a corn drier, together with a few pits and postholes: its western edge seemingly referenced the eastern side of former Routeway 8 and its southern side the position of the 'votive' deposit (Period 4.2).

South of the enclosed settlement, the remnants of a few indeterminate features were found on the north bank of Fox Brook. To the south, Enclosures 113 and 117 were retained and modified, but the other Period 4.3 enclosures in this area (Enclosures 115, 116 and 177) went out of use. The northern side of Enclosure 116 was cut by the southernmost ditch of a larger, rectangular enclosure (Enclosure 118) located immediately adjacent to Fox Brook. The eastern ditch of this enclosure, and the redefined perimeter ditch for Enclosure 117, cut into the fills of Boundary 13, but continued to reference this much earlier feature, suggesting that it remained a significant feature in the landscape. Similarly, the southern ditch of Enclosure 117 cut the edge of the northern ditch of Routeway 9, but continued to respect its position, suggesting that the trackway also remained in use.

The enclosed settlement

Enclosure 114
The north-western corner of Enclosure 114 (Fig. 4.18) was redefined by the digging of a narrow ditch, up to 0.7m wide and 0.2m deep, as it survived, just inside the line of the earlier perimeter ditch. Further south, the western ditch was re-cut on much the same line as the earlier boundary, now measuring *c*.0.9–1.8m wide and up to 0.4m deep, but the eastern side was poorly defined, perhaps surviving as a narrow ditch segment, *c*.15m long, 0.6–0.7m wide and 0.2–0.3m deep. Internally, a subsidiary sub-rectangular enclosure, with internal dimensions of *c*.12 x 9m, was located on the western edge of Enclosure 114. This was defined to the north and east by an L-shaped ditch of similar size and form to the re-cut western perimeter ditch, which defined its western boundary. The southern side may have been completely open, although a narrow, poorly preserved ditch or gully, 0.5–0.7m wide and 0.1–0.2m deep, may have been all that remained of its southern arm.

A second small, subsidiary enclosure may have been appended to the western side of Enclosure 114. This was roughly triangular in plan, *c*.16m north to south and *c*.7m east to west, at its longest and widest points. Its southern side was defined by an east to west ditch or gully, 0.5m wide and up to 0.4m deep, and it was bounded on the west by another ditch, 0.8m wide and 0.17m deep. A gap, 2.5m wide, at the junction of the two ditches suggested the existence of an entrance at the south-western corner of the enclosure. At the southern terminal (*8959*) of the western ditch, adjacent to the putative entrance, a small dog (*8960*), similar in stature to a modern dachshund, had been buried on its right side: a notable feature was the deliberate placing of a small lump of chalk over the left eye (Fig. 4.19; see also Baxter, Chapter 8.III and Fig. 8.10).

Enclosures 104 and 105
Within the northern and eastern parts of the enclosed settlement, Enclosures 104 and 105 were further modified during Period 4.3 (Fig. 4.18), and three new enclosures were subsequently established in this area (Enclosures 121–123, below). The perimeter ditch of Enclosure 104 was redefined in several places, most notably to the north and at the north-western and south-western corners. The curvilinear sub-enclosure established within the south-eastern corner of Enclosure 114 in Period 4.3 was

retained, and a segmented ditch, 0.5–0.9m wide and up to 0.56m deep, was dug c.3m inside its perimeter, concentric with the perimeter ditch. The northern boundary ditch of Enclosure 105 was also re-cut, but this enclosure otherwise remained largely unaltered from the preceding period. Approximately 2m outside the eastern ditch, a new ditch was cut, the line of which mirrored that of the eastern perimeter. This feature was 0.55–0.75m wide and 0.19–0.34m deep, and formed a junction with Boundary 106 (below) to the north.

Enclosures 121, 122, 123 and Boundary 106
Boundary 106 was an east to west aligned ditch, 1.05–1.5m wide and 0.1–0.4m deep, the western end of which cut across the eastern perimeter ditch of Enclosure 104, although the feature as a whole lay largely outside that enclosure (Fig. 4.18). It was traced for 19.1m, its western end terminating c.3.5m south of a small, sub-square enclosure (Enclosure 121), with which it may have been contemporary. Enclosure 121 lay at the north-east corner of Enclosure 104, but probably post-dated the use of that feature (as did Boundary 106), since in places its ditches cut across the infilled perimeter ditch of the earlier enclosure. It measured 20m, north to south, by 18m, enclosing an area of approximately 330m^2, and contained no surviving occupation features or deposits. Close to its north-western and north-eastern corners were opposed entranceways, c.3m wide to the west and approximately 6m wide to the east, marked by gaps in the perimeter ditches. The ditches themselves were 0.56–1.04m wide and 0.14–0.38m deep.

Further internal sub-division of the area at the extreme north-eastern corner of the enclosed settlement was suggested by a number of other narrow ditches or gullies, most notably an east to west aligned feature, up to 0.6m wide and 0.27m deep, extending eastwards from the north-eastern corner of Enclosure 121, c.12m inside (*i.e.* south of), and aligned broadly parallel with, the northern arm of Boundary 100. A few metres north of Enclosure 121, a short ditch or trench, c.6.5m long, up to 1.67m wide and 0.14–0.48m deep, cut across the east ditch of Enclosure 102 on a north-west to south-east alignment.

Boundary 106 was subsequently cut by two curvilinear ditches, interpreted as the fragmentary remains of two small, stratigraphically late, enclosures. The easternmost of these (Enclosure 122) survived as a short curving ditch segment, c.8m long, 1.17–1.8m wide and 0.34–0.54m deep, which would have formed the north-western corner of the putative enclosure. Enclosure 123, located c.7m west of Enclosure 122, was somewhat better preserved, with almost half of the perimeter ditch surviving to the north and west. As it survived, the enclosure was C-shaped, measuring c.12m, north-east to south-west and c.8m wide, but may originally have been roughly circular, its south-eastern half perhaps having been completely destroyed. Its perimeter ditch was up to 1.8m wide and 0.54m deep.

Peripheral areas

Enclosures 119 and 120
Attached to the north-western corner of the enclosed settlement was a large, roughly triangular enclosure (Enclosure 120), measuring c.39 x 37m at its widest points, formed by two ditches running off Boundary 100 (Fig. 4.18). The northernmost, which curved north-westwards from Boundary 100 before turning to run almost due west, was no more than a shallow gully, at least as it survived, only 0.16–0.18m wide and 0.24m deep. The southern ditch was slightly more substantial and ran south-westwards from Boundary 100 before turning sharply north-westwards, to run along the eastern side of Routeway 8, on the line of the trackway's eastern ditch, which must have remained visible at this time. The southern ditch skirted (and excluded) an area of wet ground that appears to have formed a focus for possible 'votive' deposition of coins and metal artefacts, principally in the 2nd century AD (Period 4.2), but conceivably also as late as the 4th century. Whether this was out of respect for the supposed 'sanctity' of the spot, or was simply to avoid a piece of wet ground, is, however, open to question.

Internally, a smaller, U-shaped enclosure (Enclosure 119), measuring c.13m, north to south by 12m, at its widest point, was located on the western side of Enclosure 120. The perimeter ditch was up to 1.9m wide and 0.7m deep, except to the north, where the top of the 'U' was closed off by a less substantial feature. Enclosure 119 itself contained no internal features or deposits, but to the north, immediately inside the northern boundary of Enclosure 120, was a cluster of eight pits, six of sub-rectangular plan and two circular features, all of which were around 0.2m deep. Some of the fills yielded charred cereal grains and chaff (predominantly spelt wheat glumes). In form and character, these features were similar to groups of sub-rectangular pits that have been noted on other Romano-British rural sites in the area, which have been interpreted as corn driers.

South of the enclosed area of settlement, relatively little activity seems to have occurred on the north bank of Fox Brook in Period 4.4, the evidence being restricted to a few, seemingly randomly-distributed, ditches of uncertain significance, some of which at least may have been drainage features. One such, which extended north-westwards for at least 15m from the northern edge of the stream channel was 0.7m wide and up to 0.44m deep, and yielded further evidence for on-site crop processing, principally in the form of spelt wheat chaff.

Enclosure 113
On the south bank of Fox Brook, Enclosure 113 of Period 4.3 remained in use and was modified (Fig. 4.18). A new timber structure (Structure 108, below) was also erected adjacent to its eastern side, although this may have occurred after the enclosure ditches had silted up. For the most part, the primary perimeter ditches of the enclosure seem to have been retained, but in the northern paddock, the eastern ditch was re-cut on a somewhat different alignment. A possible entrance was marked by a gap, c.2m wide, in this ditch. The western ditch was not redefined, but a narrow ditch or gully was cut approximately 1.7m inside it, on a parallel alignment.

Structure 108
This structure was located immediately outside and to the east of Enclosure 113 (Fig. 4.18). The precise form of the building was difficult to determine, but it appears to have been essentially rectangular (Fig. 4.20), measuring (perhaps) c.7.5 x 4m internally, with its long axis aligned roughly north to south. Its walls were marked by shallow

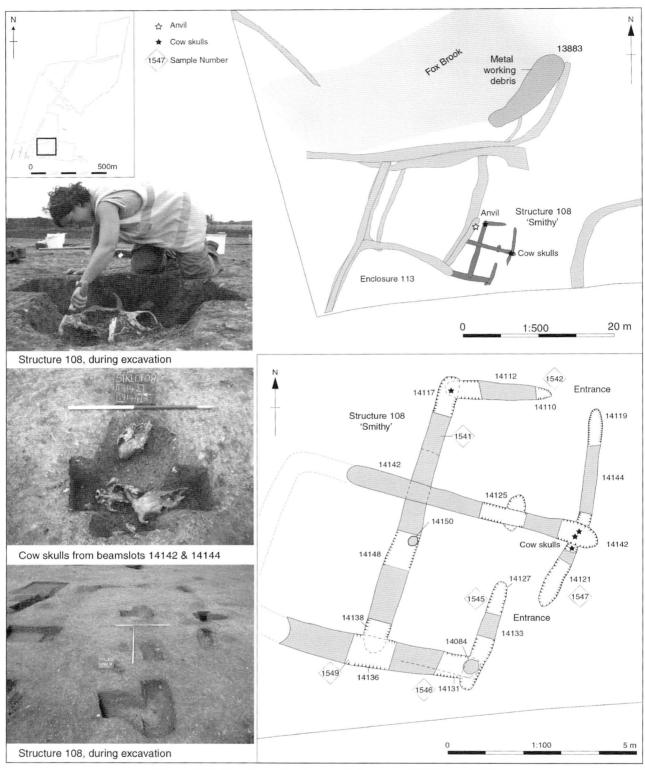

Figure 4.20 Period 4.5: Settlement 6, Structure 108. Scale 1:100

construction trenches or beamslots (*14112* to the north, *14136* to the south, offset ditches *14133* and *14144* to the east and *14148* to the west); the southern part of the east wall was offset *c.*1m to the west of the northern part. Possible doorways were marked by gaps at the north-eastern corner of the building and towards the south-eastern corner (1.1m and 0.9m wide respectively). An internal east to west aligned partition, marked by a trench (*14142*) of similar form to the others, divided the structure into two rooms or compartments, the northernmost being roughly square (*c.*4 x 3.3m internally) and the southernmost broadly L-shaped (resulting from the offsetting of the southern part of the east wall), measuring *c.*4 x 4m at its widest points. A possible oval posthole (*14125*), 1.05 x 0.45m and 0.3m deep, was located towards the eastern end of this wall, but may have been an earlier feature rather than being directly

Plate 4.9 Southern terminal (*14077*) of the eastern entrance into Enclosure 113, Settlement 6, looking south-west and showing iron anvil (SF 3760) *in situ* (Period 4.4)

associated with Structure 108. The line of the partition seems to have extended westwards for *c*.1.6m beyond the west wall, and the southern wall trench (*14136*) also seems to have extended further west, suggesting the possible existence of a third room or compartment (measuring *c*.4m, north to south and at least 2m, east to west), at the south-western corner of the structure. If this is correct, the building's ground plan may have resembled an inverted 'L' shape.

That the building may have functioned as a smithy was suggested by the recovery of hammerscale and metal flakes from the fill of its southern construction trench and of a small iron anvil (Crummy, Chapter 6.III; SF 3760), that came from the terminal of the ditch demarcating the eastern entrance into Enclosure 113, located immediately adjacent to the north-west corner of the building (Pl. 4.9). Within the building, a complete cow skull was recovered from the terminal of the northern wall trench (*14110/14117*), while three more cattle skulls were recovered at the junction of the partition wall with the east wall (*14142* and *14144*). Whether the skulls were deposited after the building had gone out of use, or relate to the building's construction and use, is not clear.

Approximately 15m north of Structure 108, a dump of material (*13883*, Fig. 4.18), *c*.13 x 3.7m in extent and containing much metalworking slag, had been deposited on the southern edge of the former channel of Fox Brook. It seems likely that this material derived from the building. Further evidence for metalworking was recovered from a long pit or trench (*13314*) situated 15m north-east of the structure. This feature measured 4.7 x 0.79m and was up to 0.64m deep, being aligned north-west to south-east. The southern side of the cut had a slight step in it, but the northern side was steeply sloping, to a slightly concave base. Four clay fills were identified, each containing charcoal, burnt clay and slag.

Enclosures 117 and 118
Towards the south-eastern corner of the settlement, Enclosure 117 was retained from Period 4.3 (Fig. 4.18), its perimeter ditch being completely redefined at this time. The recut ditch was 1.2–2m wide and 0.46–0.8m deep, and enclosed a slightly larger area (*c*.495m^2) than the primary ditch. The entrance into the enclosure was still located at the north-east corner, but access was simplified by the removal of the internal ditch that had divided the northern end of the enclosure from the rest of the area (Period 4.3; above). On the eastern side of the enclosure, *c*.10m south of the entrance and adjacent to the eastern perimeter ditch, was a long, east to west-aligned pit or trench (*13070*), 4.3 x 0.6m and up to 0.35m deep. The two clay fills of this feature yielded various small finds, including a coin of the House of Valentinian (AD 386–78; SF 3687) and another of Valentinian (AD 367–75; SF 3688), a copper alloy bracelet (Fig. 6.18, SF 3690), several nails and a quern fragment (SF 3691), together with 137 sherds of pottery – the latest of 4th-century date.

Enclosure 118 was located immediately north-west of Enclosure 117, and stratigraphically post-dated Enclosure 116 of Period 4.3, since its southern ditch cut through the north ditch of the earlier enclosure. Enclosure 118 was rectangular, measuring *c*.23m east to west and up to 13.5m, north to south, enclosing an area of approximately 281m^2. Its perimeter ditch was 1.25–1.8m wide and 0.5–0.7m deep, with a gap at its south-western corner marking the location of an entranceway, *c*.2.2m wide

VI. Period 4.5: late Romano-British (late 4th to early 5th century AD)

Introduction
(Fig. 4.21)
The last decades of the Roman period saw a reversal in the fortunes of the two excavated settlements. Settlement 7, which had expanded considerably in the 4th century (Period 4.4) after a very slow start in earlier periods, continued to flourish into the late 4th–early 5th century AD, as both stratigraphic and artefactual evidence amply demonstrate. However, the basic layout of the settlement, established in Period 4.4, did not change markedly at this time, although one of the principal boundary ditches was re-cut, largely on a new line.

In contrast, Settlement 6, which had been intensively occupied throughout the Romano-British period, appears to have been wholly or largely abandoned. No features or deposits attributable to Period 4.5 were recorded anywhere on this part of the site, and finds were restricted to one or two pieces of early Anglo-Saxon metalwork and a similar quantity of contemporary pottery (Chapter 5.II).

Settlement 7
(Fig. 4.22)

Summary
Ceramic and other artefactual evidence indicate that Settlement 7 continued to be occupied to the very end of the Roman period in the early 5th century AD, and perhaps beyond. However, the layout of the settlement does not appear to have changed radically at this time (Fig. 4.22), with much of the evidence for Period 4.5 occupation coming from pottery and other artefacts in the upper fills of earlier ditches, or in contemporary ditches that represented re-cuts of earlier features. The major exception to this was a realignment of the perimeter ditch enclosing the north and east sides of the settlement, which was re-cut, largely on a new line (Boundary 120). Internally, several of the enclosures constructed earlier in the 4th century (Enclosures 126, 131, 132, 134, 136, 137 and 138) were seemingly maintained, but only one new enclosure (Enclosure 139) was built; this contained a stone-lined well (*5387*). Two rectangular structures

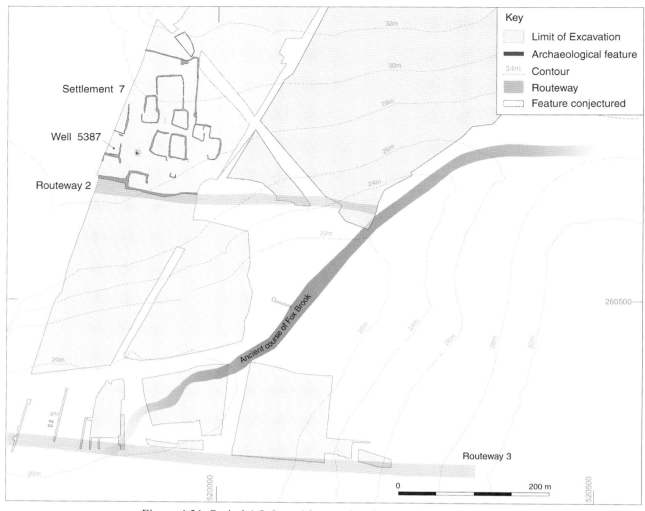

Figure 4.21 Period 4.5: Late 4th to early 5th century AD phase plan

(Structures 115 and 117) were also erected in the southern part of the settlement, although neither appears to have been located within an enclosure. A build-up of silts towards the south-east corner of the settlement, over an area that seems to have been wet since at least the late Iron Age, indicates that flooding may have been increasingly problematic in the late Roman/early post-Roman period.

Settlement boundaries
The settlement's southern boundary ditch (Boundary 20), cut in Period 4.4, appears to have been retained, but the northern and eastern boundary ditch (Boundary 110), went out of use and a new ditch (Boundary 120) was constructed (Fig. 4.22). This was 0.9m–1.6m wide and up to 0.75m deep. To the north, it followed the same line as Boundary 110, but to the east it was dug on a new line, c.10m east of and parallel with former Boundary 110. The southern end of this new ditch turned east through 90° to link up with the north side of Enclosure 134, which itself followed the line of an earlier boundary (Boundary 112) that had evidently gone out of use earlier in the 4th century.

Enclosure 139
This large, rectilinear ditched enclosure was constructed on the western edge of the site (Fig. 4.22). It measured in excess of 90m north to south, and over 19m east to west, but extended north and west of the excavated area. Its southern and eastern ditches were up to 2.2m wide and 0.65m deep; a short ditch segment of similar character also extended south-east for c.8m from the south-eastern corner of the enclosure. Internally, the enclosure was sub-divided by an east to west aligned ditch, 1m wide and 0.5m deep, located just over 30m north of the southern boundary ditch. This feature clearly referenced the substantial boundary ditch of Period 4.4 (Phase 2) that had extended west from Enclosure 133, having been dug immediately alongside the northern lip of the earlier feature. The eastern perimeter ditch survived in three segments, with gaps 12.6m and 10m wide in between; these may have been entrances, rather than the result of truncation. The southern segment had been re-cut on no less than four occasions, suggesting a long period of maintenance and use, and the central segment had been redefined at least once.

The southern terminal of the northern ditch segment (*4935*) yielded the fragmentary remains of a copper alloy 'cog-wheel' armlet (Crummy, Chapter 6.III; Fig. 6.19, SF 2235), examples of which are known from both late Roman and early Saxon burial contexts. Further south, the northern terminal of the central ditch segment contained over 400 sherds of pottery, representing nearly a quarter of the entire ceramic assemblage for Period 4.5. The group

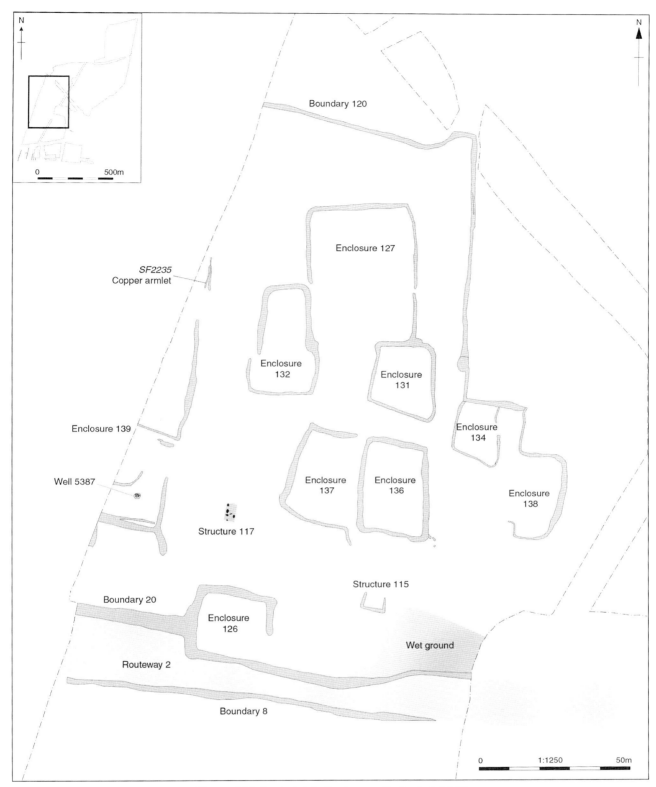

Figure 4.22 Period 4.5: Settlement 7. Scale 1:1250

comprises a mixture of storage jars, cooking vessels and tablewares, and represents a typical late Roman domestic assemblage for the region, and dates to the very end of the Romano-British period (Lyons, Chapter 7.IV). The sherds were considerably less abraded than the bulk of the pottery from earlier periods (the average sherd weight being c.17g), suggesting that they had suffered less post-depositional disturbance, probably due to the decrease in subsequent activity on the site. Only 12m to the east, another relatively large assemblage (over 50 sherds) of late Roman Shell-tempered ware (mainly dishes and jars) was recovered from an upper fill within the southern boundary ditch of Enclosure 127, which had gone out of use some time before.

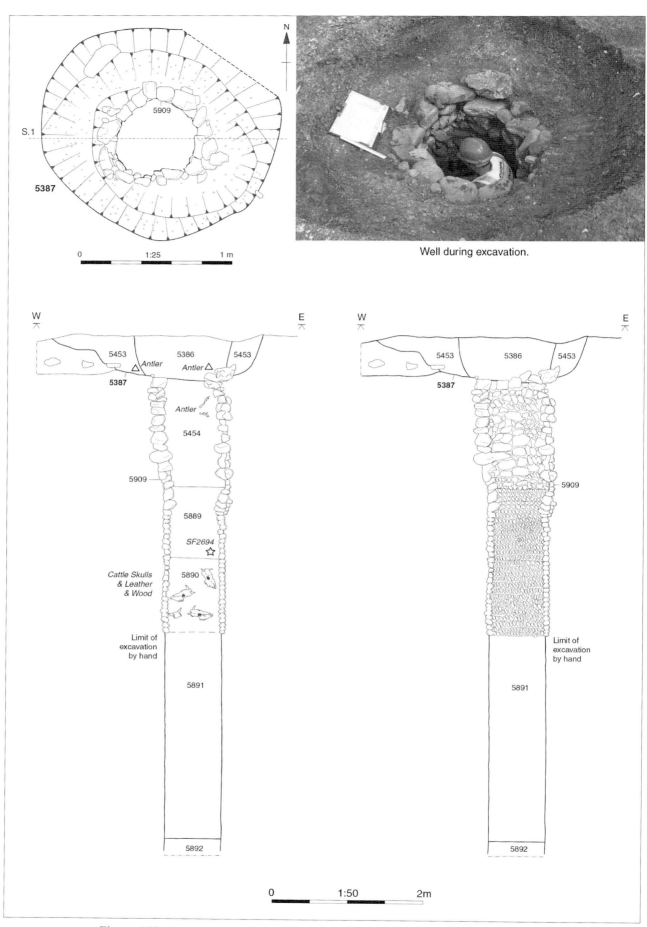

Figure 4.23 Period 4.5: Settlement 7, well *5387*. Plan scale 1:25, section scale 1:50

Internally, only two features were recorded within the limited area of Enclosure 139 that was available for investigation: a large, sub-rectangular pit or short ditch segment, and a stone-lined well (*5387*, below). The pit was located in the southern part of the enclosure, immediately south of (and aligned parallel to) the internal partition ditch, and just inside the putative southern entrance into the enclosure. It was 6m long, 1.5m wide and 0.75m deep and yielded 157 sherds of very late Roman pottery. It also contained quantities of burnt clay and oyster shell, a range of iron nails and some metalworking debris.

Well 5387
This feature, located close to the south-eastern corner of the enclosure (Fig. 4.22), was the only deep well recorded on the site, and also represented the only stone-lined feature discovered. As a solution to water supply, it represented a significant break with former practice, and one that was unsuited to the underlying geology. Earlier generations of settlers, in both the Iron Age and the Romano-British period, had collected water in large, but relatively shallow waterholes, designed to catch rainwater and surface run-off.

The well shaft, which was excavated to a depth of over 7m without reaching the bottom (Fig. 4.23), was 1.25m in diameter, and had been lined with a mixture of flattened river cobbles, glacial erratics, and limestone fragments (*5909*), laid in rough, drystone courses. The uppermost courses were constructed using rather larger, unhewn boulders, which had clearly been gathered from the same source or sources as the smaller stones in the lower lining. At the well head, the upper 0.6m of the construction cut (*5387*) was 2.24m in diameter, and had been backfilled with a gravelly clay containing frequent chalk nodules (*5453*). No datable finds were recovered from the construction fills.

Infilling of the well shaft would appear to have been a relatively rapid process. The fills, which were hand-excavated to a depth of 4m, were given five separate context numbers (earliest to latest: *5890*, *5889*, *5454*, *5386*), although this was mainly to provide some subdivision of the finds and environmental samples, since the bulk of the filling appeared very similar in character, comprising very dark grey brown clay silts. Finds and environmental samples were also retrieved from machine-excavated material lower down the well shaft (4–7m below the surface); these were allocated a separate context numbers (*5892*, *5891* and *5893*). With the exception of the uppermost deposit (*5386*), all of the shaft fills were waterlogged.

A large assemblage of animal bones was recovered from the well shaft (Baxter, Chapter 8.III, Fig. 8.15). Of the domestic species present, cattle predominate, accounting for 50% (by number of identified fragments) of the collection, although sheep are also common (43%). Smaller quantities of horse (6%) and pig (1%) were also found, together with a few examples of dog, cat, red deer (antler only), hare, wood mouse, water vole and amphibians. The assemblage includes the crania of thirteen cows (both cattle and oxen, Fig. 8.16), and the partial remains of at least twelve sheep. Most of the cattle, sheep and (possibly) horse bones probably derived from butchery waste, as no complete or partially articulated skeletons were recovered, although there was little evidence of butchery marks. None of the bones was very weathered, and very few had been gnawed, and it is probable that some were still held together by ligaments when deposited in the well.

The plant and insect assemblages recovered (particularly from fill *5893*) indicate dry, open grassland and disturbed ground, and also suggest the proximity of grazing animals. Insect taxa include a small suite of dung beetles (*Scarabaeidae*) and a small group of species associated with rotting organic matter and fouler material such as dung and rotting vegetation. Aquatic taxa are limited to families associated with ephemeral, muddy pools, which is perhaps unsurprising, since the material from which they derived was presumably deposited after the well had gone out of use and been partially backfilled. Most of the plant species recorded are typical of lighter soils. The presence of nearby dung heaps, or similar phosphate-rich deposits is suggested by the seeds of henbane (*Hyoscyamus niger*), while the presence of ragwort (*Senecio* sp) may suggest that the land was periodically over-grazed. Some evidence of crop processing, in the form of cereal grains and chaff, most frequently spelt wheat glumes, was recovered from fill *5889*. The well itself appears to have eventually become overgrown with brambles and elder.

The pollen assemblage is dominated by grass, and this may again have been derived from the surrounding pasture/meadows, but a larger proportion probably came from material deposited as rubbish within the well. It was not possible to distinguish between grass and cereal pollen due to the condition of the pollen grains. Some of the taxa identified are typical of damp conditions. Most of the herbs identified have culinary and/or medicinal applications, but this does not necessarily mean that they were put to such uses, since many of the species represented are common weeds of disturbed ground which would no doubt have been growing freely in and around the settlement. A notable exception was mistletoe pollen, which, as Green notes (Chapter 8.VII), appears out of place in an assemblage devoid of tree pollen. Mistletoe was used for its medicinal properties, but was (and is) more commonly associated with rites of fertility and renewal, and was used for ceremonial purposes. The relatively large amounts of fungal spores commonly found on animal dung indicate either that animals were grazing close to the well or, more probably, that dung formed a component of the rubbish thrown into the well following its disuse.

Artefacts from the well include a range of diagnostically very late Roman objects, such as a composite antler comb (Fig. 6.51, SFs 3157 and 3158), a piece of bone inlay decorated with triple ring-and-dot motifs, probably from a wooden box (Fig. 6.52, SF 2694), and a glass vessel fragment (SF 5387). Nine fragments from five leather sandals (SFs 2692, 3161, 3174, 3187, 3189, 3195, Fig. 6.55 and SFs 3152, 3175 and 3188, not illus.; Mould, Chapter 6.X) were also recovered, together with 120 sherds of late Roman pottery and a single sherd from a handmade vessel, the latter from fill *5891*. Once completely filled, a number of red deer antler fragments (SFs 2515–6) were seemingly deliberately placed into the top of the shaft (Baxter, Chapter 8.III).

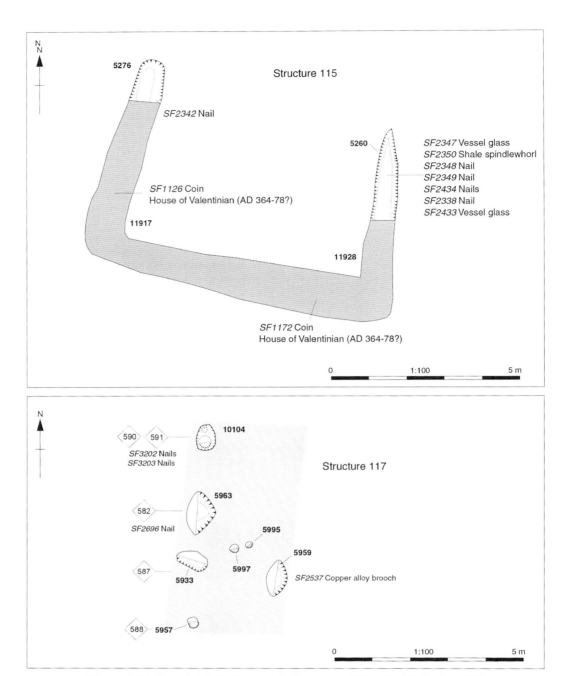

Figure 4.24 Period 4.5: Settlement 7: Structures 115 and 117. Scale 1:100

Structures 115 and 117
Only two possible timber structures were attributable to Period 4.5, both located in the southern part of the site. Structure 115 was situated towards the south-east corner of the settlement (Fig. 4.22), just under 70m south-east of Enclosure 139. It was rectangular, measuring 6–6.2m north-west to south-east, and *c.*5m wide, internally. Wall lines were represented by a square-sectioned gully or slot, 0.5–0.7m wide and 0.3m deep, which was traced on three sides, the northern side seemingly being open (Fig. 4.24). The foundation trench/slot yielded a range of artefactual materials, including late Roman pottery, two coins of the House of Valentinian (AD 364–78; SF 1126 and 1172), vessel glass, and a shale spindlewhorl, a horncore, and burnt and butchered animal bone. Their findspots are noted on Fig. 4.24.

Structure 117, located *c.*20m east of the south-eastern corner of the enclosure, was represented by an L-shaped arrangement of four postholes, and three smaller postholes or stakeholes (Fig. 4.24). It may have been roughly rectangular, *c.*5.5 x 3m, but was too poorly preserved for its character to be determined. No internal features or deposits had survived within either of these structures, and no other recorded features were obviously associated with them. Early 5th-century pottery was recovered from some of the postholes associated with Structure 117, along with various nails and a copper alloy brooch (SF 2537).

Settlement 6
No features or deposits attributable to Period 4.5 were recorded anywhere within Settlement 6, which appears,

therefore, to have been wholly or largely abandoned at the end of the Romano-British period (see Chapter 5).

VII. Discussion: Romano-British settlement

Settlement morphology

Early Romano-British (late 1st to early 2nd century AD)
Many recent excavations of Iron Age/Romano-British rural settlements have demonstrated that continuity of occupation from the late Iron Age to the early Romano-British period is entirely typical, both in Cambridgeshire (Evans *et al*. 2008, 191) and elsewhere (Booth *et al*. 2007, 42). Indeed, there are relatively few excavated examples of early Romano-British settlements that were entirely new foundations. Evidence for a more significant re-organisation of landholdings does not seem to have occurred until the late 1st to 2nd century AD, with the adoption of a larger-scale agricultural system associated with larger farmsteads.

At Love's Farm, the early Roman period was characterised by a marked reduction in the number of farmsteads, particularly on the higher ground to the north, which was effectively abandoned at this time. In fact, with the exception of Settlement 7 (which originated in Period 3.5), no trace of Romano-British occupation was found north of Routeway 2, which was itself re-defined as a ditched track or droveway at this time. This may suggest that the population gradually coalesced into more nucleated settlements, perhaps as a result of a range of social, economic and environmental factors (see further discussion in Chapter 9).

The late 1st–early 2nd century AD (Period 4.1, Fig. 4.1) saw very little change in Settlement 7, with most of the major features established in the late pre-Roman Iron Age remaining in use. With the exception of a possible hayrick (Structure 110, below), no buildings or other structures were recorded, and there was little other evidence for on-site domestic occupation at this time. As in the preceding period, the impression gained is of agricultural enclosures and boundary ditches on the periphery of a farmstead located somewhere off-site, presumably to the west. It is therefore somewhat surprising that an assemblage of over 200 sherds of pottery, including samian ware and high quality, imported Gaulish wares, many comprising complete or near-complete vessels, was recovered from the re-cut ditch of one enclosure (Enclosure 28). Whilst it has been suggested that these vessels may derive from disturbed cremation burials (above), no other evidence was found to suggest that this was the case, and the deposit is perhaps best interpreted as a dump of tablewares and other pottery derived from a fairly high status occupation area nearby.

Settlement 6 now developed into a fully enclosed farmstead, measuring up to 140 x 80m at its greatest extent, and bounded by a fairly substantial perimeter ditch. The discrete group of enclosures added to the north-western corner of the settlement in Period 3.5 (Enclosure 163) was integrated, with some minor modifications, into the new layout, but the earlier rectilinear enclosures (Enclosures 11 and 13), that had formed the principal focus of the settlement in the late Iron Age, were removed. The layout of the settlement's interior was fragmentary as it survived, but appears similar to the 'grid iron' pattern of enclosures and paddocks known from many Romano-British rural settlements in the area, including Lower Cambourne and Jeavons Lane, excavated as part of the Cambourne New Settlement project (Wright *et al*. 2009, 23, fig. 10; 44, fig. 17), and at Addenbrooke's Hospital, Cambridge (Evans *et al*. 2008, 41, fig. 2.13). Occupation appears to have been focused towards the centre of the enclosed area, where three rectilinear timber structures (Structures 100, 102, and 109) were located. These buildings are considered in more detail below – whilst few indications of their function had survived, it seems likely that some at least served as accommodation and others may have been for storage, or perhaps served some other agricultural purpose. A small, circular structure (Structure 101) located west of these buildings, just inside the settlement enclosure, may have been a hayrick, identical in character to that found in Settlement 7 (Structure 110). A horse burial lay within an enclosure in the southern part of the settlement.

Outside the farmstead, the two pre-existing ditched trackways or droveways (Routeway 8 to the west, Routeway 9 to the south) remained in use. Slight traces of a possible ditched field system (Field Systems 5 and 6) were recorded to the south, adjacent to the north bank of Fox Brook.

Middle Roman (c.2nd to 3rd century AD)
The 2nd century (Period 4.2, Fig. 4.5) saw the re-planning of Settlement 7, although traces of activity in this area remained relatively sparse and it is possible that more intensive settlement continued to be focused off site. A probable north to south aligned ditched track or droveway (Routeway 10) seems to have formed the focus of activity at this time. To the south this may have linked to Routeway 2, the major east to west route on this part of the site, whilst to the north it seemingly terminated at the entrance to a small, sub-square enclosure (Enclosure 30). Two similar enclosures (Enclosures 27 and 129) were located nearby; neither contained any occupation features, but the perimeter ditch of Enclosure 129 cut into a horse burial.

The only structural remnants found in this area indicate the presence of a small, post-built rectangular building (Structure 111), situated on the western edge of the trackway. Whilst superficially resembling a four-post structure, most of which are presumed to have had an agricultural purpose, Structure 111 may have been a dwelling, since one of several adjacent pits yielded the shells of marine molluscs, including oysters, together with animal bones and charcoal – an assemblage suggestive of nearby domestic occupation. Some distance south of this building, a large pit, possibly an extraction pit (Quarry 7) yielded a collection of misfired pottery wasters, together with fragments of kiln lining and kiln furniture, presumably rubbish derived from a nearby pottery kiln. Although no direct evidence for the kiln itself was found, this discovery adds to the increasing corpus of evidence for pottery production at, or in the vicinity of, rural settlements in Cambridgeshire during the late Iron Age/early Romano-British period, an aspect of the rural economy that is considered in more detail in Chapter 9.VI.

In the southern part of the site, the basic layout of Settlement 6 remained little changed in the 2nd century, although the configuration of ditched enclosures and paddocks within the enclosed farmstead was modified, and a ditched track or droveway (Routeway 11) now entered the settlement at its north-eastern corner. In this phase in particular, the layout of the compound bears some resemblance to the late 1st- to mid 2nd-century settlement at Haddon (Hinman 2003, 28–30, fig. 13), particularly in terms of the provision of a series of rectilinear paddocks along one side of the main enclosure (to the west in Settlement 6, to the east at Haddon). At that site, the faunal assemblage indicated the introduction of a specialised agricultural regime, with young cattle and sheep being bred and reared for their meat (Hinman 2003, 28). However, a similar development was not apparent in the faunal remains associated with Settlement 6, or indeed from elsewhere on the Love's Farm site (see below).

A single rectangular timber building (Structure 116), located towards the southern edge of the enclosure, appears to have existed within the farmstead at this time. The function of this poorly preserved structure could not be determined but, given the lack of evidence for other buildings during this period, it may have been a dwelling, unless accommodation was located off-site at this time. The only other structure recorded was a small, rectilinear timber building (Structure 103, below) of uncertain character and purpose, located west of the enclosed farmstead and adjacent to Routeway 8. Although located in reasonably close proximity to a probably votive assemblage of personal ornaments and other metalwork, which had been deposited in a wet area just outside the farmstead enclosure, there was no evidence that Structure 103 itself had any ceremonial significance. It is possible that a small, 2nd-century coin hoard (Hoard 1), buried in a pit not far from the collection of metalwork, may also have been a votive offering, as contemporary coinage was extremely rare on the site as a whole (see discussion in Chapter 9.IX).

Whilst it is possible that some of the 2nd-century elements of Settlement 7, including Routeway 10, survived into the 3rd century (Period 4.3, Fig. 4.9), most appear to have fallen from use. Over much of the investigated area, a highly fragmented pattern of predominantly east to west aligned ditches was established. The significance of these features is difficult to determine, although they somewhat resemble a north to south aligned system of 4th-century ditches, interpreted as the remains of small fields, excavated at Little Paxton Quarry, north of St Neots (Jones 2000, 137–41, fig. 11.10). There, the environmental evidence suggested an open, pastoral environment and the presence of grazing animals, dominated by cattle and sheep.

Settlement 6 once more retained its basic layout into the 3rd century, subject to further remodelling of the enclosures within the main farmstead compound and the construction of a new rectangular timber building (Structure 105). This was a substantial, possibly aisled structure, 8m wide and over 11m long, of a type well-known from Romano-British rural sites in southern England (Hingley 1989, 39–45). Although frequently interpreted as barns (see Buildings, below), some may have served as houses, whilst many are likely to have been multi-functional. South of the main farm complex, a palimpsest of small enclosures, boundary ditches, pits and other features was recorded on either side of the Fox Brook. Although peripheral to the enclosed farmstead, artefactual and environmental evidence suggest that a range of activities was being undertaken in this area, possibly including cereal processing and malting/brewing. A small timber building of uncertain purpose (Structure 106) was located within a small, ditched enclosure (Enclosure 113) on the south bank of the Fox Brook.

Late Roman (4th to early 5th century AD)
It was only during the 4th century (Period 4.4, Fig. 4.14) that intensive occupation occurred within the excavated (eastern) part of Settlement 7, with the establishment of a large enclosed farmstead, measuring 180m north to south and over 155m east to west. In its most developed form, the quite formal, 'grid-iron' plan of enclosures and paddocks within the settlement resembles a broadly contemporary settlement enclosure at Stansted, in Essex (Cooke *et al.* 2008, 162–5, fig. 8.10), and the conquest-period farmstead at Addenbrooke's Hospital, Cambridge (Evans *et al.* 2008, 41–2, fig. 2.13). As already noted, similar layouts are evident at other Romano-British farmsteads in the region, including those at Lower Cambourne and Jeavons Lane, east of Love's Farm (Wright *et al.* 2009, 23, fig 10; 44, fig. 17), and also at Prickwillow Road, Ely (Atkins and Mudd 2003, 16, fig. 12). Towards the centre of the Settlement 7 at Love's Farm, a substantial, rectangular aisled building (Structure 114) was erected within one of the ditched enclosures. It was similar in character to Structure 105 (Period 4.3) in Settlement 6, but probably somewhat larger (*c.*15 x 10m). As with Structure 105, this building was too poorly preserved for its function to be determined, but the fact that no other buildings were recorded suggests that it may have served as the main farmhouse, although it could have been multi-functional (Hingley 1989, 39–45; see also below).

The internal configuration of enclosures and paddocks continued to develop within Settlement 7, becoming ever more complex. The remains of cobbled areas at several locations, including at enclosure entrances, suggest that access was required to these areas by people and, perhaps, by wheeled transport, not just livestock (Abrams and Ingham 2008, 74). One of these surfaces yielded a large assemblage of iron objects (Crummy, Chapter 6.III), mostly nails and broken tools/agricultural equipment, although whether this was scrap metal, destined to be recycled but abandoned for some reason, or had some other significance, is unclear.

Settlement 6 remained in use into the 4th century, although activity here apparently tailed off earlier than in Settlement 7. The large ?aisled building (Structure 105) erected in the 3rd century probably remained in use, and some of the paddocks within the main farmstead enclosure were again re-defined. The only other contemporary building was an irregular rectilinear structure (Structure 108) located to the south of Fox Brook, probably within a small ditched enclosure. Associated metalworking debris suggests that this functioned as a smithy (see below), and a large deposit of iron smithing slag was also found a short distance to the north of the building, adjacent to the stream.

Ceramic and numismatic evidence demonstrate that Settlement 7 continued to be occupied to the end of the Roman period (Period 4.5), and, indeed, the associated metalwork suggests a degree of affluence during the 4th century. The remains of two structures were found: a post-built example (Structure 117) and a three-sided, trench-built example (Structure 115). In an enclosure in the western part of the site, a substantial stone-lined well was constructed, its fills yielding a significant assemblage of late Roman artefactual and ecofactual assemblage (see Ritual Deposition, below, and Chapter 9.IX).

Buildings

In the Romano-British period, rectilinear timber buildings gradually replaced the roundhouses at Love's Farm, although – with the exception of two possibly aisled buildings – the majority were small, and most were of uncertain purpose. The earliest recorded structures, attributed to Period 4.1 (late 1st–early 2nd century AD), comprised a cluster of three buildings (Structures 100, 102, and 109) located towards the centre of Settlement 6. Structures 100 and 109 were both post-built, with uprights placed in individual postholes, and were of similar size ($c.8.2 \times 4.1$m and 7×4.5m respectively), but both were so poorly preserved that little else can be usefully said about them, and their function is unknown. Structure 102 was larger ($c.12$m long, north to south, and 8.8m wide at its widest point), with side walls marked by quite substantial gullies or construction trenches, up to 0.95m wide and 0.55m deep. These were somewhat curving, giving the ground-plan of the building a distinctly bowed appearance. No structural evidence for the north wall was noted, but the south wall may have been marked by a much less substantial gully/trench, only 0.2m wide and 60mm deep, which suggests that this wall was not load-bearing. Although no internal features or deposits were recorded, and no evidence pertaining to the building's function was found, the bowed plan of the structure bears some resemblance to a somewhat larger ($c.20 \times 11$m) aisled building at Roystone Grange, in Derbyshire (Hingley 1989, 40, fig. 17), although there was no evidence that Structure 102 was itself aisled.

The only significant concentration of painted wall plaster to be recovered from the site came from two early Romano-British deposits infilling the top of an Iron Age boundary ditch (Boundary 1), located a short distance south of Structures 100 and 102. The plaster, which was mostly white with traces of red paint, also occurred (clearly residually) in the fills of two large pits or post-pits that had been dug through these fills. Despite the proximity of these deposits to Structures 100 and 102, there was no evidence that it had derived from either of these buildings; indeed, its origin is entirely unknown.

In Period 4.2, a single rectangular building (Structure 111) was constructed in Settlement 7, and another (Structure 116) was located within the main enclosed compound in Settlement 6. A third timber building (Structure 103) was also located to the west of the farmstead compound in this area. Structure 111 measured 5×3m, and resembled a large four-post structure, since it was marked only by four corner posts. Structure 116 survived only as a row of five stone-packed post-pads aligned roughly east to west. Structure 103, located $c.30$m west of Settlement 6's main compound, appears to have comprised a single room or cell, 4×3.3m, defined by a continuous construction trench. Another room, or (more probably), a partly enclosed external area, lay to the north. Although located in quite close proximity to an area of wet ground, which may have been a focus for votive deposition in the earlier Roman period (see Chapter 9.IX), there was no clear evidence that Structure 103 had any ceremonial, religious, or ritual significance, although the possibility cannot be completely discounted.

In the 3rd century, a small timber building (Structure 106) was erected south of the Fox Brook, on the southern periphery of Settlement 6, and outside the main farm compound, within which a large and possibly aisled building was erected during the same period (Structure 105, below). The remains of Structure 106 comprised a series of postholes and short slots or trenches, covering an area $c.6 \times 5$m, but little sense could be made of the building's plan, and its function is unknown. The 4th century saw the construction of a second ?aisled building in Settlement 7 (Structure 114, below), but no other structures were found in this area. In the area of Settlement 6, a single timber building (Structure 108) was erected at this time, to the south of Fox Brook. The ground plan of the structure proved difficult to reconstruct, but it may have been in the form of an inverted 'L', measuring $c.7.5 \times 4$m, internally, at its greatest extent. Its walls were marked by shallow construction trenches, and the building appears to have been subdivided into two rooms or compartments. Unusually, associated artefactual evidence made it possible to suggest a likely function for this structure, which appears to have served as a smithy (Crummy, Chapter 6.III and Starley, Chapter 6.IV).

Also in the 3rd century AD, a large rectangular timber building (Structure 105), over 11m long and 8m wide, was constructed within the main farm compound in Settlement 6. A very similar structure (Structure 114), measuring $c.15 \times 10$m, was also constructed in the 4th century towards the centre of Settlement 7. Both buildings were aligned north to south, and were composed of large, earth-fast posts set into individual postholes. They comprised a central room, running the length of the building, defined by posts on either side – on site they were identified as aisled buildings of a type well known from Romano-British settlement sites (Hingley 1989, 39), although no evidence for the outer set of posts appears to have been found, suggesting that they may have been simple, unaisled structures (a type also found at many sites; cf. Thetford, Atkins and Connor 2010, 15). If they were indeed aisled, the 3rd to 4th-century date of the Love's Farm structures is consistent with the wider evidence, which suggests that such buildings were uncommon in Britain before the mid to late 2nd century AD, although a few earlier examples are known, and it has even been suggested that the origin of this architectural form may be pre-Roman (Atkins and Connor 2010, 15). Iron Age aisled buildings appear, however, to be extremely rare in Britain, although they occur in pre- Roman contexts in northern Europe. Further discussion appears in Chapter 9.IV.

At the very end of the Roman period (Period 4.5), two small, rectangular timber structures (Structures 115 and 117) were built within Settlement 7, but nothing of similar date was found in Settlement 6, since that farmstead appears to have been largely abandoned around this time. Structure 115 measured $c.6 \times 5$m, with walls defined on three sides by a square-sectioned gully or construction trench; to the north, the building may have been open-sided, although this wall might have been constructed in a different way, leaving no trace in the archaeological record. Structure 117 was marked by an L-shaped arrangement of postholes and stakeholes, and may have measured $c.5.5 \times 3$m but was very poorly preserved. The function of neither structure could be determined, but the gully/slot for Structure 115 yielded a range of finds suggestive of possible domestic and craft activities.

Pottery from some of the postholes associated with Structure 117 indicates a likely construction date in the early 5th century AD.

In addition to the Iron Age roundhouse drip-gullies detailed in Chapter 3, two much smaller ring ditches of early Romano-British date (both attributed to Period 4.1) were recorded, one (Structure 101) in Settlement 6, the other (Structure 110) associated with the earliest Romano-British phase in Settlement 7. Both were represented by unbroken, rather than penannular or segmented, ring gullies, 3.82m in diameter, in the case of Structure 101, but only 2.6m in diameter for Structure 110. The gullies were of similar depth (c.0.1–0.15m), but that in Structure 110 was wider (0.66m) than the gully for Structure 101 (0.2–0.3m). Both structures are interpreted as possible hayricks, similar in form to a possible late Bronze Age example excavated at Addenbrooke's Hospital, Cambridge (Evans *et al.* 2008, 30). There, the structure was dated on the evidence of two potsherds recovered from the ring gully, and a parallel was noted from south Lincolnshire, associated with a late Bronze Age/early Iron Age field system.

'Ritual' deposition

Human burials
No human burials were found associated with the Roman settlements, suggesting that burial grounds lay elsewhere at this time. As noted above, pottery recovered from Settlement 7 may suggest the nearby presence of a 1st-century cremation cemetery in the vicinity.

Hoards and votive deposits
The most striking evidence for probable 'ritual' deposition at Love's Farm occurred during the Romano-British period, in the form of an apparently votive deposit of metalwork in Settlement 6 in Period 4.2 (Pl. 4.2) and in the contents of a late Roman well (Settlement 7, Period 4.5), potentially providing insights into 'religion' in the countryside at this time. These important assemblages are fully discussed in Chapter 9.IX. The two small coin hoards found in Settlement 6 (Period 4.2) and Settlement 7 (Period 4.4) may represent stashes rather than having any ritual connotations. In addition, examples of possible foundation and/or closure deposits of late Roman date were found in both Settlements 6 and 7. In the former, the foundation of Structure 108, which appears to have been a smithy, may have been marked by the deposition of cattle skulls within its construction trenches, whilst an anvil was buried in an adjacent ditch terminal. In Settlement 7, a large assemblage (over 400 sherds) of pottery, representing nearly a quarter of the entire Period 4.5 ceramic assemblage, was recovered from the northern terminal of Enclosure 139 (Period 4.5). Only 12m to the east, another relatively large assemblage of over fifty sherds of late Roman Shell-tempered ware (mainly dishes and jars) came from the southern boundary of Enclosure 127.

In the 2nd century AD, a cattle skull had been placed at the base of the perimeter ditch close to the north-western corner of Enclosure 124, within Settlement 7, attesting to the likely continuation of such 'ritual' practices at the site into the Romano-British period. It is not clear if a *denarius* of the period AD 206–10 (SF 3040), found in the westernmost terminal of the northern entrance into Enclosure 112, within Settlement 6 (Period 4.3), represents a 3rd-century example of such a rite, or was merely a casual loss.

Other indications of votive practices or spiritual beliefs during the Romano-British period were slight. An unstratified late 3rd-century radiate coin (SF 3610) had been pierced for use as an amulet, the perforation being placed so that the (illegible) deity on the reverse would have hung upright. Three Roman coins had also been deliberately abraded on both faces, a phenomenon noted on coins recovered from Romano-British religious sites, and in Anglo-Saxon burials (Crummy, Chapter 6.III). An unstratified bell fragment may, by analogy with similar items discovered elsewhere, have had a ritual significance, whilst an unstratified copper alloy hairpin (SF 1182) dating to the first/2nd century AD had been bent and its tip bent upwards, possibly indicating a votive purpose.

Possible 'ritual' deposits associated with the late Roman well are detailed in Chapter 9.IX: 'Deposition in Watery Places'.

Animal burials
Two of the three complete horse burials recorded on the Love's Farm site were both located in or near Settlement 6 and were of late 1st/early 2nd-century AD date (Period 4.1), whilst the third, associated with Settlement 7, was attributed to the 2nd century (Period 4.2). In Settlement 6, a stallion or gelding, 9–10 years of age, was buried in a large pit (*10611*) that had been dug into an earlier, infilled, enclosure ditch. The second horse buried in this area was located to the south-west, outside the enclosed settlement, where it had been buried in a large pit (*11735*) that had been dug directly into the natural subsoil. The third horse had also been buried in a pit (*4880*) dug directly into the natural clay. This was a mare, approximately 10 years old, which had been interred on the north-western periphery of Settlement 7. Similar burials are known from Iron Age and Romano-British settlements elsewhere in the region, for example at Haddon, near Peterborough (Collins 1994, 151–2). Since there was no suggestion that the Love's Farm burials had any kind of 'ritual' significance, it is presumed that they represent the disposal of farm animals that had died from natural causes (see Baxter, Chapter 8.III and Chapter 9.IX).

In the 4th century AD (Period 4.4), a male dwarf hound (*8960*), similar in stature to a modern dachshund (Baxter, Chapter 8.III), had been buried in a ditch terminal within Settlement 6. The most striking feature of this burial was that a fragment of chalk had been placed over the left eye socket, the animal having been buried on its right side. Baxter notes that the remains of brachymel dwarf hounds of this kind formed a significant proportion of the dog remains found in Romano-British contexts at Love's Farm, and suggests that these are likely to have been pets.

The partial skeletons of three ewes came from the fill of Quarry 7 in Settlement 7 (Period 4.2). In the 3rd century AD (Period 4.3), the partial skeleton of a juvenile sheep, comprising the skull and foot elements, was deposited at the north-west corner of Enclosure 113 (Period 4.3), south of the enclosed area of Settlement 6. No cut marks, indicative of butchery, were noted on any of the bones in these skeletons, meaning that a votive interpretation of their burial cannot be ruled out.

Conclusions

From their origins in the middle Iron Age, the scattered farmsteads of the area gradually coalesced, in the decades either side of the Roman invasion, to form two nucleated settlements located close to the route leading towards St Neots and Eynesbury. Despite these developments, the basic subsistence economy of the site (as detailed in Chapters 6–8 and discussed in Chapter 9.V) remained unchanged, with the rearing of cattle and sheep and the cultivation of spelt wheat dominant throughout. Unlike some of the sites nearby, there was no evidence for agricultural specialisation as a result of the Roman conquest.

The presence of traded pottery implies that at least some within the Love's Farm community were operating above subsistence level by the end of the Iron Age, a trend that continued into the Romano-British period, when modest quantities of imported goods reached the site. The fact that such artefacts were recovered from all Romano-British phases demonstrates that Roman material culture was at no stage deliberately shunned, and that at least some individuals were willing and able to acquire some of the trappings of a 'Roman' lifestyle. As in the preceding period, evidence was sought for ritual or ceremonial activities. A concentration of personal ornaments and other Romano-British artefacts was strongly suggestive of 'votive' deposition, perhaps in a 'watery place'. A full discussion of all of the findings is presented in Chapter 9.

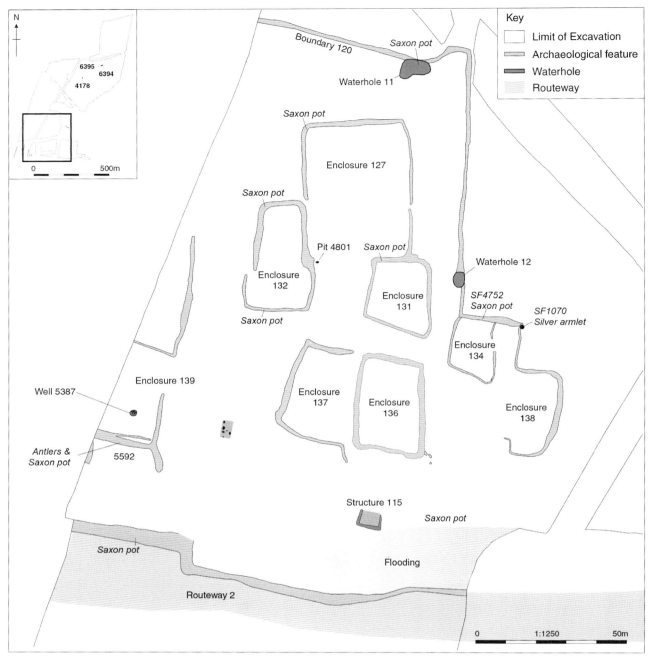

Figure 5.1 Period 5.1. Early Saxon phase plan. Scale 1:5000

Chapter 5. Post-Roman (Periods 5 to 7)

by John Zant and Mark Hinman

I. Introduction

That activity occurred on the site in the early Anglo-Saxon period (*c.*5th to 6th century AD) is indicated by the presence of relatively small quantities (205 sherds in total) of handmade, early Saxon pottery (Blinkhorn, Chapter 7.VIII), and a few other diagnostic artefacts (Crummy, Chapter 6.III). Most of this material came from the vicinity of Settlement 7 which, after a slow start, had seen a marked intensification of activity during the 4th century AD (Period 4.4), a process that had clearly been sustained into the late 4th to early 5th century AD (Period 4.5). There, the distribution of finds suggested that activity may have continued within some of the ditched enclosures that had been established during the 4th century and, therefore, that the settlement was occupied continuously from the 4th century to the 5th/6th century, throughout the period of transition from late Roman to early Anglo-Saxon traditions. However, the chronology of the early Anglo-Saxon pottery from the site is at odds with the idea of continuity, but rather points to possible abandonment from the end of the Roman period to (at least) the late 5th century.

With the exception of a handful of pottery and other artefacts, no evidence for early post-Roman activity was found within Settlement 6, which appears to have been wholly or largely abandoned in the late Roman period (Period 4.5). Elsewhere, a few finds of this period were also recovered from the uppermost fills of several earlier features in the north-eastern part of the site, which had seemingly seen little or no occupation since the 1st century AD (Period 3.5). However, no evidence for Anglo-Saxon activity after the 6th century AD was found anywhere on the site.

II. Period 5: early Anglo-Saxon (late 5th-6th century AD)
(Fig. 5.1: Pls 5.1–5.2)

Settlement 7

The distribution of early Anglo-Saxon pottery and other artefacts makes it clear that Settlement 7, which had been intensively occupied in the late Romano-British period was also a focus for activity into the early post-Roman period (Fig 5.1). Although there was no evidence that enclosure ditches or any other late Romano-British features were maintained at this time, finds from the upper fills of some of these features demonstrate that they remained partially open into the 5th/6th century. A notable example of this was recorded in the southern ditch (*5592*) of Enclosure 139, one of the latest Romano-British enclosures within the settlement. This yielded a small assemblage of 5th- to 6th-century pottery (Blinkhorn, Chapter 7.VIII), and small fragments of an imported lava quern (Percival and Shaffrey, Chapter 6.VI), which were found in association with two complete red deer antlers (Baxter, Chapter 8.III; SFs 2601–3). That the antlers had been deliberately and carefully placed within the feature seems clear (Pls 5.1 and 5.2), suggesting that the act of deposition had some ritual or symbolic significance (see Chapter 9.IX).

Elsewhere, early Anglo-Saxon pottery was recovered from the upper fills of several other late Roman enclosure ditches, including the north-western corner and southern boundary of Enclosure 127; , the southern boundary ditch of the settlement, located west of Enclosure 126, the northern and south-western boundary ditches of Enclosure 132, and Boundary 120, the settlement's outer perimeter ditch, at the point where it also formed the northern boundary of Enclosure 134. Boundary 120 also yielded, from its eastern terminal, a fragment from a 6th-century silver armlet (Crummy, Chapter 6.III; Fig. 6.42, SF 1070).

Enclosure 137 was also notable for the laying, within a segment of its silted-up southern ditch (*10139*), of a probable causeway, formed of stones laid directly over the ditch fills. Amongst the stones used were two worked, structural fragments (Shaffrey, Chapter 6.VII; SF 2453 and SF 2454), presumably robbed from a Romano-British building or monument of some architectural pretension located somewhere in the vicinity of the site.

In addition to the enclosure ditches themselves, a few other late Roman features also yielded small amounts of early Anglo-Saxon pottery. One such was the stone-lined well (*5387*) located towards the south-eastern corner of Enclosure 139, which yielded a handmade early Saxon vessel (SF 2626) from one of its upper fills.

Whilst the presence of early Anglo-Saxon cultural material in the upper fills of late Roman features provides a clear indication that people were living nearby in the early post-Roman period, probably either within the boundaries of Settlement 7 itself or close by, very few features of certain or possible 5th/6th-century date were recorded. One likely candidate was a large pit or waterhole (Waterhole 11), which had been dug through the latest phase of the settlement's northern perimeter ditch (Boundary 120), some time after that feature had largely silted up. The waterhole, which was located close to the north-eastern corner of the settlement, was irregular in plan (measuring *c.*10 x 5m and 1.9m deep), and yielded twenty-two sherds of early Anglo-Saxon pottery. Approximately 70m to the south, and also cutting into the silted up remains of Boundary 120, which here formed the eastern limit of the settlement, was a second, large pit-like feature (Waterhole 12), oval in plan, 5.2 x 3.7m and 0.55m deep. The fact that both features had been dug into the settlement's perimeter ditch suggests that this feature was still visible, and may even have continued to serve as a boundary marker. The only other possibly contemporary feature was a small pit (*4801*), which had been dug into the boundary ditch of Enclosure 127, close to the enclosure's south-west corner. This was roughly circular, 0.7m in diameter and 0.1m deep, with a dark, charcoal-rich fill from which eight early Anglo-Saxon sherds were recovered.

Plate 5.1 Enclosure 139, Settlement 7: perimeter ditch *5592* under excavation, showing deliberately placed red deer antlers (SFs 2601–3)

Plate 5.2 Detail of red deer antlers (SFs 2601–3) placed in the perimeter ditch (*5592*) of Enclosure 139, Settlement 7

Settlement 6
To the south, evidence for early Anglo-Saxon activity within the area of Settlement 6 was confined to the recovery of two potsherds from the area of Enclosure 104, near to the northern limit of the site, and two metal artefacts – a saucer brooch and a buckle (Crummy, Chapter 6.III). The brooch (Fig. 6.42, SF 2881) is datable to the later 6th century, whilst the buckle (Fig. 6.42, SF 1269) is either of 6th-century date, or slightly later; both items came from the modern ploughsoil.

Other activities
On the northern part of the site a circular pit (*4178*, not illustrated), 1.8m in diameter and 0.6m deep, was located on the side of the hill, *c*.370m north-east of Settlement 7. The base and southern edge of the pit had seemingly been crudely lined with a number of large stones, whilst its fill yielded two sherds of early Anglo-Saxon pottery. In addition, forty-eight sherds of this period were recovered from two soil layers (*6394*, *6395*) which partly overlay the northern boundary ditch (*6241*) of Enclosure 10 (Settlement 2), a rectilinear enclosure of Iron Age origin, and a further five sherds came from *6181*, which had accumulated within the upper part of a late Iron Age quarry pit within the same enclosure (Quarry 3; Fig. 3.21).

III. Periods 6–7: medieval and post-medieval field systems (*c.*1066-1800)
(Fig. 5.2)

No evidence was found for occupation on the site between the 6th/early 7th century AD and the beginning of the Anglo-Norman period in the second half of the 11th century. During the medieval period (Period 6), the entire

Figure 5.2 Ridge and furrow. Scale 1:5000

site appears to have been covered by arable fields, as evidenced by the extensive remains of ridge and furrow (represented in the archaeological record by rows of parallel furrows cutting the natural subsoil and/or earlier archaeological features), which were recorded on many parts of the site (Fig 5.2, Field System 7), together with a few contemporary boundary ditches. For the most part, there proved to be good spatial concordance between the physical remains of the field systems as recorded by excavation, and the pre-enclosure furlong boundaries depicted on the draft Inclosure plan for St Neots, produced in 1770. A few post-medieval field ditches (Period 7), which clearly post-dated the 18th-century enclosure of the medieval open fields, were also recorded. The recovery of a large assemblage of medieval and early post-medieval metal artefacts from the site, together with thirty-one medieval/post-medieval coins and nine jetons, suggests that refuse from nearby farms and settlements may have been used to manure the fields (Crummy, Chapter 6.II).

On the north-eastern part of the site, the surviving furrows were orientated predominantly north-west to south-east, which corresponds closely to the alignment of the furlong boundaries in this area. In the extreme north-eastern corner, furrows were recorded over an area in excess of 300 x 300m, but extended beyond the investigated area to the north-west and south-east. Approximately 125m to the south-west was a more limited area of survival, recorded over an area measuring $c.200 \times 125$m. Associated with this, and sharing the alignment of the furrows, was a field boundary ditch, which was traced for $c.120$m but not excavated. The position and alignment of this feature corresponds almost exactly with a post-enclosure field boundary depicted on the Ordnance Survey First Edition map of 1864 (Ordnance Survey), and there can, therefore, be little doubt that this was a post-medieval feature (Period 7). The ditch was also located $c.20$m east of, and parallel to, a furlong boundary that is shown on the draft Inclosure plan of 1770.

It is of some interest that the furrows and furlong boundaries on this part of the site had similar alignments to the principal late Iron Age features recorded in this area (Chapter 3, Settlement 1, Routeway 4, Field System 3; and Settlement 2, Enclosure 10). However, the almost total lack of evidence for Romano-British (and, indeed, Anglo-Saxon) activity in the vicinity makes it unlikely that there was actual continuity of land use from the pre-Roman to medieval periods. Rather, it is possible that the lie of the land dictated the prevailing alignment of field boundaries and other landscape features in both the Iron Age and the Middle Ages, or (perhaps more plausibly) it may be that the medieval pattern of land use was influenced to some degree by the relict remains of pre-Roman enclosure ditches and other features that survived as visible earthworks.

To the south and west, on the western part of the site, the surviving furrows were mostly aligned NNE/SSW, and survived (albeit patchily), over an area measuring up to $c.300 \times 300$m. Towards the north-eastern corner of this area, part of a boundary ditch was traced on a NNW–SSE alignment for $c.50$m. The position of this feature corresponds almost exactly with a post-enclosure field boundary depicted on both the 1770 Inclosure plan and the 1864 Ordnance Survey map, meaning that there can be little doubt that it represents the remains of a post-medieval field boundary. In centre of the area, however, was another boundary ditch, which does not appear on the post-medieval mapping. This feature shared the alignment of the furrows on either side, and was traced north to south for approximately 300m. Its absence from the post-medieval maps, together with the fact that it was cut by one of the adjacent furrows, suggests that this boundary may have disappeared at a relatively early date. Be that as it may, it is notable that, to the south, the ditch respected the position of an enclosure-period field boundary that appears on the 1770 and 1864 maps, and which survived, in the form of a hedgerow, until the excavations commenced in 2005. On the Inclosure plan, this boundary is seemingly respected by some of the earlier furlong boundaries, suggesting that it had been laid out on the line of a furlong boundary. More remarkably, it also appears to have followed the line of an excavated Romano-British trackway which itself developed out of an earlier east to west aligned track dating back to at least the middle Iron Age (Routeway 2). This suggests either that the track remained in use from the Iron Age into the medieval period – a not inconceivable possibility – or that the boundary ditch defining the northern side of the Romano-British trackway (Boundary 8) survived as a visible earthwork into the medieval period, when it was re-used or referenced as a furlong boundary. Whatever the precise details, it is clear that the line of this ancient track, fossilised in the form of the post-medieval field boundary (and the presumed medieval furlong boundary it replaced), marked the boundary between two areas of medieval ridge and furrow; the NNE/SSW block already described, to the north, and an area of north/south- and east/west-aligned furrows to the south, located towards the south-western corner of the site.

To the south of the boundary, the extant furrows were orientated more nearly north to south and east to west than those further to the north, again corresponding broadly to the alignment of the furlong boundaries in this area. On this part of the site, a block of east to west aligned furrows, up to $c.150 \times 100$m, was bounded on the west by an area of north/south furrows, measuring $c.200$m, north to south, by $c.100$m wide, and on the south by another (comparatively poorly-preserved) block of north to south aligned furrows, recorded over an area measuring up to $c.100 \times 80$m. East to west aligned furrows were also recorded on the southern edge of the site, north of, and parallel to, the modern B1428 road. Here, they were traced east to west for up to 230m, and north to south for $c.125$m.

IV. Discussion: Anglo-Saxon

Anglo-Saxon activity
The evidence for early Anglo-Saxon occupation at Love's Farm is broadly datable to the late 5th–7th centuries AD and comprises a small assemblage of pottery (Blinkhorn, Chapter 7.VIII), principally recovered from Settlement 7, and three diagnostic metal artefacts (Crummy, Chapter 6.III). For the most part, the pottery came from the upper fills of demonstrably earlier features: Romano-British enclosure ditches, wells/waterholes and pits. An assemblage of forty-eight sherds also came from a soil deposit on the northern part of the site, and five fragments were recovered from the upper fill of an Iron Age quarry pit in the same area. Features of possible or probable Anglo-Saxon origin were restricted to two large pits or

waterholes (Waterholes 11 and 12), which cut the latest Romano-British perimeter ditch (Boundary 120) enclosing Settlement 7, a small pit (*4801*) that had been dug into the ditch of one of the internal enclosures within the settlement, and an isolated partially stone-lined pit (*4178*) situated on the northern part of the site. All yielded small quantities of early Anglo-Saxon pottery, but no evidence for contemporary buildings, hearths or other occupation features was recorded, either within Settlement 7 or elsewhere. A crude stone 'causeway' laid across the silted up south ditch of Enclosure 137 is not closely dated but resembles a feature recorded at Lower Cambourne (Wright *et al.* 2009, 29), where a neat setting of large cobbles, 1.2m wide, had been laid over a hollow that had formed at the junction of several earlier ditches. Here, a 6th- to 7th-century socketed spearhead came from the upper fill of the hollow, and nearby was a pit, which yielded two sherds of early Anglo-Saxon pottery. At Haddon, south-west of Peterborough, 4th-century enclosure ditches were also infilled and levelled with considerable quantities of stone rubble (French 1994, 74), although this activity was not closely dated.

At Love's Farm, with the exception of pit *4178*, evidence for early Anglo-Saxon activity beyond Settlement 7 was largely confined to a few stray sherds of pottery that were either recovered from the upper fills of earlier features, or were unstratified. The metalwork comprised a late 6th-century saucer brooch and a 6th- to early 7th-century buckle (both unstratified finds from the area of Romano-British Settlement 6), and part of a decorated silver armlet, also of the 6th century, from the upper fill of Boundary 120, the latest ditch enclosing Settlement 7.

Conclusions

Excavations at Love's Farm have added to the corpus of information on early Anglo-Saxon settlement in the region, albeit that the evidence was confined largely to finds of pottery and a few other artefacts. Following abandonment in the 6th/7th century, the site was put under the plough, probably in the 12th/13th century, in order to feed an increasing population. Full discussion of the evidence, setting it into its wider context, appears in Chapter 9.X.

Chapter 6. The Finds

I. Worked flint
by Barry Bishop
(Fig. 6.1)

Introduction
Excavations at Love's Farm led to the recovery of 270 struck flints and a single stone artefact of prehistoric date – a polished greenstone axe. The present report summarises the key features of the assemblage and considers its wider significance.

Assemblage characteristics
The bulk of the assemblage can be regarded as residual, being recovered from Iron Age and later features. It is dominated by un-retouched flakes and blades or retouched items that individually cannot be precisely dated on strict typological grounds alone. Nevertheless, considerations of both the technological and typological aspects of the assemblage indicate that it was manufactured over an extended period, from the Mesolithic through to the Bronze Age.

Predominant amongst the raw materials is a translucent 'glassy' black, brown and grey flint, that ultimately derives from the chalk to the south, but has cortex that indicates it was primarily obtained from alluvial gravel deposits. Around 10% of the assemblage is made from an opaque and sometimes banded brittle and 'stony' cherty flint in a variety of colours and textures that rarely exhibits natural cortex, but is present in the form of large, thermally shattered angular chunks. These could have originated from sources much further north, but are present in large quantities within the Boulder Clay that occurs across most of the site. It likely, therefore, that most of the material was brought to the site, presumably from the alluvial sources in the valley below, but that the more handily available glacial flint was also used when needed.

The assemblage contains a wide range of flakes, cores and retouched implements. It represents all stages in the reduction sequence, ranging from discarded cores and decortication flakes, representing the initial stages of reduction, to used and worn-out tools (Table 6.1). Retouched implements form more than 15% of the overall assemblage and a wide variety of types is present. This number is likely to be an underestimation, as many other flakes exhibit what may be light retouch or heavy use-wear but these have been discounted due to the masking effects of post-depositional damage on residually deposited pieces. Of particular interest are two axes, one of flint and the other of greenstone, that are not commonly recovered from settlement sites.

The proportion of retouched pieces is high when compared to many lithic assemblages in the region, including some of the 'classic' Neolithic settlement sites, such as Kilverstone or Hurst Fen, both of which contained c.5–6% (Beadsmoore 2006; Clark et al. 1960). It is also higher than the 7% recorded from Hinchingbrooke (Bishop 2004) and 8.5% from Silver Street, Godmanchester (Bishop 2008), but is more comparable to some of the other assemblages recovered from within this stretch of the Great Ouse Valley, such as at Little Paxton (Bevan 1995), Eynesbury (P. Harding 2004) and Fenstanton (Chapman et al. 2005), where retouched implements formed 14–20% of what were all similarly dated, multi-period, assemblages. The most common types are edge-trimmed flakes and scrapers, which together contributed over half of the retouched implements. These frequently form the largest retouched categories at early settlement sites, including many from sites along this part of the River Ouse Valley, such as at Eynesbury (P. Harding 2004), Bob's Wood, Hinchingbrooke (Bishop 2004), Silver Street, Godmanchester (Bishop 2008) and Fenstanton (Chapman et al. 2005). This high proportion is suggestive of 'domestic' assemblages where a wide range of activities are represented, suggesting broader-based settlement rather than specialised or task-specific activity occurring at the site.

Chronology

Overview
The assemblage is clearly of mixed date and its recovery from predominantly later features means that establishing the precise chronology and the nature of occupation as represented by worked flint is problematic. Three broad phases of activity are indicated by the typological and technological characteristics of the lithic assemblage, and these are discussed separately below.

Artefact type	*No. objects*	*% of total*
Decortication flake	31	11.4
Core rejuvenation flake	5	1.8
Chip	6	2.2
Flake	98	36.2
Flake fragment	10	3.8
Blade-like flake	8	3.0
Prismatic blade	34	12.5
Non-prismatic blade	19	7.0
Core	8	3.0
Conchoidal chunk	9	3.3
Axe	2	0.7
Arrowhead	3	1.1
Bifacially worked flake	2	0.7
Denticulate	1	0.4
Edge trimmed	12	4.4
Knife	2	0.7
Notch	1	0.4
Piercer	1	0.4
Flaked pounder	1	0.4
Scraper	13	4.8
Serrate	5	1.8
Total	*271*	*100*

Table 6.1 Composition of the flint assemblage

Mesolithic and early Neolithic

The only diagnostic piece of Mesolithic date is a micro-burin recovered from an Iron Age ditch. Micro-burins are usually associated with the manufacture of microliths and this may represent an episode of microlithic equipment repair or maintenance. Although this was the only piece of certain Mesolithic derivation, blades and blade-like flakes made up over 20% of the entire assemblage, of which nearly two-thirds are prismatic and two of the eight cores recovered had produced blades. Blades are characteristic of Mesolithic and early Neolithic assemblages, although the high proportion of systematically-made prismatic types is at least suggestive of more extensive activity during the Mesolithic period than is implied by the single micro-burin.

Activity at the site continued across the transition and into the early Neolithic, as is attested by the presence of the two axes and a tip of a leaf-shaped arrowhead. Both axes are complete. The greenstone axe (Fig. 6.1, SF 3637) came from a deposit of Romano-British date (Period 4.2) within Settlement 6, in the southern part of the site. This artefact, which probably came from Great Langdale in Cumbria, has been heavily worked down from a larger implement, but retains a wide cutting edge and has been re-polished. The flint axe is recorticated, but recent damage indicates that it was made from a grey translucent flint that contains considerable cherty inclusions. It is quite thick but appears to have been finished, with all-over flaking and smoothed edges, but there are no traces of polishing on any of its surfaces. It is comparable in shape to 'Cissbury'-type axes (*e.g.* Barber *et al.* 1999, fig. 2.9) and measures 185mm long by a maximum of 63mm wide and 40mm thick.

Many of the other retouched pieces, including the serrates and a number of the edge-trimmed implements, were made on blades or narrow flakes and are characteristic of Mesolithic and early Neolithic industries. These are typical of those found on similarly-dated settlement sites, their number and variety indicating that, in addition to flint reduction, a range of other activities involving tool use were also being pursued. Struck flint was also recovered from some of the Neolithic features on the site, but only in small quantities and probably as incidentally incorporated residual material, with little evidence for any deliberate depositional practices. The largest quantities came from layer *11115* in the northern part of the site, which yielded twenty-one pieces. This mostly comprises the waste emanating from blade production and may represent a single knapping episode. The only implement present comprises a flake with very fine blunting along one edge and use-wear traces along the opposite margin, indicating that it had been used for cutting. Similarly, in the southern part of the site, pit *7444* contained seventeen struck pieces, many of which could be refitted, from three fills. It again represents knapping waste from the production of both blades and flakes and includes two cores. Also present in this feature was a large, lightly edge-trimmed, narrow flake, from fill *7445*, and a further edge-trimmed flake, possibly a worn serrate, from fill *7518*. On the same part of the site, fill *7145* of pit *7144* contained a smaller assemblage of six pieces, again including a cortically-backed utilised flake, and a finely-made side and end scraper came from another fill (*7143*) within this feature.

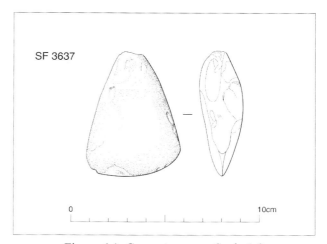

Figure 6.1 Greenstone axe. Scale 1:2

Catalogue of illustrated item
(Fig. 6.1)

SF3637 Greenstone axe. Worked down from a larger implement, it now measures 69mm long, 52mm wide and is 23mm thick. River wash, *13333*, Settlement 6, Period 4.2.

Later Neolithic and early Bronze Age

Later Neolithic and early Bronze Age flintworking activity is somewhat harder to define than that of earlier periods, but the presence of competently produced broader flakes, often with edge-trimmed or faceted striking platforms, and some of the elaborately retouched pieces, suggest that flintworking at the site continued during these periods.

No significant assemblages were present in any of the earlier prehistoric features or deposits recorded on the site, but the recovery of an oblique arrowhead and a barbed and tanged arrowhead, both residual within later contexts, indicate activity at the site during both the later Neolithic and the early Bronze Age. Also of interest is a finely and skilfully produced plano-convex knife made from grey 'stony' flint, since these artefacts were possibly of ceremonial significance and are often associated with funerary activity (*e.g.* Healey 1998). Many of the other retouched pieces, particularly a number of well-made, often symmetrical scrapers, are also most typical of later Neolithic or early Bronze Age examples.

Late Bronze Age

A sparse scatter of rudimentarily-produced struck flints was recovered from the site. These are difficult to categorise individually, but considered together, suggest that sporadic flintworking continued into the later 2nd millennium BC. These include a number of opportunistically produced thick and squat flakes with very obtuse striking platforms (*cf.* Martingell 1990) and well-developed points of percussion, and a few randomly reduced and often minimally-worked cores that had produced flakes of similar characteristics. Some of the scrapers are also made on thick, poorly struck flakes and these may also be late in date, although, in general, industries of this period are mostly characterised by a restricted range of retouched pieces, often with only scrapers being present. These pieces are comparable to other later prehistoric industries in the region, such as those at Hinchingbrooke (Bishop 2004), Silver Street, Godmanchester (Bishop 2008), or the post-barrow assemblages at Barleycroft Farm (Evans and Knight 1996) and Raunds (Ballin 2002).

Discussion
As is discussed in detail elsewhere in this volume, the Midlands claylands have, until the last few decades, been thought of as damp, thickly wooded and, prior to the advent of heavier agricultural tools in the late Iron Age, not conducive to early settlement. More recent research and survey is, however, beginning to change this picture, demonstrating that from the Mesolithic onwards, the claylands actually formed a diverse set of habitats and had witnessed equally complex patterns of settlement to other areas (Clay 2002).

The lithic assemblage from Love's Farm is not large given the size of the area investigated, but it does demonstrate that by the Mesolithic period there was an interest in the claylands beyond the river valleys and this continued persistently, if not continuously, throughout the Neolithic and Bronze Age. It adds to the emerging picture of prehistoric flint use and early settlement in the uplands as well as providing complementary evidence for the extensive Neolithic and Bronze Age settlement and ceremonial activity identified along the adjoining stretch of the Ouse Valley (Malim 2000).

Certainly by the Neolithic, this interest extended beyond simple task-specific expeditions. The assemblage was manufactured using a range of raw materials that indicate movement between the valley floors and the uplands. It also has a high and varied proportion of retouched implements, suggesting that resources were being brought back to the site and processed in what may be considered a settlement context, where populations stayed, or returned to, for sufficiently long periods to undertake a range of different activities. The presence of the axes also demonstrates the far-reaching connections of this Neolithic community. The greenstone axe had travelled a considerable distance before being finally discarded and had been worked down, perhaps more than once, and re-polished, stressing its longevity and the extensive biography it embodied. Stone axes are not commonly found within settlement contexts, although a flake struck from a similar greenstone axe was found at Hinchingbrooke (Bishop 2004). Their presence at ceremonial sites is more commonly attested. A number – some broken and burnt, others worked down in a similar way to the Love's Farm example – were found at the causewayed enclosure sites at Etton and Haddenham (Pryor 1998; Evans and Hodder 2006). Unfortunately, the circumstances surrounding the deposition of the Love's Farm specimen are not known, but at Haddenham and Etton it appears that they held considerable symbolic potential, which probably derived, in part at least, from their places of origin and their complex biographies (Whittle 1995; Edmonds 2004). Similar metaphorical properties may have extended to the flint axe recovered from Love's Farm, although in this case its history extends beyond the prehistoric period, since it was found co-incidentally during metal detecting of river wash deposits above the Fox Brook (by machine driver Nick Richardson) which lay close to one of the Roman settlements (Settlement 6, the deposit has been assigned to the Middle Roman period). Prehistoric axes have frequently been recovered from Roman contexts, and whilst in many cases, it seems likely that they became incorporated unintentionally into these contexts, in some circumstances it is probable that the axes were recognised as ancient, exotic or even supernatural objects, and were deliberately collected and re-deposited (*e.g.* Castle 1974; Greenwood 1982; Rodwell 1988; Turner 1999; Bishop 2001; Howell 2005).

Due to the difficulties in providing definitive dates for many of the pieces, discussion of chronologically specific flint-using practices is problematic. Nevertheless, some broad patterns may be recognised. The earliest definite indication of activity at the site suggests the repairing of microlithic equipment during the Mesolithic period, and this concern with projectile technology appeared to continue into the early Neolithic, as evidenced by the leaf-shaped arrowhead. Although difficult to assign specifically to either one of these periods, the number and variety of retouched implements indicates that, during these periods, the site was being used as more than just a transient hunting encampment. Raw materials were being brought in from a number of different sources, reduced at the site and the products used to process a range of resources also gathered from the wider landscape. Traditionally, axes are associated with woodland clearance (although the greenstone axe is too small for anything other than delicate woodworking), and their symbolic qualities may have been as important as any functional properties. A few features and deposits of early Neolithic date were identified on the site, and some of these contained seemingly contemporary flintwork, comprising small quantities of knapping waste and simple cutting tools, but no obvious indications of special depositional practices were noted.

The later Neolithic and early Bronze Age material is somewhat harder to categorise, but appears broadly to represent a continuation of similar kinds of activities as identified for the earlier periods. Arrowheads are still present and the use of tools such as scrapers and edge-trimmed pieces continues. The presence of the plano-convex knife is interesting and may indicate that ceremonial activities were occurring at the site. Others have also been found at nearby sites in similar locations, including Hinchingbrooke (Bishop 2004).

The presence of irregularly-reduced waste, such as chunks, crudely made thick flakes and partially reduced cores showing numerous incipient cones from failed removals, suggests that flint working continued at the site during the later 2nd millennium BC and perhaps even later (*cf.* Herne 1991; Young and Humphrey 1999; Ballin 2002; Humphrey 2007). Flint use during these periods typically involves small assemblages that are present in low densities within later contexts, and is indicative of opportunistic and short-lived episodes of tool production and use.

II. Coins and jetons
by Nina Crummy

Introduction
A substantial assemblage of 444 coins and nine jetons was retrieved from Love's Farm; a full catalogue of the three Iron Age and 402 Roman coins is presented in Appendix 2 (divided into broad period and stratigraphic groups). Most of the coins were residual in later levels, or came from the

Figure 6.2 Graph of Love's Farm (excluding the coin hoards), Haddon and Bob's Wood, Hinchingbrooke coins, by Coin Period set against the British mean (after Reece 2002, 145; Guest 2003; Crummy in prep. a)

fill of ditches that silted up only slowly and remained as negative features in the landscape for several centuries. Others are of stratigraphic pertinence, while some have been adapted in various ways and are of intrinsic interest. The coins range in date from late Iron Age to modern, with the bulk of the assemblage composed of 4th-century Roman issues, predominantly of the Houses of Constantine and Valentinian. Two small coin hoards were also discovered: a mid-2nd-century hoard (Hoard 1) from the western periphery of Settlement 6 (Period 4.2), and a late 3rd-century hoard (Hoard 2) recovered from Waterhole 9 on the southern edge of Settlement 7 (Period 4.4). The thirty-one medieval and post-medieval coins and jetons, all found unstratified, are not detailed here, although further information is available in the project archive.

Methodology

The coins are discussed below more closely by period – Iron Age and Roman – with the Roman coins further subdivided by settlement, coins with secondary adaptation, and the two hoards. Where possible, the Roman coins have been allocated to one of the coin periods defined by Reece, allowing them to be converted into relative values and compared with both Reece's Romano-British mean and the coin evidence from other sites (Reece 1995; 2002, 145–50). The data are also presented as bar charts to enable comparison with the Suffolk assemblages studied by Plouviez (2004).

The late Iron Age coins

Three Iron Age coins were recovered. A bronze of Cunobelin (SF 2711) came from the fill of Quarry 3 (Period 3.4) in Settlement 2, in the northern part of the site. The obverse shows a helmeted head facing left with CVNOBIL in front, within a pelleted border. The reverse shows a standing boar facing left, with a triangle of three pellets above, a branch before, and TASCFIL between two plain lines below, all within a pelleted border. This is Van Arsdell's 1983-1, which he dates to c.AD 10–20 (Van Arsdell 1989, 407) and Hobb's type 1952–5 (Hobbs 1996, 133). What is almost certainly another coin of Cunebolin (SF 1024), an otherwise illegible head/horse type, was also recovered from a Period 3.4 deposit within Settlement 2, in this case a fill (4047) of the western arm of the perimeter ditch for Enclosure 10. A third possible Iron Age coin (SF 1090) was found unstratified in the northern part of the site. This is very worn, however, and in such poor condition that the identification remains uncertain.

The discovery of both stratified Iron Age coins within the area of Settlement 2, together with the occurrence of a possible third coin in the same general area, may be indicative of a difference, either in chronology or status, between this settlement and the other Iron Age occupation foci on the site. Status cannot be accurately assessed on this limited evidence, only viewed against the backdrop of the absence of coins from the other settlements. As far as dating is concerned, Haselgrove (1987, 163–88; 1993, 57) has suggested that the bronze issues of Cunobelin were first placed in circulation at the major sites, such as Camulodunum, Braughing and Baldock, and only reached the smaller settlements after a prolonged period of trade and other forms of exchange. This may suggest that the coins were not deposited within Settlement 2 until well into the 1st century AD.

The Roman coins

(Figs 6.2–6.4)
Including the coins from Hoards 1 and 2, there are 402 coins of Roman date, of which 307 can be allocated to one of Reece's twenty-one coin periods (Reece 1995), the remainder being too worn or corroded for close identification. Hoard 1 is composed of *aes* coinage ranging in date from the reign of Domitian (AD 81–96) to that of Antoninus Pius (AD 138–61), while Hoard 2 comprises debased *antoniniani* from Gallienus (AD 253–68) to Carausius (AD 287–93).

When the closely dated hoard coins are removed, the general site assemblage is composed of 277 legible coins. Using Reece's method of cumulative comparison per thousand (Reece 1991; 1995; 2002, 145–50), Figure 6.2 shows the assemblage against Reece's mean for Britain,

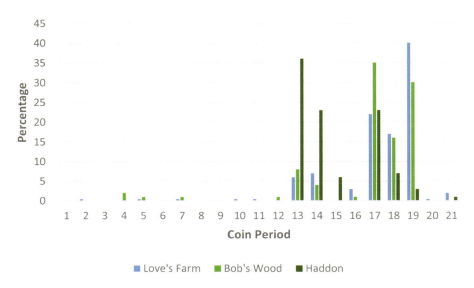

Figure 6.3 Bar chart of Love's Farm, Haddon and Bob's Wood coins by Coin Period (excluding Love's Farm coin hoards)

Coin Period	Date	Love's Farm		Bob's Wood		Haddon	
		No.	%	No.	%	No.	%
1	to AD 41	-	-	-	-	-	-
2	41–54	1	0.5	-	-	-	-
3	54–69	-	-	-	-	-	-
4	69–96	-	-	2	2	-	-
5	96–117	1	0.5	1	1	-	-
6	117–38	-	-	-	-	-	-
7	138–61	1	0.5	1	1	-	-
8	161–80	-	-	-	-	-	-
9	180–92	-	-	-	-	-	-
10	193–222	2	0.5	-	-	-	-
11	222–38	1	0.5	-	-	-	-
12	238–60	-	-	1	1	-	-
13	260–75	16	6	7	8	25	36
14	275–96	19	7	4	4	16	23
15	296–317	-	-	-	-	4	6
16	317–30	9	3	1	1	-	-
17	330–48	62	22	32	35	16	23
18	348–64	48	17	15	16	5	7
19	364–78	110	40	28	30	2	3
20	378–88	1	0.5	-	-	-	-
21	388–402	6	2	-	-	1	1
Totals		277	-	92	-	69	-

Table 6.2 Coins from Love's Farm, Bob's Wood and Haddon by number and percentage

with data from Haddon near Peterborough (Guest 2003) and Bob's Wood at Hinchingbrooke near Huntingdon (Crummy in prep.) shown for direct comparison.

The Love's Farm and Bob's Wood site assemblages behave in much the same way across all periods, only rising above the British mean in the late 4th century. The picture presented by the data using this method can, however, be misleading, as it uses cumulative values and implies, but does not necessarily reflect, a high level of coin loss in periods following a peak. Thus, Bob's Wood completes its sequence of coins in Period 19 (House of Valentinian, AD 364–78) and therefore remains above the mean despite having no coins from the later periods. In contrast, at Love's Farm the coin loss, in simple numbers, is more broadly spread, and the site does have coins from Periods 20 and 21, but the result of comparison with the British mean produces a similar flow to that from Bob's Wood. Haddon matches the early-low characteristic of Bob's Wood and Love's Farm, a feature common to most rural Romano-British sites, but rises above it in the late 3rd century and remains above until the last period, a pattern that occurs on other sites in eastern England, and that

Figure 6.4 Graph of Love's Farm coins with and without the coin hoards

Guest (2003) considered to reflect the site's location on the border between the eastern region and the East Midlands. The graph shown here differs a little from Guest's, who may have allocated coins that were not fully legible to some of the late 4th-century periods (2003, appendix 5). All three sites thus conform to patterns noted on other rural sites, while the overall flow of the graph for Love's Farm and Bob's Wood is also matched at sites of more varied types (Reece 1995, 197, fig. 22).

If Fig. 6.2 shows that Love's Farm, Bob's Wood and Haddon conform to rural patterns of coin supply, its level is more clearly shown using histograms and real numbers. Figure 6.3 and Table 6.2 show that none of the sites received coinage in any quantity on a regular basis from the conquest through to at least AD 260 (Period 13); a little reached Love's Farm and Bob's Wood, but Haddon appears to have received none at all. Similarly, Monument 97 at Orton Longueville had only one *dupondius* of Antonia minted under Claudius I (AD 41–54), the West Fen Road site at Ely had only one coin of Trajan and 3rd- to 4th-century issues, whilst no Roman coinage at all was found at Ely's Trinity Lands and Hurst Lane reservoir sites (Mackreth 2001, 39; Evans *et al.* 2007, 52, 68–9). Clearly, in the early and middle Roman periods, if not throughout the entire period of Roman occupation, at least some rural settlements in northern Cambridgeshire seem to have had economies largely, if not wholly, based on a means of exchange that did not involve the use of coinage.

Of the illegible coins, eleven can, on the basis of their size and thickness, be confidently attributed to the 1st–2nd centuries AD, considerably increasing the number of coins lost on the site in the early Roman period. Even so, coins of this date are so few that they do not substantially increase the likelihood that a cash economy was operating on the site at this time. Adding the coins from the two hoards to the total provides a greater effect (Fig 6.4), raising the line of the graph considerably and thereby presenting more reason to argue for a site economy based on coinage. However, as anomalies within the coin assemblage, the hoards should be discounted from the statistics rather than included. The date ranges of Hoards 1 and 2, and the dates at which both groups were removed from circulation, coincide with what are in effect two low peaks in the pattern of coin supply, corresponding to Reece's Periods 5–7 and 13–14. The extraction of so high a proportion of coins from the available pool, and their possible deposition as votive offerings, together imply that, while coins were recognised at Love's Farm as having a value, they were considered to be most usefully spent in religious rather than commercial transactions.

After AD 260, Love's Farm received the greatest proportion of its coins in Periods 17–19, with most dating to Period 19 (AD 364–78); it received comparatively little coinage in the late 3rd century (Periods 13–14). Bob's Wood is very similar, but with rather more from Period 17 (early House of Constantine) than Period 19. Haddon received most in Periods 13, 14 and 17, declining thereafter. Overall, the similarity between the graphs for Love's Farm and Bob's Wood is so close as to enable the two sites to form a standard against which to measure future large landscape excavations in north Cambridgeshire.

The Love's Farm and Bob's Wood pattern is also similar to that for Icklingham and north-west Suffolk in general (Plouviez 2004, fig. 60), although with a much greater emphasis on Period 19, particularly at Love's Farm. There may have been a broad regional zone of coin supply that covered all or part of northern Cambridgeshire as well as north-west Suffolk, and the validity of such a zone is worth exploring more fully with future excavated assemblages, particularly as north-west Suffolk has a different coin loss pattern to the rest of that county (Plouviez 2004). However, the site at Brandon Road, Thetford, in the north-west corner of this area, conforms more to the general Suffolk pattern in having low coin loss in Period 19 (Crummy 2010, 40), which implies that the link between Bob's Wood, Love's Farm and Icklingham/north-west Suffolk owes more to site type and history, or to external political events, than to region. This must certainly be the case with the much higher proportion of coins from Period 19 at Love's Farm than at any other within the proposed zone.

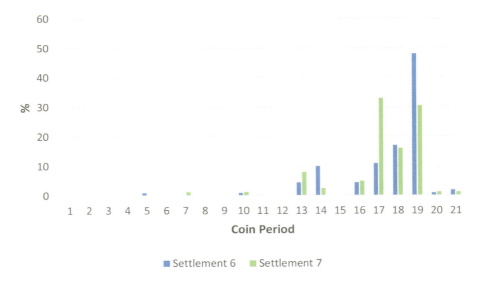

Figure 6.5 Percentages of coins by Coin Period from Settlements 6 and 7

Coin Period	Date	Settlement 7		Northern fields		Combined northern assemblage		Settlement 6		Southern fields		Combined southern assemblage	
		No	%	No	%	No	%	No	%	No	%	No	%
1	to AD 41	-	-	-	-	-	-	-	-	-	-	-	-
2	41–54	-	-	-	-	-	-	-	-	1	12.5	1	1
3	54–69	-	-	-	-	-	-	-	-	-	-	-	-
4	69–96	-	-	-	-	-	-	-	-	-	-	-	-
5	96–117	-	-	-	-	-	-	1	1	-	-	1	1
6	117–38	-	-	-	-	-	-	-	-	-	-	-	-
7	138–61	1	1.25	-	-	1	1	-	-	-	-	-	-
8	161–80	-	-	-	-	-	-	-	-	-	-	-	-
9	180–92	-	-	-	-	-	-	-	-	-	-	-	-
10	193–222	1	1.25	-	-	1	1	1	1	-	-	1	1
11	222–38	-	-	1	4.5	1	1	-	-	-	-	-	-
12	238–60	-	-	-	-	-	-	-	-	-	-	-	-
13	260–75	6	8	2	9	8	8	4	4.5	-	-	4	4
14	275–96	2	2.5	1	4.5	3	3	9	10	1	12.5	10	10
15	296–317	-	-	-	-	-	-	-	-	-	-	-	-
16	317–30	4	5	-	-	4	4	4	4.5	-	-	4	4
17	330–48	26	33	4	17	30	29	10	11	2	25	12	12
18	348–64	13	16	5	21.5	18	18	16	17	1	12.5	17	17
19	364–78	24	30.5	9	39	33	32	44	48	3	37.5	47	47
20	378–88	1	1.25	-	-	1	1	1	1	-	-	1	1
21	388–402	1	1.25	1	4.5	2	2	2	2	-	-	2	2
Totals		79	-	23	-	102	-	92	-	8	-	100	-

Table 6.3. Coins from Settlements 6 (southern) and 7 (northern), their adjacent fields, and as combined northern and southern assemblages by number and percentage. The figures do not include the two hoards.

The coins from Settlements 6 and 7: a comparison
(Fig. 6.5)
A comparison between the casually lost coins recovered from Settlements 6 and 7 is provided in Table 6.3 and Figure 6.5. Table 6.3 shows the numbers of the coins from within the defined areas of the settlements, the numbers from the adjacent fields or peripheral areas, and the combined settlement/field assemblages, together with appropriate percentages. Figure 6.5 shows only the percentages from within the settlements. As with the full site assemblage there is only a scatter of coins from before Period 13. The numbers of coins from Periods 13 and 14 are also very low at each settlement, but in Settlement 7, Period 13 coins outnumber those of Period 14, whilst this is reversed in Settlement 6. The quantities involved are very small, but this suggests some shift in emphasis between the two settlements.

There are no Period 15 coins, and only a few Period 16 coins came from either settlement. There are then marked differences in Periods 17 and 19. Period 17 coins are far more numerous in Settlement 7 than in Settlement 6, those from Period 18 are quite equally matched, whilst those of Period 19 are far more numerous in Settlement 6 than to the north. Looking at the figures from an intra-settlement perspective, the balance between Periods 17 and 19 is even within Settlement 7, with Period 17 representing 33% of its assemblage and Period 19 representing 30.5%. Within Settlement 6, however, Period 17 coins account for only 11% of the assemblage, with those of Period 19 accounting for 48%. This marked difference may reflect a change in the character of occupation within Settlement 6 between the middle and later Roman periods.

Secondary adaptation

Five Roman coins show three forms of secondary working. Firstly, a coin of either Magnentius or Decentius (SF 3665) from Settlement 6 has been cut down or clipped to minim size, a form of adaptation that may have occurred considerably later than the date of issue (AD 350–3). Secondly, an unstratified radiate (SF 3610) from Settlement 6 has been pierced and worn as an amulet. Although illegible, enough of the design remains to show that the perforation has been deliberately placed to allow the reverse image of a standing figure to hang more or less upright, whilst the emperor's bust would have hung face downwards. Thirdly, both faces of a fragmentary 3rd- to 4th-century coin (SF 2226) from Boundary 112 in Settlement 7 (Period 4.4), have been deliberately abraded until they are smooth, and both faces of an unstratified 4th-century issue (SF 3701) from the area of Settlement 6 are also abraded. An unstratified blank disc with scratch marks on the surface (SF 1160) is almost certainly also a coin.

The two latter forms of secondary adaptation may have taken place in either the late Roman or early Anglo-Saxon periods. At Colchester, perforations respecting the reverse image have been noted on coin amulets from late Roman burials (Crummy *et al.* 1993, 156, table 2.62), and two perforated and abraded 1st/2nd-century coins and two abraded half-coins have been found in the vicinity of Temple 10 and Temple(?) 7 (Crummy 2006a, 64–5, 68, fig. 32, 6–9), the latter have been interpreted as possible solar symbols. At the Anglo-Saxon village of West Stow, Suffolk, thirty-six Roman coins had been pierced, representing a substantial proportion (12.5%) of the total from the site, four of the thirty-six had also been abraded, and a further fourteen coins had just been abraded (Curnow 1985a, 77, 80–1). Perforated Roman coins have also been found in many Anglo-Saxon burials, often strung on bead festoons, such as those from Great Chesterford in Essex, and Barrington, Cambridgeshire (Meaney 1981, 213–16; Evison 1994, 27; Malim and Hines 1998, 213). Burials at Abingdon, Oxfordshire, contained pierced or abraded coins (White 1988, 62–3), whilst a cemetery at Andover, Hampshire, produced thirteen pierced coins, one of which had also been abraded (Curnow 1985b).

The coin hoards

Hoard 1

Hoard 1 was found during the evaluation phase of the project, on the western periphery of Settlement 6, held within a pottery vessel (Pl. 4.1). It consists of twenty-three copper alloy issues of the late 1st to mid-2nd centuries AD (Table 6.4): seventeen *sestertii*, four *asses*, and two worn *dupondii/asses*. Another *as* (SF 1232), found unstratified in the backfill of the evaluation trench, may also belong to this group. The coins are all worn and in some cases are illegible, although this is partly due to the conditions of burial.

The circumstances of the hoard's deposition are ambiguous. It may simply have been buried for safekeeping, but, in view of its proximity to the (probably) broadly contemporary deposit of coins and metalwork recovered from deposit *6572*, it could conceivably represent a votive offering.

Coin hoards terminating with Antoninus Pius are far fewer in number than those of Marcus Aurelius and Lucius Verus, and those composed solely of *aes* coinage are not numerous (Robertson 1974, figs 2–3; 2000, 32–47). Apart from some poorly recorded finds from the 17th to 19th centuries, there is one hoard of twenty-five coins from Langford, Bedfordshire; one of 281 buried in a pot in Croydon, Surrey; one of thirty(?) from Gowerton, Glamorgan; one of seven from Bittern Pits, Manchester; and one of nine, found with other objects, from Doncaster, Yorkshire. The Langford and Croydon finds start with Claudius I, those from Doncaster and Gowerton with Vespasian, and that from Bittern Pits with Domitian (Robertson 2000, 32, 36, 38, 44–5; Burnett 1978; Walters 1907, 353–72; Buckland and Magilton 1986, 57, 74). The distribution of hoards terminating with Antoninus Pius is very scattered, and within the eastern region as a whole there is a gap from London up to Londonthorpe in Lincolnshire, with only two coastal hoards at Snettisham in Norfolk and Benacre in Suffolk, although Fox mentions one from Doddington in Cambridgeshire that cannot be verified (Robertson 2000, xxvi, map 7; Shotter 1981, 121–2; Fox 1923, 229). The Love's Farm hoard sits west of centre of this empty area.

The absence of coins of Marcus Aurelius and Faustina II from Hoard 1 suggests that it was deposited within the reign of Antoninus Pius rather than later, but good quality 2nd-century *aes,* with their large thick flans, are thought to have remained in circulation well into the 3rd century, and hoards of both Marcus Aurelius and Commodus are well represented within the eastern region, raising the possibility that the Love's Farm hoard belongs instead within the context of this later regional phase of deposition (Robertson 2000, xxvi, maps 8–9; Reece 2002, 42–4). That the Antoninus Pius issues in Hoard 1 are as worn as those of Domitian and Trajan would support the idea of prolonged circulation, and the absence of coins of Marcus Aurelius and Commodus from the casual losses could provide a local context for long use. Although other coins would have reached the settlements and then left again,

Date range	Quantity
Domitian (AD 81–96)	1
Trajan (AD 98–117)	5
Hadrian (AD 117–38)	6
Antoninus Pius/Faustina I (AD 138–61)	6
Illegible, late 1st–2nd century AD	5
Total	23

Table 6.4 Summary composition of Hoard 1

Date range	Quantity
Gallienus (AD 260–8)	1
Gallienus(?) (AD 253–68)	1
Salonina (AD 260–8)	1
Claudius II (AD 268–70)	2
Victorinus (AD 268–70)	3
Tetricus II (AD 270–73)	2
Carausius (AD 287–93)	1
Illegible radiate *antoninianus*	1
Total	12

Table 6.5 Summary composition of Hoard 2

they are perhaps unlikely to have been very numerous. Including illegible pieces, only fourteen other coins contemporary with the 50–80 year span of the issues in the hoard were found on the site, and there are none from the next thirty years or so. The twenty-three issues in Hoard 1 therefore appear to represent a substantial proportion of the coins available for collection on the site for over 100 years.

Hoard 2
The second hoard came from the upper fill (*7476*) of Waterhole 9, which was located on the southern edge of Settlement 7 in Period 4.4. The twelve coins are all *antoniniani*, with a terminal date early in the reign of Carausius (AD 287–93); many Carausian hoards are dominated by the later and better coinage of the early AD 290s (Robertson 2000, 205–22). Eight of the coins had corroded together, suggesting that they may have been deposited in a leather purse or wrapped in cloth.

The hoard represents 26% of the total number of coins found on the site that date to the period *c.*AD 260–96, covered by Reece's Periods 13 and 14. The ten certain pre-Carausian issues form an even more striking proportion (39%) of those from Period 13 alone.

Comparable hoards have been found in Cambridgeshire, although all have some degree of uncertainty about their provenance, composition, or validity. One presented to the Cambridge University Museum by the Cambridge Antiquarian Society is said to be from Shelford, but there are no further details of the provenance. Found before 1933 in a grey ware pot, it consists of forty-four coins beginning with Gallienus and ending with one *antoninianus* of Carausius (Robertson 2000, 214–15). A remarkably similar hoard, found in a grey ware pot in the early 20th century at Peterborough, contained forty-four coins from Hadrian to Carausius; this is presumably not the same as the Shelford hoard, although its present location is unknown (Robertson 2000, 217–18). Nine coins in Wisbech Museum, starting with Salonina and ending with Carausius, were found in 1948 near Wisbech, and may be either a hoard or part of one (Shotter 1978, no. 156; 1981, 121–4; Robertson 2000, 215). Shotter's study of Fenland coinage also lists antiquarian hoard finds terminating in the reign of Carausius from Emneth, Whaplode and Welney, although there are no further details of their composition (Shotter 1981, 121; Robertson 2000, 222). In contrast to the ambiguity of the Carausian hoards from Cambridgeshire, there are many hoards that close with Period 13 issues (Shotter 1981, 120–4; Robertson 2000, maps 11–14).

Further afield, two hoards of similar size and range to Hoard 2 came from Lancaster, one hidden near the main flue in a bath-house. Both consisted of fifteen coins starting with Gallienus and ending with Carausius (Shotter and White 1977; Shotter 1978, no. 154; Robertson 2000, 207). A group of sixteen coins from Wroxeter starting with Philip I and ending with four issues of Carausius was found with other metal objects, and may have been debris from an abandoned temple (Bushe-Fox 1914, 9; Robertson 2000, 209). Many other hoards have a similar date range, a substantial proportion of them from Wales, including one of fifty-six coins from the cellar of the headquarters building in the fort at Caernarfon (Wheeler 1924, 68, 71, 115–18; Shiel 1977, 40–1; Robertson 2000, 211–13, 220–2).

Large hoards with a similar date range can more clearly be defined as savings and would have been accumulated gradually, such as that from Penard in Glamorgan, which contained 2,583 coins with a greater range of issues from both the official rulers and those of the Gallic Empire (Boon 1967, 291–7; Robertson 2000, 213). In contrast, at least some of the smaller hoards, particularly purse groups, may not have been deliberately accumulated savings but may instead represent *ad hoc* deposits containing a cross-section of coins in circulation at the time. Such an interpretation for the Love's Farm group would require a cash economy on a greater scale than is evident from the limited coin supply to the site at this period. Given that the group represents such a high proportion of the contemporary coins found on the site, it is more probable that it is a small savings hoard, formed within a community that had only a limited use for coinage, much like Hoard 1. It may have been deposited for security in uncertain times early in the reign of Carausius or may be related to votive activity, since it was deposited in the top of a waterhole; in the latter case it would have formed a substantial gift.

III. Metalwork
by Nina Crummy

Introduction and methodology
Excluding material from graves, coins, hobnails and structural nails, 290 items of metalwork of Iron Age to early Anglo-Saxon date were recovered from the site (Table 6.6). Many additional items of later medieval to modern date are listed in the archive, but have not been discussed here.

Small finds are very diverse in material, form and purpose – the methods of assemblage analysis used here (and for the non-metal items; below) are generally based on the functional categories defined by Crummy (1983), adding or omitting categories where appropriate. This approach allows the assemblage as a whole to be summarised and compared to those from other sites, but it does not allow for the mutability of function. For example, a brooch is overtly a dress accessory (category 1), but may be a type used by the Roman army (category 13) or deposited as a votive offering (category 14). A flexible approach to function is therefore essential and should be guided by archaeological context (Crummy 2007). The size of the Love's Farm excavation and its natural division into southern and northern areas, particularly in the Romano-British period (Settlements 6 and 7 respectively), provide scope for analysis by both function and area, whilst many of the items in the possible votive group deposited in context *6572* on the western periphery of Settlement 6, belong to two different functional categories, and should be viewed from two different perspectives. The site assemblage is discussed below as a complete group, then in terms of the two settlement groups (including non-metallic materials). Detailed reports of these objects, listed by material type, date and function, are presented after this overview. Full discussion of the metalwork in relation to other categories of finds is given in Chapter 9.VI. Detailed catalogues are provided for illustrated items. Selected unillustrated items (including those from burials) are also catalogued here, while others are catalogued in the project archive.

Overview
(Figs 6.6–6.7)
The standard Romano-British small finds assemblage always has high numbers of dress accessories (category 1), fittings (category 11) and miscellaneous objects (category 18), with nearly all the other categories represented by at least a few finds. The miscellaneous items usually fall into three sub-groups: multi-functional items, unidentified objects and small pieces of scrap, with the latter invariably in the majority. Rural assemblages are often more idiosyncratic than those from towns, with the overall number of objects low and many categories unrepresented, but dress accessories, fittings and miscellaneous scrap still frequently predominate.

The individual character of an assemblage often appears when a category other than the major three is unusually high, and this is generally most apparent in

Category	Category no.	Total
Dress accessories	1	63
Toilet instruments	2	6
Textile manufacture and working	3	1
Household equipment	4	10
Recreation	5	0
Weighing and measuring	6	4
Literacy	7	4
Transport	8	1
Tools	10	10
Fittings	11	34
Agriculture	12	5
Military equipment	13	8
Religion	14	26
Metalworking	15	20
Boneworking	16	0
Miscellaneous	18	98
Total		290

Table 6.6 Metalwork by function, excluding hobnails and structural nails

categories such as religion, military equipment, agriculture and animal husbandry, tools and crafts. Some examples are shown in Figure 6.6: at the Gilberd School, Colchester, militaria are comparatively well-represented and highlight the site's location within the early fortress (Crummy 1992); at Bob's Wood, Hinchingbrooke, Cambridgeshire, a number of offcuts from smith's blanks

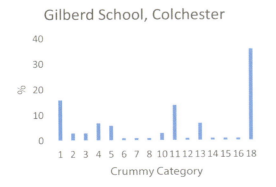
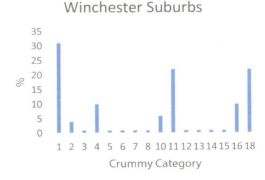

Figure 6.6 The Love's Farm small finds assemblage by function, shown as percentages. Hobnails and nails are not included. Three other sites are shown for comparison: Gilberd School (Crummy 1992); Bob's Wood (Crummy in prep.); and Winchester suburbs (Rees *et al.* 2008)

Figure 6.7 Objects from 'votive' layer *6572* by type

The small finds from Settlements 6 and 7: a comparison
(Fig. 6.8)

Selecting from the full assemblage only those objects recovered from Settlements 6 and 7 allows differences between the two areas to be defined, while combining some of the functional categories enables the data to be presented in a manner that highlights these differences. Figure 6.8 shows the assemblages divided into only six groups as percentages of the whole: personalia (dress accessories and toilet equipment, categories 1 and 2); household and fittings (categories 4 and 11, combined because objects such as keys can be justifiably placed in either category, and because most of the fittings probably come from equipment or buildings); crafts (categories 3, 10, 12, 15 and 16, covering textile manufacture, agriculture, metalworking and bone working, and general tools); religion (category 14); *varia* (shown as 'other' on relevant pie charts), which for Settlement 7 includes objects from categories 7 and 13 (literacy and military equipment), for Settlement 6 the group shown as Assemblage A includes objects from categories 6, 8 and 13 (weighing, transport and military equipment), and for Assemblage B only categories 6 and 13; the last group is miscellaneous (category 18). Settlement 6 Assemblage A shows only plain rings in the group for ritual activity, while Assemblage B shows objects found in deposit *6572* transferred into that group from those that cover their primary or overt use as personalia, *etc*. Coins are not included here.

The most striking difference between the three charts is the low proportion of objects associated with ritual in the assemblage from Settlement 7. Just over half the objects relate to the first three groups and the fifth group, which taken all together can be defined as the standard equipment used by the population that lived and worked on this part of the site. Just under half consists of miscellaneous items, principally iron scrap from the settlement's yard surface. Were the other iron objects from the yard transferred to this group, and the hobnails and nails added as well, it would completely dominate the chart. This very particular use of scrap iron presumably reflects a significant event in the settlement's history.

Craft items formed a far larger proportion of the assemblage for Settlement 6, with all the bone-working debris and all the agricultural equipment (albeit in small quantities in each case), coming from this part of the site. Iron-working debris and tools are also well represented here, although they are not exclusive to this settlement. As presented in Figure 6.8, Assemblage A shows that possible ritual behaviour was more prominent than in Settlement 7 to the north, but when the items from deposit *6572* are transferred into this group (Fig. 6.8, Assemblage B) it forms about a quarter of the total assemblage, mainly reducing the personalia and miscellaneous groups and outranking the evidence for crafts.

The three charts together suggest that Fox Brook, or perhaps a spring feeding the stream, may have formed a ritual or religious focus not only for the inhabitants of Settlement 6, but also those occupying Settlement 7 to the north. There is no certain distinction between the crafts carried out in the two settlements, as so few agricultural items and fragments of bone-working debris were recovered. An emphasis on ironworking is present in both settlements, although it is chiefly represented by reused scrap in Settlement 7.

raise the metal-working category above its usual low level because of the presence of an abandoned smithy (Oxford Archaeology East, in prep.); while in the Winchester suburbs a quantity of debris from bone-working does the same for that category (Rees *et al*. 2008). Assemblages from sanctuaries are very diverse because, depending upon local ritual practices, a wide range of objects might be used for votive deposition, blurring the distinction between functional categories (Crummy 2004, table 7). For example, brooches (category 1) formed the overwhelming majority of the votive offerings at the shrine on Nornour, Isles of Scilly, while many seal-boxes (category 7) were deposited at Great Walsingham, Norfolk (Hull 1968; Bagnall Smith 1999, 40–7).

The Love's Farm assemblage as shown in Figure 6.6 (which includes non-metal finds such as boneworking waste and spindlewhorls) conforms to the general run of small finds assemblages by having high numbers of dress accessories, fittings and miscellaneous scrap, particularly the latter, but also has five particularly striking characteristics. There are no objects relating to recreation (category 5), and only one relating to transport (category 8), but the number of tools (category 10) is high, and would be further enhanced by the addition of those listed under the craft-specific categories of textile manufacture, agriculture and metalworking. Evidence for metal-working (category 15) is the highest of all the craft-specific categories, with ironworking predominating. What is clear from the catalogue is that a large quantity of ironwork (mainly from categories 1, 11 and 18) derives from a cobbled yard in Settlement 7 and this too is pertinent to the evidence for ironworking, particularly as no copper alloy objects were found in the same context. Finally, the number of items possibly connected with ritual or votive behaviour (category 14) is high, particularly when it is considered that this figure includes none of the objects recovered from context *6572* in Settlement 6, which may have been votive in nature (Fig. 6.7). These characteristics of the assemblage are examined in more detail in Chapter 9.VI.

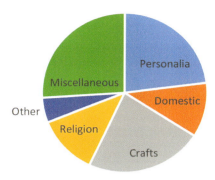

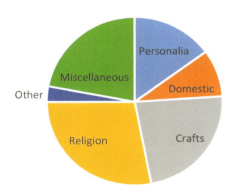

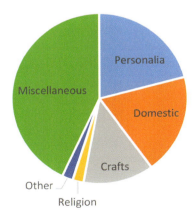

Figure 6.8 Small finds from Settlements 6 and 7 by broad functional groups. For Settlement 6, Assemblage A shows only the plain rings in the group for religion, Assemblage B shows objects from 'votive' layer *6572* (not including coins) transferred into religion.

Metalwork from late Iron Age/Romano-British burials

Metal objects were recovered from a single late Iron Age inhumation burial (grave *11729*) of Period 3.3, located on the western periphery of Settlement 6, and from three late Iron Age/early Romano-British cremations (*6804*, *6839*, *7008*) within Cemetery 3, which was established in Period 3.5 immediately to the north of Settlement 6. The finds are restricted to a number of small brooch fragments and some nails. The brooches are almost certainly worn or unworn pyre deposits while the nails probably derive either from the timber used to build the pyre or from wooden funerary deposits burnt upon it. The complete nails are all much the same size, suggesting that they might have derived from a box or small piece of furniture.

Only pin and spring fragments remain of the brooches in cremations *6839* and *7008* (the latter burial also contained a bone disc, SF 3374, see Chapter 6.IX), but at that period the most frequently used brooch was the Colchester, made in the area of Catuvellaunian influence over the period of *c*.AD 10–40, with some remaining in use to *c*.AD 50. Contemporary Gallo-Roman imports were Langton Down and Rosette brooches, all three types being typical of the period of Cunobelin. In the absence of any examples of the imported forms among the general site finds, it is most likely that the fragments in burials *6839* and *7008* came from one or more Colchester-types.

The brooch fragment from cremation *6804* is part of a Nauheim derivative, a form introduced at the conquest and continuing in use to perhaps as late as *c*.AD 80/5. The form was imported in considerable numbers following the Roman invasion and continued in use until the mid-Flavian period (Stead and Rigby 1986, 109, nos 15–22; Bayley and Butcher 2004, 53–6). They were found in considerable numbers at Baldock (Stead and Rigby 1986, 109), and there is an example in a Claudian-Neronian burial at Stansted (Havis and Brooks 2004b, 200); they are also known from Flavian burials at Winchester (Rees *et al.* 2008, 34).

These two brooch types typify the forms in use over most of the 1st century AD. Both are of one-piece construction and plain in style. The Colchester was the standard brooch type of the Catuvellauni before the Roman conquest, while the Nauheim derivative was probably the cheapest available type after it. Both forms are well represented among the general site finds, indicating that the brooches interred in the cremations were of types in common use amongst the Love's Farm population.

Grave *11729* yielded a plain copper alloy finger-ring, which cannot be closely dated. Finger-rings are rarely the only dress accessories deposited in a grave as they often form part of a suite of jewellery buried with young females (although the grave contained the skeleton of an adult male), but where only one ring is present in a burial it may be a symbol of marriage (Clarke 1979, 318–20, table 2; Crummy *et al.* 1993, 142–3; Philpott 1991, 130).

Catalogue of metalwork from cremations (not illustrated)

Cremation 6804

SF3365 The head, part of the spring and part of the pin of a Nauheim derivative **brooch**. The head is of thin flat section. Length 9mm. *6805*, fill of cremation *6804*, Cemetery 3. Period 3.5.

Cremation 6839

SF3397 Copper alloy bow **brooch** spring fragment: two coils and part of the pin or chord. Length 8mm. *6838*, fill of cremation *6839*, Cemetery 3. Period 3.5.

SF3398 A group of iron **nails** and nail fragments: a) six complete nails. Lengths 40 x 2, 39, 38, 37, 34mm; b) 15 incomplete nails. Lengths 32, 29, 26, 25, 23, 22, 20 x 2, 18 x 2, 17 x 2, 14, 10, 7mm; c) nail head, diameter 10mm; d) seven shank fragments. Lengths 34, 33, 22 x 2, 18, 17, 15mm. *6838*, fill of cremation *6839*, Cemetery 3. Period 3.5.

SF3410 Incomplete iron **nail**. Length 44mm. *6838*, fill of cremation *6839*, Cemetery 3. Period 3.5.

SF3429 Two complete iron **nails**. Lengths 36 and 33mm. *6838*, fill of cremation *6839*, Cemetery 3. Period 3.5.

Cremation 7008

SF3368 Fragment of curved copper alloy wire, probably part of the coil from a bow **brooch** spring. Diameter 6mm. *7007*, fill of cremation *7008*, Cemetery 3. Period 3.5.

SF3399 Two copper alloy wire fragments, one curved, the other straight; probably part of the pin and spring of a bow **brooch**. Lengths 5mm and 10mm. *7007*, fill of cremation *7008*, Cemetery 3. Period 3.5.

SF3433 Five tiny copper alloy fragments, two curved; probably part of a bow **brooch** spring. Lengths 6, 8, 3, 3 and 3mm. *7007*, fill of cremation *7008*, Cemetery 3. Period 3.5.

Grave 11729

SF3305 Incomplete and fragmentary copper alloy **ring** of indeterminate section. Diameter 22mm. *11728*, fill of grave *11729*. Period 3.3.

Other late Iron Age and Romano-British metalwork

Dress accessories
(Figs 6.9–6.21)

Overview

A wide range of dress accessories represents a large proportion of the general metalwork assemblage from the site. They are catalogued below by general type, and Table 6.7 presents the brooches, hairpins, armlets and finger-rings by their period and general location. Evidence for footwear is discussed separately below, with leather shoes in a separate section (Mould, Chapter 6.X). The dress accessories in general reflect the suggested early date for the establishment and development of Settlement 6, and a later foundation date for Settlement 7, but the evidence is not clear-cut.

Seven dress accessories came from contexts associated with the various Iron Age and Romano-British settlements on the site, but most are of Romano-British date, or came from negative late Iron Age features that filled up very gradually over many centuries. The only late Iron Age artefact type that occurs in a definite late Iron Age context is a finger- or toe-ring (Fig. 6.20, SF 3019), which came from the Period 3.4 fill of Boundary 1 in the area of Settlement 3. Of the other items, two are post-conquest brooches and one may be part of a Rearhook brooch that is also probably of post-conquest date, although it may perhaps be as early as c.AD 40. There are three armlets, two of which may be of late Iron Age date (but are only tentative identifications), whilst the third is a 4th-century type (Fig. 6.18, SF 3449).

Three late Iron Age Colchester brooches, dating to c.AD 10–50, were found unstratified, and a fourth came from an unphased context outside Settlement 6 (Fig. 6.9). Colchester-type brooches were the standard British-made type in use among the Catuvellauni and Trinovantes under Cunobelin, and their manufacture ceased either at his death or at the conquest. Haselgrove (1987, 163–88; 1993, 57) has suggested that bronze coins of Cunobelin were first placed in circulation at the major settlements and only reached the smaller settlements much later. The same may hold true for contemporary brooches, which would place all four of the Love's Farm Colchester-type brooches late within their period of popularity.

Nine dress accessories came from the area of Settlement 7, but none from the surrounding area. Two are brooches, one a mid 1st-century type, which was residual in a Period 4.4 deposit, whilst the other is a 3rd-century glass centre boss brooch, recovered from the fill of a Period 4.4 ditch. A strip fragment from Period 4.2 pit *5912* may be the terminal from an armlet, but the identification is far from certain. Five armlets came from Period 4.4 and 4.5 contexts: one is a mid-Roman snake's head type (Fig. 6.18, SF 2429), the other four are late types, including two typical of the late 4th- to 5th-century transition. A single late Roman finger-ring also came from Period 4.5 (Fig. 6.20, SF 2608). A degree of wealth and status is evident from the snake's head armlet and the glass centre boss brooch.

At first glance, Table 6.7 suggests that the concentration on the later Roman period evident in the assemblage from Settlement 7 may be repeated in Settlement 6 to the south, but a greater emphasis on the early–middle Roman periods (five objects compared to two in Settlement 7) shows that the reverse is true. The presence of more brooches than armlets is also a reflection of an early–middle Roman bias, with eight from Settlement 6, increasing to thirteen if the brooches from peripheral areas around the settlement are included, compared to only five from Settlement 7. None of the brooches from Settlement 6 are late Roman.

	Period	*Brooches*	*Hairpins*	*Armlets*	*Finger-rings*	*Totals*
Settlements 1–5	-	3	-	3	1	7
Settlement 7	4.2	1	-	1	-	2
	4.4	1	-	3	-	4
	4.5	-	-	2	1	3
Settlement 6	4.1	1	-	-	1	2
	4.3	1	1	1	-	3
	4.4	1	-	2	-	3
	'Votive' layer	4	2	2	-	8
	Unphased	1	-	-	-	1
	Unstratified	5	-	-	-	5
Unattributed/unstratified		10	2	10	1	23

Table 6.7 Distribution of dress accessories by location and period, excluding hobnails

Site	Hairpins as % of dress accessories		% Hairpins by material		
	No.	%	Bone	Metal	Other
Love's Farm, Cambs	10	15	50	50	-
Haddon, Cambs	1	10	-	100	-
Mantles Green, Bucks	7	33	14	86	-
Bierton, Bucks	5	17	80	20	-
Puckeridge-Braughing, Herts	31	23	67	33	-
Hacheston, Suffolk	39	13	67	33	-
Baldock, Herts	54	20	61	39	-
Castleford, Yorks	46	10	70	28	2
Colchester (Culver Street), Essex	254	64	89	8	3

Data from: Haddon (Crummy 2003a); Mantles Green (Yeoman and Stewart 1992); Bierton (Allen 1986); Hacheston (Seeley 2004); Baldock (Stead and Rigby 1986); Puckeridge-Braughing (Potter and Trow 1988); Castleford (Cool and Philo 1998); Colchester (Crummy 1992)

Table 6.8 Percentages of hairpins from Love's Farm compared to other dress accessories, and percentages of bone and metal hairpins within the complete hairpin assemblage, from sites in the eastern region and East Midlands

This early–middle Roman bias in the dress accessories in Settlement 6 is reflected in the eight objects from layer *6572* on the settlement's western periphery, which may have formed part of a votive deposit in an area susceptible to localised flooding. Many, if not all, are of early–middle Roman date, and they have therefore been shown separately in Table 6.7. Four brooches and two hairpins range in date from the pre-Flavian period to the 2nd century, while two armlets cannot be closely dated and may be contemporary with them, or possibly rather later. A Claudian-Neronian military armlet fragment found in the same deposit should also be mentioned here (see Military Equipment, below).

Although there are too few brooches from Love's Farm to provide a brooch-use profile using the methods pioneered by Plouviez for Hacheston in Suffolk and for regional British groups (Plouviez 2004, table 16; 2008, 172–6), the assemblage has several distinct characteristics. First, the presence of pre-conquest Colchester brooches (Fig. 6.9) is typical of sites in this area under the influence of the Catuvellauni in the first half of the 1st century AD. Second, a mix of imported Hod Hill (Fig. 6.10) and Nauheim (Fig. 6.11) derivatives with regional British-made forms is also typical of mid–late 1st-century sites in the eastern region, such as Baldock, Puckeridge-Braughing and Hacheston (Stead and Rigby 1986, fig. 51; Olivier 1988a, table 7; Plouviez 2004, table 16). Thirdly, several brooches dating from the mid 1st–2nd century are more unusual in this region, and it is conceivable that the examples deposited in layer *6572* may have been acquired specifically for votive use, or were deposited by non-locals.

Another feature of the assemblage is the low number of hairpins compared to other dress accessories – only five metal examples out of a total of sixty-one artefacts (8%), which increases to only ten out of sixty-six (15%) if bone hairpins and other bone artefacts are included. Although, on some sites, differences in excavation and finds retrieval methods affect both the numbers of objects recovered overall and the proportion of metal to other materials, there appears to be a distinct decline in the number of hairpins found on rural sites compared to those in both small and large Roman towns, and the proportion of bone to metal hairpins also declines away from urban centres (Table 6.8).

The cultural distinctions and socio-economic factors giving rise to this difference between urban and rural sites were no doubt complex, and may have varied between *civitates* and between different areas within *civitates*: therefore to summarise it as a facet of the greater Romanisation of urban populations would be too simplistic. It is nevertheless clear that outside urban settlements in the eastern region women did not regularly dress their hair in ways that required the use of hairpins. Within this general trend, Love's Farm lies between the rural and urban profiles, having a generally low number of hairpins, but with an equal number of bone to metal (the bone hairpins are detailed separately later in this chapter).

Brooches
The brooches are divided below into groups by type, rather than by location. The earliest are late Iron Age Colchester brooches, the latest an early 3rd-century glass centre boss brooch.

a) Colchester brooches
(Fig. 6.9)
Colchester-type brooches occur in large numbers at Verulamium and at Sheepen, Camulodunum, where they are the principal type present before the Roman conquest (Hull forthcoming, Type 90; Stead and Rigby 1986, 112; 1989, 17, 89–91; Niblett 2006, figs 9–10; Hawkes and Hull 1947, 308–10). They also have a more diffuse distribution southwards to Kent, northwards to Yorkshire and to Gloucestershire in the west, no doubt mirroring the trade routes of the period and also the expansionist policy of Cunobelin and his sons. Many would have been in use at the conquest, and those from outside the principal zone of use may also demonstrate a scattering of some elements of the tribes after the Roman invasion. None of the four Love's Farm examples is stratified in a late Iron Age context.

Catalogue of illustrated items
SF2977 Copper alloy Colchester **brooch** missing the end of the forward hook and the spring with the pin. The side-wings and bow are plain, the catch plate is fretted. Length 66mm. The general date range for this brooch type is the first half of the 1st century AD, with the elaborate catch plate perhaps indicating that it was made comparatively early in that period. Manufacture of Colchester brooches probably ceased at the conquest in AD 43, with most falling out of use and deposited in the ground by c. AD 50. Unstratified.

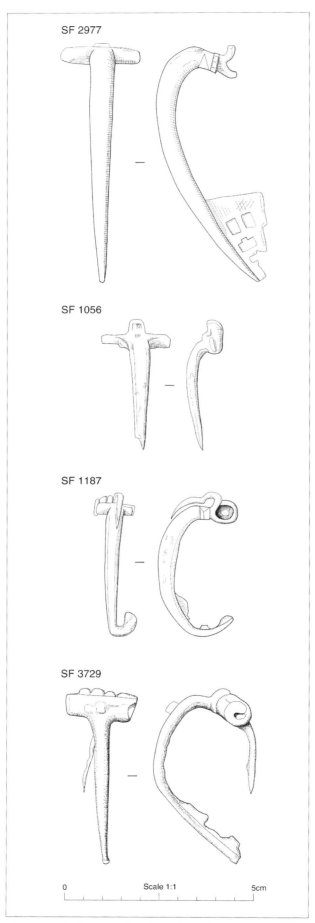

Figure 6.9 Copper alloy brooches of Colchester type

SF1056 Copper alloy Colchester **brooch**, missing the lower part of the bow, part of the forward hook and the spring and pin. The side-wings are plain, as is the bow. Length 36mm. Date-range c.AD 10–40. Unstratified.

SF1187 Small copper alloy Colchester **brooch**, missing one half of the spring with the pin. The lower part of the bow is bent and the catch plate is missing. The side-wings are very small. Length 40mm. This example may belong late in the period of manufacture, c.AD 30–40. Unstratified.

SF3729 Copper alloy Colchester **brooch**, lacking the end of the pin and part of the catch plate. The spring is of six turns. The bow is plain; it has been slightly bent and the head has been pushed downwards, damage that probably occurred before deposition. The catch plate has stepped perforations. Length 48mm. *14189*, unphased.

b) Hod Hill brooches
(Fig. 6.10)

Hod Hill brooches first appeared in Britain c.AD 43, and continued in use to c.AD 60/5; many were used by military personnel but they also occur on civilian sites such as Verulamium, Baldock, Hacheston and Stonea (Waugh and Goodburn 1972, 116, nos 14–16; Stead and Rigby 1986, 120, nos 112–20; Mackreth 1996, 319, nos 59–67, 327, nos 103–4; Plouviez 2004, 89–91). Neither of those listed below was stratified in a context contemporary with its period of use.

Catalogue of illustrated items

SF2046 Copper alloy Hod Hill **brooch**, missing the pin and the edge of the catch plate. The knobbed axial bar is iron. There is a prominent transverse moulding at the head. The bow has marginal mouldings and a central ridge for most of its length, but the marginal mouldings taper out close to the foot, which has a round foot knob. The catch plate has a triangular perforation. Length 50mm. Unstratified.

SF1043 Part of the head and upper bow of a copper alloy Hod Hill **brooch**; a fragment of the iron hinge pin survives. There are two transverse mouldings at the junction of head and bow, and the latter has marginal mouldings and a central ridge. Length 19mm. *10439*, modern.

c) Nauheim derivative brooches
(Fig. 6.11)

As with the Hod Hill brooches, the Nauheim derivatives of the types present at Love's Farm were introduced at the conquest, but they continued in use until the mid-Flavian period (Stead and Rigby 1986, 109, nos 23–44; Bayley and Butcher 2004, 53–6). The example from Settlement 6 is considerably later in date than the ditch from which it was recovered, suggesting that it was either intrusive, or (perhaps more likely), that the ditch, although middle Iron Age in origin, remained partially open into the 1st century AD.

Catalogue of illustrated items

SF3137 Copper alloy Nauheim derivative **brooch** bow of rectangular section tapering to a knife-edge foot. There are marginal grooves running to just above the foot. Length 40.5mm. *10990*, fill of ditch *10988*, Enclosure 1, Settlement 6. Period 3.2.

SF2707 Copper alloy Nauheim derivative **brooch**, missing the spring and pin. The plain, narrow, rectangular-section bow tapers to a knife-edge foot. The catch plate is solid. Length 43mm. *6181*, fill of Quarry 3, Settlement 2. Period 3.4.

SF1300 Copper alloy Nauheim derivative **brooch** with the pin, part of the spring, the foot and catch plate missing. The bow is rectangular. Length 34mm. Unstratified.

SF2047 Copper alloy Nauheim derivative **brooch** lacking the pin. The bow is square in section and tapers to a knife-edge foot. There is a group of three transverse mouldings near the top. The foot is bent. The catch plate was originally solid but has a secondary round perforation, burred on the outer side. Length (bent) 46mm. Unstratified.

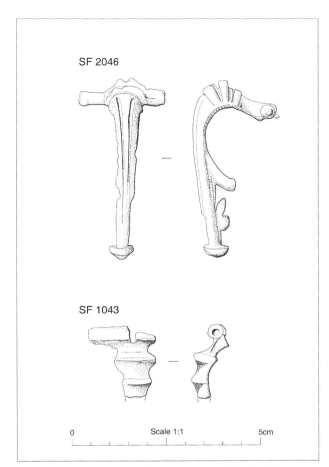

Figure 6.10 Copper alloy brooches of Hod Hill type. Scale 1:1

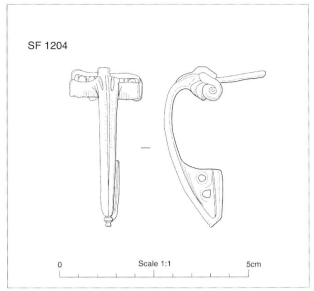

Figure 6.12 Copper alloy brooch of Colchester BB derivative type. Scale 1:1

was developed among the Iceni, probably just before the conquest, and continued in use until c.AD 60/5.

Catalogue of illustrated item

SF1204 Copper alloy Colchester BB derivative **brooch**, complete apart from the end of the pin. The spring has seven coils and the axial bar and chord are held in the doubly-pierced lug characteristic of the type. The side-wings are plain. The head has a crest derived from the Colchester's forward hook. The upper part of the bow has a central groove crossed by a zigzag line, the lower part is plain. The catch plate has one round and one triangular piercing. Length 44mm. Date-range c.AD 65–80. *7647*, modern.

d) Colchester B and BB derivatives and Rearhook brooches (Fig. 6.12)

Colchester B and BB derivative brooches, dated respectively to c.AD 50–70 and c.AD 65–80, succeed the original Colchester type as the most usual forms among the Trinovantes and Catuvellauni after the conquest. They are two-piece brooches with the spring held in a double lug behind the head. Rearhooks are also two-piece brooches, but with the spring held by a rearward-facing hook behind the head. This method of fixing the spring

e) Polden Hill/Rearhook hybrid brooches (Fig. 6.13)

On western Polden Hill brooches the spring was held on an axial bar between the returned ends of the semi-cylindrical side-wings. On both Love's Farm examples (SF 2815 and SF 2772) the spring is also secured by a rearward-facing hook, a hybridisation with the Icenian Rearhook form that also occurs in Suffolk (Plouviez 2004, 95). A date of c.AD 40–60/5, contemporary with Rearhooks, is appropriate. As both the Love's Farm examples were found in possible

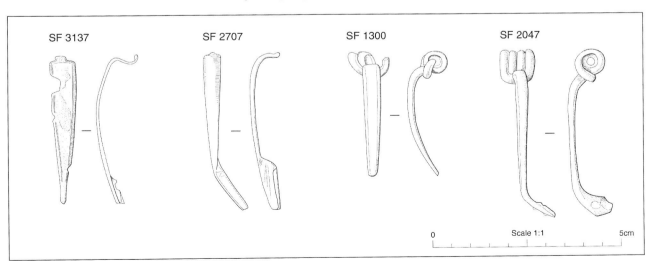

Figure 6.11 Copper alloy brooches of Nauheim derivative type. Scale 1:1

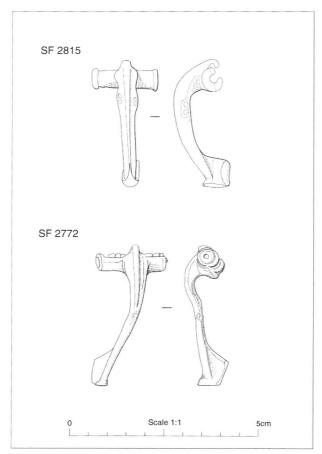

Figure 6.13 Copper alloy brooches of Polden Hill/Rearhook hybrid type. Scale 1:1

votive deposit *6572*, they may have been deposited together as a pair (Pl. 4.2).

Catalogue of illustrated items
SF2815 Small copper alloy Polden Hill **brooch**, missing the axial bar, spring and pin. The side-wings have terminal mouldings. The bow has a central ridge with rudimentary acanthus mouldings on the sides marking the turn towards the foot. Length 35mm. *6572*, alluvial deposit, Settlement 6. Period 4.2.

SF2772 Copper alloy small, light Polden Hill **brooch**, complete apart from the pin. The bow is bent to one side. The chord is secured by a stout rearward facing hook. There is a prominent crest on the head, which dips before running down the top of the bow, a vestige of the forward hook of the Colchester type. There is a tiny footknob. The catch plate is solid. Length 39mm. *6572*, alluvial deposit, Settlement 6. Period 4.2.

f) Headstud, trumpet and T-shaped brooches
(Fig. 6.14)
Only one of each of these three forms is present, two of them from deposit *6572* (Pl. 4.2). The decoration on the Lamberton Moor headstud brooch (SF 2906) is unusual, but there are two closely similar smaller examples from Dragonby, Lincolnshire, and one from Oakley Down, Dorset (Hull forthcoming, Type 149A, nos 9152, 9157 and 8999).

The trumpet-headed brooch (SF 2791) from layer *6572* is a plain example with a fixed head-loop that probably dates to the 2nd century. Also from *6572* is a T-shaped brooch (SF 2769) belonging to a western type with considerable variation in the decoration at the top of the bow. Closely similar examples to the Love's Farm brooch, distinguished by having little ornament on the crossbar and the comparatively plain V-shaped feature at the top of the bow, come from Charterhouse-on-Mendip, Avebury and Caerwent (Hull forthcoming, Type 104, nos 1206, 4502, 8855–6). The date range is late 1st century AD.

Catalogue of illustrated items
SF2906 Copper alloy hinged Lamberton Moor **brooch**, complete apart from the tip of the pin. The head-loop is plain, the side-wings flat and grooved along their full length. The head-stud is unenamelled. Below it the bow is covered with fine transverse grooves. There is a large moulded footknob, not fully half-round, with the edge of the bottom moulding covered with upright grooves. The catch plate is solid. Length 60mm. *11589*, unphased.

SF2791 Complete copper alloy Backworth **brooch** of plain form with fixed head-loop. The spring is held on a single lug behind the trumpet head. The headloop is lozenge-shaped and unpierced, although it has a small off-centre depression. The bow above and below the button is plain and light, terminating in a small foot-knob. The button is decorated with angled grooves and is flanked by plain mouldings. The catch plate is solid. Length 49.5mm. *6572*, alluvial deposit, Settlement 6. Period 4.2.

SF2769 Copper alloy hinged T-shaped **brooch**, complete apart from the end of the pin and part of one end of the crossbar. The pin is hinged on an axial bar fitted through the crossbar, which has two slight grooves at the end. The top of the bow is wide and tapering, with marginal mouldings and a central V-shaped moulding. Below these features it is plain and tapers down to a very narrow foot with a tiny terminal knob. The catch plate has a round perforation. Length 48mm. *6572*, alluvial deposit, Settlement 6. Period 4.2.

g) Plate brooches
(Fig. 6.15)
A Keyhole Rosette plate brooch (SF 3170) is an imported Claudian-Neronian form occurring in small numbers across eastern Britain and representing the final interpretation of the Iron Age series of spring-cover Rosette brooches (Crummy *et al.* 2007, 317–18). Examples from Richborough, Kent, and Burgh Camp, Suffolk, have an incised zigzag on the foot, and the latter also has an applied repoussé-decorated plate that is of smaller diameter than the base plate (Bayley and Butcher 2004, 122–3; Olivier 1988b, fig. 9, 4).

An enamelled equal-ended plate brooch (SF 1188) is a 2nd-century form with a lozenge-shaped centre and zoomorphic terminals that occurs widely across Southern Britain. Examples are particularly numerous at the shrine at Nornour, Isle of Scilly (Hull 1968, figs 19–20).

The latest brooch from the site is an ostentatious oval glass centre boss type (SF 2194). The gilding on the front and white-metal plating on the reverse are the norm for this ostentatious type. Most examples, and the round equivalent, come from Britain, where they are presumed to have been made, although an early example comes from Zugmantel, Germany, which was abandoned in AD 260 and two others from a cemetery at Regensburg, also in Germany, may date to *c*.AD 230–50, making a 3rd-century date probable for the Love's Farm brooch (*ORL* 8, 82, Taf. 10, 26; Lamprecht 1906, pl. 4, 7; Mackreth 1986, 64). There are also several known from Anglo-Saxon graves, examples of either reuse or curation of Roman objects, and one found at Newgrange, Eire, may also have made its way there as a treasured object that conferred status on the owner (White 1988, figs 14–16; Carson and O'Kelly 1977, pl. 7a, E.56:976).

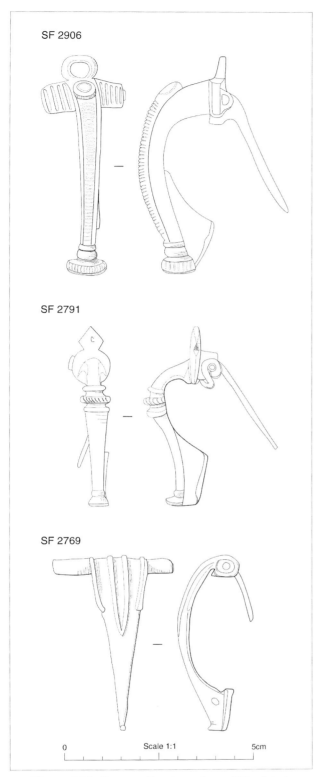

Figure 6.14 Copper alloy brooches of Headstud, Trumpet and T-shaped type. Scale 1:1

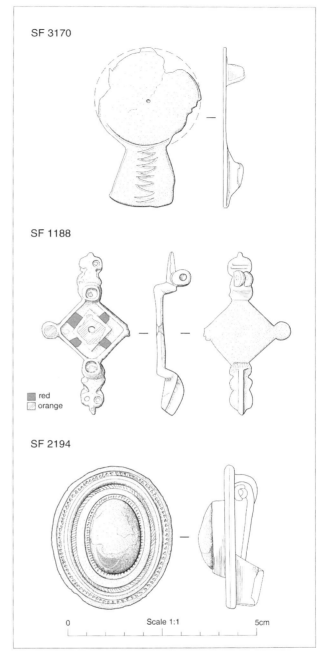

Figure 6.15 Copper alloy brooches of 'Plate' type. Scale 1:1

Catalogue of illustrated items

SF3170 Copper alloy Keyhole Rosette **brooch**, with traces of tinning on the foot and disc. The upper edges of the disc are damaged and the pin, which was held between two lugs on the back of the brooch, is missing. There is a marginal groove around the disc and on the edges of the foot. A small rivet in the centre of the disc suggests that it had an applied plate that would have been smaller than the back-plate as the tinning is visible 5mm in from the edge of the disc. The foot has a central line of incised zigzag decoration. Length 44mm. Unstratifed.

SF1188 Equal-ended enamelled plate **brooch**, complete apart from the pin, part of the catch plate, one side lug and some of the enamel. The centre is lozenge-shaped and has lugs at each corner and zoomorphic terminals at top and bottom bearing the hinge and catch plate. There are traces of orange enamel in one lug and in the central panel of the lozenge. The enamel in the border is pale green but may originally have been red. Length 45mm. *11609, unphased.*

SF2194 Complete copper alloy oval glass centre boss **brooch**, with a large green cabochon in the central setting. The glass has largely lost its original surface, but traces of colour on what remains suggest that it was originally marbled green and red. The front of the brooch is gilded and has two zones of punched decoration, set in troughs between mouldings. The outer one consists of a square around a saltire in relief, with the punchmarks set close together to produce a running spool-like effect. The inner has both a raised cabled moulding and another band of cross decoration, the latter set close at the base of the central setting. The back of the brooch is plated with white metal. The pin is sprung on a single lug. Length 40mm, width 32mm. *5838*, fill of ditch *5860*, Enclosure 126, Settlement 7 (Phase 2). Period 4.4.

i) Penannular brooches
(Fig. 6.16)
The plain penannular brooch (SF 3013) is a 1st-century AD form that occurs in contexts dated to both before and after the Roman conquest (Fowler 1960, 152). The context of this example suggests that it is of post-conquest date. Other examples from the eastern region come from Baldock, Colchester, Hacheston and Puckeridge-Braughing (Stead and Rigby 1986, fig. 49, 153–6; Crummy 1983, 18, fig. 16, 97, 99; Plouviez 2004, 205–6; Olivier 1988a, 50).

In contrast, penannular brooches with ribbed hoops tend to be from late Roman contexts, although the damage to the terminals of SF 3078 from Love's Farm does not allow it to be attributed to a particular type and its context suggests it may be middle Roman (Fowler 1983, 18–19).

Catalogue of illustrated items
SF3013 Copper alloy circular-section penannular **brooch** of Fowler Type C (1960, 152), with most of both terminals missing and only small fragments of the pin remaining. Diameter 29mm, section diameter 2mm. *8739*, fill of ditch *8740*, Enclosure 101, Settlement 6. Period 4.2.
SF3078 Distorted circular-section hoop from a copper alloy penannular **brooch**, ribbed along its length. Both terminals are damaged, Diameter approximately 27mm, section diameter 3mm. *10526*, Enclosure 114, Settlement 6. Period 4.3.

Hairpins
(Fig. 6.17)
Most of the five hairpins came from the southern part of the site and all are early forms. Two are from deposit *6572* on the western periphery of Settlement 6, and add to the substantial number of late 1st- to 2nd-century items found in that context (Pl. 4.2). One belongs to Cool's Group 5, with a grooved head (SF 1209), a widespread form that can be divided into sub-groups on the details of the decoration; most are probably of 2nd-century date (Cool 1990, 157). The other is of Cool's Group 6 (SF 1219), which dates from the mid 1st century to the early to mid 2nd century, and has a largely eastern and southern distribution, with Love's Farm lying close to the northern limit (Cool 1990, 157, fig. 15). The type was particularly popular among the Catuvellauni, occurring at both urban and rural sites, and may have been made at Verulamium, although the earliest stratified example is from Baldock (Stead and Rigby 1986, 128, no. 211).

Two other hairpins appear to have been deliberately mutilated, possibly for use as votive objects, although they are not from specifically 'votive' contexts. One (SF 2094) is another example of Cool's Group 5, recovered from the outer ditch of Enclosure 22, a Period 3.5 feature located on the northern part of the site (Chapter 3). Its tip has been flattened into a neat leaf shape, perhaps the deliberate conversion of the pin into a model spear, and the shank is bent into a double curve, perhaps the deliberate damage of a votive object at the time of deposition. It is possible that the model makes reference to the goddess Minerva, since the weapon is one of her principal attributes, and a Minerva bust handle from a wax spatula was found elsewhere on the Love's Farm site (below, p.165). Furthermore, in her sky-goddess/healing aspect, it is

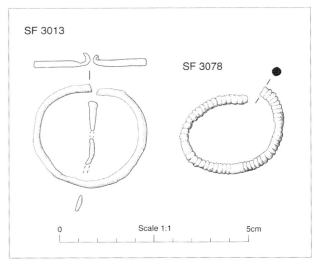

Figure 6.16 Penannular copper alloy brooches. Scale 1:1

possible that Minerva may have been associated with a local deity to which the rings in context *6572*, perhaps deposited as solar symbols, were dedicated (see below). Another possibility is that the spear refers to Mars, as was assumed for miniature spears from the sanctuaries at Harlow, Uley, Nettleton and Woodeaton, and also at the small town of Wilcote in Oxfordshire (France and Gobel 1985, fig. 44, 62; Henig 1993, figs 110–1; Wedlake 1982, fig. 96, 13; Kirk 1949, nos 40–1; Bagnall Smith 1998, no. 152; Crummy 2004, 284, fig. 6, 162). As there is no evidence of his cult at Love's Farm, the weapon's association with Minerva, or a local interpretation of Minerva, seems more appropriate here.

The second altered hairpin (SF 1182) has an idiosyncratic head form that can be related to Cool's Groups 3 and 11 (Cool 1990, 154, 160, 164). Its shaft has also been bent and its tip hooked upwards. It probably dates to the 1st–2nd century AD, but was unstratified. The fifth hairpin (SF 3600), and the only one that may not have some kind of votive association, is a variant of Cool's Group 5 that is probably of 1st- to 2nd-century date.

Catalogue of illustrated items
SF1209 Copper alloy **hairpin** of Cool's Group 5, with three grooves below a simple pointed top. The shaft is slightly bent and the tip is missing. Length 68mm. *6572*, alluvial deposit, Settlement 6. Period 4.2.
SF1219 Complete copper alloy **hairpin** of Cool's Group 6, with a flattened globular head above a single cordon. Length 92mm. The type is mainly found in eastern England and dates from the mid 1st century into the 2nd century (Cool 1990, 157). *6572*, alluvial deposit, Settlement 6. Period 4.2.
SF2094 Copper alloy **hairpin** of Cool's Group 5, with three slight grooves below a slightly rounded head. The shank is bent into a long 'S' and the tip has been flattened into a regular leaf-shape. Length 140mm. *2598*, fill of ditch *2594*, Enclosure 22. Period 3.5.
SF1182 Copper alloy **hairpin** with a comparatively long head compared to the shaft. The head is hexagonal in section, and has one long and one short bead defined by groups of grooves, topped by a small biconical knob. The shaft is bent, and towards the tip has been turned up into a hook. Length 76mm. Unstratified.
SF3600 Upper part of a copper alloy **hairpin** with a tiny conical knob above a baluster and groove. The form is close to that of Cool's Group 5 and probably dates to the late 1st–2nd century (Cool 1990, 157). Length 33mm. *13058*, fill of ditch *13060*, Enclosure 119, Settlement 6. Period 4.4.

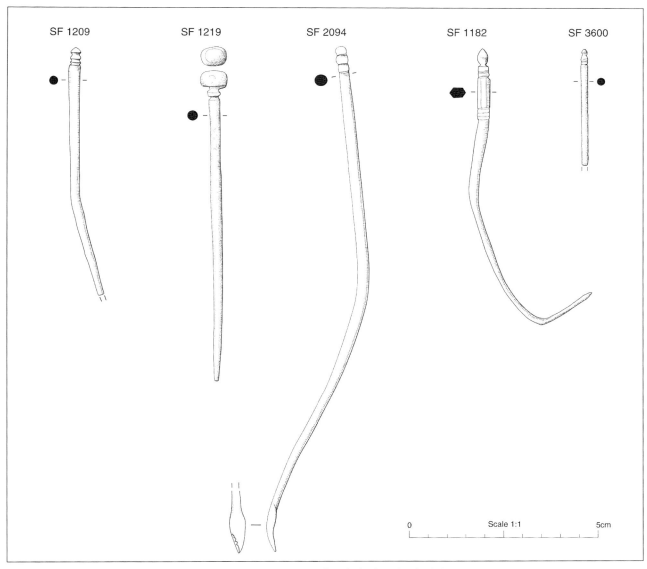

Figure 6.17 Copper alloy hairpins. Scale 1:1

Armlets
(Figs 6.18–6.19)
A large number of armlets came from a range of contexts; they are listed below approximately by date and type. The earliest examples may date to Period 3.4 (SF 2965; not illustrated) and Period 3.5 (SF 2955). Both may be late Iron Age, although the identifications are tentative, and both came from ditch fills, which could have accumulated long after the ditches themselves were first dug. Also only tentatively identified as an armlet is SF 2675 (not illustrated), from a Period 4.2 pit.

The terminal from a snake's head armlet (SF 2429) is probably of 2nd- to early 3rd-century date (Johns 1996, 110–11), and several cable armlets probably belong to the later 3rd–early 4th century. Probably only one (SF 3690) is from a context contemporary with its period of use. Two armlets came from deposit *6572* in Settlement 6 (SF 1221 and SF 2792; Pl. 4.2). Both are of the light bangle form popular in the 4th century, but the considerable number of 2nd-century objects from the layer could point to an earlier date. Many of the remaining armlets are late Roman bangle types, either penannular or with varying methods of joining the terminals. Some are stratified in late Roman contexts or come from fills of earlier landscape features that may have accumulated long after the date at which the features themselves originated.

At least four items belong to types typical of the late 4th to early 5th century. One (SF 2235), from a Period 4.5 deposit, is a cog-wheel armlet with toothing between crenellations, examples of which appear in burials post-dating *c*.AD 360 at both Lankhills, Winchester, and Colchester, and in occupation contexts of late 4th- to early 5th-century date at Neatham, Silchester and Gadebridge (Clarke 1979, 305, type D1e; Crummy *et al*.1993, tables 2.52, 2.67; Redknap 1986, fig. 73, 100–1; Crummy 2006b, 128–9; Neal and Butcher 1974, 139, fig. 60, 159). The same type occurs in early Saxon Grave 3 at Dorchester-on-Thames, dated to the first quarter of the 5th century, placing it firmly in the late Roman–early Anglo-Saxon transitional period (Kirk and Leeds 1954, fig. 29, 2, 6; White 1988, 109). The other three examples from Love's Farm (SFs 2511, 3617, 3676) are all multiple-motif (multiple-unit) armlets, a type that is also known from late 4th- to early 5th-century burials at Lankhills and

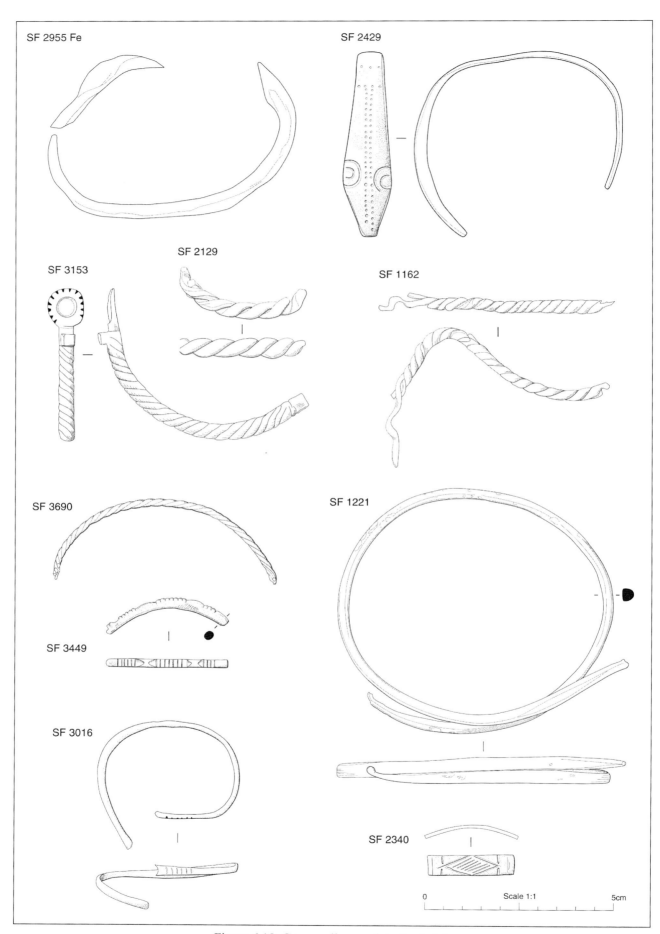

Figure 6.18 Copper alloy armlets. Scale 1:1

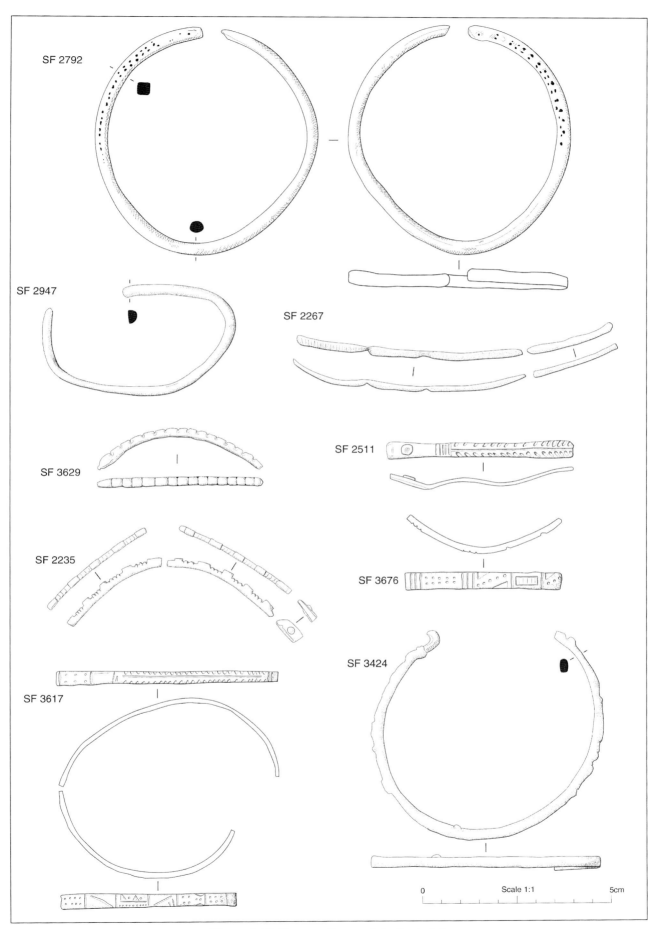

Figure 6.19 Copper alloy armlets. Scale 1:1

Colchester, and from an early 5th-century burial at *Durobrivae*, as well as from late Roman occupation contexts (Clarke 1979, 307, 309, Type E; Crummy *et al.* 1993, tables 2.52, 2.67; Crummy 1999; 2000; 2006b, 122, 129; Swift 2000, 305).

Catalogue of illustrated items

Fig. 6.18

SF2955 Two fragments of an oval iron ring, possibly a penannular **armlet**. Maximum diameter 65mm, width 7mm. *8194*, fill of ditch *8286*, Boundary 1. Period 3.5.

SF2429 Fragment of an oval copper alloy **armlet** of rectangular section with snake's head decoration on the surviving terminal. The features of the snake are shown by a double row of punched dots along the centre of the head, flanked by eyes of double ring-and-dots that overshoot the edges. Maximum diameter 55mm, height 6mm at hoop, rising to 13mm at the terminal, thickness 2mm. *4998*, fill of ditch *4999*, Enclosure 137, Settlement 7 (Phase 2). Period 4.4.

SF2129 Fragment of copper alloy two-strand cable **armlet**. Diameter approximately 60mm. *10424*, modern

SF3690 Fragment of a copper alloy three-strand cable **armlet**. Surviving diameter 59mm, section diameter 1.5mm. *13069*, fill of pit *13070*, Structure 108, Settlement 6. Period 4.4.

SF1162 Bent fragment of copper alloy three-strand cable **armlet**. Length 59mm; diameter approximately 70mm. Unstratified.

SF3153 One half of a copper alloy two-piece **armlet** with the round section grooved to imitate cabling. The terminal has a small square lug set before a large eye for a hook-and-eye fastening, with grooves around the outer edge. The inner end of the fragment narrows to a plain rebated shank, originally inserted into a socket at the end of the other half. Diameter 62mm, section diameter 4.5mm. Unstratified.

SF1221 Copper alloy plain oval **armlet** of D-shaped section, tapering to each terminal. The ends overlap for some length, and damage at each point suggests that they each originally had been coiled around the main section of the armlet to form a slip-knot fastening. Maximum diameter 74mm, height 4.5mm, thickness 3mm. *6572*, alluvial deposit, Settlement 6. Period 4.2.

SF3449 Fragment of a circular-section copper alloy **armlet** with faceted rectangular panels alternating with groups of transverse grooves. Diameter 45–55mm, section diameter 2mm. The design is similar to that on mid–late 4th-century armlets from Colchester and Portchester (Crummy 1983, 44, no. 1715; Cunliffe 1975, fig. 111, 31). *7328*, Period 3.3.

SF2340 Fragment of a narrow copper alloy **armlet** bearing a faceted rectangular panel with hatched central lozenge flanked by transverse bars. Length 23mm, height 5.5mm. See SF 3449 above. Unstratified

SF3016 Distorted fragment of a copper alloy **armlet** of 'D-shaped' section. The hoop is plain apart from a group of grooves next to a broken pierced terminal from a hook-and-eye fastening. Diameter (bent) 38mm, section 2.5mm high, 1.5mm thick. *8778*, fill of ditch *8779*, Enclosure 112, Settlement 6. Period 4.3.

Fig. 6.19

SF2792 Copper alloy penannular **armlet** of oval-section with blunt terminals. Towards one terminal a row of tiny punched dots runs along the top and bottom edges, increasing to a double row at the end. There was probably similar decoration at the other terminal, now largely worn away and obscured by corrosion pits. Maximum diameter 61mm, height 4.5mm, thickness 3.5mm. *6572*, alluvial deposit, Settlement 6. Period 4.2.

SF2947 Small plain copper alloy penannular **armlet** with blunt terminals; the section is D-shaped. Maximum diameter (distorted) 51mm, height 3.5mm, thickness 2.5mm. Unstratified.

SF2267 Two fragments of a straightened narrow copper alloy **armlet**, one with worn traces of transverse grooves. Lengths 64 and 25mm, height 2.5mm. Unstratified.

SF3629 Fragment of a circular-section copper alloy **armlet** decorated with deep transverse grooves that produced the effect of strung beads. Length 45mm, section diameter 2mm. *14189*, unphased.

SF2235 Three fragments of a copper alloy crenulated **armlet** with toothing between the crenulations; one fragment is part of a lap joint with iron rivet. Diameter 65mm. *4936*, fill of ditch *4937*, Enclosure 139, Settlement 7. Period 4.5.

SF2511 Fragment from the riveted lap-joint of a straightened copper alloy multiple-motif **armlet**. The surviving panel has a central groove flanked by angled grooves to produce a herringbone effect. It is separated from the terminal by transverse mouldings. Length 49mm. *5539*, occupation deposit, Settlement 7. Period 4.4.

SF3617 Copper alloy multiple motif **armlet**, with one terminal missing. Motifs include feathering, transverse grooves, ring-and-dots, dots, diagonal grooves and chip-carving. Maximum diameter 57mm, height 4mm, 1mm thick. *14189*, unphased.

SF3676 Fragment of a copper alloy multiple motif **armlet**. Motifs include chip-carving, ring-and-dots and transverse grooves. This fragment shares with SF 3617 the use of panels defined by transverse grooves and filled with two rows of ring-and-dots, although on this piece the panels are longer and contain more ring-and-dots. Length 41mm, height 5mm, 1mm thick. *14189*, unphased.

SF3424 Copper alloy **armlet** with one terminal missing; the other is hooked for a hook-and-eye fastening. The surface is obscured by corrosion pits, but was probably decorated. Diameter 65mm, section 3.5 by 2.5mm. *5980*, layer, Settlement 7. Period 4.5.

Finger-rings
(Fig. 6.20)

A coiled form of finger-ring found at Love's Farm (SF 3019) is typical of the late Iron Age, with several examples coming from the *oppida* at Maiden Castle and Camulodunum (Wheeler 1943, fig. 86, 10–17; Sharples 1991, fig. 139, 12–14; Hawkes and Hull 1947, pl. 99, 1). They could be worn on either the fingers or toes. A ring of this type was worn on a finger of the left hand of a late 1st-century BC skeleton at Baldock and others on the toes of skeletons at Maiden Castle (Stead and Rigby 1986, 128, fig. 54, 201; Wheeler 1943, 266, 278).

The plain copper alloy finger-ring (SF 3012) is a type that cannot be closely dated but its context, in a Period 4.1 posthole, in this instance suggests an early Roman date. Octagonal finger-rings (such as SF 1138) mainly date to the 4th century AD in Britain and often come from sanctuary sites, occurring in both silver and copper alloy, although examples on the continent can be as early as the Augusto-Tiberian period (Crummy 2006a, 64; 2006b, 123; Bertrand 2003, 41). Also belonging to the late Roman period is the wavy-edged hoop (SF 2608).

A number of plain rings were recovered from the site, including several from *6572* (Pl. 4.2), the possible votive deposit on the western periphery of Settlement 6. These are unlikely to have been used as finger-rings as they have round or polygonal sections (see Religion).

Catalogue of illustrated items

SF3019 Copper alloy **finger-** or **toe-ring** of three coils, pulled open at one end, Diameter 23mm. *8799*, fill of ditch *8800*, Boundary 1, Settlement 3. Period 3.4.

SF1138 Fragment of a silver octagonal **finger-ring**, cleanly broken on one side, slightly pulled out of shape on the other. Diameter 20mm, height 7mm, thickness 1mm. Unstratified.

SF2608 Broken and bent copper alloy **finger-ring** with wavy-edged hoop. Diameter approximately 18mm. *5658*, fill of ditch *5659*, Enclosure 139, Settlement 7. Period 4.5.

SF3012 Complete plain copper alloy **finger-ring** of 'D-shaped' section. Diameter 18mm, height 3mm, thickness 2mm. *8737*, fill of posthole *8738*, Enclosure 103, Settlement 6. Period 4.1.

Footwear
(Fig. 6.21)

Metallic evidence for footwear is represented by two iron cleats and a scatter of hobnails, although leather shoe fragments have also survived (Mould, Chapter 6.X).

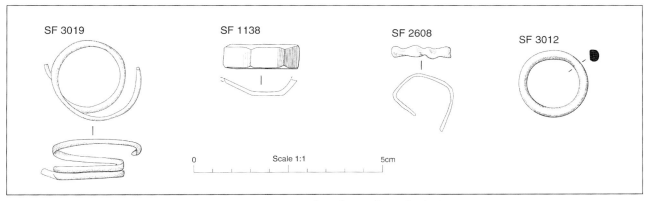

Figure 6.20 Copper alloy finger rings. Scale 1:1

Cleats of various shapes could be fitted to the heels or toes of boots or shoes and evidence from both Silchester and Winchester shows that they are more frequently found in the late Roman period, with the earliest examples from Winchester dating to the mid–late 3rd century (Richards 2000, 372–3; Crummy 2006b, 129; Rees *et al.* 2008, 60–2). Both of the Love's Farm cleats came from the fills of Period 4.4 ditches.

The iron hobnails recovered from the site are indicative of a specific technology rather than of the use of stout boots, as shoes could also have nailed soles. Those stratified in Romano-British contexts come almost exclusively from within the two Romano-British settlements (Settlements 6 and 7), not from the surrounding fields or peripheral areas, although considerably more were recovered from Settlement 7 than from Settlement 6. This distinction may be the result of a greater use of nailed soles in the late Roman period, when occupation was concentrated in the northernmost settlement.

Most hobnails were found singly or in small groups of less than ten, probably all casual losses from soles that were worn or breaking up. There are, however, larger clusters from the following five locations:

Period 4.1: ditch *5780*, Settlement 7 (group of 30);
Period 4.3: ditch *5619*, Boundary 115, Settlement 7 (group of 16);
Period 4.3: pit *15089*, Settlement 6 (two groups of 78 and 19, and one separate example, Pl. 4.7);
Period 4.4: pit *4748*, Structure 114, Settlement 7 (group of 30);
Period 4.4: cobbled yard *5344*, Settlement 7 (two groups of 33 and 25, and 11 other scattered examples).

The clusters from pits and ditches probably represent the disposal of one or more items of footwear. The number of soles represented by these clusters cannot be estimated with any certainty as patterns of nailing varied considerably, from a simple outline around the edge, perhaps with others in the centre, to almost total coverage. The groups from the cobbled yard in the northern settlement may also represent the disposal of footwear damaged beyond repair, but the presence of eleven other hobnails, mostly as single finds, together with a quantity of broken iron objects and pieces of scrap iron, as well as a large number of iron nails, suggests rather the deliberate incorporation of waste ironwork into the surface (see Fittings, Metalworking and Miscellaneous, below). The absence of copper alloy objects from the same context provides confirmation that the ironwork was specially selected. A comparison may be drawn with scrap ironwork incorporated into make-up deposits, including cobbled surfaces, at Winchester (Rees *et al.* 2008, 179).

Catalogue of illustrated items

SF2699 Iron **cleat**, with rounded plate and two spikes, both broken. Width 24mm, length of longest spike 9mm. *5771*, fill of ditch *5772*, Enclosure 126, Settlement 7 (Phase 2). Period 4.4.

SF2468 Triangular iron **cleat** with a short spike at each corner. 41 x 51mm. *5471*, fill of ditch *5472*, Settlement 7 (Phase 1). Period 4.4.

Toilet instruments
(Fig. 6.22)

The metal toilet equipment consists of three nail-cleaners, a tweezers and a mirror, all dating to the early Roman period, and a possible toilet instrument shaft fragment that cannot be closely dated.

All three nail-cleaners (SFs 1012, 3007 and 2229) are of the Baldock type, found in the tribal or *civitas* areas of the Catuvellauni and Trinovantes and dating from the mid-1st century AD into the 2nd century, with examples

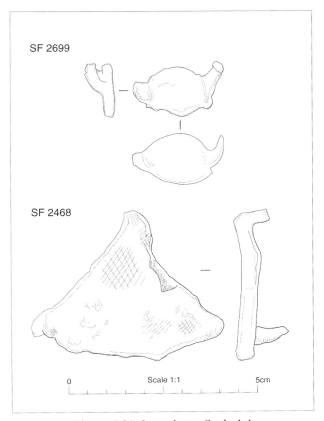

Figure 6.21 Iron cleats. Scale 1:1

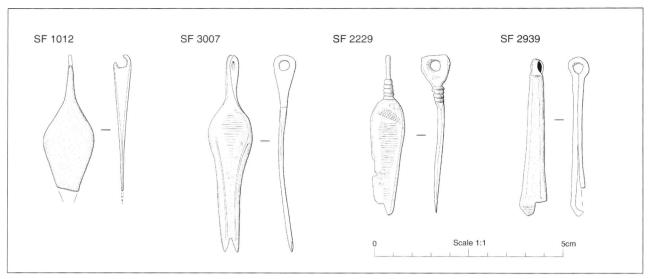

Figure 6.22 Copper alloy nail cleaners. Scale 1:1

from Longthorpe, Baldock and London demonstrating that the type was in production by the pre-Flavian period (Crummy and Eckardt 2004, 51–6; Eckardt and Crummy 2008, 119–21; Webster 1987, 91, fig. 23, 32; Stead and Rigby 1986, fig. 56, 277; Sheldon and Townend 1978, 57, 82, 156, fig. 62, 2). Its distinguishing characteristic is the way in which the upper terminal sweeps round sharply at right-angles to the blade. The standard form is either plain, as SF 1012, or has marginal grooves on the blade, as SF 3007, but a variant form has grooves or mouldings on the neck, as SF 2229. Variants form a high proportion of the total number of Baldocks from London, and there is some possibility that they were made there, while the standard type was made at one or more manufacturing centres in the eastern region (Crummy with Pohl 2008, 220–3). The tweezers (SF 2939) may also have come from a Baldock-type toilet set. Marginal grooves can occur on tweezers of various types and sizes, but those on sets with Baldock nail-cleaners from Gorhambury and Baldock are of similarly small size and general style (Stead and Rigby 1986, fig. 56, 264, fig. 57, 289; Neal *et al.* 1990, fig. 124, 110–12).

The small mirror fragment (not illustrated) is rectangular and dates to the early Roman period; it would originally have been set in a wooden frame (Lloyd-Morgan 1977, 243–52; 1981, 3–20; Rees *et al.* 2008, 66, 69–70).

Catalogue of illustrated items

SF1012 Fragment of a copper alloy Baldock **nail-cleaner**, lacking part of the suspension loop and the end of the blade with the points. There are file marks from finishing on the edges. Length 37.5mm. Unstratified.

SF3007 Complete copper alloy Baldock **nail-cleaner** with marginal grooves on both sides of the blade. Length 55mm. *8707*, fill of ditch *8708*, Enclosure 116, Settlement 6. Period 4.3.

SF2229 Copper alloy Baldock variant **nail-cleaner** missing one point. The blade is separated from the suspension loop by a grooved neck. The loop has a straight top. Length 44mm. Nail-cleaners of this type are comparatively unusual in the Baldock assemblage but at least one example was found (Stead and Rigby 1986, fig. 57, 283). *4886*, fill of ditch *4887*, Settlement 7 (Phase 1). Period 4.4.

SF2939 Copper alloy **tweezers**, one side of the grip is missing and the other is damaged. There are marginal grooves down both blades. Length 43mm. *8122*, fill of ditch *8123*, Boundary 2, Settlement 6. Period 4.1.

Textile equipment

While objects made from other materials are associated with the manufacture of textiles, such as spindlewhorls and loomweights (see Section V below) only a single iron fragment (SF 2121, not illustrated) from an unphased context provides evidence for sewing, although its identification as a needle is only tentative.

Household equipment
(Figs 6.23–6.25)

Most of the household equipment was found unstratified, meaning that the objects are listed below by artefact type rather than settlement or period. A few items are early Roman, but most are of late Roman date or were found in late Roman contexts.

The certain early pieces are a lion-headed stud (SF 1002) and a palmette hasp (SF 3748), both from jewellery boxes, and fragments of box cladding (SF 1222) from layer *6572* may also be early. Studs with lion masks, ranging from well executed relief images to rudimentary suggestions as on this example, were often used on jewellery boxes to attach the lock-plate. They symbolised the protection of the contents, but they acquired a secondary funerary importance where the boxes were used as cremation caskets (Borrill 1981, 315–16; Niblett 1985, 25–6; Philpott 1991, table A4).

Two small vessels, one of copper alloy (SF 1190) and one of lead (SF 3616), were recovered from the area of Settlement 7. Both may be cups, but the copper alloy piece is badly damaged and it may alternatively have been used as a scale pan.

Evidence of high-status dining in the late Roman period is provided by a silver spoon (SF 1527) and two spoons with decorative handles (SF 1058 and SF 3674). The former is similar to examples in the Hoxne hoard (Bland and Johns 1993, 27–8), the latter belong to a type that is found in both late Roman and early Saxon contexts (Price 2000, 55, fig. 2,12, 318; West 1985, 60, fig. 237, 4–5).

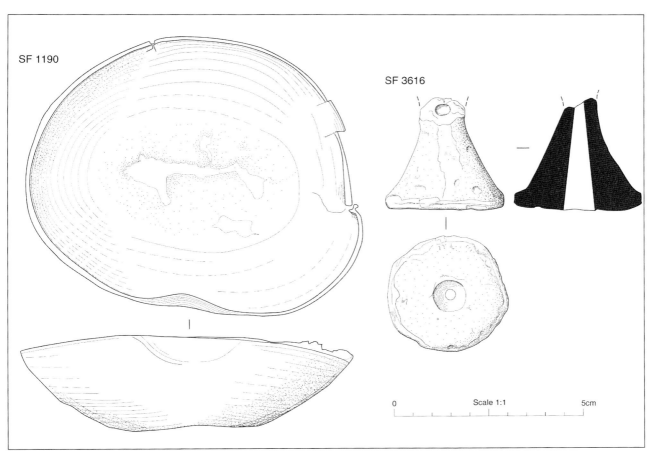

Figure 6.23 Copper and lead alloy possible cups. Scale 1:1

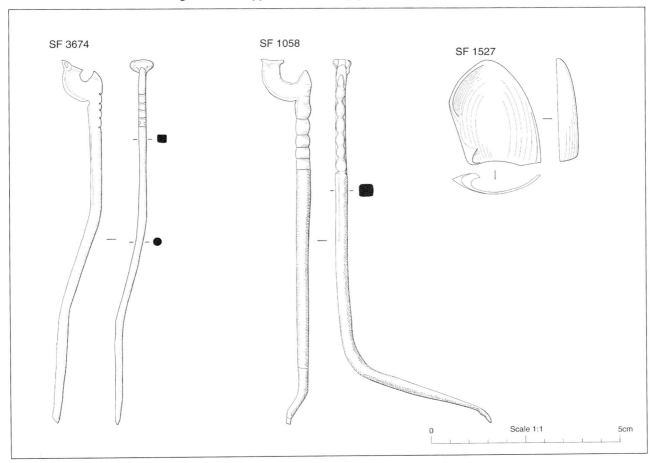

Figure 6.24 Silver and copper alloy spoons. Scale 1:1

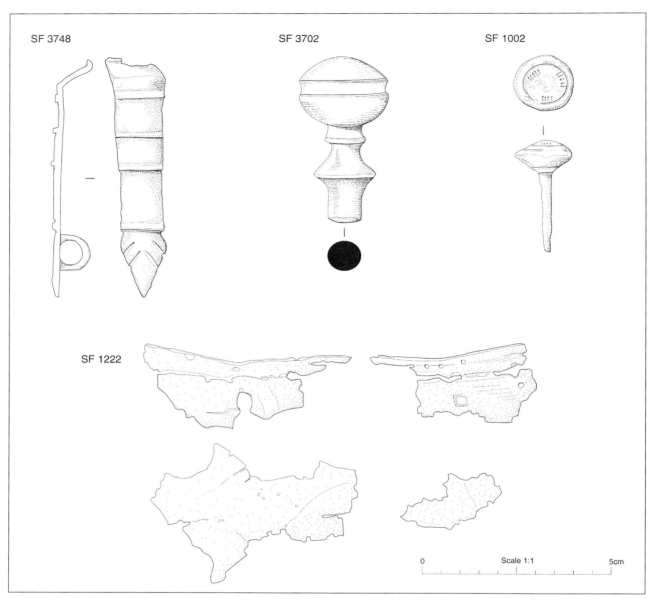

Figure 6.25 Copper alloy box fittings. Scale 1:1

Catalogue of illustrated items

Fig. 6.23

SF1190 Damaged shallow copper alloy **cup**, originally convex. Diameter 88mm, height 25mm. *9103*, fill of ditch *9104*, Enclosure 114, Settlement 6. Period 4.4.

SF3616 Conical lead-alloy vessel foot with central perforation, probably from a small **cup**. Height 30mm, diameter 32mm. *14189*, unphased.

Fig. 6.24

SF3674 Copper alloy **spoon handle** with decorative grooves and chip-carving before an offset junction. Length 100mm. *14189*, unphased.

SF1058 Bent copper alloy **spoon handle** with faceted decoration along the lower end. Length (bent) 100mm. Unstratified.

SF1527 Fragment of a silver narrow oval **spoon bowl**; the size, form and thinness of the metal suggests a date in the late Roman period. Length 28mm. Unstratified.

Fig. 6.25

SF3748 Copper alloy **hasp** from a wooden box, with a palmette terminal and transverse mouldings. The hinged upper end is broken. Length 66mm, width 14mm. The type dates from the mid 1st century AD into the 2nd century (Borrill 1981, table 46). *14189*, unphased.

SF3702 Large copper alloy knobbed **terminal**, possibly a fitting from a large box or piece of furniture. Length 48mm, maximum diameter 24mm. *13315*, fill of ditch *13316*, Settlement 6. Period 4.4.

SF1002 Copper alloy **stud** with debased lion mask decoration on the head. Three groups of short grooves are all that remain of the lion's head, defining the mane between the ears and below them on each side. The tip of the shank is missing. The head is solid and top-heavy, and, as well as grooves defining the lion head, has a group of mouldings on the underside around the top of the shank. Length 32mm. Unstratified.

SF1222 Four fragments of **sheet**, two with an original thickened straight edge (now bent). Probably cladding from a box, although no certain rivet holes for attachment remain. 58 x 23mm; 44 x 21mm; 55 x 40mm; 28 x 16mm. *6572*, alluvial deposit, Settlement 6. Period 4.2.

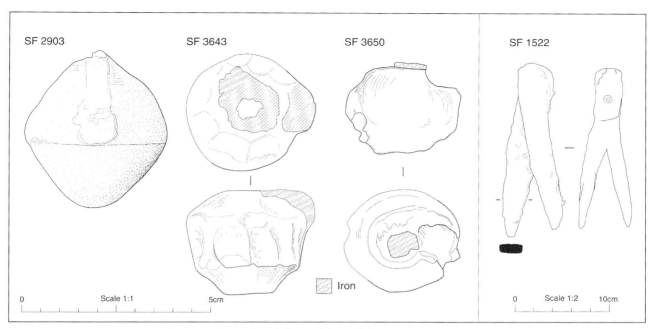

Figure 6.26 Lead weights and iron dividers. Scale 1:1 and 1:2

Weighing and measuring
(Fig. 6.26)
Three lead weights fitted with iron suspension hooks probably came from steelyards used to weigh trade goods; two came from Settlement 6. Their size varies, but without the integral iron hooks no accurate estimate of their weight in relation to either the Roman or Celtic pound can be provided. An unstratified pair of iron dividers (SF 1522) is of simpler form than most Roman examples (Manning 1985, 12) and may therefore be of medieval or later date.

Catalogue of illustrated items
SF2903 Biconical lead **weight** with traces of an iron suspension hook embedded in the top. Height 43mm, maximum diameter 38mm. *8005*, unphased deposit within Settlement 6.
SF3643 Roughly globular lead **weight** with faceted surface and flattened girth and base. There are traces of an iron suspension hook in the upper end. Height 32mm, diameter 35mm. Weight 188g. *13884*, alluvial deposit, Settlement 7. Period 4.2.
SF3650 Damaged biconical lead **weight** with the stump of an iron suspension hook embedded within it. Height 30mm, diameter 30mm. Weight 72g. Unstratified.
SF1522 Iron **dividers**, with flat (now bent) arms rounded at the upper end and fixed together by a small rivet. Length 95mm. Unstratified.

Literacy
(Fig. 6.27)
Three iron styli, two from the northern part of the site and one from the southern, provide some evidence for literacy at Love's Farm. Only one comes from a dated context, the fill of a Period 4.5 ditch in Enclosure 139 within Settlement 7. Like the weights above, the styli may have been principally used in connection with trade or other forms of record-keeping.

A copper alloy handle in the form a bust of Minerva comes from an iron-bladed wax spatula and may also be evidence for literacy. Such spatulas could be used to cut up blocks of wax and spread it on wooden writing tablets, although they could also be used in the manufacture of salves and other medicinal preparations. As goddess of learning, Minerva was an appropriate deity to preside over the preparation of wax tablets, and she also had links to the healing arts in her role as Minerva Medica (Crummy 2002). The spatula form is Feugère's type A5, on which the style of the Minerva busts ranges from elaborate and fully classical to more simplified Romano-Celtic versions (Feugère 1995; Crummy 2002). Most examples probably date to the 2nd century, with some perhaps belonging to the early 3rd century. The socket of the Love's Farm bust is less spatulate than most, and in this, and in its use of transverse linear decoration and ring-and-dots, it can be linked to a handle from Yorkshire in the form of a hunter god, unfortunately damaged, but still retaining a quiver on his back (Crummy and Holmes 2003a–b).

The only complete type A5 wax spatula from Britain was found in a grave at Ospringe, Kent (Whiting 1923, 66, pl. opposite 65; Whiting *et al.* 1931, pl. 55). The number of Minerva bust handles recorded from Britain has increased in recent years due to the reporting of casual or detector finds under the Portable Antiquities Scheme. It might be expected that objects linked so directly to literacy would occur more frequently in highly Romanised large towns and military establishments, which is indeed the case for the less decorative forms of wax spatulae, but most handles of type A5 spatulae come from rural, villa or sanctuary sites (Crummy 2003b, table 2). It is possible that they were marketed as high-quality items for the civilian population, but they may also have been recycled as votive objects especially where, as here, they are disassociated from their iron blade and often have all traces of iron removed from the socket (Crummy 2003b). Within the eastern region examples have been found at Stonea Grange and Cambridge in Cambridgeshire, and Stonham Earl in Suffolk (Jackson and Potter 1996, fig. 112, 59; Crummy 2001a; Geake 2002).

Catalogue of illustrated items
SF1514 Iron **stylus** with short point. The stem is damaged and the eraser is missing. Length 131mm. Unstratified.

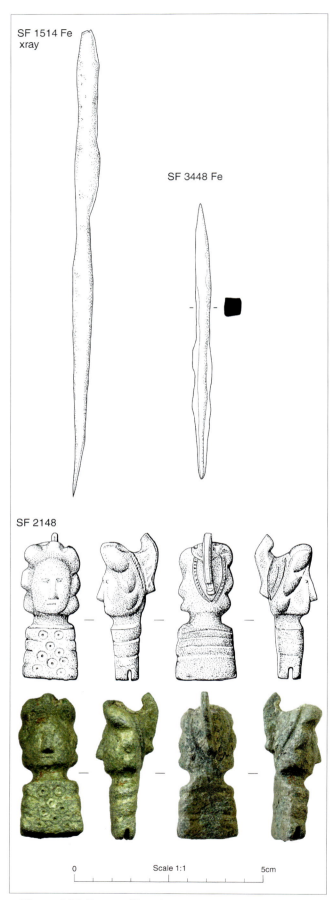

Figure 6.27 Iron stylii and copper alloy spatula handle. Scale 1:1

SF3448 Iron **stylus** fragment, with pointed round-section shank narrowing to a blunt end, which may be original or may have developed into an eraser. Length 76mm. *7318*, unphased deposit.

SF2148 Copper alloy Minerva bust **handle** from a wax spatula with an iron blade. The representation is comparatively crude, but the goddess is identifiable by her crested Corinthian helmet, which is set on the back of her head behind a high triple-peaked coiffure. Her triangular nose is prominent but her mouth is only suggested by a slight groove and her eyes by small round pits. The split socket has transverse grooves on the back that terminate in angular notches on each side at the front, which is decorated by seven ring-and-dots set as a double quincunx. Length 41mm, maximum width 16mm. Unstratified.

Transport
(Fig. 6.28)

The only item associated with transport is a lunula pendant found in layer *6572*, its amuletic purpose making it an appropriate votive deposit. The lunula was a common motif and occurred on a range of Roman metalwork, from jewellery to military equipment. The size of this example is most appropriate for a harness pendant. It is not matched among those from the German *limes* published by Oldenstein (1976) and is more likely to be a Romano-British civilian piece, probably of 2nd-century date.

Catalogue of illustrated item
SF2787 Copper alloy **lunula** with knobbed and moulded terminals. There is no obvious means of attachment, but the outer edge is very rough and may originally have had a suspension loop. Length 42mm, width 52mm. *6572*, alluvial deposit, Settlement 6. Period 4.2.

Tools
(Fig. 6.29)

All of the tools are knives or cleavers, apart from a fragment of a saw blade and a tang (iron punches are detailed under 'Metalworking' below). Two knives are of Manning's Type 23, which originated in the Iron Age but is also found in early Roman contexts (Manning 1985, 118; Curle 1911, 281, pl. 60, 2 and 7; Manning and Scott 1986, 153, fig. 66, 524). There are no marked concentrations within the settlements, although two blade fragments were among the scrap ironwork recovered from a cobbled yard (*5344*) in Settlement 7.

Catalogue of illustrated items
SF1146 Iron **knife** of Manning Type 23 (1985, fig. 29, 23), with short pointed tang, upturned tip and markedly convex edge. Length 137mm, maximum width 33mm. *4813*, unphased deposit, Settlement 7.

SF2953 Iron **knife** of Manning Type 23 as SF 1146 above. Length 146mm, maximum width 42mm. *11598*, unphased deposit, Settlement 6.

SF3030 Narrow iron **knife** blade fragment, with curved back and straight edge (as Manning 1985, fig. 28, 1a–d, 4). Length 47mm, width 9mm. *8906*, fill of ditch *8907*, Enclosure 105, Settlement 6. Period 4.4.

SF3488 Incomplete iron **knife** with the stump of a tang or handle. The back of the blade lies below the line of the tang, which itself curves downwards. The edge drops down sharply from the tang then rises rapidly to run more or less parallel to the back. Length 85mm, maximum width 26mm. This latter feature is unusual, but may be the result of much sharpening. If so, the original form may have been similar to Manning 1985, fig. 28, 9, which has an integral knob-ended handle. *8569*, fill of ditch *8572*, Enclosure 114, Settlement 6. Period 4.4.

SF2225 Incomplete iron **knife** with long tang. The back is in line with the tang for about two-thirds of its length and then angles downwards towards the missing tip. The edge is convex. Length 113mm, maximum width 23mm. *10422*, modern.

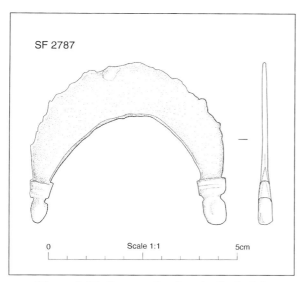

Figure 6.28 Copper alloy lunula. Scale 1:1

Fittings
(Figs 6.30–32)
The fittings are listed below by material, and within material by location and period. The only lead object is an unstratified rivet, perhaps used to repair a wooden or ceramic vessel. The copper alloy items are mainly studs but they also include an enamelled decorative piece (SF 1080) belonging to a small group of fittings from Roman Britain and Gaul. Complete examples with a freely swivelling ring fixed in the central perforation are known from Little Waldingfield, Suffolk, and Ballan, Les Aumônes, Indre-et-Loire, and there is an incomplete example from Silchester, Hampshire (Martin *et al.* 1999, fig. 94, H; Boucher 2004, 20, fig. 1, 3; Crummy 2005a; 2006b, 125). They may have been used as pivoting ring-handles on the straps of bags or small boxes – the tenons on the reverse held in tension against the leather strap when lifted (Crummy 2005a).

The iron objects include several keys from Settlement 7, indicating a degree of portable wealth of some kind and the need to safeguard it. Other items include pintles, ring-headed pins, staples and hooks, the types of fittings used in buildings or on gates.

Nails form the largest group of iron fittings, with over 600 recorded, and more from unphased, unassigned and unstratified contexts listed in the archive. Most are of Manning's Type 1b, with more or less round and slightly conical head and a shank less than 150mm in length; one nail from Structure 108 in the southern settlement may be of the longer Type 1 (Manning 1985, 134). There are a few examples of less frequently occurring types, but none were found in contexts that showed why they might have been preferred over the standard form. Five Type 2 nails, with flat triangular heads, were found: one from a Period 4.4 deposit in Settlement 7 (the fill of the perimeter ditch of Enclosure 136 in Phase 2); three in Period 4.3 contexts in Settlement 6 (from Enclosures 114 and 117, and from a minor ditch (*9120*)); and a fifth example from a medieval plough furrow (Period 6). Ten Type 3 nails, with narrow T-shaped heads no wider than the shank, were found in Settlement 7: one in association with Routeway 9 of Period 4.3; single examples in the perimeter ditches for Period 4.4 (Phase 2) Enclosures 137 and 138, and in a minor deposit (*5508*) of the same phase; three also came from Period 4.4 cobbled yard *5344*, which yielded many other scrap iron objects, and there were three unstratified examples. Two further specimens came from the southern part of the site, from Period 4.2 pit *6566* and Period 4.3 ditch *6759*. A headless nail, Type 5, was also found in yard surface *5344*, within Settlement 7 (Period 4.4, Phase 2), and another came from a Period 4.5 ditch (*4895*) in the same area. A round-headed Type 8 upholstery nail (Manning 1985, 136) was also recovered from Period 4.5 well *5387* in Settlement 7.

As with the hobnails, many more nails come from Settlement 7 than from Settlement 6. The nails from stratified Period 4 contexts in both settlements are summarised in Table 6.9. From this it can be seen that in Settlement 6, the number of nails lost was fairly consistent across the periods, apart from Period 4.5, which has none, while in Settlement 7 the number from Period 4.4 accounts for 70 % of the total, rising to 84 % for the whole of the later Roman period when those from Period 4.5 are included. A considerable number of scrap nails were included in yard surface *5344*, representing over a quarter of the total from Settlement 7 and over a third of the

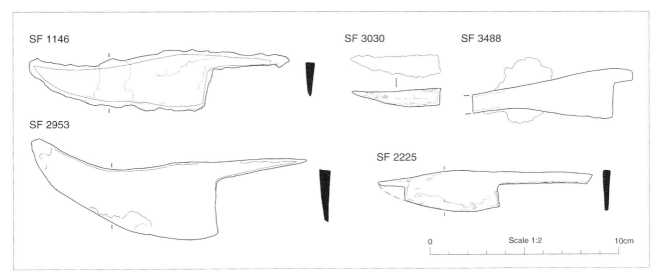

Figure 6.29 Iron knives. Scale 1:2

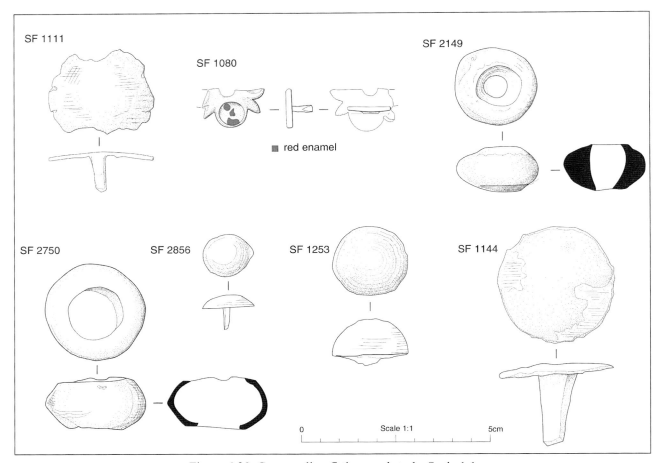

Figure 6.30 Copper alloy fittings and studs. Scale 1:1

number from the period (Table 6.9). Even without this group, and even allowing for nails residual from earlier periods, the number of nails in Period 4.4 would be the highest in Settlement 7. The implication of these figures is that occupation was consistent in Settlement 6 apart from at the very end of the Roman period, when it may have dropped away to nothing, but that it rose sharply in Settlement 7 in Period 4.4 and continued into Period 4.5. This is at variance with the coin data, which shows greater coin loss in Settlement 6 in the late 4th century than in Settlement 7. More subtle factors must have been at play, probably to do with varying styles of occupation and land use in the two settlements and the role of coinage in the late Roman period.

Period	Settlement 6		Settlement 7		Totals
	No	%	No	%	No.
4.1	37	20	7	2	44
4.2	28	15	44	13	72
4.3	57	31	1	<1	58
4.4	62	34	232 (91)	70 (28)	294
4.5	-	-	46	14	46
Totals	184		330		514

Percentages are of the total number of nails from each settlement. The nails from the yard surface in Settlement 7 are shown in brackets in the column for Period 4.4

Table 6.9 Iron nails from Settlements 6 and 7 by period

Catalogue of illustrated items

Fig. 6.30

SF1111 Copper alloy **stud** with damaged flat head. Diameter (if complete) 28mm; length 10mm. *4133*, fill of ditch *4134*, Settlement 2. Period 3.5.

SF1080 Fragment of a copper alloy **fitting** with one complete and two incomplete enamelled roundels with angular lugs between them, set around a perforation that would have been central on the complete object. The enamel in the complete roundel is largely missing; it appears to have consisted of a central motif within a field of red. There is a 'T-shaped' projection on the back of the fragment to allow it to be slotted into an incision in a leather strap and then turned to secure it in position. A second one would have existed on the opposite side of the central hole. Surviving dimensions 11 x 16.5mm; original dimensions 22 x 22mm; 7mm long. *10447*, modern.

SF2149 Copper alloy biconical **fitting** with central perforation; possibly cladding from the iron leg of a folding stool (*cf.* Croom 2007, fig. 45). Diameter 22.5mm, length 12.5mm. Unstratified.

SF2750 Copper alloy hollow biconical **fitting**; possibly a furniture fitting as SF 2149 above. Diameter 26.5mm, length 14mm. Unstratified.

SF2856 Small copper alloy **stud** with convex head. Diameter 12.5mm, length 10mm. Unstratified.

SF1253 Composite stud consisting of a convex copper alloy **boss** filled with lead-tin solder that secures an iron shank. Diameter 20mm, height 10mm. Similar studs were used on boxes in the Roman period. Unstratified.

SF1144 Copper alloy **stud** with slightly convex head and thick square-section shank. Diameter 31mm, length 24mm. Unstratified.

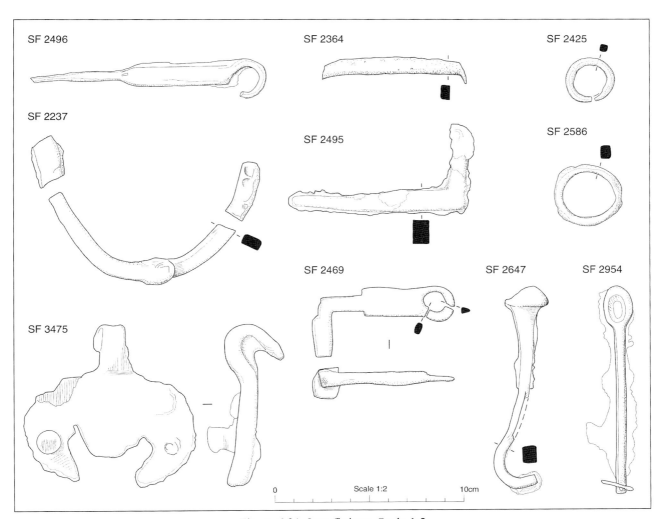

Figure 6.31 Iron fittings. Scale 1:2

Fig. 6.31

SF2496 Iron tumbler-lock **lift-key**, probably of T-shape (as Manning 1985, pl. 40, O23) but lacking the lower end of the shank with the teeth. Length 125mm. *5923*, fill of ditch *5924*, Enclosure 21, Settlement 7. Period 4.1.

SF2364 Iron **joiner's dog**, with most of the arms missing. Width 74mm, surviving length of longest arm 14mm. *5325*, fill of ditch *5326*, Settlement 7. Period 4.2.

SF2586 Iron **ring**. Diameter 36mm. *4625*, fill of Quarry 7, Settlement 7. Period 4.2.

SF2237 Three curved iron **bar fragments**, the longest including a soldered repair where it has snapped in antiquity. Length of longest 103mm, section 11 by 4mm. *4983*, fill of ditch *4984*, Enclosure 129, Settlement 7. Period 4.2.

SF2425 Iron **ring**. Diameter 26mm. *5355*, fill of ditch *5356*, Enclosure 137, Settlement 7 (Phase 2). Period 4.4.

SF2469 Iron tumbler-lock **slide key** with solid shank topped by a worn suspension loop. The bit is either solid or has very short teeth defined by grooves, as Manning 1985, pl. 41, O48–52. Length 75mm. *5481*, fill of posthole *5482*, Settlement 7 (Phase 2) Period 4.4.

SF2647 Iron **swivel** with conical head, the hooked end of the shank is missing. Length 115mm. Probably from the end of a chain, as Hawkes and Hull 1947, 383, pl. 105, 33; Manning 1985, 138, S4. *5839*, fill of pit *5840*, Settlement 7 (Phase 2). Period 4.4.

SF2495 Iron **pintle**, with broken round-section pivot and square-section spike. Length of pivot 47mm, length of spike 96mm. *5539*, occupation layer, Settlement 7 (Phase 2). Period 4.4.

SF2954 Iron ring-headed **pin**, with a round rove fitted onto the point. Length 115mm. *8287*, fill of pit *8288*, Structure 116, Settlement 6. Period 4.2.

SF3475 Hooked iron **fitting** in the form of a crescentic plaque with a rounded projection between the arms. Behind each arm is a stout riveted projection (one broken off but present). The hook descends from the centre of the outer edge. Length 91mm, width 90mm. *11337*, fill of ditch *11338*, Boundary 100, Settlement 6. Period 4.2.

Fig. 6.32

SF3520 Short iron ring-headed **pin** with pierced rounded terminal rather than a true ring. Length 50mm. *11391*, fill of ditch *11393*, Boundary 100, Settlement 6. Period 4.4.

SF3762 Small iron **pintle** with complete circular-section pivot and rectangular-section spike. Length of pivot 56mm, length of spike 28mm. *14076*, fill of ditch *14077*, Settlement 6. Period 4.4.

SF3110 Long iron ring-headed **shank** in fragments. The shank is formed from two welded bars that split and curve into the arms, where they are welded to a straight bar, leaving a triangular gap at the head. Length 473mm, width 8.3mm. *10473*, fill of ditch *10474*, Settlement 6. Period 3.3.

SF3308 Iron **staple or joiner's dog**. Width 31mm, length 71mm. *11808*, fill of pit *11809*. Unphased feature, Settlement 6.

SF2683 Iron split-spike **loop**, tips missing. Length 47mm, head diameter 15mm. *4813*, unphased deposit, Settlement 7.

SF3684 Lead strip **rivet**, with two shanks and rove intact. Length 22mm, width 8mm, height 11mm. Unstratified.

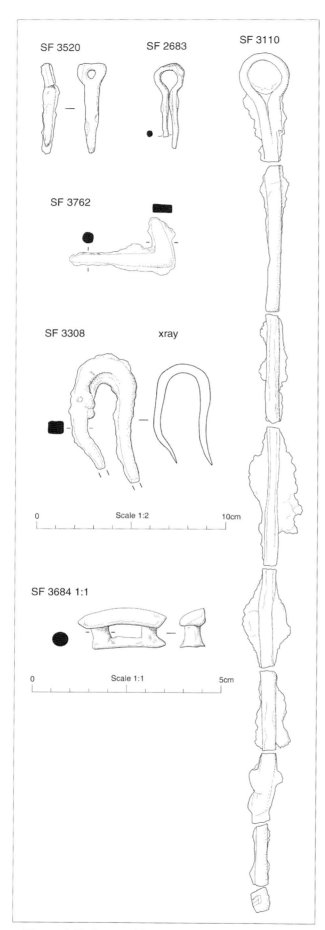

Figure 6.32 Iron and lead fittings. Scale 1:1 and 1:2

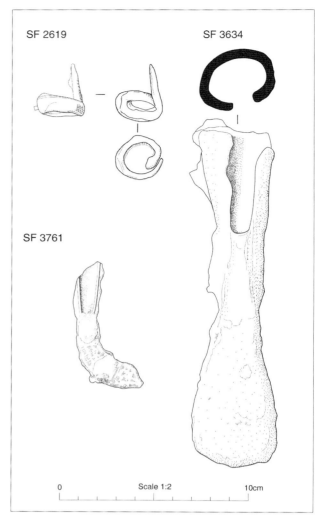

Figure 6.33 Iron agricultural equipment. Scale 1:2

Agricultural equipment
(Fig. 6.33)

Two goad pricks, one from Settlement 7 and one unstratified, would have been used to drive plough-oxen or to herd other animals to pasture or to slaughter. At some sites, animals may have been driven to ritual slaughter as sacrificial beasts; five goad pricks were found at the shrine of Apollo at Nettleton and one from the shrine of Nodens at Lydney (Wedlake 1982, 49; Wheeler and Wheeler 1932, 189). The other implements all came from Settlement 6, comprising a spud or hoe, a rake prong and a socketed-hook used in pruning and similar horticultural or agricultural tasks. Given the small size of this group of objects, it is unlikely that the apparent distinction here of animals in Settlement 7 and arable crops in Settlement 6 is meaningful, especially as the stratified goad prick came from the yard surface (*5534*) in Settlement 7 that contained much scrap ironwork (see Miscellaneous, below).

Catalogue of illustrated items

SF2619 Iron **goad-prick**, with one coil below the spike. Diameter 25mm, length 33mm. Unstratified.

SF3634 Iron **spud** or **hoe** with large open socket. Length 185mm, maximum diameter of socket 39mm. See Manning 1985, pl. 19, F14–F15. *13505*, external deposit, Settlement 6. Period 4.2.

SF3761 Small socketed **hook**; most of the blade is missing, what remains is blunt. Length 70mm. *14076*, fill of ditch *14077*, Settlement 6. Period 4.4.

Military equipment
(Fig. 6.34)
Apart from a 2nd- or 3rd-century fitting from auxiliary equipment, and possibly some or all of the Hod Hill brooches (see Dress Accessories, above), the only items from Love's Farm that have been classed as military equipment are several fragments of *armillae*, armlets awarded to ranks below centurion for force of arms in battle. This attribution is based on the Claudian-Neronian date and military context of several stratified examples and on links between the decorative motifs used on the armlets and on both military belt-plates and Hod Hill and Aucissa brooches (Crummy 2005b). For example, the terminal design on SF 1167 derives from the candelabra-and-leaves motif or crossed thunderbolts-and-spears motif, both of which occur on military belt-plates (Grew and Griffiths 1991, 57; Deschler-Erb 1999, taf. 17, 353, taf. 19; Crummy 2005b, fig. 4). These armlets are a distinctive type that occurs widely in the south-east of England and they were probably specific to the conquest of Britain, awarded after engagements in the early years of the campaign. All the examples from Love's Farm belong to Group A, which has two longitudinal rows of cabled decoration (Crummy 2005b, 96).

One terminal fragment came from layer *6572* (Pl. 4.2), on the western periphery of Settlement 6, and may be the earliest item from that context; the others are all unstratified or from the fills of earlier negative features. They form the largest collection yet recovered from one site, and raise the question of the relationship of Love's Farm to historical events running from the conquest to the Boudican revolt. The mechanisms by which military awards reached rural settlements would have been very varied, ranging from battles or skirmishes, the requisitioning of supplies, tax-gathering, votive offerings, or the settling of veterans on land where they could provide a degree of protection to the developing infrastructure (Crummy 2005b, 100). The proximity of Love's Farm to the point where Ermine Street crossed the River Great Ouse may be pertinent to several of these possibilities.

Catalogue of illustrated items

SF2803 Terminal fragment of a copper alloy *armilla* with marginal grooves and two bands of angled 'S-shaped' punch marks set across pairs of parallel grooves. As the hoop expands towards the terminal a second marginal groove is introduced on the undamaged edge. On the terminal four palmette stamps are flanked by two transverse bead-rows, probably made with a toothed wheel. Maximum diameter approximately 60mm, maximum width 18mm. Palmette stamps also occur on *armillae* from Hamperden End, Essex, Verulamium, Hertfordshire, and Hockwold-cum-Wilton, Norfolk (Crummy 2005b, fig. 3, 12, 22 and 30). *6572*, alluvial deposit, Settlement 6. Period 4.2.

SF63 Fragment of a copper alloy *armilla* with a central groove flanked by two bands of angled S-shaped punchmarks set across pairs of parallel grooves, as SF 1167 below. Length (bent) 28mm, width 14mm. *300*, fill of posthole *301*, Settlement 3. Period 3.3.

SF1030 Very worn flat fragment of a copper alloy *armilla*, retaining only traces of the pairs of parallel grooves over which are dots representing each end of the 'S-shaped' punch marks. Length 27mm, width 21mm. *4896*, fill of ditch *4897*, Enclosure 132, Settlement 7 (Phase 2). Period 4.4.

SF1167 Terminal fragment of a copper alloy *armilla*, with a central groove flanked by two bands of angled 'S-shaped' punch marks set across pairs of parallel grooves as on SF 63. The fragment widens slightly at the terminal, which bears a floret of four petals with a central ring-and-dot and a ring-and-dot in each angle. Length 25mm, maximum width 15mm. There are two similar fragments with the same motif on the terminal from Baldock, Hertfordshire (Crummy 2005b, 102, fig. 3, 16 and 18). Unstratified.

SF3000 Terminal fragment of a cast copper alloy *armilla*, with ridged and grooved section and marginal mouldings defined by grooves. There is a row of annulets down the centre flanked by two bands of angled 'S-shaped' punch marks set across rounded ridges between pairs of parallel grooves. The terminal was hammered flat to remove the ridges and grooves and is consequently slightly wider than the main part of the hoop. The deep grooves of the paired parallel grooves are still visible. There are two transverse rows of large annulets across the terminal, flanked by two rows of smaller ones. Maximum diameter about 60mm, width 17mm. Annulets occur on the terminals of *armillae* from Stansted and Harlow, Essex, Baldock, Hertfordshire, and Stonea Camp, Cambridgeshire, although the designs all differ from this example (Crummy 2005b, fig. 3, 14, 17, 11, 15 and 28). Unstratified.

SF2062 Fragment of a copper alloy *armilla*, with two bands of angled 'S-shaped' punch marks set across pairs of parallel grooves. Length 26mm, width 17.5mm. Unstratified.

SF1295 Bent fragment of a copper alloy *armilla*, with marginal mouldings and two bands of close-set angled 'S-shaped' punch marks set across pairs of parallel grooves. Length (bent) 19mm, width 18mm. Unstratified.

SF1202 Convex circular copper alloy **mount** from auxiliary military equipment. There are two riveted projections on the reverse for attachment to leather. Similar mounts are found in late 2nd- to 3rd-century contexts on the German *limes*, and Oldenstein suggests that they were purely ornamental (1976, 186, 7, taf. 56). *11615*, unphased deposit, Settlement 6.

Religion
(Fig. 6.35)
Although only a bell fragment and a group of plain rings are catalogued here as votive items, many other objects were, or may have been, used in this way, principally dress accessories and coins. All these items and their link to ritual behaviour at Love's Farm are discussed in the Small Finds overview (above), and in more detail in Chapter 9.IX.

The bell fragment is unstratified but many of the plain rings came from layer *6572* (Pl. 4.2), and therefore may have been deposited as votive offerings. Plain rings served a variety of purposes, for example as strap-junctions on harness, but as offerings they were used to represent the wheel of the sky god. They were used in this way at the sanctuary at Uley, Gloucestershire, and at several sanctuaries in Gaul (Bayley and Woodward 1993; Pommeret 2001, fig. 7, 76–7, fig. 8, 78–96; Feugère 2002). The section of the rings from Love's Farm varies, and one is penannular, made from a rolled copper alloy strip.

Catalogue of illustrated items

SF1244 Rim fragment from a small copper alloy **bell** with round mouth. Diameter (if complete) 27mm; surviving height 17mm. Unstratified.

SF2771 Plain copper alloy round-section **ring**. Diameter 22mm. *6572*, alluvial deposit, Settlement 6. Period 4.2.

SF2788 Copper alloy polygonal-section **ring**. There is a deep groove on the outer edge. Diameter 19mm. *6572*, alluvial deposit, Settlement 6. Period 4.2.

SF2800 Plain worn copper alloy **ring** with narrow round-edged section. Diameter 22mm. *6572*, alluvial deposit, Settlement 6. Period 4.2.

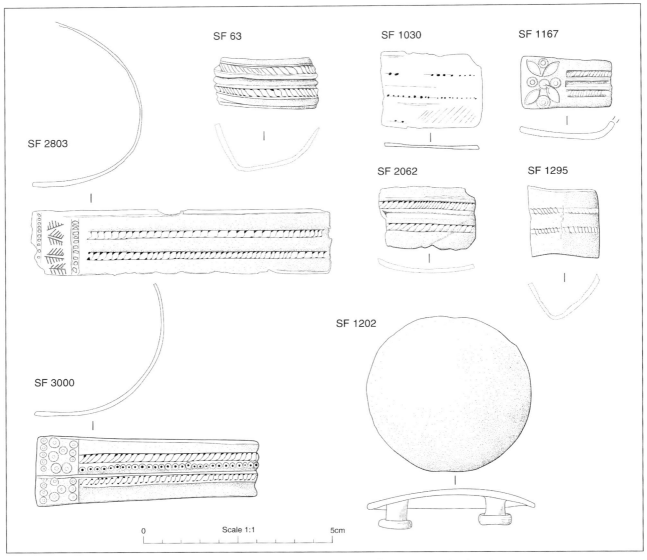

Figure 6.34 Copper alloy *armilla* and military mount. Scale 1:1

SF2802 Plain copper alloy **ring** with 'D-shaped' section. Diameter 21.5mm. *6572*, alluvial deposit, Settlement 6. Period 4.2.

SF2933 Copper alloy strip rolled into a **ring** with overlapping terminals. Both ends are cut, one on the slant. There is a short slight groove at that end. Diameter 18mm. *8013*, fill of ditch *8013*, Boundary 2, Settlement 6. Period 4.1.

SF3306 Plain copper alloy **ring** with square section. Diameter 22mm. *11803*, fill of 'oven', Enclosure 109, Settlement 7. Period 4.2.

SF1051 Plain copper alloy **ring** with 'lozenge-shaped' section. Diameter 27mm. *10438*, Enclosure 136, Settlement 7 (Phase 2). Period 4.4.

SF3700 Small copper alloy **ring** of circular section. Diameter 16mm, section diameter 2mm. *14189*, unphased deposit.

SF3605 Copper alloy **ring** of slightly faceted circular section. Diameter 30mm, section diameter 3mm. *14189*, unphased deposit.

SF1008 Plain copper alloy **ring** with flattened polygonal section. Diameter 26mm. Unstratified.

SF1256 Plain copper alloy **ring** with 'lozenge-shaped' section. Diameter 29mm. Unstratified.

SF2855 Plain copper alloy **ring** with irregular flattened polygonal section. Diameter 27mm. Unstratified.

SF1099 Plain copper alloy **ring** with 'D-shaped' section; possibly a finger-ring. Diameter 22mm. Unstratified.

SF2873 Small distorted wire **ring** with the terminals secured by interlocking hooks. Maximum diameter 12.5mm. Unstratified.

Metalworking
(Figs 6.36–6.38)

The objects associated with metalworking are divided below into tools and metalworking debris (further comments on metalworking at the site are given by Starley, below). The number of items involved is not large and they come from both Romano-British settlements (Settlements 6 and 7) and from other contexts. The debris includes both copper alloy and iron fragments, but only one of the copper alloy pieces is stratified and the others may be post-Roman. The iron debris consists chiefly of offcuts of smith's blanks, which would have been imported from outside the site, probably from quarrying and smelting sites in Northamptonshire or north Norfolk. Two of the six pieces from Settlement 6 come from the perimeter ditch of Enclosure 115 (Period 4.3) and three were recovered from a pit in Enclosure 119 (Period 4.4). Although these numbers are too low for the finds to be termed concentrations, they nevertheless provide some pointer towards to the location of smithing activity on the site.

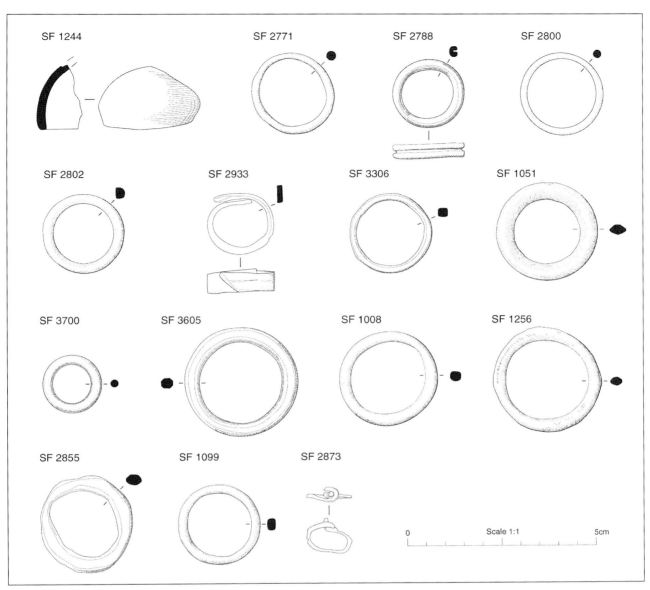

Figure 6.35 Copper alloy bell and rings. Scale 1:1

The tools consist of an anvil and five punches. The anvil (SF 3760) is most similar to a 3rd-century example from a pottery manufacturing site at Hasholme, Yorkshire (Manning 1985, fig. 1, 2), with no step to mark the depth to which it was seated into a wooden block or bench. At 25kg, the Love's Farm anvil may be described as of average weight. An anvil in the Waltham Abbey hoard, although quite large, weighed only 4.3kg, the Hasholme anvil is 13kg, while the upper end of the range is marked by a 50.5kg anvil from Sutton Walls hillfort in Herefordshire (Kenyon 1953, 64; Manning 1975; 1985, 1). At Love's Farm, the deposition of the anvil in the fill of a Period 4.3 ditch probably marked the abandonment and clearance of a smithy (see Structure 108, Period 4.4 and Pl. 4.9). Clearing out a smithy emphasises the value of the tools, bloomery iron, and iron scrap, all of which could be reused. A smithy in Southwark was only identifiable by the hearths and a little iron-working waste. Here, most debris that could not be reused was probably dumped a short distance away: four iron objects were recovered from the smithy's final phase of use (Drummond-Murray and Thompson 2002, 61–2, 67, 83, 98). Similarly, a smithy at Stanton Low, Buckinghamshire, was represented by an anvil and small dumps of scrap, the former perhaps too heavy to move and the latter perhaps of little potential for reuse, but the only tool recovered was a chisel (Woodfield and Johnson 1989, 231, 234, fig. 38). At the other extreme the large Mantles Green site in Buckinghamshire, part of a villa estate occupied for most of the Roman period, produced six anvils and a scatter of other smith's tools (Stewart and Kempster 1992, 149–51, fig. 27, nos 1–3, 5).

Catalogue of illustrated items

Fig. 6.36

SF3760 Iron block **anvil**, with rounded edges to the working face. One side is extended just below the top by an accretion of slaggy residue. No punching hole has been located. Height 240mm, maximum dimensions at top 165 by 170mm (extending to 200mm below working surface), base 120 by 90mm. Weight 25kg. *14078*, fill of ditch *14079*, Settlement 6. Period 4.3.

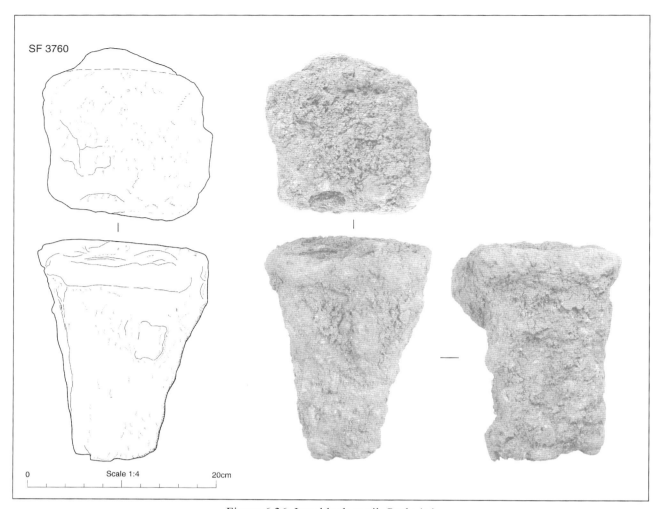

Figure 6.36 Iron block anvil. Scale 1:4

Fig. 6.37

SF2506 Iron **punch** with worn but not burred head. At the tip the shank narrows to a blunt point. Length 111mm. *10435*, Enclosure 136, Settlement 7 (Phase 2). Period 4.4.

SF2564 Iron **punch** shank fragment, narrowing to a chisel edge. Length 43mm, width at edge 6mm. *4966*, fill of ditch *4967*, Boundary 112, Settlement 7 (Phase 1). Period 4.4.

SF2366 Iron **punch** with flat round head not much wider than the square-section shank. Length 85mm. *5339*, fill of post-medieval ditch *5340*

SF3307 Iron **punch** or chisel with burred square head. The stem is round in section, the blade is shouldered. The edge is worn from use. Length 167mm, diameter of stem 14mm. The form of this tool is not matched among the Roman sets, chisels and punches in the British Museum (Manning 1985, 9–11, 21–4). *11808*, fill of pit *11809*. Unphased feature, Settlement 6.

SF3229 Iron ?**punch** tip, rectangular in section. Length 58mm, section 7 by 4mm. Unstratified.

Fig. 6.38

SF2269 Square-section **shank**, probably a fragment of bar-iron but possibly the shank of a punch. Length 42mm, section 7 x 7mm. *5076*, Enclosure 131, Settlement 7 (Phase 2). Period 4.4

SF2397 Slightly tapering fragment of **bar-iron**. Length 42mm, maximum width 14mm. *5344*, cobbled yard surface, Settlement 7 (Phase 2). Period 4.4.

Miscellaneous
(Figs 6.39–6.41)

The miscellaneous metalwork is divided below by material and within material by period. Many of the copper alloy items consist of fragments of sheet, some of which came from layer *6572* on the western edge of Settlement 6, and may perhaps be associated with the box cladding catalogued as household equipment. Much of the ironwork also consists of sheet fragments, and a large proportion of the pieces are scrap incorporated into Period 4.4 yard surface *5344* in Settlement 7.

A particularly distinctive, but unidentified, iron object (SF 3106) came from the base of Period 3.3 ditch *10747* in Enclosure 1 within Settlement 6. The identification of this object, and even its original form, is far from certain. In its present state it consists of three parallel narrow bars welded together at one end into a spike; the other ends of the bars are broken off at different lengths. They may have come together to form a second spike at the missing end, although the longest narrows towards the break, or they may have developed into any other shape. If the object was meant to be used horizontally, then the bars are too thin to support much weight, which precludes use as a fire dog or, combined with the large gap between the bars, as a gridiron. It may, however, have rested across a pair of fire dogs to form a more substantial base. The spike may have been set into a long wooden rod to form a handle. If so, the

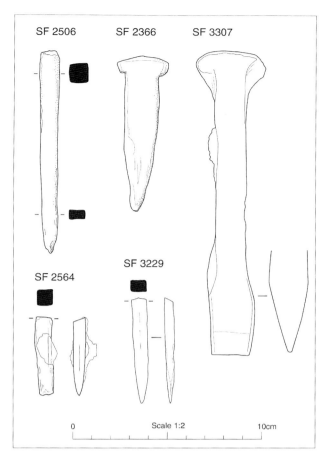

Figure 6.37 Iron punches. Scale 1:2

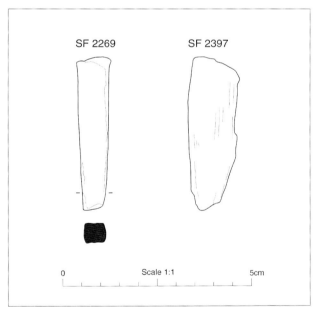

Figure 6.38 Iron bar fragments. Scale 1:1

bars are disproportionately long to be part of a working fish spear, but the object could have been mounted upright as a totem. All these suggestions are highly speculative.

Catalogue of illustrated items

Fig. 6.39: Copper alloy

SF3446 Spatulate **fragment**, with both sides of the narrower section flanged to form a socket. Length 29mm, maximum width 6.5mm. *3704*, fill of gully *3705*, Structure 2, Settlement 3. Period 3.3.

SF2774 Irregularly-shaped **fragment** with a transverse moulding at one end. Length 53mm, maximum width 12.5mm. *6572*, alluvial deposit, Settlement 6. Period 4.2.

SF2773 Hooked **bar** with broken tip. The upper end is rectangular in section and has notches on each side near the terminal. The lower end is narrower and 'D-shaped' in section. Length 39mm, maximum width 5mm. *6572*, alluvial deposit, Settlement 6. Period 4.2.

SF2942 Tapering copper alloy **strip**, flanged at one end to form a socket, as SF 3446 above. The narrower end is plain, the broader end has feathered edges and a line of small dots down the centre. Length 26mm, maximum width 4.5mm. *11596*, unphased deposit, Settlement 6.

SF1145 Damaged polygonal tubular **fitting**, tapering at each end. Length 36.5mm, maximum diameter 13mm. *4813*, unphased deposit, Settlement 7.

SF1296 Spoon-shaped **fitting** with a lug at one end and a broken concave shaft at the other. Length 33mm, width 17mm. Possibly medieval or later. Unstratified.

SF1293 A square **shank** with a thickened broken terminal and flared scoop. The scoop is triangular, with raised edges, and is fluted at the lower end. Length (bent) 73mm, maximum width of scoop 17mm. Unstratified.

Fig. 6.40: Iron

SF2386 Rectangular **sheet** fragment with one end missing. There is a rivet in the two surviving corners and a third in the centre of the broken end. Length 45mm, width 40mm. *5344*, cobbled yard surface, Settlement 7 (Phase 2). Period 4.4.

SF2569 Two figure-of-eight-shaped **chain-links**, one complete and one incomplete. Length of complete link 32mm, maximum width 12mm. *5676*, fill of ditch *5642*, Enclosure 139, Settlement 7. Period 4.5.

SF3165 Curvilinear **plaque** fragment with a clenched nail for attachment *in situ*. 44 x 24mm; nail length 24mm, clenched to give a wood thickness of 13mm. Possibly a box fitting. *5915*, unphased deposit.

Fig. 6.41: Iron

SF3106 Iron **object** consisting of three thin parallel bars (in fragments) with the outer two angled inwards at one end to meet the central one and all three then welded together to form a spike. All are square to rectangular in section and all are incomplete, but they were probably originally all the same length. The longest outer bar is now about 530mm to the angle, the other 215mm to the angle, and the central one 320mm including the spike. In total the length is about 760mm and the width 230mm. The bars range in width from about 10mm at the spiked end to about 3mm at the tip of the longest. *10748*, fill of ditch *10747*, Enclosure 1, Settlement 6. Period 3.3.

Post-Roman metalwork
(Fig. 6.42)

A saucer brooch (SF 2881), a buckle (SF 1269) and a silver strip (SF 1070) all probably date to the early Anglo-Saxon period. The brooch dates to the later 6th century and the buckle is either of 6th-century date or slightly later (Marzinzik 2003, 51, pl. 141, 1 left, pl. 142, 3 left and right). The silver strip with its stamped decoration on the margins is almost certainly part of an armlet, comparable to 6th-century silver spiral armlets from Tuddenham and Holywell Row in Suffolk, and from Norton in Cleveland (Lethbridge 1931, 8, fig. 2, 3; Kennett 1977, 40, 53, pl. 1,

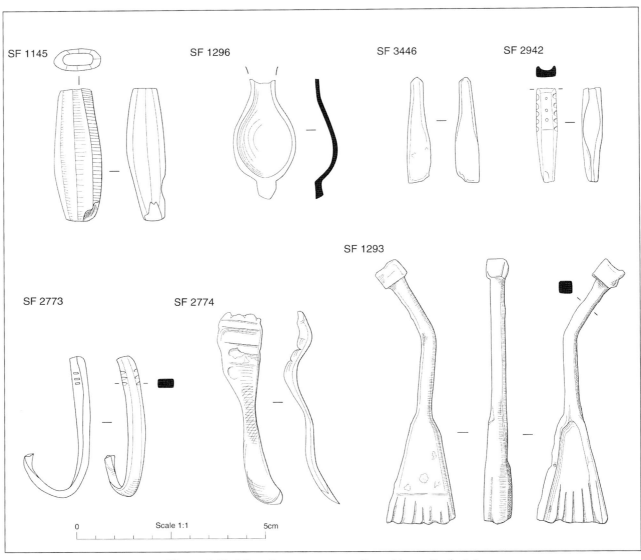

Figure 6.39 Miscellaneous copper alloy objects. Scale 1:1

fig. 1, 2; Sherlock and Welch 1992, fig. 45). The Love's Farm piece has broken at one end and has been reworked for some form of secondary use, the gap in the marginal decoration having been filled by different stamps to those around the rest of the strip.

The objects are not concentrated on one particular part of the site; the strip comes from a boundary ditch in Settlement 7 and the buckle was recovered from a post-medieval or modern context in the general area of Settlement 6, whilst the brooch is unstratified.

Catalogue of illustrated items

SF2881 Cast copper alloy **brooch**, with gilding on the upper surface. Parts of the rim, the iron pin, and the catch plate are missing. Diameter 42.5mm. The grooves on the rim are alternately two long and narrow followed by one short and wide, producing a tongue-and-double-groove effect. One plain and one knurled moulding surround the central field, which is filled with spiral decoration. This is based on the five-spiral type but is lighter and more complex, with the triangles that usually lie between the centres on the outer edge incorporated as tendrils, and with an inner group of five spirals surrounding the integral central stud. Two lugs on the reverse retain the iron axial bar for the sprung pin. Unstratified.

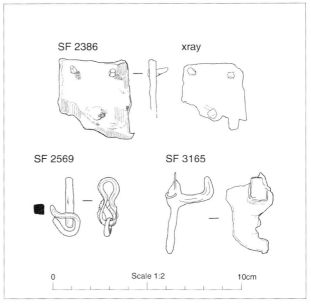

Figure 6.40 Miscellaneous metalwork. Scale 1:2

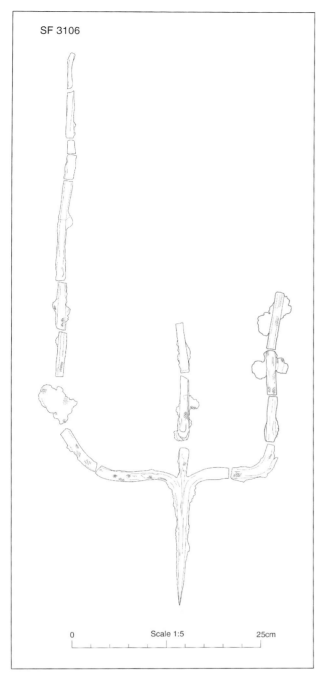

Figure 6.41 Iron object. Scale 1:5

SF1269 Small copper alloy oval **buckle** of Marzinzik's Typegroup II.24b-i, with a folded rectangular belt-plate secured at the end by two rivets. There are traces of white-metal plating on the surface. Length 22mm, width of buckle loop 12.5mm, width of belt-plate 7.5mm. *7643*, modern.

SF1070 Silver **strip**, more or less triangular in shape, with one end original, narrow and rounded, and, the other damaged, wider and straight. The widest part of the metal lies off-centre, but closer to the undamaged end, not the damaged one as would be expected if the object had been originally symmetrical. The metal on the reverse of the damaged end is covered with fine transverse striations, probably from secondary working. Along the long straight edge is a line of horseshoe-shaped stamps, and along the angled sides a line of large stamps in the form of horse heads, created by a central slightly flattened annulet with one set of transverse grooves beneath it and two above it. At the damaged end these lines of stamps do not meet as they do at the original end, and the gap is filled by two pairs of triangular stamps set apex to apex (to form angular hour-glass shapes). Length 84mm, maximum width 20.5mm. *10442*, fill of Boundary 120, Settlement 7. Period 5.

Medieval and post-medieval metalwork
A large quantity of metalwork dating to the medieval, post-medieval and modern periods was recovered from the site; the assemblage is not reported here, but is summarised in the site archive. Much of the material probably reached the site in midden waste from the nearby town of St Neots, and from Love's Farm itself.

IV. Metalworking debris
by David Starley

Summary
Analysis of the metalworking debris from Love's Farm indicates that localised iron smithing was the only significant metalworking activity that took place on the site from the late Iron Age to the late Roman period. During the 4th century AD, a smithy may have operated on the southern periphery of Settlement 6, within a small timber building (Structure 108, Fig. 4.20); a rare discovery of an anvil was also made close by (see Crummy, above, and Pl. 4.9). No hearths or floors survived within the structure, and debris was generally found within pits, ditches and other features outside the building, or within its construction trenches. Other pit hearths elsewhere on the site may also have been used for heating iron, although their primary purpose is more likely to have been domestic.

Methodology
In total, 18kg of metalworking debris were visually examined; a full catalogue of the assemblage is available in the archive. Most of the material was hand-collected during the excavation, although further debris was recovered from spoil heaps with the aid of metal detectors. Of the many environmental samples taken during the excavation, only a selection of those from Settlement 6 (in the area of the probable smithy) were systematically checked for hammerscale by passing a magnet through the sieve residues, although occasionally more of this debris was reported from routine examination of flotation residues.

The metalworking debris was classified into standard categories based on those used by the former English Heritage Ancient Monuments Laboratory. Visual observation of the exterior was supplemented by examination of fresh fracture surfaces, the use of a geological streak plate and magnet. Table 6.10 presents a summary of the findings, based on the categories used and the metalworking or other activities which are implied by the debris.

Classification of terms

Diagnostic: iron smithing
Evidence for iron smithing comes in two forms: bulk slags and micro slags. Of the bulk slags, the most easily recognisable are normally the smithing hearth bottoms which generally have a characteristic plano-convex section, typically with a rough convex base and a vitrified upper surface which is flat or slightly hollowed as a result of the downward pressure of air from the tuyère.

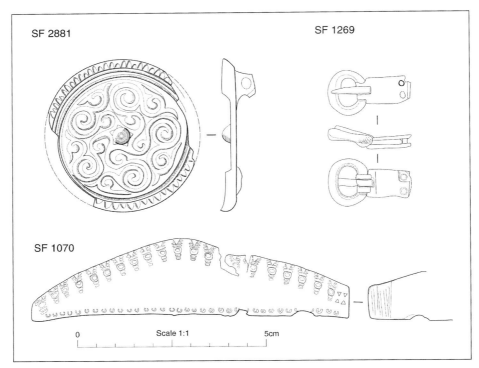

Figure 6.42 Early Anglo-Saxon metalwork. Scale 1:1

Compositionally, smithing hearth bottoms are predominantly fayalitic (iron silicate) and form as a result of high temperature reactions between the iron, iron-scale and silica from either the clay hearth lining or possibly sand used as a flux by the smith.

In addition to bulk slags, iron smithing also produces micro slag of two types (Starley 1995). Flake hammerscale consists of fish-scale like fragments of the oxide/silicate skin of the iron dislodged during working. Spheroidal hammerscale results from the solidification of small droplets of liquid slag expelled during hot working, particularly when two objects are being fire-welded together or when the slag-rich bloom of iron is first worked into a billet or bar. Hammerscale is considered important in interpreting a site not only because it is highly diagnostic of smithing but also because it tends to build up in the immediate vicinity of the smithing hearth and anvil. It may therefore give a more precise location of the activity than the bulk slags which may be transported elsewhere for disposal (Mills and McDonnell 1992).

Undiagnostic: ferrous metalworking
The largest category of metalworking material found at Love's Farm was that recorded as undiagnostic

Activity	Classification	Wt (g)	No. contexts
Smelting	Tap slag, furnace bottom, ore *etc.*	0	0
Smithing	Smithing hearth bottom	4591	11
	Flake hammerscale	Not quantified	3
	Spheroidal hammerscale	0	0
Undiagnostic ironworking	Undiagnostic ironworking slag	6010	44
	Fayalitic runs	13	1
	Iron-rich cinder	79	2
	Iron object/fragment	194	6
Non-ferrous metalworking	Crucible fragment	9	1
	Undiagnostic metalworking slag	10	1
Metalworking or other high-temp process	Vitrified hearth/furnace lining	729	21
	Cinder	341	23
	Fired clay	4	1
	Fuel ash slag/burned daub	5201	21
	Burned stone	5	1
Fuel		0	0
Non-slag	Ferruginous concretion	44	1
	Stone	761	4
Total		*17981*	

Table 6.10 Summary of metallurgical debris

ironworking slag. Such irregularly shaped fayalitic slags are produced by both the iron smelting and iron smithing processes. Given the total absence of smelting evidence from the site, however, it can safely be said that all the material from Love's Farm derived from smithing. A single, smaller dribble of similarly dense slag was classified as a fayalitic run, a type known, from experimental reconstructions, to form in both smelting furnaces and smithing hearths, but assumed here to be from smithing. Iron-rich cinder was distinguished by its significant content of iron not chemically combined as silicates, but visible as rust-orange coloured hydrated iron oxides and iron hydroxides. It would also normally be considered undiagnostic, except where other evidence points only to a single activity, in this case smithing. Certain pieces of 'slag' were shown by their cracked surfaces and testing with a magnet to contain significant amounts of metallic iron. Whilst it is possible that iron artefacts such as nails might be unrecognisable if sufficiently heat affected or corroded, these iron lumps may well include waste fragments from the smithing process.

Undiagnostic: metalworking or other high temperature process
Several of the categories of material can be produced by a wide range of high temperature activities and are of little help in distinguishing between these processes. Material identified as vitrified hearth/furnace lining may derive either from ironworking or, particularly with fragments showing brightly coloured glazes or copper alloy corrosion, from non-ferrous metalworking (only one fragment of the Love's Farm material showed this characteristic). This material forms as a result of a high temperature reaction between the clay lining of the hearth/furnace and the alkali fuel ash or fayalitic slag. It may show a compositional gradient from unmodified fired clay on one surface to an irregular cindery material on the other. A material associated with vitrified lining was classed as cinder. This comprises a porous, hard and brittle slag formed by the reaction between the alkali fuel ash and fragments of clay that had spalled away from the hearth/furnace lining, or another source of silica, such as the sand sometimes used as a flux during smithing.

The small amount of fired clay without any surface vitrification found within the assemblage could have derived from structures associated with metallurgical purposes, or from those used for other high temperature activities. A significant mass of debris was classified as fuel ash slag/burned daub – a material of lightweight porous nature which suggests a process other than metalwork, possibly the conflagration of daub-built structures. Such material has been recognised elsewhere during this period, for example at Bob's Wood, Hinchingbrooke (Oxford Archaeology East, in prep.) and has been referred to as 'Iron Age Grey' amongst some specialists (Fosberry and Eley 2005).

Fuel
Although no individual pieces of coal, coke or charcoal were seen, impressions of the latter were commonly encountered in the undiagnostic ironworking debris, suggesting that this was the usual fuel for working iron.

	Wt (g)	Length (mm)	Width (mm)	Depth (mm)
Range	103–1065	70–190	45–130	20–75
Mean	425	103	75	39
Std dev.	325	36	22	15

Table 6.11 Smithing hearth bottom dimensions, all phases

Copper alloy casting debris
A single small fragment of crucible was identified, which showed flecks of liverish red material on the interior. This was apparently a rim fragment, heated in such a way that the top and interior were more vitrified, a feature normally associated with Iron Age rather than Roman crucibles.

Other material
The category of material identified as ferruginous concretion forms as a result of the redeposition of iron hydroxides, a process similar to iron panning. On archaeological sites such material may be of relevance in identifying ironworking activities and deserves close examination, since its formation is likely to be enhanced by the nature of the surrounding archaeological deposits. In particular, examination may reveal the presence of hammerscale within concretions and help to identify the location of iron smithing.

Hammerscale
As discussed above, hammerscale provides an important indicator of the location and extent of iron smithing on the site. In relation to Settlement 6, where an anvil was recovered, a number of residues from environmental samples recovered from in and around a possible smithy (Period 4.4, Structure 108) had a magnet passed through them and this fraction was sent to the specialist. These small samples were weighed and a visual estimate made of the percentage of both spheroidal and flake hammerscale present. The material recovered from these samples provides supporting evidence for the presence of iron smithing in the form of both flake and spheroidal hammerscale. The quantities, however, are small (46g in total), the largest quantity (29g) coming from the construction trench (*14133*), which formed the south-east corner of Structure 108.

In addition, hammerscale was also noted in the flotation residues from a number of environmental samples. The results are discussed in the following two sections which examine the chronological and spatial distribution of both bulk and micro slags.

Metalworking activity by phase
(Fig. 6.43)
The total mass of bulk metalworking debris has been grouped by activity and by phase (Table 6.12 and Fig. 6.43). The results clearly demonstrate that virtually no slag was recovered from contexts pre-dating the late Iron Age or post-dating late Roman occupation and that the mass of the debris assemblage as a whole is split fairly evenly between the various Iron Age and Roman phases.

The Iron Age assemblage contains a very high proportion of undiagnostic material, particularly fuel ash slag/burned daub which may not be connected to any

Period	Non-ferrous	Smithing	Undiagnostic	Fuel ash/daub	High temp/other	Total
3.1	0	0	0	0	0	0
3.2	0	82	0	13	0	95
3.3	0	1375	225	3533	48	5181
3.4	0	0	211	343	27	581
3.5	0	0	150	1059	21	1230
Combined Iron Age	0	1457	586	4948	96	7087
4.1	0	714	387	52	76	1229
4.2	0	0	194	6	102	302
4.3	0	1454	1329	75	46	2904
4.4	9	124	2574	2	552	3261
4.5	0	139	0	0	0	139
Combined Roman	9	2431	4484	135	776	7835
Total	9	3888	5070	5083	872	14922

Table 6.12 Metalworking debris from Iron Age and Roman deposits (weight in grams)

metalworking activity. More certain evidence of Iron Age metalworking comes in the form of diagnostic smithing debris which derives almost entirely from two hearth pits (see below). The Roman assemblage indicates a greater concentration of smithing debris (and the probably associated undiagnostic ironworking debris), in Periods 4.3 and 4.4, i.e. during the 3rd and 4th centuries AD. Likewise, the hammerscale results from the vicinity of Structure 108 in Settlement 6 also span this period, although it is possible that smithing activity in this area commenced as early as Period 4.2. All the quantities are small, however, and on the basis of the slag alone the site cannot be seen as the location of more than low-level iron smithing activity.

Statistical examination of the smithing hearth bottoms in Table 6.13 shows the Roman examples to have the typical range of sizes for the period – the mean for the small number of Iron Age examples is heavily biased by a single hearth bottom of very large size (SF 3720, below).

Distribution of metalworking debris

The 18kg of metalworking debris came from a total of 104 contexts spread over the site. With few exceptions, the debris all derived from the fills of features such as ditches, gullies, postholes and beamslots. For the most part, the low quantities present within individual features do not suggest systematic filling; more probably, debris was randomly deposited within these features, together with other material detritus, and it is therefore unclear how close to the original production site they were deposited. Notably, however, some localised concentrations were evident.

The only features which might have represented structural remains associated with smithing were two hearth pits (*50143* and *73001*) associated with the Period 3.3 occupation within Settlement 4, in which hammerscale was found when processing environmental soil samples. No bulk slag came from these features, nor from the same area of the site, suggesting that these may have been domestic hearths used simply for heating iron prior to simple re-shaping without the full range of blacksmithing operations which would produce other forms of debris. West of hearth *50143*, a modest amount of ironworking debris was recovered from a few Period 3.3 ditches, together with a very large smithing hearth bottom (SF 3720). The latter is rather at odds with other evidence for this phase, but does suggest that substantial iron smithing may have taken place in the vicinity during this early period. In the late pre-Roman Iron Age (Period 3.4) there is slight evidence for ironsmithing, with hammerscale being reported in a deposit (*4279*) associated with Roundhouse 7, within Settlement 2.

More significant metalworking deposits were found in various ditches and pits associated with Settlement 6, in which low levels of various ironworking slags continued to be deposited from the late Iron Age to the 2nd century AD. The settlement then appears to have seen intensified activity in the 3rd and 4th centuries. This activity may have spread further north, to the area of Enclosures 119 and 120 (at the north-western corner of the settlement) in the 4th century, since the latter produced the single crucible sherd recovered from the site, as well as

Period	Count	Mass: mean (g)	Min. (g)	Max. (g)	Std dev. (g)
3. Iron Age*	3	513	164	1065	395
4. Roman	6	405	103	967	330
Unphased	2	352	309	394	43

* includes results from one half hearth bottom, scaled up to original dimensions

Table 6.13 Smithing hearth bottoms by site period

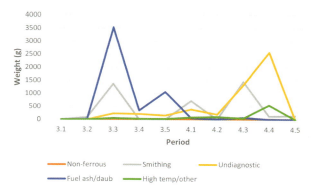

Figure 6.43 Metalworking debris through time

ironworking debris. At the south-eastern corner of the settlement, the construction trenches of Structure 108 (Period 4.4) yielded hammerscale and bulk ironworking debris, albeit in small quantities. Ditches immediately to the north also contained small amounts of debris. It should be stressed that the quantity of metalworking debris examined represents a very limited amount of metalworking, although the site's sampling strategy, the truncation of deposits and possibly removal of debris from the site are all likely to have lessened the amount of material recovered or recoverable. On the basis of examination of the debris, the identification of this as an area where iron smithing took place appears sound and is supported by the metal finds (Crummy, above). A ferrous object, interpreted as a smith's blank (SF 3813; not illustrated), came from a 3rd-century context (*13567*). More significantly, however, an extremely rare surviving ironworker's anvil (Fig. 6.36, SF 3760) had, apparently been deliberately placed in a ditch terminal, close to Structure 108. Although a number of tools which could have been used for ironworking were found on the site, including chisels (Fig. 6.37), their specific use (or uses) cannot be conclusively established.

Conclusions
Dominating the site's metalworking assemblage is evidence for iron smithing, which evidently took place from the late Iron Age through to the late Roman period, with the 3rd and 4th centuries providing most evidence quantitatively. There is no evidence for any fuel other than charcoal, which contrasts with the apparent use of coal at the site of Bob's Wood, Hinchingbrooke (Oxford Archaeology East, in prep.) only a few kilometres to the north.

No unambiguous smithing features were evident at Love's Farm, but the identification of a possible late Roman smithy delineated by construction trenches containing slag and hammerscale, provides the strongest candidate for such a specialised structure. Occasional finds of hammerscale elsewhere on the site, sometimes associated with hearths, may suggest that some working of iron might have been carried out in an otherwise domestic context. The large numbers of iron finds at Love's Farm demonstrate the importance of ferrous alloys for tools, fittings and the ubiquitous nails. How much of this could have been produced on site, perhaps using iron from the smelting sites on the nearby Jurassic Ridge, is difficult to deduce from the limited remains. The discovery of a substantial anvil, however, does suggest that the site would once have been home to a specialist smith, able to undertake the manufacture and repair of a wide range of artefacts.

Significantly Love's Farm's proximity to the Jurassic Ridge – considered to be the third most important area for Roman iron production in Britain after the Weald and Forest of Dean – brings the site into an area whose iron production and use was examined and published by Irene Schrüfer-Kolb (2004). She divides sites firstly into those in small towns, secondly into a lower level with blacksmiths' workshops on rural settlements and finally (and more frequently) into rural sites where 'domestic' smithing activities were carried out in hearths also used for other purposes. Love's Farm appears to provide evidence for both of the latter categories. Amongst the other local sites that could be added into Schrüfer-Kolb's 'domestic' category is Bob's Wood, Hinchingbrooke, only 13km to the north of Love's Farm, which has many similarities in terms of the continuity of settlement from Iron Age to Roman. Its assemblage of 36kg of metalworking debris was again dominated by evidence for small scale iron smithing, probably serving the needs of the local community and, from analytical studies of discarded bar stock, probably largely utilised iron from local Jurassic Ridge sources (Starley 2009). The Roman settlement at Sandy, Bedfordshire, which lies *c.*9.5km south of St Neots, produced just over 100kg of ironsmithing and copper alloy casting waste (Starley 1993). Finally, at Wendy, Cambridgeshire, 12km to the south-west, a 1st- to 4th-century settlement at the crossing of the River Rhee by Ermine Street, much (unspecified) iron slag was reportedly found (Wilson 1973). These studies (and smaller assemblages from other sites) provide an interesting comparison to the well known iron-producing sites of the Jurassic Ridge and presumably acted as end-users for the iron manufactured there.

V. Glass and amber objects
by Stephen Wadeson

Vessel glass
Eighty-six fragments of Roman vessel glass were recovered from across the site (largely from Settlements 6 and 7), representing a minimum of seventeen vessels. With a single exception, this was entirely produced either by mould-blowing or free-blowing, the most common method of manufacture at that time.

Within the assemblage several fragments of blue-green, mould-blown prismatic bottles (Isings 1957, form 50), produced during the 1st–2nd centuries AD, were found. The two most complete examples (SF 3631 and SF 2538) both consist of lower wall and base fragments. One (SF 3631) exhibits square moulding as part of the base design, running parallel to the edge of the bottle. Used as storage containers, rather than tablewares, square bottles were commonly in use up to the end of the 2nd century AD. A single shard of blue-green glass from the narrow neck of an unguent bottle (SF 2437) was identified. Such containers were produced to hold small quantities of perfumes and oils during the 1st and 2nd centuries AD.

The tableware assemblage consists of twenty-four fragments of glass, which represent a minimum of ten vessels. Although some of the material dates between the 1st- and 3rd centuries AD, most of these shards can be dated to the later part of the Roman period (4th century AD). The earliest vessel identified is a blue-green pillar-moulded bowl (SF 2969; Isings 1957, form 3b), from which three lower convex body shards with vertical ribs were recovered. On the lower interior of the bowl are the partial remains of two horizontal bands of abrasion, an attribute associated with deeper rather than shallow bowls (Cool and Price 1995, 19). Thought to date to the 1st century AD, this is the only example of a cast vessel identified in the assemblage. It is a high status item and could possibly be associated with military activity or trade stimulated by the construction of Ermine Street during the 1st century AD.

Also found was a single facet-cut decorated body fragment (SF 2915) dating from the late 2nd to 3rd centuries AD. This type of decoration occurs on a variety of vessels, especially cups and bowls, produced from the

2nd century until the end of the Roman period. Facet cutting was designed to exploit the ability of colourless glass to reflect and refract light in attractive patterns (Cool and Price 1995, 76).

The assemblage also contains several fragments from an out-turned tubular base ring (SF 3046), most probably associated with a tubular rimmed bowl (Isings 1957, form 44 or 45). The vessel type first appears during the late 1st century AD and is a common find on Romano-British sites; the form went out of use during the second half of the 2nd century (Cool and Price 1995, 95).

Late Roman tablewares, typical of the 4th and early 5th centuries AD (Cool and Price 1995, 220), are well represented within the assemblage. Diagnostic pieces include several out-turned, fire-rounded rims from three individual vessels (SFs 2347, 2695, 3708). In addition the partial remains of a beaker (SF 3210) consisting of the small concave base with pontil mark was also identified. The presence of the pontil scar on the base of the vessel suggests that the rim of the vessel was probably heat finished (Cool and Price 1995, 92). Also recovered was a lower body and base fragment from a late Roman drinking vessel (SF 2456). The vessel has a shallow concave base with a slight central kick around which the remains of the pontil mark are still visible. Found on a range of vessels that can be dated to between the 2nd- and 4th centuries, the base ring is created by the application of more than one spiral trail of glass to its underside. The spiral trail which formed the base has been continued, forming the spiral decoration visible on the remains of the vessel's lower body. Produced in a bubbly, pale greenish glass typical of the late Roman period, this example was found with pottery securely dated to the 4th century AD.

In addition a single shard (SF 3808) from a conical beaker (Islings 1957, form 106b) was identified. Noticeably thin-walled, the curved rim fragment of colourless glass is typical of 4th-century tablewares. A further colourless shard (SF 3481) was also identified; however, due to its fragmented condition, all that can be determined is that the fragment is part of a drinking vessel dating from the 4th century AD.

In conclusion, this is a small assemblage of vessel glass of predominantly Romano-British date (mid 1st century to late 4th/early 5th centuries AD). Tablewares form the greater part of the group, although some storage vessels are also represented. The assemblage is domestic in character and appears typical for the area and time. A similar assemblage has recently been recovered from Bob's Wood, Hinchingbrooke a short distance to the north (Oxford Archaeology East, in prep.). Situated on the western edge of Ermine Street, the site's inhabitants had access to the local market towns (such as *Durovigutum* (Godmanchester) and *Durobrivae* (Water Newton)). It is likely, therefore, that the excavated glass vessels were traded specialist items that became more widely available (or affordable) during the later Roman period.

Beads
Five glass beads and one amber example were recovered from Love's Farm. Two are Iron Age in date and represent the earliest glass artefacts recovered from site; the remaining three are Roman. Also identified within the assemblage were the fragmented remains of a small, ruby red amber bead. Amber is fossilised resin from pine trees, *Pinus succubufera*, that existed 40–60 million years ago, during the Eocene period. Warm to the touch and light in weight, amber is typically golden honey in colour, but is also less commonly found in ruby reds (Birley and Greene 2006, 50).

Catalogue of beads (not illustrated)

Iron Age beads

SF3444 A clear, colourless **annular bead** decorated with a band of opaque yellow glass irregularly applied around the inside of the perforation. 7mm thick with a diameter of 23mm, 5g. Classified by Guido as a Class 5, Hanging Langford type (Guido 1978 57/9), beads of this style were produced between the 2nd century BC and the 1st century AD. *7259*, fill of ditch *7260*. Period 3.2.

SF156 An **annular bead** with a whirl design in contrasting colours: a blue annular bead with yellow whirls emerging from the perforation. 6mm thick with a diameter of 19mm, 2g. Classified by Guido (1978, 51/2) as a Class 7a type. Beads of this type can be dated to the later Iron Age (*c.*150 BC–*c.* AD 50); their popularity ended with the Claudian conquest of southern Britain. Ditch *890*, Field System 3, Settlement 1. Period 3.4.

Roman beads

SF2135 The partial remains of a long glass **hexagonal bead**, produced in an opaque, light green glass. 5mm long by 6mm wide, 1g. *4671*, fill of ditch *4672*, Enclosure 30, Settlement 7. Period 4.2.

SF2471 An opaque, terracotta-coloured **cylinder bead**, a rarity in Britain as most cylinder beads of the time are normally green or blue. Identified throughout the Roman period, the majority of beads of this type are more typically recovered from 3rd- and 4th-century deposits. 6mm long, by 3mm wide, 1g. *5499*, fill of ditch *5500*, Enclosure 137, Settlement 7 (Phase 2). Period 4.4.

SF3470 A small glass **biconical bead**, produced in an opaque, light green glass. 3mm thick with a 5mm diameter, 1g. *9288*, fill of ditch *9289*, unphased.

SF3326 An incomplete amber **annular bead** that has been broken into several tiny fragments and was identified from the visible remains of the central perforation. Late Romano-British in date, based on the contemporaneous pottery recovered. 4mm thick. *5038*, fill of pit *5039*, unphased.

VI. Stone, shale, ceramic and fired clay objects

Querns and millstones
by Sarah Percival and Ruth Shaffrey
(Fig. 6.44)

Introduction
Excavations at Love's Farm produced an assemblage of twenty-nine querns and millstones including five saddle querns, four beehive rotary querns, five disc style rotary querns, three definite millstones and a further two possible millstone fragments. Several contexts also produced stone identified as probable quern fragments – either small weathered scraps of quern stones (particularly lava but also Millstone Grit), or small quern fragments of indeterminate type (N=4). The 2005 assemblage was catalogued by Sarah Percival using pro-forma NAU Archaeology recording sheets, while the 2008 assemblage was recorded by Ruth Shaffrey using Oxford Archaeology pro-forma sheets. The two assemblages are treated as one group in the following text and are summarised in Table 6.14.

Iron Age querns
The four saddle querns recovered from the site are fashioned either from Millstone Grit (N=1) or quartzitic sandstone (sarsen) boulders collected from the underlying

Period	Association	Possible quern	Rotary quern	Beehive rotary quern	Saddle quern	Millstone
3.2	Settlement 1			1	2	
3.3	Settlement 4	1		1		
3.5	Settlement 6			1		
4.1	Settlement 6				1	1
4.1	Settlement 7	1	1			
4.1	Field System 6				1	
4.2	Settlement 6					
4.2	Settlement 7				1	
4.3	Settlement 6	1				1
4.4	Settlement 6		2			2 (or querns)
4.4	Settlement 7	1	1	1		
US, UP		3	4			1
Total		7	8*	4	5	5

US = unstratified, UP = unphased; * = including five disc style rotary querns

Table 6.14 Querns and millstones by site period, type and association

glacial boulder clays or local streams or rivers. One example (SF 2718) came from a middle Iron Age enclosure associated with Settlement 1 (Period 3.2, Enclosure 150), perhaps having been deliberately placed in the ditch terminal. Another saddle quern (SF 2618) came from a quarry pit (Quarry 7, Period 4.2) associated with Settlement 7. Of the remaining examples, one derived from an early Roman building in Settlement 6 (SF 3055, Period 4.1, Structure 102) and the other came from Field System 6 (SF 2085). Of the group, one is a fragment (SF 2618) and three are complete or near complete; they were recorded using the typology developed at Danebury (Brown 1984, 418; Laws et al. 1991, 396). Each of the querns has a flattened grinding surface, which has been rubbed smooth during manufacture or use. Two of the complete examples (SFs 2085 and 2718) are large and roughly shaped with little working of the edges and base; these correspond to Danebury type S1. The third (SF 3055), of Danebury type S2, is thinner and more finely finished. Largely unshaped sarsen boulder saddle querns are common finds at sites in Cambridgeshire and Bedfordshire, with examples coming from the nearby sites of Fairfield Park Stotfold, Baldock and the Plant Breeding Institute, Trumpington (Shaffrey 2007a, 88; Foster 1986, 179; Percival 2004a).

Four examples of beehive rotary querns were recovered, including two pieces of igneous glacial erratics. The first (SF 2084, ditch *2226*, Enclosure 9, Period 3.3) may be a roughly fashioned rotary quern similar to examples from Bob's Wood, Hinchingbrooke (Percival in prep. a), although these were made of quartzitic sarsen. The fragment has one worked surface suggesting a bun-like form. No grinding surface survives. This piece was examined by David Williams (Southampton University) who surmised that 'the sample is of a hard, rough, hypermelanic, ultramafic plutonic rock, perhaps a perknite. The area around St Neots suffers from a dearth of good reliable stone deposits whose properties are suitable for the grinding action of quernstones, the majority of the local stone being Jurassic limestone. It seems highly likely, therefore, that the stone used for the quern was obtained as an isolated erratic from the local streams, gravels, boulder clays or drift deposits, rather than being imported to the site from some distance away. It most probably originated from Scandinavia or the North Sea Basin'.

The second beehive rotary quern fragment (SF 3537) had apparently been deliberately placed in the gully terminal of Roundhouse 14 (Settlement 6, Period 3.5). It retains evidence for a curved (concave) grinding surface, steep sides, part of the eye, and has pecked surfaces. A third beehive quern (SF 3779), from Boundary 1, is made from a coarse quartz sandstone, possibly Millstone Grit but with an apparently low feldspar content.

A semi-complete upper stone from a Yorkshire-type beehive quern (Watts 2002, 32) was found in a late 4th-century enclosure ditch in Settlement 7 (SF 2539, Enclosure 126, Period 4.4; Fig. 6.44). The quern has been broken in half and is made of Millstone Grit, with features characteristic of Yorkshire type querns including a drilled handle hole that does not pierce the V-shaped hopper (Watts 2002, 32). Yorkshire querns are widely distributed across the north of England and into Scotland (Watts 2002) but are less common in south-east England. Their main *floruit* lies between 200 BC and AD 100 (John Cruse, pers. comm.) and a recent find of a Millstone Grit upper stone from Couteenhall, Northampton was dated to *c*.AD 1–100 (Jones *et al.* 2006).

Romano-British querns
With the change from saddle querns and small beehive querns to flat disc style querns and millstones came a change in provenance, with the emphasis on a small number of imported lithologies, notably Millstone Grit, with smaller quantities of lava and glacial erratics collected from the local drift deposits. Seventeen incomplete rotary querns and millstones from the site are made of Millstone Grit, probably from sources in the Derbyshire and South Yorkshire Peak District. Petrological analysis of Millstone Grit querns found in East Anglia has indicated a Pennine origin (King 1986, 86; Ingle 1990, 60). Millstone Grit is the most common Romano-British quern material in this geographical area; its distribution has already been plotted in some detail and need not be repeated here (Shaffrey 2007b, fig. 8.17, table 8.49).

Five fragmentary Millstone Grit querns are of flat disc type (Watts 2002, fig.11 a). The querns are generally too incomplete for further identification although it is likely that one example (SF 2652), from Boundary 109 in Settlement 7, may be an upper stone, with the incomplete remains of a circular eye. The top of the stone is pecked whilst the grinding surface has the remains of dressed furrows. Similar examples have been found in late 2nd- to 3rd-century contexts from Stonea (Jackson and Potter 1996, fig. 190, 3). One fragment has a carved slot on the upper surface, although the function of the slot is uncertain. A further example (SF 3780; Fig. 6.44) has the distinctive combination of segmented radial grooves towards the perimeter of the quern and deep spaced pitting towards the eye. It was associated with Enclosure 117 in Settlement 6 (Period 4.4).

The assemblage at Love's Farm also contains two large incomplete millstones, both of Millstone Grit (SF 3003 and 3116) from Enclosure 103, Settlement 6 (Period 4.1) and unphased respectively. The larger example (SF 3116) has no surviving diagnostic features while the smaller one (SF 3003) retains a pecked upper surface and a number of rotary striations on the grinding surface. Parallels for this millstone at Stonea were of late 2nd- to 3rd-century date (Jackson and Potter 1996). Neither millstone can be related to particular structures. It is possible that they relate to a mill on the site (presumably animal powered), but it is equally plausible that the fragments were collected nearby for reuse.

A small quantity of abraded lava quern fragments was recovered from late Roman/early Anglo-Saxon contexts. Lava querns were widely imported into eastern England from sources in Rhineland Germany and, less commonly, from the Volvic region of France from around AD 50 until the end of the 5th century AD, and again from the 6th century AD into the later medieval period (King 1986, 95). Lava also occurs on a number of sites in the region, although generally with a low preservation rate (Shaffrey 2007b, fig. 8.17, table 8.49).

In common with other quern and millstone assemblages, many of the Love's Farm stones show evidence of having been burnt. The highly fragmentary rounded scraps of lava recovered from 1st- to 2nd-century hearth or oven *6531* in Pit Group 3 (Settlement 6) are extremely burnt. Broken millstones, with their flat faces, were ideal for and often reused in floors or oven bases (Watts 2002, fig. 12), such as the incomplete lava millstone recovered from the base of a 2nd- to 3rd-century corn dryer at Burnham Market, Norfolk (Percival 1999).

Discussion
Many of the querns and millstones came from ditch fills, reflecting the predominant feature type present on the site. It is possible that some of these ditch deposits might represent cases of deliberate deposition such as were found nearby at Bob's Wood, Hinchingbrooke (Percival in prep. a). This is particularly likely in cases where the querns were found in ditch terminals, as such deposits were often placed to mark boundaries or entrances (Hill 1995, 11). The Yorkshire-type quern was broken in half and may have been deliberately broken and deposited. Deliberate damage to quern stones has been noted on several sites in Cambridgeshire (Percival 2004a), Yorkshire (J. Cruse, pers. comm.) and throughout southern England (although generally in the mid–late Iron Age; Hill 1995). The example at Love's Farm was found in the same fill as two 4th-century coins and is paralleled at Bob's Wood, Hinchingbrooke, where half an East Anglian style Puddingstone upper stone was deliberately buried with a semi-articulated horse skeleton (Percival in prep. a). However, a note of caution must be sounded since querns often survive as almost exact halves and further work is needed to establish the relationship between fragment size and context/deposition type in order to determine whether the deposition of 'half' querns is significant.

Love's Farm has a markedly more limited range of sources of supply than other nearby sites of comparable date (Shaffrey 2007b, fig. 8.17) particularly during the Roman period. It is not possible to determine the popularity of lava querns due to their poor survival but their presence can be noted in addition to the Millstone Grit. Several other lithologies are notable by their absence, in particular, Hertfordshire Puddingstone and Old Red Sandstone, both of which are common on Roman sites in the area. Other sources also absent at Love's Farm but represented in smaller numbers elsewhere include Lodsworth Greensand from Sussex and Spilsby sandstone from Lincolnshire (Percival 2004). Millstone Grit may have dominated quern supply in this region during the later Roman period (as seen at Bob's Wood; Percival in prep. a) but the limited range of stone types from Love's Farm, occupied throughout the Roman period, suggests either that supply of querns to the site was tightly controlled or that its occupants did not have access to all lithologies.

Catalogue of illustrated items
SF2539 Upper Yorkshire-type beehive rotary quern. Millstone Grit. Handle measuring 36mm with V-shaped hopper. Burnt. Measures 290mm diameter x 94mm thick. *5600*, fill of ditch *5601*, Enclosure 126, Settlement 7 (Phase 2). Period 4.4.
SF3780 Upper rotary quern fragment. Millstone Grit. Worn smooth all over and with good evidence for reuse as hone. Grinding surface retains some radial grooves towards the circumference and deep pitting, irregularly spaced towards the centre. Measures approximately 500mm diameter x 40mm thick. *13063*, fill of ditch *13065*, Enclosure 117, Settlement 6. Period 4.4.

Mortars and rubbing stones
by Ruth Shaffrey
Six items have been classified as crop processors, including two shallow mortars (one unstratified, the other unphased), which would have utilised small boulders or large cobbles as rubbers. An example of the latter came from Enclosure 12, in Settlement 6 (Period 3.3) and was heavily burnt (SF 2968, not illustrated). These items probably indicate the grinding or processing of substances other than grain, for example crushing nuts, pounding roots or powdering minerals (Barker 1985, 12). Three pebbles with various levels of either percussion wear or area smoothing caused by rubbing suggest that, at some levels, processing was carried out using conveniently shaped stones gathered locally.

Whetstones and hones
by Nina Crummy and Ruth Shaffrey
(Fig. 6.45)
The small number of whetstones and hones recovered (six items) seems low considering the agricultural nature of the occupation at Love's Farm and the number of knives and other edged tools recovered. All the whetstones and hones

Figure 6.44 Quern and millstone. Scale 1:4

are made from fine-grained, probably locally available sandstone. The two primary whetstones are well used: one is a typical elongate example (SF 3736), the other is a wide flat stone of longer than usual length (>146mm, SF 3829). This suggests the sharpening of longer, possibly agricultural implements. The four hones utilise a variety of naturally shaped stones and show only limited use, either a few sharpening grooves on one side or smooth worn areas on one side or face only. None has been deliberately shaped or modified. All come from Roman contexts; the group is too small for marked concentrations to be defined in any one area of the site or in any one period.

Catalogue of illustrated items

SF3736 Elongated **whetstone** with sub-rectangular profile made from fine-grained pale brown quartzitic sandstone. Slightly tapered along length but evenly worn all over. One face is slightly reduced by use-wear has a deep sharpening groove across the original end. Length 74mm, section 20 by 15mm. *13505*, external deposit, Settlement 6. Period 4.2.

SF3829 Large micaceous sandstone **whetstone** of ovoid section. One end is broken, the other is spalled. Both faces are also spalled, and one has a large area worn flat by use. One edge is very worn and flat, with sharp angles developed at the junction with the faces. Length 147mm, width 63mm, maximum thickness 29mm. *13001*, unphased deposit.

SF2132 Sandstone **hone** of elliptical section. The surviving original end is bevelled. The surface is rough on all faces. Length 85mm, width 25mm, 15mm thick. *4625*, fill of pit *4626*, Structure 112, Settlement 7. Period 4.2.

SF3233 Slightly tapering rectangular-section **hone** of dense limestone, the narrower end is broken. One face is slightly irregular and spalled, the other is smooth; they may have been used for edge-sharpening and polishing respectively. Length 101mm, maximum width 27mm, maximum thickness 10mm. *10234*, fill of pit *10236*, Settlement 7. Period 4.4.

Loomweights
by Alice Lyons
(Fig. 6.46)

Two triangular loomweights (SF 3109 and SF 3483) were retrieved from Iron Age deposits at Love's Farm. Loomweights of this type are commonly found on Iron Age sites in this area (*e.g.* Hylton and Williams 1996, 140; Duncan and Mackreth 2005, 126). Both of the examples from Love's Farm were manufactured in the chalky clay typical of the Iron Age burnt clay within this assemblage (Fabric C1, Table 6.21). Their construction in this friable material suggests they were intended for a loom located within a structure, and indeed one of the weights is fumed as if it was suspended near a domestic hearth.

Traces of wear recorded on almost identical weights from an Iron Age and Roman enclosure at Burgh, Suffolk (Martin 1988, 63, fig. 35) indicate that the loomweights were suspended point downwards, possibly to prevent breakage if suspended from one corner only. Unfortunately no wear marks have survived on the Love's Farm examples to establish whether that was also the case here.

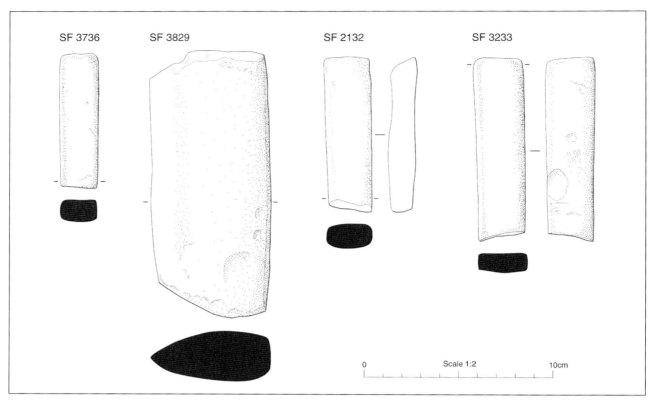

Figure 6.45 Hones. Scale 1:2

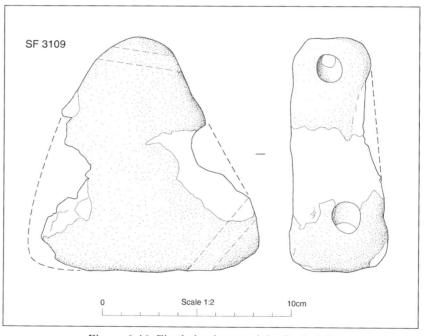

Figure 6.46 Fired clay loomweight. Scale 1:2

Catalogue of illustrated item

SF3109 Burnt clay (Fabric C1) triangular **loomweight** consisting of 31 fragments, weighing 924g, 130mm long and 45mm thick. Each corner is perforated with a diagonal circular/oval opening between 10–20mm wide. The fabric has become fumed and discoloured over time. *10753*, fill of ditch *10747*, Enclosure 1, Settlement 6. Period 3.3.

?Bobbin
by Alice Lyons
(Fig. 6.47)

The interpretation of this object as a textile bobbin is provisional and based only on its similarity to modern day coarse-thread reels. If not a bobbin then perhaps this may have been a kiln prop or spacer. No parallels have yet been found for this object.

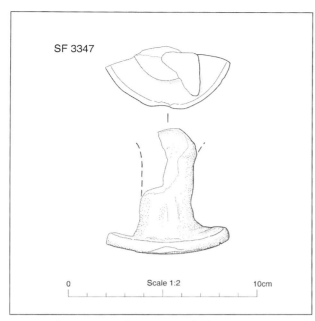

Figure 6.47 Fired clay ?bobbin. Scale 1:2

Catalogue of illustrated item

SF3347 An incomplete object that may be a large ceramic **bobbin**, possibly used to wind wool. It is 69mm long and has part of a circular disc (66mm diameter) surviving on a central stalk (30mm diameter) with a broken end that may have held another circular disc. This object was found with late Romano-British pottery. *4813*, unphased deposit, Settlement 7.

Spindlewhorls
by Nina Crummy
(Fig. 6.48)

The spindlewhorls are made in a variety of worked stone and reused ceramic materials and were found scattered across the site and across all periods. An Iron Age limestone whorl (SF 3107) came from a Period 3.3 ditch re-cut in Settlement 6, a Roman limestone whorl (SF 2971) was recovered from the fill of a Period 4.4 oven in the same settlement, and a third whorl in this stone (SF 2120) was unstratified; it may be late Iron Age, Roman, or perhaps even medieval in date.

A small pierced limestone pebble from a Period 3.3 ditch in Settlement 1 may also have been intended for use as a spindlewhorl (SF 2742). Its central perforation, drilled from both sides as was usual in the manufacture of these objects, is unfinished, suggesting that the pebble was abandoned at this stage because it was too light for use as a whorl. A second larger pebble from a post-medieval furrow also has an unfinished perforation, but in this instance the depressions drilled out on each face are much wider at the top than is usual for spindle holes and it may have been abandoned because the spindle would not sit firmly within the hole (SF 3401). A perforated water-worn sandstone pebble is perhaps too irregular to have functioned well as a whorl, but spalling around the edges of the hole on one face suggests that it has been fitted with a spindle and spun (SF 3044). The holes of all three of these pebbles bear the marks of a bow drill.

A shale spindlewhorl from the fill of a Period 4.5 ditch in Settlement 7 belongs to the late Roman period of popularity of these objects (SF 2350). They occur in a number of 4th-century female burials in Hampshire, Dorset and Somerset (Clarke 1979, 369; Philpott 1991, 184), and also in Late Roman occupation contexts on sites such as Silchester, Portchester, Cirencester and Frocester and Canterbury (Crummy 2006b, 131). One was found with a bone weaving tablet and a coin hoard with a closing date of AD 364 in the backfill of a well in Winchester (Rees *et al.* 2008, 76).

The remaining three whorls are made from recycled pottery sherds, one from a Period 3.5 deposit in Settlement 7 (no SF number, not illustrated), one from a Period 4.3 context in Settlement 6 (SF 3006) and the third from a Period 4.4 context in Settlement 7 (SF 3231).

The whorls add in a limited way to the environmental information about local agricultural practice and the economy of the site. They were probably used to spin wool, which points to the keeping of a flock of sheep and/or goats of which a considerable number were allowed to reach maturity so that they would provide wool, instead of slaughtering most in their first or second year as would be the case for a flock kept for milk and meat (Payne 1973, 292–4). The whorls may alternatively have been used to spin a vegetable fibre such as flax, but this species does not do well in waterlogged soils, making only the high ground at Love's Farm suitable for such a crop. Once harvested, the flax plants need to be retted before spinning, usually in ponds, ditches or flowing water, and in this respect Love's Farm provides an ideal environment for its processing.

Catalogue of illustrated items

SF3107 Large limestone **spindlewhorl**, approximately discoid but with two straight abutting sections. The surfaces and edges are worn but covered with linear tool marks, varying from groups of fine lines to individual grooves. The spindle hole is figure-of-eight-shaped and worn. Maximum diameter 57mm, thickness varies from 15 to 7mm; central diameter of spindle hole 11mm. *10752*, fill of ditch *10747*, Enclosure 1, Settlement 6. Period 3.3.

SF2120 Thick discoid **spindlewhorl** of limestone or hard chalk. One face and the edge are badly spalled. The spindle hole is a worn figure-of-eight shape. Diameter 37mm, 14mm thick; central diameter of spindle hole 7mm. Unstratified.

SF2742 Irregular hard chalk pebble, probably a rejected unfinished **spindlewhorl**. The surfaces are smooth but irregular and with some linear tool marks. As with SF 3401 below, the pebble has been drilled through on both faces, the large depressions meeting to form a small irregular perforation. Maximum diameter 34mm, minimum 27mm, 18.5mm thick; external diameter of both depressions 16mm. This object is too small and light to have been used as an effective spindlewhorl. *9917*, fill of ditch *9918*, Enclosure 150, Settlement 1. Period 3.3.

SF3401 Disc of hard chalk, the surfaces smooth but irregular, grooved in places by linear tool marks. A depression has been drilled into each face, but the central perforation where they meet has been left narrow and irregular. The sides of the depressions are still grooved from a bow-drill. Probably a rejected unfinished **spindlewhorl**, as the depressions are much wider on the surfaces than is usual for spindle holes. Maximum diameter 50mm, 18mm thick; external diameter of depressions 17 and 15mm. *7360*, fill of furrow *7361*, modern.

SF3044 Triangular water-worn pebble of micaceous sandstone, broken at each end and perforated at the centre, possible **spindlewhorl**. The perforation is worn, but the depressions are wide and marked with grooves from a bow drill like those on SFs 2742 and 3401. Maximum dimensions 58 x 52mm, 18mm thick; central diameter of perforation 7mm, external diameter of depressions 15 and 18mm. Unstratified.

SF2971 Discoid limestone **spindlewhorl,** with well-formed edge and faces, all worn smooth apart from a small chip on one edge. The spindle hole is worn and straight-sided. Diameter 40mm, 12mm

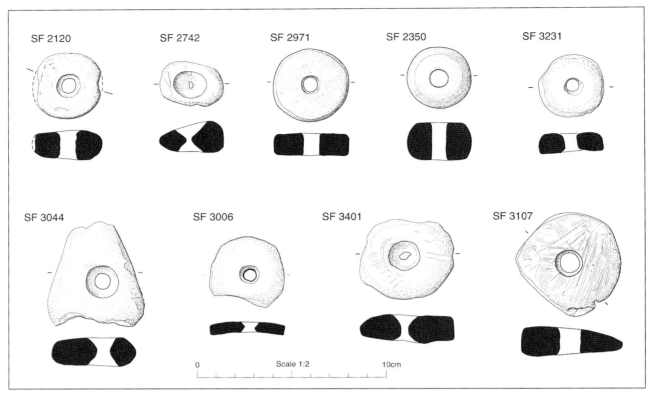

Figure 6.48 Stone and chalk spindlewhorls. Scale 1:2

thick; diameter of spindle hole 7mm. *8477*, fill of oven *8478*, Settlement 6. Period 4.4.

SF2350 Shale **spindlewhorl** with a single girth groove. The polished surface is scratched and worn around the circumference, and in antiquity flaked off entirely on both the upper and lower faces. As the exposed undersurface is also worn, the whorl continued to be used in its damaged condition. The spindle hole is straight-sided, also indicative of much wear. Diameter 34mm, height 20mm; central diameter of spindle hole 8mm. *5259*, fill of gully *5260*, Structure 115, Settlement 7. Period 4.5.

SF3006 Damaged **spindlewhorl** made from a body sherd from a large Nene Valley colour-coat jar. The surface is irregular but smooth. Both surfaces are abraded, the outer one particularly, and both have spalled around the figure-of-eight-shaped spindle hole. A ridge remaining at the centre of the spindle hole suggests that it was little used. Diameter 40mm, 6.5mm thick; central diameter of spindle hole 5mm. *8707*, fill of ditch *8708*, Settlement 6, Enclosure 116. Period 4.3.

SF3231 **Spindlewhorl** made from a pot base. The edge is slightly irregular but smooth. Both surfaces are abraded and have spalled slightly around the spindle hole, which is worn but tapers towards the centre in a narrow figure-of-eight shape. Diameter 36mm, 11mm thick; central diameter of spindle hole 6mm. *10205*, fill of pit *10207*, Settlement 7. Period 4.4.

VII. Architectural stonework
by Ruth Shaffrey

The excavations produced eighteen fragments of structural stonework, all of which came from Period 4.5 deposits in Settlement 7. The majority of the group came from surfaces *5363* and *5593*, four coming from ditches associated with Enclosure 137 (Table 6.15). The stone is a loosely cemented and porous, shelly oolitic limestone. The shell content is low although variable and there are some distinctive bands of oyster shells. The stone appears visually most like a type of Lincolnshire limestone known as Weldon stone (Hudson and Sutherland 1990, 23), the original source of which is some 40km from St Neots.

A few fragments retain no evidence of use but most are fragments of ashlar or have one or more tooled surfaces and all seem likely to have been used structurally. Three pieces are moulded but are too damaged for function to be assigned. One slab of the same stone has a tooled edge and worn surface (SF 2659). It is either largely unworked or heavily worn as it bears little other evidence of shaping. The most distinctive item is a corner fragment of moulded stone that may be a piece of architrave from a door or window surround (SF 2596). This item, together with the quantity of stone and a number of other moulded fragments, suggests that the stone was robbed from a fairly substantial building nearby.

The probable identification of Weldon stone is of particular significance here, since its occurrence in Roman contexts is unusual and it is unclear to what extent it was utilised at this time (Sutherland 2003, 82). In Kent, architectural fragments of Weldon stone have been identified at Northfleet Roman villa (Shaffrey 2011) and it was also used for a small child's sarcophagus at Springhead (Hayward pers. comm.). In London it was identified as one of two likely sources for the Lincolnshire Limestone in the London Arch (Dimes 1980, 198–200). Love's Farm therefore provides further evidence of the exploitation of Weldon stone by the Romans, although it should be noted that its identification has not been confirmed by microscopic analysis.

Context	Cut	Feature	Interpretation	With tooling	Without tooling	Other	SF nos	Total
4998	4999	Ditch fill	Enclosure 137	1	1		2453, 2454	2
5141	5142	Ditch fill	Enclosure 137		2		2682	2
5593	5593	Surface	Cobbled surface	2	1	1 (slab)	2662, 2663, 2665, 2659	4
5636	5636	Surface	-	3	7		2262, 2587–90, 2592–95, 2597	10
Total				6	11	1		18

Table 6.15 Non-diagnostic structural stonework, all from Settlement 7 (Period 4.4)

VIII. Ceramic building material and fired clay
by Alice Lyons, with Heather Wallis
(Fig. 6.49)

Introduction
A total of 5648 fragments of ceramic building material (CBM), including daub and tile, weighing 83.803kg, was recovered (Table 6.16). The material is extremely fragmentary and abraded, with few original surfaces remaining and an average fragment weight of 56g for the tile and only 12g for the daub.

The CBM was counted and weighed by form and fabric type, and any complete dimensions measured (mm). Levels of abrasion, any evidence of re-use or burning were also recorded, following guidelines laid down by the Archaeological Ceramic Building Materials Group (ACBMG 2002). The terminology used follows Brodribb (1987).

Distribution
When the CBM is examined by the associated pottery spot date (Table 6.17) it can clearly been seen that, as expected, tile was rarely found in pre-Roman deposits (and what was found is probably intrusive Roman material). A significant amount of the daub assemblage (c.11%) was, however, retrieved from pre-Roman features. Daub-covered features such as ovens, hearths and roundhouses were commonly constructed by Iron Age communities, and this form of building did not cease with the introduction of kiln-fired tile in the Romano-British period. It is noteworthy that the majority of both daub and tile recovered from the site originates from the Romano-British period. Very little post-Roman daub and tile was found.

Ceramic building material was recovered from a wide variety of features across the excavated area, largely being found residually. None of these fragments were found in direct association with a Roman building, although it is notable that a high proportion of the material originates from the area of Settlement 6. Most of the daub was recovered from pits and most of the tile from ditches (Table 6.18). This very clear differentiation in disposal patterns suggests that, as the tile survived in large pieces, it was deliberately dumped within drainage ditches to prevent them from silting up, while the daub was discarded into rubbish pits.

Tile

Fabric
Six Romano-British tile fabrics were recorded (Table 6.19). The majority of the material is formed from locally available clays and temper, the most widely used of which is the hard red sandy fabric (F1) with flint inclusions. Also fairly well represented is a less sandy fabric (F2) with the addition of brick grog inclusions. Other local fabrics consist of a hard dark red fabric (F3), a tile with a distinctive reduced core (F5) and a poorly mixed example that has distinctive pink swirls of clay (F6).

It is notable that a small amount of non-local shell-tempered tile (F4) was recovered; this is not an uncommon find in the Midlands and is generally thought to originate from the Harrold industries in Bedfordshire (Zeepvat 1987, 118), although shell-rich clay beds are found over most of the region (including Cambridgeshire) and another source cannot be ruled out. This tile-type dates from the middle to late Roman period (Hylton and Williams 1996, 154).

Form
Of the five distinct tile types identified, the majority are roof tiles, including *tegulae*, *imbrex* and undiagnostic roof tile (Table 6.20).

When combined, the roof tiles consisting of *tegula* (c.21%), *imbrex* (c.14%) and undiagnostic roof tile (c.28%) form the majority (c.63%) of this assemblage by

CBM type	Quantity	Wt (g)	Wt (%)
Tile	393	21901	26.1
Daub	5254	61902	73.9
Total	5648	83803	100

Table 6.16 Ceramic building material, listed in descending order of percentage of weight

Period	Tile (%)	Daub (%)
Prehistoric	0.3	3.3
Middle Iron Age	0.0	2.5
Iron Age	0.7	1.9
Late Iron Age	0.1	1.3
Late Iron Age to early Roman	1.9	1.5
Early Roman	3.2	4.9
Romano-British	62.9	71.0
Roman to early Anglo-Saxon	0.3	1.1
Saxon	0.0	0.1
Medieval	1.2	0.01
Post-medieval	0.8	0.7
Undated	28.4	11.6
Total	100	100

Table 6.17 Ceramic Building material by period (by percentage of weight)

CBM type	Ditch (%)	Pit (%)	Other (%)
Tile	50.0	10.0	44.7
Daub	20.5	62.4	17.2

Table 6.18 The percentage of ceramic building material (by weight) by feature type

Type	Quantity	Wt (g)	Wt (%)
Tegula	22	4515	20.6
Roof tile	89	6058	27.7
Imbrex	21	2994	13.7
Flue	14	1255	5.7
Bonding	13	2643	12.1
Undiagnostic	234	4436	20.3
Total	393	21901	100

Table 6.20 The tile types

weight. Only two examples of undiagnostic roof tile have traces of mortar (from context *4318* and one from well *5890*) which is unsurprising since mortar was not required when these tiles were used in the Roman style on a low-pitched roof. The *tegulae* measure between 16–32mm thick, with a mean measurement of 20mm. They occur in three fabrics in the assemblage (F1: 2813g/62%, F2: 1040g/23%, F3: 219g/5% and F4: 443g/10%), and are generally produced in the hard red sandy fabric F1. No complete examples were found, and the fragments have an average sherd weight of *c*.205g.

The undiagnostic roof tile (that may be *tegulae*) measure between 11–31mm thick and have a mean measurement of 14mm thickness. These fragments were produced in a wide variety of fabric types (F1: 2003g/33%, F2: 1443g/24%, F3: 1058g/17%, F4: 177g/3%, F5: 1237g/20% and F6:140g/3%), again most frequently (by weight) produced in F1. No complete examples were found and the fragments have an average sherd weight of only *c*.60g.

Imbrices are a much more unusual tile type in this assemblage and only represent *c*.14% of the total by weight. They measure between 12–27mm thick with a mean measurement of 16mm. This type of tile was found in three fabrics types (F1: 2020g/68%, F2: 787g/26% and F4: 187g/6%), although as with the other tile types the hard red sandy F1 is the most common. No complete examples were found and the fragments have an average weight of *c*.143g.

Flue tile (*c*.6%) forms a small part of this assemblage by weight. These open-ended, box-shaped tiles were intended to be built in the thickness of the walls of a room heated by a hypocaust. They are often decoratively combed, to provide a key for any mortar required to hold the tile in place, although no mortar was recorded on these examples. The flue tiles within this assemblage measure between 13–25mm thick, with a mean thickness of 19mm. This type of tile was most commonly found in the hard red F1 fabric (518g/41%), although almost as commonly occurs in the softer grog-tempered F2 (472g/38%). Flue-tile was also found in fabric F3 (47g/21%). No complete examples were found and the fragments have an average sherd weight of *c*.90g.

Bonding tiles (*c*.12%) are a flat tile used to form bands which alternated with wider sections of regular stonework; they normally run through the entire thickness of the wall, to give stability to the mortared rubble-core. They were also useful as levelling courses during construction (Gurney 1986, 45, fig. 31) and it is also possible these tiles could have been (re)used as flooring. The thirteen incomplete examples found at Love's Farm measure between 29–55mm thick, with a mean thickness between 29–36mm. These tiles were found in fabrics F1 (1966g/76%), F2 (169g/6%), F3 (196g/7%), F4 (176g/7%) and F6 (136g/4%), although most frequently in F1. No complete examples were found and the fragments have an average sherd weight of 203g. No signature marks were recorded (finger-incised wavy lines on their upper surface that may have been purely decorative or have served a practical purpose such as batch marking).

Undiagnostic fragments (*c*.20%) have only one (or no) original surfaces surviving and are therefore impossible to assign to type. They form a significant part of this assemblage by weight, but are extremely severely abraded with an average weight of only *c*.19g. These fragments are found in all fabric types, but most commonly as F1 (1586g/36%) and as F2 (1554g/36%). The other fabric types were less well represented (F3: 507g/12%, F4: 94g/2%, F5: 454/10%, F6: 152g/4%).

Fired clay
A total of 5254 fragments of burnt clay, weighing 61.902kg, was recovered from the site and four individual fabric types were recorded (Table 6.21), the most common of which (G1) is a sandy clay fabric with burnt flint fragments and brick grog inclusions. Burnt clay was found

Fabric	Fabric descriptions	Fragment count	Fragment Wt (g)	Wt (%)
F1	Hard red slightly sandy fabric, occasional reduced core, moderate flint fleck and sparse-to-medium flint inclusions, smooth to touch.	133	10906	49.8
F2	Pinky orange hard fabric, occasional flint fleck and grog inclusions (lots of lost inclusion holes), smooth to touch.	153	5554	25.4
F3	Hard dark red sandy fabric, moderate flint fleck inclusion, rough to touch.	50	2245	10.3
F4	Hard, medium-to-dark red brown, shell tempered.	10	1077	4.9
F5	Orangey red, hard, slightly sandy, reduced core, moderate flint fleck, often gritty surface.	36	1691	7.7
F6	Mainly cream but poorly mixed so some pink swirls, hard and smooth, slightly sandy with grog inclusions, some large.	11	428	2.0
Total		393	21901	100

Table 6.19 The ceramic building material fabrics, listed in numerical order

Fabric	Fabric descriptions	Fragment count	Fragment Wt (g)	Wt (%)
G1	Soft sandy clay fabric, red orange in colour, minimal inclusions, sparse fragments of burnt flint and brick grog.	1304	33309	53.8
C1	Pinky buff fabric with inclusions of chalk fragments (up to 12mm) and occasional flint fragment. Some inclusions fairly large in size. Colour can vary between yellowy off-white to red and grey.	3143	25075	40.5
C2	Hard pinky red fabric with fine chalk inclusions.	555	2250	3.6
S1	Soft and gritty, brown red fabric with sand inclusions and occasional flint fragment.	252	1268	2.1
Total		5254	61902	100

Table 6.21 The daub quantified by fabric type

in almost every type of feature, quite frequently as a residual contaminant within disuse fills and often only as tiny fragments.

This burnt clay or daub was manufactured from local materials and was evidently used in the production of ovens, kilns and houses (Rigby and Foster 1986, 184, fig. 80). It sometimes bears the impressions of wattles and withies that formed the superstructures of these buildings and helped to maintain their shape and reduce shrinkage during construction. The wattles and withies, made of twigs, then either rot, or have been burnt, away. It should be noted that daub is a soft porous substance and not as resilient as kiln fired CBM; only material that has been deliberately or accidentally burnt will survive in the soil. For example, a small (c. >1% by weight), but significant percentage of the assemblage was retrieved from gullies associated with prehistoric roundhouses and/or enclosures. Although extremely fragmentary (as a result of pre- and post-depositional abrasion) with an average fragment weight of only c.3g the widespread presence of daub in these features indicates that it would have been a common material type in use at that time, also demonstrating the types of building techniques used for these structures. A similar distribution of daub recovered from roundhouse gullies was observed at Salford, Bedfordshire (Slowikowski 2005, 118).

It is also worthy of note that fabric types C1 and C2 are both local clays with chalk inclusions. The brick grog-tempered daub (G1) is almost exclusively Romano-British. This more recent date probably accounts for the larger fragment size (26g) as opposed to an average fragment size of 7g for the other fabrics.

Most of the daub assemblage cannot be associated with specific features and was retrieved in a general distribution from ditches (c.20%) and pits (c.62%), although two features provide evidence for kiln superstructures. A significant amount of daub (c.2.3%) came from a Romano-British pit (fill *5687*, pit *4626*, see below), nearly all of which is of the chalky C1 type, perhaps suggesting an early Roman date (see above). The pottery associated with this feature dates from the both the early and late Romano-British periods, suggesting that the relevant deposit had been disturbed. Although no diagnostic daub types were found associated with this feature, numerous withy impressions were found. The diameters of these impressions measure between 12–34mm, with a mean measurement of 17mm, indicating the use of quite substantial withies or staves.

Pit *4626*, part of Quarry 7 in Settlement 7 (Period 4.2), contained a large assemblage of daub that is consistent with being the partial remains of a demolished pottery kiln (Table 6.22). Although disturbed from their original position, some of the daub fragments are recognisable as the wall (including the upper lip), floor and flue arch of a circular kiln (see Kiln Furniture, below). Most of the fragments are of fabric type G1. The small amounts of other fabrics found may represent repairs to the kiln or daub from another source.

The surviving dimensions of the wall fragments range between 34–44mm in width, with a mean measurement of 37mm. Surviving withy impressions have measurable diameters of between 8–26mm, with a mean measurement of 19mm. The upper lip of this wall (diagnostic as having at least two surfaces at a 90° angle to each other, with the same curvature as the wall) varies in width between 30–65mm, with a mean measurement of 40mm. The withy diameters within the lip fragments measure between 16–47mm, with a mean measurement of 22mm. Two of the surviving lip fragments have pinched (raised) external surfaces, which are paralleled by a kiln found at Holt, Denbigh (Swan 1984, 36, fig. IV). Swan suggests that the thickened rim indented with thumb impressions found at Holt may have been purely decorative; alternatively they could represent the point at which small flue-vents occurred at the junction of the kiln-lip and the topping load. This would have allowed oxygen into the kiln while firing took place, to produce whitewares. The only waster sherds retrieved from the Love's Farm kiln debris are Sandy greywares, perhaps suggesting that the raised /pinched sections were only decorative in this case.

The possible kiln floor fragments found within pit *4626* are flattish and one has a slight lip as if it may have formed part of a portable floor, or one that had been inserted into the kiln after the wall had been fired at least once. The fragments are unperforated and measure between 20–30mm thick, with a mean measurement of 25mm. The surviving withy dimensions measure between 15–17mm thick, although only two impressions were recorded. No complete dimensions survive on the fragments of daub that may have originated from the flue arch of the kiln. All of these fragments are diagnostic due to their curved nature (more curved than the kiln wall). Several withy impressions did survive and these measure between 11–22mm, with a mean measurement of 15mm.

In addition to the pottery wasters recovered from this deposit, fired clay and possible worked stone kiln furniture (see below) were recovered. Much of the kiln superstructure must have been deposited elsewhere, however, as insufficient material was contained within the pit to reconstruct a complete circular upright draft kiln with flue, while diagnostic kiln features such as most of

Fabric	Daub (g)	Wall (g)	Lip (g)	Floor (g)	Arch (g)	Total (g)	Total (%)
C1	1241	0	37	0	247	1525	4.8
G1	17844	5997	4500	242	1736	30319	94.68
S1	201	0	0	0	0	201	0.68
Total	19286	5997	4537	242	1983	32045	100

Table 6.22 The daub from pit *4626*, Quarry 7, Settlement 7, Period 4.2

the floor (*i.e.* the central part of the kiln) are missing. It is therefore impossible to attribute the kiln to form type.

Possible kiln furniture
(Fig. 6.49)
In addition to the debris from a possible kiln noted above, three fired clay objects from Love's Farm, only one of which is complete, have been tentatively interpreted as possible kiln props or spacers. Unless separated by a clay or stone spacer, unfired pots placed in the kiln are likely to become fused together and not fire correctly: pots are more likely to stick together if slipped with wet clay or (unusually for the Roman period) glaze. One example from Love's Farm (SF 3836) was found with pottery kiln debris in fill *4625* (pit *4626*) of Quarry 7, a Period 4.2 feature located in Settlement 7. An object which has been interpreted as a possible bobbin (Fig. 6.47, SF 3347, above), may also have been used as a kiln prop or spacer. Quarry 7 also yielded two burnt fragments of sedimentary limestone, both of which have a very similar 'crescent moon' shape (not illustrated). No direct parallels for these objects have been found and they may simply be fire-cracked stones, but the smooth internal curve of the 'crescent moon' shape, suggests that they could have served as kiln spacers (Swan 1984, 40).

Catalogue of illustrated items
SF3836 An incomplete cylindrical object, possibly a **kiln prop or spacer**. It has a flat end and smoothed sides, 9mm thick (57g). Fabric C1. *4625*, fill of pit *4626*, Quarry 7, Settlement 7. Period 4.2.
SF3349 An incomplete cylindrical object, possibly **a kiln prop or spacer**. It has a flat end and smoothed sides, no complete dimensions survive (68g). Fabric C1. *5565*, fill of pit *5596*, Settlement 7. Period 4.5.
SF3114 A complete sub-circular slightly domed oval (55mm x 60mm x 13mm) disc (49g), possibly a **kiln prop or spacer**. One surface is smoothed; the other is less uniform with one straight incised straight line – the result of pressure before firing. Fabric S1. *8929*, fill of pit *8895*, Settlement 6. Period 4.1.

Discussion
The assemblage of CBM from Love's Farm spans several hundred years between the Iron Age and Romano-British periods. The chalky daub (C1) of the Iron Age was found in the disuse and demolition fills of roundhouse gullies and enclosures, indicating that these structures were probably at least partially constructed using wattle-and-daub technology and possibly that they had burnt down, causing the daub to harden and survive in the soil. The chalky daub continued in use in the early Roman period, being largely used to construct a pottery kiln. As the Romano-British period progressed and kiln-fired tile became more common, later daub (from the 2nd century onwards) was made using tile fragments (F2) as grog. This material was used to construct the majority of the pottery kiln found in fragmentary form within pit *4626*, as well as many other structures, ditches and pits across the site. The large quantity of daub found in Romano-British features indicates that wattle-and-daub structures continued to be built even when kiln-fired tile became available to the civilian population in the early to mid 2nd century AD.

Given the extent of the excavations at Love's Farm it is remarkable that such a small amount (*c.*17kg) of kiln-fired Romano-British tile was recovered. Although the presence of roof, flue and bonding/floor tile indicates that Romano-British building(s) of the Roman style were constructed nearby, only a very small quantity of such material was found here: at most, the complete weight of the tile assemblage represents seven complete *tegulae* (Hylton and Williams 1996, 153). The low level of tile recovered indicates that it was not used as a primary construction material within the immediate vicinity of Love's Farm and perhaps only a small amount of robbed material reached the site. There was, however, a small concentration of roof tile in an outlying trench to the east of Settlement 6 which may indicate the presence of a small structure in the vicinity.

IX. Bone and antler objects
by Nina Crummy
(Figs 6.50–54)

The small assemblage of bone and antler objects recovered from the site ranges in date from late Iron Age to late Roman. The objects fall into a limited range of the functional categories defined by Crummy (1983), with a

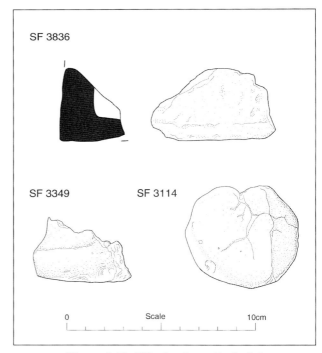

Figure 6.49 Kiln furniture. Scale 1:1

	Dress	Toilet	Household	Tools	Bone-working	Misc.
Settlements 1–5 and 8	-	-	-	3	2	-
Settlement 7	4	2	1	-	-	2
Settlement 6 and southern fields	2	1	-	2	3	-
Unstratified	-	-	-	1	-	-
Total	*6*	*3*	*1*	*6*	*5*	*2*

Apparent discrepancies between the number of catalogue entries and the number of objects in Table 6.23 can be accounted for by the use of two small find numbers for two non-joining fragments of a single comb (SFs 3157, 3158), and by one small find number covering two pieces of bone-working waste (SF 3039).

Table 6.23 Bone and antler objects by general location and functional category

number of tools and pieces of waste debris pointing to local boneworking using the skeletal remains of domesticated animals (further comments on antler working are included in Chapter 8.III). Table 6.23 presents the assemblage by settlement and function and the objects are catalogued below by function.

A small bone disc from Iron Age cremation burial *7008* within Cemetery 3, which was established in Period 3.5 immediately to the north of Settlement 6, is probably a bead or appliqué of some kind (SF 3374, Fig. 6.50). Other objects from the Iron Age settlements are restricted to two socketed and pointed tools, a possible bobbin, and two fragments of bone-working debris. One point is from Enclosure 150, a Period 3.3 feature in Settlement 1 (SF 2723, Fig. 6.53), one piece of debris and the other point are from Quarry 3, in Settlement 2 (Period 3.4) and Enclosure 12, in Settlement 6 (Period 3.3) respectively (SF 2714, Fig. 6.53; SF 3529, Fig. 6.54), and the ?bobbin and second piece of debris are from Enclosure 10 (Period 3.4) in Settlement 2 (SF 6306, not illustrated; SF 2722, Fig. 6.54). Coin evidence shows that many of the ditches on the site remained as negative features in the landscape throughout the Roman period and beyond, meaning that these bone items may be much later than their context dates suggest. Nevertheless, the three tools would not be out of place in an Iron Age milieu and it may be pertinent that both fragments of waste debris are of horse bone, while those from Roman contexts are of cattle. The socketed points were probably leather-workers' awls, and polish on the more complete example (SF 3108) is appropriate to such a use. The possible bobbin consists of a well polished tube pierced on one side. It may perhaps best be compared to the pierced and unpierced sheep/goat metapodials that occur on both Iron Age and Roman sites and that have usually been associated with weaving (*e.g.* Pitt-Rivers 1888, 175; Wheeler 1943, 306; Wild 1970, 34, 130, fig. 16; Sellwood 1984, 389, fig. 7.37, 3.177–3.180; Greep 1998, 283, nos 179–85; Price 2000, 100, fig. 6.3, 85). Like the metapodials, the tube could certainly have been used in a variety of ways in cold technologies such as textile manufacture, netting, rope-making or basketry.

The group of objects from Settlement 7 are of very different character, all being late Roman and most being dress accessories and toilet equipment (Table 6.23). Some of the objects are contemporary with coinage of the Houses of Valentinian and Theodosius (AD 364 into the early 5th century). Although the group is small, it points to familiarity with the material culture of the late Roman period, in particular with the equipment associated with the coiffure. The dress accessories consist of a bone hairpin with faceted cuboid head, a type that dates to the 4th century and perhaps the early 5th century (SF 2365, Fig. 6.50; Crummy 1983, 23, Type 4), two hairpin shaft fragments with the swelling characteristic of hairpins dating to after *c.*AD 150 (SFs 2357 and 2627, not illustrated,; Crummy 1983, 20; 1992, 144), and a bone armlet of mid/late 4th-early 5th century date (SF 2233, Fig. 6.50; Clarke 1979, 314; MacGregor 1985, 112–13). The three hairpins came from Enclosures 127 and 133 (Period 4.4), the armlet from ditch *4895* (Period 4.5). Two other shaft fragments also came from Settlement 7, both from Period 4.4 contexts. They are probably also from hairpins, but both are short and lack the swelling that would identify them as hairpins rather than needles or spoon handles. Toilet equipment is represented by two pieces of a composite antler comb from well *5387* (Period 4.5; SF 3157=3158, Fig. 6.51), and another comb fragment from cobbled surface *5344* (Period 4.4, SF 2443, not illustrated). The fragment from Period 4.4 may be intrusive, as composite antler combs first appeared in Britain *c.*AD 360–5 (Galloway 1979, 247; Crummy 2001b, 102), although this phase may well have extended into the late 4th century. One of the comb fragments from well *5387* is an end-plate with a straight central section flanked by notches. Combs with straight centres are unusual in Roman Britain, most being either convex or concave, but there are two from South Shields Roman fort, one from the Wellington Row site in York, and two from Poundbury (Allason-Jones and Miket 1984, nos 2.39 and 2.45; York Archaeological Trust, unpublished, *Wellington Row site 1988–9.24*, SF 14293; Galloway 1993, fig. 78, 2–3). The final bone object from Settlement 7 is a single rectangular piece of inlay decorated with triple ring-and-dot motifs, probably from a wooden box (SF 2694, Fig. 6.52). Its late Roman context date matches that of a piece of veneer from Richborough (Henderson 1949, 152, no. 176), and of a group of 1,709 bone veneer or inlay plaques, including pieces like SF 2694, found abandoned on a workshop floor dated to the late 4th to early 5th century and sealed by dark earth on the Market Hall site, Gloucester (Hassall and Rhodes 1975, 73, fig. 28). A complete set of veneer from a late Roman wooden box was found in a late 4th- to 5th-century inhumation at Winchester, and in Germany there are also complete boxes from a late Roman context at Heilbronn, and in a Frankish grave at Weilbach (Rees *et al.* 2008, 108–11; Goessler 1932; Schoppa 1953).

The bone objects from Settlement 6 combine the characteristics of both the above groups, being composed of tools, waste debris, hairpins and a composite antler comb fragment. Two pieces of waste debris from Boundary 2 (Period 4.1) are from cattle, in contrast to the

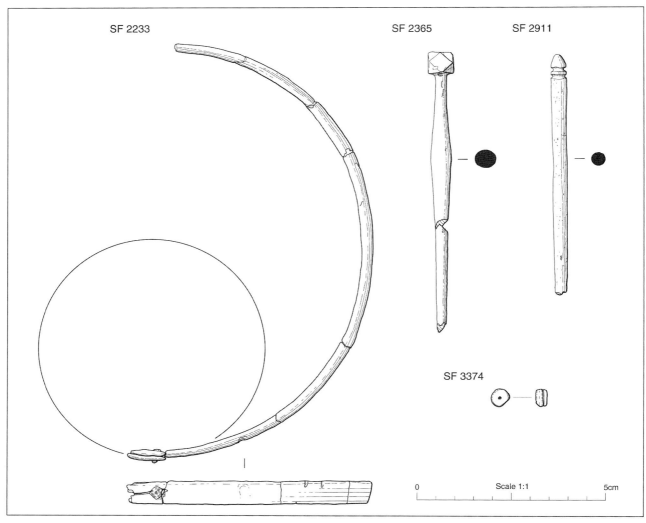

Figure 6.50 Worked bone dress accessories. Scale 1:1

utilisation of horse bones in the settlements. Both are discarded distal articulations from cattle metapodials (SF 3039, Fig. 6.54). The shafts of these bones provide strong straight sections of dense bone suitable for many objects, including hairpins and hinge units, and dumps of discarded articulations have been found in early Roman London and late Roman Canterbury (Crummy 2001b, 98, 100; Greep 1995, 1135–41). The third piece is a splinter from a long bone, perhaps utilised as a point, from Enclosure 104 (Period 4.4); the species cannot be determined (SF 3514, Fig. 6.54). The tools consist of a sheep/goat metatarsus with several groups of nicks along its length and a burnt ?handle fragment that may be from a disturbed burial or pyre feature (SFs 3505 and 2992, Fig. 6.53). As its shaft is highly polished, the metatarsus may have been a bobbin much like the tube from Settlement 2, but the many groups of nicks on the surface suggest it was used, perhaps secondarily, as a tally bone.

The hairpins from the southern area consist of an early Roman type from a Period 4.2 pit in the settlement (SF 2911, Fig. 6.50; Crummy 1983, 21, Type 2) and part of the swollen shaft from a pin later than c. AD 150, from a ditch (*11589*) outside the settlement (SF 2907, not illustrated). The final item is a late 4th- to early 5th-century damaged double-sided composite antler comb from the same ditch (SF 3104, Fig. 6.51). The comb's connecting-plates are plain apart from a pair of angled steps at each end and the one surviving end-plate is damaged and little of its decoration remains. Connecting-plates are more usually decorated than plain, but there are combs with plain plates with stepped edges from Lankhills, Poundbury, Alchester and York (Galloway 1979, fig. 31, 610; 1993, fig. 78, 2; Iliffe 1932, pl. 17, 2; York Archaeological Trust, unpublished, 1988.24, SF 14293). The steps run either along all four edges or along the two long edges, making the plates on SF 3104 unusually plain within the context of combs from Roman Britain, some of which are very highly decorated. The present author has argued elsewhere, from stylistic and stratigraphic evidence, that late Roman composite combs were made by itinerant makers of bone and antler objects who travelled from settlement to settlement or market to market as they did on the continent in the Viking period, carrying a stock of only lightly ornamented combs that could later be decorated (personalised) to suit the taste or pocket of individual purchasers (Crummy 2001b, 102–7). This is given credence by the fact that, within the substantial number of double-sided composite combs from Britain, the same examples from Poundbury and York share plain features with both SF 3104 and the comb (SF 3158) from well *5387*

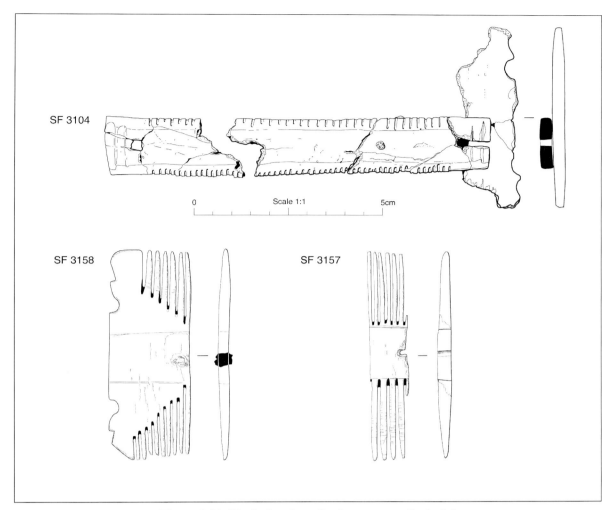

Figure 6.51 Worked antler toilet instruments. Scale 1:1

(Galloway 1993, fig. 78, 2; York Archaeological Trust, unpublished, 1988.24, SF 14293). Both the Love's Farm combs would, on this basis, belong at the lower end of the market, pointing to engagement with this aspect of personal grooming in the late Roman period but without the element of conspicuous consumption that characterises more elaborate combs.

The only item that cannot be attributed to one of the groups above is an unstratified pack-needle made from an antler tine (SF 16, Fig. 6.53). Used to tie up bales or lash them onto pack animals, this is probably of Roman date, although it may be either earlier or later (Mikler 1997, 55–6).

In summary, with variations in emphasis between the different areas and periods of the site, the assemblage of bone and antler objects provides evidence for leather-working, probably textile manufacture, the utilisation of both worked and unworked bones from horses, cattle and sheep/goats, the baling of goods and their transport, and contact with the changing grooming practices and styles of material culture of Roman Britain.

Catalogue of illustrated items

Dress accessories (Fig. 6.50)

SF3374 Small bone **disc** with two grooves around the circumference and a tiny central perforation. Diameter 4.5mm, length 3mm. *7007*, fill of cremation *7008*, Cemetery 3. Period 3.5.

SF2911 Bone **hairpin** with two grooves beneath a pointed head, a type that dates from the mid 1st century into the 2nd century AD (Crummy 1983, 21, Type 2). The end of the shaft is missing. Length 66mm. *8069*, fill of pit *8070*, Settlement 6. Period 4.2.

SF2365 Bone **hairpin** with faceted cuboid head, in two pieces (Crummy 1983, 23, Type 4). The type dates to the 4th century and perhaps the very early 5th. The shaft is broken and damaged at the break; it is very narrow immediately below the head. The tip is missing. Lengths of the individual pieces 48 and 29mm. *5334*, fill of ditch *5336*, Enclosure 133, Settlement 7 (Phase 2). Period 4.4.

SF2233 Bone **armlet**, almost complete. Made from a single strip of bone bent into a circle and secured by an iron rivet, the bone has split near the rivet, sprung apart and fragmented; a small section from close to the rivet is missing. The degree of curvature on the individual pieces varies. Surviving length of fragments: 54, 33, 28, 24, 19, 17 and 10mm; width 6mm. The original diameter was probably about 60–65mm. *4894*, fill of ditch *4895*, Settlement 7. Period 4.5.

Toilet instruments (Fig. 6.51)

SF3104 Double-sided composite antler **comb**. Most of one connecting-plate survives, together with part of the second connecting-plate, one end-plate, and part of the adjacent tooth-plate. The individual elements were secured by five iron rivets, only two of which remain. The connecting-plates are plain apart from a pair of angled steps at each end. Their sides are scored with tooth-cutting marks, with broad teeth on one side and narrow ones on the other. The sides and end of the end-plate are mainly missing, but one shallow and one deep semicircular notch remain on the edge near each terminal. Minimum length of connecting-plates 98mm, width 15mm.

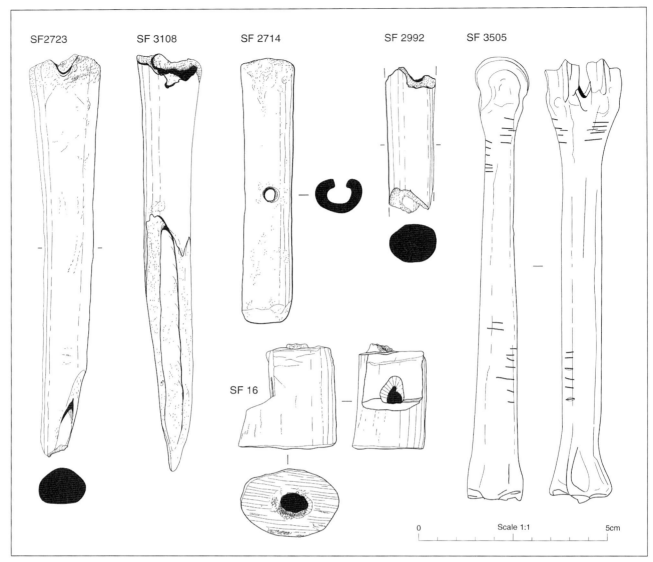

Figure 6.53 Worked bone and antler tools. Scale 1:1

Minimum width of end-plate 50mm. *11602*, unphased deposit, Settlement 6.

SF3158 End-plate from a double-sided composite **comb** of red deer antler, retaining the iron rivet that attached the missing connecting-plates. The position of the latter is marked on each face by fine incised guidelines. The decorative edge has a straight central section with a semicircular notch and a shallower angled notch on each side. The surviving corner is rounded, the other is chipped. Length 21.5mm, width 58mm, decreasing to 56–57mm where the teeth are worn from use. *5893*, fill of well *5387*, Settlement 7. Period 4.5.

SF3157 Fragment of a tooth-plate from a double-sided composite antler **comb**, broken across a rivet hole stained with iron. The teeth are intact. From the same comb as SF 3158 above, but not fitting. Length 10 mm, width 57 mm. Area 4a (*5890*), fill of well *5387*, Settlement 7, Period 4.5.

Household (Fig. 6.52)

SF2694 Bone rectangular **plaque** decorated with a large triple ring-and-dot motif; the dot is a hole that may have taken an attachment peg. The back is rough with cancellous tissue. 24 x 20mm. *5889*, fill of well *5387*, Settlement 7. Period 4.5.

Tools (Fig. 6.53)

SF2723 Socketed bone **tool** with the point, and most of the short socket, broken off. Length 111mm. *11137*, fill of ditch *11140*, Enclosure 150, Settlement 1. Period 3.3.

SF3108 Socketed bone **tool** with some damage to the upper sides of the socket and to the upper end where the articulation has been removed. The point and the lower sides of the socket are worn and polished. Length 115mm. *10753*, fill of ditch *10747*, Enclosure 1, Settlement 6. Period 3.3.

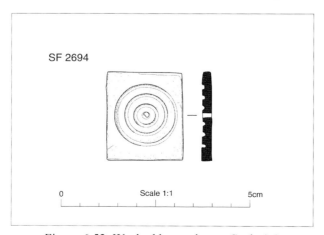

Figure 6.52 Worked bone plaque. Scale 1:1

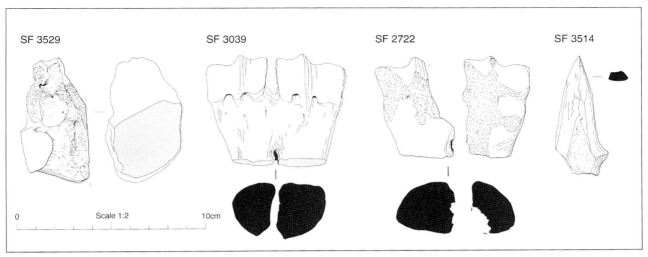

Figure 6.54 Boneworking debris. Scale 1:2

SF2714 Slightly waisted bone **tube** with a perforation in the centre of one side. The surface is very polished and the ends are both very worn and polished. Length 73.5mm, maximum diameter 15mm. *6363*, fill of pit *6338*, Quarry 3, Settlement 2. Period 3.4.

SF16 Fragment of a **pack-needle** made from an antler tine, but with the lower end cut across leaving a broken spur of the core. Length to cut edge 27mm, total length 29mm, maximum diameter 26mm. Unstratified.

SF2992 Part of a slightly tapering tubular object made of bone, probably part of a **handle**, burnt to a dark grey-black colour both internally and externally. The marrow cavity has been trimmed to form a tapering hollow. Both ends are broken. Length 40mm, maximum diameter 13.5mm. *9428*, fill of ditch *9429*, Settlement 6. Period 3.4.

SF3505 Sheep/goat metatarsus with highly **polished shaft** marked by four rows of short nicks. Near the proximal end of the shaft is a row of six nicks and there are three rows set around the shaft just above the distal articulation: two with four deep nicks and a central shallow one and one with eight nicks, some deeper than others. Length 121mm. Like SF 2714 above this bone may have been used as a bobbin. *11308*, fill of ditch *11307*, Enclosure 100, Settlement 6. Period 4.1.

Bone-working debris (Fig. 6.54)

SF3529 Distal articulation of a **horse radius** that has been sawn from the shaft. Width 67.5mm. *8118*, fill of ditch *8119*, Enclosure 12, Settlement 6. Period 3.3.

SF2772 Two distal articulations from a **cattle metapodial**, one incomplete. Both have been sawn from the shaft. Lengths 58 and 56mm. *8122*, fill of ditch *8123*, Boundary 2, Settlement 6. Period 4.1.

SF3039 Fragment of the distal end of a **horse metapodial**, trimmed slightly on one side of the articulation. Length 98mm. *6306*, fill of ditch *6225*, Enclosure 10, Settlement 2. Period 3.4.

SF3514 Utilised fragment from a shattered **long bone**. The fragment comes to a point that is slightly worn and could have been used as a piercing tool. Length 66mm. *11350*, fill of ditch *11348*, Enclosure 104, Settlement 6. Period 4.4.

X. Leather shoes
by Quita Mould
(Fig. 6.55)

A small group of leather was recovered from a well in Settlement 7. In Britain, Roman leather is dominated by large assemblages from military or urban contexts – rural groups are relatively rare and few dating to AD 350+ have been found, making this small assemblage of particular interest. Cleats and hobnails from the site are detailed by Crummy, above.

The leather was wet and washed when examined and recorded. Leather species were identified by hair follicle pattern using low powered magnification. Where the grain surface of the leather was heavily worn, identification was not always possible. The distinction between immature (calfskin) and mature cattle hides is not always easy to determine and the term bovine leather has been used when in doubt. Bottom unit components are assumed to be of cattle hide unless stated otherwise. The grain patterns of sheep and goat skins are difficult to distinguish and have been grouped together as sheep/goat when the distinction could not be made. The terminology used to describe Roman shoes and the shoe constructions employed are those most recently summarised by van Driel-Murray (2001).

Leather was recovered from four contexts (*5889, 5890, 5891, 5893*), all fills within a deep stone-lined well (*5387*; Fig. 4.23), a Period 4.5 feature located within Settlement 7. The leather comprises small fragments of Roman shoes. The shoe parts from fills *5891* and *5893* are particularly fragmentary having been excavated by machine rather than by hand. The shoes are of nailed construction, the most common method of shoe construction employed and found throughout the Roman occupation. Shoes of nailed construction have soles made of several layers held together principally by nailing. These layers, usually comprising an insole, a middle sole, middle laminae or small pieces of middle packing, and an outer sole, are known collectively as the bottom unit.

The shoe parts recovered are highly fragmentary and it is possible that four or five individual shoes are represented. While the shoe parts found are predominantly bottom units of nailed construction, two items – a sole forepart (SF 3152) and a small heel stiffener (SF 3187/3189) – have features that hint that they may come from a sandal and a stitched shoe respectively. Too little of each shoe survives to be certain.

Despite the fragmentary nature of the parts recovered, a number of constructional features are preserved. The bottom units are sparsely nailed with the individual nails widely spaced. The insoles are attached to middle laminae by constructional thonging: fragments of thong, varying

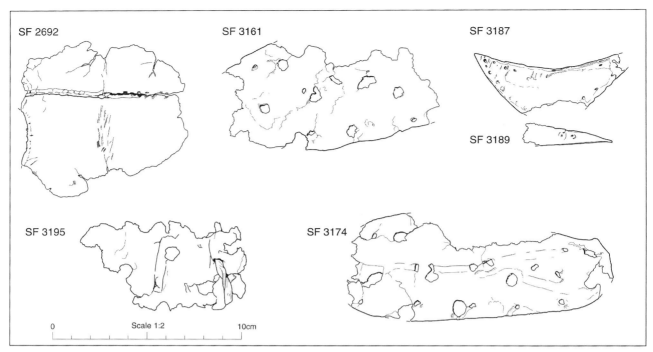

Figure 6.55 Leather shoe fragments. Scale 1:1

from 3–5mm in width, being preserved on several fragments of bottom unit (SF 3161; SF 3175, 3188 and 3195). One bottom unit fragment (SF 3174) showed that the lasting margin of the shoe upper had been whip stitched to the edge of the middle component with fine thong or thread 2mm wide.

Two pieces of shoe upper are present: a small triangular heel stiffener of cattle hide (SF 3187/3189) and the toe area from a vamp (SF 2692). The latter, a fragment torn from the toe area of a shoe vamp of bovine leather was found in context *5889*. The vamp has a false toe seam running vertically down the centre. The false seam has been formed by line of paired, angled, grain/flesh stitches sewn with a double thread pulled tightly to form a flat-topped ridge 2mm wide on the upper (grain) surface and a channel on the lower (flesh) surface (see Fig. 6.55). This is the tenth example of a mock toe seam recorded from Roman Britain that is known to the author. This is likely to be a reflection of the limited recovery of later Roman leather assemblages in Britain rather than a measure of their rarity, as they appear to have been found more frequently in other north-western provinces. The false or mock toe seam may take a number of forms including a line of tunnel stitching and a simple running stitch of thong; the stitched ridged seam of the Love's Farm shoe is finely sewn. Like the Love's Farm example, the other shoes with mock toe seams come principally, but not exclusively, from civilian contexts in south-eastern England. The most westerly, from the early/mid 4th-century boat at Magor, Gwent (van Driel-Murray 1999, 7) has a saddle stitched false seam and may be the closest parallel. Few examples come from dated contexts but those that do are of 4th-century date. Four have been found in wells, like the Love's Farm example. One was found in the basal fill of a well at the Tower Works, Peterborough (Mould 2005). Other examples have been found in a well with pottery dating after AD 250 at Rectory Farm, Market Deeping, Lincs (Mould 1996a, 1996b), in a well fill dating to *c*.AD 330–360 at Piddington, Northants (Friendship-Taylor 1997, 2), and in a 4th-century well backfill at Skeldergate, York (MacGregor 1978, fig. 28, 353).

Catalogue of illustrated items

SF2692 **Shoe vamp fragment**. Toe area of shoe vamp, broken away above the lasting margin. A curving grain/flesh closed seam, stitch length 3mm, present along the right side. A decorative false toe seam runs vertically from this curved seam toward the toe. The false seam comprises a line of paired, angled, grain/flesh stitches sewn with a double thread pulled tight to create a channel on the flesh (interior) side and a flat-topped ridge 2mm wide on the grain side. Incomplete. Leather worn, little grain pattern visible, probably bovine 2mm thick. Length 87mm, width 84mm. *5889*, fill of well *5387*, Settlement 7. Period 4.5.

SF3161 Shoe, nailed bottom unit fragments. Thong, small fragment, no grain pattern visible, 17 x 5 x 1mm. Fragment of bottom unit component of nailed shoe, probably from the forepart of a middle component. Widely spaced nailing along the edge with a second line present. A pair of thong slots present in the centre and a small piece of thong, 3mm wide, protrudes from a hole along the edge. A square iron nail shank remains *in situ*. No grain pattern visible. Length 119mm, width 165mm, 1.5mm thick. *5891*, fill of well *5387*, Settlement 7. Period 4.5.

SF3174 Shoe, nailed bottom unit fragments. The seat, waist and lower tread area of a middle component from a nailed bottom unit. Widely spaced line of nailing around the edge and down the centre. A line of smaller holes is present along the edge with the impression of fine thong, 2mm wide, by which the lasting margin of the upper was attached. Pair of thong slots with the clear impression of constructional thonging, 5mm wide, running down the centre. Leather compacted, no grain pattern visible, 1mm thick. Length 146mm, width 60mm. *5891*, fill of well *5387*, Settlement 7. Period 4.5.

SF3187 **Shoe, heel stiffener**. Small triangular heel stiffener with gently curving profile and grain/flesh stitching, stitch length 5mm, along the surviving edges. Broken into two pieces, top missing. Incomplete. Leather cattle hide. Surviving height 27mm, width 110mm, 3mm thick. *5891*, fill of well *5387*, Settlement 7. Period 4.5.

SF3189 Part of heel stiffener SF 3187 (above). *5891*, fill of well *5387*, Settlement 7. Period 4.5.

SF3195 Shoe, nailed bottom unit fragment. Fragment of nailed bottom unit component with widely spaced nail holes and thonging present. Thonging, 4mm wide, runs parallel and 10mm from the edge, the impression of constructional thonging, 5mm wide, is also visible running down the centre. Leather compacted bovine. Length 50mm, width 89mm, 2mm thick. *5891*, fill of well *5387*, Settlement 7. Period 4.5.

Chapter 7. The Pottery

I. Introduction
by Alice Lyons

Summary

Investigations at Love's Farm produced one of the largest multi-period pottery assemblages yet to have been excavated in the eastern region. The group amounts to 33,871 sherds, weighing 428.454kg and representing at least 12,000 vessels. Whilst the material spans the Neolithic (Period 1) to Anglo-Saxon periods (Period 5), most was deposited during the Romano-British period (Period 4; late 1st–4th centuries AD).

Neolithic and earlier Bronze Age pottery were found in small quantities, representing 0.4% by weight of the total assemblage. Iron Age pottery was more numerous (16.9%), spanning the middle to late Iron Age (Periods 3.1–2 and 3.3), with no diagnostic early Iron Age material present. The late pre-Roman Iron Age (LPRIA; Period 3.4), the early Roman pottery (Period 4.1) and the material transitional between these two periods (Period 3.5) represents 24.8% (by weight) of the assemblage. Pottery was, however, at its most abundant during the middle to late Romano-British period (Periods 4.2–4.5) when over half (57.4%) of the total assemblage was deposited. A small amount (0.5%) of post-Roman pottery was also found.

Throughout all periods, most vessel types were utilitarian in nature and largely locally produced (often in shell-tempered fabrics), with imported wares being relatively scarce. The only exception to this occurred in the LPRIA and early Roman periods, when pottery was generally finer and frequently imported.

Preservation

The average sherd size across the whole assemblage is *c*.13g. While this is not unusual in the context of the region, the local clay geology meant that, once in the soil, the pottery continued to degenerate due to the naturally abrasive action of the clay soil, which often removed the original surface of the sherds. This destructive process was compounded by the use of the land for ploughing and drainage. The combined result of these natural and cultural processes is that much of the pottery arrived in ditches as a result of post-depositional movement of soil, and was therefore rarely found in its primary site of deposition (with a few notable exceptions). Over the site as a whole, these factors led to the deposition of a large group of fragmentary and abraded vessels.

Methodology

The assemblage was analysed in accordance with the guidelines laid down by the Prehistoric Ceramic Research Group (PCRG 2010) and the Study Group for Roman Pottery (Darling 2004; Willis 2004). The total assemblage was studied and a catalogue prepared for the project archive.

All sherds have been counted, classified and weighed to the nearest whole gram. For the wheelmade pottery the surviving percentage of each rim was measured to provide an Estimated Vessel Equivalent (EVE) calculation. It became apparent, however, that while EVE is a useful comparative statistical tool (Tyers 1996, 205), it does not accurately represent the number of individual vessels identified (only the sum of the surviving percentage of recorded rim diameters). At Love's Farm, a total of 7,873 catalogue entries was made for the LPRIA (Period 3.4), late Iron Age to early Romano-British transitional period (Period 3.5), the early Romano-British period (Period 4.1) and the middle to late Romano-British period (Periods 4.2–4.5), each of which represents a minimum of one vessel; this figure gives a better impression of the total number of vessels analysed and the actual vessel count is estimated to be nearer 10,000 vessels. (Each catalogue entry should ideally only represent one vessel, but in practise undiagnostic body sherds from different vessels are grouped together, meaning that the number of catalogue entries represents a minimum vessel count only.) An additional 2,103 catalogue entries were made for prehistoric and Iron Age material, making an estimated total site assemblage of 12,103 vessels.

Period	Date	Sherd count	Sherd wt (g)	Estimated Vessel Equivalent (EVE)	Percentage (%) of assemblage by wt
1	Neolithic	411	1303	-	0.3
2	Bronze Age	40	302	-	0.1
3.1–3.3	Iron Age	6387	72592	-	16.9
3.4	Late pre-Roman Iron Age	3624	53001	26.08	12.4
3.5	Transitional	1857	22757	19.12	5.3
4.1	Early Roman	3144	30388	37.70	7.1
4.2–4.4	Romano-British	16365	218673	13.36	51.0
4.5	Late Romano-British	1838	27175	19.72	6.3
5	Post-Roman	205	2263	1.62	0.5
Total		33871	428454	117.60	100

The Neolithic, Bronze Age and early Saxon sherds noted in this table do not necessarily derive from features of that date, since some are residual or intrusive in other periods.

Table 7.1 The ceramic assemblage by site period

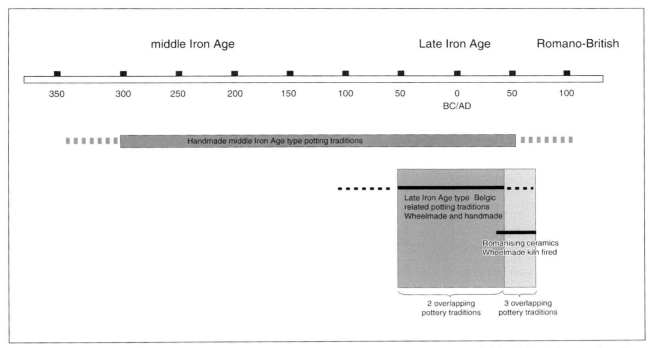

Figure 7.1 Model of the currency of later Iron Age potting tradition in southern Cambridgeshire (after Brudenell forthcoming)

All sherds were examined (if necessary using a hand lens; x20 magnification) and were divided into fabric groups defined on the basis of the dominant inclusion type present. The fabric codes are descriptive and abbreviated by the main letters of the title (*e.g.* samian, Southern Gaulish = SASG); vessel form was also recorded: a full list of the Romano-British fabrics appears in Appendix 3.I, while codes for earlier material appear in Tables 7.2 and 7.5. Decoration and abrasion were noted and a spot date has been provided for each individual sherd and context. For the Romano-British assemblage, only pottery that represents >0.4% (by weight) of each chronological group is discussed in detail here, with the exception of imported finewares.

Consideration of how the pottery was distributed within the archaeological features and how this changed through time has been achieved by using a GIS programme. Placing the pottery 'back in context' helped facilitate a dialogue between excavators and ceramic specialists (even although the general condition of the pottery is poor) and allowed the major developments in pottery supply and manufacture to be considered in direct relation to the changing site morphology. Using this process it became apparent that there were two distinct Romano-British settlements at Love's Farm: an earlier southern settlement (Settlement 6) and a later northern one (Settlement 7), an interpretation supported by evidence from the metal finds (Chapter 6.II: Coins).

Illustrating the pottery for publication has proved problematic due to the generally abraded nature of the assemblage. As a result, relatively few vessels were selected for illustration, although all are cross-referenced with other published examples within the Type Series (Appendix 3.II).

Report structure
(Fig. 7.1)
This chapter seeks to identify the characteristics of the ceramic assemblage at each stage in the site's evolution. To facilitate this, the early prehistoric pottery (Periods 1 and 2) is considered first, followed by the material spanning the middle Iron Age to the LPRIA (Periods 3.1–3.4). Analysing this latter material proved challenging as the period between the mid 4th century BC and the early 1st century AD encompasses changes in the ceramic traditions of this region which do not fit neatly into the conventional period divisions. For instance, elements of the handmade middle Iron Age-type potting tradition extend throughout the late Iron Age, up to, and sometimes even immediately beyond the Roman conquest (Fig. 7.1). Similarly, grog-tempered pottery and wheel-turned vessels of the late Iron Age tradition appear to be absent from the region's settlement sites until the mid to late 1st century BC, and when present, continue to be found alongside handmade middle Iron Age-type wares. To make matters even more confusing, some of the wheel-thrown forms allied to the late Iron Age tradition can post-date the Roman conquest by at least a decade and can still be found in Iron Age-type (or 'native') fabrics alongside Romanising wares.

In order to deal with these issues in practical terms, all pottery of Iron Age-type was separated from the LPRIA and analysed independently, although it is inevitable (given the chronological and stylistic background detailed above) that some pottery of differing ceramic traditions may actually be contemporary. In contrast, the Romano-British pottery is presented as a cohesive group, although the samian is considered both within its stratigraphic grouping, and as a separate entity spanning all periods. Finally, the Anglo-Saxon pottery is detailed and discussed.

II. Earlier prehistoric pottery
by Sarah Percival
(Fig. 7.2)

Neolithic (Period 1)

Introduction

An assemblage of 411 sherds of Neolithic (*c*.4000–2400 BC) pottery weighing 1,303g, and representing a maximum of twenty-five vessels, was collected from eight features. Most of the material came from pit *7444* (Fig. 2.3) in the southern part of the site, and soil deposits *11114* and *11115* (Fig. 2.2) to the north, which together produced 79% of the total Neolithic assemblage (1,029g). The remainder of the sherds were residual within later features. Most of the pottery is earlier Neolithic (402 sherds), generally consisting of plain bowls, although a single sherd of later Mildenhall Ware was also found, and a small quantity of later Neolithic Peterborough Ware was recovered. The condition of the majority of the sherds is poor and the mean sherd weight extremely low, at just 3.1g.

Fabric

Four fabrics were identified in three fabric groups; flint-tempered, shell-tempered and sandy with iron compounds (Table 7.2). The range of fabrics is similar to those identified within the contemporary assemblage from the prehistoric ritual complex at Eynesbury, which lies on the flood plain some 3km south-west of Love's Farm (Mepham 2004). Flint-tempered ware is the most common fabric at Love's Farm, making up 88% of the total assemblage (1,126g), including most of the plain bowls and the Peterborough Ware vessels. This fabric is highly characteristic of earlier Neolithic pottery in East Anglia, and dominates the major contemporary assemblages from Hurst Fen, Mildenhall and Broom Heath, Ditchingham, as well as recently excavated examples from Colney and Fordham (Clark *et al.* 1960; Wainwright 1972; Percival 2004b; Percival in prep. b). The flint-tempered fabric contains crushed angular flint in a range of sizes, while a second fabric (QF) contains smaller quantities of fine flint within a sandy matrix. Shell-tempered sherds make-up just under 9% of the assemblage, including the single Mildenhall Ware rim. This fabric is heavily leached, giving the sherds a pitted appearance. Shell temper was commonly used at Etton (Kinnes 1998) and was also found at Bob's Wood, Hinchingbrooke (Percival in prep. c), but is less prevalent in most other areas of East Anglia. The iron-rich fabric is unusual, but was also found at Eynesbury (Mepham 2004, 29).

Form

Rims were identified from a maximum of twenty-five vessels and were classified following the rim typology used for Hurst Fen, Suffolk, Windmill Hill, Wiltshire and Spong Hill, Norfolk (Longworth 1960, 228; Smith 1965; Healy 1988, fig. 57). Twenty-two of the vessels are plain bowls, of which thirteen have rolled or folded rims (Fig. 7.2, No. 1), seven have simple rounded rims, and two pointed rims (Fig. 7.2, No. 2). It is likely that the vessels were bag-shaped closed or neutral forms (Cleal 2004), similar to those found at Broome Heath (Wainwright 1972) and at Eynesbury (Mepham 2004, 29). At both Eynesbury and Love's Farm, however, the high fragmentation, small sherd size and low percentage of rims found prohibit precise identification of form.

A single rim sherd from a Mildenhall Ware vessel was found within deposit *11114*, which lay within a natural hollow (Fig. 2.2). This shell-tempered sherd is similar to a vessel found at Etton, and has comparable incised channels on an externally thickened rim (Kinnes 1998, fig. 181, M91).

In addition, nineteen sherds of later Neolithic Peterborough Ware from at least two vessels were recovered. Both rims are flattened and pinched-out, one being decorated with incised hatching on the rim top with fingertip impressions below (Fig. 7.2, No. 3). The second example has cord-impressed maggots on the interior of the rim with incised cross-hatched lines below and impressed decoration on the exterior (Fig. 7.2, No. 4). Again, these vessels find parallels within the Etton assemblage (Kinnes 1998, fig. 201 E1, fig. 202, E6), and are tentatively identified as being of the Ebbsfleet sub-style (Gibson 2002, 218).

Catalogue of illustrated Neolithic pottery

1   Earlier Neolithic **plain bowl** rim, Fabric F1. *7518*, fill of pit *7444*. Period 1.
2   Earlier Neolithic **plain bowl** rim, Fabric F1. *7518*, fill of pit *7444*. Period 1.
3   Later Neolithic **Peterborough Ware bowl** pinched out rim, Fabric F1. *7145*, fill of pit/gully *7146*. Period 1.
4   Later Neolithic **Peterborough Ware bowl** rim, incised on rim top, Fabric QF. *7145*, fill of pit/gully *7146*. Period 1.

Discussion

The earlier Neolithic plain bowl is characterised by simple, rolled or folded rims and slack, bag-shaped vessels, although interpretation of vessel form remains uncertain. Rim forms are very similar to those identified at Broome Heath, Ditchingham (Wainwright 1972). The pottery is likely to be broadly contemporary with the earlier Neolithic vessels from Eynesbury where a radiocarbon date of 3970–3690 cal. BC was recovered from the closing pit of a hengiform monument (Mepham 2004, 30).

Early Bronze Age (Period 2)

Forty sherds, weighing 302g, were identified as being of Bronze Age date. One sherd from a possible Beaker with a pointed rim and incised decoration in grog-tempered

Fabric	Description	Quantity	% Quantity	Wt (g)	% Wt
F1	Common to moderate small to medium angular flint	329	81.8	1126	88.0
QF	Quartz sand with sparse to common small angular flint	5	1.2	14	1.1
S	Common, soft white shell plates up to 6mm; sparse quartz sand	56	13.9	109	8.5
FE1	Quartz sand with sparse to common sub rounded iron compounds	12	3.0	31	2.4
Total		402	100	1280	100

Table 7.2 Quantity and weight of earlier Neolithic pottery by fabric

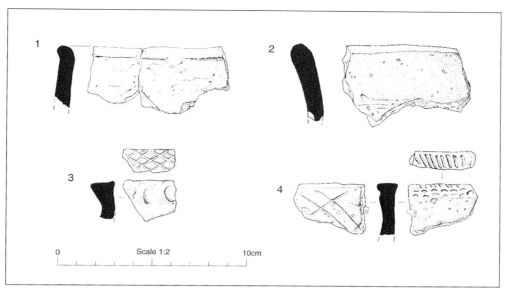

Figure 7.2 Early prehistoric pottery. Scale 1:2

fabric was recovered from soil layer *7356*, in the southern part of the site. The sherd is broadly similar to Beaker types recovered at Eynesbury (Mepham 2004, 39), and represents intermittent domestic activity at the Love's Farm site during the later Neolithic to earlier Bronze Age. Twenty-three sherds from two early Bronze Age Collared Urns were also recovered from well/waterhole *11136* (Waterhole 1; Fig. 2.2), located towards the north-east corner of the site. All are made of heavily grog-tempered fabric. These undecorated vessels are small, perhaps standing to a height of 0.3m, and have been found in funerary contexts (Ashwin and Bates 2000, 42) but are also known from non-funerary contexts in the fens (Longworth 1984). It is likely that the Love's Farm Collared Urns are domestic in origin.

A rim fragment from a large Collared Urn with cord-impressed decoration was recovered from an evaluation trench. The urn is made of a coarse, soapy, grog-tempered fabric. Again, such vessels are known from both funerary and non-funerary contexts. The Love's Farm example finds parallel with a semi-complete Collared Urn at Eynesbury, which contained a cremation burial (Mepham 2004, fig.19).

III. Iron Age and Iron Age/Romano-British transitional pottery
(Figs 7.3–7.10)

Introduction
The Iron Age to transitional pottery (Period 3) from the site is listed and quantified by site period in Table 7.3. The late Iron Age material is examined below both by ceramic phase and site period.

Iron Age pottery by ceramic phase
by Sarah Percival

Introduction
The large assemblage of Iron Age pottery contains a variety of pottery styles. No diagnostic early Iron Age pottery was recovered: the earliest material found dates to the middle Iron Age (*c*.400–100 BC), continuing through the later Iron Age (*c*.100–50 BC) and into the LPRIA, which continues into the 1st century AD. A total assemblage of 8,187 sherds, weighing 87,152g was recovered from the entire site, while a group of 11,868 sherds came from deposits assigned to Period 3 as a whole (including all residual and transitional material; see Table 7.3 and Lyons below). The breakdown of Iron Age pottery by ceramic period is shown in Table 7.4. The pottery is in an average state of preservation and, when considered by ceramic phase, has a mean sherd weight (MSW) of 11g.

Fabric
Six main fabric groups were identified, of which fossiliferous shell-tempered fabrics are the most prevalent, making up over 45.5% of the assemblage: they are shown by fabric group in Table 7.5 and in full detail in Table 7.6. Sandy fabrics are the second most common fabric and grog-tempered fabrics are the third most numerous. Small quantities of organic, calcareous and flint-tempered fabrics were also found.

Shell-tempered wares often make up a considerable proportion of Iron Age assemblages from western Cambridgeshire (Hancocks 2003, table 7.6; Abrams and Ingham 2008, fig. 2.11). The importance of shell tempering within Iron Age assemblages in south-western Cambridgeshire probably reflects the distribution of the Jurassic formations which provide the source of the clay in which fossiliferous shell occurs naturally (Williams 2003a, 169; Williams 2003b, 76). In addition to geological availability, cultural preference also influenced the choice of fabric type. This is demonstrated at sites such as Haddenham, where shell-tempered vessels were imported to the site (Hill and Braddock 2006). The preference to use coarser shelly fabrics in the production of larger storage vessels and some cooking jars observed at Love's Farm is seen at many other sites in the area, including Little Paxton, Haddenham V and Bob's Wood, Hinchingbrooke (Hancocks 2003, 76; Hill and Braddock 1999; Percival in prep. c).

The sandy fabrics are very similar to those found at Bob's Wood, being characterised by the presence of

Date	Period	Sherd count	Sherd Wt (g)	EVE	MSW (g)	Proportion (Wt %) of site assemblage
Iron Age (not closely datable)	3	541	19643	-	36.3	4.58
Earlier Iron Age (750–350 BC)	3.1	32	145	-	4.5	0.03
No pottery of diagnostic Early Iron Age date was present at the site, although a small quantity of pottery broadly dating to the Iron Age was recovered from features attributed to this phase.						
Middle Iron Age (350–100 BC)	3.2	1614	13305	-	8.2	3.10
Shell-tempered vessels dominated, although sandy fabrics were also used. Calcareous or chalk and flint-tempered fabrics were also in use, with grog-tempered fabrics present in very small quantities.						
Late Iron Age (100 BC to AD 42)	3.3	4200	39499	-	9.4	9.21
Sandy fabrics took over from shell-tempered wares and grog-tempered fabrics formed a significant component. Flint fabrics fell from use, although calcareous fabrics continued.						
Period 3 and 3.1–3.3 Total		*6387*	*72592*	*N/A*	*14.6*	*16.94*
Late Pre-Roman Iron Age (mid 1st century BC to mid 1st century AD)	3.4	3624	53001	26.08	14.6	12.38
Iron Age (handmade/bonfired pottery) was being supplemented by wheelmade/kiln fired Gaulish imports and local copies. Grog-tempered pottery became common.						
Transitional (mid 1st AD to early/mid 2nd AD)	3.5	1857	22757	19.12	12.3	5.31
Iron Age fabrics (becoming sandier) continued to be used to produce more Romanised forms (rolled rim jars *etc.*). Some vessels were wheelmade and some were handmade. Gaulish finewares, including samian, were now in use.						
Period Total		*11,868*	*148,350*		*12.5*	*34.57*

Table 7.3 Iron Age to transitional pottery (Period 3) listed and quantified by sub-period

Ceramic period	Quantity	% Quantity	Wt (g)	% Wt	MSW (g)
Middle Iron Age	1978	27.6	31544	37.5	16
Later Iron Age	2174	30.3	26584	31.6	12
LPRIA	781	10.9	11553	13.7	14
Iron Age	2235	31.2	14464	17.2	6
Total	*7168*	*100*	*84145*	*100*	*11*

Table 7.4 Quantity and weight of Iron Age pottery by ceramic period

Main inclusion	Quantity	% Quantity	Wt (g)	% Wt
Shell (fossil) (S)	2332	32.5	38282	45.5
Quartz sand (Q)	3629	50.6	34265	40.7
Grog (G)	1006	14.0	10130	12.0
Organic (O)	13	0.2	43	0.1
Flint (F)	8	0.1	56	0.1
Calcareous (C)	158	2.2	1351	1.6
Other	22	0.3	18	0.0
Total	*7168*	*100*	*84145*	*100*

Table 7.5 Quantity and weight of Iron Age pottery from the entire site, by fabric group

sparse to abundant quantities of quartz sand, iron oxide grains and complete or fragmentary flint gravel. Fabrics are usually harder and denser than those with shell (Hill and Braddock 1999). Organic tempering forms less than 1% of the assemblage. Vegetable-tempered pottery is a rare component on many later Iron Age sites across Cambridgeshire, but was used in relatively large quantities on some 3rd- to 1st-century BC sites around the southern fens and at West Stow (West 1990, 60; Hill and Braddock 1999). At Bob's Wood, organic-tempered sherds formed around 5.6% of assemblage (Percival in prep. c), perhaps indicating that this site had stronger links to the southern fen area than were present at Love's Farm.

Chalky fabrics are found in small quantities in all three Iron Age phases represented (*i.e.* middle Iron Age, late Iron Age and LPRIA), but are most common in the late Iron Age (Period 3.3). Similar fabrics were found at Bob's Wood, and may represent imports to the site, perhaps from the chalk-rich clays of the Chiltern Hills to the east and south-east (Hill and Braddock 1999). No glauconitic fabrics were found at Love's Farm, although these form a

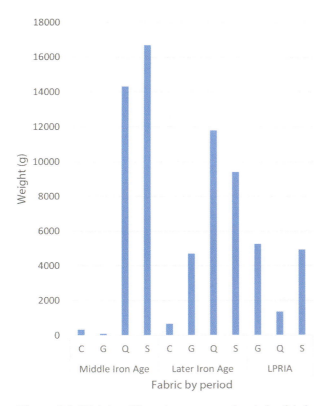

Figure 7.3 Weight of Iron Age pottery sherds by fabric type and ceramic period (excluding fabrics with less than 100g of material)

component of many Iron Age assemblages, such as Bob's Wood (Oxford Archaeology East, in prep.).

The relative quantities of each fabric type did not remain static throughout the three periods of Iron Age occupation at the site (Fig. 7.3). During the middle Iron Age (Period 3.1–3.2), shell-tempered vessels predominated, although sandy fabrics formed a significant proportion of the site assemblage. The relative proportions of shelly and sandy fabric compare well with those from nearby Little Paxton (Hancocks 2003, table 7.1). Throughout this period calcareous- or chalk-, organic- and flint-tempered fabrics were in use, together with very small quantities of grog-tempered fabrics. By the later Iron Age (Period 3.3), sandy fabrics had taken over from shell-tempered wares, and grog-tempered fabrics formed a significant component. Flint fabrics fell out of use at this time although calcareous fabrics continued. In the LPRIA (Period 3.4), grog was the most common inclusion found. Sandy fabrics declined and shelly fabrics continued to form an important component, albeit used for a restricted number of vessel types, for example storage jars. The increasing importance of grog tempering in the LPRIA is echoed at Bob's Wood (Percival forthcoming) and Little Paxton (Hancocks 2003, 75). Thompson, in her discussion of the introduction of grog-tempered wares, notes that in Cambridgeshire, which lies on the periphery of the main grog-using areas, sandy fabrics commonly form a high percentage of later assemblages (Thompson 1982), and this is certainly the case at Love's Farm in the later Iron Age. By the LPRIA, however, the use of sand declined, suggesting that, at Love's Farm, the grog fabrics replaced the sandy fabrics rather than supplementing them. This indicates that, on sites where shell tempering was prevalent during the middle Iron Age, it continued to be of importance in the LPRIA. A similar pattern of adoption is seen at Bob's Wood, where the use of shell-tempered fabrics was well established before grog tempering was introduced, and continued to be used alongside the newer grog-tempered vessels. Mixed shell and grog fabrics are found in both the Love's Farm and Bob's Wood assemblages.

Form

The vessels were recorded using the form series developed for later Iron Age pottery from Cambridgeshire by J.D. Hill (Hill and Horne 2003, 174). A minimum of 385 vessels was recovered, based on rim count, a number which is almost certainly less than the actual quantity of vessels present. The forms present are shown in Table 7.7.

Vessel forms vary at Love's Farm, showing a strong chronological progression through the three Iron Age phases (Fig. 7.4). In the site's middle Iron Age assemblage, nine vessel forms are represented, principally slack-shouldered jar forms A and D. By the later Iron Age phase the number of vessel forms present increases to fifteen, and in the LPRIA twenty-one vessel forms were in use (many of which are included in the 'Other' category in Fig. 7.4). Storage jars occur in all three ceramic periods, although the numbers decline in the LPRIA.

All three phases contain slack-shouldered jars and bowls with simple upright or near-upright rims (Type A: Fig. 7.5, No. 5; Fig. 7.6, No. 10; Fig. 7.8, No. 22) or everted rims (Type D: Fig. 7.5, Nos 1 and 7, Fig. 7.6, No. 13). This utilitarian vessel form dominates most middle to late Iron Age assemblages from Cambridgeshire (Hill and Horne 2003, 174) and is widely found throughout East Anglia (Percival 1996, 265). The slack-shouldered jars declined as the Iron Age progressed, and represent only a small component of the LPRIA assemblage. A similar fall-off in Type A vessels in the LPRIA is seen at other contemporary sites such as Bob's Wood, where, although the Type A jar forms appear to have continued in use alongside the LPRIA forms, the Type A bowls were replaced by grog-tempered cordoned forms (Types Q and R; Percival in prep. c).

Decoration is limited amongst the Type A vessels. Eleven are decorated with diagonal fingernail impressions across the flattened rim top and six have scored decoration (Fig. 7.6, Nos 9 and 10). No vessels were found with fingertip impressed decoration to the shoulder.

Tub- and barrel-shaped neckless, and sometimes rimless, vessels (Types K, P and T) – present in relatively large numbers within the contemporary assemblage from Bob's Wood, Hinchingbrooke (Percival in prep. c) – are less common at Love's Farm. A similar vessel form found at Love's Farm is a wide-rimmed straight-sided jar with bead rim (Thompson C1–3), which dates to the 1st century BC but continued in use into the 1st century AD (Thompson 1982, 217). Vessel Type K (Fig. 7.5, No. 4) is present in small numbers in the middle to late Iron Age phases but disappears completely in the LPRIA. Small numbers of Type P, flowerpot-shaped vessels are found in all three phases (Fig. 7.7, No 14), but Type T straight-sided beakers are entirely absent. Although tub- and barrel-shaped vessels were found at nearby Little Paxton (Hancocks 2003, 89), they are most common on sites in the southern fens and Lincolnshire (Pryor *et al.* 1985, fig.

Fabric	Description	Quantity	Wt (g)	% Wt
C1	Sparse sub-rounded chalk pieces; sparse quartz, organic	168	1383	1.6
F1	Speckled with angular flint	349	1200	1.4
F2	Big chunky flint inclusions	7	14	0.0
G	Grog tempered	20	40	0.0
G1	Very dark dense fabric. Abundant small rounded grog. Pimpled surface.	272	2062	2.4
G100	Common medium sub-angular grog, occasional quartz, sparse flint	25	255	0.3
G2	Common, medium pale grog pieces; some quartz sand	221	2113	2.4
G3	Moderate, large angular grog; occasional rounded chalk	49	355	0.4
G4	Moderate, small rounded grog; occasional rounded chalk, organic	43	190	0.2
G5	Buff orange; occasional orange pieces of grog; occasional white chalk	54	562	0.6
G6	Orange buff surfaces, dark grey interior and matrix; speckled with dark grey grog pieces	150	1891	2.2
G7	Grog big sparse and shell (rare)	20	424	0.5
G8	Wheelmade chalk grog, orange ext, grey interior	31	230	0.3
GS	Grog with shell	6	32	0.0
GTW	Grog-tempered ware	8	37	0.0
GTW(P)	Grog-tempered ware with pink grog	7	189	0.2
GW(G)	Greyware with grog	31	384	0.4
GW(G)(P)	Greyware with pink grog	2	15	0.0
GW(GROG)	Greyware with grog	23	88	0.1
O1	Vacuous fabric with organic voids	7	27	0.0
OW(G)	Oxidised ware	3	6	0.0
OW(GROG)	Oxidised ware with grog	3	10	0.0
PGW	Proto sandy greyware. Micaceous, grey throughout, occasional buff surfaces, dark speckled	19	207	0.2
Q	Quartz sand tempered	299	536	0.6
Q1	Common quartz sand; micaceous, dark grey throughout	898	7155	8.2
Q2	Common quartz sand; occasional angular flint, occasional rounded white quartz. Orange buff surfaces, grey matrix	870	5574	6.4
Q3	Sand and fine shell, soapy	365	2694	3.1
Q4	Common quartz sand with occasional flint	292	5493	6.3
Q5	Common quartz sand with occasional chalk	710	5800	6.7
Q6	Sandy harsh with occasional shell	156	769	0.9
Q7	Dense hard-fired sandy occasional large rounded quartz	15	94	0.1
Q8	Fine dense sandy	255	6465	7.4
QF	Quartz sand with flint	5	14	0.0
RW(G)	Grog-tempered reduced ware	111	1115	1.3
RW(GROG)(P)	Grog-tempered reduced ware with pink grog	28	277	0.3
S	Shell-tempered ware	123	243	0.3
S1	Common, soft white shell plates up to 6mm; sparse quartz sand. Dark grey to buff surface, dark grey throughout	1016	9789	11.2
S2	Abundant small shell pieces. Soft dark grey orange surface, dark grey matrix	274	6564	7.5
S3	Orange; occasional large fossil shells, sparse hard flint	113	3682	4.2
S4	Moderate medium shell 6mm or less	736	7603	8.7
S5	Common very coarse shell up to 8mm which protrude from surface	116	8839	10.1
SF	Shell with flint	9	27	0.0
SGW	Sandy greyware	19	132	0.2
SGW(FINE)	Sandy greyware	11	66	0.1
SGW(GROG)	Sandy greyware	1	4	0.0
SGW(PROTO)	Proto Sandy greyware	17	135	0.2
SRW	Sandy reduced ware	2	28	0.0
SRW(FINE)	Sandy reduced ware fine	6	61	0.1
SRW(G)(P)	Sandy reduced ware with pink grog	3	17	0.0
SRW(GROG)	Sandy reduced ware with grog	5	274	0.3
SRW(P)	Sandy reduced ware	3	24	0.0
STW	Shell tempered ware	152	1528	1.8
STW(G)	Shell tempered ware (grog)	12	314	0.4
STW(HM)	Shell tempered ware (Hand made)	3	35	0.0
U	Undiagnostic	43	78	0.1

Fabric	Description	Quantity	Wt (g)	% Wt
VOW	? Oxidised ware	1	9	0.0
Total		*8187*	*87152*	*100*

Table 7.6 Quantity and weight of Iron Age pottery from the entire site, by fabric (including intrusive Roman sherds)

Form	Description	Quantity	Wt (g)	No. vessels
1	Flat rim	29	827	27
2	Rounded rim	13	411	9
6	Square shaped exterior lip	2	12	1
A1	Slack shouldered jar with upright neck and flat rim	120	3255	105
A2	Slack shouldered jar with upright neck and rounded rim	7	62	6
B2	Dog leg profile angular shouldered jar with upright neck rounded rim	2	26	1
C3	Angular shouldered jar with tapered neck rounded rim	1	22	1
D	Outward flared rim, slack shoulder.	21	115	0
D1	Slack shouldered jar with flared neck and flat rim	46	1259	34
D2	Slack shouldered jar with flared neck and rounded rim	41	313	28
E1	Jar with high rounded shouldered upright neck flat rim	8	234	5
E5	Jar with high rounded shouldered upright neck rim with rounded external lip	3	221	1
F2	Round bodied vessel with short everted rim with rounded rim ending	9	179	8
G	Round bodied open vessel with distinct concave neck and everted rim	4	82	4
G10	Round bodied open vessel, distinct concave neck and everted elongated beaded rim	3	57	2
G2	Round bodied open vessel with distinct concave neck and everted rounded rim	50	1074	30
G9	Round bodied open vessel with distinct concave neck and everted beaded rim	1	5	1
H1	High shouldered round bodied vessel with distinct angular profile neck straight outward flaring flat rim	1	3	1
H2	High shouldered round bodied vessel with distinct angular profile neck straight outward flaring rounded rim	2	21	2
J	High shouldered open vessel with straight walls and distinct angular shoulder	4	22	1
J2	High shouldered open vessel with straight walls and distinct angular shoulder rounded rim ending	12	112	1
K	Ovoid or rounded slack shouldered vessel, no distinct rim	25	854	16
M	Round globular vessel, no neck	11	143	1
M2	Round globular vessel, no neck rounded rim	2	82	2
N	Fish bowl short neck everted rim	8	120	2
N2	Fish bowl short neck rounded everted rim	14	828	9
P6	Flowerpot-shaped vessel. Square external lip	71	7920	8
P9	Flowerpot-shaped vessel beaded rim	2	220	2
Q	Carinated open bowl,	66	730	2
Q10	Carinated open bowl tapered beaded rim	2	15	2
Q2	Carinated open bowl rounded rim	13	101	2
Q9	Carinated open bowl beaded rim	1	1	1
R	Cordoned-necked open vessel	5	116	0
R10	Cordoned-necked open vessel tapered beaded rim	4	64	4
SJAR	Storage jar	87	4241	22
Thompson E	Cup	54	545	4
WJAR	Wide-mouthed jar	48	564	21
E2-4		1	2	1
Thompson D1-4	Wide-mouthed bowl	2	23	2
Thompson C1-3	Wide-rimmed straight-sided jars with bead rims	2	115	2
Thompson B1-1	Plain everted rim necked jars	4	160	4
Thompson D3-1	Plain rounded bowls	1	39	1
Lid seated bowl	Lid seated bowl	3	50	3
Lid seated jar	Lid seated jar	79	412	3
Jar/bowl	Vessel of uncertain form	29	430	2
Lid	Lid	1	6	1
Total				*385*

Table 7.7 Number of Iron Age vessels from the entire site, by vessel form

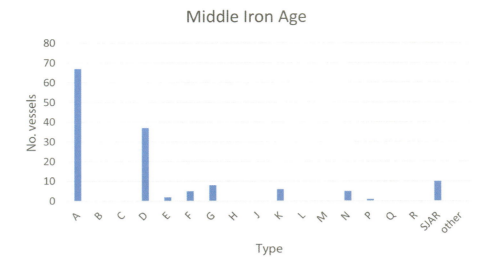
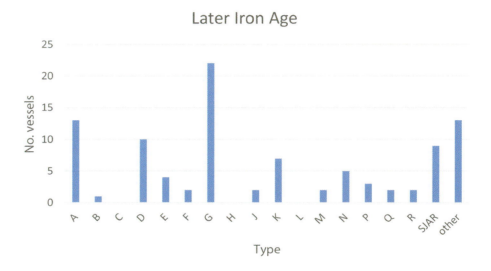
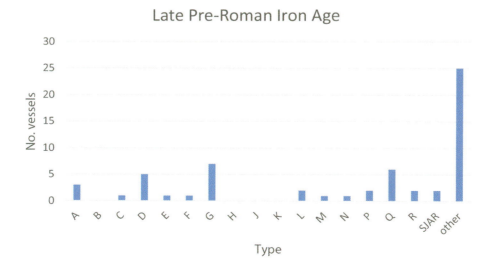

Figure 7.4 Number of Iron Age vessels from the entire site, by type

75, 10; Chowne 1986, fig. 9, 45), and were found in large quantities at Bob's Wood (Oxford Archaeology East, in prep.). It is possible that links with these easterly communities suggested by the similarity of vessel form at Bob's Wood were less strong at Love's Farm, where these vessel forms are less prevalent.

Vessels with rounded 'S-shaped' profiles and everted rims (Types F and G, Fig. 7.6, No. 8; Fig 7.9, Nos 23 and 29) were found in small numbers in the middle Iron Age assemblage but increased to become the dominant vessel form in the later Iron Age; by the LPRIA the form had declined. This parallels findings at Bob's Wood, where Type G vessels were only found in the later Iron Age assemblage (Percival in prep. c). Other coarseware jar forms include Type C (Fig.7.9, No. 24), a shouldered form with a constricted rim which is narrower than the girth of the vessel (found in small numbers in the LPRIA), and Type E, which has a high rounded shoulder and short upright neck, giving a 'dog-leg' profile (Hill and Horne 2003, 174: Fig.7.5, No. 2). This is found in all three phases but is most common in the later Iron Age (Period 3.3). No bowl or dish forms were found.

Wide-mouthed cordoned jars and bowls with bead rims (Type Q) in grog-tempered fabrics appear in the assemblage in the later Iron Age, but are found in greater numbers in the LPRIA (Fig. 7.9, Nos 26 and 27). These LPRIA vessels broadly correlate with Thompson's form B1–1, the plain everted-rim necked jars which date to the middle to late 1st century BC (Thompson 1982, 87). In the LPRIA these are joined by a range of other, finer jar forms including Thompson's forms D1–4, a wide-mouthed bowl, and D3–1, a plain round bowl (Thompson 1982, 297), dated to the late 1st century BC. Worthy of note are the four examples of small fine cups (Thompson Form E) found in the LPRIA phase. This proliferation of finer serving and tablewares in the LPRIA suggests that the occupants of Love's Farm were adopting a more Romanised style of dining which required a greater range of finewares (Hill 2002, 146).

Scored decoration occurs on only 4.9% of the sherds by weight (351g). This proportion is small, and compares well with sites demonstrating low percentages of scoring such as nearby Little Paxton, where scoring was present on only 4.88% of sherds (Hancocks 2003), Haddenham V (6.2%, Hill and Braddock 2006) and Wardy Hill (7%, Hill and Horne 2003). In contrast, western Cambridgeshire sites have a higher percentage of scored sherds. At Bob's Wood, scored sherds account for 26.7% of the assemblage (Percival in prep. c), at Werrington 44% (Mackreth 1988, 113), and at Wakerley 45% (Jackson and Dix 1987, 116). Scored decoration is most prevalent in assemblages in the East Midlands (Elsdon 1992), and the presence of scored decoration at sites such as Bob's Wood may demonstrate a trade or other cultural connection between sites in western Cambridgeshire and Lincolnshire, which is absent at Love's Farm, Little Paxton and the Ely sites (Percival in prep. c).

Deposition and distribution
The mean sherd weight (MSW) for the assemblage is 11g, a figure which recurs at many contemporary sites in Cambridgeshire (Hill and Horne 2003, table 40), including Bob's Wood (Percival in prep. c). At both Bob's Wood and Love's Farm the pottery was principally recovered from ditches. It is possible that similar

Ceramic period	Ditch	Pit
Middle Iron Age	85	7.9
Later Iron Age	78	12.0
LPRIA	65	4.9

Table 7.8 Percentages of Iron Age pottery recovered from ditches and pits by ceramic period

Feature type	Quantity	% Quantity	Wt (g)	% Wt
Ditch	4447	62.0	54419	64.7
Pit	1264	17.6	10168	12.1
Ditch terminal	86	1.2	8042	9.6
Unknown and evaluation	564	7.9	4720	5.6
Cremation	77	1.1	2067	2.5
Quarry	202	2.8	1392	1.7
Gully	257	3.6	1112	1.3
Posthole	124	1.7	847	1.0
Natural	70	1.0	814	1.0
Construction trench	29	0.4	243	0.3
Hearth/oven	21	0.3	111	0.1
Surface (external)	6	0.1	58	0.1
Waterhole	7	0.1	63	0.1
Foundation trench	2	0.03	19	0.02
Grave	2	0.03	18	0.02
Pit/posthole	7	0.1	14	0.02
Slot	1	0.01	17	0.02
Wall	1	0.01	16	0.02
Cleaning	1	0.01	5	0.01
Total	7168	100	84145	100

Table 7.9 Quantity and weight of Iron Age pottery from the entire site, by feature type (excluding intrusive Roman sherds) in descending order of weight

taphonomic processes affecting sherds within the fills of ditches led to sherds of similar size being found at so many contemporary sites.

The relative proportion of pottery found in ditches declines through the ceramic phases, being lowest in the LPRIA (Table 7.8). Pottery of middle Iron Age date has the highest MSW of the assemblage (Table 7.4), although over 85% of the sherds of this ceramic period were recovered from ditches (Table 7.8). The large MSW of this category may be explained by the presence of deliberately selected material, including larger rim and base sherds placed in the ditches, particularly ditch terminals *12060* and *12062*, flanking the entrance into Period 3.3 Enclosure 159 in Settlement 3 (Fig. 3.14). Similar depositional practices were observed within the assemblage from Bob's Wood (Percival in prep. c).

Pottery from pits makes up only 12% of the total assemblage (Table 7.9), with some 88 pits producing pottery. Pit assemblage size ranges from 2g to 1187g, the largest single group being recovered from pit *8759* of Period 3.5 (the late Iron Age to early Romano-British transitional period) in Settlement 6. This feature, one of three pits within Enclosure 11 which may have been associated with nearby Roundhouse 14, contained rim and body sherds from a large, shell-tempered jar. A more detailed consideration of the deposition of the material

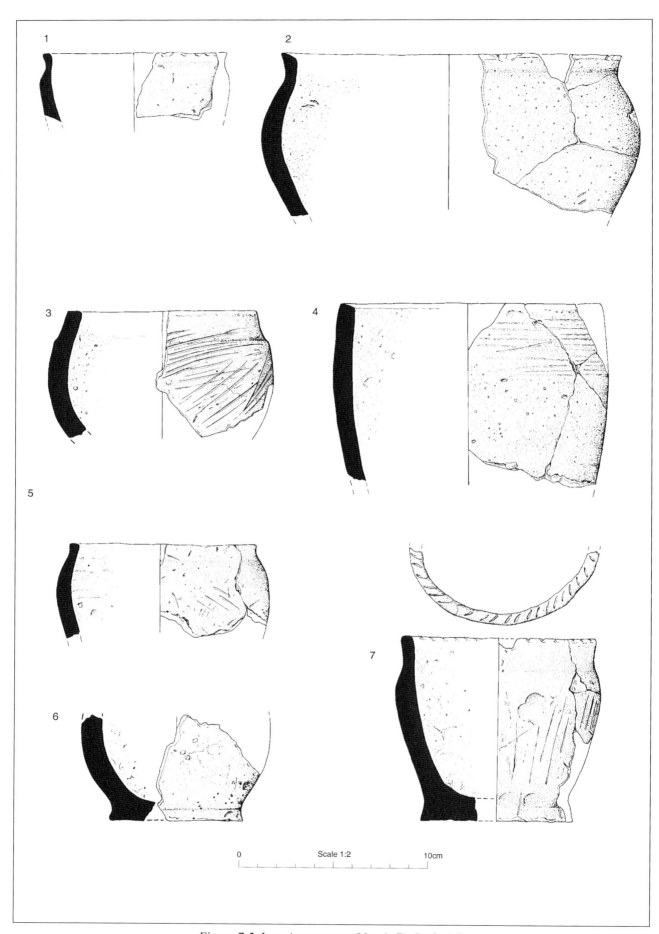

Figure 7.5 Iron Age pottery (Nos 1–7). Scale 1:2

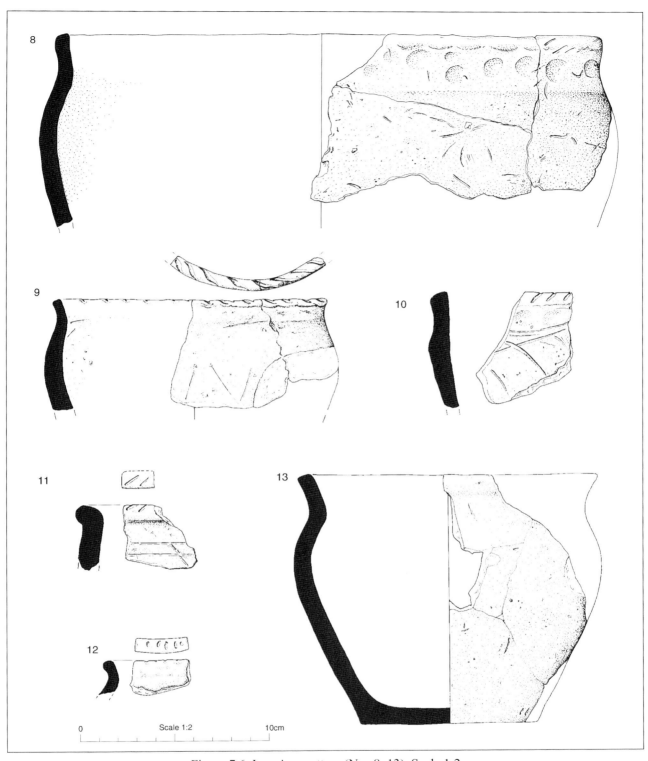

Figure 7.6 Iron Age pottery (Nos 8–13). Scale 1:2

from LPRIA and late Iron Age to early Romano-British transitional deposits (Periods 3.4–3.5) is provided by Lyons, below.

Discussion
The large assemblage of Iron Age pottery from Love's Farm is one of a growing number of contemporary assemblages from Cambridgeshire. Detailed examination of the fabrics and forms within these assemblages has suggested that, far from being composed of similar fabrics and vessel types, each assemblage has distinct characteristics which suggest different cultural preferences. The locally available Jurassic shelly clays would have provided a ready source of raw materials for local potters and, indeed, shell-tempered fabrics form the bulk of the middle Iron Age assemblage. In the later phases of occupation, however, this is not the case, with the later Iron Age having predominantly sandy fabrics,

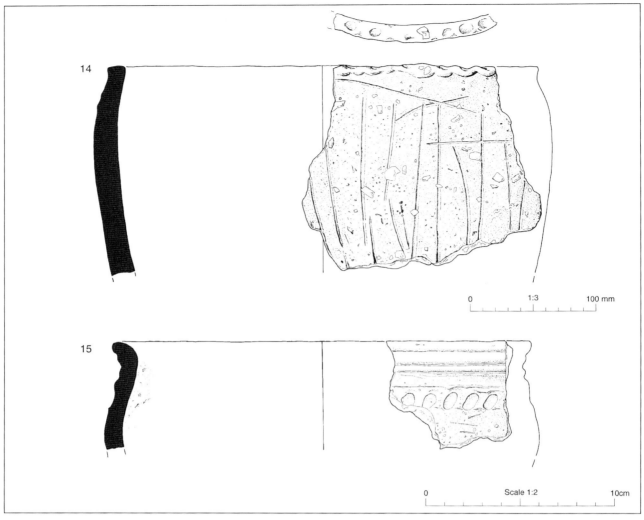

Figure 7.7 Iron Age pottery (Nos 14–15). Scale 1:2

whilst the LPRIA pottery is mostly grog tempered. A very similar pattern of exploitation of clay sources was observed at Wardy Hill where, from the 3rd century BC onwards, the local potters chose to use sandy alluvial clays in preference to the fossiliferous clays which underlay the site (Hill and Horne 2003, 171). Sandy fabrics are dominant within the Iron Age assemblages from other sites around Ely, such as Hut Lane, West Fen Road, Little Thetford and Greenhouse Farm, as well as Cambourne and Scotland Farm (Abrams and Ingham 2008, fig. 2.11). In contrast, at both Little Paxton and Bob's Wood, Hinchingbrooke, shell-tempered fabrics are dominant throughout all periods of occupation. It is likely that Bob's Wood and Little Paxton were influenced by the shell-tempered ware users of the Nene and Welland Valleys (Percival in prep. c; Hancocks 2003, 102), whereas Love's Farm may have had different connections, perhaps associated with the area around Ely. In addition, the ovoid, tub- and barrel-shaped vessels which characterise the assemblages from Little Paxton (Hancocks 2003, 73), Bob's Wood, and those from the west of the county, are much less common at Love's Farm. Here, the assemblage contains mostly slack-shouldered jars in the middle Iron Age, and sinuous bowl and jar forms in the later Iron Age, supplemented in the LPRIA by a range of grog-tempered carinated bowls, jars and cups. It is possible that the River Great Ouse formed a partial eastern boundary for users of shell-tempered wares with their westerly trading networks, whilst a group of sandy fabric users who had links with central and eastern populations were focused around Ely and the River Cam.

Despite the proposed cultural links suggested by fabric and form preference within the Love's Farm assemblage, no explicit trade links can be proven. At Little Paxton, which lies a little less than 4km from Love's Farm, thin section petrology showed the presence of glauconite within several fabrics, suggesting that a small proportion of the vessels were of non-local production (Hancocks 2003). Glauconite was also found at Wardy Hill, but only in the LPRIA or 'Belgic' forms (Williams 2003a, 76). This suggests that, at Wardy Hill, a non-local source of supply was only accessed during the later phases of occupation. Similar non-local fabrics, such as those containing chalk or glauconite, suggest that long-distance trade may have been taking place at Bob's Wood, especially in the LPRIA (Hill and Braddock 1999).

The vessel forms found at Love's Farm are typical of the range expected within a domestic assemblage. The quantity of sherds present is unusual, reflecting the large area covered by the excavation, and the density and

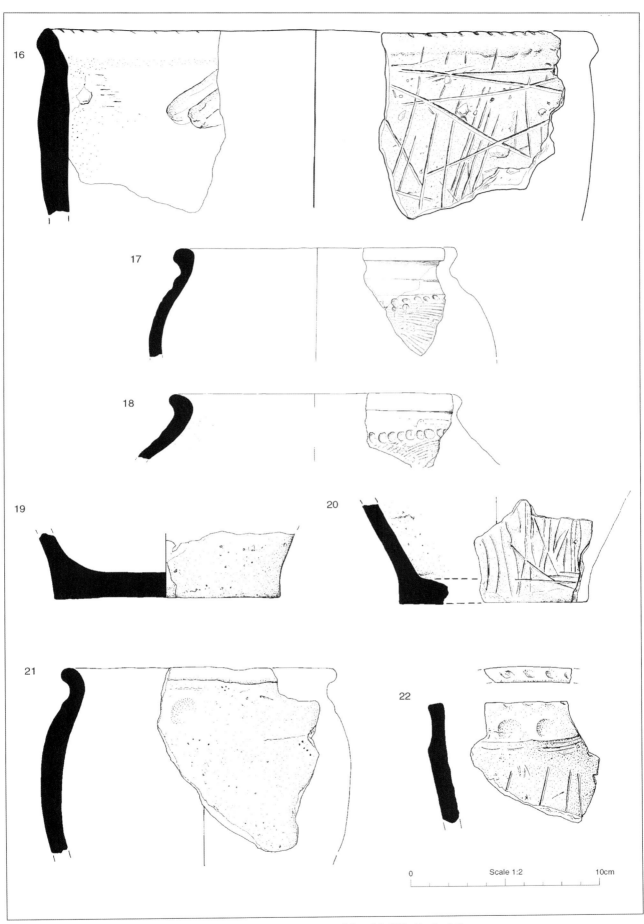

Figure 7.8 Iron Age pottery (Nos 16–22). Scale 1:2

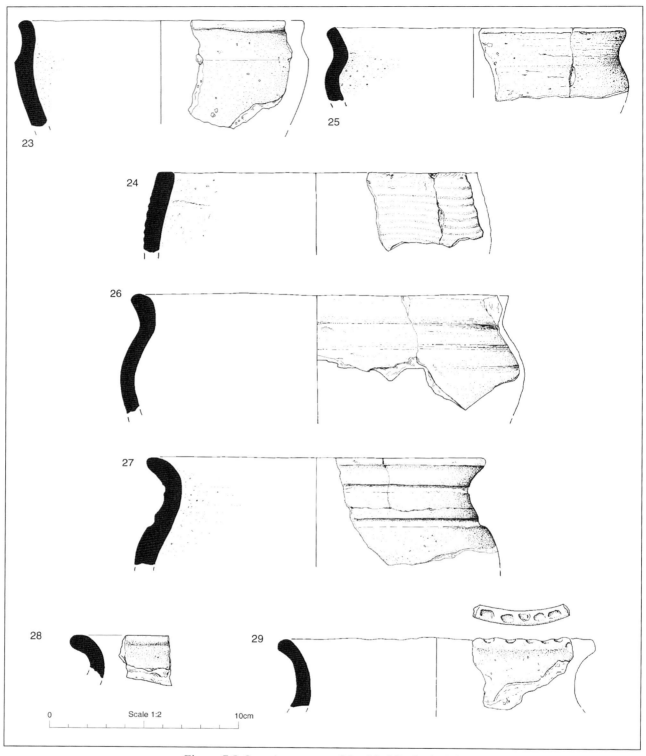

Figure 7.9 Iron Age pottery (Nos 23–29). Scale 1:2

longevity of occupation. Brief analysis of assemblage taphonomy indicates a very similar pattern of disposal at both Love's Farm and Bob's Wood. At both sites, the vessels are highly fragmentary and incomplete, and around 65% of each assemblage was found in the fills of ditches, with only 12% and 15% respectively from pit fills. The ditch deposits are composed of dumps of mixed household waste, perhaps from deposits which had been selected (Percival in prep. c). At Bob's Wood there is evidence for limited placement of pottery sherds chosen from the general assemblage in some contexts, and a similar practice is hinted at within several ditch terminals at Love's Farm.

Catalogue of illustrated Iron Age pottery
(Figs 7.5–7.9)

Fig. 7.5

1. Middle Iron Age **jar/bowl** form D1, Fabric Q5. *7279*, fill of ditch *7280*, Enclosure 151, Settlement 3. Period 3.2.
2. Middle Iron Age **jar/bowl** form E1, Fabric S8. *7279*, fill of ditch *7280*, Enclosure 151, Settlement 3. Period 3.2.
3. Middle Iron Age **bowl** form N2, Fabric S1, scored. *7418*, fill of ditch *7419*, Settlement 3. Period 3.2.
4. Later Iron Age **bowl** form K2, Fabric S2. *6633*, fill of ditch *6634*, Settlement 6. Period 3.3.
5. Middle Iron Age **jar/bowl** form A1, Fabric Q5. *6840*, fill of ditch *6841*, Enclosure 14, Settlement 3. Period 3.3.
6. Middle Iron Age **jar/bowl** base, Fabric Q3. *6840*, fill of ditch *6841*, Enclosure 14, Settlement 3. Period 3.3.
7. Middle Iron Age **jar** form D1, fingernail impressed on rim edge, Fabric Q4. *6840*, fill of ditch *6841*, Enclosure 14, Settlement 3. Period 3.3.

Fig. 7.6

8. Middle Iron Age **jar/bowl**, form F2, Fabric S5. *7315*, fill of ditch *7312*, Enclosure 17, Settlement 3. Period 3.3.
9. Middle Iron Age **jar/bowl** form A1, scored, Fabric Q5. *8184*, fill of ditch *8185*, Enclosure 13, Settlement 6. Period 3.3.
10. Middle Iron Age **jar/bowl** form A1, slashed on rim top, Fabric C1. *8184*, fill of ditch *8185*, Enclosure 13, Settlement 6. Period 3.3.
11. Middle Iron Age **jar/bowl** form K2, fingertip impressed on rim top, Fabric C1. *8184*, fill of ditch *8185*, Enclosure 13, Settlement 6. Period 3.3.
12. Middle Iron Age **flowerpot-shaped vessel** form P6, incised lines, Fabric S7. *8184*, fill of ditch *8185*, Enclosure 13, Settlement 6. Period 3.3.
13. Middle Iron Age **jar** form D2, Fabric Q1. *9135*, fill of ditch *9136*, Boundary 1, Settlement 6. Period 3.3.

Fig. 7.7

14. Middle Iron Age **jar/bowl** form P7, Fabric S5. *12061*, fill of ditch terminal *12060*, Enclosure 159, Settlement 3. Period 3.3.
15. Later Iron Age **storage jar** rim, fingertip impressed on shoulder, Fabric G2. *8631*, fill of ditch *8634*, Enclosure 1, Settlement 6. Period 3.3.

Fig. 7.8

16. Middle Iron Age **jar/bowl** form ??, incised scored, Fabric S8. *10756*, fill of ditch *10747*, Enclosure 1, Settlement 6. Period 3.3.
17. Later Iron Age **storage jar** form ??, fingertip impressed on shoulder, combed, Fabric G6. *8693*, fill of pit *8675*, Enclosure 12, Settlement 6. Period 3.3.
18. Later Iron Age **storage jar** form ??, combed stabbed, Fabric Q8. *10932*, fill of ditch *10740*, Enclosure 13, Settlement 6. Period 3.4.
19. Middle Iron Age **jar** base, Fabric S6. *10920*, fill of ditch *10921*, Enclosure 159, Settlement 3. Period 3.4.
20. Middle Iron Age **jar/bowl** base, incised scored, Fabric Q2. *10920*, fill of ditch *10921*, Enclosure 159, Settlement 3. Period 3.4.
21. Middle Iron Age **jar** form P3, Fabric S6. *10920*, fill of ditch *10921*, Enclosure 159, Settlement 3. Period 3.4.
22. Middle Iron Age **jar/bowl** form A1, fingertip impressed on rim top, Fabric S6. *12063*, fill of ditch *12064*, Enclosure 159, Settlement 3. Period 3.4.

Fig. 7.9

23. Later Iron Age **jar** form G2, Fabric Q3. *8588*, fill of ditch *8589*, Settlement 6. Period 3.4.
24. Later Iron Age **jar** form C3, combed, Fabric G2. *6244*, fill of ditch *6245*, Enclosure 10, Settlement 2. Period 3.5.
25. Later Iron Age **jar** form J2, Fabric Q5. *6987*, fill of pit *6988*, Enclosure 165, Settlement 8. Period 3.5.
26. Later Iron Age proto wide-mouthed **jar** form Q??, Fabric G1. *8499*, fill of roundhouse gully *8500*, Roundhouse 14, Settlement 6. Period 3.5.
27. Later Iron Age proto wide-mouthed **jar** form Q??, with double incised band, Fabric Q1. *8499*, fill of roundhouse gully *8500*, Roundhouse 14, Settlement 6. Period 3.5.
28. Later Iron Age proto wide-mouthed **jar** rim, Fabric Q1. *8499*, fill of roundhouse gully *8500*, Roundhouse 14, Settlement 6. Period 3.5.
29. Middle Iron Age **jar/bowl** form G2, fingertip impressed on rim top, Fabric S7. *5267*, fill of ditch *5268*, Enclosure 30, Settlement 7. Period 4.2.

Late pre-Roman Iron Age and transitional pottery, by site period
by Alice Lyons

Introduction

The LPRIA and transitional assemblage is characterised in Table 7.3.

Late pre-Roman Iron Age (Period 3.4)

A total of 3,624 sherds of pottery weighing 53,001g (*c*.26 EVE) was recovered from deposits assigned to this period, which represents *c*.15% (by weight) of the entire ceramic assemblage (Table 7.3). Only a very limited range of nine main pottery fabrics were identified (Table 7.10), reflecting the relative paucity of ceramic sources available to the population of Love's Farm at this time. Although the choice of fabrics was not extensive, this does not mean that the quality of these wares was low, and the presence of Gaulish-inspired finer coarsewares may suggest a relatively high status for the settlement at this time.

It is worthy of note that analysis of the material by ceramic phase (Percival above, Table 7.4) has identified a total of 781 handmade fragments, weighing 11,553g (EVE not recorded), as being manufactured in the LPRIA period, which constitutes only *c*.22% (by weight) of the total sherds recovered from LPRIA features. This clearly demonstrates that features of this period contained pottery of several ceramic traditions (see Fig 7.1).

In the LPRIA, pottery was generally being deposited in ditches (78% by weight), although smaller amounts were found in pits (3%) and a quarry (2%), as well as in other deposits. The pottery from these contexts has a MSW of *c*.15g – a large size for the Love's Farm assemblage, which has an overall MSW of only *c*.13g. The limited abrasion on these sherds may indicate that they did not suffer the same level of post-depositional disturbance as pottery deposited in chronologically later layers.

Coarsewares

The most common reduced fabric retrieved from LPRIA features was handmade Sandy reduced ware. Where this fabric could be assigned to form, plain everted-rim necked jars (Thompson 1982, 87, type B1–1) and carinated open bowls (Hill with Horne 2003, 174, type Q) were the most common vessel types, alongside a small number of cordoned, necked open vessels (Hill with Horne 2003, 174, type R). The style and manufacturing techniques of these pots show a strong affinity with the Iron Age tradition of potting. In addition, a less sandy version of this fabric (RW HM/WM) was commonly found and, where the form of the vessels could be identified, they proved to be a distinctive form of pedestal urn (Types 2.8 and 2.9), characteristic of the LPRIA period and often used in funerary contexts. These vessels display the developing skill of the native potters, which involved the transition from handmade to wheelmade wares. These vessels were

Fabric description	Sherd count	Sherd wt (g)	EVE	MSW (g)	Wt (%)
Sandy reduced ware (handmade) (Q1, Q2, Q3, Q5, Q6, Q8, SRW HM)	998	17649	4.53	17.7	33.3
Shell-tempered ware (handmade) (STW, S1–3, 5, 6, 8 STW(grog))	702	15407	5.05	22.0	29.1
Reduced ware (handmade) (RW HM/WM)	193	7779	1.41	40.3	14.7
Reduced ware with grog inclusions (handmade and wheelmade) (G1, G2 and G6, GW(Grog), RW(Grog))	731	4854	2.51	6.6	9.2
Proto-Sandy greyware (SGW(PROTO))	331	2489	3.39	7.5	4.7
Fine greyware (GW(Fine))	116	453	0.70	3.9	0.9
Verulamium whiteware (VOW)	52	351	0.38	6.8	0.7
Reduced ware with calciferous inclusions (C1)	20	224	0.25	11.2	0.4
Central Gaulish samian (SAM CG)	5	53	0.00	10.6	0.2
South Gaulish samian (SAM SG)	8	45	0.24	5.6	
East Gaulish samian (SAM EG)	2	10	0.05	5.0	
Poorly represented and intrusive ERB material	466	3687	7.93	7.9	7.0
Total	3624	53001	26.08	14.6	100

Table 7.10 The pottery from features assigned to the LPRIA (Period 3.4)

almost certainly intended to be an impressive form (Thompson 1982, 33), and their slightly differing (less sandy and finer) fabric may indicate that they were traded (non-local) items.

Shell-tempered wares are well represented, particularly lid-seated jars (Type 4.4), which remained little changed from the preceding late Iron Age, when this form was popular. Although shell-tempered storage jars (Type 4.14) were found, as noted above, they were not as common as in the preceding periods.

Analysis of the ceramic assemblage recovered from features assigned to the LPRIA demonstrates that this was a time of rapid change, since not only was new technology being adopted – in the form of the fast potter's wheel and the semi-permanent kiln (Swan 1984) – but also new grog-tempered pottery fabrics (Thompson 1982) were being introduced to cope with this change. Grog-tempered fabrics are the fourth most common fabric found in LPRIA features at Love's Farm, allowing the introduction of wheelmade technology and the resulting development in vessel forms to be clearly observed.

As noted by Percival above, wide-mouthed cordoned jars and bowls with bead rims (Hill and Horne 2003, type Q) in grog-tempered fabrics originated in the later Iron Age, but occur in greater numbers in the LPRIA. The latter vessels broadly correlate with Thompson's form B1–1, plain everted-rim necked jars dating to the middle to late 1st century BC (Thompson 1982, 87). In the LPRIA these forms are accompanied by a range of other finer jar forms which demonstrate that Roman (Gaulish) influence was being felt even in rural Cambridgeshire well before the Roman invasion. In addition to the grog-tempered greywares, it is at this time that proto-Sandy greywares (a ware which later became one of the most common utilitarian fabrics in use at Love's Farm) are first found in significant quantities. Where sherds can be assigned to a type, medium-mouthed lid-seated jars (Type 4.4) and high-shouldered jars with everted rims (Type 4.13) – both Iron Age forms – are found, as well as undiagnostic medium- and wide-mouthed jar rim sherds. It is interesting to note that a very 'Roman' fabric type was used to produce very 'Iron Age' forms. A small amount of greyware with distinctive calcareous inclusions (i.e. locally produced) was recovered, although only undiagnostic jar sherds were found in this fabric.

At the end of the LPRIA, more Romanised oxidised fabrics are evident, including Verulamium whitewares (c.AD 50+). These occur mostly as undiagnostic body sherds, but include a bifid jar (Type 4.8).

Finewares
Although some finer LPRIA coarsewares have been identified, imported Roman-type finewares remain very scarce, with the majority of the material being made locally, albeit influenced by Gaulish design. Exceptions to this are a fine greyware (Gaulish) poppy-head beaker (Type 3.8, Fig. 7.10, No. 2), Southern Gaulish samian vessels (Dr 15/17 and Dr 18), Central Gaulish samian (Dr 18/31, Dr 33, and Dr 38), and a small amount of (intrusive) East Gaulish samian (Dr 33). A small number of Terra Rubra sherds, in the form of a bag-shaped beaker (Type 3.6.5, Fig. 7.10, No. 1) were also found. It is possible that these early imports are an indicator of the latest LPRIA activity, broadly contemporary with the period of the Roman conquest (AD 43+), and of Roman military activity in the vicinity, as these wares are rarely found in rural settlements at this early date unless associated with the movements of the army (Tyers 1996, 56). It is possible that these vessels were especially collected or curated (by the military or civilians) for use in the cremation burial rite (introduced into South-East Britain from Gaul in the LPRIA period), which was practiced to a limited degree in this region.

Late Iron Age–Early Romano-British Transition (Period 3.5)
A total of 1,857 sherds, weighing 22,757g, and with an EVE of c.19 vessels, was recovered from features assigned to this period, representing c.6% of the entire assemblage (Table 7.3). It is apparent that a wider range of fabrics was being deposited in features at this time than was the case in the LPRIA, as eighteen main fabrics were identified (Table 7.11). A range of utilitarian coarseware vessels and fabrics formed the bulk of the pottery in use at this time. They were used for small-scale storage of dry goods, as well as for cooking and serving food.

Fabric description	Vessel form	Sherd count	Sherd wt (g)	EVE	MSW (g)	Wt (%)
Shell-tempered ware (handmade and wheelmade) (STW S1 S2)	Medium-mouthed jars, dishes	413	7023	3.13	17.00	30.87
Sandy greyware (SGW)	Medium- and wide-mouthed jars, dishes and bowls	328	3365	2.95	10.26	14.79
Greyware with grog inclusions (handmade) (GW(GROG) G2 G6 G7)	Wide-mouthed jars	188	2269	2.89	12.07	9.97
Sandy reduced ware (handmade) (SRW Q1 Q2 Q4 Q5 Q100)	Jars and dishes	240	1864	1.45	7.77	8.19
Verulamium whiteware (OW(GRITTY) SOW(GRITTY) VWW)	Bowls and mortaria	32	1093	0.67	34.16	4.80
Horningsea reduced ware (HORN)	Storage jars	12	810	0.00	67.50	3.56
Reduced ware (handmade) (RW HM)	Wide-mouthed jars	81	668	0.66	8.25	2.94
Reduced ware with oxidised surfaces and grog inclusions (RW(GROG)(P))	Jars	49	641	0.31	13.08	2.82
Proto sandy greyware (SGW(PROTO))	Jars	53	528	0.23	9.96	2.32
Sandy oxidised ware (SOW)	Medium- and wide-mouthed jars	43	380	0.56	8.84	1.67
Nene Valley oxidised ware (NVOW)	Jars and bowls	15	269	0.47	17.93	1.18
Greyware with calciferous inclusions (C1, GW(CAL))	Wide-mouthed jars	15	210	0.32	14.00	0.93
Mancetter Hartshill whiteware (MAH WH)	Mortaria	4	184	0.15	46.00	0.81
Oxidised ware with grog inclusions (OW(Grog))	Wide-mouthed jars	16	171	0.51	10.69	0.75
Nene Valley colour-coat (NVCC)	Dish	19	153	0.20	8.05	0.67
Terra Rubra (?IMP PR 6)	Dish	22	126	0.28	5.73	0.55
Amphora (AMP)	Storage jar	2	104	0.23	52.00	0.46
Reduced ware with grog inclusions (RW(grog))	Jar	18	102	0.79	5.67	0.45
Poorly represented and intrusive ERB material	-	307	2797	3.32	9.11	12.27
Total		1857	22757	19.12	12.25	100.00

Table 7.11 The pottery recovered from transitional deposits, listed in descending order of weight (Period 3.5)

The majority of pottery was recovered from ditches (74% by weight), although pits (9%) and a quarry (5%) also contained large assemblages of pottery. The material is severely abraded, with a MSW of only $c.12$g.

Coarsewares
Shell-tempered ware was common throughout the Iron Age and LPRIA, and continued to be frequently produced in Period 3.5 ($c.31$%), forming the most common fabric deposited in features at this time. Although undiagnostic storage jars and jar body sherds were still commonly found in deposits assigned to this period, the range of forms produced had begun to develop. The lid-seated jars (Type 4.4) commonly seen in the late Iron Age and LPRIA now rarely occurred, since globular medium-mouthed jars with rolled rims (Type 4.5.2 and 4.5.3) had taken their place. A wide-mouthed jar form with a plain 'S' profile (Type 5.6) was also found (including one almost complete example), along with single examples of straight-sided dishes or platters (Type 6.18 and 6.19). None of these vessels are sooted, and none is decorated.

Also found was the flat base of a single large jar in a handmade, sandy reduced ware, fabric that had been modified with at least five post-firing holes in the vessel base (Fig 7.10, No. 6). The phenomenon of perforating coarseware vessels has been seen at the adjacent site of Childerley Gate (Lyons 2008), where it was practiced on a large scale in the early Roman period. Towards the end of this period, a small amount ($c.4$%) of Horningsea-type storage jar ware began to be traded onto the site, perhaps in relation to a contained commodity (Evans et al. 2017). The increase in the availability of this product might go some way to explaining the decline in Shell-tempered storage jars at this time.

The second most common fabric is a Sandy greyware ($c.15$%). The range of forms is not extensive, but includes single examples of a jug (Type 1.10) and a beaker with an everted rim (Type 3.13), together with several medium-mouthed globular jars (Types 4.5.2 and 4.5.4) and shallow dishes or platters (Types 6.18, 6.21 and 6.22). Some earlier proto-Sandy greywares ($c.2$%) were also found, although only undiagnostic jar/bowl sherds were identified.

Grog-tempered reduced ware ($c.10$%) was used in both handmade and wheelmade vessels. The handmade examples consist of cordoned jars with beaded rims (Fig. 7.10, No. 4), and the fabric is frequently decorated with combed arcs and waves. The wheelmade wide-mouthed jars (Type 5) include carinated (Type 5.2.1) and 'S'-shaped (Type 5.6) varieties. Several of these are sooted, and one is decorated with a cordon of zig-zag burnished lines. In addition a reduced ware with grog inclusions and a distinctive oxidised surface ($c.3$%) was found, used in the manufacture of wide-mouthed jars

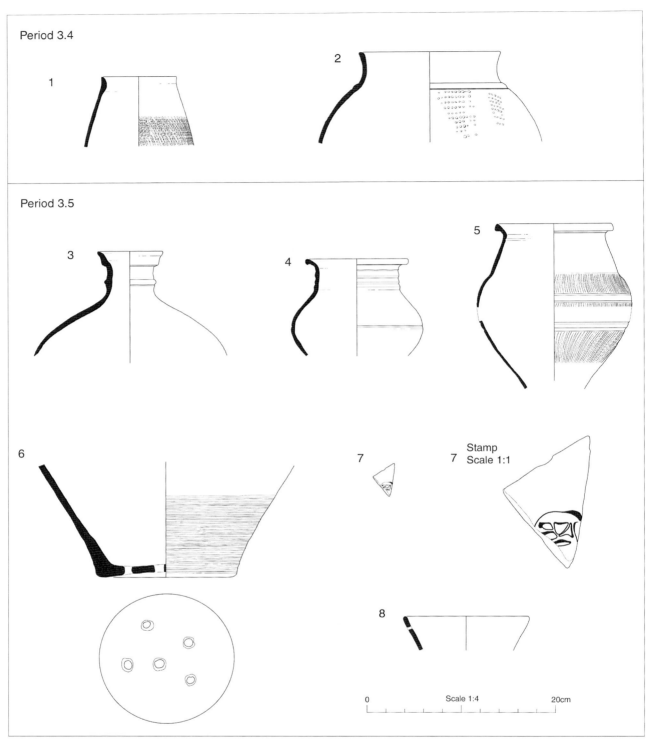

Figure 7.10 Late pre-Roman Iron Age to Romano-British transitional pottery (Periods 3.4–3.5) (Nos 1–8)

(Type 5). This ware typically occurs in the Milton Keynes area (Marney 1989), and is recorded at other sites in south and west Cambridgeshire (Lyons 2008). Intriguingly a tiny fragment from a platter base stamped with a partial (unreadable) maker's mark was also found (Fig. 7.10, No. 7). Contemporary stamps of this kind are rare but have been found elsewhere in the region notably at Broughton in Milton Keynes (Lyons *et al.* 2014, 217–18), and at Clay Farm, near Cambridge (Lyons with Rigby in prep.).

A sand-tempered reduced ware (*c.*8%), used to produce handmade and wheelmade vessels, occurred in the form of a wide-mouthed jar (Type 5), two medium-mouthed jars (Type 4.5.2), and a straight-sided dish (Type 6.19). A less sandy reduced ware (previously identified as a possible non-local product) was identified, representing *c.*3% of the period assemblage; this occurred as miscellaneous jar sherds, and may well have been largely residual by this time. As in the preceding period, a small amount of greyware, distinctive because it included calcareous material (*i.e.* locally produced), was used to manufacture wide-mouthed jars (Types 5 and 5.3).

The most common oxidised coarsewares in use during Period 3.5 were the distinctive gritty whitewares of the Verulamium industry, produced at a number of kiln sites in the St Albans area. These kilns started making pottery soon after the Roman conquest, and their products represent some of the earliest domestically produced Romano-British traded wares available in the region. In addition to some undiagnostic material, a cupped rim flagon (Type 1.9), two bifid jars (Type 4.8), two carinated bowls (Type 6.3), a lid (Type 8.1) and a large bead and flange mortarium (Type 7.51) were found. Small but significant quantities of unsourced (but probably locally produced) Sandy oxidised wares (*c.*2%) were retrieved, which generally comprise undiagnostic body sherds, although a bifid jar (Type 4.8) – perhaps copying the Verulamium product – was found, as well as a wide-mouthed jar (Type 5.3). As with the reduced wares, both grog- and sand-tempered oxidised wares were in use at this time. The grog-tempered oxidised ware constitutes less than 1% (by weight) of the assemblage, and occurs as undiagnostic medium- and wide-mouthed jar fragments.

At the end of the period whitewares began to arrive from another regional production centre located in the Nene Valley. Nene Valley whitewares are represented mostly by undiagnostic body sherds, but the standard bifid jar (Type 4.8), as well as a bowl with a flaring rim (Type 6.15) and undiagnostic flagon and mortarium sherds were also recorded. A single mortarium sherd (Type 7.15.1) from the Mancetter-Hartshill industry in the West Midlands was identified, hinting at an expansion in the traded material available at this time.

Specialist wares
In addition to the mortaria fragments mentioned above, other specialist wares from the site include two body fragments of unsourced amphorae and a black sand Campanian (CAM AM) amphora fragment (0.5%). The Campanian amphora fabric, probably from the Dressel 2–4 form (Peacock and Williams 1986, class 10) thought primarily to contain wine, together with Verulamium whiteware, suggest the consumption of wine at Love's Farm, even if it was on a fairly small scale.

Finewares
The earliest imported fineware identified in this group comprises a single, straight-sided conical cup (Type 6.13; Fig. 7.10, No. 8) in Gaulish Terra Rubra, making up *c.*1% of the assemblage. This vessel may have arrived at Love's Farm before the conquest. Contemporary with this vessel is a fine greyware butt beaker (Fig 7.10, No. 5), possibly also a Gaulish import. Chronologically later than these vessels is a very small amount of plain samian (too small to register on Table 7.11), which consists of a Southern Gaulish platter (Dr 18) and a dish (Dr 42), dated to *c.*AD 70–100. Slightly later Central Gaulish samian wares in the form of two dishes (Dr 31) and two cups (Dr 33), dated between *c.*AD 120–200 were also found, but were probably intrusive within this transitional group. At the end of the period, Nene Valley colour-coated material (*c.*1%), demonstrated by the presence of undiagnostic beaker sherds, was arriving at Love's Farm. The use of these finewares suggests that the Roman style of dining had been adopted to some extent, although in what context these wares were used remains unknown.

Catalogue of illustrated LPRIA and transitional pottery
(Fig. 7.10)

Period 3.4

1   TR2 wheelmade **bag-shaped beaker** (Type 3.6; Perrin 1996, 233). *8488*, fill of ditch *8585*, Enclosure 20, Settlement 6. Period 3.4.
2   SGW wheelmade **poppy-head beaker** with barbotine dot decoration (Type 3.8; Stead and Rigby 1986, 352, 546). *8488*, fill of ditch *8585*, Enclosure 20, Settlement 6. Period 3.4.

Period 3.5

3   RW handmade **narrow-mouthed flask** (Type 2.8). *5430*, fill of ditch *5431*, Enclosure 28, Settlement 7. Period 3.5.
4   RW handmade **narrow-mouthed jar** (Type 2.9). *5430*, fill of ditch *5431*, Enclosure 28, Settlement 7. Period 3.5.
5   GW(FINE) wheelmade **butt beaker** rouletted with a white slip (Type 3.13; Stead and Rigby 1986, 339). *5501*, fill of ditch *5502*, Enclosure 28, Settlement 7. Period 3.5.
6   SRW handmade **storage jar** (base only). Combed decoration. Five post-firing holes drilled in the base. *5501*, fill of ditch *5502*, Enclosure 28, Settlement 7. Period 3.5.
7   GW(GROG) wheelmade **base fragment,** stamped with an incomplete and unreadable maker's mark. SF 3528. *8792*, fill of ditch *8794*, boundary 12, Settlement 6. Period 3.5.
8   GAB TR2 wheelmade straight-sided **conical cup** (Type 6.13), copying samian form Dr 33. Post-firing hole on the vessel wall. *5501*, fill of ditch *5502*, Enclosure 28, Settlement 7. Period 3.5.

IV. Romano-British pottery
by Alice Lyons
(Figs 7.11–7.14)

Introduction
The assemblage of Romano-British pottery is quantified and characterised in Table 7.12 and fully detailed in the site type series in Appendix 3.

Early Roman (Period 4.1)
A total of 3,144 sherds of pottery, weighing 30,388g (*c.* 37 EVE) was recovered from early Roman deposits, representing *c.*9% of the entire assemblage (Table 7.12). In total, eighteen main fabrics were identified (Table 7.13), the same number as in Period 3.5, suggesting that levels of ceramic supply did not change significantly. It is worthy of note, however, that this is the only period group in which shell-tempered wares are not the most prolific fabric – within this group they comprise the second most common ware. Although the reasons for this remain uncertain, it is possible that changing fashions, as Roman influence grew, resulted in Iron Age-type shell-tempered wares being temporarily less desirable; however, after the early Roman period they reclaimed their dominant market share.

The majority of the pottery from Period 4.1 was found within ditches (77% by weight), with a smaller amount in pits (8%) and other features. The material is severely abraded, with a MSW of only *c.*10g, which is the smallest of any period group at Love's Farm. This may reflect the subsequent intensity of land use (and the resulting post-depositional disturbance) within the settlement during the middle to late Roman period.

Date	Period	Sherd count	Sherd Wt (g)	EVE	MSW (g)	Proportion (Wt %) of site assemblage
Early Romano-British (mid 1st to mid 2nd century AD) Pottery from this period is being produced in Roman (grey/sandy) fabrics, but generally not on an industrial scale. Gaulish finewares, with samian becoming more common, are now in use. Also present are domestically produced fine red wares which copy samian forms.	4.1	3144	30388	37.70	9.7	7.1
Romano-British (late 1st to 4th century AD) By the later 1st century, large kiln sites are becoming known and by the mid 2nd century most pottery is being produced on an industrial level. This trend continues and develops until the end of the Roman period. Samian is eventually replaced (in the late 2nd/early 3rd century) by domestic finewares.	4.2	5660	78998	72.01	14.0	18.4
	4.3	1672	19719	22.95	11.8	4.6
	4.4	9033	119956	111.87	13.3	28.0
Period 4.2–4.4 Total		*16365*	*218673*	*206.83*	*13.4*	*51.0*
Late Romano-British/Early Saxon (early 5th century) Iron Age fabrics (becoming sandier) continued to be used to produce more Romanised forms (rolled rim jars *etc.*). Some vessels were wheelmade and some were handmade. Gaulish finewares, including samian, were now in use.	4.5	1838	27175	19.72	14.8	6.3
Period Total		*21,347*	*276,236*	*264.25*	*12.7*	*64.47*

Table 7.12 Romano-British pottery (Period 4) listed and quantified by sub-period

Fabric description	Vessel form	Sherd count	Sherd wt (g)	EVE	MSW (g)	Wt (%)
Sandy greyware (SGW)	Narrow-, medium- and wide-mouthed jars, also dishes and bowls	1105	7935	12.29	7.2	26.1
Shell-tempered ware (STW, S1, S3, S4, STW(GROG))	Medium-mouthed jars, storage jars, dishes and bowls.	435	5392	5.53	12.4	17.7
Reduced ware (handmade) (RW HM)	Wide-mouthed cordoned jars	324	3636	2.64	11.2	12.0
Reduced ware with grog temper (GW(GROG), RW(GROG), G1, G6)	Wide-mouthed cordoned jars	270	3516	1.72	13.0	11.6
Sandy reduced ware (handmade) (SRW, Q1, Q3, Q5, Q8)	Medium- and wide-mouthed jars	147	1864	1.58	12.7	6.1
Verulamium whiteware (OW(GRITTY), VOW, VWW)	Medium-mouthed jars, bowls and mortaria	143	1596	2.81	11.2	5.3
Sandy oxidised ware (SOW)	Flagons, narrow-, medium-, wide-mouthed jars, also bowls and a lid	163	1179	2.90	7.2	3.9
Oxidised ware with grog inclusions (OW(GROG))	Medium-mouthed jars, bowls and lid	123	951	1.37	7.7	3.1
Nene Valley oxidised ware (NVOW)	Medium-mouthed jar and mortaria	4	487	0.33	121.7	1.6
Fine greyware (GW(FINE))	Wide-mouthed jar/bowl	40	364	0.39	9.1	1.2
Black-surfaced red ware (BSRW)	Medium-mouthed jars	58	361	0.37	6.2	1.2
Spanish amphora (BAT AM 1)	DR20	4	318	0.00	79.5	1.0
Reduced ware with oxidised surfaces with grog inclusions (RW(GROG)(P))	Storage jar	16	313	0.19	19.6	1.0
Pink grog-tempered ware (PGROG)		3	212	0.00	70.7	0.7
South Gaulish samian (SAM SG)	Dishes, bowls and platters	34	213	0.43	6.3	0.7
Proto sandy greyware (SGW(PROTO))		37	164	0.62	4.4	0.5
Italian amphora (ITA AM 1)		1	133	0.20	133.0	0.4
Reduced ware with calciferous inclusions (C1)		16	135	0.00	8.4	0.4
Poorly represented and intrusive ERB material		221	1619	4.33	7.3	5.3
Total		*3144*	*30388*	*37.70*	*9.7*	*100*

Table 7.13 The pottery from features assigned to the early Roman period, listed in descending order of percentage of weight (Period 4.1)

Coarsewares

a) Sandy greyware
This is the first period in which fully Romanised Sandy greywares (SGW) appear (*c*.26%), forming the majority of the period assemblage, although a small number of proto-Sandy greywares (*c*.0.1%) were still in use. An impressive range of forms appears to have been available as soon as SGW began to be produced, many of which are copying or derived from 'Belgic' jar/bowl and beaker forms (Thompson 1982). It is noticeable that the utilitarian medium-mouthed cooking pots, which dominated in this fabric during the middle and late Roman periods (see below), were comparatively rare at this time. The vessel types found consist of rounded narrow-mouthed jars of both a necked (Type 2.1) and neckless (Type 2.4) version, along with three beaker types, including a beaker with a funnel rim (Type 3.1), globular beakers with an everted rim (Type 3.7) and a beaker with a 'cavetto' rim (Type 3.11). Medium-mouthed jar forms are restricted to high-shouldered (Type 4.1), lid-seated (Type 4.4), globular with a rolled rim (Type 4.5) and globular with an everted rim (Type 4.13). Wide-mouthed jars are the most frequent form, mostly undiagnostic (Type 5), but including cordoned versions (Thompson 1982, class B3; Type 2.1), carinated forms (Thompson 1982, class E; Type 2.2) and jars with a reverse S-profile (Type 5.3, Fig. 7.11, No. 9). These wares are commonly decorated with grooves, some with incised wavy lines and several with barbotine dot. Less well represented, but not unusual, are open dish and bowl forms including straight-sided dishes (Type 6.19), and an open dish or platter with an internal angle (Type 6.21). Carinated bowls with a flattish rim (Type 6.3) were also found, as well as lids (Fig. 7.11, No. 11). Soot residues are rare, suggesting that these vessels were rarely used for cooking, but rather for small scale storage (especially the lid-seated vessels) and the consumption of food and drink.

Additionally, a distinctive black-surfaced red ware fabric was recorded (*c*.1%), which was only identified in the form of the medium-mouthed jar (Type 5). This may have been a misfired greyware, possibly suggesting the presence of a kiln nearby.

b) Shell-tempered ware
At this time, shell-tempered wares were only the second most prolific fabric (*c*.18% by weight). By this period most of the jar forms were manufactured on the wheel, although some of the large storage vessels were still produced using prehistoric manufacturing technology. Although shell-tempered wares were present in large numbers, the range of forms in which they were produced was conservative. By far the most common type was the medium-mouthed lid-seated jar (Type 4.4), supplemented by other globular jars with rolled rims (Type 4.5). Storage jars were common (Type 4.14), with S-profiled wide-mouthed jars (Type 5.6), dishes (Type 6.19 and 6.21) and bowls (Type 6.4) making up a small part of the assemblage. These vessels are very rarely sooted and only occasionally decorated, either with simple grooves or combed decoration.

c) Reduced ware
The handmade reduced ware that was the most common fabric in Period 3.5 was still well represented in the early Roman period (*c*.12%). The LPRIA-type narrow-mouthed urns were no longer in use. This fabric was now mainly used to manufacture wide-mouthed jars (Type 5), including cordoned (Type 5.1) and carinated types (Type 5.2). These vessels are generally not sooted and are usually plain, although several examples are combed and one is burnished. Another example has had a post-firing hole drilled in the vessel neck, demonstrating an adaptation of use, perhaps to secure a covering.

Although handmade sandy reduced wares remained in use (*c*.6%), their popularity was decreasing at this time, and they are found in a limited range of forms, including medium-mouthed jars of lid-seated (Type 4.4) and globular (Type 4.13) form, as well as miscellaneous (Type 5) wide-mouthed jars (Type 5.6). Soot residues were found on several of the sherds, which are generally plain, although a few are combed. These fabrics appear to have been replaced by the finer sandy greyware described above.

d) Grog-tempered reduced wares
Still in use alongside the Romanised sandy greywares were the grog-tempered greyware vessel types that began to be produced in Period 3.5. Found in a lesser amounts (*c*.12%) than the sandy greywares, these were produced in a more limited and slightly different range of forms. Medium-mouthed jars are rare in the site assemblage, although an everted rim form (Type 4.13) was recorded. Miscellaneous wide-mouthed jars are the most common form (Type 5), although carinated (Types 5.1 and 5.2) jars are well represented. Open forms (dishes and platters) are not generally found in this fabric at this time, only one hemispherical bowl (Type 6.4) being identified. Decoration (where present) consists of grooves, wavy incised lines, alongside both area and detail (cross-hatch and loops) burnishing. Although soot residues are not common, they are more frequently found than on the sandy greyware sherds; this, combined with the lack of tablewares (dishes and platters), may suggest that grog-tempered greywares were used more for heating food than the finer and less heat tolerant (*i.e.* less capable of withstanding thermal shock) sandy greywares. Later grog-tempered wares with a distinctive pink surface, typical of the Milton Keynes area, were found in small quantities (*c*.1%), although no specific vessel types were identified.

e) Oxidised wares
Sandy oxidised coarsewares, probably produced in the same manufacturing centres as the sandy greywares, were used in significant quantities at this time (*c*.4%). Forms include ring-necked flagons (Type 1.2), narrow-mouthed jars (Type 2.1), medium-mouthed jars of lid-seated (Type 4.4) and everted rim (Type 4.13) type, as well as a wide-mouthed jar with an S-profile (Type 5.6). Several of the sherds show signs of having been covered in a white slip, perhaps to disguise the effects of poor colour control during firing, and others are incised with combed lines. As with the Verulamium whitewares (see below), several of these sherds are fumed, indicating exposure to an indirect heat source. Moreover, as with the greywares, grog-tempered oxidised wares were used contemporaneously, although in smaller numbers (*c*.3%). No flagons were identified in this more utilitarian fabric, but medium-mouthed jars with lid seating (Type 4.4) and

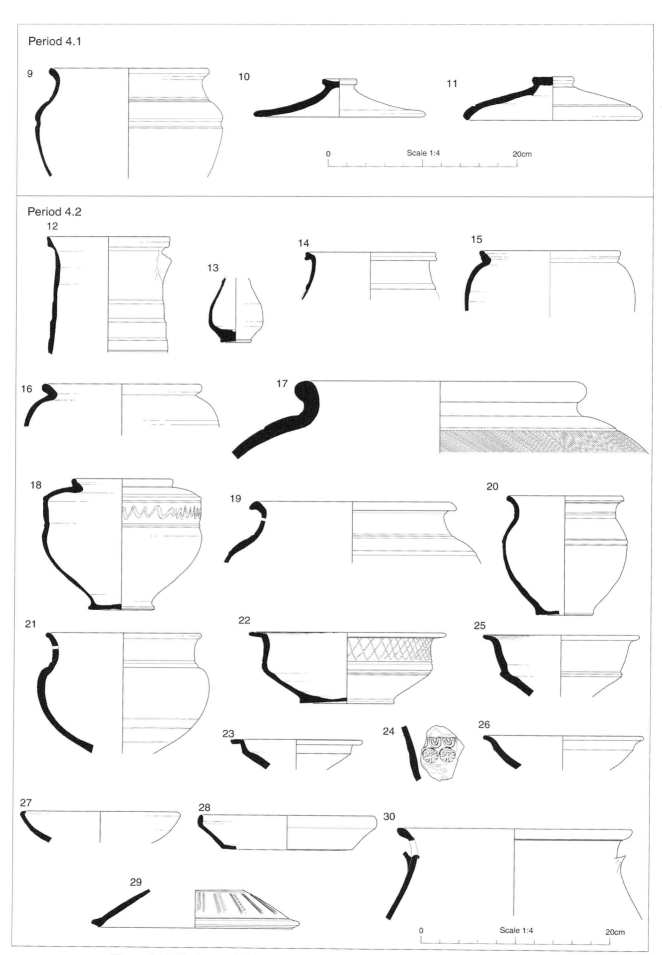

Figure 7.11 Early to middle Romano-British pottery (Periods 4.1–4.2) (Nos 9–30)

globular forms with everted rims (Type 4.13) were found, as well as miscellaneous (Type 5) wide-mouthed jars. An open form consisting of a carinated cup (Type 6.9) and a lid (Type 8.1, Fig. 7.11, No. 10) were recorded. Vessels in this fabric are frequently decorated with combed wavy lines. None of the material is sooted.

Verulamium whiteware, which started to be manufactured in the mid 1st century AD and first appears on the Love's Farm site in Period 3.5, became more common as the early Roman period progressed and the industry became established. Cupped rim flagons (Type 1.9) were in use, as well as common medium-mouthed bifid rim jars (Type 4.8) and a carinated bowl with a flattish rim (Type 6.3). Notably, bead and flange (Type 7.5.1) mortaria (mixing bowls) were introduced into the Love's Farm ceramic repertoire at this time. Several of these sherds are fumed (including the flagon sherds), possibly indicating that they had been placed near a heat source to warm wine or other contents (see Mortaria, below).

Specialist wares
A small number (*c*.1%) of Spanish amphora (BAT AM 1) sherds were recovered, probably all derived from Dressel 20 globular olive oil amphora. These, together with the presence of Verulamium whiteware mortaria, suggest that Roman-style food preparation and tastes were continuing to be adopted, or at least experimented with, at Love's Farm in the early Roman period, as they had been in late pre-Roman times.

Finewares
The main finewares found during this period are greywares (*c*.1%). The source of these vessels is uncertain, but several are certainly compatible with North Gaulish imports (Tomber and Dore 1998, 74), and the range of forms may support this theory. The fabric is recorded in a limited range of forms, comprising wide-mouthed jars (Type 5 and 5.3) with decorative motifs including burnishing and coarse rouletting. None of this material is sooted.

Samian tablewares are the second best represented fineware. Plain Southern Gaulish samian, dated between *c*.AD 50–100 (*c*.1%) is represented by platters (Dr 15/17 (stamped), Dr 18, Dr 18/31), a cup (Dr 27) and a dish (Dr 36). Later plain Central Gaulish material, datable to *c*.AD 120–200, was also beginning to be used in this period, but in very small quantities (0.2% by weight of this period group). Forms include a cup (Dr 33), dish (Dr 31 (stamped), Dr 31R, Dr 18/31) and bowl (Dr 37) forms. These vessels are quite fresh and retain no residues or signs of repair or re-use.

Found in very small quantities (and therefore not shown on Table 7.13) is an unsourced, domestically produced red fineware, apparently copying the more expensive samian forms, such as cup rim flagons (Type 1.9) and deep bowls (Type 5 and 6). Three sherds of Southern British glazed ware were also found (Tomber and Dore 1998, 213). Glazed wares are rare in Romano-British ceramic domestic assemblages and this material may represent the remains of a single vessel carried onto the site, perhaps by an individual who had travelled from the south along Ermine Street.

Catalogue of illustrated early Roman pottery
(Fig. 7.11)

9   GW(FINE) rounded **wide-mouthed jar** with a reverse S-profile and a cordon on the neck (Type 5.3; Rogerson 1977, 39; 46; 94). *5863*, fill of ditch *5666*, Boundary 109, Settlement 7. Period 4.1.

10 SOW wheelmade plain **lid** of standard type to fit cooking/storage pot (Type 8.1; Perrin 1996, 57; 58; 59). *8124*, fill of ditch *8125*, Boundary 2, Settlement 6. Period 4.1.

11 SGW wheelmade **lid** with single groove, made to fit cooking/storage pot (Type 8.1; Perrin 1996, 57; 58; 59). *8929*, fill of pit *8895*, Settlement 6. Period 4.1.

Middle to late Roman (Periods 4.2–4.5)
(Figs 7.11–7.13)

In order to prevent repetition, the presentation of this part of the pottery analysis consists of an overview of all middle to late Roman pottery (Periods 4.2–4.5), followed by a brief sub-period summary. The presence of samian is noted below as appropriate, and is fully reported on by Wadeson and Monteil.

A total of 16,365 sherds, weighing 218,673g and representing *c*.206 EVE, was recovered from middle to late Roman deposits (and is quantified and characterised in Table 7.12). Pottery from this period represents *c*.62% of the entire Roman assemblage by weight, and a total of twenty main fabrics were recorded. The key characteristics are the dominance of the three main fabrics: Shell-tempered ware, Sandy greyware and Nene Valley colour-coated ware. The range of vessel types available also expanded dramatically during this period.

Coarsewares

a) Shell-tempered wares
As with the early Roman period, shell-tempered wares remained the most common fabric at this time, here forming nearly half the assemblage (*c*.42% by weight). The majority of these wares are unsourced, but it is clear that the forms produced, and their place of manufacture, changed through time. It is probable, however, that the very thick storage jar fragments (Type 4.14, Fig. 7.11, No. 17), which form the majority of this assemblage by weight, were produced in the Lower Nene Valley between the 1st and 3rd centuries AD (Perrin 1996, 119–120). This form of jar was so durable, practical and generally successful that it remained in production alongside finer vessel types until the rise of the Horningsea storage jar industry (see below) in the 2nd and 3rd centuries. The lid-seated jar (Type 4.4, Fig. 7.12, No. 34) first seen in earlier phases was still prolific, being the most common form by sherd count, until it was replaced by the medium-mouthed globular jar with the out-turned and under-scored rim (Type 4.5.3, *cf.* Fig. 7.14, Nos 63 and 64) in the later part of the 2nd century. Other forms that became fashionable at this time include medium-mouthed globular jars with a squared, out-turned rim (Type 4.5.2) and medium-mouthed globular jars with a large rolled rim (Type 4.5.4). Many of these vessels have rilled decoration on their bodies; less common is a combed wavy line motif. Soot residue is not uncommon on these vessels, indicating that many were used as cooking pots. Towards the later part of the Romano-British period, flanged (Type 6.17) and straight-sided dishes (Type 6.19, Fig. 7.13, No. 55), thought to have been used as casseroles, became standard. These are generally plain, although some of the flanges

are decorated with an incised wavy line. These wares may have been produced at any centre in a position to exploit the local Jurassic shelly clay beds, although it is worthy of note that they are not of the Lincolnshire Dales (Tyers 1996, 190) or Bourne-Greetham (Tomber and Dore 1998, 156) type. A successful (and excavated) example of an industry producing wares of the type found at Love's Farm has been recorded at the Harrold kilns in Bedfordshire (Brown 1994, 19–107) and Earith in Cambridgeshire (Anderson 2013), although other (nearer) kilns sites probably existed (Tomber and Dore 1998, 212).

b) Reduced wares

Handmade reduced ware vessels continued to be manufactured into the 2nd century AD, and form a distinctive part of the Romano-British assemblage from Love's Farm (*c*.1%). They occur in a limited range of forms, consisting of lid-seated (Type 4.4) and everted rim (Type 4.13) medium-mouthed jars, as well as wide-mouthed cordoned (Type 5.2) and rounded (Type 5.3) forms. The rounded wide-mouthed form is the most common variety. A single example of a straight-sided dish (Type 6.19) was found. These vessels are scored or combed, and soot residue survives on some surfaces.

Wheelmade sandy reduced wares continued to reach Love's Farm (*c*.1%). The range of forms found is limited, but suggests that this ware continued in use throughout the Roman period. These vessel types include high-shouldered (Type 4.1), globular (Type 4.5) and everted rim (Type 4.13) medium-mouthed jars and miscellaneous wide-mouthed jars (Type 5). Straight-sided dishes (Types 6.18 and 6.19), flanged dishes (Type 6.17) and a lid (Type 8.1) were recorded. The dish form is the most common vessel type in this fabric, suggesting that it may have become more common in the later Roman period.

The fifth most common fabric (*c*.2% by weight) is Horningsea reduced ware. This industry, located to the north-east of Cambridge on the western fen edge, was recently the subject of a major research project (Evans 2002; Evans *et al*. 2017) which has shown the ware's influence to have been more far reaching than previously thought, particularly in supplying settlements in southern Cambridgeshire, with wares perhaps being transported down the River Ouse into Bedfordshire (S. Macaulay, pers. comm.). This industry came to prominence in the 2nd and 3rd centuries, and, although other utilitarian forms were produced, is best known for manufacturing a distinctive storage jar with a large everted rim. This form was produced in a biscuit-like fabric, often decorated with combed arcs, that allows for relatively easy identification. At Love's Farm, it was found in small quantities in the form of a ring-necked flagon (Type 1.1, Fig. 7.12, No. 31) and globular, medium-mouthed jars (Type 4.5), together with medium- (Type 4.12) and wide-mouthed jars (Types 5.3, 5.6) with an S-profile. Straight-sided dishes with a triangular rim (Type 6.18) and a lid (Type 8.1) were also found. Most of the pottery in this fabric, however, is of the distinctive storage jar vessel (Type 4.17), none of which has soot (or any other) residues.

A small amount of a distinctive black-surfaced redware (0.4%) was recovered. No flagons, narrow-mouthed jars or beakers in this fabric were noted. Medium-mouthed jars of globular (Type 4.5) and everted rim (Type 4.13) forms were found in small quantities, while medium-mouthed jars with slashed decoration on the shoulder (Type 4.10) were particularly common. Found in small quantities were undiagnostic wide-mouthed jars (Type 5), straight-sided dishes (Type 6.18), flanged dishes (Type 6.17), carinated bowls with a flattish, out-turned rim (Type 6.3) and a flanged rim bowl (Type 6.15). Some of this material has burnished decoration surviving on its surface.

c) Greywares

Sandy greywares are the most common ware by sherd count and estimated vessel equivalent, although by weight they represent only a quarter of the assemblage. They were made in the widest range of forms of any fabric found, the only forms not evident being the specialist flagons and mortaria more commonly made in oxidised wares in this region. As the range of vessel types is so large, a chronological progression within the period assemblage can be observed. A carinated jug (Type 1.10), not commonly produced after the mid-2nd century AD, was recorded, while other earlier Romano-British vessel types associated with the serving of liquid include narrow-mouthed jars (Type 2.1) and beakers, including funnel-necked (Type 3.1), globular (Type 3.7), poppy-headed (Type 3.8), cavetto-rimmed (Type 3.11), and butt beakers (Type 3.13). Other earlier greyware forms include medium-mouthed lid-seated jars (Type 4.4), wide-mouthed jars of miscellaneous type (Type 5), and carinated (Type 5.2) and reverse S-profile (Type 5.3) types, all of which were common. By the late 2nd century, medium-mouthed jars were the most abundant, including high-shouldered (Type 4.1) and globular (Type 4.5, Fig. 7.13, No. 44) forms. The most common medium-mouthed jar form in this fabric, however, is the BB2–inspired (Tyers 1996, 186–8, fig. 232: IIF5, IIF6, IIF8, IIF9) vessel with an everted rim (Type 4.13). The straight-sided dish with a triangular rim (Type 6.18), another BB2 form (Tyers 1996, 186–8, fig 232: IVH1, IVH4–H7), was also introduced and widely used at this time. In the later Roman period, thick-walled dishes became very popular, particularly flanged (Type 6.17) and straight-sided (Type 6.19) varieties. Soot residues have not survived well on the surface of these sherds, but are present in some instances. Decorative motifs are quite common, with simple single or multiple horizontal grooves and incised wavy lines the most frequently used. Burnished areas have survived on some of the sherds, together with cross-hatched and wavy lines. Other motifs found more rarely include combing, coarse rouletting, stabbing and occasional traces of white slip.

Another distinctive sandy greyware fabric with a blue hue was found in significant quantities (*c*.1%). This fabric was introduced in the early Roman period, but continued to be used until the end of the Roman period. As with the general sandy greyware fabric, many of the forms produced are inspired by BB2–type pottery. Narrow-mouthed jars (Type 2.1), beakers with everted rims (Type 3.11) and lid-seated (Type 4.4), globular (Type 4.5), grooved (Type 4.6) and everted rim (Type 4.13) medium-mouthed jars were all in use. Miscellaneous (Type 5), carinated (Type 5.2) and rounded (Type 5.3) wide-mouthed jars were the most popular vessel types in this fabric. Also found were straight-sided dishes (Types 6.18 and 6.19) including flanged (Type 6.17) varieties, and a lid (Type 8.1).

An important development in the use of greywares in the Romano-British period is marked with the introduction of the Lower Nene Valley greywares, as their manufacture established the sandy greyware fabric as the main utilitarian ware in the region. They were only produced between the late 2nd century and the early 4th century (Perrin 1999, 112), after which their range of forms was produced in colour-coated fabrics (see below), allowing the later Roman shell-tempered ware industry to flourish (see above). At Love's Farm, they represent only 0.5% (by weight) of the Romano-British assemblage and occur mainly in the form of flanged rim flagons (Type 1.4) and miscellaneous wide-mouthed jars (Type 5), although high-shouldered (Type 4.1), lid-seated (Type 4.4), globular (Type 4.5), bifid (Type 4.8) and everted rim (Type 4.13) medium-mouthed jars are also present. Straight-sided dished (Types 6.18 and 6.19) and flanged varieties (Type 6.17) were found, as were bowls with flanged rims (Type 6.15), a platter (Type 6.22) and a lid (Type 8.1). Most of these vessel forms are represented by single examples, only the high-shouldered and everted rim medium-mouthed jars, and the flanged dishes being found in larger quantities. Some of the sherds are decorated with roulette motifs, but the majority are plain. Only one sherd retains a sooty residue.

d) Oxidised wares
The range of oxidised fabrics available expanded in the middle to late Roman period, although their percentage of the market remained constant, at approximately 5%, since several oxidised fabrics were recovered only in small quantities.

e) Oxidised ware with grog inclusions
Oxidised ware with grog inclusions continued to be supplied in similar quantities to those of the early Roman period (Period 4.1), although they form a smaller part (c.3% by weight) of the larger Period 4.2–4.4 assemblage. The range of forms is both limited and plain, with the majority falling out of use around the middle of the 2nd century AD. A ring-neck flagon (Type 1.1) and a narrow-mouthed jar (Type 2.1) were found, but no beakers were recorded. Jars include medium-mouthed lid-seated (Type 4.4), globular (Type 4.5) and everted rim (Type 4.13) types, and a wide-mouthed rounded jar (Type 5.3) was also present. A dish with an internal angle (Type 6.21), a bowl with a reverse S-profile (Type 6.1), a flanged rim bowl (Type 6.15) and a lid (Type 8.1) were recovered. Most of these wares are undecorated, but there is a small sub-group of three sherds that are decorated with stamped rosettes and ovolos (two of which are illustrated: Fig. 7.11, No. 24 and Fig. 7.13, No. 48), which imitate decorative motifs more commonly seen on samian ware. The dating of these sherds is of interest, as they were found with later Roman material, and may be a local 4th- or early 5th-century imitation of samian, which had not been supplied to the region for almost 100 years by that time. It is perhaps more likely, however, that they represent copies of a late Roman redware from Oxfordshire, which was also heavily influenced by the Gaulish samian industry.

f) Verulamium whiteware
Supply of Verulamium whitewares continued in similar quantities to those found in Period 4.1 until around the middle of the 2nd century AD (Tyers 1996, 201), although these wares form a smaller proportion of the larger Period 4.2–4.4 assemblage (c.1% by weight). At Love's Farm, Verulamium wares are represented by ring-necked (Type 1.1) flagons, a Hofheim-type two-handled (Type 1.5) flagon, a funnel-necked beaker (Type 3.1) and a hemispherical bowl (Type 6.4). However, the main utilitarian forms were the bifid rim medium-mouthed jar (Type 4.8), which was often fumed or sooted, and a carinated bowl with a flattish out-turned rim (Type 6.3). A mortarium of classic Verulamium bead and flange type (type 7.5.1) was also recovered.

g) Gritty oxidised ware
As the supply of Verulamium whitewares declined, regional potteries began to manufacture similar oxidised wares with a gritty surface texture; kilns are suspected in Northamptonshire and one is known at Godmanchester (Lyons 2007; Lyons in prep. b). This ware was more common than Verulamium whitewares at Love's Farm, representing c.2% of the assemblage by weight. The range of forms includes ring-necked (Type 1.1) flagons and, less commonly, cupped rim (Type 1.9) flagons. No narrow-mouthed jar or beaker forms were recorded. Medium-mouthed jar forms, including lid-seated (Type 4.4), globular (Type 4.5) and (more commonly) bifid (Type 4.8) types were found, as well as miscellaneous wide-mouthed jars (Type 5). Present in small quantities are straight-sided dishes with triangular (Type 6.18) and flanged (Type 6.17) rims. Carinated bowls with flattish out-turned rims (Type 6.3) and bowls with flanged rims (Type 6.15) are present, as well as a lid (Type 8.1). Most of these vessels are undecorated and utilitarian in nature, and many are fumed or sooted.

h) Sandy oxidised ware
The best-represented oxidised fabric is an unprovenanced sandy oxidised ware (c.2% by weight), probably manufactured at a range of local centres (similar to the sandy greyware fabrics). This fabric occurs in a wide variety of forms, including utilitarian and specialist types. Earlier Roman (?residual) forms include globular (Type 3.7) and butt (Type 3.13) beakers, lid-seated medium-mouthed jars (Type 4.4), along with carinated (Type 5.2) and rounded (Type 5.3 and 5.6) wide-mouthed jars. Dishes with an internal angle (Type 6.21) are common, one of which is decorated with gold mica both internally and externally. In the 2nd century, two flagon types were in use, one with a thickened rim (Type 1.2) and the other with a cupped rim (Type 1.9). A limited number of narrow-mouthed jars (Type 2.1) and a funnel-necked (Type 3.1) beaker were also found. Several medium-mouthed jars, including globular (Type 4.5) and everted rim (Type 4.13) variations were in use from the mid 2nd to 4th centuries. Many of these vessels are covered in a white slip, probably to obscure the colour variations created during the firing process, and several are combed. Single examples of reeded (Type 7.9.1) and bead and flange (Type 7.10.2 and 7.10.4) mortaria were recovered. A bifid rim (Type 4.8) medium-mouthed jar, and straight-sided (Types 6.18 and 6.19) and flanged (Type 6.17) dishes were commonly used in this period. Of

particular interest are several open forms that imitate samian finewares, including the straight-sided cup (Type 6.5 – imitating Dr 30, Fig. 7.13, No. 49); these may have been produced locally in response to the shortage of Gaulish samian when importation ceased in the 3rd century. These examples appear to be earlier and more direct copies of samian forms than the oxidised grog-tempered versions described above.

i) Nene Valley whiteware
The influence of the Lower Nene Valley pottery industry can be seen with the arrival, in addition to the greywares described above, of the whiteware produced there in the later 2nd century. This fabric was used in significant quantities ($c.2\%$) and a range of utilitarian forms were found in small numbers, including narrow-mouthed jars (Type 2.1), undiagnostic beakers (Type 3), medium- (Types 4.1, 4.4 and 4.8) and wide-mouthed (Type 5.6) jars, dishes (Types 6.18, 6.19, 6.21) and bowls (Type 6.15). Two undiagnostic jar body sherds have pre-firing holes in the vessel wall, suggesting that they were purposely made as strainers of some sort. However, the main product of this fabric was an oxidised mortarium with slag trituration grits. Many of the mortaria fragments cannot be assigned to a specific type, but the majority of those that could are of the reeded-rim design (7.9.1, Fig. 7.14, No. 67) for which this factory is most well known. A small number of variations on this design (Types 7.9.3, 7.9.4, 7.9.5) were found. One mortarium base (SF 2459, Fig. 7.14, No. 68) had been adapted for another use by having a single hole punched through it. Several of the sherds are fumed, suggesting they had been placed near an open flame.

Amphora
Amphora represent $c.2\%$ by weight of the Period 4.2–4.4 assemblage. A small amount of material cannot be assigned to source, but the majority is of the globular olive oil Dressel 20 type from southern Spain, although a smaller quantity of Italian wine amphorae (Dressel 1/2) was also found. Amphorae are generally poorly represented in low order settlements in East Anglia, and their presence here in more than one fabric and vessel type may reflect the proximity of the site to the military supply route along Ermine Street.

Finewares

a) Grey finewares
A small quantity of fine greywares (0.4% by weight) was recovered. This material has a very small average sherd size ($c.6$g) and is generally of early Roman 'London Ware' type: it is therefore largely residual. The forms consist of a butt beaker (Type 3.13), a wide-mouthed jar (Type 5.3) and a dish with an internal angle (Type 6.21). Two imitation samian forms in the shape of a deep bowl (Type 6.6 – imitating Dr 37) and a conical cup (Type 6.13 – imitating Dr 33) were identified.

b) Samian
In the middle to late Romano-British period, samian was in use at Love's Farm in fairly low quantities, in total representing 0.98% by weight of the entire assemblage (see Wadeson and Monteil, below). Within this relatively small group most ($c.70\%$ by weight) originated in Central Gaul, although some Southern Gaulish material ($c.20\%$) was still in circulation. A very small amount ($c.6\%$) of later Eastern Gaulish samian, dating to $c.$AD 120–260, was also used at Love's Farm.

The Central Gaulish material consists of several cup forms (Dr 27, Dr 35, Dr 46, Dr 33 (three stamped examples)), of which Dr 33 is the most common. Several platters (Dr 79, Dr 79R), are present, and shallow dishes were in use (Dr 18/31 (one stamped example), Dr 31, Dr 31R, Dr 36, Dr 42, Curle 23). Bowl forms are common (Dr 37, Dr 38 (one stamped example), Dr 81 and Curle 11), but the deep bowl Dr 37 was the only decorated ware in use at Love's Farm. One mortarium (Dr 45, a more expensive form) was also found.

c) Nene Valley colour-coat
The third most common fabric found in this period comprises the Nene Valley colour-coated wares, which represent $c.10\%$ of the assemblage by weight. This industry was started in the mid 2nd century AD (Tyers 1996, 173–5) by workers originating from, or inspired by, industries in the Lower Rhineland (*ibid.*, 146–8). These continental wares consist of bag-shaped beakers, often decorated with barbotine figures, and folded beakers. It is worthy of note that the rough-cast decoration commonly employed by the Rhineland potters was not widely used by the Nene Valley industry. Between the mid 2nd and 3rd centuries AD a range of fineware beakers and flagons was produced. During the later Roman period, however, the industry was radically reorganised (Perrin 1999, 87–9) – fewer beakers were made and more utilitarian jars and thick-walled dishes were produced. Although still colour-coated, these wares are utilitarian in nature and do not fit so comfortably into the 'fineware' category.

At Love's Farm, Nene Valley finewares were introduced during the mid 2nd century. Bag-shaped (Type 3.6) and globular (Type 3.7) beakers, followed by later funnel-necked vessels (Type 3.1), were in use. By the end of the 2nd century flagons had been added to the repertoire, with flanged (Type 1.4), straight-necked (Type 1.7) and cupped (Type 1.9) rim versions all in use. With the demise of Lower Nene Valley greyware production and the subsequent rearrangement of the industry, a range of jars and dishes was introduced; particularly popular at Love's Farm was the high-shouldered medium-mouthed jar (Type 4.1), and the medium-mouthed jar with a large rolled rim (Type 4.5.4). Dishes were used in significant quantities, and their robust nature means they have survived well within this assemblage. At Love's Farm the simple straight-sided dish (Type 6.19) and the flanged dish (Type 6.17) were the most commonly used. Nene Valley colour-coated mortaria (one of the more expensive Nene Valley products) were present in small quantities.

d) Oxfordshire red colour-coat
Oxfordshire red ware comprised the fourth most common fabric at Love's Farm ($c.2\%$). It was traded into the area from the middle of the 3rd century AD, and appears to have continued to be imported until the early 5th century. Much of it is very abraded, and in some instances the red slip has been entirely worn away. A range of forms was found, including disc (Type 1.3) and cupped rim (Type 1.9) flagons, along with narrow-mouthed jars (Type 2.1). Medium-mouthed jars are well represented, the most common of which is the high-shouldered form (Type 4.1). Wide-mouthed jars are also common, but their

Fabric description	Vessel form	Sherd count	Sherd wt (g)	EVE	MSW (g)	Wt (%)
Shell-tempered ware (STW)	Narrow- and medium-mouthed jars, also dishes	1350	33517	14.25	24.8	42.4
Sandy greyware (SGW)	Beakers, narrow-, medium- and wide-mouthed jars, platters, dishes, bowls and lids	2492	24670	33.91	9.9	31.2
Gritty oxidised ware (OW(GRITTY))	Flagon, medium-mouthed jars and bowls	192	2074	2.38	10.8	2.6
Horningsea reduced ware (HORN)	Storage jars	61	1797	0.87	29.5	2.3
Sandy oxidised ware (SOW)	Flagon, narrow-, medium- and wide-mouthed jars, platter, dish and bowl	200	1701	3.51	8.5	2.2
Nene Valley colour-coat (NVCC)	Beakers, medium-mouthed jars and dishes	151	1679	2.67	11.1	2.1
Reduced ware (handmade) (RW HM)	Medium- and wide-mouthed jars	105	1661	1.12	15.8	2.1
Verulamium whiteware (VWW)	Flagons, beakers, medium-mouthed jars, bowl and mortaria	70	1402	1.51	20.0	1.8
Sandy reduced ware (SRW)	Medium-mouthed jars and dishes	248	1069	1.07	4.3	1.4
Grey ware with grog inclusions (GW(GROG))	Flagon, beaker, wide-mouthed jars, bowl	77	975	1.08	12.7	1.2
Spanish amphora (BAT AM 1)	Amphora	4	953	0.00	238.3	1.2
Reduced ware with oxidised surfaces and grog inclusions (RW(GROG)(P))	Wide-mouthed cordoned jar	93	844	0.41	9.1	1.1
Fine greyware (GW(FINE))	Beaker, wide-mouthed jar, dish and bowl	66	750	0.56	11.4	1.0
Sandy greyware with grog inclusions (SGW(GROG))	Wide-mouthed cordoned jars	41	694	0.47	16.9	0.9
Oxidised ware with grog inclusions (OW(Grog))		52	639	0.53	12.3	0.8
Black-surfaced red ware (BSRW)	Medium-mouthed jars, dish and bowl	50	604	0.62	12.1	0.8
Nene Valley oxidised ware (NVOW)	Narrow- and wide-mouthed jars, dish and mortaria	26	595	0.65	22.9	0.8
South Gaulish samian (SAM SG)	Cup, dish, bowl, platter	41	427	1.05	10.4	0.5
Oxfordshire red ware (OXRCC)	Flagon, medium- and wide-mouthed jar, dishes and mortaria	36	411	0.97	11.4	0.5
Central Gaulish samian (SAM CG)	Dish, bowl, platter	45	341	1.18	7.6	0.4
Poorly represented and intrusive ERB material		260	2195	3.20	8.4	2.8
Total		5660	78998	72.01	14.0	100

Table 7.14 The pottery recovered from features assigned to the Romano-British period (Period 4.2), listed in descending order of percentage of weight

fragmentary nature has made identification of individual types difficult (Type 5). A range of cups and bowls was found, several imitating samian forms. These comprise a straight-sided cup (Type 6.5 – imitating Dr 30), a conical cup (Type 6.13 – imitating Dr 33) and a flanged bowl (Type 6.14 – imitating Dr 38). The latter is one of the more common vessels types found in this fabric at Love's Farm. Other open forms include a hemispherical bowl (Type 6.4), a carinated straight-sided bowl (Type 6.7), and a bowl with a flanged rim (Type 6.15). Dishes form a significant part of this assemblage, including types seen in both the coarseware and fineware assemblages; the straight-sided dish with a triangular rim (Type 6.18), the straight-sided dish with a plain rim (Type 6.19) and the dish with an internal angle (Type 6.21). Although Oxfordshire redware mortaria were commonly recorded, much of the material could not be assigned to a specific type; however, several individual forms using high bead and small flanges are typical of the Oxfordshire industry (Young 1977; Types 7.7.1, 7.7.2, 7.7.4, 7.8.6). A reeded rim type more often seen in Nene Valley whiteware fabric (Type 7.9.1) was also recognised.

e) Hadham redware
Hadham ware, another late Roman fine redware, was identified within the assemblage (0.5%). This ware was manufactured in Hertfordshire (Tyers 1996, 168–9) and copied samian and Oxfordshire vessel types. It is distinctive however, since it is less micaceous than the Oxfordshire fabrics (Tomber and Dore 1996, 151) and was

Fabric description	Vessel form	Sherd count	Sherd wt (g)	EVE	MSW (g)	Wt (%)
Shell-tempered ware (STW)	Medium-mouthed jars and dishes	532	8702	7.73	16.4	44.1
Sandy greyware (SGW)	Medium- and wide-mouthed jars, dishes, bowls and a lid	442	3819	6.69	22.54	19.4
Nene Valley colour-coat (NVCC)	Beaker and medium-mouthed jars, dishes and bowls	131	1712	2.57	13.1	8.7
Reduced ware (handmade) (RW HM)	Wide-mouthed jars	67	854	0.74	12.8	4.3
Greyware with grog inclusions (GW(GROG))	Beaker and jars	27	429	0.16	15.9	2.2
Sandy reduced ware (SRW)	Wide-mouthed jars	36	416	0.46	11.6	2.1
Nene Valley oxidised ware (NVOW)	Mortaria	19	403	0.32	21.2	2.0
Oxfordshire red ware (OXRCC)	Wide-mouthed jar, bowls and mortaria	32	384	0.33	12.0	2.0
Fine greyware (GW(FINE))	Beaker	82	340	0.72	4.2	1.7
Red fineware (RED FW)	Medium-mouthed jar	28	239	0.10	8.5	1.2
Black-surfaced red ware (BSRW)	Wide-mouthed jar and bowl	16	232	0.10	14.5	1.2
Hadham red wares (HAD RW)	Flagon, narrow-mouthed jar and bowl	19	158	0.80	8.3	0.8
Sandy oxidised ware with flint inclusions (SOW(FLINT+))		9	158	0.00	17.6	0.8
Oxidised ware with grog inclusions (OW(GROG))		15	155	0.00	10.3	0.89
Sandy oxidised ware (SOW)	Beaker and medium-mouthed jars	41	144	0.26	10.3	0.7
Oxidised ware with chalk inclusions (C1)		10	142	0.00	14.2	0.7
Gritty oxidised ware (OW(GRITTY))	Medium-mouthed jars and bowls	19	135	0.60	7.1	0.7
Verulamium whiteware (VWW)	Bowls	7	126	0.09	18.0	0.6
Horningsea reduced ware (HORN)	Dish	11	120	0.10	10.9	0.6
Central Gaulish samian (SAM CG)	Cup, dish and bowl	12	90	0.46	7.5	0.5
Poorly represented and intrusive ERB material		117	961	0.72	8.2	4.9
Total		1672	19719	22.95	11.8	100

Table 7.15 The pottery recovered from features assigned to the Romano-British period (Period 4.3), listed in descending order of percentage of weight

commonly burnished (not slipped). Forms identified consist of two flagons, of disc rim (Type 1.3) and face mask type (1.8, Fig. 7.12, No. 32 and Fig. 7.13, No. 40), as well as a pinched-neck jug (Type 1.11). Medium-mouthed jars of the high-shouldered (Type 4.1), and globular (Type 4.5) and bifid rim (Type 4.8) varieties were in use; as were miscellaneous wide-mouthed jars (Type 5), flanged bowls (Type 6.14), flanged dishes (Type 6.17) and miscellaneous mortaria (Type 7). Of these vessels the high-shouldered jar and the flanged bowl are the most common forms.

The mid to late Roman pottery by period

Period 4.2: 2nd century
Closer examination of the pottery found in deposits assigned to Period 4.2 (Table 7.14) shows that a total of 5,660 sherds, weighing 78,998g (c.72 EVE), was recovered from features assigned to this period, constituting c.18.4% (by weight) of the entire assemblage (Table 7.12). Shell-tempered wares, supplemented by Sandy greywares, form c.74% by weight of the entire period group. This is a massive domination of the market, and suggests that local wares fulfilled the majority of the settlement's ceramic needs at this time. Although retrieved in much smaller quantities than the locally produced wares, pottery was also arriving from the domestic regional production centres at Verulamium (St Albans) and the Nene Valley (Peterborough); imported Southern and Central Gaulish samian was also in use. The range of fabrics available to the local population was widening, however, with twenty individual fabrics present in significant quantities (two more than were present in Period 4.1).

Pottery from this phase was most commonly retrieved from pits (36% by weight) and ditches (31%). The assemblage has a MSW of only 14g, and is severely abraded.

Catalogue of illustrated 2nd-century pottery
(Fig. 7.11)

12 GW(GROG) wheelmade **Hofheim-type flagon** with a single handle (Type 1.6; Martin 1988, 182, 183, 185). *10210*, fill of pit *10211*, Settlement 7. Period 4.2.

13 OW(GROG) miniature wheelmade **narrow-mouthed jar**, slim and pear-shaped (Type 2.2). *10171*, fill of pit *10172*, Enclosure 21, Settlement 7. Period 4.2.

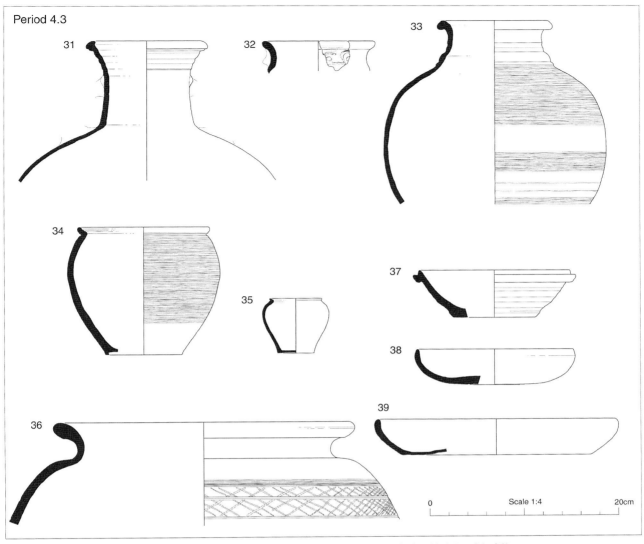

Figure 7.12 Middle Romano-British pottery (Period 4.3) (Nos 31–39)

14 SGW wheelmade **medium-mouthed bifid jar**, in this case probably the top of a butt beaker (Type 4.8/3.13). *4625* fill of pit *4626*, Quarry 7, Settlement 7. Period 4.2.

15 STW wheelmade **medium-mouthed jar** with a rounded body and simple everted rim (Type 4.13; Martin 1988, 250; 251). *4625*, fill of pit *4626*, Quarry 7, Settlement 7. Period 4.2.

16 STW wheelmade **medium-mouthed jar** with a rounded body and simple everted rim (Type 4.13; Martin 1988, 250; 251). *4625*, fill of pit *4626*, Quarry 7, Settlement 7. Period 4.2.

17 STW wheelmade **large storage vessel** with a rolled rim (Type 4.14). *5687*, layer, quarry 7, Settlement 7. Period 4.2.

18 SGW(BLUE) wheelmade **wide-mouthed carinated jar** (Type 5.1; Martin 1988, 196–21. *9043*, fill of ditch *9044*, Enclosure 107, Settlement 6. Period 4.2.

19 SOW wheelmade **wide-mouthed jar** (Type 5.2.1; Perrin 1996, 71). *4625*, fill of pit *4626*, Quarry 7, Settlement 7. Period 4.2.

20 SGW wheelmade **rounded jar** with a reverse S-profile, with a groove on the neck and mid body (Type 5.3; Rogerson 1977, 39; 46; 94). *9043*, fill of ditch *9044*, Enclosure 107, Settlement 6. Period 4.2.

21 RW handmade **rounded jar** with a reverse S-profile, with a groove on the neck (Type 5.3). Post-firing hole drilled in vessel neck. *8921*, fill of ditch *8922*, Enclosure 101, Settlement 6. Period 4.2.

22 GW(FINE) wheelmade **carinated bowl** with a flattish out-turned rim (Type 6.3; Rogerson 1977, 16; 69; 72). *8776*, fill of ditch *8775*, Enclosure 109, Settlement 6. Period 4.2.

23 SGW wheelmade **carinated bowl** with a flattish out-turned rim (Type 6.3; Rogerson 1977, 16; 69; 72). *4625*, fill of pit *4626*, Quarry 7, Settlement 7. Period 4.2.

24 OW(GROG) wheelmade **imitation samian**. *5562*, fill of pit *4626*, Quarry 7, Settlement 7. Period 4.2.

25 SGW wheelmade sharply **carinated cup** (Type 6.9.1; Perrin 1996, 91). *4625*, fill of pit *4626*, Quarry 7, Settlement 7. Period 4.2.

26 SGW wheelmade **flanged rim bowl** with curving sides, out-turned rim (Type 6.15; Rogerson 1977, 74; 76; 97). *4625*, fill of pit *4626*, Quarry 7, Settlement 7. Period 4.2.

27 SGW wheelmade **dish** with an internal angle resulting in an incurving rim (Type 6.21; Perrin 1996, 28, 29, 30). *4625*, fill of pit *4626*, Quarry 7, Settlement 7. Period 4.2.

28 SGW wheelmade **dish** with an internal angle resulting in an incurving rim (Type 6.21; Perrin 1996, 28, 29, 30). *4625*, fill of pit *4626*, Quarry 7, Settlement 7. Period 4.2.

29 SGW wheelmade **lid** of standard type to fit cooking/storage pot with grooved decoration (Type 8.1; Perrin 1996, 57; 58; 59). *9043*, fill of ditch *9044*, Enclosure 107, Settlement 6. Period 4.2.

30 SGW wheelmade **spouted jar** (Type 4.26). *4625*, fill of pit *4626*, Quarry 7, Settlement 7. Period 4.2.

Period 4.3: 3rd century
Examination of the pottery found in deposits assigned to Period 4.3 revealed that only 1,672 sherds, weighing

Fabric description	Vessel form	Sherd count	Sherd wt (g)	EVE	MSW (g)	Wt (%)
Shell-tempered ware (STW)	Narrow- and medium-mouthed jars, also dishes, lids	3194	53673	37.21	16.8	44.7
Sandy grey ware (SGW)	Beakers, narrow-, medium- and wide-mouthed jars, platters, dishes, bowls and lids	2776	26763	31.49	9.6	22.3
Nene Valley colour coat (NVCC)	Flagons, beakers, narrow-, medium- and wide-mouthed jars, bowls, dishes, mortaria and lids	1136	15684	22.28	13.8	13.1
Oxfordshire red ware (OXRCC)	Bowls and mortaria	456	3717	4.90	8.2	3.1
Nene Valley oxidised ware (NVOW)	Medium-mouthed jars, bowls and mortaria	74	2126	1.17	28.7	1.8
Sandy reduced ware (SRW)	Medium-mouthed jars and dishes	86	1672	2.01	19.4	1.4
Sandy oxidised ware (SOW)	Medium- and wide-mouthed jars, dishes and mortaria	265	1654	1.21	6.2	1.4
Spanish amphora (BAT AM 1)	DR20	11	1324	0.23	120.4	1.1
Horningsea reduced ware (HORN)	Storage jars	43	1175	0.43	27.3	1.0
Spanish amphora (BAT AM 2)	DR20	2	1033	0.00	516.5	0.9
Central Gaulish samian (SAM CG)	Dish, bowl, platter, cup	86	861	1.56	10.0	0.7
Hadham red ware (HAD RW)	Flagons, medium-mouthed jar, bowl and mortaria	109	768	1.11	7.1	0.6
Reduced ware (handmade) (RW HM)	Medium- and wide-mouthed jars, dish	52	688	0.52	13.2	0.6
Nene Valley grey ware (NVGW)	Medium-mouthed jars, platter, dish and bowls	46	654	1.40	14.2	0.6
Gritty oxidised ware (OW(GRITTY))	Medium-mouthed jars, dish and bowl	57	629	1.40	11.0	0.5
Reduced ware with oxidised surfaces and grog inclusions (RW(GROG)(P))	Storage jar	63	724	0.07	11.5	0.1
Poorly represented and intrusive ERB material		577	6811	4.88	11.8	6.2
Total		9033	119956	111.87	13.3	100

Table 7.16 The pottery recovered from features assigned to the Romano-British period (Period 4.4), listed in descending order of percentage of weight

19,719g (c.23 EVE), were recovered. This is the smallest group of pottery recovered from any one period at Love's Farm, representing only c.4.6% (by weight) of the entire assemblage.

Twenty main fabrics were identified (Table 7.15), the same types as in the preceding period, suggesting a constant and stable supply. As previously, Shell-tempered wares dominate the local market, although Sandy greywares are less well represented at this time. This change is possibly due to the increasing popularity of Nene Valley products, which claimed a significant part of the market share. Verulamium wares also declined in market share as the Nene Valley expanded, although it seems unlikely that this was the sole reason for the decline in the Verulamium industry. In addition to the Nene Valley colour-coated finewares, Central Gaulish samian tablewares were also in use.

Pottery was found in a limited number of features, mostly ditches (71% by weight), but also pits (1%) and postholes (3%). The material recovered is generally abraded, with a MSW of c.12g. Grog-tempered pottery is extremely rare (c.3% by weight), but was found in a small concentration around a large timber building (Structure 105). This might indicate an early date within this period for this structure, or could be a reflection of some kind of specialist activity (such as brewing) that was being undertaken in the vicinity.

Catalogue of illustrated 3rd-century pottery
(Fig. 7.12)

31 OW(GRITTY) wheelmade **ring-necked flagon** (Type 1.1; Perrin 1996, 90). *5651*, fill of ditch *5638*, Boundary 111, Settlement 7. Period 4.3.

32 HAD RW wheelmade **facepot** (Type 1.8). *8964*, fill of posthole *8965*, Structure 105, Settlement 6. Period 4.3.

33 SGW wheelmade **narrow-mouthed jar** (Type 2.1; Perrin 1996, 132; 222; 416). *5696*, fill of ditch *5638*, Boundary 111, Settlement 7. Period 4.3.

34 STW wheelmade **lid-seated medium-mouthed jar** with short angular neck (Type 4.4; Perrin 1996, 387). *5637*, fill of ditch *5638*, Boundary 111, Settlement 7. Period 4.3.

35 SGW wheelmade miniature **medium-mouthed jar** with a rounded body and simple everted rim (Type 4.13; Martin 1988, 250; 251). *5637*, fill of ditch *5638*, Boundary 111, Settlement 7. Period 4.3.

36 STW wheelmade **storage jar** (Type 4.18), decorated with two cordons of burnished cross-hatch motif. *5696*, fill of ditch *5638*, Boundary 111, Settlement 7. Period 4.3.

37 NVCC wheelmade **hemispherical bowl with a plain hooked flange**, copy of samian form Dr 38 (Type 6.14; Howe et al. 1980, 83; 101). *5416*, fill of ditch *5417*, Boundary 115, Settlement 7. Period 4.3.

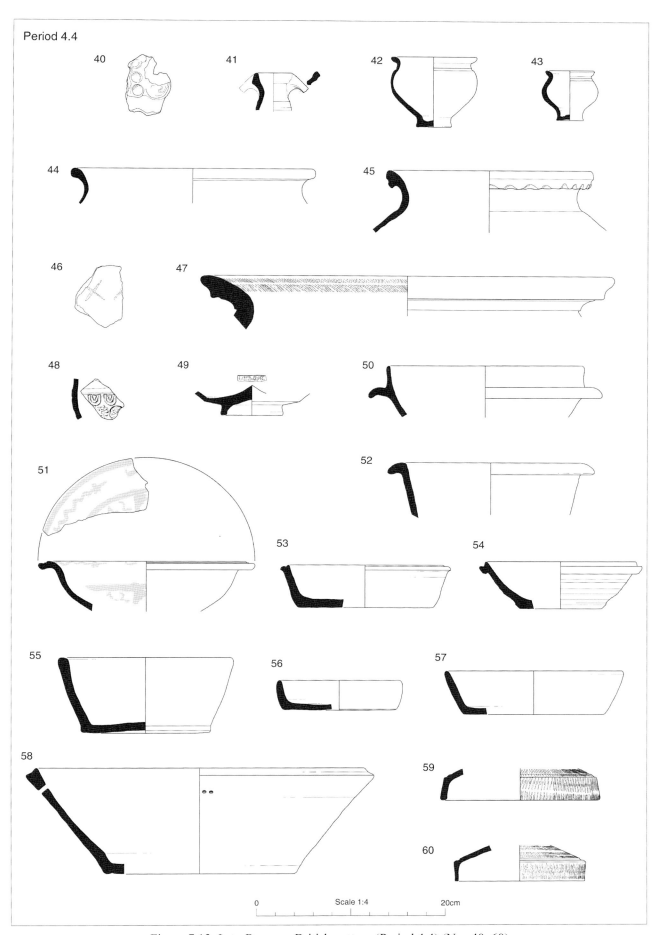

Figure 7.13 Late Romano-British pottery (Period 4.4) (Nos 40–60)

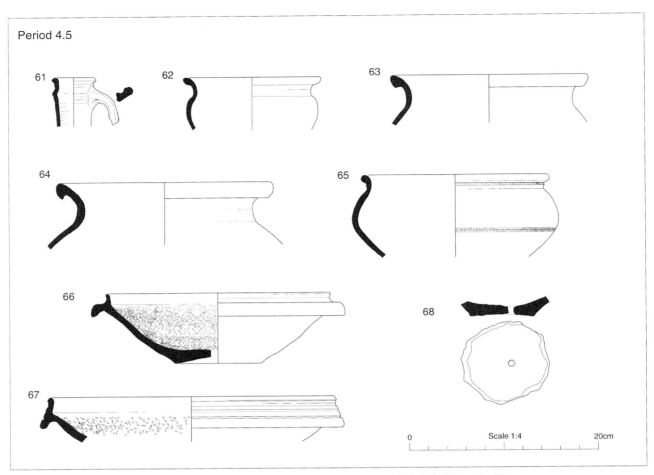

Figure 7.14 Late Romano-British pottery (Period 4.5) (Nos 61–68)

38 SGW wheelmade **dish with an internal angle** resulting in an incurving rim (Type 6.21; Perrin 1996, 28, 29, 30). *10324*, fill of ditch *10327*, Boundary 111, Settlement 7. Period 4.3.

39 SOW wheelmade **dish with an internal angle** resulting in an incurving rim (Type 6.21; Perrin 1996, 28, 29, 30). *10325*, fill of ditch *10327*, Boundary 111, Settlement 7. Period 4.3.

Period 4.4: 4th century
A total of 9,033 sherds, weighing 119,956g (*c*.112 EVE), was recovered from this period group, forming the largest period group in the entire assemblage (*c*.28% by weight). Sixteen fabrics were recorded in significant quantities, suggesting that choice was becoming limited at this time (Table 7.16). Shell-tempered wares (*c*.45% by weight), supplemented by Sandy greywares (22%), still dominated the supply of pottery to the site.

The pottery was largely recovered from ditches (57% by weight), a surface (16%) and pits (8%), with lesser amounts retrieved from postholes and other deposits. The material is generally abraded, with a MSW of only *c*.13g.

Catalogue of illustrated 4th-century pottery
(Fig. 7.13)

40 HAD RW wheelmade **facepot** (Type 1.8). *13883*, layer, Structure 108, Settlement 6. Period 4.4.

41 NVCC wheelmade plain **cupped-rim flagon** (Type 1.9; Perrin 1996, 159). *4776*, fill of ditch *120110*, Enclosure 131, Settlement 7. Period 4.4.

42 NVCC wheelmade **globular beaker with an everted rim** (Type 3.7; Perrin 1996, 18; 62; 63; 67). *4747*, fill of pit *4748*, Structure 114, Settlement 7. Period 4.4.

43 NVOW wheelmade **miniature high-shouldered jar** (Type 4.1). *5894*, fill of ditch, Boundary 116, Settlement 7. Period 4.4.

44 SGW wheelmade **medium-mouthed jar** with a short neck and rolled rim (Type 4.5). *4998*, fill of ditch *4999*, Enclosure 137, Settlement 7. Period 4.4.

45 STW wheelmade **medium-mouthed jar**, everted rim that is hollowed or with projection underneath (bifid), globular body (Type 4.8; Perrin 1996, 592; 583). *9458*, fill of ditch *9459*, Settlement 6. Period 4.4.

46 SGW wheelmade **jar** body sherd with a post-firing graffito. *5344*, cobbled surface, Settlement 7. Period 4.4.

47 HORN wheelmade **Horningsea storage jar** with an out-sized, out-turned rim (Type 4.17; Evans 1991, fig. 2, nos 1–9). *5226*, fill of ditch *5227*, Settlement 7. Period 4.4.

48 OW(GROG) wheelmade **imitation samian**. *10329*, fill of ditch *10330*, Enclosure 126, Settlement 7. Period 4.4.

49 OW(GROG) wheelmade **imitation samian** stamped base. *10234*, fill of pit *10236*, Settlement 7. Period 4.4.

50 OXRCC wheelmade **hemispherical bowl with a plain hooked flange**, copy of samian form Dr 38 (Type 6.14; Howe *et al.* 1980, 83; 101). *5907*, fill of posthole *5908*, Settlement 7. Period 4.4.

51 NVCC wheelmade **flanged rim bowl** with curving sides, out-turned rim with painted decoration (Type 6.15; Rogerson 1977, 74; 76; 97). *5919*, fill of ditch *5920*, Settlement 7. Period 4.4.

52 STW wheelmade **straight-sided dish with an out-turned rim** (Type 6.15/18; Rogerson 1977, 74; 76; 97). *5002*, fill of ditch *5003*, Enclosure 136, Settlement 7. Period 4.4.

53 NVCC wheelmade **flanged rim straight-sided dish** with a flat base (Type 6.17; Perrin 1996, 468; 469; 483). *7597*, fill of ditch *7598*, Settlement 6. Period 4.4.

Fabric description	Vessel form	Sherd count	Sherd wt (g)	EVE	MSW (g)	Wt (%)
Shell-tempered ware (STW, S1)	Narrow- and medium-mouthed jars, also dishes	772	13542	6.04	17.5	49.8
Nene Valley colour coat (NVCC)	Flagon, beaker, medium-mouthed jars, bowls and dishes	318	5326	5.88	16.8	19.6
Sandy grey ware (SGW)	Narrow-, medium- and wide-mouthed jars and dishes	376	3400	4.31	9.0	12.5
Oxfordshire red ware (OXRCC)	Flagon, medium- and wide-mouthed jar, dishes and mortaria	148	1092	1.25	7.4	4.0
Sandy oxidised ware (SOW)	Beaker, medium-mouthed jars, dish and mortaria	47	592	0.80	12.6	2.2
Nene Valley oxidised ware (NVOW)	Dish and mortaria	8	574	0.03	2.1	2.1
Oxfordshire colour coated white ware (OXWCC)	Mortaria	6	402	0.33	67.0	1.5
Sandy reduce ware (handmade) (Q2)		49	348	0.00	7.1	1.3
Red fineware (RED FW)		1	274	0.00	274.0	1.0
Horningsea reduced ware (HORN)	Storage jars	5	222	0.05	44.4	0.8
Hadham red ware (HAD RW)	Flagon	34	185	0.24	5.4	0.7
Pink grog tempered ware (PGROG)		6	185	0.00	30.8	0.7
Spanish amphora (BAT AM 1)	DR20	1	165	0.00	165.0	0.6
Reduced ware with grog inclusions (RW(GROG))		5	149	0.00	29.8	0.6
Poorly represented and intrusive ERB material		62	719	0.79	11.6	2.6
Total		1838	27175	19.72	14.8	100

Table 7.17 The pottery recovered from features assigned to the Romano-British period (Period 4.5), listed in descending order of percentage of weight

54 SRW wheelmade **flanged rim straight-sided dish** with a flat base (Type 6.17; Perrin 1996, 468; 469; 483). This example has an inverted flange which could mean it was also used as a lid. *5344*, cobbled surface, Settlement 7. Period 4.4.

55 STW wheelmade deep **straight-sided dish** with a plain rim (Type 6.19; Perrin 1996, 402; 403; 415). *4805*, fill of ditch *4806*, Boundary 117, Settlement 7. Period 4.4.

56 NVCC wheelmade shallow **straight-sided dish** with a plain rim (Type 6.19; Perrin 1996, 402; 403; 415). *4998*, fill of ditch *4999*, Enclosure 137, Settlement 7. Period 4.4.

57 SGW wheelmade **straight-sided (but angled) dish** with a plain rim (Type 6.19; Perrin 1996, 402; 403; 415). *4998*, fill of ditch *4999*, Enclosure 137, Settlement 7. Period 4.4.

58 STW wheelmade **straight-sided dish** with a lid-seated rim (Type 6.19; Perrin 1996, 402; 403; 415). Post-firing holes on vessel wall. ?Support for string handles. Similar to Perrin 1999, fig. 73, no. 483. *4807*, fill of ditch *4806*, Enclosure 127, Settlement 7. Period 4.4.

59 NVCC wheelmade **Castor box lid** (Type 6.2.1). *4998*, fill of ditch *4999*, Enclosure 137, Settlement 7. Period 4.4.

60 NVCC wheelmade **Castor box lid** (Type 6.2.1). *5272*, fill of ditch *5274*, Enclosure 133, Settlement 7. Period 4.4.

Period 4.5: late 4th/early 5th century
A total of 1,838 sherds, weighing 27,175g (*c.*20 EVE) was recovered from deposits assigned to this period. Fourteen main fabrics were deposited at this time, almost half of which are Shell-tempered wares (Table 7.17). The pottery has a MSW of 15g and is not, therefore, as abraded as some of the earlier material; presumably as activity on the site declined after this time.

In Settlement 7, the only part of the site where activity appears to have occurred in Period 4.5, Romano-British shell- and quartz sand-tempered pottery was found throughout features assigned to this period. Pottery was also retrieved from the settlement boundary ditch and a timber structure (Period 4.5, Structure 115) located towards the southern edge of the settlement.

Catalogue of illustrated late 4th to early 5th century pottery
(Fig. 7.14)

61 NVCC wheelmade straight-necked **narrow-mouthed flagon** with a single handle. (Type 1.7. Perrin 1996, 161). *5088*, fill of ditch *5089*, Enclosure 139, Settlement 7. Period 4.5.

62 OXRCC wheelmade **medium-mouthed jar with high-shouldered profile** (Type 4.1; Rogerson 1977, 1; 2; 19; 22; 44; 107). *5345*, fill of ditch *5346*, Unphased.

63 STW wheelmade **medium-mouthed jar**, short neck, rolled and generally undercut rim and globular body (Type 4.5.3). *4822*, fill of ditch *4821*, Boundary 120, Settlement 7. Period 4.5.

64 STW wheelmade **medium-mouthed jar**, short neck, rolled and generally undercut rim and globular body (Type 4.5.3). *5259*, fill of ditch *5260*, Structure 115, Settlement 7. Period 4.5.

65 OXRCC wheelmade **wide-mouthed jar/bowl with** one or two grooves mid-body (Type 5.4). *5890*, fill of well *5387*, Settlement 7. Period 4.5.

66 OXWCC wheelmade (high) bead and flange **mortarium** (Type 7.7.2). *5909*, fill of ditch *5910*, Settlement 7, Enclosure 139, Settlement 7. Period 4.5.

67 NVOW reeded rim **mortarium** (Type 7.9.1). *8942*, ditch *8943*, Period 4.1.

68 NVOW wheelmade **mortarium** base with a post-firing central hole. *5343*, fill of pit *5596*, Settlement 7. Period 4.5.

Fabric	Vessel type	Sherd count	Weight (g)	EVE	Weight (%)
Nene Valley whiteware (NVOW)	7.9, 7.9.1, 7.9.2, 7.9.3, 7.9.4, 7.9.5	96	4232	2.22	45.8
Verulamium whiteware (VWW)	7.1, 7.5.1, 7.5.2, 7.9.1	26	1274	1.09	13.8
Oxford red slipped ware (OXRCC)	7.7.1, 7.72, 7.7.4, 7.8.6, 7.11.1	44	853	0.98	9.2
Oxford white slipped ware (OXWCC)	7.7.1, 7.7.2	21	947	0.77	10.2
Nene Valley colour-coat (NVCC)	7.9.2, 7.9.4	4	255	0.41	2.8
Sandy oxidised ware (SOW)	7.9.1, 7.10.2, 7.10.4	6	505	0.26	5.5
Oxfordshire whiteware (OXWW)	7.8.1, 7.8.3, 7.9.1	15	408	0.25	4.4
Mancetter-Hartshill whiteware (MAH WH)	7.15.1	5	676	0.15	7.3
Hadham red ware (HAD RW)		3	28	0	0.3
Whiteware (WW)		3	51	0	0.6
Central Gaulish samian (SAM CG)	Dr 45	1	22	0	0.2
Total		224	9251	6.13	100

Table 7.18 The mortaria, listed in descending order of weight (%)

V. Mortaria
by Alice Lyons
(Fig. 7.14)

The assemblage
Some 224 sherds, weighing 9,251g (6.13 EVE) of mortaria were recovered. This substantial type of mixing bowl has survived in relatively large pieces with a MSW of 41g and represents a minimum 133 individual vessels. Although a small amount of mortaria was found in Period 3, the majority (82% by weight) was recovered from Period 4 deposits. The relevant fabrics are noted in Table 7.18 and the illustrated vessels are catalogued above (Fig. 7.14, Nos 66–68).

Of particular interest are the Verulamium mortaria, of which at least ten vessels were found. One large bead and flanged example, typical of this industry, is also stamped with the maker's mark. Stamped examples were made until c.AD 155/160, although production continued until c.AD 200 (Tyers 1996, 134). As such, Verulamium mortaria represent the chronologically earliest examples of this distinctive form at Love's Farm. Most numerous, with a minimum vessel count of fifty-six, are Nene Valley whiteware mortaria. These are mostly present as reeded rim types (Type 7.9.1), although bead and flange (Type 7.9.3, 7.9.4) and wall-sided (Type 7.9.5) examples were also found. Produced from the early 2nd century into the 4th century, the Lower Nene Valley factory was a major supplier throughout East Anglia (Tyers 1996, 128). In addition, a few mortarium sherds, distinctive with red-brown trituration grits, were identified as originating from the Mancetter-Hartshill kilns on the Warwickshire/Leicester border (Tyers 1996, 123), while several other vessels (SOW) could not be assigned to source.

Well represented within this group are later Roman fabrics. A minimum of twenty-five Oxfordshire red ware mortaria, with a red slip were found in a limited range of forms with a distinctive high-bead (Type 7.71, 7.7.2) and, less usually, wall-sided examples (Type 7.7.4). Examples in the same fabric but finished with a white slip were less common, as a minimum of thirteen vessels were found as high-bead types only (Type 7.7.1, 7.7.2). Also from this factory came a small number of whiteware mortaria – a minimum of ten vessels were recorded in a similar range of high-beaded types (Types 7.8.1, 7.8.3). The Oxfordshire industry began exporting vessels into East Anglia from the mid 3rd century and continued until the end of the Roman period (Tyers 1996, 129). A very few sherds of late Roman red ware mortaria from the Hadham kilns in Hertfordshire (Tyers 1996, 168–9), occurred as undiagnostic body sherds only.

In addition to the coarseware mortaria described above, a few fine tableware mortaria were found. These include a single Central Gaulish samian mortaria with a lion's head spout (Dr 45) which first appeared in Britain during the late 2nd century (Webster 2005, 56). A few examples of Nene Valley colour-coated mortarium were also found, one of which (Type 7.9.2) copies this distinctive samian type.

This mortaria assemblage, dominated by Nene Valley products and supplemented by several other regional suppliers, appears typical of the area during the Roman period (Hancocks 2003). The history of this vessel type and how they were used, however, is still being explored and is discussed in more detail below.

The wider context
Mortaria are known to have been produced in Italy from at least the 3rd century BC and examples were exported to sites around the Mediterranean, alongside Italian amphorae and coarsewares. It is not clear in what quantities these vessels were transported but, as they could not have been exchanged for the value of their contents (unlike amphora which were (Peacock and Williams 1986)), it must be assumed that these mixing bowls were recognised and valued for their own form. As the Roman Empire expanded and developed, the popularity of mortaria also spread; this was due to the association of mortaria with the military. It is likely that mortaria formed part of the basic military kit in the same way querns did (one quern to every ten men was an essential item of military equipment; Childe 1943, 25) which would have enabled each unit of men to prepare their own food. As a result, it was in the military zones of Central and Northern Gaul and along the Rhine frontier that mortaria production increased from the Augustan period (63 BC–AD 14) onwards.

Since mortaria are associated with military movements they are often some of the first Roman pottery introduced into any newly conquered area and as a result have become an indicator for 'Romanised' ceramic assemblages. For example, a few early mortaria were imported into Britain from Northern Gaul during the pre-conquest period to elite sites such as Braughing and Sheepen (Cool 2006, 43 and 166), but this was very rare. Generally mortaria were introduced to the wider population of Britain with the successful conquest in AD 43, at which time a number of factories in the Lyons area of Gaul (Hartley and Tomber 2006, 26) supplied numerous 'wall-sided' mortaria to Britain, with small military workshops (such as Longthorpe; Hartley 1987, 127–8) supplying localised need.

Although mortaria were initially consumed mostly by the military, the ability of the army to produce their own supply – as occurred at Holt on a legionary scale (Grimes 1930) – was hampered by the demands of major building schemes and military campaigns. This inconsistent level of production left a major opportunity for civilian entrepreneurs to fill the gap in the market (Hartley and Tomber 2006, 18–9). As a result large scale civilian factory (Peacock 1982, table 10) or industrial (Sinopoli 1991, 103) production was rapidly established in Britain with the effect that coarseware imports decreased, although samian fineware mortaria (Tyers 1996, 110, fig 94, Dr 45) were imported from the mid 2nd to mid 3rd centuries AD. Indeed, civilian coarseware mortaria production became a thriving industry throughout the Romano-British period with Britain eventually consuming more of this vessel type than other parts of the empire (Hartley 1998, 209). From the AD 50s, large factories were founded in south-east Britain. These production centres produced mortaria in Gaulish-type fabrics and forms, which suggests that immigrant potters helped with the foundation of these potteries. The Verulamium industry was based in various workshops around London and St Albans (Tyers 1996, 132–4) as well as Colchester (*ibid.*, 119–20), providing examples of early mortaria manufacturing centres. In the early 2nd century, as the conquest became more secure and the Roman influence spread, factories in the Midlands such as Lincolnshire (Tyers 1996, 122–3) and Mancetter Hartshill (*ibid.*, 123–4), and also to the north at Rossington Bridge (*ibid.*, 129–30), became established. By the mid 2nd century another large industry had been set up in the East Midlands in the Lower Nene Valley (*ibid.*, 127–9), probably instigated by potters from the Rhineland (Perrin 1999, 87). During the later Roman period mortaria formed part of the output of the major industries such as those in the New Forest (Tyers 1996, 125), Oxfordshire (*ibid.*, 129) and at Crambeck (*ibid.*, 188–89) which were producing mortaria alongside colour-coated wares and coarsewares. Colour-coated mortaria were produced for the first time by these manufacturers. By this later period forms had developed to include flanged, hammer-headed and wall-sided types.

Many local potters produced a few mortaria among their repertoire, often alongside flagons (Lyons 2003, 50–51), which were both forms that were more difficult and time-consuming to make than the average cooking pot. Larger industries, however, were clearly specialists and the mortaria are often the most widely distributed of their products, (or at least the most visible of the coarseware products to be distributed) and possibly therefore of real commercial value. Specialist mortaria production centres such as Colchester were shipping large numbers of mortaria vast distances up to the Antonine and Hadrian's walls from *c*.AD 140 onwards.

The interpretation of mortaria as grinding bowls is convincing:

'In the classical Roman kitchen envisaged by the recipes of Apicius, mortars were needed to grind a variety of ingredients to produce either a puree that could be poured, or a solid mass which has then been shaped by hand. Amongst the finds from most Romano-British sites there are utensils that seem ideally suited to perform this function. The commonest are the coarse pottery mortaria which normally have a wide spout at one point, and grit embedded in the interior surface' (Cool 2006, 42).

There are, however, aspects of mortaria use that are still far from understood, such as why so many examples are sooted and burnt, since surely these were mixing bowls rather than cooking pots – how could they be both? Another question is: 'why if mortaria are so closely connected to the Roman way of cooking are they relatively rare finds at Pompeii?' (Stefani 2005). More considered analysis suggests that mortaria use changed both with time (as described above) but also with the social group that they were being used by. Early Roman rural (non-Romanised and non-military) communities have been recorded curating mortaria, as well as samian and glass, but using them only as bowls (Cool 2006, 45), while the elite early Roman societies of south-east England were importing coarseware mortaria as high status items (*ibid.*, 43). Other recent research by Lloyd Jones (2005, 139) on rural Welsh communities suggests that mortaria were used to produce many novel food stuffs, made possible by the wider supply introduced by the Romans, including sausages, cheese and leavened bread. Is it possible that mortaria became heated during the rising and resting process of making bread with yeast, a process not necessary in the warmer climate of Italy? As it is unlikely that mortaria arrived in British markets with an instruction booklet, all these uses are possible, rather than necessarily the simple function of a herb grinding that has previously been assumed.

VI. Samian
by Stephen Wadeson, with contributions from Gwladys Monteil
(Figs 7.15–7.16)

Summary
An assemblage of 403 sherds of samian, weighing 3,597g (6.48 EVE) was recovered from 174 contexts during both field walking and excavations at Love's Farm. The majority of the assemblage consists of small, fragmentary, abraded sherds, with an average weight of *c*.9g. Many sherds are too small to identify or date closely, indicating a high level of post-depositional disturbance, such as middening and/or manuring. The quantities of samian by fabric source are shown in chronological order in Table 7.19.

Production centre and dating

Southern Gaul
The earliest material recovered from Love's Farm is from La Graufesenque, with 170 sherds, 34.1% by weight (2.11 EVE) of the total assemblage (Period 4.1). The samian in this phase is not closely datable due to its fragmentary

Fabric	Code	No. sherds	% no. sherds	Wt (g)	% Wt	EVE
South Gaulish Samian	SASG	170	42.2	1225	34.1	2.11
Central Gaulish Samian (Les Martres)	SAMV	10	2.5	52	1.5	0.21
Central Gaulish Samian (Lezoux)	SACG	211	52.4	2145	59.6	4.06
East Gaulish Samian	SAEG	12	2.9	175	4.8	0.10
Total		403	100	3597	100	6.48

Table 7.19 Samian quantified by fabric source

nature, and can only be approximately dated to c.AD 50–100. The majority of the material, however, is most likely to be Flavian (c.AD 70–100), as samian is rarely found in Britain on sites away from forts and major urban centres before c.AD 70 (Willis 2003). A small number of pre-Flavian (c.AD 50–70) sherds from Dr 15/17 platters and Dr 29 decorated bowls are nevertheless present in the assemblage, as well as a single sherd from a Ritterling 8 cup, which is earlier. Of the pottery from La Graufesenque, 45.3% (by weight) are dishes, most of which are Dr 18/31 and Dr 36. This includes a dish of indeterminate form stamped on its basal interior: 'OF.VIT[AL]' (*Officina* Vit[al]) (Fig. 7.16, SF 2940) and can be attributed to Vitalis ii whose work dates to c.AD 70–100. As yet, no exact match has been found for this version of the stamp, but one possibility is that it refers to Vitalis ii whose work can be dated to c.AD 70–90. A further 4.2% of the assemblage could not be identified with certainty and could be either a dish (Dr 18/31) or a platter (Dr 18).

Platters, specifically Dr 15/17 and Dr 18, account for a further 29.1% of the assemblage. The most complete example of a platter, a late Flavian Dr 15/17 contains a partial maker's stamp on the basal interior: 'OF[VI]RILI' (*Officina* [Vi]rilis) (Fig. 7.15, SF 3536). This stamp is associated with the potter Virilis ii, whose work can again be dated to c.AD 80–105 at La Graufesenque.

Decorated bowls are well represented within the assemblage (10.3% by weight), with sherds from Dr 29, Dr 30, Dr 37 and Kn 78 forms having been identified. These include a single sherd from a Dr 30 bowl with panel decoration; contained within horizontal and vertical beaded borders are the partial remains of figure type Os 1582, 'bear with cupid' (Fig. 7.15, SF 3056). Although no exact match could be found for the design, Os 1582 is found on a Dr 29 base stamped by the potter Licinus (AD 45–65) (Knorr 1919 (K19), taf 46, C). Cups represent a further 7.2% of the assemblage and, with the exception of a single sherd from a pre-Flavian Ritterling 8, the majority of the cups are Dr 27. The latter includes the remains of a Dr 27g cup (SF 3245) with an illegible maker's stamp on its basal interior (not illustrated). Due to the nature of the assemblage, the remaining 2.7% (c.15% by count) of the sherds from Southern Gaul are too small and fragmentary to be identified or dated more closely.

Central Gaul
The majority of the samian recovered from the site comes from Central Gaul, and accounts for 61.1% by weight (4.27 EVE) of the total assemblage. The earliest is Trajanic in date and was manufactured at Les Martres-de-Veyre, c.AD 100–120 (Periods 4.1 and 4.2). Only ten sherds (1.5% by weight) were positively identified, comprising both decorated and plain forms. These include two sherds from Dr 37 decorated bowls (Fig. 7.15, SF 3356 and SF 3535). Both sherds use the replacement ovolo of twin dolphins, tail to tail (Stanfield and Simpson 1990, fig. 4, no. 4), as used by Drusus I. Although found in separate contexts, it is highly likely that both sherds, while not joining, come from the same vessel. Plain forms present include dishes (48.1% by weight) and cups (9.6% by weight). A further 7.7% of the samian is too small and abraded for identification.

The majority of samian from Central Gaul (211 sherds, 59.6% by weight, EVE 4.06) is Hadrianic to Antonine in date, and was produced at Lezoux; c.AD 120–200 (Period 4.2). As with the Southern Gaulish samian, the range of vessel types is primarily limited to bowls, cups and dishes. Earlier forms include fragments from several Dr 18/31 dishes, while later forms include a Ludowici Tg dish and Walter 79R platter, both of Antonine date (c.AD 160–200).

Bowls constitute the bulk (44.2%) of the samian identified from Lezoux, and include both decorated and plain forms. The majority of the plain bowls are fragments of Dr 38, a form typical of the second half of the 2nd century. Amongst these are three sherds from the base of a Dr 38 displaying a complete maker's stamp on the internal surface (Fig. 7.16, SF 2667). The stamp reads CINTVSMVSF (Cintusmus *Fecit*) and can be associated with the products of Cintusmus i (c.AD 140–80).

Only five decorated sherds, all from Dr 37 bowls, were identified in the assemblage, including two joining sherds (Fig. 7.15, SF 2168) in panel decoration. The design uses ovolo B103, while below is a small bird (Os 2316 [s]) in a double circled medallion. On the right can be seen the partial remains of a 'nude man with cloth' (Déch 344, Os 638 as shown on Stanfield and Simpson 1990, pl. 114, no. 33). Dating to the middle to late Antonine period, the ovolo and figure types used are those commonly associated with the potter Advocisus (c.AD 160–90).

Almost a quarter of the Lezoux assemblage is made up of cups, primarily Dr 33. Three examples (Fig. 7.16, SF 2442, SF 3271 and 3504) have makers' stamps on their basal interior and can be dated fairly precisely. The earliest of these is a partial stamp, [F]ELIX[.]F ([F]elix *Fecit*), which can be associated with Felix ii (c.AD 135–65). The second vessel, which has been reworked (see below), contains a complete stamp, PECVLIAR.F. (Peculiar *Fecit*) and refers to potter Peculiar i (AD 145–170). The latest of the three stamps (by date), can be attributed to Tituro of Lezoux (c.AD 170–200), the partial stamp reads, TITVRO[NISOF] (Tituro *Officina*).

A further 20.2% of the assemblage is represented by dishes, which are dominated by forms Dr 31 and Dr 36. Again, the majority of these vessels cannot be dated closely, with the exception of a single basal sherd from a Dr 31 (Fig. 7.16, SF 2764), with a partial, abraded maker's stamp for which no exact match has been found. Reading MASC[II]LLIO, the stamp is credited to Mascellio i, whose work is dated to the late Antonine period (*c*.AD 160–200).

A rim sherd from a Dr 42 dish variant (SF 2507, not illustrated), recovered from ditch *5619*, is the only example of a vessel retrieved from site which has been decorated using incised 'cut glass' decoration. While the majority of the curved rim is plain, where the lip overhangs (Detail A, Webster 1976, 52), the outside face has been decorated using a simple, incised line pattern. Attached to the rim are the partial remains of a strap handle of double spiral twist design. On the underside of the handle, at the join with the body of the vessel, pre-firing graffiti is visible, the only example of a graffito recovered from the assemblage.

The single sherd of samian mortarium identified within the assemblage is a fragment from a Dr 45. Introduced in the second half of the 2nd century, Dr 45 is the most frequently encountered samian mortaria type (Hartley 1969, 248). It is suggested that samian mortaria are often absent on rural sites, generally occurring in towns, and may be seen as an indicator of social status (Mills 1998). Generally smaller than their coarseware counterparts, specialised mortaria such as these were designed for the purpose of mixing and grinding. In the absence of samian mortaria, the occurrence of worn interior surfaces in some samian vessels, especially small plain bowls such as Dr 38, indicates that these vessels were used as an alternative for mixing and grinding, despite lacking interior gritted surfaces (Willis 2005). As with the material deriving from La Graufesenque, 2% of the samian from Lezoux consists of small, fragmentary sherds, frequently found to be residual and not closely datable.

Eastern Gaul
The latest material recovered is from Eastern Gaul, and accounts for just 4.8% by weight (0.10 EVE) of the total assemblage (Periods 4.1 and 4.2). This is a small assemblage of mainly abraded, fragmentary sherds which are not closely datable; consequently, a broad date range of *c*.AD 140–230 has been assigned to most sherds. None of the sherds identified can be assigned with any certainty to a specific centre of production. Of the twelve sherds identified, the range of vessel types is limited to bowls (48.6% by weight), cups (31.4%) and dishes (14.9%). The remaining 5.1% of the samian is too small and abraded for identification.

Vessel condition

Wear patterns
Within the assemblage, several dishes (Dr 36), bowls (Dr 37 and Dr 38) and a single cup (Dr 27) exhibit internal wear and are heavily abraded, resulting in the removal of the slip. This type of abrasion is normally attributed to the use of the vessel for mixing and grinding, often in place of a mortarium (Willis 2005). Willis suggests that the cup form Dr 27 and the small plain bowl Dr 38 are the most likely forms to show internal wear. Two of the best examples from the Love's Farm assemblage are the partial remains of a Dr 27 cup (*8399*, a cobbled surface in Settlement 6, Period 4.1) and a Dr 38 hemispherical bowl (*10186*, a pit fill associated with Settlement 7, Period 4.2).

The remains of the Dr 38 bowl show heavy, localised abrasion on the curve of the vessel at the point where the base becomes the wall. Here, all of the slip has been completely removed in a consistent pattern graduating up the wall until the point where the slip has been untouched. From this pattern it is possible to suggest that the user was right-handed, having held the bowl in their left hand, using the vessel's flange to assist in a stronger grip on the bowl (Willis 2005), and with the pestle in their right hand. Towards the centre of the vessel the slip is less well-worn; a partial, but illegible maker's stamp is still visible in the centre of the base.

While only four base sherds were recovered from the Dr 27 cup, all are completely void of slip due to its probable use for mixing or grinding. One of these sherds shows evidence of secondary use, consisting of four small abrasion marks of roughly circular shape (4mm in diameter) in the fabric of the vessel. These small hollows are possibly the result of the samian being used to provide a source of red pigment for the manufacture of rouge. This was achieved by a repeated drill-like action, using a small implement, into the fabric of the vessel to produce a red powder (Geoff Dannell, pers. comm.). The use of this vessel for mixing and grinding, together with the amount of wear seen on the base, corresponds closely to the results of experimental work by Biddulph, which indicate that the Dr 27 cup was frequently used in the kitchen as a mortar (Biddulph 2008).

Also identified within the assemblage are the remains of a Dr 37 decorated bowl (Fig. 7.15, SF 2168), which is partially worn on its interior surface. Only a small percentage of decorated samian bowls show signs of internal wear, suggesting that the majority were used for serving food, or possibly as drinking vessels, and not in ways which would cause wear on the interior (Willis 2005). Unfortunately, due to the small amount of wear on the Love's Farm sherd, it is not possible to establish with certainty the specific process that caused the wear pattern within this vessel.

Secondary use
The remains of two vessels show evidence of trimming; a Southern Gaulish Dr 18/31 dish (*c*.AD 90–110) and a stamped Central Gaulish Dr 33 cup (*c*.AD 160–170, SF 2442). Both have had their walls removed at the junction of the base and vessel wall, indicating a secondary function either as gaming counters or vessel lids.

Repaired samian
Only two examples of repaired vessels were identified within the assemblage; a small fragment (SF 3338) from the rim of a Dr 18 platter (*c*.AD 50–100) and a rim sherd (SF 3340) from a Dr 31/31R bowl (*c*.AD 140/60–200). In both cases, repairs were carried out using rivets, which involved the drilling of holes through the fabric of the vessel either side of the break for the insertion of metal rivets (Willis 2005). In both examples only the partial remains of a single hole exist, while none of the rivets were recovered during excavation. The repaired sherds account for only 0.2% (by weight) of the entire assemblage, which is comparable to, if not lower than, the low percentages encountered on many rural sites (Willis 2005).

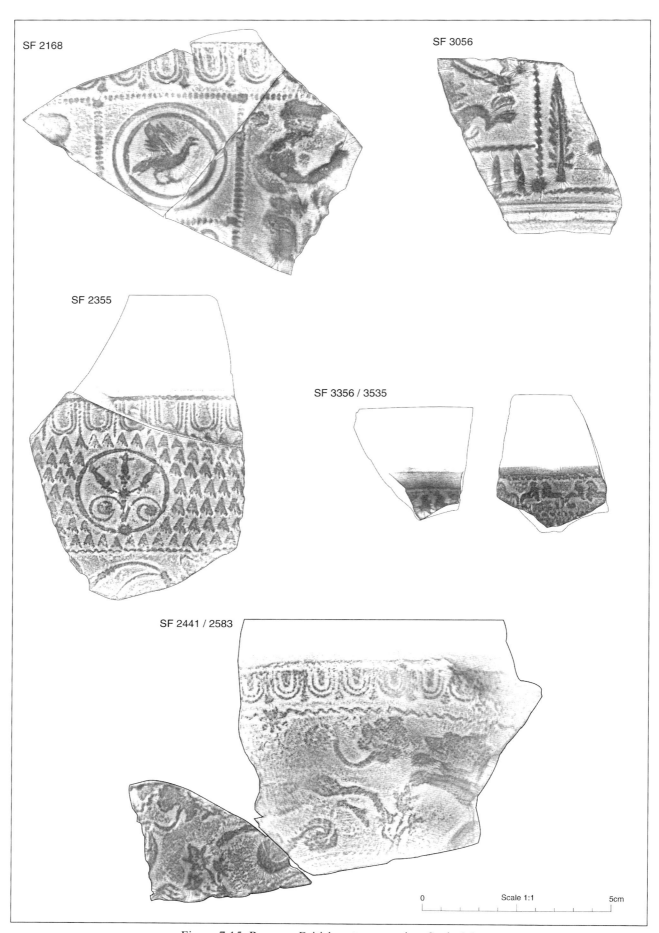

Figure 7.15 Romano-British pottery: samian. Scale 1:1

Figure 7.16 Romano-British pottery: samian stamps. Scale 1:1

Discussion

Samian was in constant use at Love's Farm throughout the Roman period, although in low quantities, in total representing 0.84% (by weight) of the entire pottery assemblage. Within this relatively small group of pottery the majority of the samian (61.1%) originated from Central Gaul, primarily from Lezoux (c.AD 120–200), although a much smaller amount was identified from Les Martres-de-Veyre (c.AD 100–120). The earliest material is Southern Gaulish (c.AD 50–100), produced at La Graufesenque and accounting for 34.1% of the total assemblage. A very small amount (4.8%) of later Eastern Gaulish samian was also recovered. This small assemblage, mainly recovered from ditch fills or pit fills, is consistent with the low frequency of samian found on many rural sites (Willis 2003; 2005). The small size of the majority of the sherds, and their low average sherd weight, points to a high level of post-depositional disturbance, which is consistent with much of the pottery being residual.

Catalogue of illustrated samian
(Fig. 7.15)

SF2168 Dr 30. Two joining body sherds, one worn on the inside from use. Panel design, ovolo 103, small bird in a double circled medallion Os 2316 (s). Nude man with cloth, Dec 344, Os 638 as on S&S 90, pl. 114, no. 33. Potter possibly ?Advocius. Lezoux, Central Gaul. Period: Mid to late Antonine. Unstratified.

SF3056 Dr 30. Panel decoration with horizontal and vertical beaded borders. Partial remains of Os 1582, bear with cupid in the upper left of sherd. Long triangular leaf has no match in K19 or K52. Os 1582 is on a Dr 29 base stamped by Licinus (K19, taf 46, C). La Graufesenque, Southern Gaul. Period: AD 50–10. Unstratified.

SF2355 Dr 30. Four adjoining sherds, the ovolo is 000153 as found on a Dr 30 from Le Mans (ser no. 1001682) and two Dr 30s La Graufesenque (Mainz Database ser no. 1001619 and 1001101). Apart from this ovolo all Dr 30s have similar decorative details of bottle bud and leaf tip. La Graufesenque, Southern Gaul. Period: AD 50–100. *5296*, fill of ditch *5297*, Settlement 7. Period 4.2.

SF2441 Dr 37. Ovolo B109 (S&S 90, fig. 13, no. 2) above wavy line.
/2583 Leaf could be H146, but no exact match in Rogers 1999, pl. 17, no.21 including the tail ending in a rosette. The dog or bear figure is similar to Os 1981, S&S pl. 109, no. 4 but there is no good match in Oswald. Potter possibly ?Butrio. Lezoux, Central Gaul. Period: Hadrianic. *5344*, cobbled surface, Settlement 7. Period 4.4.

SF3356 Dr 37. Plain upper exterior with line below, ?bead row below which is an ovolo of twin dolphins, tail to tail, S&S, fig. 4, no. 4 double dolphin motif used by Drusus I. Possibly same vessel as SF 3535. Les Martres-de-Veyre, Central Gaul. Period: Trajanic. *6586*, fill of pit *6588*, Settlement 6. Period 4.2.

SF3535 Dr 37. As SF 3356. *8122*, fill of ditch *8123*, Boundary 2, Settlement 6. Period 4.1.

Samian potters' stamps
(Fig. 7.16)

The catalogue lists the potters identified in alphabetical order. Each entry gives the catalogue number, the potter's name (i, ii *etc.*, where homonyms are involved); die form; form type, reading, published example (if any), pottery of origin, date; context information. Ligatured letters are underlined. All periods noted refer to site periods assigned to each context and not ceramic period.

SF2667 Dr 38. Cintusmus i (die 6a) **CINTVSMVSF** Lezoux, Central Gaul. Period: *c*.AD 140–180. *5983*, fill of well-cut *5387*, Settlement 7. Period 4.5. (Hartley *et al.* 2008, 38–43)

SF3271 Dr 33. Felix ii (die 2d) **[F]ELIX[.]F** Lezoux, Central Gaul. Period: *c*.AD 135–165. *10169*, fill of pit *10170*, Enclosure 21, Settlement 7. Period 4.2. (Hartley *et al.* 2009a, 35–36)

SF2764 Dr 31. Mascellio i (die 4a) **MASC[II]LLIO** Lezoux, Central Gaul. Period: *c*.AD 160–200. *6528*, fill of ditch *6529*, Settlement 6. Unphased. (Hartley *et al.* 2009b, 338–339)

SF2442 Dr 33. Peculiar i (die 5a) **PECVLIAR.F** Lezoux, Central Gaul. Period: *c*.AD 145–170. *5344*, cobbled surface, Settlement 7. Period 4.4. (Hartley *et al.* 2011, 116–19)

SF3504 Dr 33. Tituro (die 1a) **TITVRO[NISOF]** Lezoux, Central Gaul. Period: *c*.AD 170–200. *11312*, fill of ditch *11311*, Enclosure 104, Settlement 6. Period 4.3. (Hartley *et al.* 2012, 67–70)

SF3536 Dr 15/17. Virilis ii (die 6c) **OF[VI]RILI** La Graufesenque, Southern Gaul. Period: *c*.AD 80–105. *10943*, fill of ditch *10944*. Unphased. (Hartley *et al.* 2012, 270–77)

SF2940 Dish. Vitalis ii (die 6a?) **OF.VIT[AL]** La Graufesenque, Southern Gaul. Period: *c*.AD 70–100. *8120*, fill of ditch *8123*, Enclosure 12, Settlement 6. Period 4.1. (Hartley *et al.* 2012, 299–321)

VII. Discussion of the late pre-Roman Iron Age and Romano-British pottery
(Fig. 7.17)

A very large amount of pottery (over 350kg), was deposited at Love's Farm during the LPRIA and the Romano-British period, representing one of the largest pottery assemblages thus far excavated in the region. It adds significantly to the dataset already formed by other recent excavations in the vicinity, from which contemporary pottery has been published (Table 7.20). It is important to note that the main characteristics of this assemblage are the use of local shell-tempered clays to produce utilitarian jar forms throughout the Romano-British period (Fig. 7.17) and the secondary role played by

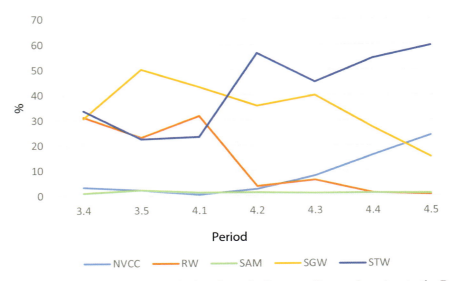

Figure 7.17 Changes in pottery supply through time from the Late pre-Roman Iron Age to the Romano-British period (by sub-period) using weight (%) as a ceramic measure

Site	Date	Wt	Main characteristics	Publication
A428 corridor	IA/RB	80kg	Primarily a quartz temper user with shelly clays playing a secondary role.	Lyons 2008
Bob's Wood, Hinchingbrooke	IA/RB	301kg	Primarily shell user in the IA that converts to mainly sand-tempered wares with shell playing a secondary role.	Lyons in prep d; Percival in prep c
Caldecote Highfields	LIA/RB	19kg	Shell and quartz temper are found in fairly even quantities in the IA, followed by LPRIA grog to primarily quartz with some shell in the RB period.	Sealey 2011a
Cambourne	IA/RB	252kg	Primarily use quartz tempered fabrics with some shell in the M/LIA, with grog temper in the LIA and quartz with shell in a secondary role in the RB period.	Seager Smith 2009
Little Paxton	IA/TRANS	38kg	Primarily shell user, with quartz- and grog-tempered wares in the IA which continues into the RB period.	Hancocks 2003
Love's Farm	IA/RB	351kg	Primarily shell user in the IA that continued to use shell-tempered fabrics supported by quartz-tempered fabrics in the RB.	This report
Werrington	IA/RB	56kg	Primarily shell user in the IA that coverts to shell superseded by mostly quartz-tempered fabrics in the RB. The small number and late appearance of coin on the site would seem to reflect the low economic status of the site.	Mackreth 1988
Wardy Hill	IA/ERB	60kg	The local populations chose to make quartz-tempered wares when shelly clays were readily available.	Hill and Horne 2003
Haddenham V	LIA/LPRIA	175kg	Shell most common temper (over 75% of the assemblage), with quartz fabrics much rarer (only 10% of the group).	Hill and Braddock 2006

Table 7.20 List of comparative sites, their main ceramic characteristics and publication (in alphabetical order)

grog- and then quartz-tempered fabrics, along with other imported or traded wares. Love's Farm was not a known market place, and the assemblage therefore reflects a settlement that accumulated and used pottery, but was not a centre for production or trade. The location of Love's Farm in a rural but busy landscape, close to both Ermine Street and the River Ouse, means that the people who lived there could have been exposed to a number of native potting traditions, while having limited exposure to a range of traded goods that were initially imported for use by the army, but which later became available more widely through the influence of the mighty Nene Valley production centre (Perrin 1999).

In the LPRIA (Period 3.4), Iron Age-type, handmade shell-tempered lid-seated jars and storage jars were commonly still in use, alongside new, locally produced, reduced fabrics heavily influenced by continental technology and pottery style. Aspects of Gallo-Belgic culture, including the introduction of imported and domestically-copied, wheelmade kiln-fired finewares (Rigby 1986; Tyers 1996, 52–5), were prevalent in southern and eastern Britain well before the arrival of the Roman army in AD 43 (Hill 2002; Tyers 1996, 55–66). Indeed, this 'Belgic' influence so ably described by Thompson (1982) can be seen in both the LPRIA and 'transitional' (Period 3.5) ceramic phases at Love's Farm. One visible aspect of this change is the reintroduction of

Fabric	Code	Vessel types	Quantity	Wt (g)	Wt (%)
Baetican (early) amphorae 1	BAT AM 1	DR1/2, DR20	28	3363	62.6
Baetican (late) amphorae 2	BAT AM 2	DR20	6	1243	23.2
Unsourced amphorae	AMP		7	239	4.5
?Italian (Feldspathic) amphorae 2	ITA AM 2	DR1/2, DR2/4	2	222	4.1
Italian amphorae	ITA AM 1		1	133	2.5
Rhodian (Pink) amphorae 1	RHO AM 1		1	80	1.5
Peacock and Williams Class 47 amphorae	P&W AM 47		1	45	0.8
Peacock and Williams Class 16 amphorae	P&W AM 16		1	26	0.5
Catalan amphorae	CAT AM		1	19	0.4
Total			48	5370	100

Table 7.21 The amphora fabrics

grog (crushed up pre-fired pottery) used as a temper (or clay mixer), that had not been widely in use in this region since the early Iron Age. The increasing importance of grog tempering seen at Love's Farm in the LPRIA is also echoed at Bob's Wood, Hinchingbrooke (Percival in prep. c) and Little Paxton (Hancocks 2003, 75). New Gaulish-inspired vessel shapes were also introduced, including cordoned and carinated jars and the pedestal urn, which was an impressive form characteristic of this time (Thompson 1982, 33).

Until fairly recently it was thought that southern Cambridgeshire formed the northern limit of Gallo-Belgic influence in south-eastern Britain, and that the adoption of new ceramic fabrics and forms, and the technology used to produce them, only occurred after the Roman invasion of AD 43 (Hill 2002, 159). Hill (2002, 157–8) suggested that strong indigenous cultural traditions prevented the widespread adoption of pre-invasion Roman (Gallo-Belgic) ceramics and technology in northern East Anglia, which occurred in the rest of south-eastern Britain (Pollard 1988) during the 1st century BC. However, re-assessment of the adoption of Gallo-Belgic culture across the region (Lyons 2011), has suggested that these new Gallo-Belgic influences travelled northwards at least as far as Cambridge, along the River Granta corridor, since accompanied 'Aylesford-Swarling' type cremation sites are now known at Bartlow, Duxford (Lyons 2011), Hinxton (Lyons in prep. a), Trumpington (Lyons in prep. c), Addenbrookes (Evans et al. 2008, 139) and even as far as Milton Keynes (Lyons et al. 2014). Furthermore, wheelmade pottery is known at Earith (Monteil 2013; Anderson 2013), Haddenham (Chris Evans, pers. comm.) and at numerous other sites in Cambridgeshire, including Bob's Wood and Love's Farm itself. Hill has in fact recently reprised his view of the extent of Gallo-Belgic influence to extend up to the eastern watershed of the Great Ouse (Hill 2007, 24).

Although much of the pottery in use during the LPRIA is of a utilitarian (shell-tempered) character, and therefore of 'low status', it may be argued that the introduction of finer, wheelmade, Gaulish-inspired grog-tempered wares reflects an aspect of higher status activity at Love's Farm, which cannot be seen in later deposits. At Haddon near Peterborough, where another low order late Iron Age/early Roman rural settlement was excavated, Jerry Evans (2003, 103) argues that the presence of such vessel types indicates a higher status of living than would have been produced by subsistence farming alone. These changes in ceramic use may reflect a difference in how pottery was perceived at this time, with material culture generally (Hill 2002) – and pottery specifically – more closely associated with the new Gaulish cultural changes affecting all areas of society. This change in perception may have resulted in the decision to invest more surplus (time/money) in the production and/or procurement of 'new' types of pottery. It is possible that such new wares were seen as more desirable than older types and this resulted in their initial popularity – an effect which declined over time as their novelty diminished. This means, therefore, that the low-to-middle status of the people at Love's Farm was unchanged, but how they chose to use their surplus resources did develop at this time.

This trend towards the 'Romanisation' of ceramics continued to gain momentum throughout the 1st century AD at Love's Farm, as well as in the wider community (Willis 1996, 219), and is suggestive of a broad social process. As a result, in addition to locally-produced Gaulish-inspired pottery, plain Southern Gaulish samian started to arrive around the middle of the 1st century AD, as did Italian amphorae and Verulamium whiteware flagons. A combination of imports and traded wares suggests that at least some of the people at Love's Farm were adopting a more Romanised method of eating and drinking, and could afford good quality ceramic wares

Form	EVE	EVE %
Wide-mouthed jar	63.82	28.08
Dish	37.62	16.55
Miscellaneous jar	27.22	11.98
Flanged dish	14.92	6.56
Flagon	13.59	5.98
Narrow-mouthed jar	13.28	5.84
Bowl	12.42	5.46
Beaker	12.19	5.36
Lid	6.84	3.01
Mortarium	6.13	2.70
Storage jar	6.09	2.68
Cup	4.33	1.91
Platter	1.72	0.76
Amphora	0.00	0.00
All other vessel forms	7.11	3.13
Total	227.28	100

Table 7.22 A list of the broad Romano-British vessel forms found in this assemblage and their Estimated Vessel Equivalent (EVE)

with which to do so. These changes may have been directly influenced by the arrival of the Roman army during the construction of Ermine Street. In the case of amphorae, however, another view is that these vessels had a worth separate from their contents, and might have been traded as storage vessels (Callender 1965, 23–41). The amphorae are characterised in Table 7.21, while the range of vessel forms reaching the site appears in Table 7.22.

By the mid 2nd century, the sandier, more Romanised, greyware fabric was gradually growing in popularity. This was in fact the only time at which sandy greywares out-supplied the shell-tempered pots (Fig. 7.17). As a result, they started to be produced on a large scale, although the range of forms was limited at first, until by the end of the 2nd century the versatility of the fabric, heavily based on the Thames Valley BB2 style of production (Tyers 1996, 186–8), had been fully exploited.

Throughout the Romano-British period, exploitation of the local shell clay beds continued. Firstly, the use of Lower Nene Valley-type storage jars and unprovenanced lid-seated jars (which were both forms similar to their Iron Age predecessors) continued until the end of the 2nd century AD. These pots were then followed by a new range of shell-tempered wares that was introduced in the later Roman period, with under-scored hooked rim globular jars and the straight-sided and flanged rim 'oven-to-table' casserole bowls becoming very popular. These later wares are very similar to the range of products produced at Harrold in Bedfordshire (Brown 1994). At this time it is unknown how much of the shell-tempered later Roman pottery was made at Harrold and how much was supplied by as-yet unlocated local sources. At present, we have very little idea of where the majority of both sandy and shell-tempered coarsewares found at Love's Farm were being produced. Only discarded kiln-bars and possibly fragments of kiln structure were found at Love's Farm, hinting at local production (see Fired Clay, Chapter 6.VIII). It is interesting that Morris (2002) suggests that the available evidence points to predominantly local production in eastern England at this time. If this is true, several coarseware production centres must be waiting to be discovered, perhaps in the area around Sandy (to the south) and Godmanchester (to the north). It is tempting to speculate that pottery produced on a large scale in the vicinity of Love's Farm could have contributed to the successful, self-sufficient nature of marginal claylands-living in the Romano-British period.

Although no petrological work has been carried out on shell-tempered wares from Love's Farm, where this type of analysis has previously been carried out (at Wardy Hill, Haddenham V and close by at Little Paxton) the results have consistently shown that all the material is rich in fossilised shell but that there is a variety of fabrics from different (unlocated) sources present (Williams 2003a, 76). This suggests that shell-tempered wares, even if locally-produced, were being sourced from a variety of clay beds, and may have been traded (or their contents may have been traded) as a valuable surplus.

Non-local wares found their way to the site at Love's Farm throughout the Romano-British period. During the early Roman period (Period 4.1), Verulamium wares continued to be used with the range expanding to include the mortaria mixing bowl. Amphora of the Southern Spanish globular olive oil variety was beginning to be used, while Northern Gaulish greywares were imported more commonly than the Southern and Central Gaulish samian being traded at that time. A small quantity of Southern British glazed ware was also found, although this may represent a single vessel being carried onto the site.

During the middle to late Romano-British period (Periods 4.2–4.4), the range of non-local fabrics expanded. Verulamium whitewares continued to be traded until the mid 2nd century, when local production of similar wares at Godmanchester (Martin and Wallace 2002, 3.7.1, iii and iv) filled the market demand. Other traded wares largely originated from the massive entrepreneurial domestic production centres that had developed by this time; most significant to the Love's Farm community was the rise of the Lower Nene Valley pottery industry (Perrin 1999), located on Ermine Street, only twenty Roman miles to the north. The Fen Basin would have been its local market place and Love's Farm is situated on its southern edge. From the mid 2nd century this industry provided fineware beakers, then specialist whiteware flagons and mortaria, followed by greywares throughout the 3rd century. After a massive reorganisation of the Nene Valley industry in the later 3rd century (Perrin 1996, 87–8), large quantities of durable dishes and jars in a colour-coated fabric reached the site (Fig. 7.17). These wares were supplemented by late Roman red wares from the Oxfordshire and (to a lesser extent) Hadham production centres. At Love's Farm, these late Roman red wares were sometimes found with handmade early Anglo-Saxon pottery, suggesting continuity of settlement from the end of the Roman period into the early Anglo-Saxon period, although this is not borne out by the dating of the early Anglo-Saxon pottery itself (Blinkhorn, below), which suggests a possible break in activity between the end of Romano-British occupation and (at the earliest) the late 5th century. It should also be noted that the amount of pottery being deposited in features at the very end of the Roman period (Period 4.5) declined dramatically (Table 7.12).

Continental imports during the Romano-British period included a relatively small amount of undecorated Central Gaulish samian, with an even smaller amount of plain Eastern Gaulish samian. Italian and Spanish amphorae were still present in small quantities. The percentage of samian (Fig. 7.17) was always very low, even for a rural site (Cooper and Lyons 2011), which must indicate that Love's Farm was of a fairly low status, this sparse use of imported wares being typical of low order settlements in the region (Evans 2003, 105).

Shell versus sand

As has already been noted, the prevailing characteristic of this assemblage is the use of shell-tempered clay, when sandier versions appear to have been the norm in other settlements at this time. Where this has been observed in the Iron Age assemblage (Percival, above), it is suggested that the River Great Ouse formed a partial eastern boundary for users of shell-tempered wares with their westerly trading networks, whilst a group of sandy fabric users who had links with central and eastern populations were focused around Ely and the River Cam. It is worth considering whether this is also true for pottery use at Love's Farm in the Romano-British period. Did Love's Farm look more to its western hinterland than to the east? Currently, no influential nearby towns are known to the west in Roman period (although the presence of a possible centre at Eynesbury is acknowledged); only the kilns producing shell-tempered ware pots at Harrold in Bedfordshire were a known influence in the later Roman period. It is interesting to note that shell-tempered wares were also the most common coarseware used in the Milton Keynes area in the Romano-British period (Marney 1989); is this because they shared a similar geology or close trade links? At the present time, however, Romano-British Love's Farm would seem to have been more closely linked to the towns of Sandy (to the south) and Godmanchester (to the north), while in the middle to late Roman period the settlement fell into the sphere of the huge Nene Valley ceramic industry based to the north at Water Newton. Ermine Street connected all these settlements and perhaps provided the dominant connecting force at this time, possibly replacing (or at least extending) the influence of the River Ouse (which ran parallel to Ermine Street between Love's Farm and Godmanchester) that dominated the landscape in prehistoric times.

While in the Iron Age the use of shell was a cultural/tribal choice, this changed with the introduction of Roman pottery manufacturing methods whereby the choice between shell-tempered and sandy-tempered coarsewares – although changing through time with variations in supply – seems to have become less culturally based and more a reflection of status. The basis for this argument is grounded on the acceptance that shell-tempered wares were the cheapest, most readily available local product and, even where widely available, finer sand-tempered greywares required a greater level of clay preparation and skilled potters' time to produce (Lyons 2009). Sandy greywares would, therefore, have been significantly more labour intensive and relatively expensive. The wider use of shell-tempered wares seen at some of the marginal sites on the clay edge, such as Love's Farm and Little Paxton, may indicate that they held a lower status than other nearby settlements, demonstrating how hard it was to produce a surplus in such economic conditions. Other slightly topographically marginal but more successful settlements, such as the sites along the A428 corridor (Cambourne, the A428 and Caldecote Highfields) and Bob's Wood, Hinchingbrooke to the north, could evidently afford to use more of the finer sandy greyware products, as was the norm in the Romano-British period (Hamilton 2002, 38). This argument could perhaps be supported by the evident decision not to use shell-tempered clay at the higher status (although chronologically earlier) site at Wardy Hill (Hill and Horne 2003, 171), which was directly located above suitable shell-rich clay beds.

Although ideally situated (close to both Ermine Street and the River Ouse) to receive traded ceramic wares from almost anywhere in the Roman Empire, it appears the population of Love's Farm in the Romano-British period was generally quite conservative in its selection of wares. It was Fox (1923, 212–3) who first noticed the lack of imported material in use in the region, and he who interpreted this as a form of 'retardation' or 'survivalism'. This derogatory perspective has since been replaced by other views, such as that the economic restrictions of an agricultural lifestyle did not provide enough surplus for the more expensive items, or equally that a rural community generally had less need of fine tablewares.

Perhaps the local clay beds provided such a good supply of both shell- and sand-tempered wares that imported pottery was not seen as necessary, resulting in a strong indigenous culture resisting change (Hill 2002, 158).

It does appear, however, that the Romanised way of eating, drinking and cooking was adopted (at least partially) at Love's Farm, and that as a result, pottery usage changed with the adoption of finer grog-tempered wares. Only the wealthiest members of the community may have used fine tablewares imported from abroad, and then only occasionally. There is evidence that when these wares came into the ownership of a family they were kept much longer that other coarser pottery types.

Previous research has referred to settlement in this area as 'farming on the edge' (Abrams and Ingham 2008), settlement on clay-rich marginal land – largely self sufficient but needing some additional traded goods to survive. The ceramic evidence fits well within this picture. It seems likely that, for most of this period, the inhabitants at Love's Farm could be regarded as of lower middling status. They were able to acquire some traded goods, but most of their needs were met locally with shell-tempered utilitarian wares. The ceramic evidence suggests that life at Love's Farm between the LPRIA and the end of the Romano-British period was of a low to middle status whereby the use of shell-tempered wares was the norm. As at other sites in the region, the pattern of LPRIA acceptance of grog-tempered pottery, the slow (piecemeal) introduction of wheel production and kiln firing and the limited nature of a fairly standard range of jar/bowl vessels forms has also been observed. Perhaps the most interesting conclusion on the shell versus sand debate is that the decision to use shell- or quartz-tempered pottery was a significant one. At other sites in this region shell-tempered pottery continued to dominate the assemblages after the late Iron Age – this may suggest a prevalence of coarser pottery and therefore, a lower status, than sites which used finer (?more Romanised) sandy greywares. This may explain why Love's Farm and Little Paxton primarily used shell-tempered vessels and other sites, such as Cambourne, A428 and Bob's Wood, used sand-tempered wares.

VIII. Post-Roman pottery
by Paul Blinkhorn
(Fig. 7.18)

Summary

The post-Roman pottery assemblage comprises 205 sherds with a total weight of 2,263g. The estimated vessel equivalent (EVE) is 1.62. The collection contains a range of handmade early/middle Anglo-Saxon wares, which are fairly typical of sites in the region, and includes two sherds with stamp impressions which are likely to be of late 5th- to 6th-century date. Granitic fabrics are very well represented and, when the geology of the area of the site is given consideration, it seems likely that the pottery of this type was manufactured locally.

Fabrics

F1: *Calcitic Sandstone*. Angular lumps of white, calcite-cemented sandstone up to 3mm, moderate 'free' sub-angular quartz grains up to 1mm, rare shell fragments up to 2mm. 28 sherds, 490g, EVE = 0.28.

F2: *Calcitic*. Angular pieces of calcite up to 2mm, sparse sub-angular limestone up to 1mm. 67 sherds, 684g, EVE = 0.19.

Context	F1		F2		F3		F4		F5		F6		Date
	No.	Wt	No.	Wt	No.	Wt	No.	Wt	No.	Wt	No.	Wt	
4176							2	10					E/MS
4735	12	128	6	45			4	25					E/MS
4769			35	244					1	41			E/MS
4800							1	7					L5th/6th c?
4808									1	4			E/MS
4816							2	21					E/MS
4820	1	17	1	3			6	66	3	16			E/MS
4822							5	13					E/MS
4896	6	109	2	60	8	207	2	4	8	97			E/MS
4898			1	20									E/MS
4942											1	5	E/MS
5591	9	236	17	240	4	32	4	27					E/MS
5839			1	15									E/MS
5866			1	18									E/MS
5897							1	3					E/MS
5898			2	34					1	22			E/MS
6181			1	5			2	17	2	14			L5th/6th c?
6394							2	24					E/MS
6395							28	202	18	173			E/MS
9151											1	1	E/MS
10370							1	44					E/MS
11352									1	7			E/MS
120231							1	7					E/MS
Total	28	490	67	684	12	239	61	470	35	374	2	6	

Table 7.23 Anglo-Saxon pottery by fabric type

F3: *Fine quartz*. Moderate to dense sub-angular quartz less than 0.5mm. 12 sherds, 239g, EVE = 0.

F4: *Granitic*. Sparse to moderate sub-angular granite up to 2mm, free flakes of biotite mica and quartz grains. 61 sherds, 470g, EVE = 0.40.

F5: *Quartz and ironstone*. Moderate to dense sub-rounded quartz up to 1mm, sparse rounded red ironstone up to 5mm. 35 sherds, 374g, EVE = 0.75.

F6: *Chaff*. Moderate to dense chaff voids up to 10mm, few other visible inclusions except for rare ironstone up to 1mm. 2 sherds, 6g, EVE = 0.

The pottery occurrence by number and weight of sherds per context by fabric type is shown in Table 7.23. Each date should be regarded as a *terminus post quem*.

The granitic wares

The presence of a high proportion of granitic sherds (Fabric F4) in this assemblage is worthy of comment, particularly in the light of the findings of the geological survey of the area (Appendix 1). Early/middle Anglo-Saxon granitic pottery is well-known in Cambridgeshire, at sites such as Orton Hall Farm (Mackreth 1978), and is found throughout central England as far south as the Thames Valley, with the Charnwood Forest area of Leicestershire thought to be the source of much of the material (Williams and Vince 1997). Certainly, at sites close to there, such pottery is relatively common (Blinkhorn 2000), and is usually by far the major ware in places such as Leicester (Blinkhorn 2004). However, the proportion of such pottery at some sites in Cambridgeshire, such as Love's Farm, is high when compared to relatively nearby sites in adjoining counties. Here, nearly 21% of the hand-built early/middle Anglo-Saxon pottery is in the granite-tempered fabric F4. At the other sites in Cambridgeshire that have produced granitic pottery, there is variation in the amounts present, although chronological factors may at least be partially the cause of this. For example, at Oakington (Blinkhorn 2007a), around 11% of the hand-built assemblage of 259 sherds was of granitic types, although over half the hand-built pottery was recovered from features of middle Anglo-Saxon or later date, and it is thus likely that a sizeable proportion of the hand-built assemblage at this site dates to the middle Anglo-Saxon period, a time when the Charnwood industry is seen to be in decline (Williams and Vince 1997, 219). This means that the actual proportion of granitic wares may have originally been higher, as it is impossible to differentiate undecorated early and middle Anglo-Saxon hand-built wares. Certainly, just two hand-built sherds from Oakington had any sort of decoration and thus were datable to the early Anglo-Saxon period. One of these was in a granitic fabric.

Granitic sherds are present in even quite small assemblages in parts of Cambridgeshire. For example, at Chatteris, four of the thirteen sherds present were of this type, and the site produced middle Anglo-Saxon wares, with over half the hand-built sherds stratified in features of that date (Blinkhorn 2008). At Peterborough, twenty of the fifty hand-built sherds were granitic, and middle Anglo-Saxon pottery was again present, although only six sherds of hand-built pottery were stratified in features of that date (Blinkhorn 2007b). Only one sherd was noted from an assemblage of forty fragments found at Stow Longa, despite most of the assemblage coming from a single feature of 6th-century date (Blinkhorn 2010a).

In Bedfordshire, at Tempsford (Blinkhorn 2005a), less than 10km to the south of Love's Farm, only one sherd from an assemblage of 116 had a granitic fabric, although Tempsford appears unlikely to have been occupied until the early part of the middle Anglo-Saxon period, with most, if not all the hand-built pottery there dating to the 7th century or later. Granitic sherds were not noted amongst the assemblage of 159 hand-built early and middle Saxon sherds from the Bedford Castle site (Williams 1979). The picture is not dissimilar in Northamptonshire. At the Chalk Lane site in Northampton, which produced 1,265 sherds of early/ middle Anglo-Saxon pottery, around 11% were granitic (Gryspeerdt 1981, 110), and at Kings Meadow Lane, Higham Ferrers, just 49 sherds from an assemblage of 1,339 (3.7%) were in such fabrics (Blinkhorn 2007c). To the south, in Buckinghamshire, the sites at Pennyland and Hartigans both produced large assemblages of early Anglo-Saxon hand-built pottery, but granitic wares were rare, comprising 1% of the assemblage at the former, and 2% at the latter (Blinkhorn 1993, tables 55 and 57).

In Norfolk, the site at Brandon Road, Thetford produced 418 sherds of hand-built pottery, of which just fifteen (3.6%) were granitic (Blinkhorn 2010b, 70–79). Middle Anglo-Saxon pottery was present in quantity, but well over 50% of the hand-built pottery came from early Anglo-Saxon features. At nearby Redcastle Furze in Thetford, none of the 375 early Anglo-Saxon sherds was granitic (Andrews 1995, 101), and they were similarly absent from an assemblage of 139 sherds from another site in Brandon Road (Dallas 1993, 124). None of the early Anglo-Saxon sites excavated during the Fenland Management Project produced sherds of this type, although the largest assemblage of hand-built pottery from any one site was just thirty-five sherds, from Tilney St Lawrence (Blinkhorn 2005b, 53). Charnwood Forest wares were present at the Lincolnshire sites excavated during the course of that project, but not generally in such large quantities as seen at this site.

The large amount of granitic pottery at the Love's Farm site – and the relatively high proportions in the area generally – suggests either that the inhabitants had stronger trade links to the Leicestershire area than the surrounding counties, including some nearer to the Charnwood Forest area, or, more likely, that there is a granitic clay source nearer to this site which was exploited by the local Anglo-Saxon potters (see Spoerry 2016 for the latest thoughts on granitic pottery in Cambridgeshire).

A local source for granitic clays in Cambridgeshire has been postulated in the past. Hall (2000) has suggested that the Till Drift is one possible relatively local source. The fact that degraded granitic pebbles were 'locally abundant' at this site and in the local Lodgeman Tills does suggest very strongly that the pottery is of local manufacture, and that (as suggested) the potters at the site were selecting such pebbles and crushing them to add as temper. The suggestion that they are unlikely to be Charnwood types due to the direction of the glaciation, but perhaps originally Scandinavian or Scottish, is an interesting one (*ibid.*), and it should be possible to resolve the issue. Williams and Vince in their original (1997) paper on the problem of attribution of the granitic wares, noted that such pottery was known from Scandinavia and the Baltic region, and that it is not only visually very similar to the Charnwood Forest types, but also little different in thin-section. However, when they subjected the foreign and Charnwood wares (from the settlement site at Catholme, in Staffordshire) to ICPS analysis, the latter were, chemically, quite different from their foreign counterparts, and each of the foreign types was also chemically different from the other. If the glacial pebbles used as the temper for the granitic pottery from this site are of Scandinavian origin, and clay used for the pots of local origin, it seems highly likely that ICPS analysis of the Cambridgeshire pottery will show that they are different chemically to those from the Charnwood Forest area, and thus of local manufacture. Such analyses, which are relatively low-cost, would be extremely useful in enhancing current understanding of early Anglo-Saxon pottery in both the region and at a national level.

Chronology

The relationship between the Romano-British and early Saxon features on the Love's Farm site suggests that there may have been continuity between the two periods. Unfortunately, the Anglo-Saxon pottery offers little to support this, as there is scarce evidence in terms of the form and decoration of the vessels to suggest an early date. Vessels which can be diagnostically early, such as the sharply carinated bowls known as *Schalenurnen* (Myres 1977), are entirely absent. All the rim sherds are from simple jar forms and, where it is possible to ascertain the overall form of the vessels, they appear to be simple globular forms which could date to any time within the early/middle Saxon period.

Decorated sherds, the most reliable of chronological markers in the early Anglo-Saxon period, are scarce here, with just two noted. Such a paucity of decorated pottery is not unusual at early Anglo-Saxon domestic sites. For example, decorated hand-built pottery only usually comprises around 5% or less of domestic assemblages, as was the case at sites such as West Stow, Suffolk (West 1985) and Mucking, Essex (Hamerow 1993), and just two sherds from an assemblage of 259 hand-built sherds at Oakington (Blinkhorn 2007a) were decorated. The two decorated sherds from this site both have stamp impressions, with one of them also having a fragment of an incised line. They are a little difficult to date. Myres (1977) saw stamping as a largely 6th-century decorative technique, although 5th-century stamped vessels are known. More recent work by Leahy (2007) has indicated that the picture is not perhaps as clear as Myres suggested, with the different styles having variable life-spans, and some having been used at a number of different times throughout the period. The sherds from Love's Farm are too small to allow the overall decorative scheme to be defined, and Leahy's sequence shows that vessels with incised decoration and stamps could date to anywhere between the 5th and early 7th centuries, although they generally appear to be more common from the later 5th to 6th century (Leahy 2007, 89–129 and fig. 116).

The only possible evidence that would support an early date for the Anglo-Saxon pottery at Love's Farm is the presence of a relatively high proportion of grantic pottery. As noted above, this is a pattern that was seen at Orton Hall Farm near Peterborough, a site which is said possibly to show continuity from the Roman to Anglo-Saxon periods. This may not be generally the case, however. Granitic-tempered pots were present at Cleatham, but only ever formed a small percentage of the

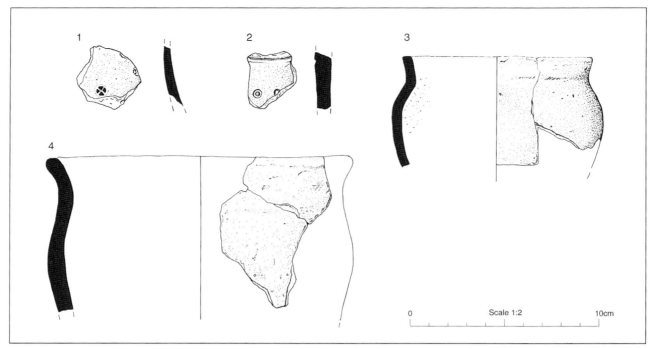

Figure 7.18 Post-Roman pottery. Scale 1:2

assemblage, and were at their most common in Phase 5, the latest phase of the cemetery (Leahy 2007, 83–4). Thus, there is no positive chrono-typological evidence from the Anglo-Saxon pottery of continuity from the Romano-British to early Anglo-Saxon periods, with the only datable sherds almost certainly belonging to the late 5th to 6th centuries.

Spatial distribution
The correlation of Anglo-Saxon pottery with many of the late Roman features on the Love's Farm site is potentially interesting but, as noted above, there are no Anglo-Saxon sherds from the excavations which can be said with certainty to be early on decorative/stylistic grounds, and the two decorated sherds which are present are highly likely to be around a century later than the latest Romano-British occupation. Evidence for continued occupation from the Roman to the early Anglo-Saxon period in south-eastern England, and, indeed early to mid 5th-century Anglo-Saxon activity generally, on the basis of pottery, is rare in a rural context, and the cases where there is such evidence, either the Roman or Saxon occupation, or sometimes both, usually have a funerary component involved. For example, the Roman temple-mausoleum complex at Bancroft in Milton Keynes, Buckinghamshire produced an Anglo-Saxon pottery assemblage which appears to date to the earliest part of the period, with carinated *Schalenurnen* and slashed/line-decorated pottery being the only datable wares present (Blinkhorn 1994a, 513). The coin evidence from the Romano-British phase of occupation showed that the site was occupied right up to the end of the period (Davies 1994, 275), and a small cemetery which was radiocarbon dated to the earliest decades of the 5th century was also present. There seems little doubt that there was continuity of occupation at this site.

One site in Milton Keynes which did produce early 5th-century pottery on an area of Romano-British domestic occupation was the Berrystead site at Caldecotte. Here, a carinated bowl and line-decorated wares were present, suggesting early to mid 5th-century occupation, with the best assemblage of such material coming from the upper fill of a Romano-British ditch (Blinkhorn 1994b). The Romano-British assemblage from that feature and the rest of the site generally, however, indicates that occupation during that period did not extend much beyond the 2nd century (Parminter 1994).

Correlation between early Anglo-Saxon and Iron Age activity is fairly well documented, however, and appears to be related to a need for a similar range of resources and soil types in each period. For example, at Pennyland in Milton Keynes, a large Anglo-Saxon settlement of at least thirteen sunken-featured buildings, three timber halls and associated enclosures was sited in an area of dense Iron Age occupation, but Romano-British activity was very sparse. The Anglo-Saxon pottery all appeared to be no earlier than the late 5th century (Blinkhorn 1993). In Cambridgeshire, early Anglo-Saxon pottery which can be dated to the earlier 5th century is extremely rare. Four carinated bowls from Barrington are listed in the Myres corpus, accessioned as having been discovered in the late 19th century (Myres 1977, 172 and figs 95 and 96). Another vessel of this type is known from Haslingfield, again discovered in the 19th century (*ibid.*). Both were cemetery sites. As far as this analyst is aware, early to mid 5th-century Anglo-Saxon pottery is entirely absent from this area of Cambridgeshire; this may be for chronological reasons, although a cultural/social explanation could equally be possible.

The distribution of the different early/middle Anglo-Saxon fabric types around this site may be evidence of settlement drift over time, such as that demonstrated at Mucking in Essex (Hamerow 1993), but a case can also be made that it is representative of the social affinities of the inhabitants of the site. It is worthy of note that the two stamped sherds from the site, both in fabric F5, were both found at the northern end of the excavations, and at quite a distance apart. This would suggest that the Anglo-Saxon activity in this part of the site (Settlement 7) is of late 5th- to 6th-century date, casting further doubt on the possibility that the pottery from the area of the Roman enclosures provides evidence of continuity from that period, although all these comments must remain tentative due to the paucity of the evidence. It is clear from the other evidence on the site that any settlement drift occurred from the south (Settlement 6) to the north (Settlement 7).

Analysis of the early/middle Anglo-Saxon pottery from Raunds in Northamptonshire showed that there were concentrations of different fabric types in various areas of the site, and that the clusters represented the manufacturing technique employed by the potters, in the sense of temper preparation either by the addition of sand or crushed rock to the clay (Blinkhorn 1997, 119). Utilising a similar methodology at Love's Farm, the crushed rock group would cover fabrics F1, F2 and F4, and the sand-tempered group F3 and F5, with the chaff-tempered F6 sherds forming a third group, although one represented by just two sherds. The distributions of the three fabric groups show that the crushed rock sherds are confined to the central and northern areas of the site, the sand-tempered sherds to all areas, and the chaff-tempered sherds to the central and southern area. This clustering of the pottery around the site may thus represent the areas exploited by groups within contemporary society with different social practices, although it could also be evidence of settlement shift. The lack of datable Anglo-Saxon pottery from the site means that the question must remain unresolved. The apparent correlation of the granitic fabric F4 with late Iron Age features is worthy of comment, and may be further evidence of the similarity of the range of resources exploited by people in the Iron Age and Anglo-Saxon periods, as discussed above.

Catalogue of illustrated early Anglo-Saxon pottery
(Fig. 7.18)

1   Body sherd with single stamp impression. Black fabric (F4) with lighter brown patch on the outer surface. *6181*, layer within partially infilled quarry pit, Quarry 3, area of Settlement 2.

2   Body sherd with two stamp impressions and two parallel incised lines. Black fabric (F4) with brown outer surface. *4800*, fill of pit *4801*, Settlement 7.

3   Large fragment of small **jar**. Uniform black fabric (F5). *6395*, layer within Enclosure 10, Settlement 2.

4   Rim sherd from a **jar**. Black fabric (F5) with pale brown patches on both surfaces. *4769*, fill of ditch *4770*, Enclosure 127, Settlement 7.

Chapter 8. Zooarchaeological and Botanical Evidence

I. Human skeletal remains
by Natasha Dodwell

Introduction
Thirteen inhumations and nine features containing cremated human bone were identified during the excavations, all of which were assigned to the Iron Age (Period 3). They came from small cemetery groups (Cemeteries 1–4) or were isolated burials. Bone samples from two inhumations were selected for radiocarbon dating (see Table 8.3 below), demonstrating that the dated burials were of the middle Iron Age and the late pre-Roman Iron Age to Early Roman period. Three further deposits recorded on site as cremations were associated with the ditches of Enclosure 22, although examination of the samples (see Fryer, below) revealed that they contained burnt animal bones, rather than human skeletal remains. These animal bones, along with those from the cremation burials, proved to be too fragmented for identification.

Methods of recovery and analysis
All soil from the deposits containing cremated bone was subject to 100% recovery as whole earth samples. These were then wet sieved, the residues passed through 10mm, 5mm and 2mm sieves and all bone >5mm extracted for analysis. The 2mm residues were scanned (and have been retained) and identifiable bone and any artefacts extracted. Osteological analysis followed procedures for cremated human bone outlined by McKinley (2002 and 2004).

General methods used in the osteological evaluation of all the human skeletal material are those of Bass (1992) and Buikstra and Ubelaker (1994). An assessment of age was based on the stages of dental development and eruption (Brown 1985; Ubelaker 1989) and epiphyseal union, on the degree of dental attrition (Brothwell 1981) and on changes to the auricular surfaces (Lovejoy *et al.* 1985). The age categories used in this report are:

infant	0–4 years
juvenile	5–12 years
sub-adult	13–18 years
young adult	19–25 years
middle adult	26–44 years
mature adult	45 years +

There may be overlaps between categories or a broad category, such as adult, where insufficient evidence is present. This is particularly true as regards the cremated material.

In keeping with standard practice, no attempt was made to sex immature individuals. The sex of adult individuals was ascertained where possible from sexually dimorphic traits of the skeleton (Buikstra and Ubelaker 1994) and metrical data but amongst the cremated remains any determinations should be treated with caution – hence ?M and ?F, as both the quantity and quality of the deposits meant that only one or two traits could be observed. The sex of the individual was ascertained where possible from sexually dimorphic traits on the pelvis and the skull and from metrical data.

The inhumation burials
Both the completeness of the skeleton, and the condition of the surviving bone affects the information that can be gleaned from each inhumation: the information is summarised in Table 8.1. At Love's Farm, the completeness and the condition of the bone is generally very poor. All of the graves were shallow having been truncated by ploughing and ranged in depth from 0.03–0.25m, with eight being 0.1m deep or less. In addition, field drains and ditches had cut through several of the graves disturbing and/or truncating many of the bodies. Skulls and pelves (the primary elements used in sexing and aging individuals) are poorly represented and this is undoubtedly due to the shallowness of the graves and the severity of truncation. The skull is missing from four skeletons (*5810, 5904, 5940* and *6353*). In addition, the skulls of skeletons *5813* and *6272* are represented only by loose teeth and jaw fragments, and that of skeleton *6906* by a single tooth. None of the long bones are complete, with many surviving only as splinters of bone. This prohibited an estimate of stature. The majority of joint surfaces are missing or damaged and the surfaces of many of the surviving shafts have been etched by insects and roots. Both of these factors may have led to the under-diagnosis of pathologies. Even amongst the more complete skeletons (*e.g. 7594* and *8098*) the vertebrae and ribs are fragmentary and many of the extremities are missing. Only one of the inhumation burials (*11730/11729*), a middle adult male, had grave goods in the form of a fragmented copper alloy ring (SF 3305), which was perhaps a finger ring (see Crummy, Chapter 6.III).

In addition to the inhumations, an adult 3rd mandibular molar, exhibiting no wear, was recovered from a layer machined for finds retrieval in Settlement 7 (*5917*, Period 4.4).

The cremation burials
The nine features containing cremated human bone were shallow and ranged in depth from 0.1m to 0.35m: the results are summarised in Table 8.2. They had all been truncated, although to what degree is unknown and it is impossible to determine how much bone, if any, has been lost. There was one urned burial with bone contained inside the vessel – a greyware beaker (SF 3430) of late 1st- to early to mid 2nd-century date. This vessel was damaged/truncated and it seems likely that the bone from

Period	Cemetery/ Settlement	Sk.	Grave	Burial type/ position	Orient.*	Grave depth (m)	Age	Sex	Pathology	Finds
3.1/3.2	Settlement 6 (Fig. 3.8)	8098	8100	Crouched on left side	N–S	0.13	mature adult	F	OA in R. wrist, shoulder, spine; AMTL, caries, calculus, abscess	
3.3	Cemetery 1, Settlement 2 (Fig. 3.13)	6272	6273	Crouched on right side	E–W	0.04	young adult	?	Calculus	
		6297	6298	Semi-flexed	NW–SE	0.10	young adult	?	None observed	
		6353	6354	Semi-flexed on right side	N–S	0.10	adult	F	None observed	
	Settlement 6 (Fig. 3.16)	11730	11729	Semi-flexed on right side	E–W	not known	adult	M	NSPI on legs; caries, calculus	Cua ring frag. (SF 3305)
3.5	Settlement 6 (Fig. 3.35)	6906	6907	Crouched? on left side?	N–S	0.07	adult	?	None observed	
	Settlement 6 (Fig. 3.33)	7594	7593	Supine, extended, arms crossed over chest	N–S	0.10–0.25	mature adult	M	OA in spine and finger; AMTL, calculus	
	Cemetery 2, Settlement 7 (Fig. 3.30)	5810	5809	Semi-flexed on left side	NE–SW	0.12	middle adult	F	Fractured R. radius	
		5813	5812	Crouched on left side	NE–SW	0.05	young adult	F	None observed	
		5816	5815	Flexed on left side	NE–SW	0.05	mature adult	?M	OA in spine, hand; caries, AMTL	
		5901	5900	Supine	NE–SW	0.12	middle adult	F	Calculus and rotten tooth	
		5904	5903	Flexed? on ?left side		0.05	adult	?	None observed	
		5940	5939	Flexed? on ?left side	W–E	0.03	adult	?	None observed	

* position of the skull referred to first. OA = osteoarthritis, AMTL = ante mortem tooth loss, NSPI = non-specific infection

Table 8.1 Inhumation burials (by period, cemetery and settlement)

Cemetery/ Settlement	Fill	Cut	Age/Sex	Wt (g)	Depth (m)	Pathology	Grave/pyre goods and possible capping
Cemetery 1, Settlement 2	6218	6219	MA/older adult ?male	537	0.16		
Cemetery 3, Settlement 6	6675	6676	Older subadult/ adult	45	0.10		
	6778	6781	Y/MA, ? F	646	0.12	NSPI on limb bones	Burnt ?animal bone
	6804	6805	Infant/ juvenile	95	0.11		Cua Nauheim derivative brooch (SF 3365)
	6838	6839	Subadult	166	0.20		Cua brooch spring frag. (SF 3397), iron nails (SF 3398, 3429, 3410)
	6910	6911	Adult	123	0.35		Burnt ?animal bone from fill of cremation pit, surrounding cremation vessel (SF 3430)
	6990			357	?		Cremation contained within a fragmented greyware bag-shaped ?beaker (SF 3430) of late 1st/early-mid 2nd century date. Burnt ?animal bone
	7007	7008	Adult	98	0.20		Cua wire, bow brooch spring and pin frags? (SF 3368, 3433, 3399), bone disc (SF 3374)
Cemetery 4, Settlement 6	9242	9243	Subadult/ young adult	42	0.13		Imported Pompeiian red ware dish/platter (x 22 sherds) of c.AD 40–80, placed above the cremation. Possible grave capping
	9244	9245	5/6 yr	50	0.15		Flat stone placed above the cremation. NSPI = non-specific infection; Cua – copper alloy

NSPI = non-specific infection; Cua – copper alloy

Table 8.2 Period 3.5 cremations (by cemetery and settlement)

Lab. no.	Skeleton	Grave	Settlement	Period	δ13C (‰) relative to VPDB	Radiocarbon age (BP)	Calibrated date (95.4% probability)
SUERC-21982 (GU-17895)	8098	8100	Settlement 6	3.1/3.2	-20.5%	2165±30	360–110 cal BC
SUERC-21978 (GU-17891)	5816	5815	Cemetery 2, Settlement 7	3.5	-19.9%	1965±30	50 cal BC–cal AD 90 (94.5 % probability)

The calibrated age ranges are determined from the University of Oxford Radiocarbon Accelerator Unit calibration program (OxCal3 v3.10)

Table 8.3 Results of radiocarbon dating

the fill around the vessel was originally contained within it. Determining the feature type of the other deposits containing cremated human bone is rather problematic; they were probably disturbed unurned burials but some, particularly those with very little bone, could be deposits of redeposited pyre debris. No mention is made in the site records of a concentration of bone within any of the features.

The bone from most of the features is buff-white in colour with a few blue/black fragments, indicative of complete oxidation. However, the bone from cremation *6218* is black/brown with fragments of humerus barely scorched, suggesting that the pyre was poorly constructed/tended or that the cremation process was curtailed for some reason. The bone from all of the deposits is highly fragmented and this has implications when attempting to identify skeletal elements. With the exception of the urned burial more bone (by weight) was recovered from the 5mm residue than from the 10mm residue. The bone from the urned burial is likely to have been protected by the vessel. McKinley (1994) has highlighted the numerous factors that may lead to the fragmentation of cremated bone including the cremation process itself, collection from the pyre, burial, excavation and post-excavation treatment. Although the fragments are generally small there is no evidence of deliberate breakage of bones before burial.

The features contained between 42g and 646g of cremated human bone. Whilst more bone will be in the unsorted 2mm residues it is unlikely that all of the body will have been interred in any of the features. Observations in modern crematoria have shown that the weight of collectable (>2mm fraction) cremated bone from an adult ranges from just over 1000g to 2400g with an average of c.1600g (McKinley 1993). This suggests either that not all of the bone that survived the cremation process was interred (which is a feature seen in all periods where cremation was practiced) or that bone has been lost to truncation.

Pyre and possible grave goods were identified in four of the features, all associated with Cemetery 3 in Settlement 6 (Table 8.2). Burnt and unburnt animal bone was identified in two of the burials (*6778* and *6910/6990*) and it is possible that more animal bone could exist amongst the fragments of unidentifiable bone. Fragments of copper alloy, possibly the remains of brooches, were identified in three of the burials in Cemetery 3 (*6804*, *6838* and *7007*). The only identifiable brooch is a Nauheim derivative from cremation *7007* dating to c.AD 43–80/5 (SF 3365), while a bone disc (Fig. 6.50, SF 3374) from the same cremation may have come from clothing (see Crummy, Chapter 6.III). The iron nails recovered from burial *6838* could derive from an object such as a box placed on the pyre or from reused timbers used to construct the pyre. The two cremations assigned to Cemetery 4 may both have been capped/marked by the placement of stones or pottery above them. Cremation *9243* was sealed by a Pompeian red ware dish/platter which was probably imported between c.AD 40–80. The fact that the vessel is burnt may indicate that it had been used in the cremation ceremony.

II. Radiocarbon dating

Two samples of human bone were submitted for radiocarbon dating to the Scottish Universities Environmental Research Centre (SUERC). The results appear in Table 8.3.

III. Animal bone
by Ian Baxter
(Figs 8.1–8.19)

Introduction
A total of 5,161 identifiable animal bone fragments were recovered by hand-collection from features dating from the early Iron Age to late Romano-British periods. Included in this figure are 789 bones from partial skeletons or articulating limbs counted as one specimen in Table 8.4. A further 1,211 identifiable fragments were isolated from the sifted environmental sample residues (Table 8.5). Undated specimens and the few animal bones from later periods have also been recorded. The largest assemblages date from the Iron Age (Period 3) and Romano-British (Period 4) periods. For the purpose of analysis these main periods have been subdivided into middle Iron Age (3.1–3.2), later Iron Age (3.3–3.4), late Iron Age/Romano-British transition (3.5), early Romano-British (4.1–4.2) and later Romano-British (4.3–4.5), but are primarily discussed below as Iron Age and Romano-British. The substantial faunal assemblage recovered from a late Roman well is reported on separately, although the data are also included in the more general overview of the Romano-British material.

Methods
Most of the animal bones from Love's Farm were recovered by hand-collection. However, a significant number of environmental samples were taken from various features across the site. While these produced a wide range of microfauna, the remains of the common domesticates are comparatively scarce in the samples, except in the case of skeletons already identified during hand-collection. The mammal bones were recorded on an Access database following a modified version of the

Taxon	3.1	3.2	3.3	3.4	3.5	4.1	4.2	4.3	4.4	4.5	Total
Cattle (*Bos* f. domestic)	1	51	206[1]	172	110	127	177	104[2]	847	301	2096
Sheep/goat (*Ovis/Capra*)	-	39	157[3]	115	168	139[4]	149[5]	86[6]	475	223[7]	1551
Sheep (*Ovis* f. domestic)	(-)	(9)	(27)	(30)	(22)	(44)	(34)	(17)	(74)	(77)	(334)
Goat (*Capra* f. domestic)	-	(-)	(+)	(-)	(3)	(-)	(-)	(-)	(3)	(-)	(6)
Red deer (*Cervus elaphus*)	-	(*)	5(*)	1(*)	(*)	1	-	-	+(*)	(*)	7
Roe deer (*Capreolus capreolus*)	-	-	-	-	(*)	-	-	-	1	-	1
Pig (*Sus scrofa*)	1	11	26	30	41	11	15	16	45	22	218
Equid (*Equus* sp.)	-	7	33	40	18[8]	20[9]	33[10]	21[11]	130	30	332
Dog (*Canis familiaris*)	-	5	9	12[12]	4[13]	9	7[14]	9[15]	34[16]	12	101
Dog/Fox (*Canis/Vulpes* sp.)	-	-	-	1	-	-	1	-	-	-	2
Fox (*Vulpes vulpes*)	-	-	1	-	-	-	1	-	-	-	2
Cat (*Felis catus*)	-	-	-	1	-	-	1	1	2	1	6
Badger (*Meles meles*)	-	-	-	-	-	-	-	-	-	+	+
Hare (*Lepus* sp.)	-	-	-	-	-	-	-	-	2	1	3
Rabbit (*Oryctolagus cuniculus*)	-	-	-	-	-	-	-	-	-	2	2
Mole (*Talpa europaea*)	-	-	-	-	-	-	-	-	1	-	1
Mouse/vole (Murid/Microtine)	-	-	-	-	-	1	-	-	1	-	2
Chicken (*Gallus* f. domestic)	-	-	+	1	1	1	1	2	11	2	19
Goose (*Anser/Branta* sp.)	-	1	-	-	1	+	-	-	3	-	5
Duck (*Anas platyrhynchos*)	-	-	-	-	-	-	-	-	-	1	1
Duck (*Anas* sp.)	-	-	-	-	-	-	-	-	2	-	2
Duck sp. (cf. *A. Penelope/acuta*)	-	-	-	-	-	-	-	-	-	1	1
Duck sp. (cf. *A. strepera/acuta*)	-	-	1	-	-	-	-	-	-	-	1
cf. Wigeon (*Anas Penelope*)	-	-	-	-	-	-	-	-	1	-	1
Tufted duck (*Aythya fuligula*)	-	-	-	-	+	-	-	-	+	-	+
Raven (*Corvus corax*)	-	-	2	-	-	+	1	-	1	-	4
Rock dove (*Columba livia*)	-	-	-	-	-	-	-	2	-	-	2
cf. Plover (*Pluvialis* sp.)	-	-	-	-	-	-	-	+	-	-	+
Passerine (*Passeriformes* sp.)	-	-	-	-	-	-	2	-	-	-	2
Anuran (*Rana/Bufo* sp.)	-	-	-	-	-	-	-	1	5	4	10
Frog (*Rana* sp.)	(-)	(-)	(-)	(-)	(-)	(-)	(-)	(-)	(+)	(-)	(+)
Total	2	114	440	373	343	309	388	242	1561	600	4372

'Sheep/goat' and 'Anuran' also include the specimens identified to species. Numbers in parentheses are not included in the total of the period. Unquantified presence of deer antler indicated by '(*)' '+' means that the taxon is present but no specimens could be 'counted' (see text). Skeletons and associated bones counted as '1'.

[1] Includes 4 bones from a foot
[2] Includes 8 bones from a partial skeleton
[3] Includes 71 bones from partial skeletons
[4] Includes 7 bones from a foot
[5] Includes 10 bones and 57 bones from partial skeletons
[6] Includes 31 bones from a partial skeleton
[7] Includes 4 bones from a partial skeleton
[8] Includes 146 bones from a partial skeleton
[9] Includes 7 bones from a hind leg
[10] Includes 67 bones and one hundred and twenty-three bones from partial skeletons
[11] Includes 14 bones from a fore leg
[12] Includes 5 bones from a partial skeleton
[13] Includes 3 bones from a partial skeleton
[14] Includes 4 bones, 10 bones and 4 bones from partial skeletons
[15] Includes 24 bones and 13 bones from partial skeletons
[16] Includes 67 bones, 6 bones and 136 bones from partial skeletons

Table 8.4 Number of hand-collected mammal, bird and amphibian bones (NISP) by site period

Taxon	3.3	3.4	3.5	4.1	4.2	4.3	4.4	4.5	Total
Cattle (*Bos* f. domestic)	-	1	-	-	+	-	2	1	4
Sheep/goat (*Ovis/Capra*)	91[1]	2	1	-	+	-	-	13	107
Red deer (*Cervus elaphus*)	-	-	-	-	-	-	+	-	+
Pig (*Sus scrofa*)	-	2	1	-	-	-	-	-	3
Dog (*Canis familiaris*)	-	-	1	-	-	-	1	5[2]	6
Cat (*Felis catus*)	-	-	-	-	-	-	-	1	1
Stoat (*Mustela erminea*)	-	-	1	-	-	-	-	-	1
Stoat/weasel (*M. erminea/nivalis*)	-	-	4	-	-	-	-	-	4
Weasel (*Mustela nivalis*)	-	-	1	-	-	-	-	-	1
Lagomorph (*Lepus/Oryctolagus* sp.)	-	-	-	-	-	-	1	-	1
Mole (*Talpa europaea*)	-	-	+	-	-	-	-	-	+
Shrew (*Sorex* sp.)	-	-	-	-	-	-	+	-	+
Common shrew (*Sorex araneus*)	-	-	1	-	-	-	9	-	10
Pygmy shrew (*Sorex minutus*)	-	-	2	-	-	-	-	-	2
Mouse/vole (Murid/Microtine)	-	7	243	1	2	12	46	14	325
House mouse (*Mus* sp.)	(-)	(-)	(6)	(-)	(-)	(-)	(-)	(-)	(6)
Wood mouse (*Apodemus* sp.)	(-)	(-)	(5)	(-)	(-)	(1)	(-)	(2)	(8)
Water vole (*Arvicola terrestris*)	(-)	(-)	(4)	(-)	(-)	(-)	(-)	(1)	(5)
Field vole (*Microtus agrestis*)	(-)	(1)	(39)	(-)	(-)	(1)	(19)	(-)	(60)
Bank vole (*Clethrionomys glareolus*)	(-)	(-)	(1)	(-)	(-)	(-)	(-)	(-)	(1)
Chicken (*Gallus* f. domestic)	-	-	-	-	-	1	-	-	1
Passerine (*Passeriformes* sp.)	-	-	6	-	-	1	-	-	7
Bird (*Aves* sp.)	-	-	-	-	-	-	+	+	+
Anuran (*Rana/Bufo* sp.)	6	5	8	-	1	654	27	10	711
Frog (*Rana* sp.)	(-)	(-)	(1)	(-)	(-)	(17+)	(3)	(-)	(22+)
Toad (*Bufo bufo*)	(-)	(-)	(-)	(-)	(-)	(-)	(2)	(-)	(2)
Fish (*Pisces* sp.)	-	-	-	1	-	3	1	-	5
Pike (*Esox luscius*)	-	-	-	-	-	-	-	1	1
Cyprinid sp.	-	-	2	-	-	-	-	1	3
Eel (*Anguilla anguilla*)	-	-	1	-	-	-	15	-	16
Total	97	17	272	2	3	671	102	6	1211

'Sheep/goat', 'Mouse/vole' and 'Anuran amphibian' also include the specimens identified to species. Numbers in parentheses are not included in the total of the period. '+' means that the taxon is present but no specimens could be 'counted' (see text). Some Anuran amphibian totals are estimated.
[1] Includes elements belonging to hand-collected skeletons
[2] Includes four bones from a foot

Table 8.5 Number of mammal, bird amphibian and fish bones (NISP) in the sieved assemblage by site period

method described in Davis (1992) and used by Albarella and Davis (1994). In brief, all teeth (lower and upper) and a restricted suite of parts of the skeleton were recorded and used in counts. These are: horncores with a complete transverse section, skull (*zygomaticus*), atlas, axis, scapula (glenoid articulation), distal humerus, distal radius, proximal ulna, radial carpal, carpal 2+3, distal metacarpal, pelvis (ischial part of acetabulum), distal femur, distal tibia, calcaneum (*sustenaculum*), astragalus (lateral side), centrotarsale, distal metatarsal, proximal parts of the 1st, 2nd and 3rd phalanges. At least 50% of a given part had to be present for it to be counted.

The presence of large (cattle/horse size) and medium (sheep/pig size) vertebrae and ribs was recorded for each context but not used in counts. Where practicable, these elements have been attributed to taxon and numbers present estimated on the basis of vertebra centra and the heads of ribs. For birds, the following were always recorded if present: scapula (articular end), proximal coracoid, distal humerus, proximal ulna, proximal carpometacarpus, distal femur, distal tibiotarsus and distal tarsometatarsus.

The separation of sheep and goat was attempted on the following elements: horncores, lower dP3, lower dP4, distal humerus, distal metapodials (both fused and unfused), distal tibia, astragalus, and calcaneum using the criteria described in Boessneck (1969), Kratochvil (1969), Payne (1969, 1985) and Schmid (1972). The shape of the enamel folds (Davis 1980; Eisenmann 1981) was used for identifying equid teeth to species. Equid postcrania were checked against criteria summarised in Baxter (1998a).

Wear stages were recorded following Grant (1982) for all lower P4s and dP4s as well as for the lower molars of cattle, sheep/goat and pig, both isolated and in mandibles. Measurements in general follow von den Driesch (1976). All pig measurements follow Payne and Bull (1988). Humerus HTC and BT and tibia Bd measurements were taken for all species, as suggested by Payne and Bull (1988) for pigs. The crown heights of equid teeth were measured following Levine (1982). Shaft diameter (SD) on dog long bones is measured as suggested by Harcourt (1974) and represents the midshaft diameter (msd).

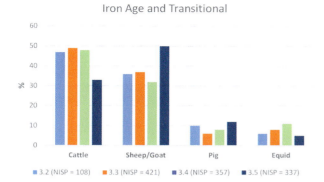

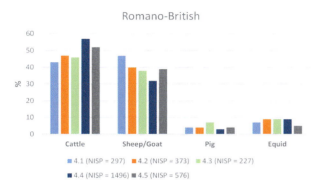

Figure 8.1 Frequency by NISP of the main domestic mammals by period. Total NISP for major domesticates = 4192

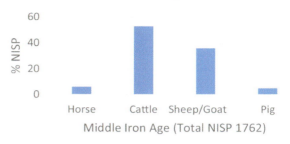

Figure 8.2 Frequency of the main domestic mammals compared with other Iron Age sites in Cambridgeshire (with additional data from Baxter 1999 and 2009, and Rielly 2008)

The survival of skeletal elements for the main taxa (cattle, sheep/goat and pig) is compared with the sequence of survival suggested by Brain (1976) based on experimental work carried out on goat skeletons near the Kuiseb river in Namibia. This sequence is used simply to facilitate an easier comparison between the survival of body parts of the three main domesticates.

Suitable equid long bones have been compared with modern reference material in a series of discriminant analysis plots following the method of Johnstone (2004, 2006). A number of pathological specimens from Love's Farm have been previously published on the ICAZ Bone Commons website (Thomas and Baxter 2007).

Provenance and preservation
The animal bones were excavated from ditches, pits, gullies, postholes and a well. Distribution plots reveal very little in the way of meaningful distribution of animal bones across the site in any of the main periods of occupation. Little information was obtained from a comparison of the assemblages from Settlements 6 and 7 in the Romano-British period, which demonstrate differences in terms of some of the other material categories.

Bone condition varies from good to poor. Much of the bone is highly fragmented. In addition to large numbers of unidentifiable fragments resulting from intensive butchery, trampling and canid gnawing, bone has also become fragmented *in situ* within the clay matrix due to cycles of expansion and contraction, during excavation and during finds processing. Skeletons and bones in articulation were not uncommon and these suggest that some material comes from primary deposits.

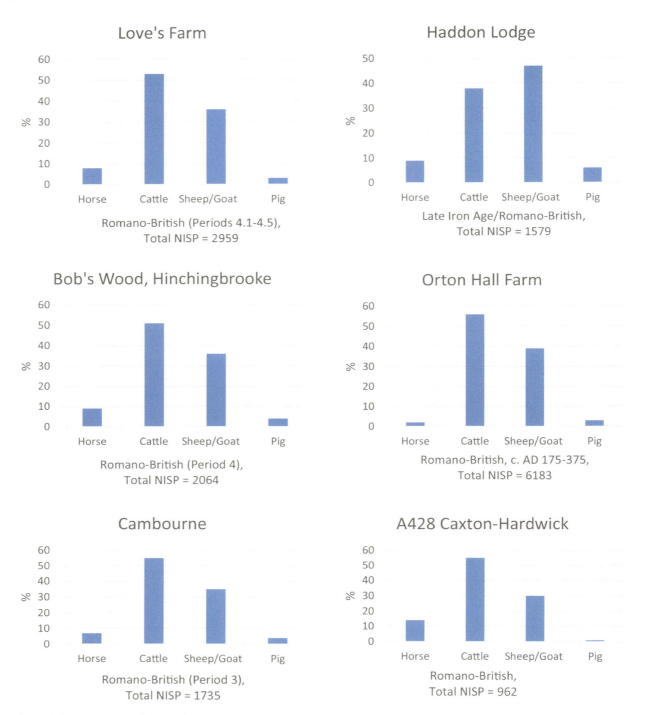

Figure 8.3 Frequency of the main domestic mammals compared with other Romano-British sites in Cambridgeshire (with data from Hamilton-Dyer 2009; Baxter 2003 and Rielly 2008)

A significant assemblage of red deer antler off-cuts and craft waste came from Period 4.4 ditch *5075* (*5074*; Enclosure 131, Settlement 7), while a key group of well-preserved material came from the late Roman well (*5387*) in Settlement 7 (Period 4.5).

Frequency of species
(Figs 8.1–8.3)
The site's animal bone assemblage is dominated by the remains of the main domestic mammals: cattle, sheep, pig and horse (Table 8.4). Domestic birds (fowl, goose and duck) are uncommon, although their numbers are liable to under-estimation due to a recovery bias against smaller bones. With the exception of red deer antler the remains of wild animals are scarce, suggesting that hunting played a minimal role in the provision of food.

Cattle is the most common species according to the number of identified specimens (NISP) in all periods except Periods 3.5 and 4.1 (Fig. 8.1), although when calculated on the basis of minimum number of individuals (MNI) sheep are much more numerous in both the Iron Age and Romano-British periods (Table 8.6). Equid remains are more common than those of pigs, both in terms of NISP and MNI, except in Periods 3.2 and 3.5.

Taxon	3. Iron Age		4. Roman		Total		Total	
	NISP	%	NISP	%	NISP	%	MNI	%
Cattle (*Bos taurus*)	540	48	1556	57	2096	54	81	33
Sheep/goat (*Ovis/Capra*)	479	42	1072	39	1551	40	151	61
Pig (*Sus scrofa*)	109	10	109	4	218	6	16	6
Total	*1128*		*2737*		*3865*		*248*	

Table 8.6 Frequencies of the three major domesticates by number of identified specimens (NISP) and by minimum number of individuals (MNI)

NISP numbers are adversely affected by differential preservation and recovery. MNI is a system less affected by these biases and probably provides a more accurate estimate of the frequencies of species at Love's Farm.

On the basis of NISP the relative frequencies of the main domestic mammals at the site during the Iron Age (Period 3, Fig. 8.2) are broadly similar to those at Greenhouse Farm, Fen Ditton (Baxter 1999), Bob's Wood, Hinchingbrooke (Baxter 2009) and the A428 sites (Rielly 2008). In the Roman period (Period 4) the sites most closely resembling the distribution pattern found at Love's Farm are Bob's Wood, Hinchingbrooke and Cambourne (Hamilton-Dyer 2009), which is situated close to the A428 sites (Fig. 8.3).

Periods 3 and 4: Iron Age and Romano-British
(Figs 8.4–8.14)

Cattle

As noted above, cattle remains are the most numerous by NISP, but not by MNI, in most of the main periods at the site. Also, on account of the much greater carcass weight, beef would have been the main source of meat in all periods. Some of the cattle skulls had been deliberately placed in ditches or other features (see for example, Fig. 8.4).

The Iron Age cattle found at Love's Farm belong to small horned and short horned types as classified by Armitage and Clutton-Brock (1976), with short horns almost twice as frequent as small horns. While the majority are adult, based on the horncore morphology (Armitage 1982), sub-adults are also represented. The main difference in the Romano-British period is a reduction in the frequency of small horns with only one specimen (out of a total of 32) recovered. Cattle classifiable as medium horned occur in Period 4, accounting for 13% of the total (*i.e.* four out of 32). Analysis of size and shape indicates that some Romano-British cores attained greater size and were, in general, different in shape from those of the Iron Age. This may be due to differences in husbandry, possibly the introduction of new breeding stock, and/or sexual composition with a relative increase in the number of castrates (oxen) in the Roman sample. Cattle crania from all periods are generally highly fragmentary with the exception of those recovered from well *5387* (Period 4.5) in Settlement 7 which are exceptionally well preserved (see further details below). The Iron Age cattle crania from Period 3 tend to

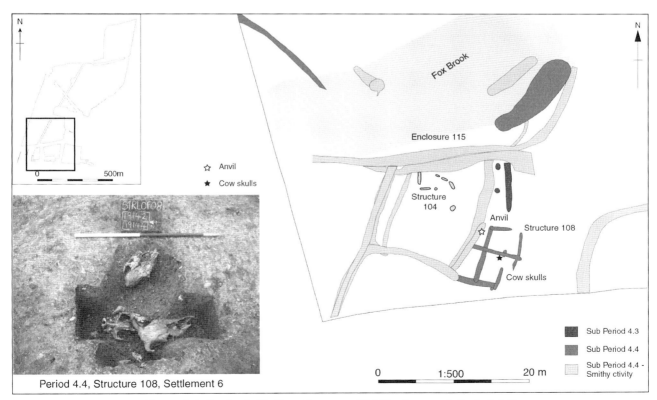

Figure 8.4 Cattle skulls from Structure 106 (Settlement 6, Period 4.4)

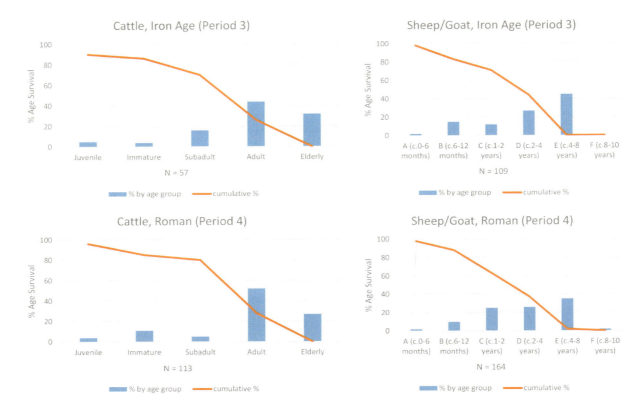

Figure 8.5 Distribution of cattle and sheep/goat mandibles by age stage (as defined by O'Connor (1998) and Crabtree (1989))

have convex frontal profiles, a typology that continues into the Roman period, but by the later Romano-British period (Periods 4.4 and 4.5) crania with prominent or pointed bosses become increasingly frequent and account for half of the sample recovered from well *5387* (see below). The frontal profile was found to be closely related to breed in a study of modern cattle crania (Grigson 1976) and this, together with a tendency towards increased horncore length during the later Roman period, is highly suggestive of the introduction of new breeding stock.

Withers heights calculated from complete long bones using the multiplication factors of Matolcsi (1970) range between 100–132cm with a mean of 113cm (N = 25) for the Iron Age assemblage, and 102–137cm with a mean of 124cm (N = 74) for the Romano-British assemblage. Of six bones yielding withers height estimates above 130cm, one dates from Period 3.5, one from Period 4.2 and four from Period 4.4. Analysis of the size of the cattle metapodials and astragali also indicates a general increase in the size of cattle during the Roman period, while examination of the shape of the same bones independent of size also suggests differences in herd composition.

Cattle of all ages are represented in the Iron Age and Romano-British features indicating that they were being bred on site. Perinatal and young cattle remains are present in both Iron Age and Romano-British features at low frequency. Analysis of the wear stages of the cattle teeth (following Grant 1982 and O'Connor 1988) indicates that most cattle were not slaughtered until fully adult (Fig. 8.5). This is largely confirmed by the fusion state of the available long bone and other epiphyses.

Butchery patterns have not been analysed in detail but, in general, carcasses were dismembered using sharp knives in the Iron Age, with more frequent use of axes or cleavers in the Roman period. Recordable butchery marks were in any case comparatively few in number, as is frequently the case with rural sites of these periods. For example, no specimens suggestive of the curing of meat for storage or consumption off-site were seen in the Love's Farm assemblage. Comparison of cattle skeletal parts with Brain's (1976) Kuiseb river goat survival sequence clearly demonstrates that all parts of the cattle skeleton are represented at the Love's Farm site. The vertebrae and ribs of cattle are widespread in the features of both periods, clearly indicating that animals were slaughtered and consumed on site.

Dental anomalies of possible genetic significance present in the Love's Farm cattle assemblage include absence of lower P2 and reduction or absence of the lower M3 hypoconulid or third pillar (Andrews and Noddle 1975; Albarella and Davis 1994 and 1996). Without destructive analysis it is difficult to be certain that the lower P2 is congenitally absent or has simply been lost with the alveolus healed over. No such examination was undertaken with the Love's Farm assemblage, as earlier attempts have proved inconclusive (Baxter 2009). Experience with cattle remains of recent date has, however, demonstrated that absence of lower P2 may be associated with extreme wear on the lower M3 hypoconulid and consequent abnormal wear on the corresponding upper M3. Examples of cattle mandibles with lower P2 absent, lower M3s with reduced or missing hypoconulids and upper M3s with abnormal wear were found. A set of three incisors found in Period 4.1 (*10522*, ditch *10523*, Boundary 103, Settlement 6) have grooves below the crown on the mesial surface caused by grass being pulled between the teeth during grazing (Miles and Grigson 1990, 494). A cattle mandible from Period 4.2 (*10321*, ditch *10323*, Boundary 111, Settlement 7) has uneven wear typical of 'wave mouth' a condition more frequently observed in horses (Baker and Easley 2005, 240–1; see also below, under equids).

Pathologies associated with the use of cattle for draught purposes (Bartosiewicz *et al.* 1997) were observed in the assemblages from both periods but were much more frequent in the Roman assemblage. These primarily affect the metapodials and result in broadening of the distal epiphyses and/or palmar depressions. Cattle phalanges from Period 3.4 (*10935*, ditch *10740*, Enclosure 13, Settlement 6) and Period 4.2 (*10624*, ditch *10625*, Boundary 1) have high ring bone. More severe pathologies also typical of draught animals include ankylosed joints and degenerative changes typical of osteoarthritis found in Period 4.1 (*8894*, pit *8895*, Enclosure 104, Settlement 6), Period 4.4 (*8078*, isolated ditch *8879*; *9324*, pit *9323*, Settlement 6; *13315*, ditch *11314*, Enclosure 104, Settlement 6) and Period 4.5 (*5658*, ditch *5659*, Enclosure 139, Settlement 7 and *5890*, well *5387*, Settlement 7).

A cut-off cattle horncore was found in Period 4.1 (*13798*, ditch *13799*, Settlement 6), a sawn cattle horncore fragment was recovered from Period 3.3 (*11418*, ditch *11411*) and a cattle horncore from an unphased deposit (*11268*) has a transverse saw cut across its posterior surface. These examples provide evidence for the utilisation of horn which is itself only preserved under exceptional circumstances. A large distal metacarpal with a broadened distal epiphysis found in Period 4.1 (*8122*, ditch *8123*, Boundary 2) has been sawn from the shaft and represents waste from bone-working. Further evidence for bone-working at the site is discussed by Crummy (Chapter 6.IX).

Sheep/goat
The remains of caprines constitute the most common taxon at Love's Farm by MNI and the second most frequent by NISP in both the Iron Age and Romano-British assemblages (see above). Where the species could be identified with certainty, sheep bones and teeth (22% identified) are much more numerous than those of goats (0.4% identified) which were only observed in Periods 3.5 and 4.4 (Table 8.4). Recent research has questioned a number of the most widely used dental characters for distinguishing between sheep and goats (Zeder and Pilaar 2010) and goats may well be less frequent. At Love's Farm, horncores of both male and female sheep were recovered from features dating from the Iron Age and Romano-British periods. Where they could be sexed, the sheep pelves derive almost exclusively from ewes. Two sheep frontal fragments, from Period 4.4 (*8570*, ditch *8572*, Enclosure 14, Settlement 6) and an unphased context (*8574*) have undeveloped or polled horncores.

Withers heights for the Iron Age sheep, calculated using the multiplication factors of Teichert (1975), range between 52–66cm with a mean of 57cm (N = 18). For the Romano-British assemblage the range is 55–71cm with a mean of 59cm (N = 34). These sheep are small compared with early Roman sheep from Great Chesterford Temple Precinct which had an average withers height of 62cm (Baxter 2011a) and contemporary sheep from Elms Farm, Heybridge (Johnstone and Albarella 2002). No significant increase in the size of the sheep over time at Love's Farm is discernable. However, this was also the case at Great Chesterford in terms of withers height, although measurement of the lower dP4 and M1 teeth confirmed an anticipated increase in size of sheep in the 2nd century AD, as previously identified at Elms Farm and other sites. Unfortunately this method requires a larger sample size than was available at Love's Farm to pinpoint changes in relative size. Based on mandibular wear, proportionately more sheep were slaughtered at 1 and 2 years during the Roman period and comparatively fewer survived after 4 to 8 years compared to the Iron Age period (Fig. 8.5). The overall kill-off pattern is typical of Iron Age and Roman assemblages and quite different from more specialised patterns associated with concentrations on the production of meat, milk or wool (Payne 1973).

Comparison of sheep/goat skeletal parts with the Kuiseb river goat survival sequence (Brain 1976) demonstrates that all parts of the skeleton are represented at the Love's Farm site, although heavily biased in favour of the more robust elements. Caprine-sized vertebrae and ribs are widespread in the Iron Age and Roman features at Love's Farm, clearly indicating that animals were slaughtered and consumed on site. Butchery of the sheep carcass was generally performed with knives in both periods.

Several dental anomalies were observed affecting the sheep population, particularly in the Iron Age assemblage. They include a mandible from Period 3.3 (*8391*, ditch *8392*, Roundhouse 14, Settlement 6) with an abscess and swelling between the 1st and 2nd molar teeth, a mandible from Period 3.4 (*6337*, Quarry 3, Settlement 2) with marked alveolar resorption due to periodontal disease, and a maxilla from Period 3.3 with the upper P4 rotated 45°. Humeri from Period 4.4 (*5773*, ditch *5772*, Enclosure 126, Settlement 7 and *8958*, ditch *8959*, Settlement 6) have early stage ossification of the lateral collateral ligament caused by repeated minor traumata, often age-related. Frequently described as 'penning elbow' (Baker and Brothwell 1980), this is a misnomer as the condition is not related to single event trauma, but is progressive and related to osteoblastic activity stimulated by repeated minor stress. A sheep metacarpal found in Period 4.2 (*14011*, pit *14012*, near Enclosure 108, Settlement 6) has a broadened distal epiphysis, exostoses on both epicondyles and periostitis affecting the area above the epiphysis on the posterior side. This animal was suffering from sesamoiditis, inflammation within and around the sesamoids at the point of insertion of the suspensory ligament. More often associated with cattle and horses it is caused by repeated trauma on the fetlock joint. The associated articular extension suggests an animal of some age (Kate M. Clark, pers. comm.). These kinds of injuries to the front legs may be expected to be more prevalent in old rams.

A partial juvenile sheep buried in Period 4.3 (*13968*, ditch *13995*, Settlement 6) consists exclusively of head and foot elements. The partial skeletons of three ewes were recovered from Period 4.2 (*5945*, pit *4626*, Quarry 7, Settlement 7). No cut marks were seen on the bones of any of these skeletons. A sheep metatarsal from Period 4.1 (*11308*, ditch *11307*, Enclosure 100, Settlement 6) is polished with multiple transverse cut marks above the distal articulation on the anterior and posterior sides and

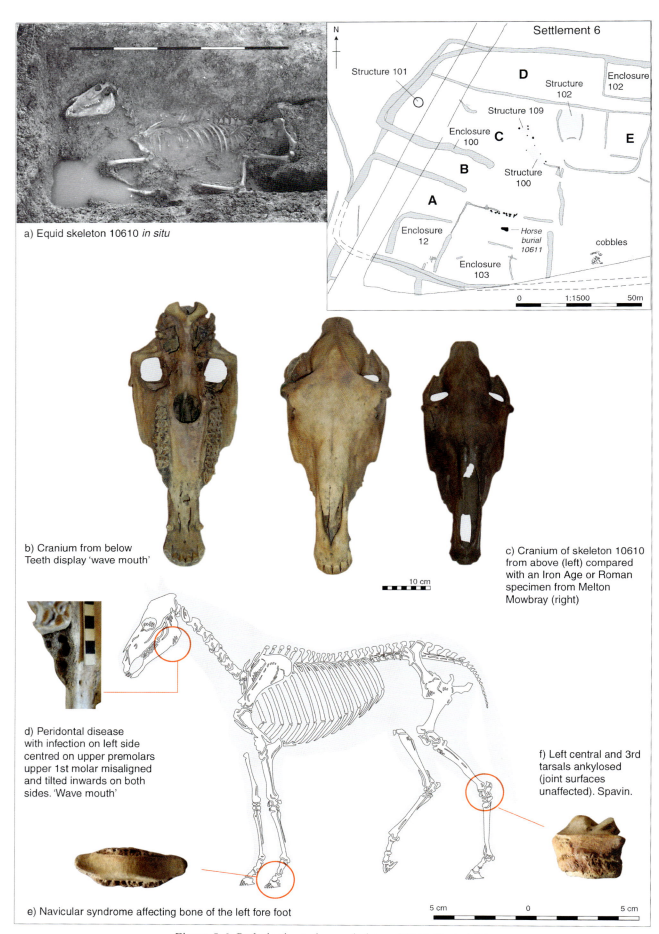

Figure 8.6 Pathologies to horse skeleton *10610*, Period 4.1

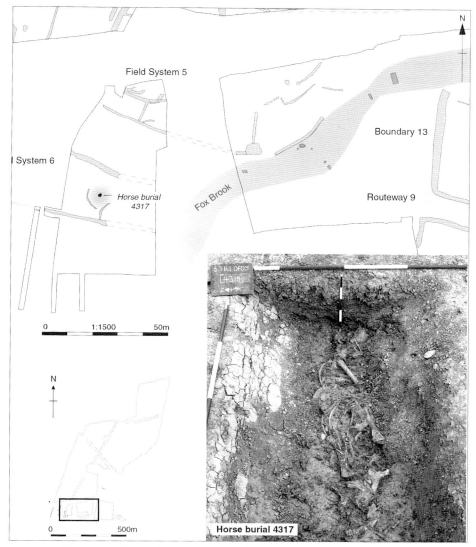

Figure 8.7 Horse burial *4317*, ditch *4318*, Settlement 6, Period 4.1

on the upper medial shaft. These marks do not appear to relate to butchery but to the utilisation of this bone as a tool of some kind. The burial of a sheep in Period 3.3 (*13275*, pit *13276*, Settlement 4) is that of an adult ewe.

Pig
The remains of pigs are not particularly frequent in the Iron Age and Romano-British deposits at Love's Farm, accounting for 9% of domestic food species by NISP in Period 3 and less than 4% in Period 4 (Table 8.4, Figs 8.1–8.3). The few mandibles available suggest that most pigs in both periods were generally slaughtered as sub-adults and young adults with the lower M3 coming into wear, and were kept as porkers and baconers. Very little further information is added by the preserved epiphyseal ends of bones. As with cattle and sheep/goat, all parts of the pig skeleton are represented in both main periods. A pig distal tibia from Period 3.2 (*7261*, ditch *7262*) has part of the fibula shaft fused to it, and a proximal 5th metatarsal from Period 4.4 (*7479*, pit *7476*, Settlement 7) has exostoses indicating fusion with the adjacent 4th metatarsal. A pig distal radius with metaphysis unfused, found in Period 3.5 (*9055*), is large compared with other specimens recovered from the site and could belong to a wild or stall-fed pig.

Other domestic mammals

Equid
Equid remains are fairly frequent at the Love's Farm site, accounting for 15% of cattle and equids combined in Period 3 and 13% in Period 4. This frequency is within the expected Iron Age range of Maltby (1996) and below the 20% at Haddon (Baxter 2003), 21% at Vicar's Farm (Clarke in prep.) and 24% at Hinxton Road, Duxford (Baxter 2011b, fig. 43). In common with other Iron Age and Romano-British sites in the region the majority of equid specimens can be confidently attributed to pony-sized horses (*Equus caballus*). Discriminant analyses of complete equid radius, metacarpal, metatarsal and tibia from Love's Farm following the method of Johnstone (2004, 2006) provides no clear indication of the presence of donkeys or mules in the assemblage.

Withers heights based on the multiplication factors of May (1985) range between 113–141cm (11 to 14 hands) with a mean of 125cm (12 hands) for the Iron Age (N = 9)

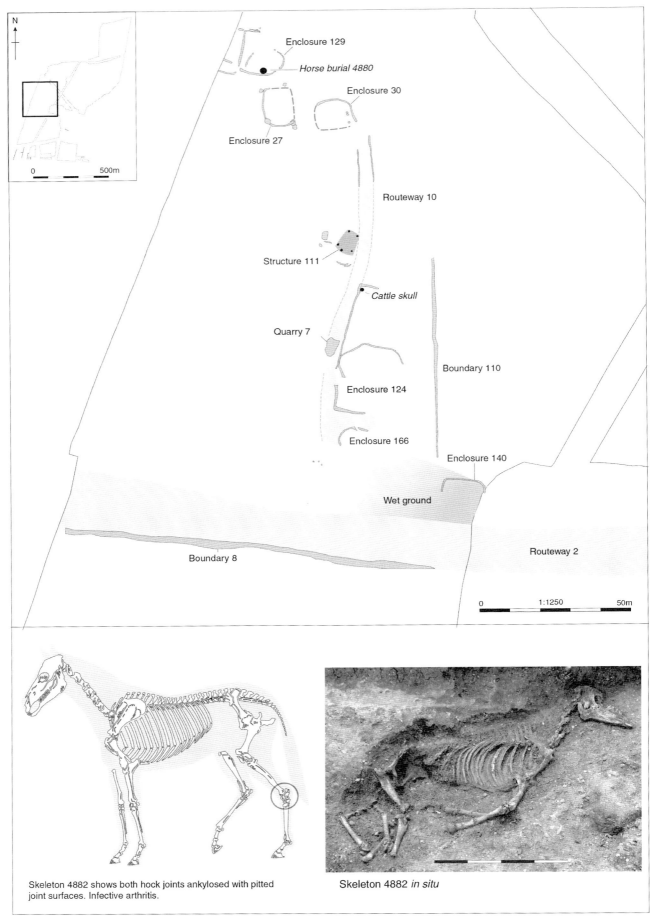

Figure 8.8 Pathologies to horse skeleton *4882*, Period 4.2

260

and 120–147cm (12 to 14½ hands) with a mean of 136cm (13 hands) for the Romano-British period (N = 19). The teeth of the horses have been aged following the method of Barone (1980) for incisors, and crown height of the grinding teeth following the comparative wear curves of Levine (1982). Mortality generally occurred after 2 years of age with very few animals surviving after 15 years. A perinatal posterior third phalanx (hoof bone) was found in Period 4.2 (*11460*, pit *11461*, Settlement 6).

Three horse burials were excavated at the site. A stallion or gelding was buried on its right side with the legs contracted under the body in Period 4.1 (*10610*, pit *10611*, Enclosure 103, Settlement 6, Fig. 8.6). This animal was 9–10 years of age and stood around 140.5cm (*c*.14 hands) high and in life suffered from a range of dental and arthropathic conditions. There was periodontal disease with infection on the left side of the maxilla centred on the upper premolars, and the upper first molars are misaligned and tilted inwards on both sides. The grinding teeth are worn in an uneven fashion typical of a condition known as 'wave mouth'. This can lead to periodontal disease and excessive wear of some of the teeth, eventually leading to discomfort or trouble with mastication (Baker and Easley 2005, 240–1). The same animal also suffered from navicular syndrome as evidenced by the degeneration of the articular surface of the distal sesamoid or navicular bone of the left fore foot (*cf.* Baker and Brothwell 1980). Navicular syndrome is a complex condition involving muscles, tendons, navicular bursa and nerve supplies (Ramey 1997). The central and 3rd tarsals of the left hock joint are ankylosed in a spavin with joint surfaces displaying no degeneration.

The scattered remains of a horse of indeterminate sex were recovered from Period 4.1 (*4317*, ditch *4318*, Settlement 6). This animal was aged approximately 12 years and stood 145cm or 14 hands high. The disordered state of the remains as excavated (Fig. 8.7) suggests that the burial had been disturbed in antiquity. Several bones from this skeleton have curious holes in them of uncertain, although most probably taphonomic, origin (A. Legrand, pers. comm.). The third horse burial is that of a mare aged approximately 10 years with a withers height of 142cm (14 hands) found in Period 4.2 (*4882*, burial *4880*, Settlement 7, Fig. 8.8). This animal had both the left and right hock joints ankylosed with pitting of the joint surfaces suggestive of infective arthritis. Infective arthritis is infection in the fluid and tissues of a joint usually caused by bacteria, frequently *Brucella abortus* (Baker and Brothwell 1980, 125). Post-medieval horse hocks with infective arthritis from Market Harborough in Leicestershire have been previously published by the present author (Baxter 1996).

Other pathologies observed among the equid remains from Love's Farm include an astragalus from Period 3.2 (*7335*, ditch *7336*) with exostoses, including a particularly large one affecting the distal tuberosity combined with destruction of the joint surfaces; an astragalus from Period 3.4 (*571*, Quarry 3, Settlement 2) with extensive exostoses and pitted joint surface typical of infective arthritis; an astragalus with eburnated and pitted distal articulation found together with central and 3rd tarsals with pitted surfaces in Period 4.1 (*5787*, ditch *5789*, Boundary 109, Settlement 7); an ankylosed hock joint from Period 4.4 (pit *7479*, Settlement 7); a metatarsal from Period 4.4 (*8571*, ditch *8572*, Enclosure 114, Settlement 6) with proximal exostoses and pitted articular surface; and a thoracic vertebra centra with spondylotic spurs found in Period 4.1 (*11734*, burial *11735*, Settlement 6). An unphased equid thoracic vertebra fragment found in a modern ditch has a massive ventral exostosis attached to the centrum, presumably part of an ankylosed series.

Ankylosed equid metacarpals found in an unphased cleaning layer (*10693*) have cut marks on the posterior shaft; a 4th metatarsal from Period 4.2 (*11337*, ditch 11338, Boundary 100, Settlement 6) has cut marks and signs of polishing; a proximal metatarsal from Period 4.4 (*13727*, pit *13720*, Settlement 6) and a femur from Period 4.4 (*13883*, dump layer, Structure 108, Settlement 6) have been butchered in similar fashion to cattle bones; and a sawn equid distal radius fragment recovered from Period 3.3 (*8118*, ditch *8119*, Boundary 2, Settlement 6) represents a bone-working off-cut.

Figure 8.9 Isolated dog burial *4395/4394*, Period 3

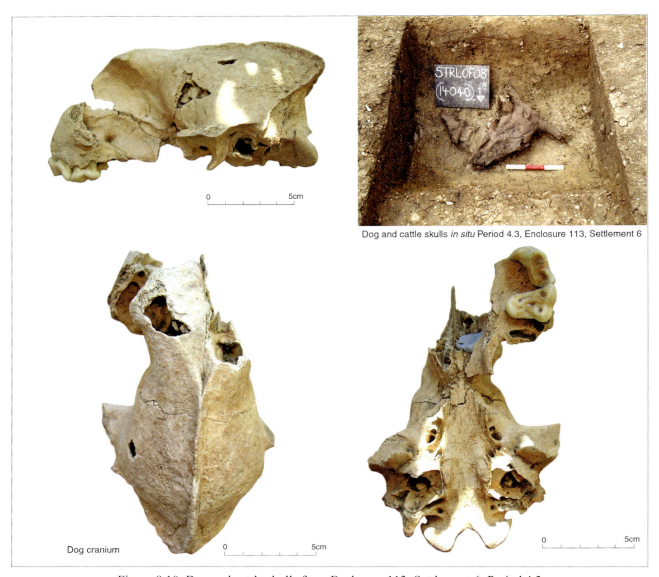

Figure 8.10 Dog and cattle skulls from Enclosure 113, Settlement 6, Period 4.3

Dog

The dogs include several partial skeletons derived from burials (Table 8.4). Withers heights of the dogs, based on the multiplication factors of Harcourt (1974) and Clark (1995), range between 41–58cm for the Iron Age (Period 3) and 25–57cm for the Romano-British period (Period 4). The presence of larger animals is indicated by an unphased proximal femur found in context *10926* which must have belonged to a dog 60cm or more at the shoulder. Iron Age specimens include the burial of a medium sized dog 54cm high (*4395*, burial *4394*, near Settlement 2, Fig. 8.9), a juvenile mandible from an animal aged under 4 months found in Period 3.4 (*8566*, ditch *8567*, Boundary 1) and the partial skeleton of another juvenile aged 5–9 months from Period 3.5 (*10571*, ditch *10572*, Enclosure 11, Settlement 6). The partial cranium of a medium sized dog (*14040*, Enclosure 113, Settlement 6, Period 4.3,) was found buried in a ditch and tucked beneath the horn of a cattle skull (Fig. 8.10). This animal had worn teeth and was female on the basis of the basicranial morphology (The and Trouth 1976).

The remains of brachymel dwarf hounds comprise a significant proportion of the Roman dog remains found at Love's Farm. These include the skeleton of a large male with a shoulder height of around 34cm that was buried in Period 4.4 (*8960*, ditch *8959*, Settlement 6). The animal lay on its right side with, apparently, a piece of chalk covering the eye (Fig. 8.11). This individual is significantly larger than a male dwarf hound from York Road, Leicester published by the present author (Baxter 2006a), indicating a high degree of variability in these chondrodystrophic types. A second smaller specimen with a withers height of 29cm whose fragmentary remains were recovered from Period 4.4 (*5434*, ditch *5433*, Settlement 7) lacks the sagittal cresting and markedly bowed limb bones of that from (*8960*) and was most probably a female of the same type on the basis of comparison with a more complete specimen found at Linton in Cambridgeshire. Several bones of a brachymel puppy were found in Period 4.4 (*5886*, surface finds, Settlement 7). Although generally compared to the modern dachshund, it may be that in life the Roman dwarf dogs looked more like the modern corgi which in origin is

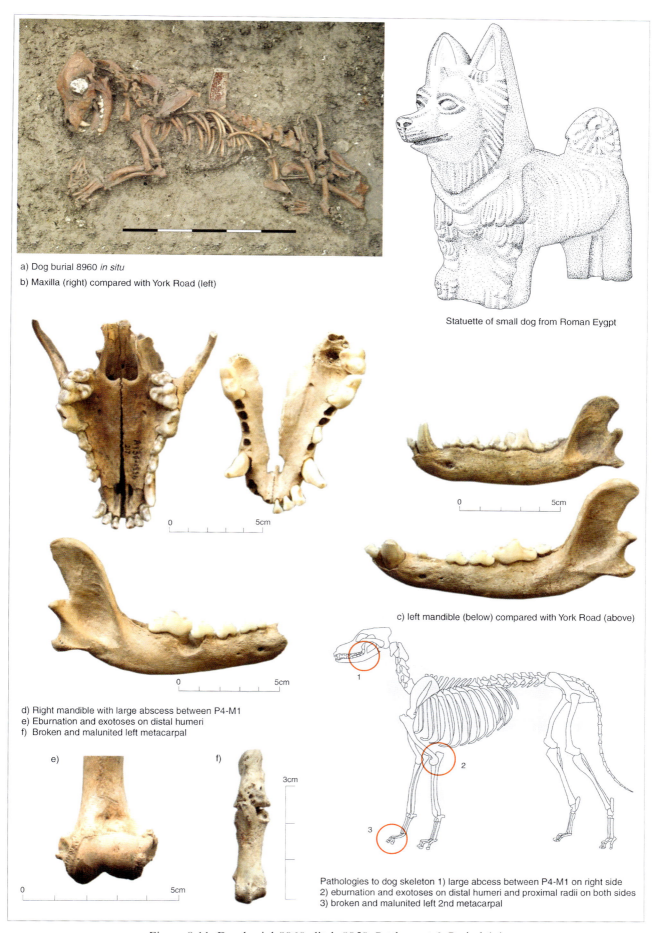

Figure 8.11 Dog burial *8960*, ditch *8959*, Settlement 6, Period 4.4

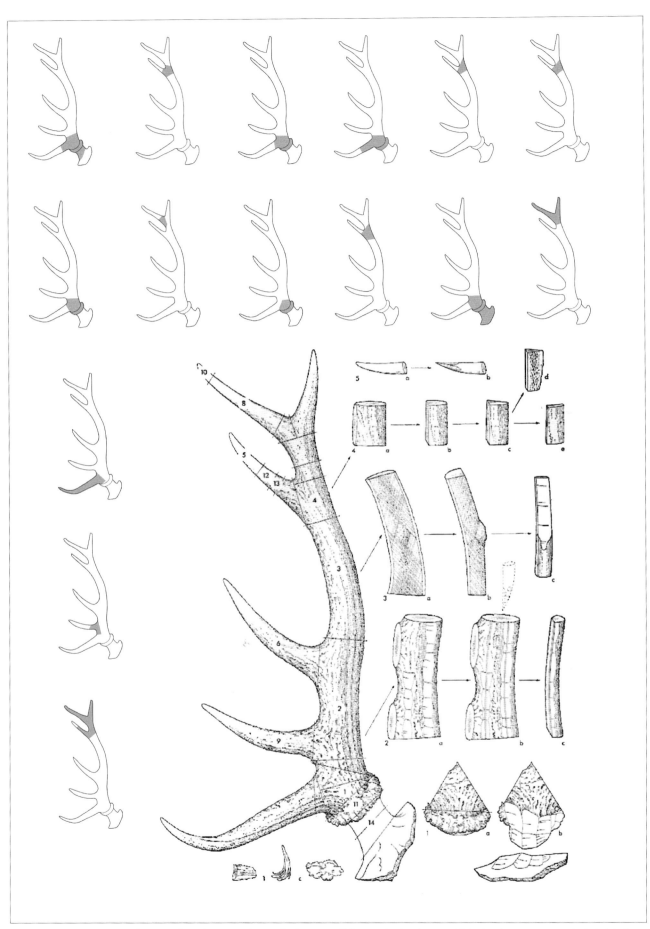

Figure 8.12 Antler offcuts and craft waste from ditch *5075* (fill *5074*), Enclosure 131, Settlement 7, Period 4.4 (after Ulbricht 1978, abb. 3)

also a herding dog (an indication of their possible appearance is given in Fig. 8.11). Infrequent remains of small non-brachymel dogs at Love's Farm include a proximal femur found in Period 4.5 (*5591*, ditch *5592*, Enclosure 139, Settlement 7) which is similar to, but slightly larger than, a specimen recovered from the High Street in Leicester (Baxter 2006a) and several bones belonging to a very young, apparently, short-faced puppy found by hand-collection in Period 4.5 well *5387* (fill *5893*, Settlement 7) and in sample residues from well fill *5889* (see below). This may possibly have been a Maltese-type lap dog (Baxter 2006a; MacKinnon and Belanger 2006). Some of these small dogs from Love's Farm and other Cambridgeshire sites are discussed in greater detail elsewhere (Baxter 2010a).

Pathologies affecting the dwarf hound (skeleton *8960*, Fig. 8.11) include a large abscess between the right lower P4 and M1, a broken and malunited 2nd metacarpal, and exostoses and eburnation typical of osteoarthritis on the distal humeri with corresponding exostoses on the proximal radii on both sides. The partial skeleton of a dog of around 34cm at the shoulder found in Period 4.3 (*13568–9*, ditch *13571*, Enclosure 115, Settlement 6) has a false joint medial to the trochlear notch of the left ulna resulting from an old dislocation of the articulation with the proximal radius. The partial skeleton of a dog with a withers height of 56cm found in Period 4.3 (*8004*, ditch *8003*, Enclosure 111, Settlement 6) has an impacted femur head, eburnated with exostoses at the junction of head and shaft, indicative of osteoarthritis following trauma. Many of these injuries are consistent with those to be expected from kicks or trampling delivered by domestic farm stock during herding.

Cat

Isolated cat bones were recovered from features dating from Periods 3.4 and 4.2–4.5 (Table 8.4). All of these are of domestic size when compared with published ranges (Kirk 1935; Kratochvil 1973, 1976; O'Connor 2007).

Domestic birds

The bones of domestic fowl (*Gallus* sp.) were recovered by hand from features dating from Periods 3.3 to 4.5 (Table 8.4) but are absent from the sample residues (Table 8.5). It is evident that chickens formed a minor element of domestic species in all periods. The infrequent remains of geese and ducks belonging to the genera *Anser* and *Anas* may include some domestic birds but, as they are indistinguishable from wild species, they are considered below.

Wild species

The most economically significant wild mammal remains recovered at Love's Farm are those of red deer (*Cervus elaphus*). Isolated bones and teeth were found in features dating from Periods 3.3, 3.4, 4.1 and 4.4. They include a mandible from a young animal aged around 10 months recovered from Period 3.3 (*10825*, ditch *10829*, Enclosure 1, Settlement 6). Antlers and antler off-cuts from craft working are much more frequent and occurred throughout the middle Iron Age to late Iron Age-Roman transition (Periods 3.2–3.5) and are particularly abundant in the later Romano-British period (Periods 4.4–4.5) (Table 8.4). The antlers derive from large forest-dwelling stags and include royals and imperials of 12 and 14 or more points respectively. Included amongst the assemblage are complete shed red deer antlers from imperials of 14 and 16 points found in Period 5 ditch *5592* (fill *5591*, Enclosure 139, Settlement 7; Pls 5.1 and 5.2).

A particularly large assemblage of red deer antler off-cuts came from Period 4.4 ditch *5075* (fill *5074*, Enclosure 131, Settlement 7). Figure 8.12 shows a comparison with a series published by Ulbricht (1978) illustrating the parts of antlers used in the manufacture of combs and smaller items, such as needles, at Haithabu in Schleswig-Holstein. Although some antler bases found at Love's Farm are still fixed to cranial fragments and probably derive from hunted animals, most antler bases have been cast and were seasonally collected as raw material. The much smaller roe deer (*Capreolus capreolus*) has always been of much less economic significance. A roe antler was found in Period 3.5 (*6233*, ditch *6223*, C-shaped Enclosure 6, Settlement 2) and a metatarsal in Period 4.4 (*9240*, ditch *9241*, Enclosure 104, Settlement 7).

Red fox (*Vulpes vulpes*) bones came from features dating from Periods 3.4 and 4.2. A fragmentary fox cranium was found in Period 3.3 (*13266*, ditch *13267*, Field System 1, Settlement 4), while a fox maxilla fragment and a slightly bowed juvenile dog or fox tibia from Period 4.2 (*8581*, ditch *8592*, Enclosure 12, Settlement 7). A fox 4th metacarpal found in Period 4.2 (*8550*, ditch *8551*, Enclosure 106, Settlement 6) has an oblique knife cut on the proximal joint surface. Isolated hare (*Lepus* sp.), mole (*Talpa europaea*) and badger (*Meles meles*) fragments were recovered from features dating from Periods 4.4 and 4.5 (Table 8.4). Rabbit (*Oryctolagus cuniculus*) bones found in two Period 4.5 contexts are certainly intrusive to these features.

Significant numbers of small mammal bones were found in environmental sample residues from Period 3.5 Enclosure 22, consisting of a penannular ditch encircling a smaller enclosure (Fig. 8.13). The assemblage from the inner northern terminal (Sample 725) principally consists of mouse and vole bones and teeth, with smaller numbers belonging to small fish, frogs, passerine birds, shrews and weasels. The bones do not appear to have been significantly fragmented or altered by digestive acids and both this fact and the species composition mean that the assemblage resembles what might be expected from the pellets of an owl (Andrews 1990; Martin 1992, 147). In Fig. 8.14 the relative frequency of taxa are compared with a Roman assemblage derived from barn owl pellets (*Tyto alba*) from the Drayton II villa site in Leicestershire (Baxter 1993). The passerines in the Love's Farm Enclosure 22 assemblages as a whole derive from sparrow to thrush-sized birds. The mustelids fragments certainly include both stoat (*Mustela erminea*) and weasel (*M. nivalis*) although several cannot be positively attributed to either species as female stoats and male weasels overlap in size.

The considerable assemblage of anuran amphibian, principally frog (*Rana* sp.), bones recovered from Period 4.3 (*13058*, ditch *13060*, Enclosure 117, Settlement 6) may represent animals trapped in a waterlogged feature during the breeding season, *i.e.* early February to the end of March (Burton 1960).

Wild bird remains recovered at low frequency by hand from Iron Age and Romano-British features include goose (*Anser/Branta* sp.), duck (*Anas* and *Aythya* sp.), raven

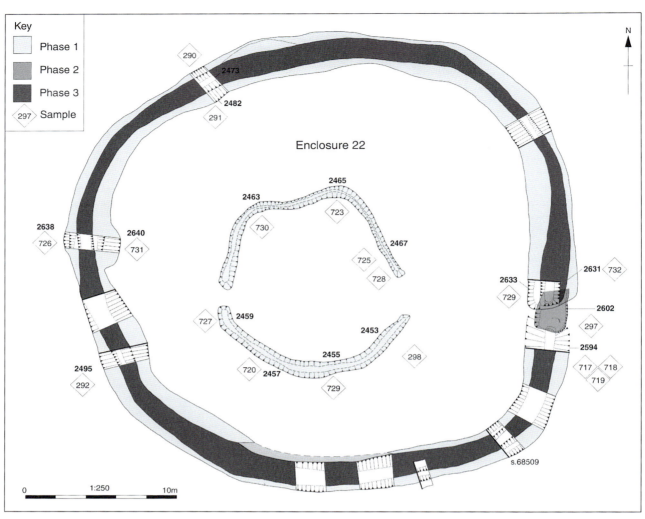

Figure 8.13 Location of samples taken from Enclosure 22, Period 3.5

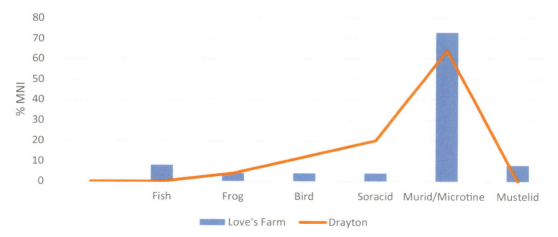

Figure 8.14 Enclosure 22 (*2466*), Period 3.5. Relative frequency of taxa compared with bones derived from owl pellets at Drayton II villa, Leics

(*Corvus corax*), rock dove (*Columba livia*), plover (*Pluvialis* sp.) and indeterminate passerines (Table 8.4).

The Late Roman well assemblage

Introduction
A total of 232 'countable' animal bone fragments came from the late Roman (Period 4.5) well *5387* in Settlement 7 (Table 8.7) and a further 37 fragments from the sieved environmental samples (Table 8.8). The well is located in Fig. 8.15, which also indicates the depositional sequence. Most of the bones are very fresh in appearance with very little fragmentation or canid gnawing. There is a much smaller number (<5%) of darker, more mineralised and fragmentary cattle bone fragments residual to the feature. None of these are sufficiently complete to be counted.

Frequency of species
Cattle are the most frequent taxon in the well deposits, accounting for 50% by number of identified fragments (NISP) of the main domestic species (Table 8.7). Sheep are next frequent at 43% of domesticates. No teeth or bones attributable to goat are present in the assemblage. Horse is more common than pig at 6% compared with 1%. Domestic dog, cat, red deer (antler only), hare, wood mouse, water vole and anuran amphibians are also present at low frequency.

Cattle
Cattle remains dominate the well assemblage both in terms of number of fragments and weight. The cattle are generally similar in their type and proportions to those recovered from other Romano-British sites in Cambridgeshire. Primarily short-horned beasts, some castrates (oxen) have horncores within the range of medium horns in the classification of Armitage (1982); the most complete crania (labelled A–F) are illustrated in Fig. 8.16. The horncores of skulls A, D and E are grooved. The morphology, age and sex estimations of the six most complete crania are presented in Table 8.9. The Love's Farm well cattle crania are equally divided into cows and oxen with the cows having pointed or prominent bosses when viewed from above and the oxen slightly convex frontal profiles (Grigson 1976). On the basis of the surface texture of the horncores (Armitage 1982) and the state of fusion of the parietal (Grigson 1982), all of the oxen and one cow were young adults and the other two cows were old adults.

Due to their completeness it was possible to take a number of measurements on the cattle crania. In the main they form a relatively homogenous group with the few noticeable differences probably attributable to sex. In Fig. 8.17 the cattle horncores from the well are compared with those from a sample of Iron Age and Romano-British sites in Cambridgeshire. In terms of both size and shape the oxen tend to form a distinct cluster. This figure also compares the same specimens with a large sample from Elms Farm, Heybridge, Essex. Two middle Iron Age crania from Lime's Farm, Landbeach (Baxter 2006b) provided a few measurements within the Love's Farm well range. The length of the molar row (von den Driesch 1976, measurement 21) for the five sufficiently complete Love's Farm well crania was compared with the same measurement for six cattle crania found at Springhead in

Taxon	Total
Cattle (*Bos* f. domestic)	115
Sheep/goat (*Ovis/Capra* f. domestic)	97
Sheep (*Ovis* f. domestic)	(44)
Red deer (*Cervus elaphus*)	+
Pig (*Sus scrofa*)	3
Horse (*Equus caballus*)	13
Dog (*Canis familiaris*)	2
Cat (*Felis catus*)	1
Hare (*Lepus* sp.)	1
Total	232

'Sheep/goat' also includes the specimens identified to species. Numbers in parentheses are not included in the total of the period. '+' means that the taxon is present but no specimens could be 'counted' (see text).

Table 8.7 Number of hand-collected mammal bones (NISP) from well *5387* (Settlement 7, Period 4.5)

Taxon	Total
Cattle (*Bos* f. domestic)	1
Sheep/goat (*Ovis/Capra* f. domestic)	11
Sheep (*Ovis* f. domestic)	(1)
Dog (*Canis familiaris*)	2[1]
Cat (*Felis catus*)	1
Mouse/vole (Murid/Microtine)	13
Wood mouse (*Apodemus* sp.)	(2)
Water vole (*Arvicola terrestris*)	(1)
Anuran amphibian (*Rana/Bufo* sp.)	9
Frog (*Rana* sp.)	(1)
Total	37

'Sheep/goat', 'Mouse/vole' and 'Anuran amphibian' also include the specimens identified to species. Numbers in parentheses are not included in the total of the period. '+' means that the taxon is present but no specimens could be 'counted' (see text).
[1] Includes 4 bones from a foot

Table 8.8 Number of mammal and amphibian bones in the sieved assemblage (NISP) from well *5387* (Settlement 7, Period 4.5)

Skull	Frontal profile	Intercornual ridge	Horncore	Age	Sex
A	Pointed boss	High single arch	Short horn	Young adult	Cow
B	Slightly convex	Low single arch	Medium horn	Young adult	Ox
C	Prominent boss	High double arch	Short horn	Old adult	Cow
D	Prominent boss	High double arch	Short horn	Old adult	Cow
E	Slightly convex	Low double arch	Short horn	Young adult	Ox
F	Slightly convex	High single arch	Short horn	Young adult	Ox

Table 8.9 Morphology, age and sex of the cattle crania from well *5387*. Based on Armitage and Clutton-Brock (1976), Armitage (1982) and Grigson (1976, 1982)

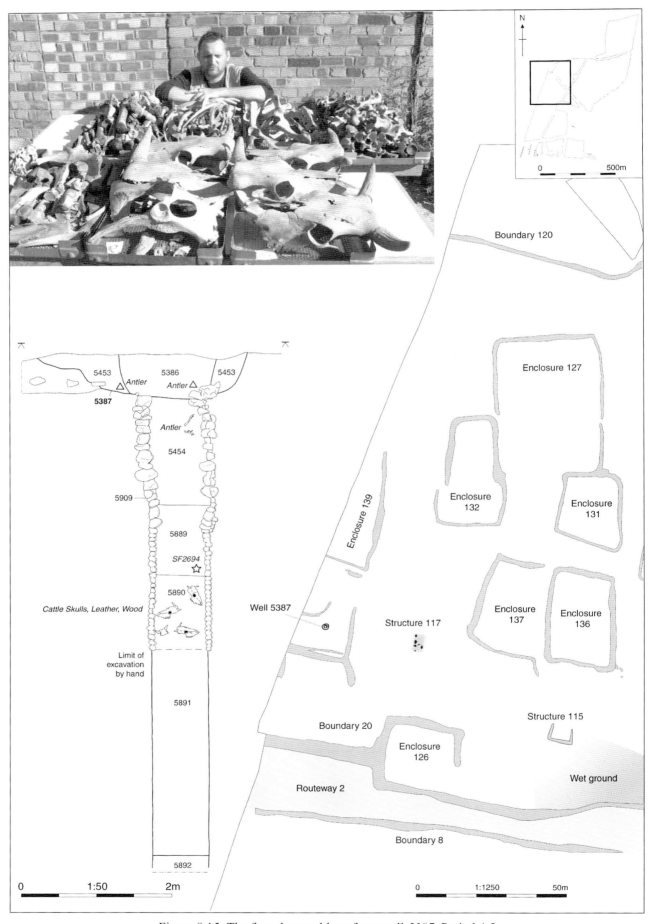

Figure 8.15 The faunal assemblage from well *5387*, Period 4.5

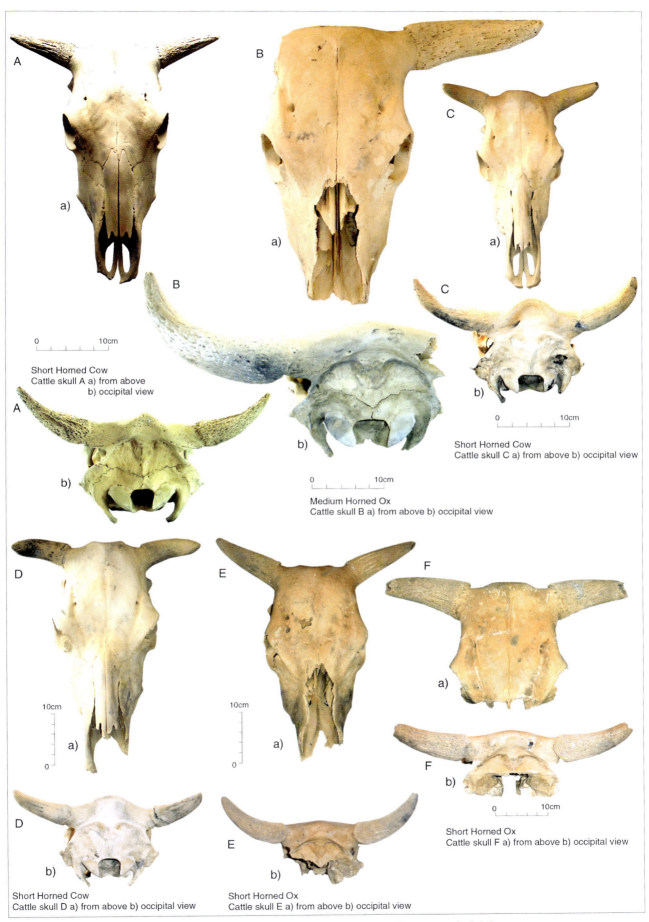

Figure 8.16 Cattle skulls from fill *5890*, well *5387*, Period 4.5

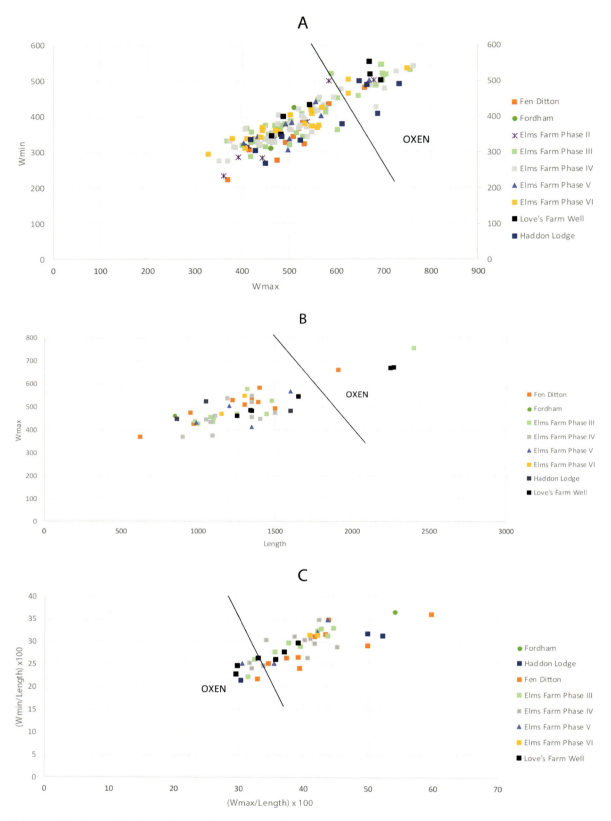

Figure 8.17 Well *5387*. Size (A and B) and shape (C) of cattle horncores compared with other Iron Age sites in Cambridgeshire. Haddon Lodge (A605/H and MSA 99), Landwade Road, Fordham (EIA) and Greenhouse Farm, Fen Ditton (MIA)

Kent, revealing that the Love's Farm cattle display a greater variation in size (Fig. 8.18).

The cattle mandibles from the well fall into two distinct groups comprising one juvenile and three immature, four adult and two elderly. The second grouping corresponds with the age estimations of the six crania given above. The postcrania suggest that most animals represented were aged over 2½ years and less than 3½ to 4 years based on epiphyseal fusion data collated by Grigson (1982) and Amorosi (1989). Most of the vertebral epiphyses are either unfused or in the process of fusing, confirming ages of less than 4–5 years for most of the animals present (Fig. 8.19). Sexable innominates (Grigson 1982) comprise two with male characteristics and five female (including four belonging to the same two individuals). Withers height estimations based on complete limb bones (Matolcsi 1970) range between 104cm to 128cm with a mean of 115cm (N = 19). The size and shape of the Love's Farm well cattle metapodials was compared with a selection of Iron Age and Romano-British from sites in Cambridgeshire. The Love's Farm well metacarpals closely group together with regard to both size and shape. There is more diversity in the size of the metatarsals which comprise two separate groups that probably represent cows and oxen. While there are some differences in metatarsal shape the sample size is small and the Love's Farm well cattle probably represent a single population or herd.

The minimum number of individuals (MNI) present in the well is seven (Table 8.10). When compared with the expected number of bones present in seven cattle skeletons it is evident that the well assemblage contains proportionately more head elements than any other part of the body and that vertebrae, appendicular limb bones and pelvic elements are half as frequent than they would be if whole, un-butchered skeletons had been deposited. Phalanges, carpals and tarsals are particularly under-represented. This situation is not improved in the residues of the environmental samples.

Pathologies include two cattle crania with occipital perforations (skulls B and C) and four metatarsals with broadened distal epiphyses. One distal metatarsal from fill *5890* has grooving and eburnation typical of osteoarthritis (Baker and Brothwell 1980) in addition to a broadened epiphysis and posterior exostoses. The left and right mandible of a single individual has the lower M3 3rd pillar or hypoconulid absent on both sides. Occipital perforations and absence of the lower M3 hypoconulid are congenitally determined and occur at variable frequencies in cattle populations (Manaseryan *et al.* 1999; Baxter 2002; Andrews and Noddle 1975; Davis 1997). Broadening of the distal epiphyses of cattle is typical of draught animals (Bartosiewicz *et al.* 1997). Crania B and E have depressions in their frontal bones possibly caused by a poleaxe or hammer. Butchery marks are scarce or absent on the postcranial bones.

Sheep

All of the caprid teeth and bones from the well that can be identified to species, amounting to 45% of the total, belong to sheep. It is therefore probably safe to assume that only sheep are represented in the assemblage. The sheep were horned and no polled or hornless crania were seen. One ewe cranium has rounded horncores, a variant occasionally seen in Romano-British assemblages. On

Figure 8.18 Well *5387*. Length of the molar row in the cattle crania, compared with those from Springhead, Kent. Springhead data supplied by Jessica Grimm

the basis of the horncore morphology, two rams and five ewes are present. However, all of the twelve innominates that could be sexed (Clutton-Brock *et al.* 1990) belong to ewes.

The eight ageable mandibles recovered primarily belong to sheep at wear stage C with lower M3 unworn, very approximately 2 years of age (six mandibles out of eight; or 75% of the total). Two mandibles belonging to younger animals were also recovered. No mandibles belonging to older sheep are present in the assemblage. On the basis of epiphyseal fusion (Fig. 8.19), approximately half of the sheep in the assemblage were aged less than 1½ to 2½ years and around a third were at least 2½ to 4 years of age (Zeder 2006). Many of the sheep vertebrae centra recovered have unfused epiphyses. It should be noted that, out of five specimens, no distal radii are fused and four out of thirteen distal femorae are fused or fusing, although fusion of the distal epiphyses of these bones would be expected to occur within the same time frame. However, the tooth and bone data is generally consistent in identifying the majority of the sheep in the well assemblage as aged around 2 years. In addition to the two mandibles referred to above, young sheep are represented by several perinatal fragments in fill *5890*, probably originating from a single individual. Withers height estimates based on complete bones (Teichert 1975) range between 55cm and 60cm with a mean of 58cm (N = 8). No pathologies or anomalies were seen on any of the sheep bones and teeth. Based on the innominate, which is the most numerous skeletal element in the well assemblage, a minimum (MNI) of twelve sheep are represented. Elements from the head and hind leg are half as frequent: vertebrae, carpals, tarsals and phalanges are well below numbers to be expected from complete skeletons.

Pig

Perinatal pig remains, probably belonging to the same individual, consisting of a humerus metaphysis and distal epiphysis and a tibia metaphysis were recovered from fill *5893*.

Element	Cattle			Sheep/goat			Pig		
	NISP	MNI	%	NISP	MNI	%	NISP	MNI	%
Upper deciduous + permanent incisors	-	-	-	-	-	-	-	-	0
Upper deciduous + permanent canine	-	-	-	-	-	-	-	-	0
Upper deciduous + permanent premolars	19	4	57	16	3	43	-	-	0
Upper M1/2	27	7	100	18	5	71	-	-	0
Upper M3	10	5	71	2	1	14	-	-	0
Lower deciduous + permanent incisors	2	1	14	-	-	0	-	-	0
Lower deciduous + permanent canine	-	-	-	-	-	-	-	-	0
Lower deciduous + permanent premolars	25	5	71	17	3	43	-	-	0
Lower M1/2	18	5	71	15	4	57	-	-	0
Lower M3	8	4	57	1	1	14	-	-	0
Horncore	14	7	100	13	7	100	-	-	0
Cranium	7	7	100	6	6	86	-	-	0
Atlas	4	4	57	3	3	43	-	-	0
Axis	4	4	57	4	4	57	-	-	0
Scapula	5	3	43	1	1	14	-	-	0
Humerus dist	8	4	57	7	4	57	1	1	100
Radius dist	8	4	57	5	3	43	-	-	0
Ulna prox	3	2	29	1	1	14	-	-	0
Carpal	1	1	14	-	-	0	-	-	0
Metacarpal dist	5	3	43	3	2	29	-	-	0
Pelvis acetabulum	8	4	57	13	7	100	-	-	0
Femur dist	5	3	43	13	7	100	-	-	0
Tibia dist	7	4	57	13	7	100	1	1	100
Astragalus	2	1	14	-	-	0	-	-	0
Calcaneum	4	2	29	1	1	14	-	-	0
Centrotarsale	-	-	0	-	-	0	-	-	0
Metatarsal dist	7	4	57	4.5	3	43	-	-	0
Phalanx 1 prox	3	1	14	-	-	0	-	-	0
Phalanx 2 prox	1	1	14	-	-	0	-	-	0
Phalanx 3 prox	2	1	14	-	-	0	-	-	0

Unfused epiphyses are not counted. Only hand-collected material is included. The MNI has been calculated as follows: incisors have been divided by 8 for cattle and sheep/goat and by 6 for pig, deciduous + permanent premolars by 6, M1/2 by 4, phalanges by 8 and all other elements, except metapodials and vertebrae, by 2. Metacarpal = (MC1 + MC2/2 + MP1/2 + MP2/4) / 2; Metatarsal = (MT1 + MT2/2 + MP1/2 + MP2/4) /2, where: MC1 = complete distal metacarpal; MC2 = half distal metacarpal; MT1 = complete distal metatarsal; MT2 = half distal metatarsal; MP1 = complete distal metapodial; MP2 = half distal metapodial. Pig metapodials are considered the equivalent of cattle and sheep/goat half metapodials. % = frequency of an element in relation to the most common one (by MNI).

Table 8.10 Body parts of the main domestic mammals from well *5387*, by number of fragments (NISP) and minimum number of individuals (MNI)

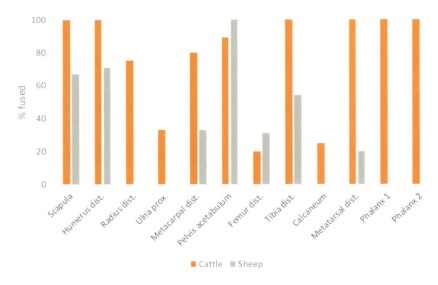

Figure 8.19 Well *5387*. Percentage of fused epiphyses for cattle and sheep

Other domestic mammals

Horse
Horse bones are relatively frequent in the well deposits. They derive from at least two individuals: an animal of around 13½ hands (134–136cm) represented by two metacarpals, and a larger horse of 14 hands (138–140cm) represented by a radius and metacarpal (May 1985). One of the smaller 3rd metacarpals has the 4th metacarpal fused to it with exostoses, probably the result of trauma.

Dog
Several bones belonging to a very young short-faced puppy were found by hand-collection in fill *5893* and in sample residues from fill *5889*. This would appear to be a Maltese type lap dog (Baxter 2006a; MacKinnon and Belanger 2006). The toothless mandible of a medium sized dog was recovered from fill *5889* and an isolated I1 from a sample residue from the same context, probably belonging to the same animal.

Cat
The fibula of a cat was found in fill *5893* and there was a 1st phalanx in a sample from fill *5889*.

Wild species
Red deer (*Cervus elaphus*) antlers (SF 2515 and 2516) were placed on top of the well deposits (fills *5453* and *5386*, see Fig. 8.15). These are very fragmentary but include four cast bases. An antler base and beam fragment from fill *5454* has several cut marks posterior to the base of the brow tine. An indication of the type of products being made comes in the form of an antler comb from the well itself (SF 3158, see Crummy, Chapter 6.IX), while an assemblage of antler working off-cuts was retrieved from a Period 4.4 ditch, also in Settlement 7 (see above). Red deer shed their antlers in spring between mid March and mid May (Legge and Rowley-Conwy 1988) and this may have been when the well deposit was closed. Although antler was almost certainly conserved for use as a raw material, the presence of neonatal sheep and pig bones may be taken as further evidence for spring closure.

An isolated hare (*Lepus* sp.) proximal ulna was found in well fill *5889*. This has a small canine puncture caused by a cat or small dog. Sample residues from fill *5889* include the bones and teeth of wood mouse (*Apodemus* sp.) and water vole (*Arvicola terrestris*). Like the small rodents, anuran amphibians comprise pit-fall victims in the sample residues of fills *5434*, *5889* and *5890*. Where identified, the remains belong to frog (*Rana* sp.).

Discussion
Throughout its occupation, the husbandry regime at Love's Farm was that of mixed farming with no significant evidence of specialisation in terms of animal products. In all the main periods of occupation sheep were the most numerous animals, followed by cattle. Pigs were kept on a relatively minor scale. Horses were an important item of stock in both the Iron Age and Roman periods and, together with dogs, were most probably primarily employed in herding the food species. While from the zooarchaeological evidence there is no obvious change in the status of the Love's Farm site from the Iron Age to the Romano-British periods, improvement in the cattle stock certainly occurred in the Roman period either through more efficient husbandry methods, the introduction of breeding stock, or most probably a combination of these. Any increase in the size of the horses at the site is much less significant and for sheep the evidence is lacking. Whilst the remains of dwarf hounds and other small dogs do occur sporadically in the British Iron Age they become significantly more numerous during the Roman period. Lap dogs of 'Maltese'/Melitean type (possibly represented by the puppy skeleton found in Period 4.5 well *5387*) are certainly an introduction from the Mediterranean. They are mentioned by Roman authors, including Pliny, and frequently illustrated by the Greeks and Romans (Brewer *et al.* 2001, 94, figs 5.4 and 5.5). However, the 'breed' (*sensu lato*) identification of the *5387* puppy is extremely tenuous and based entirely on the qualitative diagnosis of the partial maxilla as 'short faced'.

In terms of evidence for 'ritual' deposition at the site, the dog, cattle and horse crania deposited in ditches and other features are fairly convincing examples of placed deposits and may be plausibly interpreted as part of foundation or closure rituals associated with the god Terminus (*cf*. Merrifield 1987). The same may be the case with Period 4.5 well *5387* in Settlement 7. There are numerous examples of wells and shafts infilled with inclusions suggestive of ritual deposition dating from Roman times, usually including dogs: *e.g.* Springhead, Kent (Grimm 2012), Baldock, (Chaplin and McCormick 1986), High Street, Leicester (Baxter 1993), Great Holme Street, Leicester (Gouldwell 1991), and Thistleton, Rutland (Baxter 2010b). These have been interpreted as ritual deposits with the dogs acting as messengers to the chthonic powers (*cf*. Green 1997; Merrifield 1987).

Whilst the hunting of deer for meat is infrequently attested and was very much a marginal activity economically, red deer antler was a valuable natural resource and is frequently found on Cambridgeshire sites during the Iron Age and Roman periods in both unmodified form, most frequently as seasonally collected shed antlers, and as off-cuts from working. There is evidence for the utilisation of antler for craft-working throughout the occupation of the Love's Farm site from the middle Iron Age onwards, but red deer antler off-cuts and craft waste are particularly concentrated in Period 4.4 ditch *5075* (*5074*; Enclosure 131, Settlement 7), possibly suggesting that a specialised workshop was located in the vicinity at this time. It is also possible that antler products (such as combs, metal-working hammers, pins and needles *etc*.) may have been produced here for trading with other centres as well as for use within the settlement. The deposition of particularly large cast antlers in Period 4.5 ditch *5592* (*5591*, Enclosure 139, Settlement 7) and on top of the Period 4.5 well *5387* deposits (*5453* and *5386*) also in Settlement 7 may represent a form of closure ritual or, more prosaically, the disposal of unwanted conserved raw material for craft-working.

Conclusions
In common with other sites in the region, the husbandry regime at Love's Farm throughout its long occupation was that of mixed farming with no significant evidence of specialisation in terms of animal products. In both the Iron Age and Roman periods sheep were the most numerous animals kept, followed by cattle. Pigs were kept on a relatively minor scale. No information is available concerning the export of surplus stock to consumer sites as

such animals will almost certainly have been transported on the hoof. The proximity of the Love's Farm site to the major artery of Ermine Street would have facilitated the transport of animals to military and urban sites for slaughter during the Roman period. The lack of investigation of what may be assumed to be related local markets in the towns of Godmanchester and perhaps *Dubrobrivae* (Water Newton) and *Duroliponte* (Cambridge) is a considerable handicap to the elucidation of the local economy at this time.

IV. Plant remains
by Val Fryer

Introduction and methods
A total of 1,152 samples for the retrieval of the plant macrofossil assemblages were taken from a variety of features at Love's Farm. All were bulk processed by Oxford Archaeology East, with the flots being collected in a 300 micron mesh sieve. All flots were dried prior to an initial evaluation of their content (Fryer 2009), which showed that sixty-four assemblages (approximately 5% of the total number of samples taken) contained a sufficient density of material for quantification (*i.e.* 100+ specimens). The remaining assemblages were mostly small (0.1 litres in volume or less), sparse and principally composed of charcoal/charred wood fragments. Some 287 flots were completely devoid of either charred or de-watered plant remains.

The flots were sorted under a binocular microscope at magnifications up to x16 and the plant macrofossils and other remains noted in selected assemblages are listed in Tables 8.11–8.12, where counts of cereal grains include only whole grains and/or embryo ends. Nomenclature within the tables follows Stace (1997) and identifications were made by comparison with modern reference specimens. Tabulated remains were charred unless otherwise indicated. Six assemblages contained de-watered macrofossils.

Sample composition
Although most of the recorded macrofossils are reasonably well preserved, some assemblages show evidence of extremely high temperatures of combustion, which resulted in severely puffed, distorted and fragmented grains. In other instances, chaff elements are heavily abraded and fragmented, possibly as a result of either prolonged exposure prior to burial or post-depositional disturbance. The de-watered macrofossils are generally well preserved, although some remains are distorted as a result of the compaction of the deposits.

Cereal grains and/or chaff are present throughout all of the quantified samples, forming a major component of many of the assemblages studied. Oat (*Avena* sp.), barley (*Hordeum* sp.) and wheat (*Triticum* sp.) grains are present, along with a single possible specimen of rye (*Secale cereale*) from a Roman rubbish pit (*14008=13265*) in Settlement 6 (Period 4.3). However, wheat is predominant throughout, presumably because of its suitability for production on the heavier clay soils of the St Neots area. Most grains are of an elongated 'drop-form' shape typical of spelt (*T. spelta*) or emmer (*T. dicoccum*), although a number of more rounded hexaploid form grains of probable bread wheat (*T. aestivum/compactum*) type were also recorded, most notably within pit *14008* noted above. Germinated wheat grains with attached sprouts, some possibly derived from the malting of grain prior to brewing, were also noted within the assemblages from Sample 1521 of the same rubbish pit along with Sample 1503 (from boundary ditch *13781*, Period 3.3, Settlement 4) and Sample 1266 (oven *11801*, Period 4.2, Settlement 6). Possible gristed or roughly milled wheat grains, with rounded broken surfaces, were found within the ditch and pit assemblages. Double-keeled spelt glume bases are particularly abundant throughout, although more slender emmer glume bases are also present, along with occasional bread wheat type rachis nodes with diagnostic crescentic glume inserts.

Oat grains and/or awn fragments occur within thirty-four assemblages, although in only one instance (Sample 499, ditch *5718*, Period 4.4, Settlement 7) can the remains be closely identified as wild oat (*A. fatua*) floret bases, with diagnostic 'sucker-mouth' basal abscission scars. Barley occurs relatively infrequently, with possible asymmetrical lateral grains of the six-row variety *H. vulgare* being noted in only two samples (Sample 319, ditch *4967*, Boundary 112, Period 4.4, Settlement 7 and Sample 738, posthole *8362*, Structure 116, Period 4.2, Settlement 6). The only other cultivated food crop remains noted are large, angular seeds of field beans (*Vicia faba*) and cotyledon fragments of indeterminate large pea/bean type pulses (Fabaceae).

Charred seeds of segetal weeds and grassland herbs occur within many of the assemblages studied, although rarely at a high density. The taxa noted most frequently include stinking mayweed (*Anthemis cotula*), corn cockle (*Agrostemma githago*), orache (*Atriplex* sp.), brome (*Bromus* sp.), small legumes (Fabaceae), medick/clover/trefoil (*Medicago/Trifolium/Lotus* sp.), grasses (Poaceae), knotgrass (*Polygonum aviculare*), dock (*Rumex* sp.) and vetch/vetchling (*Vicia/Lathyrus* sp.). Macrofossils within the six de-watered assemblages indicate that, from the later Iron Age (Period 3.5) through to the late Roman period (Period 4.5), rough, grassland conditions were locally predominant, with species recorded including fool's parsley (*Aethusa cynapium*), great burdock (*Arctium lappa*), musk thistle (*Carduus* sp.), hemlock (*Conium maculatum*), wild carrot (*Daucus carota*), fairy and perennial flax (*Linum catharticum* and *L. perenne*), mallow (*Malva* sp.), meadow/creeping/bulbous buttercup (*Ranunculus acris/repens/bulbosus*), sow thistle *(Sonchus asper* and *S. oleraceus*), chickweed (*Stellaria media*), hedge parsley (*Torilis japonica*) and stinging nettles (*Urtica dioica*). Of particular interest within the de-watered assemblages are the seeds of sainfoin (*Onobrychis viciifolia*), a plant which was once thought to have been only an occasional post-glacial relict and re-introduced from the Low Countries in the post-medieval period, but which has been recorded from an increasing number of medieval, Roman and now Iron Age deposits.

Evidence from the waterlogged and dewatered assemblages indicates that some features may have been sufficiently wet to sustain limited aquatic flora, including plants such as duckweed (*Lemna* sp.), water crowfoot (*Ranunculus* subg. *Batrachium*) and horned pondweed (*Zannichellia* sp.). This is, perhaps, not surprising, given the high water table across the excavated area. The late Iron Age quarry within Settlement 2 (Quarry 4, *120062*) probably became overgrown with trees and woody shrubs including maple (*Acer* sp.), hawthorn (*Crataegus* sp.), sloe (*Prunus spinosa*), brambles (*Rubus* sect. *Glandulosus*) and elderberry (*Sambucus nigra*). Examination of the pollen from the same quarry (Green and Boreham below) indicates the presence of hazel, juniper, birch, alder and ivy. The insect remains provide a well-preserved and interpretable assemblage, indicating dry open pasture and nearby hedgerows and/or wood pasture (Tetlow below).

Charcoal/charred wood fragments are present throughout, although rarely at a very high density. Other plant macrofossils occur infrequently, but include indeterminate de-watered moss fronds, twig fragments and thorns, and charred pieces of root/stem, inflorescence fragments and tubers.

Given the extended period of site use it is, perhaps, surprising that so few other remains were recorded within the assemblages. The pieces of black porous and tarry material are probable residues of the combustion of organic remains (including cereal grains) at very high temperatures. Possible domestic midden residues include fragments of bone (some of which are burnt), eggshell and fish bone. Water flea eggs (*Cladoceran ephippia*), ostracods and de-watered arthropod remains were recorded within the de-watered assemblages. Other remains include small pellets of burnt or fired clay, splinters of burnt stone, siliceous globules, small mammal and/or amphibian bones and small pieces of coal, although it is assumed that some or all of the latter were intrusive within the contexts from which the samples were taken.

The Iron Age (Period 3)

Settlements and miscellaneous Iron Age features
Eight potential Iron Age settlement areas were identified during excavation. However, although features were extensively sampled, only seven assemblages from Settlements 2, 4 and 6 (together with a further four from miscellaneous contemporary features) contain a sufficient density of material for quantification. Perhaps surprisingly, this is not particularly unusual, as it would appear that Iron Age habitation areas were frequently kept scrupulously clean, with refuse being deposited either in pits or in any nearby open feature (most notably within ditch fills, *cf.* Colchester Garrison, Fryer 2004a). This latter practice is certainly the case within Settlements 1, 3, 5, 7 and 8, where the few charred remains recorded (primarily charcoal/charred wood fragments but including some grain and chaff) are predominantly from the enclosure ditch fills and well away from the domestic foci. Within the few charred assemblages which have been quantified from Settlements 4 and 6, only two are from structural features of middle to late Iron Age date. Sample 134 (hearth *50144*, Period 3.2, Settlement 4), contains an extremely low density of cereals, chaff and charcoal/charred wood fragments, all of which are probably derived from domestic hearth waste. Although the small assemblage from Sample 866 (posthole *8825*, Structure 6, Period 3.3, Settlement 6) is grain dominant, only 133 whole grains were recorded along with a moderate density of indeterminate grain fragments. It is, perhaps, most likely that these are the remains of foodstuffs, which were accidentally spilled and charred during culinary preparation.

Cereals, chaff and weed seeds are also present within the remaining five quantified assemblages of Iron Age date, although mostly at a low to moderate density (that is, between three and thirty specimens per litre of soil sampled). No one category of material is consistently predominant and, as most of the recorded detritus is probably derived from the burning of waste generated by the day to day processing of cereals for immediate consumption (*cf.* van der Veen 2006), there is insufficient data to ascertain the precise agricultural status of the site. However, evidence from the de-watered plant macrofossil assemblages and the pollen samples (see Green and Boreham, below), appears to indicate that rough grassland conditions were locally prevalent, possibly suggesting that a mixed economy of agriculture and pastoralism was in operation during the later Iron Age.

Enclosure 22
Samples for the retrieval of the plant macrofossil assemblages were taken from segments of the inner and outer ditches and from burnt deposits, which had been placed within or adjacent to the entranceways of both parts of a large double-ditched enclosure (Enclosure 22, Period 3.5, Fig. 8.13). It was suggested on site that these burnt deposits (originally thought to be cremations) might relate to acts of closure. The material within twenty of these assemblages was scanned and the plant macrofossils and other remains noted are listed on Table 8.11. All plant remains are charred. Modern contaminants, including fibrous roots, seeds and arthropods, are present throughout.

With the exception of charcoal/charred wood fragments, plant macrofossils are relatively scarce, only occurring at a higher frequency within the burnt deposits. Preservation is generally quite poor, with a high density of the grains and seeds being severely puffed and distorted, probably as a result of combustion at very high temperatures. Plant remains within a number of the assemblages are also heavily abraded, possibly indicating that they were exposed to the elements for some considerable time prior to burial.

Oat (*Avena* sp.), barley (*Hordeum* sp.) and wheat (*Triticum* sp.) grains are present, mostly as single specimens within an assemblage. Cereal chaff is exceedingly rare, but spelt wheat (*T. spelta*) glume bases are present in Samples 298 (inner ditch segment *2453*) and 732 (outer ditch segment *2631*). Seeds of common weeds and grassland herbs are also rare, occurring exclusively within the burnt deposits or their adjacent fills. Taxa noted include small legumes (Fabaceae), black bindweed (*Fallopia convolvulus*), goosegrass (*Galium aparine*), grasses (Poaceae), ribwort plantain (*Plantago lanceolata*), dock (*Rumex* sp.) and vetch/vetchling (*Vicia/Lathyrus* sp.). A single sedge (*Carex* sp.) nutlet found in Sample 724 is the sole wetland plant macrofossil recorded. Charcoal/charred wood fragments are present throughout, although rarely at a high density. Other plant macrofossils include pieces of charred root or stem and indeterminate seeds and tuber fragments.

Twelve samples were taken from fills within the outer ditch. With the exception of Sample 719 (from the lower fill of the southern ditch terminus), the assemblages all contain a low density of cereals and/or weed seeds, with a

Sample no.	298	720	723	725	727	728	729	730	290	291
Context no.	2452	2456	2464	2466	2458	2641	2454	2462	2472	2481
Feature/cut no.	2453	2457	2465	2467	2459	2467	2455	2463	2473	2482
Ditch	Inner	Inner	Inner	Inner	Inner	Inner	Inner	Inner	Outer	Outer
Cereals										
Avena sp. (grain)	x	-	-	-	-	-	-	-	-	-
Hordeum sp. (grains)	xcf	-	-	xcf	-	-	-	-	-	xcf
Triticum sp. (grains)	xx	-	-	xcf	-	xcf	-	-	-	-
(glume bases)	x	-	-	-	-	-	-	-	-	-
T. spelta L. (glume bases)	x	-	-	-	-	-	-	-	-	-
Cereal indet. (grains)	xxx	-	-	xx	-	-	-	x	xcf	-
Herbs						-	-	-	-	-
Chenopodiaceae indet.	-	-	-	x	-	-	-	-	-	-
Fabaceae indet.	xx	-	-	x	-	-	-	-	-	-
Fallopia convolvulus (L.) A.Love	-	-	-	-	-	-	-	-	-	-
Galium sp.	-	-	-	x	-	-	-	-	-	-
G. aparine L.	x	-	-	-	-	-	-	-	-	-
Lapsana communis L.	xcf	-	-	-	-	-	-	-	-	-
Medicago/Trifolium/Lotus sp.	xcf	-	-	-	-	-	-	-	-	-
Plantago lanceolata L.	x	-	-	-	-	-	-	-	-	-
Small Poaceae indet.	x	-	-	-	-	-	-	-	-	-
Large Poaceae indet.	-	-	-	x	-	-	-	-	-	-
Polygonaceae indet.	-	-	-	x	-	-	-	-	-	-
Rumex sp.	-	-	-	-	-	-	-	-	-	-
Rumex acetosella L.	-	-	-	x	-	-	-	-	-	-
Sheradia arvensis L.	x	-	-	-	-	-	-	-	-	-
Valerianella dentata (L.) Pollich	x	-	-	-	-	-	-	-	-	-
Vicia/Lathyrus sp.	-	-	-	-	-	-	-	-	-	-
Wetland plants										
Carex sp.	-	-	-	-	-	-	-	-	-	-
Other plant macrofossils										
Charcoal <2mm	xxxx	x	x	xxxx	x	xxx	x	x	xxx	x
Charcoal >2mm	xx	-	-	x	-	x	-	x	x	-
Charred root/stem	xx	-	-	x	-	x	-	-	x	-
Characeae indet.	x	-	-	-	-	-	-	-	-	-
Indet. seeds	x	-	-	-	-	-	-	-	-	-
Indet. tuber	x	-	-	-	-	-	-	-	-	-
Other materials										
Black porous 'cokey' material	xxx	-	-	x	-	x	-	x	x	-
Black tarry material	x	-	-	x	-	-	-	-	-	-
Bone	x xxb	-	x	x xb	-	xb	x	x	xx xxb	-
Burnt/fired clay	x	-	-	-	-	-	-	-	x	-
Small mammal/amphibian bone	x xb	-	-	x	-	-	x	-	x	x
Volume of flot (litres)	0.1	<0.1	<0.1	0.1	<0.1	<0.1	<0.1	<0.1	<0.1	<0.1
% flot sorted	100%	100%	100%	100%	100%	100%	100%	100%	100%	100%

Table 8.11 Plant macrofossils from Enclosure 22 (Period 3.5). See Fig. 8.13 for sample locations

small concentration of material within burnt deposit *2602* (Sample 297). Charcoal/charred wood fragments are relatively scarce. The composition of the mollusc assemblages (see Fryer and Fosberry, below) appears to indicate that although the outer ditch was at least seasonally water filled, the enclosure itself was probably situated within an area of predominantly short-turfed open grassland.

Although charred plant remains are present within all of the outer ditch assemblages, in most cases there is insufficient material to be indicative of deliberate deposition. The abraded condition of the macrofossils may well indicate that they are primarily derived from wind-blown detritus, which was accidentally incorporated within the ditch fills. The only possible exception to this is a burnt deposit (Sample 297), which appears to have been deliberately placed between the ditch termini as part of the closure of the eastern entranceway to the enclosure during the later Roman period.

The assemblages of the eight samples from the inner ditch are of particular interest, their composition being noticeably different from those of the outer ditch. The two

Sample no.	292	297	717	718	719	724	726	731	732	733
Context no.	2496	2516	2593	2599	2601	2634	2637	2639	2630	2632
Feature/cut no.	2495	2602	2594	2594	2594	2633	2638	2640	2631	2633
Ditch	Outer	Outer	Outer	Outer	Outer	Outer	Outer	Outer	Outer	Outer
Cereals										
Avena sp. (grain)	-	-	-	-	-	-	-	-	-	-
Hordeum sp. (grains)	-	-	-	-	-	-	-	-	-	-
Triticum sp. (grains)	-	x	-	-	-	-	x	-	-	-
(glume bases)	x	-	-	-	-	-	-	-	-	-
T. spelta L. (glume bases)	-	-	-	-	-	-	-	-	x	-
Cereal indet. (grains)	x	x	x	x	-	x	-	-	-	-
Herbs	-	-	-	-	-	-	-	-	-	-
Chenopodiaceae indet.	-	-								
Fabaceae indet.						x				
Fallopia convolvulus (L.) A.Love	-	x	-	-	-	xtf	-	-	-	-
Galium sp.	-									
G. aparine L.	-	-	-	-	-	-	-	-	-	-
Lapsana communis L.	-	-	-	-	-	-	-	-	-	-
Medicago/Trifolium/Lotus sp.	-	-	-	-	-	-	-	-	-	-
Plantago lanceolata L.	-	-	-	-	-	-	-	-	-	-
Small Poaceae indet.	-	-	-	-	-	x	-	-	-	-
Large Poaceae indet.	-	x	-	-	-	-	-	-	-	-
Polygonaceae indet.	-	-	-	x	-	-	-	-	-	-
Rumex sp.	-	x	-	-	-	-	-	-	-	-
Rumex acetosella L.	-	-	-	-	-	-	-	-	-	-
Sheradia arvensis L.	-	-	-	-	-	-	-	-	-	-
Valerianella dentata (L.) Pollich	-	-	-	-	-	-	-	-	-	-
Vicia/Lathyrus sp.	-	x	-	-	-	-	-	-	-	-
Wetland plants										
Carex sp.	-	-	-	-	-	x	-	-	-	-
Other plant macrofossils										
Charcoal <2mm	x	x	x	x	x	xxx	x	-	xx	x
Charcoal >2mm	x	x	-	x	-	x	-	-	-	-
Charred root/stem	-	-	x	-	-	-	-	-	-	-
Characeae indet.	-	x	-	-	-	-	-	-	-	-
Indet. seeds	-	-	x	-	-	-	-	-	-	-
Indet. tuber	-	-	-	-	-	-	-	-	-	-
Other materials										
Black porous 'cokey' material	x	xx	-	-	-	xx	-	-	-	-
Black tarry material	-	-	-	-	-	x	x	-	-	-
Bone	-	xb	-	-	-	x xb	-	-	x xb	-
Burnt/fired clay	-	-	-	-	-	-	x	-	-	-
Small mammal/amphibian bone	-	-	-	-	-	-	-	-	-	-
Volume of flot (litres)	<0.1	<0.1	<0.1	<0.1	<0.1	<0.1	<0.1	<0.1	<0.1	<0.1
% flot sorted	100%	100%	100%	100%	100%	100%	100%	100%	100%	100%

Table 8.11 cont.

burnt deposits (Samples 298 and 725), from the termini of the ditches flanking the east-facing entrance to the central area, are the only samples of those studied from within the inner ditch which contain assemblages of charred plant remains. Both yielded a moderate to high density of cereals and grassland plant seeds, the latter possibly being indicative of the use of dried plant material for kindling or fuel. Charcoal/charred wood fragments are also marginally more abundant. The mollusc assemblages (see below) are dominated by open country species, with freshwater taxa only occurring within the deposits close to the eastern entrance. While they indicate that the central area was dry and open, the east-facing ditch termini both contain small numbers of freshwater snails, possibly suggesting that these parts of the ditch were deeper and wetter.

Four-post structures

Three four-post structures were associated with Settlement 3 (Period 3.3). Such structures appear very frequently on sites of Iron Age and Romano-British date, yet their purpose is still far from fully understood with interpretations varying from grain stores to funerary platforms. The assemblages from four-post Structure 3 (Samples 805–806) both contain some chaff and grain but are, perhaps, more of note for the number of seeds of grassland plants, particularly vetch/vetchling. The assemblage from the second structure is similarly composed (Structure 4, Samples 807, 809 and 816) and it is therefore tentatively suggested that both of these structures may have served as supports for hay ricks. That the material within the postholes is charred may indicate that both structures were destroyed by fire.

Romano-British (Period 4)

Settlement 6
As with the Iron Age contexts, although extensive sampling of features associated with Settlement 6 was undertaken, only thirty-eight assemblages contain sufficient material for quantification. Of these, eight are pit assemblages assigned to Periods 4.1 and 4.2 (1st to 2nd century AD). The assemblage from Sample 897 (pit *8895*) is somewhat unusual as, although small (0.1 litres in volume), it is weed-dominant with seeds, particularly those of grasses and grassland herbs, outnumbering the other remains by approximately 2:1. A small number of entire spelt spikelets, with the grains still tightly enclosed within the glumes, are also present and it is, perhaps, most likely that this assemblage is derived from a small deposit of mixed refuse including burnt flooring or bedding materials and cereal processing/parching waste, although it must be said that evidence for the latter is scant.

The assemblages from Samples 1498 and 1499, both from pit *13817* (Period 4.1), contain moderately high densities of chaff and are probably derived from cereal processing waste, which was either burnt immediately after it was generated or subsequently used as fuel. High densities of chaff are also present within two pits (Sample 1200, pit *11445* and Sample 1504, pit *13851*, both Period 4.2), although, unlike the previous two samples, grains and a number of detached cereal sprouts are also present. It is tentatively suggested that these assemblages are derived from detritus generated by the deliberate germination of cereals during the malting process. Similar assemblages were recorded from a slightly later Roman granary/maltings at Beck Row, Suffolk (Fryer 2004b). The remaining pit assemblages contain a far lower density of material, much of which is probably derived from scattered or wind-blown refuse, which accidentally accumulated within the feature fills.

Small deposits of charred waste also appear to have accumulated or been placed within the various enclosure, drainage and boundary ditches associated with Settlement 6. Sample 1511 (from enclosure ditch *13931*, Period 4.1) is of particular interest as it contains a high density (approximately 94 grains per litre of soil sampled) of very poorly preserved wheat grains. Most of the grains are missing some or all of the dorsal surface and many are also distinctly concave in profile or totally hollow. The broken surfaces of the cereals are often covered with a tarry substance, making the grains appear 'melted', and it is assumed that this assemblage is derived from a batch of germinated or malted grain, some of which may have been roughly milled prior to charring. Burning obviously occurred at an extremely high temperature, and may have been the result of an accidental fire during the malt drying process. Cereal processing waste, in the form of chaff-rich assemblages, came from ditches *13528* (Sample 1470, Period 4.1), *11480* (Sample 1253, Period 4.2) and *13815* (Sample 1497, Period 4.4), although this may not necessarily be indicative of on-site processing since such waste was commonly traded as fuel throughout the Roman period (van der Veen 1999).

A number of structures were also located within Settlement 6. The abundance of cereal sprouts within the Period 4.2 oven assemblages (ovens *9567* and *9836*, Samples 1266, 1267 and 1268) may indicate that, at least in their latter stages, the ovens were used for malt drying, possibly prior to brewing. However, it should be noted that such structures were probably multi-functional, serving a number of domestic and light industrial purposes. The ovens appear to have been at least partly fuelled by cereal processing waste, although dried grasses and grassland herbs may have been used as kindling. Similarly, samples from the Period 4.2 corn drier (fills *6706=6710=6717*, corn drier *6727*, Samples 601, 602 and 609) may have been used for purposes other than the drying and parching of grain prior to threshing. Wheat chaff is abundant within the drier contexts, probably indicating that yet again, the principal fuel used within the structure was cereal processing waste, although in this instance, charcoal/charred wood fragments are also common.

The postholes of two structures (Structure 116: a post-built building of 2nd-century date, Sample 669, Period 4.2; and Structure 105: a large timber building dating to the 3rd century, Sample 893, Period 4.3), produced assemblages which are moderately grain-rich. Both assemblages also contain charred seeds of grasses and grassland herbs, charcoal/charred wood fragments and small pieces of burnt bone, and in addition the samples from Structure 116 include fragmentary large pulse (pea/bean type) seeds. It is, perhaps, most likely that these assemblages are derived from small quantities of domestic hearth waste or culinary detritus.

Four of the most striking assemblages recovered from Settlement 6 came from the fills of a shallow rubbish pit (*14008=13625*, Period 4.3), which was dug into an existing drainage ditch terminus (*13822*). All four assemblages are particularly grain-rich, containing oats, barley, elongated and rounded wheat grains and a single possible specimen of rye. Complete spelt spikelets are recorded within Samples 1478 and 1520, and the grain to chaff ratio of approximately 1:1, noted within Samples 1520 and 1521, is also consistent with the presence of two-grained spikelets. However, within Sample 1478, the grain to chaff ratio is 5:1, possibly suggesting the presence of a batch of grain at a more advanced stage of processing. A high proportion of the wheat grains in all four assemblages have distinct hollow embryo ends, dorsal grooves and concave profiles and appear to have germinated prior to charring. In addition, detached cereal sprouts are abundant in all four assemblages. The samples also contain moderately high densities of weed seeds, most notably specimens of brome including, within Sample 1519, a number of germinated seeds. Although most seed contaminants were probably a nuisance, brome appears frequently within batches of Iron Age and Romano-British grain (*cf.* St Osyth, Essex, Fryer 2007) and was probably tolerated, as it neither detracted from the palatability of the crop nor affected its storage potential. The precise origin of the material within the Love's Farm pit is a little unclear, as the material represents a secondary deposit of detritus from another source. However, it would appear most likely that the assemblages are derived from either a mixture of malted grain and fuel waste, or from batches of semi-processed cereal, some of which was possibly being stored in spikelet form. Whether this grain was being placed in underground pit stores, where germination of the outermost 'skin' of grain was acceptable and the pits were cleansed by seasonal firing (*cf.* Reynolds 1974 and Murphy 1991), or in inappropriate over-ground facilities, where a high degree of accidental germination occurred and the dross was subsequently being burnt, is not known, although underground pit stores are unlikely to have been present at Love's Farm due to the high water table.

Two assemblages from Samples 1552 and 1553 (Waterhole 8, Period 4.3), appear to be derived from a small quantity of cereal processing and/or storage waste, which was probably subsequently used as fuel. All stages of processing appear to be represented, from the awns and glumes removed by parching and winnowing through to the larger contaminant weed seeds hand-picked immediately prior to consumption or use, and although grains are virtually absent, detached sprouts are present in both assemblages.

Settlement 7

Compared to Settlement 6, plant macrofossil evidence from Settlement 7 is particularly sparse, with few specific activities being indicated. Of the four pit fills studied, only one (Sample 479, pit *5572*, Period 4.4) contains what appears to be a moderate density of cereal processing waste, with the remaining three assemblages almost certainly being derived from scattered or wind-blown refuse of uncertain origin. As with Settlement 6 and the earlier Iron Age contexts, much of the waste generated by the occupants of Settlement 7 appears to have been dumped within the enclosure and boundary ditches. Of the eight ditch assemblages studied, six appear to be largely derived from low to moderate densities of processing waste, much of which was probably used as fuel. However, the two samples from Period 4.4 ditches *5165* and *5718* (Enclosures 138 and 131; Samples 425 and 499 respectively) are somewhat unusual as they contain high densities of cereals and, in the case of Sample 499, a very high density of chaff (approximately 1100 specimens per litre of soil sampled). Given that both assemblages also contain a number of detached cereal sprouts, it is perhaps most likely that this material provides further evidence for the malting of grain at the Love's Farm site.

Among the latest deposits studied from the site are the two de-watered fills of well *5387* (Period 4.5, Table 8.12). This feature appears to have been in use for a relatively short period (the pottery is late Roman) and included the possible 'ritual' deposition of finds (including leather shoes; see Mould, Chapter 6.X) and animal bones (see Baxter, above), as well as plants with possible medicinal/spiritual significance (see Green and Boreham, below). The three plant macrofossil assemblages obtained from fills of the well are broadly similar in composition, containing species indicative of predominantly dry, rough grassland conditions with minimal areas of cultivated ground, a situation generally reflected by the insect remains (Tetlow, below). Somewhat surprisingly, most of the plant species present are commonly found on lighter soils, although the site itself is situated on clay. However, most are shallow rooted and were probably growing in the well-broken topsoil layer. The presence of nearby dung heaps, or similar phosphate-rich deposits, is indicated by the seeds of henbane (*Hyoscyamus niger*) whilst the presence of ragwort (*Senecio* sp.) may suggest that the land was periodically over-grazed. The insect remains confirm the presence, albeit at low levels, of dung beetles and other species associated with rotting organic matter. The well itself appears to have been muddy rather than permanently water-filled, and the well-head may have become overgrown with brambles and elderberries by the end of the Roman period. Both de-watered and charred cereal chaff (as well as some grains) are present within both of the late Roman fills, but as such material appears to have been spread over much of Settlement 7, this is perhaps not surprising.

Conclusions

Despite the large size of the settlement area and the extended period of occupation of the various elements of the site, plant macrofossils are scarce, occurring at a high density within only 5% of the features sampled. There would appear to be at least three possible reasons why so little material was recovered, namely: much of the waste being generated by the occupants of the site was deposited in features which were beyond the area of excavation; the intermittent drying, wetting and cracking of the clay soil caused severe mechanical damage to the macrofossils and the overall assemblage is now incomplete; the occupants of the site were operating a subsistence agricultural economy, producing sufficient for their own needs with little surplus. Cereals were processed on a day to day basis with minimal waste and much of the bi-product (*i.e.* chaff) was being utilised as fuel for domestic and other purposes.

It certainly is the case that the few high density plant macrofossil assemblages recorded are frequently from peripheral contexts, for example the enclosure and boundary ditches. Other assemblages appear to be the result of accidental fires which, presumably, happened relatively infrequently. As for the agricultural status of the site, it would appear most likely that it was operating a mixed economy throughout its entire existence, relying heavily on the husbandry of all the major species of domestic animal, and producing sufficient grain for its own requirements from the areas of the site which were most suitable for crop production.

There is, unfortunately, little to indicate how any of the cereal crops were being stored. The assemblages examined from the four-post structures appear to indicate that they had been used as hay ricks (see also the two possible circular hayrick bases, Structures 101 and 110, both of Period 4.1, in Settlements 6 and 7, Chapter 4) and, although the charred cereal remains within the Settlement 6 rubbish pit may be related to pit storage, it is, perhaps, unlikely because of the locally high water table. Granary stores, such as those recorded at St Osyth (Fryer 2007) and Verulamium (Fryer 2006), can only easily be identified if destroyed by fire, and as this appears not to have occurred at Love's Farm, no such structures are indicated here.

The malting of grain, presumably for brewing, was almost certainly occurring on or near the site, although again, probably only on a small scale, meeting the needs of individual family groups. Little can be deduced from the

Sample no.		586	577	578
Context no.		5893	5889	5890
Feature no.		5387	5387	5387
Period		4.5	4.5	4.5
Cereals and other food plants	**Common names**			
Avena sp.(awn frags.)	Oat		8fg	
Triticum sp. (grains)	Wheat		48	8
(glume bases)			24+32w	8w+16
(spikelet bases)				64
(rachis internodes)			56	16
T. spelta L. (glume bases)	Spelt		96	104
Cereal indet. (grains)			24	
(basal rachis nodes)			16	
Herbs				
Aethusa cynapium L.	Fool's parsley	4+3fgw	32fgw	40+48fgw
Agrimonia eupatoria L.	Agrimony			8w
Anagallis arvensis L.	Scarlet pimpernel	2w	16w	32w
Anthemis cotula L.	Stinking mayweed	1w+3	8	8w
Apiaceae indet.		1w	8	64w
Arctium lappa L.	Great burdock			24w
Arenaria sp.	Sandwort	1w		
Asteraceae indet.		3w	8w	
Atriplex sp.	Orache	19w	304w	192w
Brassiaceae indet.		77w	40+8tfw	24tfw
Bromus sp.	Brome		16	8
Carduus sp.	Musk thistle	34w	32w	8fgw
Centaurea sp.	Cornflower	6cfw	40w	16cfw
Cerastium sp.	Mouse-ear chickweed	4w	8cfw	24cfw
Chenopodium album L.	Fat hen	5w	80w	16w
C. rubrum/glaucum	Goosefoot		8w	
Chenopodiaceae indet.			24w	8w
Cirsium sp.	Thistle		104w	16cfw
Conium maculatum L.	Hemlock	3+1fgw	104+56fgw	40+56fgw
Conopodium majus L.	Pignut		56w	
Daucus carota L.	Wild carrot	25w	304w	16+56fgw
Foeniculum sp.	Fennel		8cfw	
Galium palustre L.	Marsh bedstraw	4cfw		
Hyoscyamus niger L.	Henbane	1+1fgw	8w	8w
Lamium sp.	Dead nettle	10w	8w	8w
Leontodon sp.	Hawkbit	11w	152w	80w
Lepidium sp.	Pepperwort	2cfw		
Linum catharticum L.	Fairy flax	15w	104w	320w
L. perenne/angustifolium type	Perennial flax type	20w	184w	96w
Malva sp.	Mallow	22w	16+32tfw	56w
Medicago/Trifolium/Lotus sp.	Medick/cover/trefoil		24	
Onobrychis viciifolia Scop.	Sainfoin	3+1fgw	40+32fgw	8+8fgw
Papaver argemone L.	Prickly-headed poppy		8w	8w
P. dubium L.	Long-headed poppy	1cfw	8w	
P. somniferum L.	Opium poppy	1w		
Plantago lanceolata L.	Ribwort plantain			8w
Small Poaceae indet.	Grasses	2w	8	8
Large Poaceae indet.		2w	56w	24w
Polygonum aviculare L.	Knotgrass	13w	288w	200w
Potentilla sp.	Cinquefoil	19w	80+24cfw	112w
Prunella vulgaris L.	Self-heal	15w	544w	384w
Ranunculus acris/repens/bulbosus	Meadow buttercup type	24w	152w+8	104w
Rumex sp.	Dock	8w	136w	96w
R. acetosella L.	Sheep's sorrel		16w	
Senecio jacobaea L.	Ragwort	3cfw	72w	24cfw

Sample no.		586	577	578
Context no.		5893	5889	5890
Feature no.		5387	5387	5387
Period		4.5	4.5	4.5
Sinapis sp.	Charlock		8cfw	
Solanum sp.	Nightshade			8fgw
Sonchus asper (l.)Hill	Spiny sow-thistle	3w	24w	8w
S. oleraceus L.	Milk thistle	4fgw	8w	8+24fgw
Stellaria graminea L.	Stitchwort	3w	24w	8w
S. media (L.)Vill	Chickweed	83w	56w	88w
Taraxacum sp.	Dandelion	2w	8w	
Thalictrum flavum L.	Meadow rue	1w	24w	16w
Thlaspi arvense L.	Field penny-cress			24w
Torilis japonica (Houtt)DC	Hedge parsley	53w	16w	16+8fgw
Urtica dioica L.	Stinging nettle	94w	40w	376w
U. urens L.	Annual nettle	19w	136w	168w
Verbascum sp.	Mullein	2w	32w	
Viola sp.	Pansy		8w	
Wetland/aquatic plants				
Carex sp.	Sedge	20w	72w	152w
Filipendula ulmaria L.	Meadow sweet		8w	
Oenanthe aquatica (L.)Poiret	Water dropwort	5w	72	64w
Ranunculus subg. *Batrachium* (DC)A.Gray	Water crowfoot	4w	8w	
R. sceleratus L.	Celery-leaved crowfoot		16w	
Tree/shrub macrofossils				
Corylus avellana L.	Hazel			18cffgw
Rubus sect. *Glandulosus* Wimmer & Grab	Bramble		16w	8w
Sambucus nigra L.	Elderberry	14w	48+8fgw	152w
Other plant macrofossils				
Charcoal <2mm		x	xx	x
Charcoal >2mm		x	x	xx
Waterlogged root/stem		xxx	xxxx	xxxx
Indet.moss		xw	xw	
Indet.seeds		7w	152	104w
Other remains				
Black tarry material			x	
Bone		x	x	x
Cladoceran ephippia		x		x
Fish bone			x	x
Waterlogged arthropod remains			xx	x
Volume of flot (litres)		<0.1	0.8	0.4
% flot sorted		100%	100%	100%

Table 8.12 Plant macrofossils and other remains from well *5387* (Settlement 7)

plant macrofossil assemblages about the status of the individual settlements during either the Iron Age or Romano-British periods, although it would appear that Settlement 6 was more intensively used, with evidence for a number of defined specific activities. It should be noted, however, that this picture may be due to the variable preservation of the plant remains within individual features.

V. Mollusca
by Val Fryer and Rachel Fosberry

Sample composition
An assemblage of 10.833kg of both marine and freshwater molluscs was recovered from the site, most of which (75%) came from Roman contexts. Some 17% of the material came from Iron Age deposits, while the remainder was from later or undated deposits. Oyster shells predominate in the marine assemblage (89%, 10.390kg) along with occasional mussel shells (10%, 0.380kg) and a single cockle shell. Occasional freshwater molluscs in the form of Swan mussels, *Anodonta cygnea* (0.060kg) were also found. All of the species present are

bivalves although none of the specimens are preserved hinged. The majority of the shells are well preserved with only occasional evidence of infestation by the parasitic worm *Polydora* sp. It is possible that the mussel shells and the single cockle shell are contaminants that were harvested and imported with the oysters. Swan mussels are freshwater molluscs and could have been collected locally. At Love's Farm, they occurred as single and generally fragmented specimens.

Oyster shells predominate throughout all periods. The majority of contexts contained single specimens, although four contexts yielded relatively large quantities (> 0.200kg). These concentrations occurred in ditch fill *11272* (0.351kg, Boundary 1, Period 3.4, Settlement 3.3), *13449* (0.528kg, Routeway 9, Period 3.5, Settlement 4), ditch fill *5637* (0.214kg, Boundary 111, Period 4.3, Settlement 7) and pit fill *5343* (0.242kg, pit *5596*, Period 4.5, Settlement 7). A single oyster valve from context *7475* (Waterhole 9, Period 4.4, Settlement 7) has a central hole approximately 1cm in diameter: this may have been accidental damage or a deliberately worked object. Mussels were generally found alongside oyster shells. The only assemblages of any size came from Enclosure 1 (0.169kg, Period 3.2, Settlement 6) and a pit fill (0.149kg, pit *8895*, Period 4.1/4.2, Settlement 6); in these instances, mussel shells predominate over other shell species.

Although specific sieving for molluscan remains was not undertaken, twenty bulk samples taken from the inner and outer ditches of Enclosure 22 (Period 3.5, Fig. 8.13) were assessed for mollusc shells. The resultant assemblages are dominated by open country species, with freshwater taxa only occurring within the deposits flanking the eastern entrance of the double-ditched enclosure. Some of the shells retain excellent surface structuring and colouration, suggesting that they are probably modern contaminants. Most of the shells are, however, fragmented with distinctive surface pitting, suggesting that they were contemporary with the contexts from which they came. Three of Evans' (1972) ecological groups of terrestrial taxa are represented, with open country species occurring most frequently. The samples from the outer ditch, along with the samples from the terminus of the inner ditch, also contain a high density of freshwater obligate species, most notably specimens of *Anisus leucostoma* and *Armiger crista*, both of which frequently occur in marshes or small bodies of water which are prone to seasonal drying.

Discussion
The Love's Farm molluscan assemblage provides limited evidence for the importation of edible shellfish to the site. Although shellfish were clearly never a significant contribution to the diet, they may have been a dietary supplement which increased in the Roman period. The oysters were presumably transported from the east coast in salt-water tanks and would have been a seasonal resource. Oysters as a dietary constituent are, however, rare in the Iron Age period, since fishing and the consumption of fish seems not to have occurred on inland sites throughout the Iron Age (Dobney and Ervynck 2007). The recovery of shellfish from Iron Age contexts is rare and has been disputed in the published evidence (Winder 1993, 10). A similar proportion of shell from Iron Age contexts to that from Love's Farm (17% of the total site assemblage) was, however, found at Cambourne (17%; Wyles 2009, 134), albeit from later Iron Age deposits.

It should be noted that certain shells, and particularly oysters, can be put to a range of uses and their presence cannot therefore be taken as direct evidence for consumption (Winder 1993, 5). Their high lime content makes them suitable for fertilisation of crop fields and use in mortar, while they were also crushed for shell-tempered pottery and other uses (Winder 1993, 5). In general terms, there is a well-documented 'randomness' to shell survival and recovery. At Love's Farm, 65% of the shell came from ditches, 20% from pits and 5% from postholes: this may suggest that the majority of the marine shell found its way into ditches as a result of activities such as manuring of fields, rather than as domestic waste.

The material from Enclosure 22 suggests that it lay within an area of short turfed grassland. The outer ditch had been excavated to a sufficient depth to hold water on at least a seasonal basis, while the terminus of the inner ditch also appears to have been sufficiently deep to be seasonally wet.

VI. Insects
by Emma Tetlow

Introduction
Insect remains were recovered from two features, a quarry pit assigned to the late Iron Age/early Romano-British transitional period (Quarry 4, *120062*, Settlement 2, Period 3.5, Fig. 3.28) and a late Romano-British well (*5387*, Settlement 7, Period 4.5, Fig. 4.23).

Methods
The samples were processed at the University of Birmingham using the standard method of paraffin flotation outlined by Kenward *et al.* (1980). The insect remains were then sorted from the paraffin flot and the sclerites identified under a low power binocular microscope at x10 magnification. Where possible, identifications were made by comparison with specimens in the Gorham and Girling collections housed at the University of Birmingham. The taxonomy used for the Coleoptera (beetles) follows that of Lucht (1987). To aid interpretation, where applicable, the taxa have been assigned ecological groups following those of Kenward and Hall (1995).

The insect assemblages

The Iron Age quarry pit
The sample from Quarry 4 produced an exceptionally well-preserved and interpretable assemblage (Table 8.13). The Carabidae or 'ground beetles', *Leistus fulvibaris* and *Nebria brevicollis*, the elaterid, *Adelocera murina* and the cantharid, *Cantharis rustica* are all found in on shaded ground at the margins of woodland or in hedgerows (Lindroth 1974, 1986; Koch 1989a), the latter also occurring in swarms around lone trees in open environments (Koch 1989a). Indicators of more open ground include a further suite of Carabidae, *Amara aenea* and *Dromius linearis;* both are xerophilous taxa found on sandy, sparsely vegetated ground (Lindroth 1974, 1986). Further species of dry, open ground, sparsely vegetated and weed dominated scrub are the carabid, *Brachinus crepitans*, and the curculionid, *Sitona tibialis*. The latter is

Feature	Quarry 4	Well	Well	Ecology	Host plants
Fill	120188	5890	5893		
Cut	120062	5387	5387		
Processed weight (kg)	5kg	5kg	5kg		
Processed volume (l)	5l	5l	5l		
Carabidae					
Leistus fulvibarbis Dej.	1			Under trees, hygrophilous	
Nebria brevicollis (F.)	2			Woodlands and open country	
Nebria spp.	3				
Trechus quadristriatus (Schrk)/striatulus Putzeys.	2			Xerophilous, open country, heaths and moorland	
Trechus spp.	1				
Bembidion unicolor Chaud.	2			Moist soils, bogs and woodland	
Bembidion spp.	4				
Harpalus rupicola Sturm.	1			Open ground on sands and gravels	
Harpalus rufipes (Geer.)			1	Dry, open country	Fat hen, knapweed
Pterostichus nigrita (Payk.)	1			Damp places near water	
Pterostichus spp.	2				
Amara aenea (Geer.)	1			Xerophilous amongst sparse vegetation	
Amara familiaris (Duft.)	1			Xerophilous in open country	
Amara spp.	2		1	Dry, open ground	
Dromius linearis (Ol.)	1			Dry, open country on sandy substrates	
Dromius spp.	2				
Brachinus crepitans (L.)	1			Dry, open country	
Dytiscidae					
Hydroporous spp.	1			Deep, permanent water bodies	
Graptodytes spp.	1				
Agabus spp.	1			Deep, permanent water bodies	
Gyrinidae					
Gyrinus spp.	1			Large areas of open water	
Hydraenidae					
Octhebius minimus (F.)	3			Most kinds of shallow water with vegetation	
Octhebius spp.	9				
Limnebius spp.	1		1	Ephemeral muddy pools	
Helophorus spp.	16		1	Ephemeral muddy pools	
Hydrophilidae					
Cercyon impressus (Sturm.)	1			Decaying organic material, dung	
Cercyon analis (Payk.)	3			Decaying organic matter	
Cercyon spp.	3		1	In vegetation at the periphery of standing, stagnant water	
Hydrobius fuscipes Leach	1			Deep, permanent water bodies	
Histeridae					
Hister spp.	1			Decaying organic matter and animal dung	
Liodidae					
Agathadium atrum (Payk.)	1			Rotting and mouldy vegetation	
Staphylinidae					Waterside
Lesteva longelytrata (Goeze)	14				
Trogophloeus spp.			1	Rotting organic material and dung	
Oxytelus rugosus (F.)	1			Rotting organic material and dung	
Platystethus arenarius (Fourcr.)	1			Rotting organic material and dung	
Platystethus nitens (Salhb.)	1				
Stenus spp.	2				
Lathrobium spp.	1				
Gryohpnus fracticornis (Mull.)	1			Rotting and mouldy vegetation	
Xantholinus spp.	11				
Philonthus spp.	6		1		
Staphylinus spp.	1				
Quedius spp.	2		1		
Tachyporus spp.	6				

Feature	Quarry 4	Well	Well	Ecology	Host plants
Fill	120188	5890	5893		
Cut	120062	5387	5387		
Tachinus rufipes (Geer.)	1			Rotting organic material and dung	
Tachinus spp.	1				
Aleocharinae gen. & spp. Indet.	3	1			
Elateridae					
Agriotes spp.		1		Meadows and woodland margins	
Adelocera murina (L.)	2			Meadows and weedy places	
Athous spp.	2			Meadows, woodlands and woodland margins	
Dryopidae					
Dryops spp.	2	1			
Cryptophagidae					
Atomaria spp.	3				
Lathridiidae				Drier rotting material such as hay and straw	
Encimus minutus	33		4		
Corticaria spp.	27	1			
Cantharidae				Meadows, woodlands and woodland margins	
Cantharis rustica Fall.	13			Meadows, woodlands and woodland margins	
Cantharis rufa L.	3				
Cantharis spp.	7				
Rhagonycha spp.	1				
Anobiidae				Dry and seasoned wood	
Anobium punctatum (Geer.)	3				
Anthicidae				Dry, open countryside and sandy pastures	
Anthicus antherinus (L.)	1				
Scarabaeidae				Dung of various animals and decaying organic material	
Geotrupes spp.			1	Dung of various animals and decaying organic material	
Onthophagus spp.	1			Decaying organic material	
Oxymous silvestris (Scop.)		1		Dung of various animals and decaying organic material	
Aphodius haemorrhoidalis (L.)	1			Dung of various animals and decaying organic material	
Aphodius sphacelatus (Panz.) or *Aphodius prodromus* (Brahm.)	3			Dung of various animals and decaying organic material	
Aphodius contaminatus (Hbst.)	2		1	Dung of various animals and decaying organic material	
Aphodius granarius (L.)	1				
Aphodius spp.	5	1	1	Meadows and grassland	
Phyllopertha horticola (L.)	3				
Chrysomelidae					Brassicas
Chaetocnema concinna (Marsh.)	3				
Chaetocnema spp.	1				
Phylotreta spp.	12		1		
Curculionidae					
Apion urticarium (Hbst.)	5				Nettles
Apion radiolus (Marsh.)	1			Disturbed ground, waysides and hedgerows	Mallows
Apion aeneum (F.)	1	2	1	Disturbed ground, waysides and hedgerows	Mallows
Apion ervi Kirby.	1			Hedgerows	Vetches
Apion spp.	18	1	2		
Polydrusus spp.	1				Dogs mercury
Barynotus moerens (F.)	1				Vetches
Sitona suturalis Steph.	1				Clover
Sitona tibialis (Hbst.)	1				Broom and gorse

Feature	Quarry 4	Well	Well	Ecology	Host plants
Fill	120188	5890	5893		
Cut	120062	5387	5387		
Sitona puncticollis Steph.	1				Vetches, clover, trefoil
Sitona spp.	2	1			
Tanysphyrus lemnae (Payk.)	1				Duckweed
Notaris acridulus (L.)	2				Sedges
Notaris spp.	3				
Hypera spp.	1				
Ceutorhynchus contractus (Marsh.)	3				Brassicas
Ceutorhynchus spp.	2	1			
Mecinus pyraster (Hbst.)	2				Plantain
Gymnetron cf. *beccabungae*	1				Brooklime
Gymnetron spp.	4	1			

Table 8.13 Insects (Coleoptera) from Iron Age Quarry 5 (Settlement 2) and the Late Roman well (5387, Settlement 7), Period 4.5

a phytophagous taxa found on gorse (*Ulex* spp.) and broom (*Cytisus scoparius*) (Bullock 1993).

A large number of taxa strongly associated with disturbed or waste ground, weeds and ruderal forbs were also recovered. The cantharid, *Cantharis rufa*, and the carabid, *Amara familiaris* are associated with generic disturbed and waste ground colonised by a variety of ruderal herbaceous species (Koch 1989a; Lindroth 1974, 1986). A second carabid, *Harpalus rufipes*, feeds upon the seeds of fat hen (*Chenopodium album*) and various knapweeds (*Polygonum* spp.), which are both herbaceous taxa and are weeds of arable crops, waste and disturbed ground: the presence of fat hen is confirmed by the analysis of pollen samples from the quarry (Green and Boreham, below). Recent research suggests that fat hen may have been a cultivar during the later prehistoric period (Stace 1997; Stokes and Rowley-Conwy 2002).

Other phytophagous beetles associated with a variety of plants commonly found in both meadows and disturbed ground include the Curculionidae or weevils of the *Apion* and *Sitona* genera. *Apion urticarium* is found on nettles (*Urtica* spp.), *Apion aeneum* and *Apion radiolus* are found on mallows (Malvaceae), in disturbed ground, waysides and hedgerows, while *Apion ervi* is found in hedgerows with vetches (*Vicia* spp.) (Bullock 1993; Koch 1992). *Sitona puncticolis* is found with vetches, clovers (*Trifolium* spp.) and trefoils (*Lotus* spp.) (Koch 1992). Finally, *Mecinus pyraster* is found on plantains, particularly ribwort plantains *(Plantago lanceolata)* (Bullock 1993).

A small suite of Scarabaeidae or 'dung beetles' was recovered from the quarry sample. None of the Scarabaeidae recovered are specific to the dung of a particular beast, although *Aphodius contaminatus*, *Aphodius granarius* and *Aphodius haemorrhoidalis* prefer the dung of cattle and horses (Jessop 1986; Koch 1989b). Coleoptera associated with rotting manure and other foul, rotting, organic material are very restricted: the assemblage consists of small numbers of the Staphylinidae *Gryohypnus fracticornis*, *Tachinus rufipes*, *Platystethus arenarius* and *Oxytelus rufipes* (Koch 1989b; Tottenham 1954).

Aquatic and semi-aquatic taxa are also limited, being represented by the Dytiscidae, *Agabus* spp., *Hydroporus* spp., and the hydrophilid *Hydrobius fuscipes* which are all found in deep, permanent water bodies (Hansen 1987; Nilsson and Holmen 1995). The gyrinid, *Gyrinius* spp. cannot be identified to species level but generally live in standing, relatively deep, open waters (Friday 1988). Further hygrophilous taxa are restricted to the semi-aquatic Hydraenidae family, a tribe associated with muddy ephemeral pools and similar muddy conditions at the fringes of permanent water bodies and found in a variety of wetland and terrestrial environments (Hansen 1987).

The majority of taxa from the quarry sample indicate dry open pasture with hedgerows or an area of wood pasture close by (Rackham 1986), along with areas of disturbed ground colonised by weeds and ruderal species. There are two possible explanations for the latter group, which dominates the quarry assemblage: the first is animal agency, and the second is quarrying activity itself. Disturbance as a result of animal agency seems unlikely since, whilst dung beetles are present, they are not found in sufficiently large numbers to suggest unequivocally that the land surrounding the quarry was used for pastoral purposes. 'Decomposer insects' found with foul, decaying organic material such as dung are also restricted. At contemporary sites in the Thames Valley, such as Miniges Ditch, Farmoor (Robinson 1993) and Heathrow (Tetlow 2006), and at other sites such as Goldcliff (Smith *et al.* 1997, 2000), evidence of grazing is emphatic, since comprehensive dung beetle assemblages have been recovered from all four sites. Dung beetles are ready fliers and their source at the Love's Farm Iron Age quarry is likely to be allocthonous and represent 'background' fauna (Kenward 1978). The progenitor of the localised ground disturbance is therefore more likely to have been quarrying activity itself, or as the quarry fell into disuse, the re-colonisation of the quarry head by weeds and other ruderal species. The herbaceous taxa indicated by the phytophagous coleoptera, such as plantains and mallows, are associated with earliest phases of vegetative succession, the natural process of vegetation change, and are ready colonisers of bare, nutrient poor, disturbed ground. Evidence of later stages of the successional process are also found in the form of phytophages associated with nettles and vetches.

Many of the coleoptera favour open, sparsely vegetated, sand and gravel substrates; the type of conditions that would have existed around the quarry head during and directly after gravel extraction. Further support for this hypothesis is provided by the relatively large size of the fauna, 314 individuals and no less than eighty-seven different species, which would suggest that deposit accumulation was a lengthy process and that the environment surrounding the quarry changed little during its formation.

It is also unlikely that the deposit formed under waterlain conditions. The aquatic and semi-aquatic faunas are extremely limited, as are hygrophilous taxa associated with damper conditions at the fringes of ponds and pools. Only three species indicate ponds or pools larger than shallow, seasonal pools. Similarly, coleoptera indicative of riparian, aquatic and semi-aquatic vegetation are limited to a single specimen of *Gymnetron beccabungae* which is found on brooklime (*Veronica beccabungae*), a semi-aquatic plant which prefers shallow water at the margins of a variety of water bodies (Haslam *et al.* 1975). The hygrophilous species, although present, are limited to taxa associated with damp, muddy substrates and seasonal pools. This would suggest that the quarry was only seasonally wet and that any standing water disappeared rapidly, leaving patches of muddier ground.

The late Roman well
The insect assemblages recovered from the well deposits in Settlement 7 (well *5387*, Period 4.5) are more restricted than those from the quarry. Despite their limited size, the samples are extremely interesting since they are strikingly similar to those from the quarry and suggest dry, open grassland or disturbed ground with grazing animals nearby. The 'ground beetles' or Carabidae, from these samples, such as *Harpalus rufipes,* and *Amara* spp., are xerophilous species found on dry, open ground. The former is particularly associated with herbaceous taxa of disturbed ground such as fat hen and knapweeds (Lindroth 1974, 1986). A further species found with vegetation characteristic of waste and disturbed ground is the weevil, *Apion aeneum*, which is found on mallows (Koch 1992).

Once again, a small suite of 'dung beetles' or Scarabaeidae was recovered from the well. Specimens of the 'Dor beetle', *Geotrupes* spp. and several species from the *Aphodius* genus, including *Aphodius contaminatus*, a species common in sandy pastures with the dung of a variety of large herbivores (Jessop 1986; Koch 1989b). A small group of species associated with rotting organic matter and fouler material such as rotting dung include a further scarabaeid, *Oxyomus silvestris*, found in a variety of decaying material including dung and rotting vegetation (Jessop 1986). Also found amongst this type of material is the staphylinid, *Oxytelus rugosus* (Tottenham 1954). Surprisingly, distinctly aquatic taxa are limited to families associated with ephemeral, muddy pools and expanses of mud such as Hydraenidae *Limnebius* spp. and *Helophorus* spp., and the curculionid or weevil, *Tanysphyrus lemnae* which feeds upon duckweed (*Lemna* spp.) (Koch 1992).

The environment surrounding the well, which was divorced from the quarry both spatially and temporally, was very similar, dry, open grassland with some evidence of grazing and disturbance, commensurate with activity by either humans or animals around the well shaft itself. As the numbers of Scarabaeidae or dung beetles in both the well samples are limited, it is difficult to determine whether the land around the well was grazed or, as these species are ready fliers, whether this component was a result of accidental allocthonous incorporation. What is apparent is that both these deposits appear to have accumulated relatively rapidly, in the case of the well perhaps as a result of ritual activity (as is indicated by some of the other material categories recovered from the feature).

In comparison to assemblages from other contemporary wells such as those at Inveresk Gate (Smith 2004), Skeldergate and the legionary fortress, York (Hall *et al.* 1980; Kenward *et al.* 1986) and Mancetter, Warwickshire (Smith 1997), material from the well at Love's Farm is restricted. Wells act as natural 'pitfall traps' for the surrounding environment and will, over time, accumulate large assemblages of insects unfortunate enough to 'fall in'. The Romano-British wells at Inveresk Gate, York and Mancetter all produced large and diverse assemblages, clearly indicative that these well deposits formed as a result of this 'pit-fall' phenomenon and the dumping of waste material associated with human housing, stabling and foodstuffs into the well.

There is no evidence on the basis of the insects present that refuse was being dumped into the Love's Farm well, since it would have been detected in the archaeo-entomological evidence. There is, however, some similarity between the well at Love's Farm and those at Wheatpieces, Tewkesbury (Tetlow 2006) and Piddington, Northamptonshire (Simpson 2001). Sedimentary, artefactual and entomological evidence from both sites, indicates that the well fills here formed rapidly and contained material potentially associated with ritual activity. At Wheatpieces a virtually complete juvenile human skeleton was recovered from the upper fill. The insect assemblage associated with this fill is very limited, which would suggest rapid, natural sedimentation, possibly the result of run-off (Tetlow 2006). Similar sedimentation has also been recorded in middle to late Iron Age pits and ditches at Heathrow Terminal 5, which appeared to be associated with less intensive pastoral activity than previous and later periods at Heathrow (Framework Archaeology 2005; Tetlow 2006). At Piddington, the majority of species recovered were indicators of the environment immediately surrounding the well, with a restricted synanthropic and decomposer component. The origin of this fill may be the result of dumping or the 'pit-fall trap' effect, the exact nature of deposit formation remaining ambiguous. A further theory is that this well was subject to ritual activity as large numbers of oyster shells, unbroken pots and animal skulls were recovered from the upper fills of the feature (Simpson 2001).

Conclusions
Archaeo-entomological evidence indicates that the environment surrounding both the late Iron Age quarry pits and the late Romano-British well at Love's Farm was very similar and was subject to little change during the

formation of both deposits. The quarry deposit was not formed under waterlain conditions. Evidence of disturbed and waste ground around the quarry head is clearly evident, and is perhaps an indication of vegetative succession as the early colonisers of waste and disturbed ground such as mallow and plantain were replaced by nettles and vetches. Evidence from the well is less clear, the exact nature of the processes which led to the formation of this deposit remaining uncertain.

VII. Pollen
by F.M.L. Green and Steve Boreham

Introduction
Pollen preservation at Love's Farm was generally poor with the best preservation limited to deeper, water-filled features. An initial assessment was carried out (by Green) on six samples from an Iron Age quarry (Quarry 3, Period 3.4, Settlement 2, located in Fig. 3.21) and the Romano-British well (*5387*, Period 4.5, Settlement 7, Fig. 4.23). Four samples from a series of features within an Iron Age field system (Field System 3 and Routeway 4, Settlement 1, Period 3.4, Fig. 3.20) incorporating lazy beds were also examined. Both the quarry sample and that from the well showed potential for analysis (by Boreham) which was subsequently carried out, incorporating analysis of samples from a second Iron Age quarry. Unfortunately, in the short period of time between their assessment and analysis, the samples from the well deteriorated and were unsuitable for further study. The results from both pieces of work have therefore been combined for publication.

Methods
Pollen preparations at the assessment stage used techniques based on the method of Hunt (1985). The sediments were desegregated by boiling in 5% NaOH for 5–10 minutes, sieved through 120µm and 10µm wire and nylon sieves to remove the sand- and clay-sized fractions. The remaining silt-sized fraction was removed by swirling (panning) on a large watch glass. The remaining material was stained and mounted on slides with a semi- permanent mountant 'aquamount'. Pollen identifications were assisted by reference to Moore *et al.* (1991) and Andrew (1984). Fungal spores referred to van Hoeve and Hendrikse (1998). References to ecological preferences principally use Stace (1997). Some of the plant nomenclature would normally be updated to Stace (1997), although an older nomenclature (Fitter *et al.*, 1985) has been used for ease of comparison with other published sites.

The subsequent full pollen analyses was conducted on sixteen sub-samples of sediment taken from discrete samples and monolith samples from two quarries and the late Roman well:

Samples 546, 547, 548 and 549 were discrete samples taken from Iron Age Quarry 3. Sub-samples for pollen analysis were taken from each of these samples.

Sample 702 was a single discrete sample taken from another possible quarry (Quarry 5) in Settlement 2. A sub-sample for pollen analysis was taken from this sample.

Samples 578 (discrete) and 584 (monoliths) were from the Romano-British well (*5387*). These samples produced a series of eleven sub-samples for pollen analysis.

The sixteen sub-samples were prepared using the standard hydrofluoric acid technique, and counted for pollen using a high-power stereo microscope.

Results

Iron Age Quarry 3 (Period 3.4)
The pollen sample from the basal fill (*6365*) of quarry *6368* (Sample 549, Table 8.14) was assessed. It was from a grey sticky clayey silt which was virtually stone free. These sediments were below the modern water table and probably accumulated below the water table when the feature was open. The stone-free fine sediments encountered at the base of the pit are consistent with sediments accumulating in an aquatic ponded environment with limited in-wash of sediments. When sieved through a 120µm sieve, the pollen sample produced small clasts of chalk and frequent fine fragments of charcoal. The resultant pollen preparation contains sparse but moderately well preserved pollen. The soil fungus *Glomus* is present, indicating the in-washing of surrounding bioactive soil into the sediments.

Only 115 pollen grains were recovered, which are dominated by grasses (Poacaea) (81% of total land pollen, TLP). It was not possible to distinguish cereal pollen from the grass pollen due to the poor condition of the grains and the slide. Trees are represented by pine (*Pinus*) and oak (*Quercus*) with small amounts of alder (*Alnus*) and birch (*Betula*), accounting for 18%TLP. A single grain of *Corylus* (hazel) was also identified. Interestingly pollen of *Reseda lutea* type was identified, which accounts for 13%TLP. This pollen type includes that of weld (dyer's rocket), wild mignonette and corn mignonette. All these plants grow on disturbed and arable land with weld being used specifically as a dye plant producing a yellow dye (see discussion below). A single grain of *Taraxacum* (dandelion type) suggests open disturbed ground, whereas *Ranunculus* 2.6%TLP is indicative of grassland or possibly aquatic environments since *Ranunculus* type also includes some aquatic buttercups such as the crowfoots. Fungal spores of the *cf.* Sordiariaceae were encountered at moderate frequency and are commonly coprophilous and associated with animal dung and the presence of grazing animals.

Analysis of three samples (547–9) from two fills of pit *6368* in Quarry 3 (Table 8.15) produced similar pollen signals, dominated by grass (Poceae; 48.8–58.8%) with a range of herbs including the lettuce family (Asteraceae (Lactuceae); 7.9–10.2%), the fat hen family (Chenopodiaceae; 1.3–3.4%), the cabbage family (Brassicaceae; 2.0–5.3%) and buttercup (*Ranunculus*; 1.4–3.1%). The disturbed ground indicator, strapwort plantain (*Plantago lanceolata*) is also present at a relatively low level (1.4–2.6%). Cereal pollen is present at 0.7% and mignonette/weld (*Reseda lutea* type) occurs at 1.3%, both occurring only in fill *6365*. Arboreal taxa include pine (*Pinus*; 1.3–2.7%), with birch (*Betula*; 0.3–0.7%), alder (*Alnus*; 0.7–1.3%) and nightshade (*Solanum*; 0.7%). Bur-reed (*Sparganium*; 1.3–5.9%) is the only aquatic taxon represented. Fern spores together account for 7.9–16.3% which, taken with the slightly elevated proportion of Asteraceae (both are resistant to destructive soil processes), may indicate that this pollen spectrum has been modified by post-depositional oxidation.

Feature group	Quarry 3	Field system 3			Routeway 4	Well
Sample	549	1217	1222	1232	1229	584
Context	6365	9625	9865	9887	9833	5889
Feature	6368	9626	9866	9888	9834	5387
Settlement	2	1	1	1		7
Period	3.4	3.4	3.4	3.4	3.4	4.5
Trees						
Alnus (alder)	2					
Betula (birch)	1					
Pinus (pine)	10					3
Quercus (oak)	8				1	
Shrubs						
Corylus (hazel)	1	1				6
Salix (willow)						2
Herbs (terrestrial)						
cf. *Centaurea nigra* (black knapweed)	3					3
Chenopodiaceae (goosefoot family)	1					1
Compositae tub. (daisy family)						10
Cruciferae (*Sinapsis* type) (cabbage family)						18
Cyperaceae (sedges)						10
Poaceae (grasess)	75	5	3	60	35	135
Polygonum (bistorts)						3
Ranunculus (buttercup family)	3			1	3	
Reseda lutea type (weld, wild mignonette and corn mignonette)	13					
Taraxacum-type (dandelion type)	1					14
Viscum (mistletoe)						1
Spores						
Equisetum (horsetails)						3
Filicales (undifferentiated fern spores)	2			1		14
Fungal remains						
cf. Sordariaceae	10					55
Total pollen excluding spores	115	5	4	61	39	154

Table 8.14 Pollen recorded at assessment stage

Iron Age Quarry 4 (Period 3.5)
Analysis of the sub-sample from quarry pit *120062* (fill *120188*, Sample 702, Table 8.15) produced a pollen signal dominated by grass (Poaceae; 37.2%), with an exceptionally diverse range of herbs including the lily family (Liliaceae; 10.2%), the lettuce family (Asteraceae (Lactuceae); 3.7%), the thistle family (Asteraceae (Asteroidea/Cardueae); 2.8%), buttercup (*Ranunculus*; 3.3%), the fat hen family (Chenopodiaceae; 2.3%) and strapwort plantain (*Plantago lanceolata*; 1.9%). Arboreal taxa include hazel (*Corylus*) and juniper (*Juniperus*) (both 1.9%), with birch (*Betula*), alder (*Alnus*) and ivy (*Hedera*). Bur-reed reaches 2.3% in this sample and fern spores together account for 19.0%. This relatively high figure for fern spores, in the absence of elevated Asteraceae, may indicate damp conditions.

Iron Age field system (Field System 3, Settlement 1, Period 3.4)
Four samples taken from elements of Field System 3, which incorporated 'lazy beds', were assessed (Table 8.14). The field system comprised parts of two small, square fields located at the extreme north-east corner of the site, adjacent to Routeway 4 in Settlement 1.

The northernmost field was bounded on the south by a narrow, ditched track (Routeway 6), the position of which the lazy beds broadly respected. Sample 1229 was taken from the ditch (*9834*) defining the north side of the track. The fill was silty. The slides contain abundant fine organics and the pollen is very sparse (39 grains). The assemblage is dominated by grasses (90%) with a single oak and three *Ranunculus* (buttercup) pollen grains. There are abundant soil fungal bodies of *Glomus* showing that a bioactive soil had weathered into the fill of this ditch. A rhizopod (*Centropyxis eromis* Type 530; van Hoeve and Hendrikse 1998) was identified, indicating the presence of water since it only lives in very wet and usually mossy conditions. Occasional fungal spores of Type 714 (van Hoeve and Hendrikse 1998) were also found, again indicative of wet marshy conditions.

Sample 1217 came from the fill lying 15cm above the base of a flat-bottomed ditch/planting trench (*9626*) from the southern central area of a block of similar ditches. This deposit was a mid to light grey slightly ginger mottled (gleyed) clay with silt and a trace of sand. The fills of these ditches/trenches appear to be an impoverished gleyed soil which indicates that the sediments have at some point been waterlogged. They contained rare terrestrial snail

Feature group	Quarry 3	Quarry 3	Quarry 3	Quarry 4
Sample	547	548	549	702
Context	6364	6364	6365	120188
Cut	6368	6368	6368	120062
Settlement	2	2	2	2
Period	3.4	3.4	3.4	3.5
Trees and Shrubs				
Betula	0.7	0.0	0.3	0.9
Pinus	2.7	1.3	1.3	0.0
Alnus	0.7	1.3	1.0	0.5
Corylus	0.0	0.0	6.9	1.9
Hedera	0.0	0.0	0.0	0.5
Juniperus	0.0	0.0	0.0	1.9
Solanum	0.0	0.0	0.7	0.0
Herbs				
Poaceae	49.0	58.8	48.8	37.2
Cereals	0.0	0.0	0.7	0.0
Cyperaceae	1.4	1.3	0.7	0.9
Asteraceae (Asteroidea/Cardueae) undif.	1.4	1.3	0.7	2.8
Centauea nigra type	0.0	0.0	1.3	1.4
Asteraceae (Lactuceae) undif.	10.2	8.1	7.9	3.7
Centaurea cyanus	0.0	0.0	0.0	0.5
Caryophyllaceae	1.4	0.0	0.7	1.4
Chenopodiaceae	3.4	1.3	1.3	2.3
Cirsium	0.7	0.0	0.0	0.0
Brassicaceae	2.0	4.4	5.3	1.4
Filipendula	1.4	0.3	0.7	1.9
Helianthemum	0.7	1.3	0.0	0.5
Lamiaceae	0.7	0.0	0.7	0.5
Fabaceae	0.0	1.3	1.3	0.5
Plantago lanceolata type	1.4	2.5	2.6	1.9
Ranunculus type	1.4	3.1	2.6	3.3
Rosaceae	0.0	0.6	0.7	0.5
Rumex	0.0	0.0	0.0	1.4
Thalictrum	0.0	1.9	0.7	0.0
Apiaceae (Umbelliferae)	0.7	0.6	1.3	0.9
Urtica	0.0	0.0	0.0	1.4
Reseda lutea type	0.0	0.0	1.3	0.0
Sanguisorba minor	0.7	0.0	0.0	0.0
Liliaceae	0.7	0.0	0.0	10.2
Veronica type	2.0	3.1	2.0	0.5
Valeriana dioica	0.7	0.0	0.0	0.0
Polygonum persicaria type	0.0	0.0	0.0	0.5
Lower plants				
Pteropsida (monolete) undif.	12.2	6.6	6.6	16.7
Pteropsida (trilete) undif.	4.1	1.3	2.0	2.3
Aquatics				
Sparganium type	1.3	5.9	3.2	2.3
Sum trees	4.1	2.5	2.6	1.4
Sum shrubs	0.7	0.0	6.9	4.2
Sum herbs	78.2	89.7	81.2	74.9
Sum spores	16.3	7.8	8.6	19.1
Main Sum	294	320	303	430
Concentration (grains per ml)	43606	50254	107858	49913

Table 8.15 Pollen recorded at analysis (percentage data)

shell and rare charcoal flecks. The slide for this sample is very poor and, despite the fact that it contains abundant organic debris, only five grains of grass pollen were identified.

A second sample (Sample 1222) came from another planting trench (*9866*) to the north-east (8–10cm above the base). The fill was similar to that of Sample 1217, being a slightly gleyed silty clay. Three grains of grass and a single grain of hazel were counted after counting four coverslips. The slides are moderately rich in unidentifiable organic debris and also contain a large amount of soil fungal hyphae, including a fungal body of *Glomus*.

Further north, a third sample (Sample 1232) came from the terminus of one of the lazy bed ditches (*9888*) in the northern field. This feature cut the north ditch (*9834*) of Routeway 4. The sample was taken from a relatively well sealed deposit 16–18cm above the base of the 'ditch'. The pollen is again very sparse and sixty grains of grass were recorded, together with a single grain of *Ranunculus* (buttercup) and an undifferentiated spore of fern (Filicales). *Glomus* was also found in moderate amounts.

The late Roman well (Period 4.5)
The sample from well *5387* (Sample 584; Table 8.14) was sub-sampled from a monolith at a depth of 2.87m within fill *5889*. The deposit was a dark grey silty clay with occasional small clasts of chalk and frequent small fragments of charcoal. The pollen is moderately well preserved although the slide was difficult to count due to the large amounts of woody debris and charcoal within the sample. A total of 154 grains of pollen were counted from this sample. The assemblage is dominated by grass pollen (87%TLP) with almost no tree pollen at all – 2%TLP pine, 3%TLP hazel and 1%TLP willow. A range of terrestrial herbs was encountered, including potentially edible plants such as Chenopodiaceae (possibly fat hen) 0.6%TLP, *Sinapsis* type 12%TLP which could include some of the edible cabbage family and Polygonum (bistort) 2%TLP. Other taxa are weedy species of disturbed ground, *Taraxacum* (dandelions), although dandelions are also edible. Plants of damper places include the Cyperaceae (sedges) 6.5%TLP, Polygonum and horsetails. Plants from drier grassy places are represented by *cf. Centaurea nigra* (black knapweed; 1.9%TLP). A relatively large number of fungal spores of the *cf.* Sordiariaceae were identified which are commonly coprophilous and associated with animal dung and the presence of grazing animals. A single grain of a most unusual pollen type in this context was identified as *Viscum* (mistletoe), the potential significance of which is discussed below.

Discussion and conclusions

The Iron Age quarries
The lower clayey, virtually clast free, sediments within Quarry 3 probably accumulated below the water table and in conditions where there was limited run-off from the land surface. This is supported by the presence of rare soil fungal bodies (*Glomus*) which indicate limited in-wash of bioactive soils from the land surface. Limited erosion of surrounding soils suggests that the surface was stabilised, perhaps by grassland. Dominated by grasses, the pollen assemblage indicates the presence of grassland, probably pasture, in the immediate environs of the quarry, a situation confirmed by the plant macrofossils and insects. Fungal spores associated with animal dung are moderately abundant and suggest grazing by herbivores such as sheep or cattle. Tree pollen suggests the presence of localised stands of woodland, perhaps in areas not suitable for agriculture: this woodland consisted of pine and oak, perhaps with oak growing within the hedges. Pollen of birch, alder and hazel are sparse in the samples and probably derived from a limited area of damp, open scrub perhaps along the edges of the drainage channels or streams.

Potentially the most interesting aspect of this pollen assemblage is the identification of a significant amount of pollen of *Reseda lutea* type (which includes weld (dyers' rocket), wild mignonette and corn mignonette). All these plants grow on disturbed and arable land with weld being used specifically as a dye plant producing a yellow dye. Unfortunately it is not possible to distinguish between the pollen of *Reseda lutea* type without type slides and it remains only a possibility that weld was being grown in the fields adjacent to the quarry or that dyeing was carried out close to or within this probably water-filled quarry as a secondary function. Even if the pollen was not of weld, all the plants of *Reseda lutea* type are indicative of disturbed and arable land. The presence of charcoal within the fill indicates its proximity to human activity and suggests either the in-washing of charred material from surrounding agricultural activities or the intentional dumping of fire waste within the disused quarry.

When combined, analysis of the sub-samples from Quarry 3 (Samples 547, 548 and 549) indicates a post-clearance grassland and meadow environment with tall herb communities. This was presumably a largely pastoral rather than arable landscape since, although some arable weeds and disturbance indicators are found, these could easily be attributed to trampling and poaching by animals. Although ostensibly tree-less, the sub-sample from Sample 549 yielded sufficient hazel pollen to suggest local scrub, perhaps managed for coppice. This sub-sample also contains a little cereal pollen and a little mignonette/weld pollen, although not at the levels detected during the pollen assessment. However, neither of these signals is enough to suggest cultivation, at least in the immediate vicinity.

The sub-sample from Quarry 4 (Sample 702) shows a similar post-clearance assemblage with a particularly diverse range of herb taxa. The presence of lily pollen (perhaps bluebells) and fern spores may indicate damper conditions, although the herb taxa still suggest a grassland and meadow environment with tall herb and riparian (bank-side) communities. Low proportions of stinging nettle (*Urtica*) may indicate areas of faecal eutrophication nearby. Pastoral rather than arable activity is again the most likely scenario. Both quarries seem to have been surrounded by similar open grassland environments. There was clearly a diversity of habitats (*e.g.* damper, drier, deep soil, shallow soil, high nutrients, low nutrients) within these areas. The paucity of aquatic taxa, apart from bur-reed, suggests that open water was scarce or only seasonally present in these features.

The Iron Age field system
Although they contained no countable pollen, there was some evidence that the 'lazy bed' ditches (Samples 1217 and 1222) contained a bioactive soil, either *in situ* or

infilling shallow ditches. The sediments were those of an impoverished, at times waterlogged soil. Any significant amounts of pollen had been lost, probably due to oxidation of the pollen grains. It is possible, given the apparent waterlogging of the soils on these slopes, that these ditches were indeed part of a 'lazy bed' system, whereby soils are piled up in between the ditches resulting in better drained soils for growing crops. The pollen from the third 'lazy bed' type ditch (Sample 1232) is better preserved than in the other ditches, probably due to its greater depth and the pollen having survived better in this more sealed context. The pollen assemblage is almost entirely that of grass and although there was probably some differential preservation of loss of pollen grains it is likely that grasses were derived from the local grassland and pasture. The presence of *Glomus* attests to the bioactive nature of the soil which infilled the ditch, however, there was no evidence from the pollen record of whatever crop was being grown. Similar Roman field systems found elsewhere have been tentatively interpreted as relating to vineyards or for growing other crops such as asparagus, for example those in Cambridgeshire at Milton and Caldecote (Kenney 2007), with another at Wollaston, Northants (Brown *et al.* 2001).

The sample (1229) from the trackway boundary ditch (Routeway 4) located on the south side of the northern field, was impoverished but suggests areas of open grassland (although it was not possible to distinguish between grass and cereal grains). The ditch was probably filled with water, at least seasonally, as indicated by the presence of a Rhizopod and fungal spores, both characteristic of damp to very wet locations. There was also in-washing of soils from the adjacent field and possible track as indicated, once again, by the presence of the soil fungus *Glomus*.

The late Roman well
It is not clear how the sediment within the late Roman well accumulated and this has a significant bearing on the interpretation of the pollen assemblage. Other categories of evidence suggest possible ritualised deposition within the feature. It is likely much of the pollen is derived from the material dumped or placed within the well, but there may be a very low background of pollen which entered the well from the surrounding environment. For example it is likely that the low values of tree pollen represented only by pine (2%TLP) are part of this background pollen.

The sediment sampled is full of charcoal, indicating that a large amount of burnt material was placed or dumped into the well. The pollen assemblage is dominated by grass pollen and this may in part be derived from the surrounding pasture/meadows, but a larger proportion is likely to be derived from material deposited within the well from another source. It was unfortunately not possible to distinguish between grass and cereal pollen due to the condition of the pollen grains, meaning that some of this grass pollen was in fact derived from cereals. Some of the herbs identified are from a damp or aquatic source such as the sedges, bistorts and horsetails but none of these plants could have grown *in situ* since the amount of light penetrating to 2.8m down the well (the depth at which the samples were taken) would have prevented such plant growth. However, they may have been plants growing in a wet area close to the edge of the well, or were derived from such material and used to backfill the well when it fell from use.

It may be significant that most of the herbs identified within the well fills have a culinary and/or medicinal use. The edible herbs include dandelions, fat hen, some of the cabbage family and bistorts, with medicinal use potentially being made of all of these plants, including horsetails and black knapweed. The plant macrofossil assemblage from the well is similarly dominated by a wide range of grassland herbs, with some evidence for overgrowth by hazel, bramble and elderberry (see Fryer, above, and Table 8.12). Mistletoe pollen is not commonly found on archaeological sites and its presence in the Love's Farm well does not tally with the otherwise treeless pollen assemblage. Mistletoe was used for its medicinal properties but was much more commonly associated with connotations of fertility and renewal and was used in a ceremonial way. Given the character of the well fills, it seems possible that mistletoe was intentionally placed into the well as a ritualised act, along with other plants, burnt matter, animal bones and other items.

The relatively large quantity of fungal spores from the well, commonly found on animal dung, suggests either that animals were grazing close to the well and that the rain washed these spores into the feature, or that part of the infill included animal dung; similar possibilities are attested by the insect assemblage (see Tetlow, above).

Conclusions
The overall impression given by the pollen is of an open pastoral landscape with cereal cultivation as a minor component. This is comparable to the findings at Cambourne where pollen preservation was better but similar results were obtained (Scaife 2009). The Love's Farm results do not provide an insight into any change in landscape use from the Iron Age through to the later Roman period. The Romano-British well has an interesting pollen spectrum, which may in part result from the ritualised closure of this feature incorporating the deliberate deposition of significant plants linked to medicinal and possibly spiritual uses. However, it is important not to over-interpret the pollen signal, and in general the pollen assemblages from the site fit comfortably within the types of Iron Age and Roman landscapes known from the claylands west of Cambridge.

Chapter 9. Discussion and Conclusions
by John Zant

I. Revisiting the research objectives

Introduction
It is appropriate in this final chapter to revisit the project's research objectives, as outlined in Chapter 1.V, and to explore the degree to which the various aims and objectives have been fulfilled in light of the new information provided by the excavations at Love's Farm. A brief overview of the research themes is given below, while each of the various strands of evidence is drawn out and developed in later sections of this chapter.

National research objectives
In accordance with English Heritage's draft *Research Agenda* (English Heritage 1997), national research themes of potential relevance to the Love's Farm project were arranged under a series of thematic headings, namely 'Processes of change', 'Chronological priorities', and 'Themes and landscapes'.

Under the first heading, three themes were identified, relating to evidence for the change from Neolithic/early Bronze Age 'monument-dominated' landscapes to the settlement-dominated landscapes of later prehistory; the interaction between 'Roman' and 'native' in the early Roman period; the development of a 'Romanised' infrastructure; and the nature of society in the period of transition from late Roman to early medieval traditions.

Whilst some evidence for Neolithic/early Bronze Age occupation was noted and a great deal of later prehistoric settlement evidence was recovered, the project did not significantly advance understanding of the processes of change between these two periods, since no clear trace of occupation during the intervening period was found (*i.e.* the middle/late Bronze Age and the early Iron Age). The possibility that the site's earliest field system may have originated in the Bronze Age is, however, discussed below.

The wealth of evidence recovered for occupation during the late Iron Age and the early Romano-British period has allowed the project to address the topic of Roman/native interaction successfully, and in particular the degree to which the indigenous population took advantage of the opportunities presented by the development of a Romanised infrastructure. The local settlement pattern evidently changed significantly at around the time of the Roman conquest, from a relatively dispersed pattern in the late Iron Age, to a much more nucleated arrangement in the Romano-British period. However, it is not clear to what extent this development was a direct result of the conquest, since there are hints that it may already have begun somewhat earlier. Evidence for the processes of Romanisation is discussed in Section VII below, with a key aspect being possible military/civilian interaction. The Love's Farm community had clearly become increasingly Romanised by the 4th century AD, although what happened to the local population in the 5th century AD remains uncertain; one of the two excavated Romano-British settlements appears to have been wholly or largely abandoned, but the other may have continued to be utilised into the late 6th century. However, little evidence for the character of occupation at this time was found and nor were there any significant traces of the processes of change from late Roman to post-Roman traditions, since most of the data came from distributions of pottery and artefacts, often in the tops of earlier features.

Under the heading of 'Chronological priorities', the site had the potential to contribute to current understanding of landscape changes on the clay uplands east of the River Great Ouse in later prehistory, and the reasons behind such changes. The establishment on the site of small farming communities in the middle Iron Age is consistent with the wider regional evidence, which suggests that 'permanent' colonisation of many clayland areas in southern and central England occurred during this period, probably as a consequence of population increase. A wealth of evidence was found to demonstrate how this nascent agricultural landscape developed during the late Iron Age and the Romano-British period. There was clearly an intensification of settlement in the late Iron Age, marked by an increase in the number of farmsteads, followed by a shift towards nucleation by the beginning of the Roman period. During this process, the dispersed settlements of the Iron Age gradually coalesced into two adjacent enclosed settlements that lay close to the road running between *Duroliponte* (Cambridge) and St Neots/Eynesbury. Despite their increased size and the more formalised character of their layout, the *raison d'être* of these settlements as farmsteads based on a mixed farming economy appears to have been essentially the same as that of their Iron Age antecedents.

The research heading 'Themes and landscapes' encompassed such topics as settlement hierarchies, rural settlement patterns, craft and industry, and the improvement of regional chronologies. The recovery of large and generally well-stratified assemblages of pottery, coins, metalwork and other closely datable artefacts from this multi-phase settlement has provided a significant contribution to each of these aspects, as discussed throughout the following text.

Other research objectives
Paramount amongst the project's regional research objectives was the need for further analysis of the origins, character and development of settlement on the region's claylands, which remained poorly understood at the time the original research agenda for the eastern counties of England was compiled (Brown and Glazebrook 2000). In view of past perceptions of the west Cambridgeshire clay uplands, which were assumed to have been largely avoided by ancient farming communities due to the perceived unsuitability of the local clay soils (Chapter 1.III), one of the most important results of the Love's Farm project has been to add to the growing corpus of evidence which demonstrates that this landscape was intensively settled and farmed in both the Iron Age and the

Romano-British period – and potentially the Bronze Age. The results reinforce the findings of other, recently published, excavations undertaken in the area (*e.g.* Abrams and Ingham 2008; Wright *et al.* 2009). As detailed in Sections II–V below, the excavated evidence demonstrates the way in which human communities exploited and changed the local landscape from the Mesolithic to the post-medieval period. A striking feature of the site is the presence of three broadly parallel routes that divided the land into roughly equal blocks from at least the middle Iron Age and possibly the Bronze Age, running between which was a series of linear fields. The evidence is explored further below in Section IV.

Compared with other recent archaeological projects located on the west Cambridgeshire clay uplands, Love's Farm is somewhat unusual in that the excavations encompassed several adjacent Iron Age and Romano-British settlements within a single site area. Comparative data were therefore available from these various farmsteads, both in terms of their character (size, morphology, function, and so on), and the ways in which each developed over a period of several centuries: comparisons between the various settlements are presented below in Section IV. Overall, the excavated settlements appear to have been of low to middle order and of very similar character and economy to contemporary farmsteads excavated elsewhere on the local claylands, and more widely within the region and southern England as a whole. Artefactual evidence suggests that at least some members of the community may have experienced increasing affluence in the Romano-British period, especially from the 4th century AD, which in turn perhaps reflects an intensification of agricultural production to generate a surplus. A full discussion of the findings relating to aspects of economy, production, trade and status is given in Sections V–VIII below, supplementing the specialist reports presented in Chapters 6–8. Various craft and 'light industrial' activities were carried out within the various settlements in both the Iron Age and Romano-British periods, over and above the agricultural practices that must have dominated the lives of most of the inhabitants. Evidence for most of these activities (including textile working, metalworking, quarrying, pottery manufacture, bone-, horn- and woodworking, and perhaps brewing) was comparatively slight, and it seems likely that all were undertaken on a sporadic basis, in the context of home or craft production designed to meet the bulk of the community's everyday needs. The crafts represented are all within the usual range of activities at such rural sites and there is no particular evidence for specialisation, either on the site as a whole or within the individual farmsteads.

Another key research theme was to examine evidence for ritual and religion in the countryside. The small cemetery groups or isolated burials of Iron Age to early Roman date associated with the farmsteads and discussed in Section VIII below add to this research aspect in general terms. While there were no monuments, structures or individual features to which an overtly ceremonial or religious function could be attached, a large square enclosure (Enclosure 8) constructed on the highest part of the site and its possible successor – a circular enclosure represented by two concentric ring ditches (Enclosure 22) – may have had a non-utilitarian function. Regrettably, the precise significance of these enigmatic monuments cannot be established on the available evidence (see below, Section IX), but they nevertheless make an important addition to the corpus of monument types in the region. In addition, the site provided insights into 'religious' practice in the countryside, in the form of various non-funerary deposits that suggest ritualised behaviour, such as placed deposits, hoards and animal burials. The most notable examples comprise an assemblage of Romano-British metalwork seemingly deposited in a 'watery place' and other material associated with a late Roman well. These are discussed below in Section IX.

II. Origins

Mesolithic

The middle Holocene, which encompasses the late Mesolithic period, was seemingly a time of climatic and environmental stability in Britain, dominated by the spread of deciduous woodland, which replaced the pine-dominated landscape of the earlier Holocene (Scaife 2000, 20). Pollen evidence from Britain as a whole suggests that different types of woodland developed on different soils. In west Cambridgeshire, it seems likely that mixed woodland – predominantly oak, elm and hazel – covered much of the clay uplands, with the better-drained river terraces perhaps being more conducive to the growth of lime, and the wetter valley bottoms dominated by alder carr and willow (Scaife 2000, 20). Overall, evidence for Mesolithic sites in Cambridgeshire remains fairly limited (Austin 2000, 7), with little progress having been made in recent years in terms of advancing understanding of even the broad pattern of Mesolithic occupation across the county and the wider region (Medlycott 2011, 6). Notable recent discoveries in Cambridgeshire itself include a possible flint working site at Somersham, in the fens, and a large flint assemblage from wind-blown soils at Over Quarry, also in the north of the county (*ibid.*). Such scatters of lithic material may mark the locations of 'core sites', which were repeatedly visited during the Mesolithic, and where a wide range of activities was undertaken (Clay 2002, 26).

Evidence for Mesolithic occupation in the Great Ouse Valley has been summarised by Dawson (2000b), who noted that, whilst riverside locations were seemingly preferred for Mesolithic occupation in the Middle Ouse Valley, the adjacent claylands are also likely to have been exploited (Dawson 2000b, 49), although little evidence for this had yet been found at the time of writing. In the vicinity of Love's Farm, Mesolithic flints have indeed been recovered in recent years from commercial archaeological investigations in the Ouse Valley near St Neots, although most assemblages are small, and usually residual, as at Eaton Socon to the west of the town, where two possible Mesolithic flints were found (Gibson 2005, 21), and to the north at Little Paxton Quarry where a few stray Mesolithic tools were recovered (Jones 2000, 131). Similarly, at Eynesbury, south of St Neots, excavations in 2000–1 yielded a single long blade of possible late Palaeolithic/early Mesolithic date from a Neolithic cursus ditch (Ellis 2004, 99), although more extensive scatters of late Mesolithic/early Neolithic flints are known from the vicinity (Ellis 2004, 6). On the clay uplands east of the Ouse, evidence for Mesolithic activity remains extremely sparse (Wright *et al.* 2009, 65), and the few artefacts recovered by excavation are invariably either residual within later features, or unstratified. A flint pick of Mesolithic/early Neolithic date was found during excavations associated with the upgrading of the A428 road, which traverses the clay plateau west of Cambridge (Abrams and Ingham 2008, 17), and, nearby, an incomplete Mesolithic microlith came from a layer of colluvium at Scotland Farm, Dry Drayton (Ingham 2008, 31). In the same area, a tranchet axe and a blade were found at Caldecote Highfields (Kenney 2007, 123–4), a short distance east of Lower Cambourne and immediately south of the A428, and excavations at Cambourne New Settlement yielded a single Mesolithic bladelet core (Wright *et al.* 2009, 65).

Whilst the lack of evidence for Mesolithic activity on the clays must be due, in part, to the lack of archaeological investigation in these areas (Chapter 1.III), it may also reflect – as Dawson suggested – a preference for river valley locations, where a greater variety of plant and animal resources was perhaps available. However, studies of the distribution of Mesolithic artefacts in the East Midlands found no evidence to indicate that the claylands of the region were avoided by Mesolithic hunter-gatherer groups, although exploitation of these areas may have been of fairly low density (Clay 2002, 28, 46, 109). The distribution of 'core area' sites and individual stray finds in the region suggest a possible model, which would see hunting camps located in preferred locations on the fringes of clayland areas, perhaps adjacent to watercourses, animal migration routes, or other important resource locations with intermittent/opportunistic 'procurement activities' taking place on the clay uplands, in order to exploit the woodland and other resources available there (Clay 2002, 110, 117). A similar situation may have pertained on the west Cambridgeshire claylands, with the discovery of single artefacts or, as may possibly be the case at Love's Farm (if the prismatic blades from the site are indeed of Mesolithic date), small collections of material on clay sites suggesting that these areas were subject only to relatively brief visitations by Mesolithic peoples, in search of game or other woodland resources, with more intensive activity confined largely to the river valleys.

Neolithic and Bronze Age
In Britain as a whole, the Neolithic saw the first incidences of woodland clearance for agriculture, although such episodes were frequently short-lived and were followed by regeneration of secondary woodland (Scaife 2000, 20). This may be because, initially at least, the subsistence strategies adopted by early Neolithic communities were similar to those followed by their Mesolithic predecessors, with fairly unintensive horticultural regimes and some animal pasturing supplementing, rather than replacing, the pre-existing range of hunting and gathering activities (Clay 2002, 111). As with the Mesolithic, studies in the East Midlands suggest that there was no deliberate avoidance of clay areas in the Neolithic and earlier Bronze Age: indeed, initial clearance of the 'natural' woodland that seemingly covered most of the claylands at this time would have made available relatively fertile woodland soils that are likely to have been eminently suitable for agriculture (Clay 2002, 112–3). Having said that, in Essex, Neolithic and early Bronze Age sites are more commonly found on the lighter soils along the coast or in the major river valleys, rather than on the clays (Timby *et al.* 2007, 20), while at Stansted, the first significant colonisation of the Boulder Clay appears to date to the late Bronze Age (Havis and Brooks 2004b, 514).

Although there is limited pollen evidence for early Neolithic woodland clearance and probable agricultural activity at some sites in East Anglia – including Etton, north of Peterborough (Scaife 1998) and Haddenham, in the fens south-west of Ely (Simms 2006) – much of the region appears to have remained largely wooded in the Neolithic and early Bronze Age (Hall and Coles 1994), and there is evidence for regeneration of secondary woodland in the late Neolithic/early Bronze Age at various sites (Wright *et al.* 2009, 61). Closer to Love's Farm, the area around Eynesbury, in the Ouse Valley immediately south of St Neots, may have been largely cleared of woodland by the late Neolithic, although large-scale forest clearance did not commence over most of the region until the early to middle Bronze Age, with wider-scale clearances occurring in the middle to late Bronze Age (Wright *et al.* 2009, 61). Environmental evidence for this period from the clay uplands is extremely slight, due partly to the lack (until recently) of investigation in these areas, and partly to poor preservation. Further afield, the results of the National Mapping Programme for Northamptonshire suggest that the claylands in that area may have remained largely wooded during the Neolithic and early Bronze Age (Deegan 2007, 114, 118). In west Cambridgeshire, the limited evidence from Cambourne New Settlement suggests that the immediate area may have been largely cleared of woodland by the middle to late Bronze Age (Wright *et al.* 2009, 64). A probable Bronze Age pit excavated at one of the sites associated with the A428 upgrade contained a few cereal grains, including examples of hulled emmer or spelt wheat and charcoal from oak, blackthorn, hazel, field maple and the hawthorn group (Abrams and Ingham 2008, 17). The range of taxa represented in the charcoal assemblage was very similar to that recorded during the Cambourne New Settlement project (Wright *et al.* 2009, 64), where it was suggested that wood was collected locally from remnants of mixed, open woodland.

The fact that almost all the evidence for early Neolithic, late Neolithic and early Bronze Age activity on the Love's Farm site (detailed in Chapter 2) was concentrated in two restricted locations focused on natural hollows is intriguing. It is not known if this points to continuous occupation of these sites from the early Neolithic into the early Bronze Age – a period spanning, at the very least, well over 1000 years – or rather indicates the periodic re-use of these favoured locations over this period. Given the scanty nature of the archaeological remains, the latter hypothesis seems more likely, and would accord with the idea that, for the greater part of this period, settlement remained semi-permanent (Brown and Murphy 2000, 10), although the lack of remains at Love's Farm could be due to later disturbance. Either way, the evidence seemingly supports Bishop's view (Chapter 6.I) that these sites functioned as 'settlements' rather than transient 'camps', albeit with occupation probably characterised by periodic visitations over an extended period.

While slight compared to the data available for later periods, the evidence for Neolithic/Bronze Age activity at Love's Farm is better than that recovered from many of the other recently-excavated sites on the clay uplands of west Cambridgeshire. Excavations in and around Papworth Everard, c.9km north-east of the site, have revealed evidence of Bronze Age occupation (Casa Hatton 2002; Hatton and Kemp 2002; Kenney 2000), including a middle Bronze Age cremation cemetery of forty-one burials, one of the largest known from the region (Gilmour et al. 2010). Whilst sites such as Papworth Everard indicate the potential of the claylands for future research into the Neolithic and Bronze Age occupation of the area, it remains the case that few data relating to the Neolithic/Bronze Age are currently available from these areas, despite the recent upsurge in development-driven investigations. Excavations associated with the A428 upgrade, on the clay plateau east of Love's Farm, yielded a handful of residual Neolithic/early Bronze Age flints, including a Bronze Age barbed and tanged arrowhead (Abrams and Ingham 2008, 17). One of the sites along the route (at Ash Plantation) exposed two small pits, one of which yielded probable Bronze Age pottery and two probable Bronze Age sherds also came from a colluvial layer at a second site (Scotland Farm, Dry Drayton). The nearby work at Cambourne New Settlement produced two early Neolithic leaf-shaped arrowheads (Wright et al. 2009, 65), a late Neolithic/early Bronze Age plano-convex knife, and a possible flint scraper, together with other scrapers, flakes and debitage that may be of broadly similar date (Wright et al. 2009, 14, 65). Most of this material came from Lower Cambourne, although one of the arrowheads was recovered from Knapwell Plantation. Middle to late Bronze Age activity was indicated by a few features at Mill Farm, including gullies, postholes and hearths, which yielded small assemblages of flint and abraded middle to late Bronze Age pottery (Wright et al. 2009, 34).

The existence of a possibly Bronze Age track on or close to the line of the present A428 has been postulated, but little direct archaeological evidence for this has been found (Wright et al. 2009, 65). It is suggested that this route, seemingly one of a number of east to west aligned tracks linking the Ouse Valley to the west with the River Cam and the line of the later Icknield Way to the east, was maintained throughout the Iron Age, and was later followed by a Roman road (Margary Road 231) which, in the medieval and post-medieval periods, developed into the present-day road linking Cambridge and St Neots (Fig. 1.3). It is possible that the western end of this track follows the line of the old Cambridge road (now the B1428), leading east from St Neots, which formed the southern boundary of the Love's Farm development site (Chapter 1.II). No direct evidence for its existence was found during the investigations, although an unmetalled track of late Iron Age origin, flanked by parallel ditches, was recorded just to the north of the B1428 (Settlement 4, Routeway 9): it appears, however, that this early track ended within the excavation area, rather than extending westwards.

At Lower Cambourne and at North Caxton bypass (another site associated with the Cambourne New Settlement project), two post-built roundhouses were recorded. Although these structures were undated, their small size (c.5–5.5m in diameter) and method of construction contrasted with the numerous Iron Age roundhouses investigated during the course of the project, which were invariably larger (mostly in excess of 10m diameter) and characterised by drip-gullies (Wright et al. 2009, 65). Since it has been asserted that small, post-built roundhouses of this type are generally earlier than their larger Iron Age counterparts, these structures were tentatively attributed to the Bronze Age, as was a fenced pen seemingly associated with the North Caxton roundhouse (Wright et al. 2009, 10, 14). Whilst this interpretation may be correct, it should be noted that a post-built roundhouse excavated at Love's Farm (Settlement 1, Roundhouse 1) was almost certainly of middle Iron Age date, since pottery of this period was recovered from several of its postholes, and from a nearby pit. At c.8–9m in diameter, the building was somewhat larger than the Cambourne structures. Early Bronze Age roundhouses defined by eaves-drip gullies are also known from the area, for example at Little Paxton, north of St Neots (Jones 2000, 134), where two structures, defined by gullies c.8m and 15m in diameter, were recorded.

The paucity of evidence for Neolithic and early Bronze Age settlement on the claylands of west Cambridgeshire, although probably more apparent than real, contrasts markedly with the data available from the gravel terraces of the Ouse Valley. There, extensive Neolithic and Bronze Age landscapes, including some of the most significant concentrations of ritual or ceremonial monuments in the county, are known from excavation and survey at many sites (Malim 2000). These include several located between Huntingdon and St Neots, such as Fenstanston (Chapman et al. 2005), Rectory Farm, Godmanchester (McAvoy 2000; Lyons in prep. b), Little Paxton Quarry, Diddington (Jones 2000), and Eynesbury (Ellis 2004). In the vicinity of Love's Farm, excavations at Eynesbury, south of St Neots, revealed a complex prehistoric ritual landscape, the principal features within which included (for the Neolithic) two cursus monuments, a hengiform enclosure, a long barrow and a number of pit groups, together with several Bronze Age cremations and a large, rectilinear enclosure, defined by pit alignments, which may date to the late Bronze Age/early Iron Age (Ellis 2004). At Little Paxton Quarry, to the north of St Neots, the bulk of the evidence indicates settlement rather than ceremonial activity during the late Neolithic/early Bronze Age (Jones 2000, 131–4, 139; 2001, 19). However, the deliberate placement of flint knives and other artefacts at the base of some of the features found in three pit clusters at the site, one of which was tentatively interpreted as a possible pit circle (Jones 2000, 131), was also suggestive of some kind of ritual activity, and a substantial early Bronze Age ring-monument and cremation burials were excavated nearby (Evans 1997). It seems highly likely that the inhabitants of the Love's Farm settlements were not only familiar with many of these ritual monuments, but formed part of the wider Neolithic/early Bronze Age community that was responsible for both their construction and use.

III. The local and regional context

Middle to late Iron Age

In East Anglia and south-east England as a whole, the middle Iron Age (c.400–100 BC) is characterised by a general intensification and expansion of settlement

(Cunliffe 2005, 432), which seemingly included the infilling of 'gaps' in earlier settlement patterns and the exploitation of 'marginal' areas (Hill 2007, 23). This phenomenon, perhaps the result of increased population pressure, has been noted elsewhere in Britain – for example in the Thames Valley (Lambrick and Robinson 2009, 378–9), the East Midlands (Clay 2002, 41–3), and on the Boulder Clay at Stansted, Essex (Havis and Brooks 2004b, 521; Cooke et al. 2008, 80) – and continued throughout the later Iron Age and into the early Romano-British period.

For the Iron Age and Romano-British periods, most of the archaeological evidence for occupation in eastern England consists of small rural settlements and associated enclosures (Rees 2008b, 61). During the Iron Age, morphological diversity is a feature of the smaller, farmstead-type settlements of the region, with both open and enclosed sites attested, for example in the Nene and Great Ouse valleys (Knight 1984), and considerable variation is also evident in the form and layout of enclosures (Dawson 2000c). However, to attempt to group settlements by enclosure shape, or on the basis of whether they appear to have been open or enclosed, can be potentially misleading, since what is visible archaeologically may not have been apparent for much of the lifetime of a particular settlement (Rees 2008b, 74). For example, many excavated enclosure ditches show evidence for re-cutting, and it is often clear that the primary ditch had silted up completely before this occurred. Prior to redefinition of the perimeter ditch, therefore, such a settlement may have been effectively open rather than enclosed. Furthermore, in instances where ditches were re-cut on several occasions, as was frequently the case at Love's Farm, settlements may have fluctuated between open and enclosed forms several times during the period of occupation, although the likelihood is that some enclosures would have continued to be defined by a denuded bank, perhaps surmounted by a palisade or hedge.

In the vicinity of Love's Farm, some of the earlier prehistoric sites identified on the lighter alluvial soils of the Ouse Valley were also occupied during the Iron Age. With the exception of a large, possibly early Iron Age, rectilinear enclosure defined by pit alignments, little evidence for Iron Age occupation was noted at Eynesbury (Ellis 2004), although the site lay within a Romano-British field system. At Little Paxton Quarry, the middle Iron Age was characterised by an irregular, 'pentagonal' ditched enclosure, with seemingly contemporary boundary ditches and other features elsewhere on the site (Jones 2000, 134). In the later middle Iron Age, two sub-rectangular enclosures were appended to one of the earlier boundary ditches, and a new ditched enclosure was constructed to the north in the late Iron Age (Jones 2000, 134–5). To the north-east, a middle Iron Age farmstead comprising a cluster of fairly irregular, conjoined enclosures was superseded in the late Iron Age by a more extensive, and increasingly irregular, complex of small, curvilinear and rectilinear enclosures, bounded on the north by a large, north-west to south-east-aligned boundary ditch (Jones 2001, 19–23). At other sites in the valley, settlement appears to have commenced in the middle Iron Age, with little or no evidence for earlier activity. At Eaton Socon, for example, investigations at Bushmead Road exposed part of a middle Iron Age rectilinear enclosure and associated (largely external) features (Stansbie 2008).

As already noted, it was during the middle Iron Age that widespread exploitation of the region's clay uplands appears to have begun (Evans et al. 2008, 179, 193), a process paralleled in other parts of Britain (Haselgrove et al. 2001, 29), including the East Midlands (Clay 2002, 43, 115). Settlement of what may previously have been regarded as unsuitable or 'marginal' areas may have resulted from increased population pressures. Certainly, at a later date, population increase appears to have been responsible for the widespread cultivation of these same clay areas during the 12th to 13th centuries, although for the Iron Age it has also been tentatively suggested that a rise in the water table, attested in the fens from the late Bronze Age and seemingly persisting into the late Iron Age, may have led to the abandonment of some low-lying sites and the establishment of new settlements on higher ground (Abrams and Ingham 2008, 30).

With the exception of the mostly very limited indications for Mesolithic, Neolithic and Bronze Age activity, the earliest archaeological evidence for settlement at virtually all of the recently excavated clayland sites in west Cambridgeshire, including Love's Farm, is attributable to the middle Iron Age, or later. An evaluation at Wintringham Park (Rees 2008a), directly south of Love's Farm (Fig. 1.3), clearly demonstrated that the local landscape was quite densely settled in the Iron Age, with numerous farmsteads and rural settlements being present, usually occupying favoured south- or south-east-facing slopes in proximity to a watercourse or other reliable water supply. Further north, the extensive remains of a middle to late Iron Age settlement have been investigated at Bob's Wood, Hinchingbrooke (Oxford Archaeology East, in prep.), which was established on a hilltop on the heavier soils overlooking Alconbury Brook, a tributary of the Ouse.

The Longstanton evaluation survey, covering an area of approximately 650ha on the clays north-west of Cambridge, found that middle to late Iron Age enclosures were the most frequent site type, representing what Evans (2008, 179) has described as the main 'colonisation horizon' within this landscape. In this area, which lies c.20km to the north-east of Love's Farm, the type site of this period commonly comprised small (c.0.2–0.5ha) settlements made up of interlinked rectilinear and curvilinear ditched enclosures. These sites were located at intervals of c.200–500m, with distances being generally greater on the clays, as opposed to gravel subsoils. Romano-British farmsteads were fewer and larger than those of the Iron Age, and clustered along a gravel ridge, although spacing maintained a c.200–400m distance interval (Evans et al. 2008, 179). However, whilst the Longstanton sites appear similar in most essentials to those found at Love's Farm, comparisons between the two must be treated with caution, given the present lack of excavation at Longstanton and the fact that the character of the landscape is markedly different to that at Love's Farm.

Papworth Everard is currently unusual for a clayland site in this area in that is has produced evidence for late Bronze Age/early Iron Age activity, including field boundaries and stockades (Kenney 2000; Hatton and Kemp 2002). At Lower Cambourne, Knapwell Plantation and Little Common Farm, a few ceramic vessels exhibited features suggestive of a possible early Iron Age (c.800–400 BC) date (Wright *et al.* 2009, 66), although no stratigraphic evidence for early Iron Age occupation was found. What is clear is that intensive occupation at these sites commenced during the middle Iron Age. On the A428, the settlement at Scotland Farm, Dry Drayton again originated in the middle Iron Age, as may also have been the case with the irregular enclosure at Bourn airfield (Abrams and Ingham 2008, 14, 33–5). At Scotland Farm, the focus of settlement seemingly shifted northwards in the late Iron Age, when a sub-rectangular enclosure containing at least one roundhouse was established adjacent to the Dam Brook (Ingham 2008). In the same general area, excavations at Caldecote Highfields found no evidence for middle Iron Age settlement, although a late Iron Age banjo enclosure was found (Kenney 2007; Kenney and Lyons 2011).

Romano-British
(Fig 9.1)
In the late pre-Roman Iron Age, the St Neots area is thought to have been located near the northern limit of the territory of the Catuvellauni (Fig. 9.1), one of the most powerful tribes in southern Britain at the time of the Roman conquest, and one of the foremost in the initial resistance to the Roman invasion (Webster 1980). Catuvellaunian influence may have extended some 150km north of the River Thames, and is traditionally held to have included the Middle and Upper Ouse Valley. Branigan (1985, 1, 100) envisaged a densely populated Romano-British landscape containing a range of settlements, principally villages and farmsteads but also including small towns, with complex 'social, tenurial and agricultural relationships' linking the various communities. Love's Farm itself may have been located in close proximity to the tribal boundary with the Iceni (who controlled the Cambridgeshire Fenland, Norfolk and Suffolk), and the Corieltauvi (whose territory possibly incorporated parts of northern Cambridgeshire, Northamptonshire and Lincolnshire).

The likely impact of the Roman military campaigns on the native rural population of west Cambridgeshire and the wider region is unclear. There is, however, no evidence that the area was 'laid waste' by the Roman army, either during the initial conquest or in the aftermath of the Boudican rebellion of AD 61. The invading forces apparently met little resistance north of the Thames, and the catchment of the Lower Ouse was rapidly taken under military control (Webster 1980). The Roman army had established a fort at *Durobrivae* (Water Newton) by AD 47, controlling a crossing of the River Nene, while a larger, vexillation fortress was located at nearby Longthorpe (Dannell and Wild 1987), and forts were also established at Godmanchester and Cambridge (Millett 1990, 62).

Although some late Iron Age farmsteads were seemingly abandoned around the time of the Roman conquest (such as that at Scotland Farm, Dry Drayton, to the east of Love's Farm; Ingham 2008), it is clear that most of the region's Iron Age farmsteads and settlements on the claylands and elsewhere continued to be occupied, seemingly without interruption, at this time. Indeed, there are few known examples of conquest-period settlements that were wholly new foundations. Whilst the character of occupation at some sites changed markedly during the

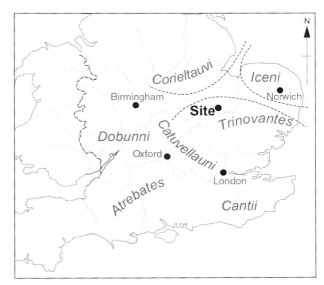

Figure 9.1 Late Iron Age tribal boundaries in eastern England, showing the location of St Neots

Romano-British period, both in terms of settlement morphology and the adoption of new agricultural strategies, this does not generally appear to have occurred in the immediate aftermath of the Roman occupation, but began in the late 1st to 2nd century AD (Evans *et al.* 2008, 191).

As in the Iron Age, rural 'native' settlements of the early Roman period tend to be characterised by conjoined, ditched enclosures (although now mostly rectilinear, rather than curvilinear), often associated with extensive ditched field systems, trackways or droveways, and other elements of a rural, agricultural landscape. In the Ouse Valley, an extensive system of such features at Eynesbury (Ellis 2004, 106–7) was presumably associated with one or more nearby farmsteads. One such may have been the settlement at Eaton Socon, immediately to the west, occupied from the late 1st to 4th centuries AD, which was largely characterised by rectilinear enclosures associated, in some phases, with field boundaries and droveways (Gibson 2005). At Little Paxton Quarry, a considerable degree of continuity is apparent in the morphology of the northernmost settlement from the late Iron Age to the early Romano-British period, although enclosures were re-planned, boundaries replaced and new features added (Jones 2001, 21–22, figs 10–11). The settlement was abandoned by the mid 2nd century AD at the latest, but it is possible that occupation merely shifted to the southern part of the site, where a settlement established in the later 2nd century was also found (Jones 2001, 26), with late Roman occupation seemingly being focused on a ladder-type settlement further to the south still (Jones and Ferris 1994). East of these settlement foci was a circular Romano-Celtic temple situated within a rectangular, ditched *temenos* (Jones 2001, 5–17). Although definitely in use during the late 3rd to mid 4th century, the precise date at which this complex was established is not clear.

A broadly similar sequence of development appears to have pertained on the clay uplands to the east of Love's Farm, where the late Iron Age banjo enclosure at Caldecote Highfields was replaced by a Romano-British farmstead of 1st- to 2nd-century AD date (Kenney 2007, 127–8). This may have been located within a rectilinear ditched enclosure, and was approached from the south by a ditched track or droveway. The latter feature post-dated a series of parallel gullies or ditches that were tentatively interpreted as the remains of a vineyard; both these features and the droveway respected the position of the earlier banjo enclosure. Several sites excavated as part of the Cambourne New Settlement project showed a similar pattern of development, with curvilinear ditched enclosures of late Iron Age/early-Romano-British date being replaced in the middle to late Roman period by more regular systems of rectilinear enclosures. At Lower Cambourne, a settlement comprising two principal, roughly D-shaped, enclosures associated with droveways, subsidiary enclosures and ditched boundaries (Wright *et al.* 2009, 17, 20, figs 7, 9), was replaced in the 2nd century AD by a more formalised pattern of rectilinear enclosures and paddocks (Wright *et al.* 2009, 23, fig. 10). Rectilinear ditched enclosures of middle to late Roman date replaced late Iron Age to early Romano-British curvilinear enclosures containing roundhouses at Knapwell Plantation (Wright *et al.* 2009, 38, fig. 15). At Jeavons Lane, an earlier, D-shaped enclosure was overlain by a regular, 'grid iron' system of rectangular fields or paddocks associated with droveways (Wright *et al.* 2009, 44, fig. 17). A similar situation was observed at Addenbrooke's Hospital, Cambridge, where a small, late Iron Age settlement of conjoined, largely curvilinear enclosures developed, around the time of the Roman conquest, into a seemingly larger settlement comprising a quite formal arrangement of small, rectilinear enclosures delimited by a larger perimeter ditch (Evans *et al.* 2008, 40–4, fig. 2.13). On sites associated with the A428 upgrade, by contrast, comparatively little evidence of direct continuity was found. A very irregular late Iron Age enclosure at Ash Plantation was replaced by two rectilinear enclosures, perhaps in the early Romano-British period, which were in turn superseded by a settlement composed of further rectangular enclosures in the later Roman period (Wright *et al.* 2009, 82, fig. 4.3). At Scotland Farm, Dry Drayton, however, the latest of the two excavated Iron Age settlements was abandoned by the later 1st century AD (Ingham 2008, 36), although an early/middle Roman droveway crossed the site of the earlier settlement (Abrams and Ingham 2008, 43, 47, fig 3.9). At Ash Plantation, a 2nd-/3rd-century farmstead appears to have been established on a previously unoccupied site (Abrams and Ingham 2008, 41, fig. 3.4, 48–53), whilst at Childerley Gate, early/middle Roman field systems were superseded by a farmstead that was in use from the late 2nd century AD to the end of the Roman period.

A new development was the rise of the villa estate, the epitome, perhaps, of 'Romanisation' in the countryside. Many villas are known in the Ouse Valley but they are absent from marginal areas and evidently avoided exposed locations, seemingly favouring south-facing slopes near to a watercourse: it has been suggested that their existence relied upon a specific agricultural system that was sufficiently profitable either to develop a pre-existing farm into a villa estate, or to maintain a newly-founded establishment (Dawson 2000c, 124–5). At Haddon, near Peterborough, the development during the late 1st to early 2nd century AD of an extensive system of large stockyards, which the faunal evidence suggested were geared to the breeding of young cattle and sheep for their meat (Hinman 2003, 28), was tentatively linked to the establishment nearby of a small villa complex. However, there were indications that the shift to this specialised agricultural regime may have begun earlier, in the mid–late 1st century AD; it is possible, therefore, that, rather than this resulting from the establishment of the villa, the villa was in fact built with the profits generated by the new enterprise.

In terms of the broader military and civil infrastructure of the region, as detailed in Chapter 1, Love's Farm lay at a significant point within local road and river networks (Fig. 1.3). Larger settlements linked by these networks (such as *Durovigutum* and Sandy) are likely to have developed into commercial, social and religious foci for the local 'native' population, including the inhabitants of the farmsteads excavated at Love's Farm, during the course of the Roman period, such as may also have been the case at the putative 'small town' or estate centre at Eynesbury, adjacent to St Neots (Spoerry 2000, 146–148). Whatever its precise status, the existence of such a focus for intensive Romano-British occupation, in close proximity to Love's Farm, is likely to have provided significant stimulus to the adoption of a more 'Romanised' way of life for the inhabitants of the Love's Farm settlements. It was previously thought that a series of earthworks between Eynesbury village and the river were the remains of a Roman fort (Spoerry 2000, 146). Much of the evidence for this had, however, already been destroyed by gravel extraction by the early 19th century, and whilst excavation during the 20th century confirmed their Roman date, too little is known of these earthworks for the existence of a fort to be proven.

IV. Iron Age and Romano-British settlement

Settlement morphology

The developing character of settlement at the Love's Farm site in the Iron Age and Romano-British periods has been detailed and discussed in Chapters 3 and 4.

Intensive occupation evidently commenced during the middle Iron Age (or possibly slightly earlier) with the establishment of a ditched field system and associated trackways (Period 3.1). This was apparently soon followed (Period 3.2) by the creation of two or three small farmsteads, characterised by unenclosed roundhouses associated with generally small and seemingly unoccupied ditched enclosures, the latter presumably having a largely agricultural purpose. A substantial square enclosure (Enclosure 8), located on the higher ground on the northern part of the site, contrasted with the others of this period in terms of its scale, shape and the size of the perimeter ditch. As such, it may have had a specialised function, although its purpose remains unclear (see Section IX).

Both the farmsteads and the square enclosure continued in use into the late Iron Age (Periods 3.3–3.4), during which time occupation appears to have expanded and intensified, with at least two new settlements being established. This period saw the construction of ditched settlement enclosures, some containing roundhouses and associated features, others probably of an agricultural nature. Roundhouses and other structures continued to be built outside these enclosures. The late Iron Age/early Roman transitional period (Period 3.5) saw the beginning of a trend towards settlement nucleation, which culminated in the Romano-British period, when two substantial enclosed farmsteads occupied the site, one to the north (Settlement 7) and the other to the south (Settlement 6), with associated fields, trackways and other occupation-related features situated beyond their perimeter ditches. A seemingly short-lived, sub-circular, double-ditched enclosure (Enclosure 22) was also built on the higher ground to the north, possibly as a direct replacement for the middle Iron Age square enclosure nearby, which went out of use at this time. Long, ditched boundaries seemingly radiated from this enclosure which, like its predecessor, may have had a particular, non-domestic/agricultural purpose, although what this was remains unclear (see further discussion in Section IX).

Decline of the outlying settlements may have been relatively gradual, perhaps with a slow process of stagnation. Why Settlement 6 should have continued to flourish well into the Roman period whilst other settlements vanished is uncertain, although it is possible that its position adjacent to the main route to the south of the site (Routeway 3) that linked nearby Roman towns, and/or its location on the bank of the Fox Brook, proved significant. Alternatively, its success may have been due to economic or social factors that are not evident in the archaeological record. Settlement 7 did not reach its peak until the 4th century, when it formed a well-ordered settlement adjacent to Routeway 2, neighbouring the more organic Settlement 6 to the south. The now dominant Settlement 7 continued to be occupied into the early Saxon period while the long-lived Settlement 6 appears to have been wholly or largely abandoned in the later 4th century AD.

The regular, 'grid iron' pattern of both Settlements 6 and 7 in the late Roman period, replacing the previous organic layout, is typical of rural sites in the region, and, indeed, more widely in southern England, and presumably reflects changes in the management of agricultural resources. In the case of the settlements at Love's Farm, the network of enclosures, paddocks and tracks appears to have been much more integrated than was the case in the Iron Age, perhaps indicating that agricultural practices were now more closely managed and regulated. The principal concentration of features was also, in both cases, contained within an all-encompassing perimeter ditch, although numerous 'subsidiary' enclosures were also located outside the core area of Settlement 6. However, whilst the layout of these settlements appears very different to that of their Iron Age antecedents, there does not appear to have been any significant change in their economy, which continued to be based on a mixed farming regime of stock rearing and cereal cultivation.

Land division and allotment
The earliest evidence for land division at Love's Farm comprised the remains of a coaxial field system (Period 3.1; Field System 1), fragments of which were recorded over the greater part of the site. This seems to have been laid out with reference to three parallel tracks (Routeways 1–3) aligned east to west, that were perhaps created during the middle Iron Age or conceivably somewhat earlier. Although no settlements directly contemporary with the fields were found within the excavated area, the tracks were clearly significant features in the local landscape, exerting considerable influence on the developing pattern of land use through the middle to late Iron Age and the Romano-British period and, in some cases, well beyond. For the most part, the earliest settlements recorded on the site, attributed to the middle Iron Age (Period 3.2), respected the position of the tracks and one later settlement (Settlement 2, Period 3.3) lay within an elongated enclosure that apparently originated as one of the early fields.

With the exception of the tracks themselves, the most important middle Iron Age boundary on the site was a north to south aligned ditch (Boundary 1), which appears to have run between Routeways 2 and 3, over a distance of approximately 330m. Although this feature ran close to one of the north to south aligned ditches of the earlier field system (Field Line 3), it did not follow its line precisely, and the settlements which were established along Boundary 1 (Settlements 3, 4, and 6) also failed to reference this earlier feature. However, it may be significant that, with the possible exception of Settlement 4 (only a small part of which could be excavated), the remains of these three settlements appeared to be restricted to a zone no more than 120m wide (and generally considerably less) that straddled Boundary 1, bounded to the west and east by two other early field boundaries (Field Line 1 to the west and Field Line 2 to the east, both also part of Field System 1). If this is correct, it would suggest that some elements of the old coaxial system continued to exert an influence on the pattern of land use at this time. It is notable that this pattern, with settlements or areas of occupation apparently strung out along a major linear boundary, is also attested elsewhere in southern England (Lambrick and Robinson 2009, 110–11; Cooke *et al.* 2008, 82).

The precise significance of Boundary 1 is uncertain, but it was presumably constructed in order to demarcate areas of land use and/or tenure. Elsewhere in southern England, it has been suggested that long Iron Age boundaries of this kind may have separated areas of open pasture, perhaps used in common by several communities, from zones of more intensive livestock management and/or arable cultivation represented by complexes of small fields, enclosures and other features of a managed rural landscape (Lambrick and Robinson 2009, 68). Following this model, the Iron Age enclosures at Love's Farm, most of which appear to have been closely linked to individual settlements (represented by one or more roundhouses) might have been developed by each community in order to control and manage stock rearing and/or crop production, whilst the seemingly 'open' areas elsewhere on the site may have been used for pasture. The fact that Boundary 1 did not extend north of Routeway 2 suggests that the area to the north, between Routeways 1 and 2, might have been part of a separate 'landholding', and it is conceivable that the extreme northern part of the site, north of Routeway 1, might have lain within a third landholding. Although there can be no direct proof of this, the different ways in which these three areas developed subsequently (see below) might support the hypothesis.

In the central and northern parts of the site, the extent to which the earlier system of coaxial fields and routeways influenced subsequent patterns of settlement is less clear than to the south. What is certain, however, is that Routeways 1 and 2 retained their importance, as is indicated by the fact that several significant middle to late Iron Age features were laid out with reference to them.

Once established, the general pattern of land use that emerged during the middle Iron Age does not seem to have changed greatly in the late Iron Age (Periods 3.3–3.4), presumably reflecting broad continuity in terms of land management and tenure. The linear aspect of the settlements in the southern part of the site, adjacent to Boundary 1, was maintained, with the most intensive activity occurring adjacent to the boundary ditch (which was redefined on more than one occasion). To the north, Settlement 2, and very probably also Settlement 1, continued to develop. The most significant changes to the late Iron Age 'infrastructure' occurred late in this period, during Period 3.4, when a system of rectilinear fields (Field System 4) and an associated trackway (Routeway 8) were established in the seemingly open area west of Settlement 6.

During this period, land between Routeways 2 and 3 (adjacent to Settlement 6) was evidently being given over to more intensive stock management and/or arable cultivation, represented by the construction of fields and smaller enclosures. To the north, the construction of a trackway (Routeway 4) leading north-westwards from Settlement 1 and the subsequent establishment to the east of this track of rectilinear fields or plots also suggests a possible expansion in the area of actively managed or controlled land in the vicinity of this settlement. This period also saw the beginnings of a shift in the alignment of enclosures, tracks and field ditches, from the broadly north–south and east–west orientation established in the middle Iron Age, to a north-east to south-west or north-west to south-east alignment. This appears to have been a broadly site-wide phenomenon, although some major pre-existing features on the original alignment (such as Boundary 1 and the middle Iron Age routeways), continued in use without any shift in alignment.

The first indications of more substantial changes to land allotment and use occurred in the late Iron Age/early Romano-British transitional period (Period 3.5), although there is no evidence that this was in any way a direct result of the Roman conquest. The most noteworthy aspect of Roman-period land allotment was the apparent abandonment, at least for intensive settlement, of most of the northern part of the site, allied to an evident focus of occupation at two comparatively large, nucleated settlements in the central and southern areas. The reasons for this change are not readily apparent, although it may well have been due to a complex range of factors, including social, economic or environmental changes. Land ownership perhaps gradually became concentrated in fewer hands, as a result of inheritance or other means of acquisition, or perhaps differences in land tenure across the site may have been a factor.

Marked contrasts in land use are also apparent in the Roman period, when the northern part of the site was abandoned and settlement between Routeways 1 and 2 was minimal. Here, activity within Settlement 7 remained at a low level until the 4th century, when the farmstead seems to have developed rapidly, although there was virtually no evidence for surrounding activity. South of Routeway 2, by contrast, Settlement 6 saw intensive occupation for most of the Roman period, and extensive remains of fields, tracks and enclosures were found to the south and west of the main settlement enclosure.

Buildings
(Fig. 9.2)

Iron Age roundhouses and structures

Date and duration
Throughout British prehistory the roundhouse represents the archetypal architectural form for living and farming accommodation. By the Iron Age, it was virtually ubiquitous on settlement sites throughout the country and continued in use into the Romano-British period (Harding 1974, 37–53). Although in some areas of the south, such as the Upper Thames Valley (Booth *et al.* 2007, 35), circular structures seem to have disappeared as an architectural form around the time of the Roman conquest, or possibly even earlier, roundhouses remained common in rural contexts throughout the 1st and 2nd centuries AD (Hingley 1989, 30), and continued to be built in some areas even after this. In the Fens at Littleport, for example, the late continuation of the building form is evident: here, a roundhouse of late 2nd- to early 3rd-century date had been lime-plastered, perhaps in an attempt to resemble masonry/marble, or as a defence against moisture (Macaulay 2002, 20 and 76). In northern England, Wales, and Cornwall roundhouses continued to be built and occupied more generally throughout the entire Roman period and beyond (Hingley 1989, 30), as they did in Scotland (Harding 2004). Late Roman roundhouses are also known from some sites in south-eastern England, for example at Stansted in Essex, where circular structures continued to be built into the second half of the 4th century AD (Cooke *et al.* 2008, 165–9, figs 8.11–8.12).

At Love's Farm, roundhouses do not appear to have been built after the 1st century AD (Period 3.5; see further discussion in Chapter 3.VI). However, Romano-British roundhouses are attested at nearby sites, including one of probable 2nd-century AD date at Ash Plantation, on the A428 (Abrams and Ingham 2008, 48), early Romano-British examples at Lower Cambourne and middle to late Roman structures at Lower Cambourne and The Grange (Wright *et al.* 2009, 19–23, 61). Of the twenty-three certain or possible examples recorded at Love's Farm, six were of middle Iron Age date (Period 3.2), whilst fifteen could be attributed to the late Iron Age (thirteen in Period 3.3 and two in Period 3.4, with another three retained or rebuilt from Period 3.2 to 3.3), and two were in use during the transitional period (Period 3.5, with one more retained from Period 3.4). Additionally, a small, sub-circular structure (5.78m in diameter) represented by a curvilinear ring gully and two postholes (Structure 5) was recorded in Settlement 2, where it was attributed to Period 3.4.

Despite their generally poor preservation, several of the Love's Farm roundhouses had evidently been rebuilt or modified during their lifetimes, as evidenced by multiple phases of intercutting ring gullies. There is little certainty as to the precise life-span of a roundhouse, which must, to an extent, have been governed by the materials used, the condition of the ground on which it was built, the use to which it was put and the care with which it was built. Evidence from dendrochronological studies (Barber and Crone 2001) indicates that the wooden elements of timber structures needed to be replaced on average every 7–15 years, perhaps giving a minimum indication of the duration of certain roundhouses. Hill (2007, 22) has suggested a far more dynamic model for late Iron Age rural life than hitherto envisaged, with long-distance travel forming an important element of a semi-pastoral life. Taking this into consideration, it is quite possible that any individual roundhouse could well have been abandoned and reoccupied by the same or different groups, on a number of occasions. Alternatively, buildings may have been cleared and rebuilt as a traditional site was reoccupied, a model which might well be reflected in the serial renewal of some roundhouses, notably Roundhouse 14 at Love's Farm. The scale of this particular building and its longevity (being rebuilt five times, spanning Periods 3.2–3.5), together with its position in a separate enclosure, may suggest that it housed the head of the settlement.

Function
Although encompassed by the generic term 'roundhouse', it is clear that not all circular structures served as houses; some may have been used for storage (Hingley 1989, 31), whilst others may have served as animal pens (Noble and Thompson 2005, 30), as has been suggested for a late Iron Age structure at Scotland Farm, Dry Drayton (Ingham 2008, 31), or even as cattle byres (Haselgrove 1982, 81). Examples of circular buildings used for industrial purposes are also known (Hingley 1989, 31), and it seems likely that many 'roundhouses' were in fact multi-functional. Indeed, it has been suggested (Lambrick and Robinson 2009, 109) that some ring gullies may not represent the remains of roundhouses at all, but may have held fences demarcating work or storage areas; this may apply particularly to semi-circular or otherwise 'incomplete' curvilinear gullies, often interpreted as partially destroyed ring gullies, which may never have been circular at all (Havis and Brooks 2004b, 531). Unfortunately, preservation of the Love's Farm buildings was so poor, with structures marked merely by truncated ring gullies and (occasionally) a few other negative features, that no direct evidence indicating their functions was recovered.

Pope (2003; 2007) has summarised the various theoretical approaches that have been developed in recent years to analyse the ways in which roundhouses might have been used, in terms both of function and use of social space, and also the possible religious or 'ritual' aspects of use (*e.g.* Oswald 1997; Parker-Pearson 1996; 1999; Parker-Pearson and Richards 1994). These include studies of perceived gender-specific activities within the domestic sphere, and what has been called the 'ritualisation trend' in Iron Age studies, where evidence is sought for ritual influences in 'everyday' domestic activity (Pope 2003, 47–8). Perhaps the most influential of the 'ritualisation' approaches has been the 'cosmological model', where roundhouse orientation, and internal use of space, are linked to cosmological references, specifically the movement of the sun (Pope 2003, 48). However, on balance, Pope argues for a more prosaic interpretation for the orientation of roundhouse entrances, which were orientated to maximise light and minimise drafts, although this is not to say that other, less practical factors, did not have some form of influence. The entrances of the buildings found during the course of the Love's Farm project, where preserved, conformed to the norm, in facing broadly towards the east or south-east. In the case of one middle Iron Age roundhouse, however (Settlement 3, Roundhouse 10), a pair of opposed entrances was indicated. Other roundhouses with opposed entrances are known, as, for example, in the defended settlement of Walesland Rath in Pembrokeshire (Cunliffe 1975, 193, fig. 12.12), occupied from the late 1st century BC into the 3rd century AD, and at a number of Bronze Age and Iron Age settlement sites in the Thames Valley (Lambrick and Robinson 2009, 141). In most cases, the opposed entrances were on the east to west axis of the buildings, as in Roundhouse 10.

Four-post structures
In addition to the roundhouses, three four-post structures were found at Love's Farm, all of which were associated with Settlement 3 (Period 3.3), and were of the common type often interpreted as granaries/hayricks or excarnation platforms (see Chapter 3.VI). A reconstruction of such features appears in Fig. 9.2. Two of the Love's Farm structures are tentatively interpreted as possible hayricks, on the evidence of the charred seeds of grassland plants recovered from some posthole fills (Fryer, Chapter 8.IV), although it is possible this material entered the postholes accidentally during construction or demolition, and was unrelated to the structures' function. At Stansted, in Essex, and elsewhere, the association of four-post settings with curvilinear gullies has led to the suggestion that some may have formed roof supports for circular buildings (Cooke *et al.* 2008, 101), although nothing of the kind was evident at Love's Farm. In the vicinity of Love's Farm, similar structures are known from several sites, including a middle Iron Age settlement at Little Paxton, Diddington (Jones 2001, 20), and at Little Common Farm, investigated as part of the Cambourne New Settlement project, where a middle to late Iron Age four-post structure, 2.6m square, was recorded (Wright *et al.* 2009, 56). Such structures were seemingly uncommon by the Romano-British period (Booth *et al.* 2007, 288), but a rectangular example, measuring 5.1 x 3.8m, was attributed to a middle to late Romano-British phase at Lower Cambourne (Wright *et al.* 2009, 27).

Romano-British buildings
Love's Farm saw a clear transition from roundhouses to rectangular structures, as is familiar at many sites (see Chapter 4.VII). The larger buildings (Structure 105 in Settlement 6 and Structure 114 in Settlement 7), which were constructed in the 3rd and 4th centuries respectively and probably continued in use into the late 4th century, were of the type sometimes referred to as 'aisled barns' or 'aisled houses', although such terms may in the past have been applied too readily to structures that had a wide range of functions, in the same way that 'roundhouse' has become a generic term for all prehistoric circular structures, irrespective of their possible function. In fact, it seems likely that many aisled buildings were multi-functional (Hinman 2003, 61). Some certainly had a predominantly domestic function (Hingley 1989, 39–45), whilst others may have been largely agricultural in nature. At Haddon, near Peterborough, two post-built, aisled buildings were probably constructed during the first half of the 2nd century (Hinman 2003, 33–6, fig. 14). The largest was of similar size to Structure 114 at Love's Farm (measuring 15 x 12m, with a nave 6m wide and aisles 3m in width), whilst the smaller structure *(c.*13 x 8m, with a nave, 4m wide, flanked by 2m-wide aisles) may have been comparable to Structure 105. As at Love's Farm, both

Figure 9.2 Reconstruction of an Iron Age settlement similar to those found at Love's Farm, showing a four-post structure in the foreground

structures were post-built, with uprights mostly set in individual stone- or clay-packed postholes, although in the north wall of the larger building, rectangular post-pads had been used. The absence of internal hearths or other 'domestic' internal features suggests that both of the Haddon buildings may have had a utilitarian agricultural purpose, an hypothesis supported by phosphate analysis of the interiors, which suggested the presence of animals: conversely, phosphate analysis of a similar aisled barn at Vicar's Farm, Cambridge, found no obvious concentrations of phosphates (Hinman 2003, 33–6). Another, possibly late 3rd- to 4th-century example, measuring 12.65 x 8m, at Kilverstone, Norfolk (Lucy and Challands 2006, 164) was also interpreted as a barn for housing livestock, whilst at Dorney, Buckinghamshire, clear evidence for crop processing was found in association with another, similar structure (Booth *et al.* 2007, 289).

There can be no doubt that, in a mixed farming economy of the kind that clearly operated in most rural areas during the Romano-British period, individual farmsteads would have needed facilities to store crops, including a proportion for domestic consumption, taxation, and seed corn (Garrow *et al.* 2006, 163), together with barns and shippons to accommodate livestock. In many instances, however, only part of an aisled structure may have been utilised in these ways, the remainder providing accommodation for a nuclear or extended family (Hingley 1989, 41–5). At Love's Farm, although Structures 105 and 114 were too poorly preserved for their function to be determined, their scale and the fact that each appears to have been the only building within their respective farmsteads (excluding, in the case of Settlement 6, smaller structures located outside the enclosed settlement compound), suggests that they may have been farmhouses, although this would not preclude their use for storage, and/or animal housing, as well as accommodation. Perring, however, argues (2002, 54–5) that the scale and design of such buildings could also be interpreted as a manifestation of agricultural abundance, emphasising the production and storage of agricultural wealth, and notes possible parallels with the role of the medieval tithe barn. Whilst there was no evidence for the existence of a range of rooms at one end of the Love's Farm buildings, as is found in so-called 'developed' aisled buildings (Perring 2002, 53; Hingley 1989, 41–2), both structures were so poorly preserved that the existence of such a range cannot be completely discounted (although this range often contained a heating system and/or mosaic floors, traces of which might have been expected to survive). It is perhaps noteworthy that wall plaster was associated with the possible gate (Structure 107, Period 4.3) in the vicinity of Structure 105. In the absence of definitive evidence, it is not possible to establish with certainty whether Structures 105 and 114 were of the developed type, in which, it has been argued, the 'headman' of an extended family (and, presumably, his own nuclear family) occupied the well-appointed separate range (Hingley 1989, 41–2), or were of simple, undivided form. The latter, it has been suggested, may have accommodated some form of extended family group living in common (Hingley 1989, 43).

At Haddon, the lack of evidence for houses or other domestic structures in the 2nd to 3rd centuries AD suggested that the site essentially comprised a series of paddocks and agricultural storage buildings, with people being accommodated elsewhere (Hinman 2003, 41). There, however, it was argued that the site had a highly specialised agricultural function (see above), perhaps as part of a small villa estate, whereas the evidence suggests that Settlements 6 and 7 at Love's Farm were non-specialised farmsteads operating a 'normal' Romano-British mixed farming economy. The lack of associated roofing tile at Haddon suggested that both buildings were roofed with organic materials (Hinman 2003, 34), presumably thatch, and it seems likely that this was also the case at Love's Farm since ceramic or stone roofing material was also conspicuously absent. That substantial Roman stone buildings were present in the vicinity is, however, attested by earlier discoveries, notably including evidence for a possible villa close to the river at Eynesbury (CHER 00396a; see Chapter 1.III).

V. The agricultural economy

Introduction
The palaeobotanical and faunal evidence from Love's Farm (detailed in Chapter 8) demonstrates that the excavated farmsteads practised mixed farming throughout the Iron Age and the Romano-British period. This is consistent with the wider evidence from central and southern England (Clay 2002, 45, 115–6; Cunliffe 2005, 407–18), which indicates that arable cultivation and the management of livestock formed vital elements of the economy of most settlements throughout these periods. However, the relative importance of cereal production and animal husbandry varied considerably, not only from region to region, but also more locally, as did the detailed production strategies adopted by individual communities. The latter were conditional upon a wide range of variables, principally relating to differences in climate, topography and soils, but also including such things as technological capabilities and economic opportunities (Cunliffe 2005, 407).

In recent years, various excavations – most notably those undertaken during upgrading of the A428 (Abrams and Ingham 2008), and as part of the Cambourne New Settlement project (Wright *et al.* 2009) – have yielded a considerable body of comparative data relating to the agrarian economy of the Iron Age and Romano-British periods on the west Cambridgeshire clay uplands. Additional information is also available from contemporary settlements located on the alluvial silts and gravels of the Great Ouse Valley, and others on the chalk of south Cambridgeshire, as well as more widely in East Anglia and across southern England. In common with the majority of contemporary rural settlements in the area, the Iron Age and the Romano-British community at Love's Farm probably operated a largely self-sufficient, subsistence economy, producing enough foodstuffs and other basic goods to meet their everyday needs, but little else. Having said that, there are indications that at least some individuals were generating sufficient wealth, presumably in the form of an agricultural surplus, to fund the purchase of non-utilitarian goods, albeit in small quantities. In the late Iron Age, this is evidenced in the archaeological record principally by the acquisition of fine, Gaulish-inspired pottery, and perhaps also by the presence of oysters, whilst the Romano-British community was able to afford glassware, imported samian and other finewares, olive oil, wine, and a few items of high status metalwork. Other than the distinctive field systems associated with Settlement 1 (Field System 3, see below) there is, however, no particular evidence for agricultural specialisation in any period, as is evident at some other sites in the region.

Environment
The limited evidence from pollen samples at Love's Farm points to a largely open landscape dominated by grassland, which was presumably used as pasture (Green and Boreham, Chapter 8.VII). This suggestion is supported by evidence from the plant macrofossils from both Iron Age and Romano-British contexts (Fryer, Chapter 8.IV), attesting to the predominance of rough grassland conditions on the site, and the mollusca present in the ditches of Enclosure 22 (Period 3.5) – the only assemblage of land molluscs analysed – which were generally indicative of open country, specifically short-turfed grassland (Fryer and Fosberry, Chapter 8.V). The insect remains from a quarry and well proved less diagnostic, with the former dominated, as might be expected given the character of the features in question, by taxa indicative of disturbed or waste ground (Tetlow, Chapter 8.VI).

The evidence from Love's Farm is entirely consistent with that recovered from the clayland sites immediately to the east. Pollen evidence from several of the Cambourne sites was suggestive of a late Iron Age and Romano-British landscape dominated by open grassland, presumably used to pasture livestock, with limited evidence for cereals or mature woodland (Wright *et al.* 2009, 69, 84). Molluscan evidence, charcoal samples and charred plant remains complemented the pollen data (Wright *et al.* 2009, 70–1, 84), with most of the charcoal and charred material comprising small roundwood and other remains of scrubland taxa. The pollen and charcoal did, however, indicate the continuing existence of areas of mixed woodland or stands of larger trees in the general area, probably with alder in wetter areas (Wright *el al.* 2009, 70–1, 85). The molluscan assemblage and charcoal from the nearby site at Scotland Farm suggested that this largely open landscape of grassland interspersed with areas of scrub and mature woodland was already in existence by the middle Iron Age (Abrams and Ingham 2008, 30–1). Little evidence for coppicing or other forms of woodland management was noted in the Iron Age at Cambourne or at any of the A428 sites, but at Lower Cambourne, The Grange and Jeavons Lane, the charcoal assemblages provided evidence for the coppicing of fast-grown oak in the Romano-British period (Abrams and Ingham 2008, 84), and this was also noted in the contemporary settlement at Childerley Gate (Gale 2008).

Animal husbandry

The faunal remains
Although stock rearing and cereal cultivation appear to have been practised at most rural settlements in the region, it seems clear that animal husbandry dominated the agricultural economy of Love's Farm, as it did at all of the excavated clayland sites to the east, in both the Iron Age and the Romano-British period (Wright *et al.* 2009, 88; Abrams and Ingham 2008, 120). The evidence from Love's Farm and the adjacent sites takes the form of environmental data which illustrates the character of the

local landscape, the physical remains of the stock animals themselves and circumstantial indicators of stock management, such as the presence of droveways, probable stock enclosures and waterholes (see below). The only artefacts recovered from the Love's Farm site that have any likely association with livestock are two iron goad pricks (one from a Romano-British deposit in Settlement 7, the other unstratified; Crummy, Chapter 6.III): such items would have been used to drive plough-oxen or to herd other animals.

The faunal remains from Love's Farm indicate that sheep/goat were more numerous than cattle in both the Iron Age and the Romano-British period (based on MNI), although as cattle are considerably larger beasts, both may have had roughly equal importance in the site economy (Baxter, Chapter 8.III). This is consistent with the evidence from most of the adjacent clayland sites, where cattle and sheep/goat were fairly evenly represented in all periods from the middle Iron Age to the late Roman period (Wright *et al.* 2009, 82; Abrams and Ingham 2008, 32; Ingham 2008, 36), with cattle being slightly more common in most assemblages. However, at Jeavons Lane, cattle were clearly predominant in the late Iron Age, and cattle also dominated the Roman-period faunal assemblage at Childerley Gate, with evidence for increased numbers there in the 3rd century AD, although both cattle and sheep were seemingly bred at this time (Abrams and Ingham 2008, 120). At Love's Farm, other domesticates were present in much smaller numbers, with horse, pig and dog attested in all periods, but chicken, goose, and duck restricted to only a few bones, mostly in Roman-period deposits. At both the Cambourne sites and Scotland Farm, horse remains, which were present in low numbers, were often articulated, and exhibited little evidence for butchery (Wright *et al.* 2009, 83; Rielly 2008), suggesting that they may have been selected for ritual use.

Elsewhere in the area, cattle and sheep dominate Iron Age and Romano-British faunal assemblages at most excavated rural sites, for example in the middle Iron Age settlement at Eaton Socon, west of St Neots (Strid 2008), in a late Iron Age/early Romano-British context at Addenbrooke's Hospital, Cambridge (Evans *et al.* 2008, 126), and from the middle Iron Age onwards at Prickwillow Road, Ely (Atkins and Mudd 2003, 50). Unlike Love's Farm, however, all these sites show a predominance of cattle over sheep/goat, with the former comprising approximately half the bone assemblages and the latter around 35–40%. Conversely, the faunal assemblage associated with the late Iron Age banjo enclosure at Caldecote Highfields was dominated by sheep/goat, followed by cattle, pig, and horse (Kenney 2007, 126; Baxter 2011c). On the chalk of south Cambridgeshire, the economy of the late Iron Age settlement at Edix Hill, Barrington was also dominated by cattle and sheep/goat, with the former probably representing the dominant meat animal, although the latter were present in greater numbers (Malim 1997, 47).

Cattle of all ages are represented in the Love's Farm faunal assemblage, including perinatal and young specimens, indicating on-site breeding, although seemingly in small numbers. However, most cattle were not slaughtered until fully adult, suggesting that they were kept principally for their secondary products (*e.g.* dairy products and leather), and doubtless also for traction.

Evidence for the use of cattle as draught animals came from both the Iron Age and Romano-British faunal assemblages, but was much more common on Roman-period bones. Where the species could be certainly differentiated, the bones of sheep were far more common than those of goat (22%, as opposed to only 0.4%). Although horn cores from both male and female sheep were found in deposits of both main periods, sexed pelves derived almost entirely from ewes. Fewer young or aged animals are present in the Roman-period bone assemblage, compared to that from Iron Age deposits, but otherwise the remains indicate a typical Iron Age/Romano-British kill-off pattern, with animals exploited for both meat and wool (and probably also for milk), and as breeding stock. Since all parts of the skeleton are represented in the faunal assemblage, most animals were probably slaughtered, processed and consumed on site (Havis and Brooks 2004b, 533). Pigs were generally slaughtered as sub-adults or young adults, and were evidently kept for pork and/or bacon.

At the Cambourne sites and at Scotland Farm, the kill-off patterns of the principal Iron Age livestock were comparable, suggesting that similar regimes of stock management were practised. Cattle were seemingly kept mainly for milk and traction, with most of the bones coming from mature adults and few younger animals or calves present, whilst sheep were kept for their wool and for breeding, being culled before their meat became too tough (Wright *et al.* 2009, 83; Abrams and Ingham 2008, 32). Likewise, at Haddon, near Peterborough, the faunal assemblage associated with a small, late pre-Roman Iron Age enclosed farmstead indicated that most sheep survived into maturity, suggesting they were exploited for wool and milk, as well as meat (Hinman 2003, 18). Many of the cattle were also mature when slaughtered, again indicating exploitation for traction and secondary products.

Iron Age cattle at Love's Farm were somewhat smaller than those of the Romano-British period, when there was an apparent increase in size from the 2nd century AD. New breeding stock may have been introduced in the later Roman period, perhaps during the 4th century AD (Period 4.4). There was some evidence to suggest an increase in the size of cattle during the Roman period at the Cambourne sites (Wright *et al.* 2009, 82), and relatively small cattle were also a feature of the faunal assemblage at Scotland Farm (Rielly 2008). No significant increase in the size of the sheep was discernible at Love's Farm. The mechanisms by which new bloodstock were introduced to individual farming communities during the Roman period is poorly understood, but it was presumably undertaken either through social and economic ties with neighbouring communities, or as a commercial transaction with specialised breeders.

Whilst animal husbandry was probably the most important element of the mixed farming economy practised by the Iron Age and Romano-British inhabitants of Love's Farm, there was no indication in any period for specialised production to supply a particular market. Rather, livestock appear to have been managed largely at a subsistence level to meet the basic needs of the local community, both for foodstuffs such as meat, milk and (presumably) butter and cheese, and for raw materials such as wool and leather, as well as where appropriate for traction. Such subsistence economies appear to have operated at the majority of Iron Age and Romano-British sites in the region, both in the area of stock rearing and in cereal production. However, during the Romano-British period, some settlements in the region appear to have been developed into 'producer' sites, where specialised forms of stock management were carried out in order to supply 'consumer' populations – presumably groups such as the army or the inhabitants of the burgeoning urban centres. At Haddon, for example, the middle to late 1st century AD saw the beginning of a shift away from the typical mixed farming strategy of the late Iron Age to a new, specialised agricultural regime, with young cattle and sheep being bred and raised for their meat (French 1994, 176; Hinman 2003, 28). This process accelerated in the late 1st to early 2nd century, when the site was extensively re-planned, perhaps in association with the establishment of a small villa complex nearby (Hinman 2003, 28), and continued to around the mid 3rd century. A droveway provided direct access to nearby Ermine Street at this time, presumably to enable livestock to be transported to market 'on the hoof'. Little evidence for domestic activity was found during this period, and it seems that the excavated remains may have served primarily as a stock yard, with accommodation located off site. A similar system may have been developed in the Roman period at Bob's Wood, near Huntingdon (Oxford Archaeology East, in prep.), where stock enclosures located adjacent to Ermine Street suggested that the livestock formed a significant part of the economy, with animals perhaps being reared to supply the nearby Roman town at *Durovigutum* (Godmanchester).

Closer to Love's Farm, a Romano-British site at Eaton Socon yielded evidence of a mainly pastoral economy, with an emphasis on the intensive rearing and movement of livestock from the 3rd century AD (Gibson 2005, 31–2). This period saw the construction of large, rectilinear ditched enclosures and associated droveways, suggestive of a change from small-scale mixed farming to large-scale pastoral management. As at Haddon, little direct evidence for domestic occupation was associated with this phase, and both sites may have functioned primarily as stock yards rather than settlements. Unlike Haddon, however, the faunal remains here indicated that many of the cattle were of some age when slaughtered, although the presence of calves and juvenile animals suggests that at least some cattle were bred at the site. The paucity of evidence for prime-aged animals may have been due to the fact that they were also exported as live animals to 'consumer' sites, although it is also possible that these animals were retained for milk production, being slaughtered only when past their prime.

Droveways and enclosures
Indirect evidence for stock management is provided by the morphology of many of the ditched enclosures found at Iron Age and Romano-British settlement sites across southern England, together with the presence of other landscape features, including waterholes (Wright *et al.* 2009, 89) and ditched trackways, which are conventionally interpreted as droveways for livestock (*e.g.* Applebaum 1966, 100). Whilst enclosure ditches, together with any associated banks, fences and hedges, would doubtless have been constructed for a variety of reasons (Collis 1996), it is likely that many were concerned with livestock control. At Love's Farm, the presence of roundhouses, pits and other features within some of the excavated enclosures can be taken as evidence that these areas were given over primarily to domestic activity, but in many enclosures very few, if any, internal features were noted, suggesting that they may have functioned as livestock pens, paddocks, or horticultural plots.

Ditched tracks or droveways such as those found at Love's Farm are a common feature of Bronze Age, Iron Age and Romano-British rural landscapes in many parts of Britain, attesting to the importance of stock-rearing in the agrarian economy during these periods. Movement of flocks and herds around the landscape would have prevented over-grazing (Abrams and Ingham 2008, 46), and the use of droveways would have facilitated and regulated such movements, as well as preventing stock from straying, possibly into adjacent cultivated fields (Neal and Fraser 2004, 85). In the vicinity of Love's Farm, late Iron Age and Romano-British droveways are attested at the Cambourne sites of Lower Cambourne, Poplar Plantation and Jeavons Lane (Wright *et al.* 2009, 16–23, figs 7–10; 32, fig 13; 44, fig 17), and at Ash Plantation and Bourn airfield, on the A428 (Abrams and Ingham 2008, 35). The late Iron Age banjo enclosure at Caldecote Highfields is also indicative of an economy based on stock rearing (Kenney 2007; Baxter 2011c), and the presence of fields and droveways at Eynesbury suggests, unsurprisingly, that the Ouse Valley adjacent to Love's Farm was also intensively managed for stock during the Romano-British period (Ellis 2004, 106–7).

At some sites, circumstantial evidence for livestock management is provided by environmental evidence for the possible existence of 'stockproof' thorn hedges, which may have supplemented the bank and ditch systems of many Iron Age and Romano-British settlement enclosures. Locally, evidence of this kind has been recovered from a late Iron Age enclosure ditch at Little Common Farm, a late Romano-British enclosure ditch at Lower Cambourne, and Roman-period deposits at Childerley Gate, where waterlogged remains of bramble and thorns from either hawthorn, buckthorn, or blackthorn were present (Wright *et al.* 2009, 71, 85; Abrams and Ingham 2008, 60, 63). The presence in enclosure ditches of land molluscs indicative of shaded environments has also been taken as possible evidence for hedges adjacent to these features (Wright *et al.* 2009, 85).

Cereal production and consumption
Palaeoenvironmental analysis at many rural settlement sites in the region has demonstrated that cereal cultivation was widespread during the Iron Age and early Roman period, and a picture of crop regimes has begun to emerge. At some sites, evidence for cereals is scarce and it is often difficult to determine whether this is a consequence of poor preservation, or genuinely reflects a low level of arable cultivation close to these particular farmsteads.

In common with most of the adjacent clayland sites, evidence for the production, processing and consumption of cereals at Love's Farm was relatively sparse. Whilst this was doubtless due in large part to poor preservation, it may also be the case that arable cultivation was not particularly intensive, with cereals being produced as part of a largely subsistence economy which yielded sufficient grain for the everyday needs of the community, but little surplus (Fryer, Chapter 8.IV). For the most part, the pollen analysed was too poorly preserved for cereal pollen to be differentiated from that of other grasses (Green and Boreham, Chapter 8.VII), although a small amount of cereal pollen was identified in a late Iron Age quarry pit (Quarry 3, Period 3.4) located within Settlement 2. It was not, therefore, possible to establish with certainty that cereals were being cultivated on or near the site in the Iron Age or the Romano-British period, although it seems likely that some grain was produced at a subsistence level. Limited pollen evidence from some of the Cambourne sites pointed to the possible cultivation of cereals in the vicinity in the late Iron Age and the Romano-British period, although it was noted that pollen is also released during cereal processing, meaning that its presence cannot be taken as definitive evidence for cereal production at these sites (Wright *et al.* 2009, 110). However, the presence of seeds of stinking mayweed (*Anthemis cotula*) in Roman-period deposits at several sites has been regarded as potentially significant, since this plant is associated with the cultivation of heavy clay soils, being first recorded in middle to late Roman contexts (Wright *et al.* 2009, 111). It is therefore of some interest that charred seeds of this plant were also found at Love's Farm (Fryer, Chapter 8.IV).

Charred grains of wheat (*Triticum* sp.), barley (*Hordeum* sp.) and oats (*Avena* sp.) were all found at Love's Farm, in deposits of all periods from the middle Iron Age (Period 3.2) to the end of the Roman period (Period 4.5), although wheat, and in particular spelt (*Triticum spelta*), predominates in all periods. Grains of free-threshing wheat, probably bread wheat (*Triticum aestivum/compactum*) were also present in a few deposits, most notably in a 3rd-century AD pit (Period 4.3) in Settlement 6, and a single possible example of rye (*Secale cereale*) also came from this feature. Emmer (*Triticum dicoccum*) was recorded, although its status in the middle and later Iron Age is unclear. Over most of south-eastern Britain, emmer was the main type of wheat cultivated during the 2nd millennium BC, although it began to be replaced by spelt (which is hardy and grows better than emmer on heavy soils) from the late 2nd/early 1st millennium BC (Cunliffe 2005, 408). Elsewhere, including the north-east of England (van der Veen 1992; Hall and Huntley 2007), and in the Upper Thames Valley (Lambrick and Robinson 2009, 277), spelt had certainly replaced emmer as the principal grain crop by the middle Iron Age, although the presence of emmer in late Iron Age and (especially) Romano-British deposits at some sites suggests that it remained as a casual invader among the main crop (*e.g.* Wright *et al.* 2009, 110; Lambrick and Robinson 2009, 277). However, it has also been suggested that the presence of emmer and spelt together in the same Iron Age deposits might indicate that they were sown as a mixed crop (Wright *et al.* 2009, 80). Spelt and emmer glume bases dominated the middle to late Iron Age assemblages recovered from the Cambourne sites, to the east of Love's Farm (Wright *et al.* 2009, 78–9), and spelt was present in middle Iron Age deposits at Scotland Farm (Abrams and Ingham 2008, 32); it also formed the bulk of a rich deposit of grain found in a pit of similar date at Eaton Socon (Druce 2008), which additionally contained emmer, barley and probable bread wheat.

Barley, probably of the six-row variety (*Hordeum vulgare*), was scarce at Love's Farm, being recorded in only two Roman-period samples. Although barley was present in Iron Age and Romano-British deposits at some of the Cambourne New Settlement sites, and at Scotland Farm (Abrams and Ingham 2008, 32), at the former it was less well represented than spelt or emmer wheat, and was poorly preserved (Wright *et al.* 2009, 80). It was suggested that, as a probable fodder crop, barley was less likely to have been charred, which may explain its poor showing (Wright *et al.* 2009, 110), but its extreme scarcity at Love's Farm suggests that it may not have been extensively cultivated or used in any period. Its presence is, however, attested at other sites in the immediate area, including in a middle Iron Age context at Eaton Socon (Druce 2008) and in Romano-British levels at Eynesbury (Allen 2004, 94). Only one of the oat grains from Love's Farm could be precisely identified, and in that case it was clearly of the wild variety (*Avena fatua*), as were all the identifiable oats recovered from the Cambourne sites (Wright *et al.* 2009, 80).

At Love's Farm, cereal chaff was present in deposits of all periods from the middle Iron Age to the end of the Roman period, but usually in small quantities. No particular concentrations were evident on any part of the site, or in any chronological period, although a few individual features contained noticeably larger quantities (Fryer, Chapter 8.IV), presumably representing discrete dumps of processing waste (or rather, hearth sweepings, since the surviving chaff was invariably charred). Whilst this suggests that final processing of grain was being undertaken on site, this probably took the form of de-husking of small batches of wheat that had been stored with the grains still enclosed within the spikelets. The presence of charred chaff in deposits of all types and of all periods suggests that this material was routinely disposed of by being thrown onto domestic hearths, although it was seemingly also used as kindling, both for hearths and for corn drying ovens/kilns. At the Addenbrooke's Hospital site, spelt chaff was extensively used as tinder in a series of conquest-period pottery kilns (Evans *et al.* 2008, 126).

At Cambourne, the high proportion of weed taxa represented by large seeds suggested that, in both the Iron Age and the Romano-British period, grain had been well processed prior to storage, with the smaller seeds having already been removed by threshing, winnowing and sieving off-site (Wright *et al.* 2009, 81). The fact that most of the charred cereal assemblages were dominated by glumes, rather than grains, also indicated that final processing took place within the settled areas, with at least some of the resultant waste being thrown onto domestic hearths. Spelt chaff from a Roman-period ditch at Childerley Gate also pointed to the de-husking of wheat at that site (Abrams and Ingham 2008, 55), and wheat chaff was again present in middle Iron Age deposits at Scotland Farm, albeit in small quantities. There, the paucity of evidence for cereals meant that it was not clear if cereals were being cultivated in the vicinity of the farmstead, or were imported to the site in a semi-processed state (Abrams and Ingham 2008, 32), a possibility that was also raised on the basis of similar evidence (or lack of evidence) in the late Iron Age settlement at Stansted, Essex (Havis and Brooks 2004b, 533; Cooke *et al.* 2008, 90).

Germinated wheat grains were recovered from several deposits at Love's Farm, possibly attesting to the malting of grain for brewing. Malting is well attested at Romano-British rural settlements in the region, although it is rarely found at Iron Age sites (Wright *et al.* 2009, 113). The presence of sprouted wheat grains in a late Iron Age (Period 3.3) ditch associated with Settlement 4 (Fryer, Chapter 8.IV) could therefore be potentially significant, although it is possible that the grain had accidentally germinated, as may also have been the case with an assemblage of partly germinated spelt grain from a middle Iron Age context at Eaton Socon (Druce 2008). At Love's Farm, germinated wheat grains also came from several Romano-British features, mostly associated with Settlement 6, ranging in date from the late 1st to early 2nd century AD (Period 4.1) to the 4th century (Period 4.4). These were mainly pits and ditches, but also included a 2nd-century oven (Period 4.2, *11801*). In the farmstead at Childerley Gate, on the A428, an assemblage of spelt wheat recovered from a pit included a significant proportion of sprouted grains, and at Cambourne, germinated grains and coleoptiles (the protective sheath covering the new shoot) were well represented in Roman-period environmental samples (Wright *et al.* 2009, 113). However, as at Love's Farm, it is impossible to tell whether this points to the deliberate germination of grain during the malting process, or merely represents the disposal of spoiled grain (Abrams and Ingham 2008, 93). That some of the sprouted grain at Love's Farm was associated with an oven is suggestive, and several other ovens and corn driers were recorded in Romano-British phases on the site, principally in association with Settlement 6, where most of the evidence for germinated grain was recovered. Such features are likely to have been multi-functional, being used, perhaps, for corn-drying/parching, malting, pottery production and other domestic and light industrial purposes (Abrams and Ingham 2008, 63; Fryer, Chapter 8.IV). At Haddon, near Peterborough, an L-shaped malting oven associated with a late Roman farmstead yielded a concentration of charred spelt wheat grains, many of which had sprouted, and also cereal processing waste which had probably been used as kindling (Hinman 2003, 52). Unfortunately, with the exception of the charred grain associated with oven *11801*, no direct evidence for the use(s) to which the Love's Farm ovens and corn driers may have been put was found, although many of the excavated features yielded wheat chaff, indicating that crop processing waste was routinely used as kindling.

In addition to palaeobotanical remains, evidence for cereal production/consumption at Love's Farm is provided by the presence of four-post structures (above), two possible hayricks and the recovery of quern stones. Querns, used for grinding cereal grains into flour, occur commonly at Iron Age and Romano-British sites of all kinds throughout Britain, attesting to the fundamental economic and dietary importance, then as now, of flour and bread. In the early Iron Age the saddle quern was the form normally used, with rotary querns becoming widespread from the middle Iron Age (Cunliffe 2005, 509). However, saddle querns dominate most Iron Age assemblages in East Anglia (Wright *et al.* 2009, 81), and it seems clear that their use persisted in the region well into the late Iron Age. Locally, the production of flour, which was probably undertaken within the household, is attested by the presence of querns at many clayland sites in the vicinity of Love's Farm, including the middle Iron Age settlement at Scotland Farm, on the A428, where only saddle querns were present (Duncan 2008). Several saddle and rotary quern fragments were recovered from Iron Age and Romano-British deposits at Lower Cambourne, Knapwell Plantation and Little Common Farm (Wright *et al.* 2009, 23, 26, 41, 54, 75), and fragments of an imported lava quern stone came from a middle to late Roman ditch at Poplar Plantation (Wright *et al.* 2009, 36). Excavation of a late Iron Age banjo enclosure at Caldecote Highfields recovered several quern fragments from the enclosure ditches (Kenney 2007, 126; Percival 2011), and a fragmentary rotary quern had been placed on the base of a pit or well within the enclosure (Kenney 2007, 125). Here, as elsewhere, querns or quern fragments were seemingly used as votive or symbolic items, their combined agricultural and domestic associations perhaps imbuing them with a special power or significance. As is detailed below, this practice is apparent at Love's Farm.

With the exception of the quern stones, artefacts with horticultural connections were restricted to an iron spud or hoe, a rake prong, and a socketed-hook used in pruning or general similar tasks (Crummy, Chapter 6.III), all of which came from the area of Settlement 6. The paucity of such implements is unsurprising, since broken or worn out iron tools are likely to have been melted down and their valuable iron recycled.

Other foodstuffs

In addition to cereals, environmental evidence for the production of other crops during the Romano-British period at Love's Farm was restricted to a few examples of the seeds of field beans (*Vicia faba*) and fragments of indeterminate large pea/bean pulse type (Fryer, Chapter 8.IV). Celtic beans (*Vicia faber* var. *minor*) were also recorded at Lower Cambourne and The Grange, together with garden pea (*Pisum sativum*) and beet (*Beta vulgaris*), although the latter was represented by a single seed and may have been growing wild (Wright *et al.* 2009, 110). Peas and Celtic beans are also attested in a Romano-British context at Eaton Socon (Gibson 2005, 31–2), and peas only at Eynesbury (Allen 2004, 93).

Probably the best evidence for the production of a crop other than grain at Love's Farm was, however, provided by the remains of two rectilinear fields (Field System 3) located at the north-east corner of the site. These fields, established in the late Iron Age (Period 3.4), contained a series of shallow, parallel trenches closely resembling a system of Romano-British ditches at Caldecote Highfields, which were tentatively interpreted as the remains of a vineyard (Kenney 2007, 127–8), almost identical to one known from Wollaston, Northamptonshire (Brown *et al.* 2001). Some twenty-four examples of similar field systems of late Iron Age to late Roman date have been recorded across eastern England as part of the ongoing Rural Roman Settlement Project (Alex Smith, pers. comm.). These are mainly in Cambridgeshire (x 6), Bedfordshire and north-west Essex, with a few in the Nene Valley and Buckinghamshire and single examples in Oxfordshire and Hertfordshire. In view of the apparent late Iron Age date of the Love's Farm examples, however, and the absence of evidence for vines at the base of the trenches, it is perhaps more likely that the Love's Farm fields were used for some kind of 'lazy bed' cultivation, or were used to grow asparagus, as has also been suggested for a similar Iron Age system at Milton, north-east of Cambridge (Connor 1999; Kenney 2007, 128, 130). Pollen analysis of samples taken from the trenches at

Love's Farm provided no clue as to the type of crops grown, the remains being dominated, as were all the pollen samples from the site, by grasses (Green and Boreham, Chapter 8.VII).

Perhaps surprisingly, the hunting of wild animals and gathering of other wild resources to supplement the Iron Age and Romano-British diet is poorly attested in the local archaeological record, and wild animal bones are also relatively rare finds on rural settlement sites of these periods elsewhere in southern England (Grant 1984; Albarella 1998). Love's Farm was no different, with few wild animal bones being recovered. With the exception of antlers, which could have been collected as cast specimens for use in craft working (below), only a handful of red deer bones were found, in late Iron Age (Periods 3.3–3.4), early Romano-British (Period 4.1) and late Roman (Period 4.4) deposits. Other potential food species represented by a few (or even single) bones include roe deer, hare, tufted duck and widgeon.

Locally, wild species played little part in the economy of the late Iron Age/early Romano-British settlement at Addenbrooke's Hospital, Cambridge (Evans *et al.* 2008, 126), or at the late Iron Age farmstead at Scotland Farm, on the A428 (Ingham 2008, 36). The remains of deer were entirely absent from the middle Iron Age settlement located close by (Rielly 2008) and, with the exception of antler fragments, only one roe deer bone was recovered from Iron Age deposits at the Cambourne New Settlement sites (Wright *et al.* 2009, 72). However, a small quantity of roe and red deer bones came from Romano-British levels at Lower Cambourne and Jeavons Lane, together with antler fragments, and the bones of mallard, widgeon and other unidentified duck species, all of which were presumably hunted (Wright *et al.* 2009, 86). Hazelnut shell fragments and sloe stones, both the residues of potential food resources, were relatively abundant in Iron Age deposits at several of the Cambourne sites and were also present in some Romano-British deposits (Wright *et al.* 2009, 80, 85).

A few fish bones, including those of pike and eel, were recovered at Love's Farm, mainly from later Roman deposits. Oysters and mussels, the latter generally in smaller quantities, were clearly being imported to the site throughout the Romano-British period, since small amounts were recovered from features ranging in date from the late 1st to early 2nd century AD (Period 4.1) to the 4th century (Period 4.4) (Fryer and Fosberry, Chapter 8.V). That these marine resources were also reaching the site in the Iron Age was, however, indicated by the presence of relatively large quantities of oyster shells in a late Iron Age (Period 3.4) fill of Boundary 1, in the vicinity of Settlement 3, and a Period 3.5 ditch associated with Routeway 9, in Settlement 4. A concentration of mussel shells, weighing 169g, was also recovered from a middle Iron Age (Period 3.2) fill of the perimeter ditch for Enclosure 1 (Settlement 6). In the Romano-British period at Lower Cambourne, the presence of mussel and oyster shells indicated that these foodstuffs were being imported to the site (Wright *et al.* 2009, 114).

VI. Craft and 'industry'
by John Zant, with Nina Crummy

Introduction
Most of the goods and equipment required by the inhabitants of Iron Age and Romano-British rural settlements are likely, as with foodstuffs, to have been produced on site – such home production probably met the bulk of a community's everyday needs (Cunliffe 2005, 485). At Love's Farm, evidence was found for a wide range of craft and 'industrial' activities, including textile production, horn, bone and antler working, iron smithing, pottery production, and probably also wood and leather working. However, given the size of the site and the long period of occupation under consideration, none of these activities is represented by large quantities of material, nor was there any evidence for particularly intensive production in any period, or in a specific area of the site.

Textile manufacture
In Britain as a whole, one of the most widely practised home crafts was the manufacture of textiles, which is presumed to have been undertaken on a part-time basis within the household. At Love's Farm, spinning of yarn was evidenced by ten certain or possible spindlewhorls – seven of stone and three fashioned from reused pot sherds. These items came from Iron Age and Romano-British deposits across the site, or occurred residually in later levels. Most of the stone examples are limestone, but a shale specimen came from a late 4th- to early 5th-century (Period 4.5) ditch fill in Settlement 7, and a possible sandstone whorl was also found. Whilst most are probably indicative of woollen textile manufacture, the spindlewhorls could have been used to spin vegetable fibres, such as flax or nettle. Similar objects are known from several sites in the area, including the middle Iron Age settlement at Scotland Farm, where two chalk spindlewhorls or weights came from an enclosure ditch, together with a fragment of a clay loomweight (Abrams and Ingham 2008, 24). Two ceramic spindlewhorls, a shale lathe core (which had probably been used as a spindle whorl) and two bone spindles, were found in Romano-British contexts at Lower Cambourne (Wright *et al.* 2009, 106).

Weaving was also indicated at Love's Farm by the presence of triangular, fired clay loomweights. These distinctive Iron Age objects would probably have been used on an upright, warp-weighted loom, although the precise nature of the loom used in Iron Age Britain remains uncertain (Cunliffe 2005, 485). The friable nature of these objects suggests that they were intended for use within a structure, not in the open air (Chapter 6.VI). A fragment of a similar weight was recovered from a pit located within a middle Iron Age ditched enclosure at Eaton Socon, south-west of Love's Farm (Stansbie 2008, 44), and fragments were also found in association with a late Iron Age banjo enclosure at Caldecote Highfields (Sealey 2011b), and within the settlements at Lower Cambourne and Knapwell Plantation (Wright *et al.* 2009, 106). Triangular, fired-clay weights are also attested at numerous other Iron Age sites in East Anglia, for example at Stansted, Essex where a large assemblage of spindlewhorls was also recovered (Major 2004, 168–73, fig. 116). Loomweights of this type disappear from the archaeological record soon after the Roman conquest

(Wild 1970, 63), and no other form of weight appears to take their place. Whilst this could be taken to indicate a rapid switch from home production of textiles to the 'industrial' production of cloth in the emerging urban centres or on imperial estates, there is a similar absence of loomweights in Romano-British towns. It may, therefore, have been caused by a change in weaving technology, although the vertical two-beam loom that needs no weights which is known to have been used in Roman Gaul seems not to have reached Britain before the 10th century at the earliest (Walton Rogers 1997, 1759–61; 2001, 160–1).

No shears were found at the Love's Farm site, but these would not be expected in Iron Age contexts, since they are absent from all but the latest Iron Age deposits in Britain (Cunliffe 2005, 485). The lack of these implements in Romano-British contexts at Love's Farm is not necessarily surprising, since such valuable iron tools are unlikely to have been discarded unless broken beyond repair, at which time they might well have been melted down and recycled. A pair of shears was, however, recovered from the excavations at Lower Cambourne (Wright *et al.* 2009, 106). The absence of bone or antler 'weaving combs', which might (in the absence of evidence for Iron Age shears) have been used for plucking wool from sheep as well as for combing the cleaned wool preparatory to spinning (Cunliffe 2005, 485) is slightly more unusual, since such combs are not infrequent finds on Iron Age rural sites in the region, for example at Highwood Farm, west of Great Dunmow, in Essex (Timby *et al.* 2007, 49), as well as more widely in southern Britain. However, the presence of spindlewhorls clearly demonstrates that the early stages of cloth production were being carried out on the site, meaning that the lack of weaving combs is unlikely to be significant.

Other evidence for textile production at the site was extremely limited. A ceramic object recovered from an unphased deposit in Settlement 7 is of uncertain purpose, but might possibly have been a textile bobbin, and a second possible bobbin, fashioned from bone, came from a late Iron Age (Period 3.4) deposit in Settlement 2. Although these objects could have been used in textile production, they might also have been utilised for other activities, such as rope making, basketry, or netting (Crummy, Chapter 6.IX). Possible evidence for sewing was provided by a tentatively identified iron needle from an unphased deposit. In the middle Iron Age settlement at Scotland Farm, various clay-lined pits were found, similar in form to broadly contemporary features at Twywell, Northamptonshire, which were interpreted as possible wool dyeing pits (Abrams and Ingham 2008, 22). At Love's Farm, a clay-lined pit (*8759*) formed part of a group of three pits located within Settlement 6, to the north-east of Roundhouse 14, which was attributed to the late Iron Age/early Romano-British transitional period (Period 3.5). This was the only clay-lined pit recorded on the site, but its precise purpose is not known. The possible presence at Love's Farm during the Iron Age of weld (dyers' rocket) is notable, since it was used to produce yellow dye: it was found associated with Quarry 3 in Settlement 2 during Period 3.4 (Green and Boreham, Chapter 8.VII).

Metalworking

The most notable evidence of metalworking at Love's Farm came in the form of a possible late Roman smithy (Structure 108) associated with Settlement 6. This 4th-century timber building lay to the south of Fox Brook, on the periphery of the settlement. Even here, quantities of metalworking waste were generally small, although the recovery of spheroidal and flake hammerscale from features associated with this structure, together with the presence of an anvil in an adjacent ditch, support the interpretation of this building as a smithy.

Other evidence for metalworking was confined to a small collection of tools, bar iron and both iron and copper alloy offcuts, all of the stratified material coming from Romano-British deposits. The offcuts and tools (including five iron punches) were fairly evenly distributed between deposits in Settlements 6 and 7, with those that could be phased all being attributed to the 4th century AD.

Metalworking debris from the site confirms that localised iron smithing was being undertaken here in both the late Iron Age and the Romano-British period, although quantities were generally small, only 18kg of material being recovered from the entire site. Small-scale casting of copper alloys was also suggested by the discovery of a crucible fragment, recovered from the perimeter ditch of Enclosure 120 which was added to the western side of Settlement 6 in the 4th century (Period 4.4), but no other evidence for this process was recovered (Starley, Chapter 6.IV). Fragments of charcoal adhering to much of the ironworking debris suggest that this was the fuel normally used for working iron in all periods.

With no local source of ore for smelting, the smiths working at Love's Farm would have primarily used bloomery iron imported onto the site in the form of smith's blanks (bar iron), a few fragments of which were found in Romano-British contexts at the site, mostly from 3rd- to 4th-century deposits in Settlement 6, but a few also from 4th-century levels in Settlement 7. This would doubtless have been supplemented by scrap iron collected for recycling. A large collection of such scrap iron, mostly comprising nails and sheet fragments, was recovered from a 4th-century cobbled surface (*5344*) in Settlement 7. Whether this was debris from an (unlocated) smithy somewhere within the settlement, or had some other significance is, however, unclear: this one group dominates the assemblage of metalwork recovered from Settlement 7, and clearly represents a significant event in the settlement's history. On balance, the complete absence of copper alloy artefacts and the presence of a fragment of bar iron suggest that this material may indeed have derived from a smithy. A similar assemblage of scrap and unforged iron was found in a late Roman context at Winchester, in the Roman town's northern suburb (Rees *et al.* 2008, 179–80, 381).

The closest major iron-producing area to Love's Farm is represented by the ironstone quarries along the Jurassic ridge in Northamptonshire, where late Iron Age and Roman smelting furnaces have been found at Gretton, Bulwick, Byfield, Wakerley and Laxton (Jackson 1979; 1998; Jackson and Ambrose 1978, 151–66; Jackson and Tylecote 1988). The furnaces at the latter site were unusually large and capable of producing enough iron to supply a hinterland that extended well into Cambridgeshire. An alternative source may have been west Norfolk, where iron-smelting sites dating from the late Iron Age to the late Roman period have also been found. Possibly the largest was located at North Wootton and South Wootton, near King's Lynn, where a bloomery exploiting the iron-pans and limonite nodules in the sand and gravels of the area seems to have extended over about 5ha and may have held over 100 furnaces (Smallwood 1989).

Starley (Chapter 6.IV) notes that, regionally, much Iron Age and Romano-British ironworking was carried out on a small scale at rural settlement sites, either in small workshops operated by specialist smiths or at a domestic level. The evidence from Love's Farm is wholly consistent with this, as is the discovery of small quantities of metalworking debris at other settlements in the locality, including Lower Cambourne, where limited evidence for iron smithing in the late 1st to 3rd centuries AD was found (Wright *et al.* 2009, 99) and in a 2nd- to 3rd-century context at Ash Plantation and Childerley Gate, on the A428 (Abrams and Ingham 2008, 50, 55). A similar pattern was found at Bob's Wood, Hinchingbrooke, 13km to the north, where analysis of bar iron suggested that iron ore from local sources on the Jurassic Ridge was being exploited (Starley 2009).

Pottery production
Three ceramic objects that were tentatively interpreted as props or spacers from a pottery kiln came from Romano-British deposits at Love's Farm (Lyons, Chapter 6.VI). One of these was found in association with misfired pottery wasters and other kiln debris in a 2nd-century AD quarry pit (Quarry 7) in Settlement 7, where the material had seemingly been dumped as rubbish. The two other items were found residually in pits within Settlements 6 and 7 assigned to Periods 4.1 and 4.5 respectively.

Although slight, the Love's Farm evidence adds to the increasing body of excavated data for local pottery production at rural settlement sites in Cambridgeshire in the late Iron Age and the early Romano-British period (Willis *et al.* 2008, 74). As elsewhere in the region, it seems probable that pottery production at the site was not a specialist activity, but was undertaken on a small scale by the local community for its own needs, and perhaps also to produce a commodity that could be used for exchange (Lambrick and Robinson 2009, 202). Such small-scale craft production, embedded within the local agricultural economy, is typical of the late Iron Age and early Romano-British period in many other parts of southern Britain. Very similar evidence to that recovered from Love's Farm was found at Prickwillow Road, Ely, where a few kiln bar fragments from Romano-British contexts attested to local pottery production, although no kilns or wasters were found (Atkins and Mudd 2003, 51). Kiln furniture provided the only evidence for possible pottery manufacture at Manor Farm, Harston (Malim 1993, 38), perhaps as late as the 4th century AD. Closer to Love's Farm, a perforated, fired clay plate, interpreted as a probable item of portable kiln furniture, was recovered from a late Iron Age/early Romano-British hearth at Little Common Farm, excavated as part of the Cambourne New Settlement project (Wright *et al.* 2009, 56), whilst pottery wasters found at Childerley Gate, also on the A428, suggested the likely existence nearby of a pottery kiln, perhaps dating to the late 2nd-century AD (Abrams and Ingham 2008, 58, 61), but no kiln furniture or other evidence was recovered. By contrast, no less than eleven mid–late 1st-century AD kilns were excavated at Addenbrooke's Hospital, Cambridge (Evans *et al.* 2008, 57–62), and a contemporary kiln group is also known from Greenhouse Farm, north-east of Cambridge (Gibson and Lucas 2002). Most of the Addenbrooke's kilns were located on the margins of the main conquest-period enclosure, a situation paralleled at Greenhouse Farm and at Haddon, near Peterborough (Hinman 2003). Although several slightly different forms were noted, all the Addenbrooke's kilns were broadly similar to the 'Belgic' or 'late La Tène-derived'-type kilns of the 1st–2nd century AD defined by Swan (1984). These were either entirely surface-built or slightly sunken, with removable kiln furniture, and are commonly found in eastern England (Swan 1984, 63). At Addenbrooke's, it was suggested that the smaller kilns may have been intended for use over a very short period (Evans *et al.* 2008, 62).

At Haddon, mid to late 1st-century AD kilns, kiln furniture and pottery wasters were recorded (Rollo 1994; Evans 2003, 75–81; Hinman 2003, 26). It was suggested that some or all of the kiln furniture and wasters had been deliberately deposited within certain features in an act of closure, possibly associated with the wholesale relocation of the population prior to the comprehensive re-ordering of the site and introduction of a new agricultural regime (Hinman 2003, 27–8). One or two kilns and kiln debris of late Iron Age/early Romano-British date were also found at Swavesey, north-west of Cambridge, where the evidence suggested production on the periphery of a large settlement, or an occasional market/production node (Willis *et al.* 2008, 74).

Other activities
Although crafts such as basketry, woodworking and rope making would almost certainly have been carried out routinely on a largely self-sufficient Iron Age and Romano-British site such as Love's Farm, these activities commonly leave little trace in the archaeological record. Bone working is also likely to have been commonly practised, although direct evidence for this at Love's Farm was restricted to five fragments of bone-working debris, two from Iron Age deposits and three from Romano-British levels. Four of the five pieces were associated with Settlement 6, although they were mostly widely dispersed, both spatially and temporally (one from Period 3.3, two from Period 4.1 and one from Period 4.4); the fifth fragment was recovered from a late Iron Age (Period 3.4) context in Settlement 2. It is reasonable to assume that simple tools, such as the two socketed bone points (probably leather workers' awls; see below) recovered from Period 3.3 deposits in Settlements 1 and 6, were probably made on the site. Off-cuts and other waste derived from the craft working of red deer antler were found in deposits of all periods from the middle Iron Age (Period 3.2) to the end of the Romano-British period (Period 4.5). Whilst, for the most part, this material was thinly scattered, a particular concentration was found in the perimeter ditch of a 4th-century enclosure (Enclosure 131) located within Settlement 7, possibly suggesting the existence of a specialist workshop nearby.

The working of horn in the late Iron Age was suggested by the presence of a cut cattle horncore fragment from a Period 3.3 ditch (Baxter, Chapter 8.III) and, in the late 1st to early 2nd century AD (Period 4.1), of a complete cut off cattle horncore in a ditch within

Settlement 6. An unphased deposit also yielded a horncore with a transverse cut across its posterior surface. Horn itself only survives in the archaeological record in exceptional circumstances, making its absence from the site unsurprising.

Whilst it is highly probable that wooden objects of many kinds were manufactured and used at Love's Farm in both the Iron Age and the Romano-British period, the lack of waterlogged preservation on the site – with the exception of the lower fills of a late Roman well (well *5387*, Period 4.5; which yielded small quantities of waterlogged organic material) – meant that none had survived. Indeed, the only direct evidence for wood-working was provided by an iron saw blade fragment (Crummy, Chapter 6.III). Similarly, the production and use of leather items must also have been widespread, although all these had also perished, except for a few fragmentary shoes recovered from the late Roman well (Mould, Chapter 6.X). Evidence for possible leather-working was, however, provided by two socketed bone points, probably leatherworkers' awls (Crummy, Chapter 6.IX), similar in character to a bone gouge and a bone awl found in association with a late Iron Age 'banjo' enclosure at Caldecote Highfields (Kenney 2007, 126; Kenney and Lyons 2011).

VII. Trade, exchange and status

Iron Age
Beyond the spheres of agriculture and 'craft' production, both of which appear to have been geared to meeting the community's basic needs, there is little indication of other economic activity at Love's Farm during the Iron Age. What limited evidence there is generally points to a low-status, largely subsistence-based economy heavily reliant upon local production and supply, with the few traded items presumably being procured through a system of barter or exchange. Having said that, the presence of finer, Gaulish-inspired pottery in late Iron Age deposits suggests that at least some members of the community were operating above mere subsistence level during this period.

The presence of three late Iron Age coins (Crummy, Chapter 6.II) does not provide evidence for the existence of a market economy in the late pre-Roman Iron Age, since such coins may have been frequently used for social transactions and some appear to have remained in circulation after the Roman conquest (Haselgrove 1979; 1996). The significance of the fact that all three coins were found in or around Settlement 2 is difficult to assess. Whilst most of the Iron Age quarrying/extraction activity that took place on the site occurred within this area, there were no other indications that this settlement was in any way different or of superior status to its neighbours.

Iron Age pottery recovered from Love's Farm represents a domestic assemblage typical of similar sites in the area. In common with other Iron Age sites in the locality, including those excavated during the A428 upgrade (Abrams and Ingham 2008), the assemblage is dominated by locally produced shell-tempered wares, which make up over 45% of the material recovered by weight (Percival, Chapter 7.II). However, the incidence of these wares is almost matched by those in sandy fabrics, which account for over 40% of the assemblage by weight, although these fabrics occur most commonly in the earlier part of the late Iron Age (Period 3.3), declining in importance later, when grog-tempering became popular. The importance of sandy fabrics in the late Iron Age is reflected at other local sites, including Cambourne (Wright *et al.* 2009) and Scotland Farm (Abrams and Ingham 2008, fig. 2.11), but these fabrics also dominate assemblages from sites around Ely and the Cam Valley, suggesting possible trading and/or cultural links between these areas. However, shell-tempered wares remained popular at Love's Farm throughout the Iron Age and indeed the Romano-British period, presumably reflecting the fact that much of the utilitarian pottery required for everyday, domestic use continued to be produced locally.

Organic-tempered wares were scarce, forming less than 1% of the assemblage, but their presence suggests a possible link to the area around the southern fens, where the use of such fabrics was more widespread, as does the incidence of certain vessel forms. Similarly, chalky fabrics may indicate trading links with communities on the chalk-rich clays of the Chilterns, to the south and south-east; again, the amount of such pottery recorded at Love's Farm is small.

From the later part of the Iron Age (Period 3.4), a range of finer traded pottery, inspired by Gaulish imports was reaching the site. These vessels – which include jars, bowls and cups – are suggestive of a more Romanised style of dining (Percival and Lyons, Chapter 7.III), probably related to the widespread adoption of Gallo-Belgic cultural influences across the south-east in the decades prior to the Roman invasion of AD 43. Distinctive late Iron Age pedestal urns also appear at this time, and these too are likely to have been non-local products acquired through trade. The presence of these ceramic forms at Love's Farm demonstrates that at least some elements of the community were not only open to such influences, but were also sufficiently affluent to acquire pottery beyond the range of locally produced utilitarian vessels. The transitional period (Period 3.5) saw the first incidence at the site of truly Romanised wares, including products of the Verulamium industry at St Albans, which began operating soon after the conquest, and imported tablewares, such as samian and Gaulish Terra Rubra, albeit in limited quantities. Notable amongst the transitional assemblage is a sherd from a Campanian 'black sand' wine amphora, which probably originated in the Bay of Naples, and two undiagnostic amphora body sherds. Whilst these fragments probably attest to the consumption of wine at the site in the 1st century AD (unless the empty amphorae were themselves traded as storage containers; Lyons, Chapter 7.IV), the presence of so few sherds suggests that this expensive commodity was not available to the bulk of the community.

Two Iron Age glass beads were recovered from the site (Wadeson, Chapter 6.V). The rarity of glass in Iron Age contexts in Britain suggests that beads and bracelets were prestige items (Cunliffe 2005, 504), and the Love's Farm examples may therefore be indicative of status, although the presence of only two items (and in contexts that were probably deposited several centuries apart) does not suggest a sustained high status presence. The few other personal ornaments of definite Iron Age date support this view, being essentially cheap, probably locally-produced, trinkets, indicative neither of high status nor of wide-ranging contacts (Crummy, Chapter 6.III). The assemblage is restricted to a few simple brooches, mainly of the Colchester-type, the most common pre-Roman Iron Age form in the region (in use *c.*AD 10–50), and two plain copper alloy finger/toe rings, both recovered from late Iron Age deposits (Periods 3.3 and 3.4). In addition, two armlet fragments – one of copper alloy, the other of iron – came from deposits attributed to the Iron Age (Periods 3.3 and 3.5 respectively), and a copper alloy hairpin was found in the outer ditch of Enclosure 22, the enigmatic monument of uncertain purpose located on the northern part of the site. Since the armlets cannot be independently dated, their possible Iron Age attribution rests upon their context, although it is possible that both were intrusive Romano-British items, or were Roman objects that had been deposited in the tops of earlier, partially-filled, features. The hairpin, which may have been modified to create a 'votive' model spear, perhaps dates to the 2nd century AD (Crummy, Chapter 6.III), and is therefore also likely to have been deposited in the ditch long after Enclosure 22 had gone out of use. Most of the items were recovered as stray finds, but a finger ring was found in a late Iron Age inhumation burial (Period 3.3), and three brooches were associated with cremation burials of the late Iron Age/early Romano-British transitional period (Period 3.5). The most notable item amongst the stratified Iron Age metalwork is an enigmatic, three-pronged iron object found in an enclosure ditch terminal (Period 3.5). This item is of uncertain purpose, but may have been deliberately placed as part of a ritual or votive act (see below).

The lithology of the Iron Age quern stones sheds some light on wider-ranging trade links, since one of the five saddle querns recovered is fashioned from Millstone Grit, derived from Pennine quarries, as are at least one, possibly two, of the typologically later rotary beehive querns (Percival and Shaffrey, Chapter 6.VI). One of the latter is a Yorkshire-type quern, which are attested in small numbers on other late Iron Age/early Romano-British sites in south-eastern England, although the Love's Farm fragment was residual in a late Roman context. The other saddle querns are made from locally-occurring sarsen boulders, and are common finds on Iron Age sites in the region, whilst the other two rotary querns may also have been fashioned from locally sourced glacial erratics.

Romano-British

Overview

As might be expected, evidence for economic contact with the wider world increased considerably in the Romano-British period, albeit that the occurrence of traded goods appears to have remained at a fairly low level for some time. Overall, it seems likely that, as in the Iron Age, the Love's Farm community worked hard to achieve self-sufficiency in terms of their basic, everyday requirements and the lack of finds associated with Roman styles of recreation or leisure is consistent with the evidence from similar rural settlements in the region in suggesting that most people had little time for recreation (Crummy, Chapter 6.III). The presence of Romanised artefacts in all of the Romano-British phases at the site, including a few relatively high status items, demonstrates that at least some individuals acquired some of the trappings of a Roman lifestyle. Various items indicate potential contact with the military and may simply reflect the proximity of the site to Ermine Street, and thereby related trade, or may suggest a closer connection in terms of the individuals who settled at the Love's Farm site. Of particular note is the significant group of military armlets (discussed below).

It appears that the Roman-period settlements at Love's Farm were of low to middling status and, like many similar rural settlements, would have presented a picture of reasonable prosperity with a 'veneer of Romanisation' (Malim 1993, 35). As in the Iron Age, the ubiquity of such settlements demonstrates that they formed a vital part of the regional economic and social system, despite their 'low status' designation (Jones and Ferris 1994, 65). The ability of such communities to produce an agricultural surplus no doubt became increasingly important in a society in which significant numbers of people (including administrators, artisans and those involved in the industrial-scale production of pottery and other commodities) were unable to produce their own food (Hingley 1989, 9–10). The resultant demand for surplus produce would have stimulated agricultural innovation and intensification, although, with the exception of evidence for the probable introduction of new breeding stock in the assemblage of cattle bones (Baxter, Chapter 8.III), there was little sign of this at Love's Farm.

Whilst many of the Romano-British artefacts recovered from Love's Farm (including all the glass, much of the metalwork and the majority of the querns) were clearly not manufactured on site, it seems highly likely that most were obtained locally, either at local Romanised market centres such as Eynesbury, *Durovigutum* (Godmanchester) and Sandy, or perhaps from itinerant traders. Similarly, the community would undoubtedly have looked no further than these local sources for the purchase of more exotic imports, such as samian tablewares and amphorae, although these products of course had their origin not only outside the region but in other parts of the Roman Empire.

Coinage and commercial activity

For at least two centuries after the Roman conquest, coin use appears to have been extremely limited at Love's Farm, with only seventeen coins of the period *c.*AD 43–260 being recovered as stray finds (of which only six were legible; Crummy, Chapter 6.II). A further twenty-three late 1st- to mid 2nd-century coins, deposited together in a pot that had been buried in the ground to the west of Settlement 6 (Hoard 1) may either represent a votive offering or a small savings hoard. Either way, they are perhaps unlikely to have been money used in everyday market transactions by the settlement's inhabitants, but may have been collected specially, possibly by a single individual, for a very particular purpose. The paucity of early/middle Roman coins at Love's Farm is entirely consistent with the pattern of low rural coin loss elsewhere in the region, and indeed nationally (Crummy, Chapter 6.II) – at Cambourne, for example, only sixteen coins of this period were recovered – suggesting that most of the rural population was not engaged in a cash-based economy during the first two centuries of Roman rule (Wright *et al.* 2009, 93) but presumably continued to use barter and exchange to obtain basic staples that could not be produced at home. If coinage was occasionally required for the purchase of more exotic goods or to facilitate the payment of taxes, it was doubtless possible to obtain coin at the local, Romanised market centres, where most of it would also have been spent.

At some rural sites in Cambridgeshire, the paucity of Roman coinage of any date suggests that some settlements in the region may not have developed a cash-based economy at all during the Roman period (Crummy, Chapter 6.II). Whether this was due to cultural conservatism, or was because of the inability of most native communities to take advantage of the economic opportunities presented by the development of towns and other nucleated Romanised settlements is, however, unclear (Dawson 2000c, 127). In the early Romano-British period, many settlements in the region were seemingly slow to take-up other aspects of Romanised material culture; a lack of samian and amphorae is evident, for example, at Eaton Socon (Gibson 2005, 32), whilst at Prickwillow Road, Ely, the excavators noted the absence of amphorae and oyster shells, these often being taken as indicators of a Romanised diet (Atkins and Mudd 2003, 52). Whilst it could be argued that such evidence points to the deliberate rejection of Roman goods, perhaps as a cultural statement (Hill 2002, 159), it is perhaps equally likely that these communities were simply unable to access and/or afford such material.

The everyday use of coinage did eventually take off at Love's Farm, where an increase in coin loss from the late 3rd century AD accelerated considerably during the course of the 4th century, peaking in the Valentinianic period (AD 364–78). A similar pattern was observed at Bob's Wood, near Huntingdon (Oxford Archaeology East, in prep), and at Cambourne (Wright *et al.* 2009, 102). This has also been noted elsewhere in the south (and, indeed, more widely in Britain), for example in the Thames Valley (Booth *et al.* 2007, 276–7). It seems likely, however, that this reflects changes in the Roman coinage itself, rather than in the nature of the rural economy. In particular, the production of vast quantities of small copper alloy coins in the late Roman period is likely to have resulted in significantly increased availability of, and familiarity with, coinage. Furthermore, the coins themselves may have been of sufficiently low monetary value to be of practical use for everyday transactions, which may not have been the case with the earlier Roman coinage. At Love's Farm, the particularly high Valentinianic coin loss, together with the presence of small numbers of the very latest coins (AD 378–402), suggests that a high level of activity continued into the last decades of the 4th century, a pattern that was also apparent at Cambourne, but which was not nearly so evident at Bob's Wood, Hinchingbrooke.

In addition to the coinage, generic indicators of possible commercial activity and/or record-keeping took the form of three lead steelyard weights, three iron styli and a copper alloy handle from an iron-bladed wax spatula, depicting a bust of the goddess Minerva (Crummy, Chapter 6.III). Although unstratified, it is possible that the latter object was recycled for use as a votive object (see further comments below).

Pottery supply
In the early Roman period (Period 4.1), the utilitarian pottery used at the site was dominated by fully Romanised sandy greywares in a wide range of forms, although local shelly wares continued to be produced and used in a restricted number of forms, principally storage jars. The availability of Verulamium whitewares, which first appeared at the site in the transitional period (Period 3.5), increased in the early Roman period, but the incidence of more exotic imported wares (which in this period included samian tablewares, probable North Gaulish greywares and probable South Spanish olive oil amphorae) remained low, the quantities present being typical of low status rural settlements in the region.

From the 2nd century AD (Period 4.2) until the late 4th/early 5th century (Period 4.5), shell-tempered wares, supplemented by sandy greywares, dominated the site's ceramic assemblage (Lyons, Chapter 7.IV) and, when combined, represented over two-thirds (*c.*67%) of the total pottery assemblage by weight (*c.*42% for shelly wares, *c.*25% for sandy greywares). In certain periods (*e.g.* Period 4.2) this proportion rose to almost three-quarters, indicating that local production centres satisfied most of the community's ceramic needs. Whilst this presumably reflects the fact that much of the utilitarian pottery required for everyday, domestic use continued to be produced locally, it has also been suggested that the preponderance of shell-tempered wares is indicative of the site's low status, even when compared to similar sites in the area, where the use of finer (and presumably more expensive) sandy greywares was the norm throughout the Roman period. Given the evidence for the craft production of pottery at rural settlement sites in the region, it is possible that the local trade in such vessels (and/or their contents) may have represented an important aspect of the rural economy, supplementing agricultural production. Additionally, smaller quantities of pottery from the major regional production centres (principally Verulamium and the Nene Valley), and from some of the smaller domestic industries (such as Oxfordshire and Hadham), continued to reach the site: the relative importance of each production centre fluctuated in line with periodic changes to, and re-organisation of, regional trade networks, especially in the later Roman period. Imported samian ware and amphorae continued to be used throughout the 2nd century and probably into the early 3rd century, although the quantities of such vessels remained low. Where identifiable, most of the amphorae appeared to comprise Spanish olive oil containers (Dressel 20), although a few Italian wine amphorae (Dressel 1/2) were also found. Amphorae of any kind are rare on most rural sites in the region, meaning that their presence in more than one fabric here is notable, perhaps reflecting the site's proximity to a possible Roman road junction and the fact that it lay reasonably close to Ermine Street, one of the principal arterial roads of the entire province.

Personal possessions
As in the Iron Age, most of the items of personal ornament recovered from Love's Farm are low status objects of base metal and simple form, all doubtless relatively cheap and easily obtainable. In addition to the native Colchester-type brooches, a small assemblage of early Roman-period brooches was recovered, which – with its mix of British-made forms and imported types including Hod Hill and Nauheim derivative brooches – is typical of rural sites in the region (Crummy, Chapter 6.III). However, the four brooches included amongst the possibly votive assemblage of metalwork recovered from alluvial deposit *6572*, to the west of Settlement 6 (Period 4.2), are notably different, comprising two mid 1st-century AD Polden

Hill/Rearhook hybrid brooches, perhaps deposited as a pair, a late 1st-century T-shaped brooch and a 2nd-century trumpet-headed brooch. No other examples of these forms were found elsewhere on the site, and it therefore seems likely that these brooches had either been specially selected for use as offerings, or they were deposited by non-local visitors. The only other unusual brooch is an ostentatious, glass-centred boss brooch of 3rd-century or later date, which came from a late 4th-century (Period 4.4) ditch fill in Settlement 7. The presence of this artefact, together with a snake's head armlet from a contemporary deposit and a late 4th-century cog-wheel armlet in a late 4th-/early 5th-century context (Period 4.5), suggests a degree of affluence and, perhaps, enhanced status amongst the inhabitants of Settlement 7 towards the end of the Romano-British period. A small group of late 4th-century bone dress accessories from this settlement (including several hairpins, an armlet and fragments from two combs) also reflects an appreciation and adoption of contemporary fashions and styles of grooming amongst elements of the community in the latter part of the Roman period. With the exception of a comb fragment and two hairpins (one of which is an earlier Roman form), similar material was absent from the area of Settlement 6.

Of the four Roman beads recovered, three are of glass, including a cylinder bead in an unusual (for Britain) opaque terracotta colour, and one is of amber (Wadeson, Chapter 6.V). The raw material for the latter may have derived ultimately from the Baltic, although fragments of amber can be collected from the shore in certain locations on the east coast of England. Like the dress accessories, there is little evidence for wide-ranging economic contacts in the assemblages of other small finds from the site. For the most part, the items recovered could all have been produced and/or obtained locally, and there is little indication of affluence or high status living. The presence in the glass assemblage of a pillar-moulded bowl fragment and a fragment from a late 2nd-/3rd-century facet cut vessel, suggests that a few individuals had access to high status glassware as early as the 1st century AD. More generally, however, the availability, affordability and/or desirability of Roman cultural items appears to have increased in the 4th century, as evidenced by a marked rise in the quantities of several different artefact types during this period. Notable amongst the assemblage of metalwork are three spoons, comprising one silver and two copper alloy examples, the latter with decorative handles (all unfortunately unstratified), which attest to high status dining on the site in the late Roman period (Crummy, Chapter 6.III).

Worked stone and shale objects
By comparison with other Romano-British settlements in the region, including those excavated as part of the Cambourne New Settlement project (Wright *et al.* 2009, 107), the assemblage of querns and millstones from Love's Farm exhibits a restricted range of lithologies. One of the principal sources of the Romano-British querns found in East Anglia was Millstone Grit from the Pennines and/or the Peak District (Percival and Shaffrey, Chapter 6.VI): it is therefore unsurprising that many fragmentary querns and millstones fashioned from this stone were found at the site. Lava querns, imported mainly from the Rhineland, are widely distributed across eastern England, and, indeed, elsewhere in Britain, but only a few abraded fragments were found at Love's Farm. Other types of stone commonly utilised for the production of Romano-British querns and millstones in the region (such as Hertfordshire Puddingstone and Old Red Sandstone) are absent from the Love's Farm assemblage, suggesting that the inhabitants did not have access to the full range of lithologies that was available in the wider area. It has been suggested that the frequent occurrence of Millstone Grit querns in the region is indicative of traditional links with the Pennine area and, by association, with the Brigantian groups who controlled access to the sources of this stone (Heslop 2008, 49).

Similarly, all six of the hones or whetstones recovered appear to have been fashioned from locally available sandstone (Crummy and Shaffrey, Chapter 6.VI), and could conceivably have been produced on site. The raw material for the single shale spindlewhorl, which came from a late 4th- to early 5th-century (Period 4.5) context in Settlement 7, probably derived from the Kimmeridge area of Dorset, although such objects are widely distributed across southern England (Crummy, Chapter 6.VI). Importation of stone to the site in the late Roman period was indicated by the presence of eighteen fragments of dressed stone, possibly derived from an off-site structure, that had been reused in a Period 4.5 surface laid over an infilled enclosure ditch in Settlement 7. The stone is thought to be Weldon stone, a type of limestone originating in Lincolnshire, *c.*40km to the north-east, which has previously been attested at only a few Romano-British sites in the south-east (Shaffrey, Chapter 6.VI).

Ceramic building materials
Just over 17kg of Roman brick and tile was recovered from the site, mostly in the form of small, abraded fragments. The small size of the assemblage (amounting, in total, to the weight of only seven complete *tegulae*; Lyons and Wallis, Chapter 6.VIII) and the abraded nature of the material suggest that it was re-used, having probably been brought to the site from elsewhere, perhaps for use as hardcore. Fabric analysis suggests that most of the material was made locally; one shell-tempered fabric may have derived from the area of the Harrold pottery industry in Bedfordshire, but another, more local, origin cannot be ruled out.

Comparisons between Settlements 6 and 7
Before the 4th century, Settlement 6 was the pre-eminent of the two Romano-British settlements both in terms of size and intensity of occupation, although the possibility that the main focus of occupation in Settlement 7 lay outside the investigated area has already been noted. For the most part, the assemblages of metalwork from the two settlements are not markedly different, with the bulk of the material representing standard equipment used by the two communities (Crummy, Chapter 6.III). Unsurprisingly, Settlement 6 yielded most of the stratified early Roman brooches and other early items of personal ornament, but a relatively high status glass centre boss brooch of 3rd-century date came from a 4th-century deposit in Settlement 7. The only other significant difference noted was the relative abundance of items certainly or possibly associated with ritual activity from Settlement 6, and the paucity of such material in Settlement 7. This has led Crummy to conclude that Settlement 6 may have been a

focus for ritual not only for the settlement's own inhabitants, but also for the community living in Settlement 7. Taken at face value, the economic and social status of the two settlements seems to have been broadly similar. As in the Iron Age, both communities seem to have operated largely at subsistence level, with stock rearing and arable cultivation forming the mainstays of the economy. The presence of small quantities of imported luxury items, such as samian tablewares, glass, wine and olive oil amphorae, together with a few items of relatively high status metalwork, suggests that some individuals, if not the entire community, were benefiting from the production of an agricultural surplus, at least occasionally (Chapter 9.V), but there is no clear distinction between the two settlements in terms of the distribution of these materials.

Evidence for military/civilian interaction?
A potentially significant aspect of the Love's Farm finds assemblage is the small collection of objects with certain or possible links to the Roman military. Principal amongst these is the group of seven fragments of early Roman military armlets (*armillae*), probably of Claudio-Neronian date, which served as military decorations for junior ranks (Crummy, Chapter 6.III). The group is the largest recovered from any one site in the region, and it is therefore particularly unfortunate that four of the objects were found unstratified, whilst another was intrusive in a late Iron Age (Period 3.3) feature and a sixth was residual in a late 4th-century deposit. The remaining specimen formed part of the probable votive assemblage of metalwork recovered from an alluvial deposit (see below), which largely dates to the 2nd century AD, although 1st-century artefacts were also present.

With the exception of a late 2nd- to 3rd-century copper alloy decorative mount, derived from Roman auxiliary equipment (which came from an unphased deposit in Settlement 6), the *armillae* are the only certainly military items recovered. Other artefacts with possible or probable Roman military connections include two Hod Hill brooches (one unstratified, the other from a modern context; Crummy, Chapter 6.III), and two fragmentary Terra Rubra vessels – a bag-shaped beaker and a conical cup (Lyons, Chapter 7.IV). Hod Hill brooches were introduced to Britain at the time of the Roman conquest, remaining in use to *c*.AD 60–65. Although they were certainly popular with the Roman military, they are also found on civilian sites. The Terra Rubra, which came from a ditch associated with the earliest phase of Settlement 7 (datable to late Iron Age/early Roman transitional period; Period 3.5), is broadly contemporary with the brooches, but is rarely found on 'native' rural sites of this date, usually being associated with early Roman military activity in the region.

The mechanisms by which these objects came to be deposited at Love's Farm remains a matter for conjecture and it is particularly interesting to speculate on why so many *armilla* fragments should have been found here. As military decorations, it might be supposed that these would have been cherished possessions, not given up lightly, which raises the possibility that they represent trophies of war, testifying to conflict between elements of the native population and the Roman army, presumably (given the suggested dating of the *armillae*), during the initial Roman conquest of the region and/or during the Boudican revolt almost a generation later. Theoretically, a similar explanation could also be offered to account for the presence of most of the other 'military-related' items at the site, with the exception of the auxiliary equipment mount which is of considerably later date than the other pieces. This item could have been lost by a serving soldier visiting the site on official or other business, or might even attest to the presence of a retired veteran within the community.

That major conflicts between elements of the region's native population and the Roman invaders did occur during the 1st century AD cannot be doubted, and it is therefore impossible entirely to discount the notion that at least some of the Love's Farm artefacts reached the site as a result of warfare. However, it is perhaps more likely that most were acquired through trade or exchange, either directly, from Roman soldiers stationed in the area, or engaged (for example) in road building, or indirectly, with items being sold on to civilians at local market centres, or by itinerant traders. In view of the site's suggested location, at the junction of two Roman roads and in reasonably close proximity to an important river crossing (Fig. 1.3), either of these scenarios is possible. Admittedly, the *armillae* do not fit so neatly into this peaceful scenario, since, as military decorations, it might be imagined that they would not be so readily traded. Whilst this might be true, it should be borne in mind that, even today, modern campaign medals are not infrequently offered for sale, sometimes only a few years after they were issued, meaning that it is not impossible that the *armillae* were also acquired through trade, being viewed, perhaps, by the 'native' community as nothing more than affordable dress accessories. This does not, however, explain why so many should have been found at Love's Farm. One fragment was seemingly part of a votive offering, perhaps deposited in a 'watery place' (see deposit *6572*, below), and, as such, may have held particular significance for the individual who made the offering, perhaps being deliberately selected or acquired for this purpose. Unfortunately, the contexts of the other pieces offer no clue to the circumstances of their deposition. As Crummy notes (Chapter 6.III), the possibility that the *armillae* derive from the settlement of army veterans here cannot be entirely dismissed, although no other evidence was found to support such an hypothesis.

VIII. Burial practices

Excavations at Love's Farm revealed a range of burials grouped in small cemeteries or placed in isolated graves. A single unaccompanied middle Iron Age inhumation was found (Period 3.2), whilst the late Iron Age evidence (Period 3.3) comprised four inhumations, all essentially unfurnished albeit that one of the graves contained a plain copper alloy finger ring. Of the seventeen burials attributable to the late Iron Age/early Romano-British transitional period (Period 3.5), eight were inhumations and nine were cremations. All were poorly furnished, although most of the cremations contained a few grave goods, principally dress accessories and pottery vessels (see Table 8.2). All the recorded burials were formal, in the sense that they had been laid in discrete grave cuts, and (in the case of the inhumations) comprised complete bodies that had seemingly been laid out with some care. No semi-articulated or disarticulated human remains, of the kind commonly encountered on Iron Age settlements sites across southern England, were found. The paucity of infant burials is a notable feature of the site, given the likelihood of high mortality amongst the newborn. Only one of the 22 recorded burials was that of an infant or juvenile, although a second grave (like the infant, a cremation burial of the late Iron Age) contained the remains of a 5–6 year-old child. Whilst this may well have been the result of differential preservation (given that even the more robust adult remains were mostly very poorly preserved), it is conceivable that the very young were either interred elsewhere, or were in some other way treated differently in death to the rest of the community.

Broadly speaking, the archaeological record for the Iron Age in Britain lacks formal burial evidence, especially for the early to middle Iron Age (Bradley 2007, 262), although formal rites are evident in certain areas and at certain times (Whimster 1981; Madgwick 2008, 99). In southern England, human remains were often disposed of in or adjacent to settlements, either through what might be viewed as 'formal' burial in discrete graves or in other ways, with burial or deposition of remains particularly frequent in boundary/enclosure ditches and storage pits (Cunliffe 2005, 552; Bradley 2007, 262). The general paucity of burial evidence for the Iron Age has led to the suggestion that the 'normative' burial rite afforded to the great majority of the population for most of the Iron Age may have involved rites that leave little trace in the archaeological record, such as excarnation or disposal in rivers or other 'watery' places (Lambrick and Robinson 2009, 319). The corollary to this argument is that those whose remains are found during excavation, either in 'formal' graves or elsewhere, were singled out for special treatment, although why this should be the case is usually far from clear.

In south-east England as a whole, cremation became increasingly common during the 1st century BC (Cunliffe 2005, 559), but the co-existence of cremation and inhumation rites in cemeteries of the late Iron Age/early Romano-British transitional period, as recorded at Love's Farm, is well attested (Evans *et al.* 2008, 57; Lyons 2011). A reconstruction of such cremation is given in Fig. 9.3. Normally, as at Addenbrooke's Hospital, and probably in the isolated late Iron Age/early Romano-British cremation at Blackhorse Lane, Swavesey (Willis *et al.* 2008, 56), the cremated remains were placed in an urn for burial; however, all but two of the Love's Farm cremations were seemingly un-urned. In the late Iron Age cremation cemetery at Westhampnett, West Sussex, where most of the 161 burials were un-urned, it was suggested that the remains may have been interred in fabric or leather containers (Cunliffe 2005, 559). The simplest graves of the transitional period contained no grave-goods, although some were provided with brooches or other personal items (Cunliffe 2005, 559); the Period 3.5 cremations at Love's Farm can therefore be seen to conform very closely to the broader regional picture. The placing of pottery, personal ornaments and (possibly) animal bones in some of these cremation burials presumably indicates belief in an afterlife, whilst the fact that some of these items were heavily burnt suggests that placing of personal possessions, and possibly also food, on the funeral pyre formed part of the ceremony.

Although the general absence of grave goods associated with the inhumation burials makes it impossible to reconstruct any aspect of the burial ceremony, each of the excavated individuals had been carefully laid in their graves. Of the twelve inhumations where orientation could be determined, nine were aligned predominantly north to south (head to the north), including three north-east/south-west-aligned graves and one aligned north-west/south-east, which might reflect a concern with orientation or alignment with the adjacent routeways/boundaries. Most of the bodies had been placed in crouched (N=4), flexed (N=3) or semi-flexed (N = 4) positions, reflecting a trend towards such burials at rural farm sites in south-eastern Britain during the late Iron Age and Romano-British period. These burials are essentially an indigenous tradition that persisted in parts of Roman Britain, declining significantly after the 1st century AD: ongoing analysis by the Roman Rural Settlement Project shows major concentrations of such burials in parts of Gloucestershire, Oxfordshire and in particular southern Wiltshire and Dorset (the 'Durotrigian burials'), with significant concentrations also evident in parts of Cambridgeshire and the East Midlands (Alex Smith, pers. comm.).

Poorly furnished inhumation burials of probably similar date to those from Love's Farm (detailed and discussed in Chapter 3) and Addenbrooke's Hospital (Evans *et al.* 2008) are known from Hinxton and Duxford (Lyons in prep. a; Lyons 2011), south of Cambridge, and Baldock, near Letchworth, Hertfordshire (Stead and Rigby 1986, 57), and elsewhere in southern Britain (Cunliffe 2005, 552), including Stansted, Essex (Cooke *et al.* 2008, 111). Closer to Love's Farm, three early Romano-British inhumations were found in association with the settlement at Lower Cambourne (Wright *et al.* 2009, 21).

IX. Ritual and votive practices

?Ceremonial enclosures

One of the principal aims of the Love's Farm project was to examine any evidence for ritual or ceremonial activity on the site (in addition to the human burials already discussed) and to attempt to identify more subtle ritual or superstitious practices occurring within an 'everyday' domestic context. Of particular interest in this regard are two enigmatic enclosures of distinctive character which lay adjacent on the north-western part of the site, on the crest of the hill adjacent to Routeway 1. The earliest was a substantial middle to late Iron Age square enclosure (Enclosure 8). Similar enclosures have been found at other Cambridgeshire sites, although interpretation of function remains problematic. At Hinxton, an enclosure associated with the Icknield Way clearly served a mortuary purpose (Lyons in prep. a), as did a possible three-sided example at Addenbrookes (Evans *et al.* 2008, 137, fig. 2.58.1), while others may have served agricultural or other functions, perhaps with ritual connotations, as at Chatteris (Thatcher forthcoming) and Trumpington (Percival in prep. d). Square enclosures of similar size associated with settlement are relatively common in the eastern region, as at Haddon V, Willingham, Werrington and Colne Fen, Earith (all illustrated in Evans and Hodder 2006, fig. 6.27).

A potentially ceremonial function might also be advanced for the later adjacent sub-circular enclosure at Love's Farm (Enclosure 22; measuring *c.*31–33m in

Figure 9.3 Reconstruction of a late Iron Age/early Romano-British rural settlement similar to those found at Love's Farm, showing a cremation in progress

diameter externally and *c.*26–27m internally), defined by two concentric ditches, which was constructed in the late Iron Age/early Romano-British period (Period 3.5; see Chapter 3.VI). It could be suggested that this feature formed, for example, an enclosed shrine, although it has not proved possible to find a direct comparator for this monument in a late Iron Age or early Romano-British context within the region. A broadly similar double-ditched enclosure (*c.*26m in diameter) has recently been found at Clay Farm, Trumpington, although this example appears to date to the 3rd to 4th century (Tom Phillips, pers. comm.). A multi-ditched, circular enclosure of probable Iron Age date, excavated at Kempsford Stubbs Farm, in Gloucestershire (Cromarty *et al.* 2007), bears some slight resemblance. However, this was larger (*c.*55m in diameter, externally, and *c.*35–40m internally), and was defined by three closely-spaced, concentric ditches, unlike Enclosure 22, where the two ditches were widely spaced (*c.*6–7m apart). Internally, a possible small (*c.*5 x 3m) rectangular structure of posthole construction was located towards the centre of the Kempsford enclosure, whilst along the eastern edge were five pits, forming a curved alignment concentric with the perimeter ditches. Nothing similar was found within Enclosure 22, which was devoid of internal features, except for the inner ring ditch.

The fact that Enclosure 22 was of seemingly unusual form might support the idea that it had a very specific, specialised function, as might the fact that it was located on the highest part of the site, some distance from the contemporary settlements. The surviving remains provided very little indication of what purpose the enclosure might have served. The possibility that it may have had a defensive purpose has already been discussed (Chapter 3.VI), but is considered unlikely. In the primary phase of the monument, the single entrance through the outer ditch, located on the east side of the enclosure, was only 0.6m wide, suggesting that access to the interior was deliberately restricted. Whilst this could have had a ceremonial significance, allowing people to enter the enclosure only in single file, it is equally possible that the narrow entrance was designed to control tightly the movement and management of livestock. Having said that, even this narrow causeway seems to have been subsequently blocked by a pit, whilst later still, the entrance was reinstated. How the enclosure was accessed during the period in which the entrance was closed is not known.

The faunal assemblage from the enclosure ditches is unusual for the Love's Farm site in that, whereas the remains of cattle dominate the Iron Age and Romano-British faunal assemblages from all the excavated settlements (Baxter, Chapter 8.III), cattle bones were absent from the Enclosure 22 ditches. A considerable number of sheep mandibles and teeth were recovered from the inner ditch, together with small quantities of pig bone and several wild bird and small mammal species: it should be noted, however, that many of the latter may have derived from owl pellets rather than resulting from human activity (hinting at the presence of a post/tree for the owl to perch on while regurgitating).

During the second phase of the enclosure, the terminals flanking the eastern entrance in the inner ditch received deposits containing large amounts of charcoal, ash and burnt animal bones, the latter in tiny fragments too small to identify to species; these were initially believed to be cremation residues, but subsequent examination of the sample residues proved that they contained burnt animal remains rather than human bone (Fryer, Chapter 8.IV and Table 8.11). The contemporary pit that had been dug across the eastern entrance of the outer ditch at this time contained a very similar deposit. The positioning of these distinctive deposits in the ditch terminals echoes the placing of other 'structured' or 'special' deposits, usually comprising collections of certain animal bones and/or artefacts, that were recorded elsewhere on the site (considered in more detail below), and which are known from Iron Age and Romano-British settlement sites across southern England and beyond. Whilst such deposits are frequently considered to have a ritual or symbolic significance, their regular occurrence in domestic contexts suggests that they were the result of 'everyday' ritualised behaviour. The presence of the burnt deposits in the inner ditch of Enclosure 22 cannot, therefore, be taken as evidence that this feature had an overtly ritual or ceremonial purpose.

Having said that, a copper alloy hairpin (SF 2094; Fig. 6.17), which may date to the 2nd century AD, was recovered from the final phase of the outer enclosure ditch, in the vicinity of the southern terminal of the primary eastern entrance which had been removed by this time. This hairpin had apparently been modified to represent a model spear and was perhaps an object of votive significance (Crummy, Chapter 6.III), adding to the general air of 'otherness' that surrounds Enclosure 22. Crummy considers that, in the context of Love's Farm, this 'model spear' may have referenced Minerva, particularly since she was also represented on the site by a depiction on a spatula handle. In her sky-goddess/healing aspect, she may have been the local deity associated with a number of copper alloy rings interpreted as solar symbols, found amongst a range of metalwork deposited, probably in the 2nd century AD, in a wet area of the site on the western periphery of Settlement 6 (below). In this respect, the ring-like form of Enclosure 22 itself might also be significant.

'Special' deposits

In recent decades there has been an increasing recognition that evidence for a wide range of ritual activity, superstitions and spiritual beliefs may reside in certain 'special' deposits, that are frequently encountered during the excavation of prehistoric and Roman-period settlement sites in Britain (Fulford 2001; Morris 2008, 91–2; Lambrick and Robinson 2009, 283–6). Types of deposits that might be thought of as 'special' vary widely (*e.g.* Cooke *et al.* 2008, 118–20), but commonly include animal bones (usually whole or partially complete skeletons, articulated limbs and crania; *e.g.* Madgwick 2008, 100; Phillips and Grassam 2006, 180–1), complete human burials or disarticulated bones (especially skulls and long bones), complete or semi-complete pottery vessels, quern stones (often broken), and a wide range of other artefacts. These can occur singly, or in mixed groups of material, sometimes with burnt stones, charcoal, and other debris, and are often found in 'distinctive' locations, particularly within ditch terminals flanking enclosure entrances (Rees 2008b, 71), in the terminals of roundhouse ring-gullies, and in pits, although they can also occur almost anywhere within enclosure ditches, or in other types of features. Various examples of such patterns of deposition found at Love's Farm are discussed in Chapter 3.VI and Chapter 4.VII.

The problem with the identification of such deposits is that there are no consistent criteria that can be employed to differentiate between 'symbolic' deposition and, say, the casual dumping of domestic refuse, or – in the case of complete animal skeletons – between animals that may have been 'ritually' deposited and those that died of natural causes and were simply disposed of (Atkins and Mudd 2003, 51). It is also unclear to what extent it is possible to separate the sacred from the profane when dealing with ancient societies (Fitzpatrick 1997b) whose belief systems are, to say the least, imperfectly understood, whilst the very idea of 'ritual' as an abstract concept has proved notoriously difficult to define (Morris 2008, 92). Consequently, various scholars (*e.g.* Wilson 1992; Haselgrove *et al.* 2001) have urged caution, pointing out that rigorous recording and analysis of the evidence is needed in order satisfactorily to identify ritual behaviour. It has also been stressed that, in the absence of a 'litmus test' for the identification of ritual activity, each deposit must be considered individually, with regard to its own context and associations (Morris 2008, 94). Despite this, there appears to have been an increasing tendency in recent years to attribute symbolic significance (either explicitly or by implication) to anything that broadly 'fits the bill', such as a single cattle skull located centrally on the base of a pit (Malim 1997), and pottery rim sherds placed in ditch terminals (Stansbie 2008, 46). It is also the case that there has been a tendency to conflate, consciously or unconsciously, the ideas of 'ritual' and 'structured' deposition, although in fact not all of the latter need necessarily be of ritual or symbolic significance, since many other kinds of human behaviour can result in the creation of 'structured' deposits. Butchery and bone working, for example, can generate large quantities of material, comprising the same skeletal elements (Morris 2008, 91), whilst deposits of heavily burnt material, such as those found in the ditch terminals in Enclosure 22 at Love's Farm, could simply derive from domestic hearths or ovens. 'Special' deposits located in ditch terminals have sometimes been interpreted in terms of rituals associated with the liminality between different social and economic spaces (Lambrick and Robinson 2009, 286), or the passage from the 'safe', humanly-controlled environment, represented by the settlement enclosure, to the realm of 'wild nature' beyond (Rees 2008b, 70–1). Whilst this is doubtless true, it may also be worth considering that, in some cases at least, material could have been deposited in other ways. For example, ditch terminals, being located immediately adjacent to enclosure entrances, could have been regarded as convenient places into which refuse was thrown as people passed from the settled area within the enclosure, where the rubbish was generated, to the fields and paddocks beyond.

Notwithstanding these issues, there is now a general consensus that ritual acts within a domestic context were a normal part of life in Iron Age and Romano-British settlements and that deposits generated by such practices are identifiable in the archaeological record (Rees 2008b, 69). The domestic context and agricultural nature of most of the deposits – the majority of which comprise animal bones, with some also containing charred cereal grains and objects (such as spindlewhorls and loomweights) associated with the processing of wool – suggests a practical and pragmatic motivation, perhaps involving propitiatory rites associated with fertility and the agricultural cycle, issues fundamental to people dependant upon agriculture (Rees 2008b, 71, 76). There is, however, no evidence that these practices formed part of any kind of widespread or organised belief system. Rather, it may be that, in Iron Age and Romano-British rural society generally, a shared 'practical-ritual' consciousness prevailed, based on shared life experiences, which was expressed through a range of both practical and ritual activities that were integrated into everyday life (Rees 2008b, 75–6; Madgwick 2008, 111; Morris 2008, 86). Such deposits were not necessarily made frequently, or even on a regular basis, but probably occurred over a period of years, as and when the circumstances of the community, household or individual concerned demanded (Lambrick and Robinson 2009, 287; Hill 1996, 28).

Many 'special' deposits appear to have been associated with the recutting of enclosure ditches and other boundaries, an act which, in itself, may have been both practical and symbolic. The periodic redefining of boundaries, both within settlement enclosures and elsewhere, would, of course, have been necessary to prevent ditches silting up and to repair any associated banks, fences, or hedges. However, the act of redefinition (allied with the placing of 'special' deposits) might also have significant social and ritual meanings, serving to establish a renewed spiritual connection with the land and with the ancestors, and to redefine possession of the land, thereby strengthening social ties within the community (Chadwick 1997, 7; 1999; Rees 2008b, 70–1). It is even possible that seemingly mundane decisions, such as the choice of ditch profile, might have been influenced by a series of pre-existing beliefs, both practical and symbolic, rather than being entirely random or irrational (Rees 2008b, 73).

Excavated examples of 'special' deposits on Iron Age settlement sites are widespread in southern England (*e.g.* Wait 1985; Hill 1995; Lambrick and Robinson 2009, 283–7), and the practice clearly continued into the Romano-British period in many areas (*e.g.* Booth *et al.* 2007, 216–7), as it did at Love's Farm. The phenomenon is well attested in Cambridgeshire, and more widely in East Anglia, where – in common with other regions – a wide range of deposit types has been identified. Examples recorded at sites located no great distance from Love's Farm include two chalk spindlewhorls/weights, recovered from the terminal of a middle Iron Age enclosure ditch at Scotland Farm, Dry Drayton (Abrams and Ingham 2008, 33). There, the excavators considered that the deposition of humanly-worked natural material may have been symbolic of the boundary between the domesticated interior of the enclosure and the 'wild' exterior, and several other possible 'structured' deposits of animal bones and other artefacts were found in enclosure ditches and pits at the same site. Nearby, at Little Common Farm, possible 'placed' deposits of late Iron Age date included the base and body sherds of a pottery vessel placed at the bottom of a pit and large sherds of pottery and an upturned cattle skull on the base of another pit (Wright *et al.* 2009, 56–7). At Caldecote Highfields, just south of the A428, several quern fragments found in the ditches of a late Iron Age 'banjo' enclosure were also thought to have possible symbolic significance (Kenney 2007, 126; Percival 2011), and a near-complete, but fragmentary, rotary quern and a large quartzitic boulder had been placed on the base of a pit or well located in the southern part of the enclosure (Kenney 2007, 125).

Slightly further afield, at Bassingbourn, on the chalk of south Cambridgeshire, a cattle skull had been placed upright near the base of, and facing, a ditch terminal of possible middle Iron Age date (Phillips 2008, 80). At Edix Hill, Barrington, another cattle skull had been placed on the base of an Iron Age pit, and a dog skeleton with a cattle skull placed above it was found in a secondary deposit in another pit (Malim 1997, 48). In Essex, excavations at Highwood Farm, west of Great Dunmow, found a concentration of cattle mandibles, together with other bones and an antler weaving comb, deposited in a ditch terminal adjacent to the eastern entrance to a late Iron Age enclosure (Timby *et al.* 2007, 49). Another terminal flanking the western entrance of the same enclosure yielded parts of a spindlewhorl and a loomweight – artefacts, like the comb, associated with textile production.

Of particular note amongst the apparently deliberately deposited items at Love's Farm was a curious three pronged object (Period 3.3; Fig 6.40, SF 3106) which lay on the base of a ditch terminal associated with Enclosure 1 in Settlement 6. The purpose of this object is not clear, but it might have been a tool used in conjunction with fire-dogs, or even a totem. Crummy (Chapter 6.III) notes that the context of the find is reminiscent of some finds of middle Iron Age iron currency bars (Hingley 1990; 2005; 2007). Iron Age iron artefacts of any size are rare site finds, outside of hoards and overtly votive contexts, presumably due to fact that iron, as a valuable commodity, would normally have been recycled (Lambrick and Robinson 2009, 288). The deposition of this object is therefore likely to have been of ritual significance, perhaps representing the community's respect for iron as a source of social and cultural power.

That similar activities continued into the Romano-British period is evidenced at numerous sites in Cambridgeshire and East Anglia, and elsewhere in southern England, for example in the Thames Valley (Booth *et al.* 2007, 216–17). This suggests that the underlying belief systems on which these ritual practices were based persisted from the Iron Age into (and indeed throughout) the Romano-British period, which in turn might indicate continuity of population (Booth *et al.* 2007, 217, 220). At Haddon, near Peterborough, a cattle skull, pottery, and a Colchester brooch were recovered from the terminal of a roundhouse gully dating to the mid–late 1st century AD and as late as the early 4th century, a pair of iron shears and a coin of Diocletian had been placed at the base of a small pit (Hinman 2003, 26, 52), subsequent to the construction of a malting oven. Even later examples of 'special' deposits, mostly composed of selected animal bones but some also containing pottery, were recorded in 4th-century contexts at Stansted, Essex (Cooke *et al.* 2008, 176–7), including a seemingly 'structured' deposit of bones and pottery found in a pit dated as late as the second half of the 4th century (Cooke *et al.* 2008, 168–9). Three rather more unusual 'placed' deposits were found in 4th-century contexts at Lower Cambourne; these comprised an assemblage of five glass vessels contained within a large ceramic storage jar, which had been placed in a ditch, a group of three pewter vessels recovered from a pit, and an iron tanged bar share and a coulter (both implements associated with cultivation), that were found together at the base of a second ditch (Wright *et al.* 2009, 105).

Animal burials
Other potentially 'special' deposits found at Love's Farm included a number of complete animal burials of both Iron Age and Romano-British date, and possible deliberately 'placed' deposits of animal bones and other artefacts (detailed and discussed in Chapters 3 and 4). Most of the animal burials had been placed in discrete burial pits, whilst the other deposits were found in pits, enclosure ditches and roundhouse gullies, particularly, as elsewhere, in the ditch and gully terminals. An association with foundation or closure rituals associated with the god Terminus appears likely (Baxter, Chapter 8.III). The complete animal burials comprised three horses and three dogs, while several complete or partial sheep skeletons were also found. In contrast to some other rural sites in the region, no whole or near-complete cattle skeletons were discovered, and sheep were also comparatively scarce. There is, however, no good evidence that this was in any way due to economic or social factors, since the deposition of complete cattle crania was fairly widespread, in both Iron Age and Roman contexts, in some cases with two or more skulls being placed together in a ditch terminal or pit and, in the case of the late Roman well, a number of cattle and sheep (see below).

Horses and dogs are species known to have been afforded 'special' treatment on Iron Age sites in Wessex, perhaps due to their social proximity to humans (Hill 1995, 103). Horses, in particular, had military, economic, religious and prestige value, and were also associated with fertility and the deity Epona (Green 1986, 171–6). At the sites investigated during the Cambourne New Settlement project, and at the middle Iron Age settlement at Scotland Farm, on the A428, horse remains were often articulated and exhibited little evidence for butchery, suggesting that they may have featured in 'special' deposits of ritual significance (Wright *et al.* 2009, 83; Rielly 2008). At Love's Farm, two of the three complete horse burials (both located in or near Settlement 6), were of late 1st- to early 2nd-century AD date (Period 4.1), whilst the third (associated with Settlement 7) was attributed to the 2nd century (Period 4.2); they appear to have died from natural causes. A complete horse burial recorded at Haddon (Collins 1994, 151–2) also exhibited no evidence for ritual practice, and was similarly interpreted. An exceptional example of a probable Romano-British votive offering was found at Haddenham, where a specially dug ditch or trench contained six complete horses and eight cattle, mostly buried nose-to-tail. Probable stock enclosures of 2nd- to 4th-century date were located nearby, and it was speculated that the offering may have been related to local environmental changes, which may have reduced the amount of available grazing land (Phillips and Grassam 2006, 181).

Dog burials are common finds on Iron Age and Romano-British sites across the region; five, for example, were found in association with the middle Iron Age settlement at Prickwillow Road, Ely (Atkins and Mudd 2003, 52), although it is often difficult to establish whether they represent some propitiatory rite or simply the disposal of animals that had died of natural causes. The most noteworthy of the Love's Farm examples appears to have been a pet, buried with a stone marking its eye.

Deposition in watery places?
In addition to the 'special' deposits described above, a notable collection of thirty-two Romano-British artefacts, principally copper alloy items and coins, was recovered from a deposit of alluvial silt (*6572*), which sealed a late Iron Age waterhole (Waterhole 5, Period 3.3) located on the western periphery of Settlement 6 (Crummy, Chapter 6.III and Pl. 4.2). This area appears to have been damp and/or susceptible to flooding throughout the Romano-British period, and it is therefore possible that the artefacts represent votive offerings made in a watery place. The only other possible interpretation is that they were part of a small metalwork hoard, deliberately concealed rather than 'offered', that had been subsequently scattered, but in view of their context a ritual or votive interpretation seems more probable. Indeed, the use of coins, brooches and other dress accessories as votive offerings within demonstrably religious contexts, such as temple sites, is so widespread in Roman Britain that the occurrence of similar assemblages in less overtly ritual locations, as at Love's Farm, is also likely to indicate ritual activity (Booth *et al.* 2007, 214).

The majority of the datable artefacts in the collection are attributable to the 2nd century AD (Period 4.2), and five of the eight coins are also of late 1st- to 2nd-century date, with a sixth possibly attributable to the reign of Septimius Severus (AD 193–211). However, the presence of several 1st-century items, including a fragment of a Claudian/Neronian military *armilla*, two mid 1st-century Polden Hill/Rearhook hybrid brooches and a late 1st-century T-shaped brooch, suggests that deposition of the metalwork may have occurred over a prolonged period, with individual items perhaps being offered only occasionally, as circumstances demanded. Alternatively, it is possible that the earlier items were heirlooms, incorporated into an important votive assemblage that was deposited in a single act. That the former hypothesis may be correct is suggested by the presence of two coins of the late 3rd to 4th century, which could provide confirmation that the location retained a spiritual or ceremonial significance for much of the Romano-British period. However, it is also possible, in view of the large number of late Roman coins found elsewhere on the site (Crummy, Chapter 6.II), that these were merely casual losses that had been incorporated incidentally into deposit *6572*. In addition to the coins, a large proportion of the assemblage comprises dress accessories, including four brooches, three armlets (one of which is a fragment of an early Roman military armlet), and two hairpins, perhaps representing personal offerings made by individuals. Eight plain, copper alloy rings were also recovered. These were not designed as items of personal ornament, like finger or toe rings, and may have had a variety of uses; however, in view of their context, the examples from deposit *6572* are considered, by analogy with similar items found in overtly religious or 'ritual' contexts elsewhere (Crummy, Chapter 6.III), to have probably had a votive purpose, symbolising the solar wheel, an attribute of the sky god. A copper alloy *lunula*, probably a horse harness pendant, probably had a similar symbolic meaning.

The context of the Love's Farm assemblage appears similar to that of a series of late 4th-century 'votive' deposits, including coins and pewter plates, found in deposits of 'bog mud' at Verulamium (Abrams and Ingham 2008, 77). Many other examples of votive deposition in watery contexts are known from Iron Age and Roman Britain (Merrifield 1987, 23–30), including assemblages from the Middle Walbrook Valley in London (Merrifield 1995; Merrifield and Hall 2008), Springhead in Kent (Andrews 2008), the sacred spring at Bath (Cunliffe 1988) and Coventina's Well, at Carrawburgh on Hadrian's Wall (Allason-Jones and McKay 1985). The deposits can sometimes be linked to a particular local deity, as at Bath and Carrawburgh, and in the case of the precious metal hoard dedicated to Senuna (represented as Minerva), found close to the River Rhee near Ashwell, in Hertfordshire (Jackson and Burleigh 2007). The watery context of the Love's Farm deposit suggests veneration of a deity of spring or stream, but the inclusion of several solar symbols, in the form of the copper alloy rings, the lunula and (possibly) the coins, might indicate worship of a sky-deity. In view of the evidence from elsewhere on the site, the latter may have been Minerva, as seems to have been the case at nearby Godmanchester (Green 1986, 45).

Approximately 25m north-west of the metalwork deposit, a small coin hoard (Hoard 1), comprising twenty-three copper alloy issues of late 1st- to mid 2nd-century AD date, had been buried in a pottery vessel. Although the proximity of the hoard to the putative 'votive' deposit is suggestive, the fact that the coins were not found within the area of alluvial silting means that a ritual explanation for their deposition remains uncertain, and they may simply represent a small savings hoard. Either way, it is likely that they represented a significant proportion of the coinage circulating on the site in the 1st to 2nd century AD, since only fourteen casually lost coins of this period were recovered from the entire site (Crummy, Chapter 6.II). In the late 3rd to early 4th century AD, a second small hoard (Hoard 2), comprising twelve coins of the late 3rd century, was buried in the top of a disused waterhole (Waterhole 9) within Settlement 7. Here too, votive deposition in association with a watery place is a possible interpretation, although it is perhaps equally likely that the partially infilled waterhole formed a convenient hollow in which to conceal the coins. The fills of the feature also yielded 280 sherds of pottery, principally the remains of kitchen and table wares, although, being distributed throughout the sequence of filling, this was presumably the result of rubbish disposal in a disused feature, rather than evidence of any ritual activity.

One of the latest Romano-British features to be constructed on the site was a stone-lined well (*5387*, Period 4.5), the only feature of its kind found, which was located within Enclosure 139 in Settlement 7. The infilling of the well shaft, which appears to have occurred quite rapidly, contained a large assemblage of animal bones, including thirteen cattle crania and the partial remains of at least twelve sheep. Whilst these remains, together with other cattle and sheep bones and small quantities of horse and pig, may have been butchery waste, the possibility of some ritual or symbolic significance cannot be discounted, particularly since the assemblage also contained small quantities of bone from non-food species, including dog, cat, water vole and wood mouse, together with red deer antler. The presence of remains relating to two dogs may be particularly significant, since examples of possible or probable votive deposits that include the complete or partial remains of two dogs are well attested in Iron Age and Romano-British contexts (Merrifield 1987, 30). Examples of wells and other deep features containing possible votive deposits of animal bones and other material are widespread in Roman Britain (Baxter, Chapter 8.III; Merrifield 1987, 46–8), although, as Merrifield notes (1987, 46), it can be extremely difficult to distinguish ritual deposits from domestic rubbish, unless they are associated with more overtly symbolic items such as human skulls.

In addition to the faunal assemblage from the well, there were hints from the pollen assemblage that ritually significant plants may have been deposited here (Green and Boreham, Chapter 8.VII). It was noted that many of the taxa recorded have well attested culinary and/or medicinal uses. However, the same can be said for many British plant species (*cf.* Grieve 1971), and many of those recorded in the well are so common that they could easily have been incorporated into dumps of earth or refuse used to infill the feature, rather than forming part of a votive offering. Having said that, the presence of mistletoe pollen in the well is clearly unusual, particularly in view of the almost complete absence of associated tree pollen, and it is difficult to avoid the conclusion that this plant – with its well-known symbolic and ceremonial attributes – had been deposited in the well intentionally as part of a ritualised act. The placing of several fragmentary red deer antlers in the top of the well suggests ritual activity, in this case associated with closure of the feature, an hypothesis supported by the presence of what was clearly a deliberately placed deposit, comprising two complete red deer antlers, in the top of the southern perimeter ditch of Enclosure 139, which was located only a few metres south of the well. That both deposits may date to the early Anglo-Saxon period (Period 5) was suggested by a few sherds of 5th- to 6th-century pottery and small fragments of a probably contemporary quern, found in association with the antlers in the ditch.

X. The Anglo-Saxon period

Settlement 7, the northernmost of the two Romano-British farmsteads excavated at Love's Farm, was occupied to the very end of the Romano-British period, as the assemblages of pottery, coins and other diagnostic artefacts clearly demonstrate. Indeed, on artefactual and ceramic evidence, activity reached a peak of intensity during the 4th century, and continued into the early 5th century. Since this is precisely the area of the site from which the great bulk of the early Anglo-Saxon pottery assemblage was also recovered, it would not be unreasonable to expect continuity of occupation through the late Roman/early Saxon transitional period and into the 6th century, with the settlement finally being abandoned sometime in the late 6th to early 7th century AD. However, the dating of the early Anglo-Saxon pottery from the site is seemingly at odds with this neat hypothesis, since the few chronologically diagnostic vessels almost certainly date to the late 5th to 6th century, with earlier forms being entirely absent (Blinkhorn, Chapter 7.VIII).

The difficulties inherent in attempting to identify (and date) 5th-century occupation on Romano-British sites of all types are well known (*e.g.* Esmonde-Cleary 2001; Gerrard 2004, 66–7), and the problems are only likely to be exacerbated on relatively small, plough-truncated rural sites located well away from late Roman population centres (Abrams and Ingham 2008, 101). The collapse of the late Roman pottery industry in Britain sometime after the end of the 4th century resulted in the latest Roman pottery vessels remaining in use long after their period of production, and the use of organic containers, which rarely survive in archaeological contexts, is also likely to have increased at this time, as supplies of pottery dwindled. Most of the other major industries in Britain also went into decline, as the withdrawal of Roman administration and the termination of the coin supply resulted in the collapse of the province's partly monetary-based economy. The resultant contraction in the range of material culture, combined with probable social changes, population decrease and a broad shift from arable cultivation to pasture (Abrams and Ingham 2008, 101; Wright *et al.* 2009, 115), means that 5th-century settlement is far more difficult to identify archaeologically than those of most earlier or later periods. However, despite the lack of evidence, it is clearly illogical to suppose that all, or even most, late Roman settlements were abandoned in the early 5th century. Furthermore, if, as is the case at Love's Farm, there is good evidence for occupation in both the early 5th-century and the late 5th–6th century, common sense would suggest that settlement was continuous throughout, even when the case for continuity cannot be proven.

The evidence from Love's Farm is similar in character to that recovered from the nearby excavations at Cambourne New Settlement (Wright *et al.* 2009), where early Anglo-Saxon occupation was also evidenced largely by the recovery of pottery and a few other objects from the tops of earlier features. At Lower Cambourne, over 100g of pottery was recovered from the dark, upper fill of two Romano-British enclosure ditches and a single sherd came from a layer of dark soil above a later Roman cobbled surface (Wright *et al.* 2009, 24–27). More significantly, three circular, vertical-sided pits were found, which cut through silted Romano-British ditches and were associated with early Anglo-Saxon pottery (Wright *et al.* 2009, 29). These were interpreted as possible wells, dug to collect water draining along what remained of the ditches, and resemble the putative wells/waterholes that cut into the perimeter ditch in Settlement 7 at Love's Farm. Also found was a socketed spearhead of 6th- to 7th-century date (Wright *et al.* 2009, 116), and a few other features and deposits were also assigned to this period, although the precise character of the occupation could not be determined. Elsewhere, small amounts of early Anglo-Saxon pottery were recovered at Knapwell Plantation, Monk Field Farm, Jeavons Lane and The Grange (Wright *et al.* 2009, 115). At the former and latter sites, most of the material came from the upper fills of Iron Age/Romano-British ditches (Wright *et al.* 2009, 40, 62), as at Love's Farm. An early Anglo-Saxon copper alloy girdle hanger of 6th-century date was also recovered from the top of a Roman ditch at The Grange (Wright *et al.* 2009, 62, pl. 26). At Monk Field Farm, however, Anglo-Saxon pottery was found towards the base of what was either a ditch or waterhole, although the sherds were heavily abraded, suggesting that they may have been residual within that feature (Wright *et al.* 2009, 53). Further sherds were also recovered from a probable hedge-line, otherwise undated, and the upper fill of a Romano-British ditch. On the basis of the spatial and stratigraphic distribution of the finds from Lower Cambourne, it was suggested that early Anglo-Saxon occupation may have been focused on one of the ditched enclosures that had been occupied into the late Romano-British period. As at Love's Farm, no contemporary structures were found, although a single early Anglo-Saxon sherd was recovered from a late Roman building, hinting at the possibility of continued occupation within that structure well into the 5th century (Wright *et al.* 2009, 115).

No direct evidence for early Anglo-Saxon occupation was found at any of the sites excavated in advance of the A428 upgrade. However, at Childerley Gate, a fairly homogeneous layer of dark soil filled the upper parts of most of the major features, which mainly comprised the large enclosure ditches of a Romano-British farmstead (Abrams and Ingham 2008, 99). This deposit was likened to the late Roman/post-Roman 'dark earths' that are frequently encountered in Roman urban centres (Esmonde-Cleary 1989, 147), and on other types of Romano-British sites, including rural settlements (Macphail 1981, 312; Macphail and Linderholm 2004, 37). It was suggested that the dark soil may once have formed a continuous layer across the site, but that, except where it infilled the tops of earlier features, it had been incorporated into the overlying subsoil by ploughing (Macphail and Linderholm 2004, 37). With the possible exception of a small pendant, which could have been of either Roman or early Anglo-Saxon date and a small amount of possibly 'proto-Saxon' grog-tempered ware (Macphail and Linderholm 2004, 100), no Anglo-Saxon artefacts or pottery were recovered from the 'dark earth', nor from any other deposits on the site, although the dark soil did contain a fairly high proportion of the very latest Roman colour-coated fine wares and red wares, suggestive of a date at the end of the 4th century or into the 5th century (Macphail and Linderholm 2004, 99), and a coin of AD 388–94 was also found. Furthermore, it is from morphologically similar 'dark earths', filling the upper parts of enclosure ditches and other features, that most of the early Anglo-Saxon artefacts recovered from the Cambourne New Settlement sites came (Wright *et al.* 2009, 115), and this was also demonstrably the case at Love's Farm. At Childerley Gate, the faunal assemblage from the dark soils was dominated by sheep/goat, a characteristic of sub-Roman/early medieval assemblages in the region (Abrams and Ingham 2008, 101), in contrast to the earlier periods, where cattle bones were always more numerous. No animal bones were recovered from analogous deposits during the Cambourne New Settlement Project (Wright *et al.* 2009, 116). At Love's Farm, the only significant finds were red deer antlers, set above the late Roman well.

On Romano-British sites in general, the precise significance of 'dark earths', and the process or processes responsible for their formation, remain a matter for debate (Ottaway 1992, 71). At some sites, agricultural or horticultural activity has been suggested as the possible cause (Perring 1991, 78–9), with material from the latest Roman levels being mixed into a deliberately dumped soil by the spade or the plough. There are, however, problems with such an hypothesis, not least the fact that micromorphological analysis of the deposits and studies of the associated artefactual assemblages have provided contradictory evidence (Macphail 1981; Watson 1998, 103; Vince 1990, 27). On balance, it seems likely that, at the majority of sites, late Roman/early post-Roman 'dark earth' formation was caused by a variety of taphonomic processes, often in combination, and that circumstances varied not only from site to site but also from area to area within a particular settlement. At some sites cultivation activity may have occurred at some point during the early medieval period, although it seems that natural soil accretion and refuse disposal may also have been significant factors (Macphail 1991, 22; Macphail and Linderholm 2004, 39). Rubbish dumping of course implies the existence of occupied areas, presumably close to the sites where refuse was being tipped. At Love's Farm and the other clayland sites, it is possible that the old enclosure ditches were being used as convenient dumping grounds for domestic refuse generated elsewhere, although the lack of direct evidence for contemporary structures or other occupation features remains problematic, and early Anglo-Saxon activity on these sites therefore remains extremely difficult to characterise. Certainly, there is as yet no evidence from rural sites on the west Cambridgeshire clay for 'typical' structures of the period, such as the sunken-featured buildings known from sites located on the chalklands in the south of the county, including Hinxton (Lyons in prep. a), Harston (Malim 1993, 38–9) and Bassingbourn (Phillips 2008, 80), or post-built, rectangular buildings of the kind known, for example from Kilverstone, in Norfolk (Lucy 2006).

Away from the claylands, however, an early Anglo-Saxon settlement is known at Eynesbury, in the Ouse Valley immediately south of St Neots and south-west of Love's Farm (Ellis 2004, 107). This comprised seven sunken-featured buildings, associated with pits and a possible enclosed area, and was occupied during the 6th to 7th centuries AD. As in earlier periods, the faunal and palaeobotanical evidence indicated a mixed farming economy with an emphasis on livestock, mainly cattle and sheep, raised primarily for non-meat products, although bread wheat, oats, rye and peas were all seemingly cultivated (Ellis 2004, 107; Allen 2004, 94). Spinning and weaving were practised in one of the sunken-featured buildings, and the presence of a smithing hearth, slag and furnace lining indicated, perhaps unsurprisingly that iron smithing was carried out on the site (Ellis 2004, 108). The presence of small quantities of 5th-century pottery suggested that occupation may have been continuous from the late Roman period, when Eynesbury may have been the site of a significant estate centre, or possibly even a small town (Spoerry 2000, 146). However, within the area of investigation, 5th-century activity seemed ephemeral at best and there was no evidence that any of the Romano-British field boundaries or ditched droveways on the site continued in use (Ellis 2004, 107–8). The abandonment of the Love's Farm settlement may have been linked to the growth of nearby late Anglo-Saxon centres at Eaton, Eynesbury and St Neots (Addyman 1965; 1973; Spoerry 2000, 150–5), which may have resulted in a shift in population (Ellis 2004, 108). It is possible that this also explains the lack of evidence for occupation at Love's Farm beyond the late 6th to early 7th century.

XI. Medieval and beyond

Although there was no evidence that any part of the Love's Farm site was settled during the medieval period, the whole area had clearly once been cultivated, since the extensive remains of medieval ridge and furrow were recorded over large parts of the investigated area (Field System 7). On the clay plateau east of Love's Farm, similar remains were noted at most of the sites investigated in advance of the upgrading of the A428 (Abrams and Ingham 2008, 103), and at those excavated as part of the Cambourne New Settlement project (Wright *et al.* 2009, 50). Ridge and furrow was also recorded at Caldecote Highfields, east of Lower Cambourne and immediately south of the A428 (Kenney 2007, 128–9). Indeed, it is clear that large areas of the clay uplands of central and eastern England were once covered by ridge and furrow, with substantial areas surviving as visible earthworks in pasture until well into the 20th century (Mills and Palmer 2007, 12). Since then, much of the upstanding ridge and furrow has been ploughed flat, as at Love's Farm, leaving, for the most part, only the remains of the furrows scoring the underlying subsoil (and also disturbing any earlier archaeological deposits). At Love's Farm, the recovery of a large assemblage of medieval and early post-medieval metal artefacts, together with thirty-one coins, nine jetons, and an assemblage of pottery, suggested that midden waste obtained from nearby farmsteads and settlements may have been used to manure the fields (*cf.* Jones 2005).

In the Bourn Valley, which lies to the south of the A428 road, along which much of the recent archaeological work on the clay uplands of west Cambridgeshire has been undertaken, studies by Oosthuizen (1997; 2003; 2006) have suggested that the layout of medieval common fields may have been influenced by surviving elements of Iron Age and Romano-British rural landscapes, particularly field boundaries and trackways. A similar study has also been carried out in an area of south-east Cambridgeshire (Harrison 2002), and another in the south-west of the county (Hesse 2000), although the latter yielded inconclusive results. In west Cambridgeshire, little direct archaeological evidence in support of Oosthuizen's work had been recovered prior to the commencement of the Love's Farm project, and none was forthcoming from either the Cambourne New Settlement Project, nor the investigations associated with the upgrading of the A428. At Caldecote Highfields, however, a medieval plough headland respected the position of an Iron Age ditched trackway, to the extent that it changed direction at the same point as the track, suggesting that the earlier feature survived as a route or a boundary into the medieval period, when it was preserved beneath the bank of the headland (Kenney 2007, 128–9). To this can now be added the data from Love's Farm, where the line of a modern, east to west aligned hedgerow (*cf.* Fig. 1.6) can be traced back, through direct archaeological evidence, to a trackway of Iron Age (possibly even late Bronze Age) origin (Routeway 2). This track remained in use throughout the Iron Age and Romano-British period and, as at Caldecote Highfields, must have either remained in use as a route into the medieval period, or survived as a visible earthwork, since its line was respected by a medieval furlong boundary. This was in turn followed by a post-medieval field boundary, shown on an Inclosure Plan of 1770, which was represented in the modern landscape by the hedgerow. An analysis of the evidence for the development of local field boundaries was conducted as part of the post-excavation stage of the Love's Farm project (Chester-Kadwell 2009), relevant aspects of which have been integrated into earlier chapters.

As in the Iron Age and Romano-British periods, the spread of arable agriculture onto the clays of west Cambridgeshire testifies to a period when population increase necessitated the cultivation and/or habitation of marginal lands that might not otherwise have been considered suitable (Abrams and Ingham 2008, 13). Although the excavated ridge and furrow at Love's Farm and elsewhere cannot be closely dated archaeologically, by means of associated pottery or other finds, it probably dates to the 12th to 13th centuries, when the population of much of medieval England was increasing (Abrams and Ingham 2008, 105; Wright *et al.* 2009, 118). As the population declined during the 14th century, due in large part to the effects of the Black Death, pressure on the land decreased, and these upland areas reverted to pasture, under which they remained until modern times, when advances in farming techniques meant that they could once more be profitably cultivated.

In common with claylands elsewhere in England, the west Cambridgeshire uplands were subjected to extensive improvement schemes from the 18th century to the 20th century, following the enclosure of the medieval open fields, which, at Love's Farm, occurred during the mid to late 18th century, and resulted in the establishment of the farm itself. Archaeologically, this period at Love's Farm was marked principally by the construction of extensive systems of ceramic land drains, which were present on all parts of the development area, as well as most of the sites on the A428 (Abrams and Ingham 2008, 1), and those undertaken as part of the Cambourne New Settlement Project (Wright *et al.* 2009, 30).

XII. Conclusions

The countryside around St Neots was once thought to owe its appearance to the 18th and 19th centuries, having all the hallmarks of a modern post-enclosure agricultural landscape. A major outcome of the Love's Farm project has been the revelation that the local pattern of fields and routeways in fact originated in the middle Iron Age, if not the Bronze Age. Until recent years it had long been held that the 'cold claylands' of the Ouse Valley were inhospitable to early populations, being unforgiving to work and therefore remaining largely uninhabited. New work at Love's Farm and its adjacent sites has revealed a previously unseen, diverse and densely populated landscape. The evidence clearly demonstrates that the process of conquering the claylands for agriculture and settlement required skilled management of the land, in an area that was prone to localised flooding. The archaeological findings are supplemented by new data from sources such as geophysical survey and aerial photography – when combined the evidence permits a wider consideration of the evolution of the landscape.

In conclusion, the excavations were highly successful in addressing all of the research aims formulated at the beginning of the project, and updated subsequently. The work established the nature of the landscape in all chronological periods, and provided highly detailed information on changing patterns of land-use, and the changing character and role of the site. A large body of data relating to the economic status of the site in the Iron Age and the Romano-British periods was recovered, and evidence for a wide range of activities was recorded. The investigations also illuminated aspects of the spiritual beliefs and customs of the inhabitants, through the identification of deposits with possible 'ritual' significance. Overall, analysis, interpretation and presentation of the excavated data from Love's Farm has greatly enhanced understanding of the character and chronology of ancient settlement on the west Cambridgeshire clay uplands, and has provided a fascinating insight into the lives and beliefs of the people who inhabited this landscape in the remote past.

Appendix 1. Geological Survey
by Steve Critchley

I. Overview

No exposures of the solid geology within the area covered by the excavations are known from published sources and field observations. The local 1:50,000 geological map (British Geological Survey 1987) confirms the underlying geology to be of mudstones belonging to the Oxford Clay Formation assignable to the Callovian and Oxfordian Stages of the Middle and Upper Jurassic. These are overlain by a substantial thickness of glacial till deposited during the Quaternary mid-Pleistocene Anglian Stage Glaciation that masks the solid geology almost everywhere within the Great Ouse basin. The till also conceals the underlying pre-Anglian topography and is regionally recorded as varying in thickness from a few metres to as much as 70m. The south-western portion of the excavation area also contained a limited exposure of coarse fluvial sands and gravels representing a distal part of the River Ouse Second Terrace gravels. Field observations indicate that the latter deposits extend further to the east than the published geological map would suggest. A number of subsequent climate-controlled glacial and interglacial periods have extensively modified and reworked the till exposures throughout the late Pleistocene, producing a complex of periglacial near surface 'permafrost active zone' erosive structures and associated sedimentation.

II. Field observations

Glacial tills

Tills deposited during the Anglian Glaciation (Oxygen Isotope Stage 12, equal to 478,000 to 424,000 years BP), underlie the majority of the excavation site and were exposed over large areas following the mechanical removal of the soil horizons. Although weathered and modified by periglacial processes in the upper layers, extensive fresh exposures of the tills were available for examination within several deeper excavations, notably those in Area 4a (Fig. App. 1.1) which provided good detail of their composition and depositional complexity.

In fresh exposures the Anglian tills (often referred to as 'chalky boulder clays') were seen to consist of stiff dark grey to light grey clays with a highly variable lithological content and clast size as well as incorporated patches of locally derived Jurassic mudstones and fluvial gravels. In machine-cut sections the effects of surface weathering could be seen as a variable depth colour change to light brownish clay exhibiting some areas of decalcification. These were also useful for examining periglacial features in section to aid classification, as well as assess depth of penetration and complexity. The freshness of the clast content below the weathered horizons was remarkable and proved helpful in the petrological identification of individual rock types and in an assessment of their frequency of occurrence.

The clasts within the till ranged in size up to 50cm, often with a well rounded to irregular form depending upon the hardness and competency of the rock type and its predepositional origin. The lithological content reflects the multiple source areas for material incorporated into the tills from eroded outcrop material and reworked older glacial and fluvial deposits as well as the direction of advance of the parent ice sheets. There is a dominance of locally derived chalk, carstone, limestone, flint and derived Jurassic fossils along with subordinate non-local sandstones, quartz arenites and more exotic igneous and metamorphic rock types. The Anglian Tills belong to a series of glacial tills assigned to the Lowestoft Till (Perrins *et al.* 1979; Lewis 1999; Bowen 1999) and detailed studies of the clast lithologies have indicated origins for some as far afield as the Scottish Highlands, Wales and the north and west of England (Sabine 1949; Lewis *et al.* 1991; Langford and Briant 2004). However, more recent studies in eastern England have indicated a locally more complex origin for some of these tills among an equally complex picture of coalescing Anglian Stage Scandinavian as well as British ice sheets (Fish and Whiteman 2001). Whether tills of differing provenance are a reflection of different glaciations and time periods or simply represent ice sheet dynamics and lateral variations within one glacial episode is unclear.

Individual clast morphology reflects the effects of erosive mechanisms on the hardness and competency of individual rock types. The softer lithologies such as chalk are well-rounded, exhibiting frequent micro-striations, whilst the flint clasts are frequently angular, reflecting their overall hardness and brittle fracture in response to mechanical and freezing stresses. The less common igneous, metamorphic and some of the sandstone clasts (in particular the quartz arenites) were frequently well-rounded, exhibiting a degree of textural maturity concurrent with their hardness, more distant source areas and the multiple periods of erosion they have been subjected to. Basic intrusive and extrusive basalts dominate the igneous rock types along with diorites and gabbros and subordinate acid intrusive granites, granodiorites and extrusive ryholites. Metamorphic rock types were more variable with epidiorites, basic and acid gneisses, amphibolites and garnet mica schists noted.

The luxury of having large areas of tills exposed for examination allowed an appreciation of the depositional complexity of the whole to be gained, as well as the extent and detail of the subsequent modifying periglacial processes to be examined with some precision. Despite extensive post-depositional modification and erosion, decalcification was variable and the high degree of depositional compaction of the tills (from the weight of the overlying ice sheet) had prevented degradation of the clasts and a number of contemporary depositional features from groundwater or weathering effects. Tills accumulating beneath continental ice sheets are termed lodgement tills and are deposited in discontinuous layers sub-glacially as debris is released directly from the sole of the ice sheet. Additionally, occasional large incorporated patches of locally derived Jurassic clays, chalk-rich patches of till and orange brown fluvial sands and gravels up to several metres in length were observed. The latter

Fig. A1.1 Site areas, showing related field numbers

would be incorporated into the tills as rip-up rafts of frozen ground during the advance of the Anglian ice sheets.

Fluvial sands and gravels
A number of such deposits were exposed within the excavation area and can be subdivided into three types depending upon their mode of formation and occurrence. The most enigmatic were a series of discontinuous lenses and large patches of locally unsorted very coarse chalk-rich gravel present in Field 3 and running obliquely in a north-east to south-west direction across the face of the slope. Compositionally these are dominated by well-rounded soft chalk and angular flint clasts, suggesting a local derivation directly from the tills, in direct contrast to the texturally mature rounded to irregular petrologically complex clasts seen within the Devensian Ouse Terrace outwash gravels. The latter were produced during multiple phases of fluvial reworking of the tills under an arctic nival regime derived from an extensive regional material source area (Gao *et al.* 2007). The chalk-dominated gravels are topographically unrelated to the Terrace gravels, whilst the post-depositional modification/erosion of the outcrop indicates that they are of some age. Machine-cut sections into these gravels, which had in part been damaged by former ancient quarry pits, showed them to infill a channel incised into the surrounding till with sharp edges and evidence of undercutting. These features – along with the irregular morphology of the deposit, material composition and lack of textural and mineralogical maturity – would suggest a sub-glacial origin perhaps contemporary with ice sheet decay.

A deeper and formerly more extensive fluvial channel underlies the modern stream (Fox Brook), which flows through the southern portion of the excavation area, observed in evaluation trenches in Field 7 and open excavation in Field 1, to be infilled with coarse brown to orange brown silty sands and gravels typical of those observed within the Ouse Terrace gravels. Mapping by the British Geological Survey has shown them to be a part of that system although the 1:50,000 scale of Sheet 187 does not indicate their true extent. The present and much-managed watercourse serves a limited catchment and has contributed a series of finer argillaceous alluvium layers observed to overlie the older gravels in machine-cut sections.

Relict patches of both glacial and fluvial gravels of varying size occur over the excavation area. Some can be related to periglacial processes or slope wash whilst others are the eroded remnants of the entrained gravel rafts seen within the tills.

Periglacial processes
The Anglian Tills show extensive modification by periglacial processes that operated during the late Pleistocene Devensian Stage (25,000 to 10,000 years BP), a period of substantive glacial re-advance. Active ice sheets existed some distance to the north and north-east whilst their maximum advances during the Dimlington Stadial (26,000 to 13,000 years BP) reached north Norfolk. Accompanying the ice sheets were intense cold climatic conditions in which periglacial processes were active with the development of abundant thermokarst features such as polygons, thermal cracks and cryoturbation. Many of these ground ice features remain preserved within the Anglian Tills represented by the contemporary and end stage infill of orange brown aeolian sands and fine grained fluvial sands and gravels.

Periglacial processes operating during such cold periods have induced extensive terrain modification with much local variability dependant upon such features as the existing slope morphology and aspect, as well as ground moisture content, permeability and the underlying geology. These processes take place within a surface layer that freezes in winter and thaws in the brief arctic summer and was observed on this excavation to extend to between 0.5m and 1.0m in depth. The repeated freezing and thawing of this layer resulted in the formation of a series of distinctive small scale localised landforms and sedimentary structures.

Within the excavation area the most dominant periglacial features are an extensive development of polygons formed in response to the tensile stresses induced by thermal contraction during intense winter cooling events. These open cracks fill with ground ice and the subsequent incremental seasonal growth of further ice development slowly expands the cracks. During the summer thaws some of the ice can be replaced by in-washed or wind-blown sand and silts and the final relict form of these features can be observed within the tills picked out by a polygon pattern of orange-brown silty sandy infills. Although observed over most of the excavation area the most extensive and visual development of polygons was to be seen in Area 1 of Field 7, where well-formed polygons with 1–1.5m amplitude occur. Here, a north-facing low gradient slope had aided formation and preservation from Holocene modification. Elsewhere polygons had suffered erosion, blurring and modification by later post-glacial slope processes particularly on south-facing areas. Large areas of complex periglacially patterned ground were observed in many areas of the excavation, such as in Field 2.

Elsewhere, some remnant ice cracks were noted particularly on south-facing slopes where they had been widened by gravity slippage in the active permafrost layers. Similar slippage processes had modified polygons on some higher gradient areas to a series of stripes with a transition between the two occasionally observed. Sediment infill within these was more variable with a greater predominance of fine chalky sands and gravels. Accumulations of slope wash sedimentation, a mixture of solifluction and colluvium, were a common feature along the base of the south-facing slopes where they overlay periglacial polygon and ice crack features, in parts themselves overlain by more recent sandy alluvial silts, as in Field 3.

In general the till exposures, particularly those which were south-facing, displayed a locally complex variability in their surface composition. Stone-rich areas, from which fines had been removed by slope wash and aeolian action, were common along with those produced by permafrost active layer sorting and cryoturbation processes. Areas where gravity-induced slope failure had occurred in the active permafrost layers were noted, along with the truncated remnants of probable incipient solifluction lobes at points with higher slope angles.

A number of natural thermokarst depressions of varying diameter were observed across the upper slopes of Field 3 (Areas 2 and 3) and Field 4 (Area 6a), containing accumulations of in-washed silty clays. Such features occur on till plateaus and form during the localised thawing of till areas with a higher ground ice content developed through favourable compositional/permeability regimes. It is likely that a combination of processes contributed to their development with more acidic groundwater chemistries contributing to the process by preferential decalcification of the underlying tills, whilst local degradation of permafrost beneath small ponds could also have been a factor. The release of latent heat during freezing of the latter can reduce the onset severity of winter ground cooling, degrading the underlying permafrost. Any accompanying subsidence would increase the volume of the pond in subsequent years, with a greater latent heat release potential to further the permafrost degradation, and so on, to aid the development of these depressions.

Appendix 2: Catalogue of Roman Coins
by Nina Crummy

All dates are AD. For reference abbreviations see p. xi.   All coins are copper alloy unless stated otherwise.

SF	Context	Feature	Group	Period	ID	Diam. (mm)	Wt (g)	Mint	Reference	Date	Coin period
Settlement 2											
2711	6337	quarry 6338	Quarry 5	3.4	Cunobelin, bronze issue, head/boar type	17	1.87	-	as Hobbs nos 1952–5; van Arsdell 1983–1	early 1st c.	-
2713	6352	quarry 6367	Quarry 5	3.4	House of Constantine copy, rev. Fel Temp Reparatio, falling horseman	15	0.76	-	-	350–60	18
1024	4046	ditch 4047	Enclosure 10	3.5	illegible Iron Age issue, head/horse type	16	1.58	-	-	first half 1st c.	-
Settlement 3											
2987	8795	ditch 8796	Boundary 12	3.5	Constantinopolis, rev. Victory on prow	16.5	2.53	Trier	HK 59	330–5	17
Settlement 6											
2944	8543	ditch 8541	Roundhouse 14	3.3	fragment; House of Valentinian, rev. Gloria Romanorum	16	1.03	-	-	364–78	19
1216	7636	-	Enclosure 20	3.4	Constantine I, rev. VOT XX in wreath	18	1.93	-	-	c.320	16
1258	7648	-	Field System 4	3.4	Valens, rev. Securitas Reipublicae	17.5	2.22	-	-	364–78	19
Settlement 8											
2136	4679	ditch 4658	Roundhouse 22	4.2	illegible	11	0.54	-	-	3rd–4th c.	-
Settlement 7											
2192	4655	gully? 4656	Enclosure 129	4.2	illegible	9.5	0.68	-	-	4th c.	-

Table A2.1. Roman coins from the Iron Age settlements

SF	ID	Diam. (mm)	Wt (g)	Mint	Reference	Date	Coin period
102	Hadrian, *sestertius*, rev. Aequitas Avg S C	31	23.08	Rome	as RIC 1481	117–38	6
103	illegible *sestertius*	33	16.71	-	-	(late) 1st–2nd c.	-
104	Hadrian, *sestertius*, rev. standing female, patera in right hand	31.5	20.93	-	-	117–38	6
105	Trajan, *sestertius*, rev. illegible	32.5	21.13	-	-	98–117	5
106	Antoninus Pius, *sestertius*, ...IIII, AVG S C in field	30	23.56			138–61	7
107	illegible *as*	27	8.25	-	-	late 1st–2nd c.	-
108	Antoninus Pius, *sestertius*, rev.illegible	30	20.50	-	-	138–61	7
109	?Trajan, *sestertius*, rev. illegible	34	19.56	-	-	98–117?	5
110	Antoninus Pius, *sestertius*, rev. Minerva	32	25.94	Rome	RIC 1909	151–2	7
111	illegible *dupondius/as*	27.5	9.18	-	-	late 1st–2nd c.	-
112	Faustina I (Diva), *sestertius*, rev. Juno	31.5	21.57	Rome	as RIC 1531	138–41	7
113	Antoninus Pius?, radiate, *as*, rev. illegible	27.5	10.12	-	-	138–61	7
114	Hadrian, sestertius Rev. standing female	32.5	25.92	-	-	117–38	6
115	Hadrian, *as*, rev. standing male	27	8.75	-	-	117–38	6
116	Trajan, *sestertius*, rev. emperor Haranguing soldiers	33	19.65	Rome	as RIC 1017	114–15	5
117	Faustina I (Diva), *sestertius*, rev. Aeternitas, Juno standing left	32	23.46	Rome	RIC 148	138–41	7
118	Trajan, *dupondius/as*, rev. standing female	25.5	12.64	-	-	98–117	5?
119	Hadrian, *sestertius*, rev. seated female	32	21.95	Rome	as RIC pl. 77, 1–2	118?	6
120	illegible *as*	25.5	7.11	-	-	late 1st–2nd c.	-
122	Domitian, *sestertius*, rev. illegible	33	22.28	-	-	81–96	4
123	Trajan, *sestertius*, rev. standing female holding cornucopia left	32	21.44	-	-	98–117	5
124	Trajan/Hadrian, illegible *sestertius*	35	21.89	-	-	late 1st–2nd c.	-
125	?Hadrian, *sestertius*, rev. standing female holding cornucopia left	33	22.55	-	-	117–38?	6

Table A2.2. Hoard 1, pit fill *260*, Settlement 6, Period 4.2

SF	Context	Feature	Group	Period	ID	Diam. (mm)	Wt (g)	Mint	Reference	Date	Coin period
Settlement 7											
1088	5475	ditch 5746	Enclosure 28	3.4	fragment; House of Valentinian, rev. Securitas Reipublicae	16	1.19	-	-	364–78	19
2139	5512	ditch 5513	Enclosure 28	3.4	Postumus, *antoninianus*, rev. Herc Devsoniensi	21	2.69	Lyon	RIC 137	259–68	13
1089	5784	ditch 5789	Boundary 109	4.1	Constans, rev. Gloria Exercitus, 1 standard	15	1.34	Trier	as HK 133	335–41	17
2141	5934	ditch 5935	Boundary 109	4.1	Constantius II, rev. Victoriae DD Avgg Q NN	16	1.37	Trier	HK 139	341–6	17
1097	11903	-	Boundary 109	4.1	Contantine II, rev. Gloria Exercitus, 2 standards	16.5	1.74	Trier	HK 49	330–5	17
2127	5858	ditch 5859	boundary/ enclosure	4.1	illegible	20	2.06	-	-	3rd c.	-
1079	10446	-	Enclosure 124	4.2	illegible *antoninianus*	20.5	3.31	-	-	3rd c.	-
2197	5168	ditch 5169	Boundary 110	4.2	illegible	11.5	0.82	-	-	4th c.	-
1166	11927	-	Boundary 111	4.3	illegible	17	1.50	-	-	4th c.	-
2510	5547	ditch 5548	Boundary 111	4.3	Valentinian I, rev. Securitas Reipublicae	17.5	1.87	Arles	CK 508	367–75	19
1123	11916	-	drainage ditch	4.2	House of Valentinian, rev. illegible	17	1.33	-	-	364–78	19
1124	10179	ditch 10181	drainage ditch	4.2	House of Constantine copy, rev. Victoriae DD Avgg Q NN	14	1.09	-	-	341–50	17
1047	10440	-	enclosure / drainage	4.2	House of Constantine copy, rev. Gloria Exercitus, 1 standard	12.5	0.45	-	-	335–45	17

SF	Context	Feature	Group	Period	ID	Diam. (mm)	Wt (g)	Mint	Reference	Date	Coin period
1053	10440	-	enclosure / drainage	4.2	House of Constantine copy, rev. Gloria Exercitus, 1 standard	13.5	1.34	-	-	335–45	17
2458	5451	posthole 5452	surface find	4.2	House of Constantine copy, rev. Fel Temp Reparatio, falling horseman	10	0.75	-	-	350–60	18
3207	10179	ditch 10181	drainage ditch	4.3	Tetricus I, *antoninianus*, rev. Laetitia Avgg N	20	1.94	-	RIC 90	270–3	13
1112	11908	-	Enclosure 126	4.4	Valentinian I?, rev. Securitas Reipublicae	18	2.21	Rome	CK 724	367–75	19
1113	11909	-	Enclosure 126	4.4	House of Constantine, rev. Fel Temp Reparatio, falling horseman	11	0.45	-	-	350–60	18
1263	7641	-	Enclosure 126	4.4	illegible	14.5	0.98	-	-	4th c.	-
2198	5600	ditch 5601	Enclosure 126	4.4	Constans, rev. Victoriae DD Avgg Q NN	17	1.03	-	-	341–6	17
2199	5600	ditch 5601	Enclosure 126	4.4	illegible	19	1.49	-	-	4th c.	-
2200	5774	ditch 5925	Enclosure 126	4.4	Valens, rev. Securitas Reipublicae	19	2.12	-	-	364–78	19
3402	7428	ditch 7429	Enclosure 126	4.4	Constantine II, rev. Beata Tranquillitas	20	2.35	London	RIV VII (London) 236	321–2	16
3389	120233	ditch 120234	Enclosure 126	4.4	House of Constantine copy, rev. Fel Temp Reparatio, falling horseman	13	0.83	-	-	350–60	18
3392	120233	ditch 120234	Enclosure 126	4.4	Valens, rev. Securitas Reipublicae	18.5	2.37	Lyon	CK278	364–7	19
3418	120233	ditch 120234	Enclosure 126	4.4	Urbs Roma, rev. wolf and twins	18	1.79	Lyon	HK 184	330–5	17
3420	7632	-	Enclosure 126	4.4	Antoninus Pius, *dupondius*, rev. standing female with cornucopia	31.5	25.28	-	-	138–61	7
1283	7641	-	Enclosure 126	4.4	House of Valentinian, rev. Securitas Reipublicae	13	0.84	-	-	364–78	19
157	734	ditch 736	Enclosure 127	4.4	?House of Theodosius, rev. Victoria Auggg	12.5	0.92	-	-	388–402	21
2133	4637	ditch 4638	Enclosure 129	4.4	House of Valentinian, rev. Gloria Romanorum	19	2.45	-	-	364–78	19
1063	5100	ditch 5101	Enclosure 130	4.4	House of Constantine copy, rev. Fel Temp Reparatio, falling horseman	12	0.81	-	-	350–60	19
1084	4942	ditch 4943	Enclosure 131	4.4	House of Valentinian, rev. Gloria Romanorum	17.5	1.67	Siscia	as CK 1418	364–75	19
2137	4975	ditch 4976	Enclosure 131	4.4	Valentinian I, rev. Securitas Reipublicae	17	2.45	Lyon	CK 363	364–78	19
3257	4531	ditch 4532	Enclosure 131	4.4	fragment; House of Constantine copy, rev. Fel Temp Reparatio, falling horseman	8	0.37	-	-	350–60	18
2140	4699	ditch 4700	Enclosure 131	4.4	Constans, rev. Victoriae DD Avgg Q NN	14	0.84	-	-	341–6	17
1037	4762	ditch 4763	Enclosure 131	4.4	Constantine II, rev. Gloria Exercitus, 1 standard	15	1.38	Trier	HK 88	335–7	17
2196	4762	ditch 4763	Enclosure 131	4.4	Constans, rev. Fel Temp Reparatio, phoenix on pyre	17.5	2.82	-	-	346–50	18
1091	11901	-	Enclosure 132	4.4	Gratian, rev. Gloria Romanorum	16	1.85	Lyons	as CK 296	367–75	19
1031	4896	ditch 4897	Enclosure 132	4.4	House of Constantine, rev. illegible	14	1.59	-	-	330–60	17
2234	4898	ditch 4897	Enclosure 132	4.4	very worn, ?Carausius, antoninianus, rev. ?Pax Aug	23	2.50	-	?as RIC 98	287–93	14

SF	Context	Feature	Group	Period	ID	Diam. (mm)	Wt (g)	Mint	Reference	Date	Coin period
1102	10338	ditch 10341	Enclosure 133	4.4	Constantinopolis, rev. Victory on prow	17.5	1.59	Trier	as HK 48	330–5	17
1101	11904	-	Enclosure 133	4.4	House of Constantine, rev. Gloria Exercitus, 2 standards	12.5	2.24	-	-	330–5	17
1105	11905	-	Enclosure 133	4.4	Constantine I, rev. Beata Tranquillitas	19	2.67	Trier	RIC 368	322–3	16
2190	10429	-	Enclosure 133	4.4	illegible *sestertius* (?Trajan)	33.5	20.47	-	-	2nd c?	-
1074	4838	ditch 4839	Enclosure 134	4.4	House of Constantine, rev. Fel Temp Reparatio	15	1.51	-	-	350–60	18
1040	10366	ditch 10367	Enclosure 136	4.4	Constantinopolis copy, rev. Victory on prow	12	0.72	-	-	330–45	17
1052	120115	120116	Enclosure 136	4.4	House of Constantine, rev. Victoriae DD Avgg Q NN	14.5	1.52	-	-	341–6	17
1069	10441	-	Enclosure 138	4.4	Constans, rev. Victoriae DD Avgg Q NN	16	1.22	Trier	HK 149	341–6	17
1076	10445	-	Enclosure 138	4.4	Constantinopolis, rev. Victory on prow	19	1.92	Trier	as HK 59	330–5	17
1133	10134	ditch 10135	C-shaped enclosure 100	4.4	illegible	13	1.19	-	-	4th c.	-
1045	120113	ditch 120114	Boundary 110	4.4	illegible	16.5	1.71	-	-	4th c.	-
2170	4742	ditch 4743	Boundary 110	4.4	minim; illegible	7	0.52	-	-	4th c.	-
1130	11921	-	Boundary 112	4.4	House of Valentinian, rev. Securitas Reipublicae	17.5	1.83	-	-	364–78	19
1131	11922	-	Boundary 112	4.4	illegible	16.5	1.20	-	-	4th c.	-
2226	120133	ditch 120134	Boundary 112	4.4	fragment; blank disc with scratch marks	15	0.40	-	-	3rd–4th c?	-
1110	11907	-	Boundary 113	4.4	House of Constantine, rev. Fel Temp Reparatio, hut	17	2.06	-	-	346–50	18
1115	11910	-	Boundary 113	4.4	?Victorinus, *antoninianus*, rev. illegible	21	2.13	-	-	268–70?	13
1119	11912	-	Boundary 113	4.4	Valens, rev. Securitas Reipublicae	18.5	2.53	-	-	364–78	19
1120	11913	-	Boundary 113	4.4	Gratian, rev. Gloria Novi Saeculi	18.5	2.14	Arles	CK 523a	367–75	19
1121	11914	-	Boundary 113	4.4	Gratian, rev. Gloria Novi Saeculi	18	1.95	Arles	CK 523a	367–75	19
1109	11906	-	Boundary 115	4.3	Constantinopolis, rev. Victory on prow	14	1.15	-	-	330–5	17
2488	5525	ditch 5523	Boundary 118	4.4	Claudius II, *antoninianus*, commemorative issue, rev. Consecratio, altar	17	1.80	-	as RIC 260	270	13
2615	5211	ditch 5212	enclosure /drainage	4.4	illegible *follis*	22	3.17	-	-	late 3rd–early 4th c.	-
2172	4740	pit 4741	Structure 114, barn	4.4	House of Valentinian, rev. Securitas Reipublicae	17.5	1.70	-	-	364–78	19
1093	5540	floor	cobbled surface	4.4	barbarous radiate	12.5	0.74	-	-	270–90	14
1094	5540	floor	cobbled surface	4.4	House of Constantine copy, rev. Fel Temp Reparatio, falling horseman	10.5	0.71	-	-	350–60	18
1095	5540	floor	cobbled surface	4.4	Claudius II, rev. Consecratio, altar	17.5	2.02	-	as RIC 260	270	13
1096	5540	floor	cobbled surface	4.4	House of Constantine copy, rev. Fel Temp Reparatio, falling horseman	10.5	0.85	-	-	350–60	18
2143	5540	floor	cobbled surface	4.4	illegible *antoninianus*	17	2.11	-	-	late 3rd c.	-

SF	Context	Feature	Group	Period	ID	Diam. (mm)	Wt (g)	Mint	Reference	Date	Coin period
2335	5507	yard surface	cobbled surface	4.4	Constans, rev. Fel Temp Reparatio, phoenix on globe	18.5	2.40	Trier	as CK 35	346–50	18
2514	5539	occupation build-up	-	4.4	illegible	12	0.78	-	-	4th c.	-
2145	5661	ditch 5660	pit group	4.4	Magnentius, rev. Felicitas Reipublice	17.5	2.38	Trier	CK 50	350–1	18
2645	5839	pit 5840	-	4.4	fragment, ?base silver; illegible *denarius* (?Severus Alexander)	16	2.01	-	-	early 3rd c.	-
2126	5269	pit 5270	isolated pit	4.4	House of Valentinian, rev. Gloria Romanorum	18	2.06	-	-	364–78	19
1041	10126	ditch 10127	-	4.4	House of Valentinian, rev. Securitas Reipublicae	16	1.51	-	-	364–78	19
2260	5038	pit 5039	-	4.4	Urbs Roma, rev. wolf and twins	16	1.77	Trier	HK 58	330–5	17
1062	5636	occupation build-up	-	4.4	Tetricus II, *antoninianus*, rev. Laetitia Augg	16.5	2.27	-	as RIC 238	270–3	13
1042	5636	occupation build-up	-	4.4	Constantius II, rev. Gloria Exercitus, 2 standards	18	1.42	Arles	HK 354	330–5	17
1046	5636	occupation build-up	-	4.4	Constans, rev. Victoriae DD Avgg Q NN	16.5	1.50	-	-	341–6	17
1075	5636	occupation build-up	-	4.4	House of Constantine copy, rev. Gloria Exercitus, 2 standards	13.5	0.76	-	-	330–45	17
1038	5636	occupation build-up	-	4.4	Valentinian I, rev. Gloria Romanorum	18	1.78	-	as CK 279	364–75	19
1039	5636	occupation build-up	-	4.4	House of Valentinian, rev. Securitas Reipublicae	17	1.77	-	-	364–78	19
1048	5636	occupation build-up	-	4.4	House of Valentinian, rev. Securitas Reipublicae	17.5	2.25	-	-	364–78	19
1033	5636	occupation build-up	-	4.4	illegible	11.5	0.61	-	-	3rd-4th c.	-
1034	5636	occupation build-up	-	4.4	illegible	12	0.92	-	-	4th c.	-
1036	5636	occupation build-up	-	4.4	illegible	16	1.46	-	-	4th c.	-
1049	5636	occupation build-up	-	4.4	illegible	12.5	1.08	-	-	4th c.	-
1125	5818	ditch 5817	-	4.4	House of Constantine copy, rev. Fel Temp Reparatio, falling horseman	11	1.11	-	-	350–60	18
1163	5508	surface layer	-	4.4	House of Constantine copy, rev. Fel Temp Reparatio, falling horseman	9	0.61	-	-	350–60	18
2512	5508	surface layer	-	4.4	House of Constantine copy, rev. Gloria Exercitus, 1 standard	13	0.88	-	-	335–45	17
2513	5508	surface layer	-	4.4	Urbs Roma, rev. wolf and twins	17	1.73	-	-	330–5	17
1072	4808	ditch 4809	Boundary 120	4.5	illegible	12.5	1.12	-	-	4th c.	-
1071	10443	-	Boundary 120	4.5	Constantine I, rev. Beata Tranquillitas	19	2.27	Trier	RIC 368	322–3	16
1126	11917	-	Structure 115	4.5	House of Valentinian?, rev. Securitas Reipublicae?	17	1.67	-	-	364–78?	19?
1172	11928	-	Structure 115	4.5	House of Valentinian, rev. Gloria Romanorum	16	1.58	-	-	364–78	19
3375	5980	layer in pond	pond	4.5	Constantine II, rev. Beata Tranquillitas	20	3.17	London	RIC VII (London) 219	321	16
3423	5980	layer in pond	pond	4.5	Constantinopolis copy, rev. Victory on prow	15.5	1.43	-	copy as HK 52	330–45	17
2144	5943	posthole 5944	pit group	4.5	Constantine I, rev. Gloria Exercitus, 2 standards	16	1.31	Trier	HK 62	330–5	17

SF	Context	Feature	Group	Period	ID	Diam. (mm)	Wt (g)	Mint	Reference	Date	Coin period
2130	4751	pit 4752	isolated pit	4.5	illegible *as*	29	7.15	-	-	1st–2nd c.	-
2169	4735	cistern 4817	isolated pit	4.5	base silver; Julia Domna, *denarius*, rev. P M TRP II COS II, standing male figure	18.5	2.13	-	-	193–211	10
1077	10352	ditch 10353	Boundary 121	7	illegible fragment	16	1.35	-	-	4th c.	-
3252	4519	ditch 4522	-	-	illegible	11	0.64	-	-	4th c.	-
1027	120109	ditch 120110	-	-	House of Valentinian/House of Theodosius, rev. ?Virtus	13	0.91	-	-	383–408	20/21
Adjoining fields											
1073	10444	furrow	furrows	7	Constantinopolis, rev. Victory on prow	17	1.48	-	-	330–5	17
1083	10450	furrow	furrows	7	fragment; House of Valentinian, rev. Gloria Romanorum	18	1.42	Arles	-	364–78	19
1129	11920	furrow	furrows	7	House of Valentinian, rev. Gloria Romanorum	19	2.11	-	-	364–78	19
1128	11919	furrow	furrows	7	illegible	16.5	2.07	-	-	4th c.	-
1144	11925	furrow	furrows	7	illegible	15	0.83	-	-	4th c.	-
1143	11924	furrow	furrows	7	James I/Charles I farthing token	17.5	-	-	-	1613–44	-
3168	10421	-	-	9	House of Constantine copy, rev. Fel Temp Reparatio, falling horseman	8	0.46	-	-	350–60	18
2214	10430	-	-	9	Valentinian I, rev. Securitas Reipublicae	17	2.08	Lyon?	-	364–78	19
1082	10449	-	-	9	illegible	13	1.14	-	-	4th c.	-
1090	11900	-	-	9	illegible (?Iron Age issue)	11	1.44	-	-	early 1st c. AD?	-
1118	11911	-	-	9	Valens, rev. Securitas Reipublicae	18	1.93	-	-	364–78	19
1127	11918	-	-	9	illegible	15	1.32	-	-	late 3rd–4th c.	-
1132	11923	-	-	9	illegible	17	2.06	-	-	4th c.	-
3155	10421	-	-	9	House of Constantine, rev. Fel Temp Reparatio, falling horseman	18	1.63	-	-	350–60	18
3156	10421	-	-	9	House of Constantine copy, rev. Fel Temp Reparatio, falling horseman	16	1.85	-	-	350–60	18
3169	10421	-	-	9	House of Valentinian, rev. Securitas Reipublicae	18.5	1.80	-	-	364–78	19
3163	5966	yard/floor surface (spoil heap find)	-	-	House of Valentinian (Valens?), rev. Securitas Reipublicae	18	1.88	-	-	364–78	19
22	560	unstrat	-	-	illegible	15	-	-	-	late Roman?	-
69	600	unstrat	-	-	illegible	18.5	-	-	-	3rd–4th c.	-
1149	4813	unstrat	-	-	silver-washed/plated; Severus Alexander, denarius, rev. ?Spes	19	2.60	-	-	222–35	11
1151	4813	unstrat	-	-	Gallienus, antoninianus, rev. Abundantia Avg	19.5	1.75	-	RIC 157	260–8	13
1157	4813	unstrat	-	-	Carausius, antoninianus, rev. Pax Avg, in field	23	4.28	London (F|O in field)	RIC 101	289–90	14
1154	4813	unstrat	-	-	Urbs Roma, rev. wolf and twins	14	0.91	-	-	330–5	17
1525	4813	unstrat	-	-	Urbs Roma, wolf and twins	16.5	1.20	-	-	330–4	17

SF	Context	Feature	Group	Period	ID	Diam. (mm)	Wt (g)	Mint	Reference	Date	Coin period
1139	4813	unstrat	-	-	House of Constantine, rev. Gloria Exercitus, 1/2 standards?	16	1.00	-	-	330–40	17
1148	4813	unstrat	-	-	House of Constantine copy, rev. Fel Temp Reparatio, falling horseman	8.5	0.35	-	-	350–60	18
1150	4813	unstrat	-	-	Valens, rev. Securitas Reipublicae	18	2.31	-	-	364–78	19
1523	4813	unstrat	-	-	Valens, rev. Securitas Reipublicae	17	2.09	Lyon	CK 322	367–75	19
1526	4813	unstrat	-	-	House of Valentinian, rev. Gloria Romanorum	17	1.80	-	-	364–78	19
1153	4813	unstrat	-	-	minim, House of Theodosius?	11	0.39	-	-	388–402	21
1152	4813	unstrat	-	-	illegible	15	2.27	-	-	4th c.	-
3171	99999	unstrat	-	-	Victorinus, *antoninianus*, rev. Invictus	20	3.25	-	-	268–70	13
3201	99999	unstrat	-	-	House of Constantine, rev. Fel Temp Reparatio, falling horseman	16	2.15	-	-	350–60	18
3200	99999	unstrat	-	-	illegible	11	0.76	-	-	4th c.	-

Table A2.3. Coins from Settlement 7 and adjacent fields

SF	ID	Diam. (mm)	Wt (g)	Mint	Reference	Date	Coin period
3421	Gallienus, *antoninianus*, rev. Aequitas Aug	17.5	2.34	-	RIC 159	260–8	13
3376	?Gallienus, *antoninianus*, rev. Spes	18	1.87	-	-	?253–68	12/13
3421a	Salonina, *antoninianus*, rev. Iunoni Cons Aug, (doe worn)	21	2.54	-	as RIC 14-15	260–8	13
3437	Victorinus, *antoninianus*, rev. Providentia Aug	20	2.27	-	RIC 61	268–70	13
3421b	Victorinus, *antoninianus*, rev. Provid(entia) Aug	18.5	2.99	-	a RIC 61	268–70	13
3421f	Victorinus, *antoninianus*, rev. Pax Aug, with split flan and sprue	22	3.52	-	as RIC 55	268–70	13
3421c	Tetricus II, *antoninianus*, rev. sacrificial implements (barbarous)	16.5	2.48	-	-	270–3 (+)	13
3421e	Tetricus II, *antoninianus*, rev. ?Fides Militum	19	2.07	-	?as RIC 229	270–3	13
3438	Claudius II, *antoninianus*, rev. illegible	17	1.81	-	-	268–70	13
3421h	Claudius II, *antoninianus*, rev. Laetitia Aug	21	3.06	-	RIC 56	268–70	13
3436	Carausius, *antoninianus*, rev. Pax Aug	21.5	3.80	-	-	287–93	14
3421d	illegible radiate *antoninianus*	16	1.88	-	-	mid–ate 3rd c.	13

Table A2.4. Hoard 2, pit *7476*, Settlement 7, Period 4.4

SF	Context	Feature	Group	Period	ID	Diam. (mm)	Wt (g)	Mint	Reference	Date	Coin period
Settlement 6											
134	61	ditch 62	Enclosure 101	4.1	Gratian, rev. Gloria Romanorum	18	1.93	-	-	367–78	19
2945	8399	external surface	cobbled surface	4.1	illegible	13.5	0.92	-	-	4th c.	-
3148	11263	ditch 11264	Enclosure 104	4.2	barbarous radaiate, rev. illegible	15	1.74	-	-	270–90	14
127	31	ditch 32	Enclosure 105	4.2	Constantine I, *follis*, rev. Soli Invicto Comiti	20	2.77	Trier	RIC VII (Trier	317–18	16
3621	13088	ditch 13089	Enclosure 110	4.2	Constantine II, rev. Gloria Exercitus, 2 standards	18	2.18	Thessalonica	HK 836	330–5	17
3695	13333	river wash	natural features	4.2	Claudius II, *antoninianus*, rev. Fides Exerci	18	2.27	-	-	268–70	13
3671	13333	river wash	natural features	4.2	House of Constantine, rev. wreath, VOT XXX	17	1.54	-	-	324–30	16

SF	Context	Feature	Group	Period	ID	Diam. (mm)	Wt (g)	Mint	Reference	Date	Coin period
3696	13333	river wash	natural features	4.2	House of Constantine copy, rev. Victoriae DD Avgg Q NN	15	1.23	-	-	341–45	17
3670	13333	river wash	natural features	4.2	House of Constantine copy, rev. Victoriae DD Avgg Q NN	13	1.27	-	-	341–45	17
3669	13333	river wash	natural features	4.2	Constantius II, rev. Fel Temp Reparatio, falling horseman (3)	16	1.35	Lyons	as CK 256	353–60	18
3668	13333	river wash	natural features	4.2	minim; House of Constantine copy, rev. Fel Temp Reparatio, falling horseman	9	0.60	-	-	350–60	18
3693	13333	river wash	natural features	4.2	House of Constantine copy, rev. Fel Temp Reparatio, falling horseman	14	0.91	-	-	350–60	18
3697	13333	river wash	natural features	4.2	illegible copy, ?House of Constantine	11	0.92	-	-	4th c.	-
3665	13333	river wash	natural features	4.2	Magnentius/Decentius, rev. ?Victoriae DD NN Aug et Caes, minim, cut down from a larger coin	9	0.57	-	-	350–3	18
3764	13333	river wash	natural features	4.2	Valens, rev. Gloria Romanorum	17	2.0	Aquileia	CK 993	364–7	19
3666	13333	river wash	natural features	4.2	Gratian, rev. Securitas Reipublicae	18	1.78	-	-	367–78	19
3667	13333	river wash	natural features	4.2	House of Valentinian, rev. Gloria Romanorum	13	1.07	-	-	364–78	19
3765	13333	river wash	natural features	4.2	House of Valentinian, rev. Gloria Romanorum	16	1.92	-	-	364–78	19
3767	13333	river wash	natural features	4.2	House of Valentinian, rev. Securitas Reipublicae	17	1.50	-	-	364–78	19
3649	13333	river wash	natural features	4.2	illegible	20	1.97	-	-	3rd–4th c.	-
3766	13333	river wash	natural features	4.2	illegible	17	1.42	-	-	3rd–4th c.	-
3648	13333	river wash	natural features	4.2	illegible	18	1.88	-	-	4th c.	-
3672	13336	river wash	natural features	4.2	Helena copy, rev. Pax Publica	14	1.17	Trier	As HK 119	337–45	17
3673	13336	river wash	natural features	4.2	illegible fragment	12	1.01	-	-	3rd–4th c.	-
3694	14181	river wash	natural features	4.2	House of Valentinian, rev. Gloria Romanorum	16	1.79	-	-	364–78	19
3645	14181	river wash	natural features	4.2	House of Valentinian, rev. Securitas Reipublicae	16	1.76	-	-	364–78	19
3638	14184	river wash	natural features	4.2	Valentinian I, rev. Securitas Reipublicae	17	1.69	-	-	364–75	19
3639	14184	river wash	natural features	4.2	Valens, rev. Securitas Reipublicae	18	2.17	Siscia	CK 1428	367–75	19
3682	14184	river wash	natural features	4.2	House of Valentinian, rev. Securitas Reipublicae	15	1.57	-	-	364–78	19
3683	14184	river wash	natural features	4.2	illegible, House of Constantine/Valentinian	13	2.27			4th c.	-
3653	14182	river wash	natural features	4.2	illegible minim	12	1.45	-	-	3rd–4th c.	-
3699	13505	river gravel	natural features	4.2	fragment; barbarous radiate	14	0.73	-	-	270–94	14
3662	13924	river wash	natural features	4.2	Magnentius, rev. Felicitas Reipublice	22	4.94	Trier	-	350–1	18
3663	13924	river wash	natural features	4.2	House of Valentinian, rev. Securitas Reipublicae	16	1.32	-	-	364–78	19
3750	13884	river wash	natural features	4.2	House of Valentinian, rev. Securitas Reipublicae	16	1.27	-	-	364–78	19
3622	14180	layer	natural features	4.2	fragment; House of Valentinian, rev. Gloria Romanorum	17	1.36	-	-	364–78	19
3010	8733	unstrat; ditch 8734	-	4.2	Constantinopolis copy, rev. Victory on prow	13	1.32	-	copy as HK 51	330–45	17

SF	Context	Feature	Group	Period	ID	Diam. (mm)	Wt (g)	Mint	Reference	Date	Coin period
3457	8940	posthole 8941	Structure 105	4.3	House of Constantine copy, rev. Fel Temp Reparatio, falling horseman	7.5	0.29	-	-	350–60	18
3040	9117	ditch 9118	Enclosure 112	4.3	Caracalla, *denarius*, rev. Vota Suscepta X	19	2.53	Rome	RIC 524	206–10	10
2952	8707	ditch 8708	Enclosure 114	4.3	Constantius II, rev. Fel Temp Reparatio, falling horseman	18	2.03	Lyon	CK 249	353–4	18
3656	13247	ditch 13248	Enclosure 116	4.3	Valens, rev. Gloria Romanorum	19	2.09	Arles	-	364–78	19
3719	13434	pit 13435	isolated pit	4.3	House of Theodosius, rev. Victoria Avggg	12	1.07	-	-	388–402	21
3687	13069	pit 13070	Structure 108	4.4	House of Valentinian, rev. Gloria Romanorum	18	1.95	-	-	364–78	19
3688	13069	pit 13070	Structure 108	4.4	Valentinian, rev. Securitas Reipublicae	16	1.90	Aquileia	As CK 1030, wreath on left	367–75	19
3726	13883	dump	Structure 108	4.4	House of Constantine copy, rev. Gloria Exercitus, 1 standard	13	0.94	-	-	341–45	17
138	87	ditch 88	Enclosure 114	4.4	House of Valentinian rev. Gloria Romanorum	11	0.68	-	-	364–78	19
3651	13044	ditch 13046	Enclosure 117	4.4	House of Valentinian, rev. Gloria Romanorum	16	1.67	-	-	364–78	19
3608	13219	ditch 13218	Enclosure 118	4.4	House of Valentinian copy, rev. Securitas Reipublicae	16	1.94	-	-	364–78	19
1217	6744	ditch 6745	Enclosure 119	4.4	Valens, rev. Securitas Reipublicae	17	1.94	-	-	364–78	19
150	75	ditch 76	Enclosure 120	4.4	House of Valentinian copy, rev. Gloria Romanorum	17	1.55	-	-	?364–78	19
3455	11232	ditch 11233	Enclosure 123	4.4	House of Constantine copy, rev. Fel Temp Reparatio, falling horseman	7.5	0.40	-	-	350–60	18
3506	120278	ditch 120281	Boundary 100	4.4	House of Valentinian, rev. illegible	18	1.71	-	-	364–78	19
3070	9462	ditch 9463	boundary/ enclosure	4.4	House of Valentinian, rev. Securitas Reipublicae	16	1.64	-	-	364–78	19
2798	6572	ritual deposit	-	4.4	illegible *sestertius*	32.5	18.11	-	-	1st–2nd c.	-
2770	6572	ritual deposit		4.4	Trajan, *as*, rev. illegible	26.5	9.61	-	-	98–117	5
2789	6572	ritual deposit	-	4.4	illegible *as* (?Trajan)	26	9.51	-	-	1st–2nd c.	-
2790	6572	ritual deposit	-	4.4	illegible *as* (?Trajan)	27.5	7.86	-	-	1st–2nd c.	-
2794	6572	ritual deposit	-	4.4	illegible sestertius, (?Septimius Severus)	32	18.20	-	-	late 2nd–e. 3rd c.	-
2796	6572	ritual deposit	-	4.4	illegible	19	1.64	-	-	3rd–4th c.	-
2813	6572	ritual deposit	-	4.4	illegible as	24	11.84	-	-	1st–2nd c.	-
2817	6572	ritual deposit	-	4.4	illegible	16.5	1.39	-	-	4th c.	-
2762	6532	ditch 6533	-	4	illegible	13	1.10	-	-	4th c.	-
2763	6532	ditch 6533	-	4	Constantine I, rev. Sarmatia Devicta	19	1.84	-	-	323–4	16
1108	5730	ditch 5729	-	4	illegible radiate *antoninianus*	16	1.89	-	-	late 3rd c.	-
1114	5730	ditch 5729	-	4	House of Valentinian?	13	1.15	-	-	364–78	19
3422	5730	ditch 5729	-	4	illegible *antoninianus*	20	2.41	-	-	mid–late 3rd c.	-
2818	7629	small find	-	9	illegible	14	1.42	-	-	4th c.	-
1203	11205	ditch 11207	-	-	Magnentius, rev. Victoriae DD NN Avg et Cae	16	1.46	Lyon?	as CK 217	351–3	18
1183	11605	finds unit	-	-	Allectus, *antoninianus*, rev. Virtvs Avg, galley	19	2.21	London	RIC 56	293–6	14

SF	Context	Feature	Group	Period	ID	Diam. (mm)	Wt (g)	Mint	Reference	Date	Coin period
1184	11606	finds unit	-	-	Constans, rev. Gloria Exercitus, 1 standard	17	1.41	-	as HK 131	335–41	17
1189	11610	finds unit	-	-	illegible	17	2.87	-	-	4th c.	-
1196	11611	finds unit	-	-	illegible	13.5	1.25	-	-	4th c.	-
1198	11613	finds unit	-	-	illegible	12	0.43	-	-	3rd–4th c.	-
1199	11614	finds unit	-	-	Victorinus, *antoninianus*, rev. Providentia Avg	19	1.75	-	RIC 61	268–70	13
1214	11616	finds unit	-	-	House of Valentinian, rev. Securitas Reipublicae	17.5	1.94	-	-	364–78	19
1233	11618	finds unit	-	-	?barbarous radiate	14.5	1.42	-	-	270–90	14
1234	11619	finds unit	-	-	Magnentius, rev. Victoriae DD NN Avg et Cae	18	2.78	-	as CK 217	351–3	18
1235	11619	finds unit	-	-	Tetricus I, rev. Pax Aug	18	2.30	-	RIC 106	270–3	13
1260	11622	finds unit	-	-	James I, Charles I farthing token	17.5	-	-	-	med/e. post-med	-
2904	11587	finds unit	-	-	Gratian, rev. Gloria Romanorum	16.5	2.29	-	-	367–78	19
2905	11588	finds unit	-	-	illegible	18	1.55	-	-	3rd–4th c.	-
2912	11591	finds unit	-	-	House of Constantine, rev. VOT V MULT X in wreath	18	2.00	-	-	318–19	16
2929	11593	finds unit	-	-	Carausius, *antoninianus*, rev. Iovi Victori(a)	22.5	2.75	London	as RIC 46	287–93	14
2934	11594	finds unit	-	-	House of Constantine, rev. Fel Temp Reparatio, falling horseman	13.5	0.96	-	-	350–60	18
2936	11595	finds unit	-	-	barbarous radiate, obv. Claudius II	13	0.72	-	-	270–90	14
2989	11599	finds unit	-	-	House of Constantine copy, rev. Fel Temp Reparatio, falling horseman	9.5	0.29	-	-	350–60	18
2991	11599	finds unit	-	-	House of Constantine copy, rev. Fel Temp Reparatio, falling horseman	10	0.86	-	-	350–60	18
2990	11599	finds unit	-	-	House of Valentinian, rev. illegible	15	0.94	-	-	364–78	19
2988	11599	finds unit	-	-	illegible	11	0.92	-	-	4th c.	-
3051	11600	finds unit	-	-	House of Valentinian, rev. Gloria Romanorum	17	2.08	-	-	364–78	19
3115	11603	finds unit	-	-	House of Constantine copy, rev. Fel Temp Reparatio, falling horseman	11	0.86	-	-	350–60	18
1200	120262	120263, machine slot	-	-	Claudius II, *antoninianus*, rev. female with cornucopia left and patera right	20	2.39	-	-	268–70	13
1291	11624	finds unit	-	-	Valentinian I, rev. Gloria Romanorum	18.5	1.71	Arles	?CK 500	367–75	19
3701	14187	unstrat	-	-	illegible, House of Constantine/Valentinian, both sides worn and severely scratched	13	1.00	-	-	4th c.	-
3610	14189	unstrat	-	-	pierced; illegible radiate antoninianus, rev. standing figure	15	2.21	-	-	mid–late 3rd c.	-
3611	14189	unstrat	-	-	barbarous radiate, obv. Tetricus I, rev. Salus Augg	17	1.37	-	-	270–94	14
3614	14189	unstrat	-	-	barbarous radiate, rev. standing figure	14	1.04	-	-	270–94	14
3753	14189	unstrat	-	-	barbarous radiate, rev. Salus Augg?	13	1.34	-	-	270–94	14
3613	14189	unstrat	-	-	House of Constantine copy, rev. Gloria Exercitus, ?2 standards	15	1.43	-	-	330–45	17
3642	14189	unstrat	-	-	House of Constantine copy, rev. Gloria Exercitus, 1 standard	14	1.11	-	-	335–45	17

SF	Context	Feature	Group	Period	ID	Diam. (mm)	Wt (g)	Mint	Reference	Date	Coin period
3678	14189	unstrat	-	-	House of Constantine copy, rev. Gloria Exercitus, 1 standard	13	0.82	-	-	335–45	17
3751	14189	unstrat	-	-	House of Constantine, rev. Fel Temp Reparatio, hut 2	21	3.14	-	-	346–50	18
3677	14189	unstrat	-	-	House of Constantine copy, rev. Fel Temp Reparatio, falling horseman	11	0.75	-	-	350–60	18
3644	14189	unstrat	-	-	Valentinian I, rev. Securitas Reipublicae	17	2.29	Arles	CK 521–2	367–75	19
3647	14189	unstrat	-	-	Valens, rev. Securitas Reipublicae	18	1.92	Arles	CK 516 (?)	367–75	19
3728	14189	unstrat	-	-	Valens, rev. Securitas Reipublicae	15	0.86	?Lyons	-	354–78	19
3749	14189	unstrat	-	-	Valens, rev. Securitas Reipublicae	16	1.91	Lyons	CK 285	364–78	19
3752	14189	unstrat	-	-	Valens, rev. Securitas Reipublicae	16	1.94	Arles	-	364–78	19
3612	14189	unstrat	-	-	Valentinian I, rev. Gloria Romanorum	18	2.00	?Lyons	As CK 279	364–75	19
3681	14189	unstrat	-	-	Valentinian II, rev. Securitas Reipublicae	16	1.66	-	-	375–8	19
3646	14189	unstrat	-	-	House of Valentinian, rev. Securitas Reipublicae	17	1.73	Arles	-	364–78	19
3680	14189	unstrat	-	-	House of Valentinian, rev. Securitas Reipublicae	16	2.42	-	-	364–78	19
3730	14189	unstrat	-	-	House of Valentinian, rev. Securitas Reipublicae	17	1.54	-	-	364–78	19
3618	14189	unstrat	-	-	fragment, ?copy; House of Valentinian, rev. Gloria Romanorum	17	0.99	-	-	364–78	19
3619	14189	unstrat	-	-	fragment, ?copy; House of Valentinian, rev. Gloria Romanorum	16	1.25	-	-	364–78	19
3606	14189	unstrat	-	-	House of Valentinian copy, rev. Securitas Reipublicae	17	1.79	-	-	364–78	19
3679	14189	unstrat	-	-	Gratian, rev. VOT XV MVLT XX in wreath	14	1.20	Lyons	CK 377 (S)	381–3	20
3675	14189	unstrat	-	-	House of Theodosius, rev. Victoria Auggg	12	0.82	-	-	388–402	21
3607	14189	unstrat	-	-	illegible halfpenny	27	7.40	-	-	18th–e. 19th c.	-
3601	99999	unstrat	-	-	Gratian, rev. Gloria Novi Saeculi	19	2.07	Arles (T)	As CK 511 (N on left not right)	367–75	19
Southern fields											
3698	14185	furrow	Furrows	6	Constans, rev. Victoriae DD Avgg Q NN	14	1.31	Trier	As HK 154, ?copy	341–6	17
3623	13182	plough scar	Plough scars	7	House of Valentinian, rev. Gloria Romanorum	17	1.45	-	-	364–78	19
2804	6573	ditch 6574	-	7	illegible halfpenny	27	-	-	-	18th–19th c.	-
3419	7573	ditch 7574	-	7	House of Valentinian, rev. Securitas Reipublicae	15	1.85	-	-	364–78	19
1227	7639	small find	-	9	illegible	15	0.67	-	-	4th c.	-
1268	7642	small find	-	9	Claudius I, *as*, rev. Minerva	23	3.91	-	-	41–54	2
2847	7630	small find	-	9	illegible *sestertius*	33	21.51	-	-	1st–2nd c.	-
136	59	ditch 60	-	-	Allectus, rev. (Laetitia Aug) galley	18.5	2.38	-	as RIC 124	293–6	14
1195	11591	finds unit	-	-	Constantinopolis copy, rev. Victory on prow	14.5	1.27	Trier	copy as HK 52	330–45	17
1201	11592	finds unit	-	-	House of Constantine copy, rev. Fel Temp Reparatio, falling horseman	8.5	0.58	-	-	350–60	18

SF	Context	Feature	Group	Period	ID	Diam. (mm)	Wt (g)	Mint	Reference	Date	Coin period
1290	11623	finds unit	-	-	illegible minim	8	0.46	-	-	mid–late 4th c.	-
1185	11607	finds unit	-	-	illegible fragment	14	0.75	-	-	3rd–4th c.	-
1232	99999	unstrat Trench 47 (site of Hoard 1)	-	-	illegible *as*	26	7.97	-	-	1st–2nd c.	-
1122	11915	unstrat	-	-	Valentinian I, rev. Securitas Reipublicae	17.5	2.32	-	-	364–75	19

Table A2.5. Coins from Settlement 6 and adjacent fields

SF	ID	Diam. (mm)	Wt (g)	Mint	Reference	Date	Coin period
5	Claudius II, *antoninianus*, rev. Consecratio, eagle	15	1.04	-	RIC 265	270	13
131	Claudius II, *antoninianus*, rev. Consecratio, altar	17	2.15	-	-	270	13
3404	?Claudius II, *antoninianus*, rev. illegible	18.5	2.36	-	-	?268–70	13
11	Tetricus I, *antoninianus*, rev. Spes (Publica?)	18	1.83	-	as RIC 135	270–3	13
18	barbarous radiate, rev. illegible	18	1.55	-	-	270–90	14
1104	barbarous radiate, rev. Virtus	10	0.77	-	-	270–90	14
1193	barbarous radiate	12	0.72	-	-	270–90	14
1242	barbarous radiate	14	1.58	-	-	270–90	14
2178	barbarous radiate	15	1.24	-	-	270–90	14
4	fragment; Carausius, *antoninianus*, rev. illegible	13.5	1.11	-	-	287–93	14
40	Urbs Roma copy, rev. wolf and twins	16.5	1.86	-	-	330–45	17
1174	Urbs Roma copy, rev. wolf and twins	14	1.37	-	-	330–45	17
1238	Urbs Roma, wolf and twins	17	1.95	Trier	HK 65	330–35	17
2161	Urbs Roma, wolf and twins	18	1.61	-	as HK 51	330–35	17
10	Constantinopolis, rev. Victory on prow	16	2.50	-	-	330–37	17
1057	Constantinopolis, rev. Victory on prow	16	0.83	-	-	330–35	17
1061	Constantinopolis copy, rev. Victory on prow	14	0.90	-	-	330–45	17
1065	Constantinopolis, rev. Victory on prow	13	1.69	-	-	330–35	17
1085	Constantinopolis copy, rev. Victory on prow	12	0.98	-	-	330–35	17
1173	Constantinopolis, rev. Victory on prow	12	1.18	-	-	330–45	17
1170	House of Constantine, rev. Gloria Exercitus, 2 standards	16	1.09	-	as HK 197	330–35	17
1210	House of Constantine copy, rev. Gloria Exercitus, 1 standard	12.5	0.81	-	-	335–45	17
2124	House of Constantine copy, rev. Gloria Exercitus, 1 standard	14	0.81	-	-	330–45	17
2202	House of Constantine, rev. Gloria Exercitus, 1 standard	15	1.22	-	-	335–45	17
8	House of Constantine, rev. Gloria Exercitus, worn, ?copy	16	1.51	-	-	330–45	17
1264	Constans, rev. Victoriae DD Avgg Q NN	16	1.47	-	-	341–6	17
2203	House of Constantiae copy, rev. Victoriae DD Avgg Q NN	14	1.16	-	-	341–50	17
2888	House of Constantine copy, rev. Victoriae DD Avgg Q NN	13.5	0.82	-	as HK 139	341–50	17
2216	House of Constantine copy, rev. standing female	12	0.96	-	-	337–45	17
2179	House of Constantine, rev. Fel Temp Reparatio, phoenix on globe	16	2.51	-	-	346–50	18
41	House of Constantine copy, rev. Fel Temp Reparatio, falling horseman	12	1.18	-	-	350–60	18
1054	House of Constantine copy, rev. Fel Temp Reparatio, falling horseman	11	0.87	-	-	350–60	18
1100	fragment; House of Constantine, rev. Fel Temp Reparatio, falling horseman	15.5	1.02	-	-	350–60	18
1236	House of Constantine copy, rev. Fel Temp Reparatio, falling horseman	8.5	0.37	-	-	350–60	18
1249	House of Constantine copy, rev. Fel Temp Reparatio, falling horseman	9	0.72	-	-	350–60	18
1251	House of Constantine copy, rev. Fel Temp Reparatio, falling horseman	11	0.70	-	-	350–60	18

SF	ID	Diam. (mm)	Wt (g)	Mint	Reference	Date	Coin period
1265	House of Constantine copy, rev. Fel Temp Reparatio, falling horseman	15	0.77	-	-	350–60	18
2997	House of Constantine, copy, rev. Fel Temp Reparatio, falling horseman	8	0.29	-	-	350–60	18
2999	House of Constantine copy, rev. Fel Temp Reparatio, falling horseman	9	0.80	-	-	350–60	18
1098	Magnentius, rev. Victoriae DD NN Avg et Cae	14	1.18	-	-	351–3	18
3441	Magnentius, rev. Fel Temp Reparatio, emperor and standard	17.5	1.86	Lyon	-	350–51	18
2949	Valentinian I, rev. Gloria Romanorum	18	2.58	Lyon	CK 338	367–75	19
1239	Valens, rev. Gloria Romanorum	17	1.82	-	-	364–78	19
1022	Valens, rev. Securitas Reipublicae	20.5	2.18	-	-	364–78	19
1087	Valens, rev. Securitas Reipublicae	18	2.32	Lyon	as CK 280	364–75	19
1116	Valens, rev. Securitas Reipublicae	18	2.73	-	-	364–78	19
1171	Valens, rev. Securitas Reipublicae	16.5	1.84	-	-	364–78	19
1261	Valens, rev. Securitas Reipublicae	16	2.28	Lyon?	-	364–78	19
1289	Gratian, rev. Gloria Novi Saeculi	17	2.10	Arles	CK 523a	367–75	19
1106	Gratian, rev. Gloria Romanorum	17	2.29	-	-	367–8	19
2162	House of Valentinian, rev. Gloria Romanorum (18)	16	1.68	-	-	364–8	19
1044	House of Valentinian, rev. Gloria Romanorum	18	1.78	-	-	364–78	19
1067	House of Valentinian, rev. Gloria Romanorum	17	1.18	-	-	364–78	19
1117	House of Valentinian, rev. Gloria Romanorum	17.5	1.66	-	-	364–78	19
1137	House of Valentinian, rev. Gloria Romanorum	16	1.54	-	-	364–78	19
2215	House of Valentinian, rev. Gloria Romanorum	16.5	2.04	-	-	364–78	19
1016	House of Valentinian, rev. Securitas Reipublicae	16	1.33	-	-	364–78	19
1026	House of Valentinian, rev. Securitas Reipublicae	18	1.79	-	-	364–78	19
1066	House of Valentinian, rev. Securitas Reipublicae	17	1.65	-	-	364–78	19
1136	House of Valentinian, rev. Securitas Reipublicae	16.5	1.16	-	-	364–78	19
1175	House of Valentinian, rev. Securitas Reipublicae	18	1.74	-	-	364–78	19
1178	House of Valentinian, rev. Securitas Reipublicae	15	0.98	-	-	364–78	19
1180	Valens, rev. Securitas Reipublicae	18	1.94	Lyon	CK 285	364–78	19
1186	House of Valentinian, rev. Securitas Reipublicae	15.5	2.80	Lyon	as CK 344	367–75	19
2156	House of Valentinian, rev. Securitas Reipublicae	18	1.88	-	-	364–78	19
2160	House of Valentinian, rev. Securitas Reipublicae	18.5	1.34	-	-	364–78	19
2173	House of Valentinian, rev. Securitas Reipublicae	18	1.44	-	-	364–78	19
2201	House of Valentinian, rev. Securitas Reipublicae	17	1.86	-	-	364–78	19
3049	House of Valentinian, rev. Securitas Reipublicae	18	1.43	Arles	-	364–78	19
2937	Honorius, rev. ?Victoria Avgg	11.5	0.89	-	-	394–402	21
1159	illegible, *dupondius*?	26.5	10.29	-	-	1st–2nd c.	-
2753	illegible *as*	26	8.64	-	-	1st–2nd c.	-
1035	illegible *antoninianus*	15	1.58	-	-	3rd c.	-
1023	illegible *antoninianus*	20	1.95	-	-	3rd c.	-
1019	illegible	20	2.66	-	-	3rd c?	-
1003	illegible	13.5	0.77	-	-	3rd–4th c.	-
1011	illegible	15	1.40	-	-	3rd–4th c.	-
1107	illegible	15.5	0.92	-	-	3rd–4th c.	-
1181	illegible	17	1.99	-	-	3rd–4th c.	-
1192	illegible fragment	16	1.33	-	-	3rd–4th c.	-
1252	illegible fragment	16	0.88	-	-	3rd–4th c.	-
2505	illegible	11.5	0.46	-	-	3rd–4th c.	-
2775	illegible	12.5	0.75	-	-	3rd–4th c.	-
1028	illegible ?copy	11	0.56	-	-	4th c.	-
1055	illegible	13	1.21	-	-	4th c.	-
1059	illegible copy	11	0.66	-	-	4th c.	-
1078	illegible fragment	14	0.77	-	-	4th c.	-
1086	illegible	14	0.77	-	-	4th c.	-
1103	illegible	15	1.36	-	-	4th c.	-
1301	illegible fragment	16.5	0.83	-	-	4th c.	-
2064	illegible	14	1.10	-	-	4th c.	-

SF	ID	Diam. (mm)	Wt (g)	Mint	Reference	Date	Coin period
2157	fragment; illegible	15	1.14	-	-	4th c.	-
2159	illegible	15.5	0.90	-	-	4th c.	-
2841	illegible	14	1.20	-	-	4th c.	-
2842	illegible	15	0.49	-	-	4th c.	-
2998	lead; imitation coin, illegible	8	0.49	-	-	mid-late 4th c.	-
1207	illegible (?House of Valentinian)	17.5	1.95	-	-	4th c.	-
1177	illegible	17.5	1.23	-	-	4th c.	-
1160	blank disc with scratch marks	23	-			Roman	-

Table A2.6. Unstratified Roman coins (context 99999)

Appendix 3. Romano-British Pottery Fabrics and Forms
by Alice Lyons

I. Abbreviations

AMP	Amphora
BAT AM 1	Spanish amphora
BAT AM 2	Spanish amphora
BSRW	Black surfaced red ware
GW(CAL)	Greyware with calciferous inclusions
GW(FINE)	Fine greyware
GW(GROG)	Greyware with grog inclusions
GW(GROG)(HM)	Greyware with grog inclusions (handmade)
HAD RW	Hadham red wares
HORN	Horningsea reduced ware
IMP PR 6	Terra Rubra
ITA AM 1	Italian amphora
MAH WH	Mancetter Hartshill whiteware
NVCC	Nene Valley colour-coat
NVGW	Nene Valley greyware
NVOW	Nene Valley oxidised (white) ware
OW(GRITTY)	Gritty oxidised ware
OW(GROG)	Oxidised ware with grog inclusions
OXRCC	Oxfordshire red ware
OXWCC	Oxfordshire colour coated whiteware
PGROG	Pink grog-tempered ware
RED FW	Red fineware
RW (HM)	Reduced ware (handmade)
RW(GROG)	Reduced ware with grog temper
RW(GROG)(P)	Reduced ware with oxidised surfaces with grog inclusions
SAM CG	Central Gaulish samian
SAM EG	East Gaulish samian
SAM SG	South Gaulish samian
SGW	Sandy greyware
SGW(GROG)	Sandy greyware with grog inclusions
SGW(PROTO)	Proto Sandy greyware
SOW	Sandy oxidised ware
SOW(FLINT+)	Sandy oxidised ware with flint inclusions
SRW	Sandy reduced ware
SRW(HM)	Sandy reduced ware (handmade)
STW	Shell-tempered ware
STW(Grog)	Shell-tempered ware (grog)
STW(HM)	Shell-tempered ware (handmade)
VOW, VWW	Verulamium whiteware

II. Fabrics

Amphorae
(48 sherds, weighing 5370g, 0 EVE, 1.47% of the entire assemblage by weight)
Self-coloured large storage vessels used for transporting luxury goods (Tyers 1996, 87; Tomber and Dore 1998, 82–113). Several different fabric and form types were found on the site (Table 7.21), consistent with the importation of wine and olive oil.

Black surfaced red ware
(265 sherds, weighing 2150g, 2.84 EVE, 0.59% of the entire assemblage by weight)
A broad fabric group of sandy coarsewares that have a red fabric and black surface. This may be the result of inefficient firing, but a sufficiently large number of these types of sherds were found to suggest it may have been a deliberate attempt to imitate the vessel shapes and surface finish of BB1 forms (Marney 1989, 177, fabric 9a).
Vessel types: 4.5, 4.10, 4.13, 5, 6, 6.3, 6.15, 6.17, 6.18

Greyware (fine)
(351 sherds, 2215g, 2.95 EVE, 0.61% of the entire assemblage by weight)
A dark brownish grey fabric with a similar or darker surface; it is hard with a smooth fracture and has a smooth to soapy feel. Some of this material may be imported Gaulish greywares (Tomber and Dore 1998, 74), however the majority is of a type sometimes referred to as 'London ware' (*ibid*, 159). This fabric was made at several centres

including West Stow and Wattisfield in Suffolk, the Nene Valley and also in London. It is a fine fabric used to make good quality vessels in the early Roman period. Some of the vessels copied samian and other Gaulish pot shapes.
Vessel types: 3.7, 3.13, 5, 5.3, 6.6, 6.13, 6.21

Greyware (grog)
(988 sherds, 10782g, 6.69 EVE, 2.96% of the entire assemblage by weight)
A dark brownish grey fabric with a similar or darker surface. It is quite a hard, soapy, hackly-fractured fabric with frequent very coarse (larger than 1mm) grog inclusions. This fabric was initially used to produce handmade forms in the 'Belgic' style, however its suitability for wheel production quickly established it as the main early Roman utilitarian ware.
Vessel types: 2.4, 3.6, 4.1, 4.4, 4.5, 4.13, 5, 5.1, 5.2, 5.3, 5.6, 5.12, 6.4, 6.13

Gritty buff ware
(624 sherds, 5812g, 6.52 EVE, 1.60% of the entire assemblage by weight)
A white to pale yellow fabric (Cameron 1996, 449) with significant amounts of quartz, giving it a gritty appearance. This pottery is rarely decorated and is nearly always found fumed or sooted, suggesting it was a utilitarian form that was frequently used for cooking. This ware is visually identical to 1st- and early 2nd-century Verulamium whiteware (Tyers 1996, 199–201), but is known to have been produced into the 2nd and 3rd centuries in the Northampton region and at Godmanchester in Cambridgeshire (Martin and Wallace 2002, 3.7.1, iii and iv). The fabric went out of fashion before the end of the Roman period.
Vessel types: 1.1, 1.9, 4.4, 4.5, 4.8, 5, 6.3, 6.15, 6.17, 6.18, 8.1

Hadham red ware
(199 sherds, 1402g, 2.43 EVE, 0.38% of the entire assemblage by weight)
Typically orange-brown, with quartz and sandstone inclusions, occasionally with a darker core (Tomber and Dore 1998, 151). Where intact, the external surface is burnished in narrow horizontal bands. Common in the late Roman period, its forms are similar to those of the Oxfordshire red ware industry and the combinations of decorative 'Romano-Saxon' bosses, dimples and grooves are diagnostic.
Vessel types: 1.3, 1.8, 1.11, 2.1, 4.1, 4.5, 4.8, 5, 6.14, 6.17, 7

Horningsea reduced ware
(201 sherds, 6342g, 1.98 EVE, 1.74% of the entire assemblage by weight)
Usually brown-grey, often with thin red-brown sub-surface margins or occasionally as a thick core (Tomber and Dore 1998, 116). The fabric can have a 'biscuit' feel, as the abundant quartz, sparse iron and limestone with mica has a distinctive open texture. Often decorated with combed arcs. Sherds are commonly thick and are generally associated with large storage jars with a distinctive out-turned rim, although thinner-walled wide-mouthed jars were also identified.
Vessel types: 1.1, 4.5, 4.12, 4.17, 5, 5.3, 5.6, 6.18, 8.1

Nene Valley colour-coat
(2044 sherds, 29137g, 38.89 EVE, 8.0% of the entire assemblage by weight)
Pale cream to orange sherds with a wide range of coloured slips (Tomber and Dore 1998, 118). This assemblage contains many of the 4th-century utilitarian dishes and jars, which are thicker and more substantial than the early continental-type beakers, with darker colour-coats (mainly brown and dark grey).
Vessel types: 1.4, 1.7, 1.9, 2, 2.1, 3, 3.1, 3.6, 3.7, 3.13, 4.1, 4.5, 4.8, 4.13, 5, 5.3, 5.6, 6.2, 6.4, 6.5, 6.7, 6.13, 6.14, 6.15, 6.17, 6.18, 6.19, 7.9.2

Nene Valley greyware
(88 sherds, 6342g, 1.98 EVE, 1.74% of the entire assemblage by weight)
Pale cream to pale grey sherds with a grey surface (Perrin 1999, 78–87), not dissimilar to the colour-coat fabric described above. This material was first produced in the second quarter of the 2nd century, continuing throughout the 3rd century, but appears to have ceased production in the 4th century.
Vessel types: 1.4, 4.1, 4.4, 4.5, 4.8, 4.13, 5, 6.15, 6.17, 6.18, 6.19, 6.22, 8.1

Nene Valley whiteware
(180 sherds, 5786g, 4.53 EVE, 1.59% of the entire assemblage by weight)
A white fabric with cream surfaces and some variation (Tomber and Dore 1998, 119). It was frequently used in the production of mortaria.
Vessel types: 2.1, 3, 4.1, 4.4, 4.8, 5.6, 6.15, 6.18, 6.19, 6.21, 7, 7.9, 7.9.1, 7.9.3, 7.9.4, 7.9.5

Oxfordshire red ware with a red colour-coat
(827 sherds, 7007g, 8.58 EVE, 1.92% of the entire assemblage by weight)

Oxfordshire red ware with a white colour-coat
(27 sherds, 1063g, 0.77 EVE, 0.29% of the entire assemblage by weight)
These fabrics are oxidised, normally red or orange with either a red/brown or a white slip, and frequently have a reduced core and pink margins (Tomber and Dore 1998, 176). The fabric contains well-sorted inclusions and is characterised by common fine, silver (sometimes gold) mica and common to abundant quartz. It is particularly common in the late Roman period in the 4th and early 5th centuries.
Red colour-coat vessel types: 1, 1.3, 1.9, 2.1, 4.1, 4.5, 4.8, 5, 5.4, 5.6, 5.13, 6, 6.4, 6.5, 6.7, 6.13, 6.14, 6.15, 6.18, 6.19, 6.21, 7, 7.7.1, 7.7.2, 7.7.4, 7.8.6, 7.11.1
White colour-coat vessel types: 7, 7.7.1, 7.7.2

Oxfordshire whiteware
(15 sherds, 415g, 0.25 EVE, 0.11% of the total assemblage by weight)
The surfaces of this fabric are generally cream to yellow, buff or white, with pale pink or orange margins (Tomber and Dore 1998, 174). It was usually used to manufacture mortaria. The fabric is quite variable, with differing amounts of quartz. Occasional iron-rich inclusions can also be present.
Vessel types: 6.14, 7, 7.8.1, 7.8.3, 7.9.1

Oxidised ware (grog)
(311 sherds, 3091g, 3.57 EVE, 0.85% of the entire assemblage by weight)

A sandy oxidised ware but with frequent very coarse (larger than 1mm) grog inclusions. This fabric is early Roman.
Vessel types: 1.1, 2.2.2, 4.1, 4.4, 4.5, 4.13, 5, 5.4, 5.1/2, 5.2/3, 6.1, 6.9, 6.15.1, 6.21, 8.1

Pink grog-tempered ware
(39 sherds, 1234g, 9 EVE, 0.34%of the entire assemblage by weight)
This is a Romano-British grog-tempered ware with a soft pale fabric with a grey core and pinkish surface. The fabric is typical of the Milton Keynes area, manufactured between the mid 2nd and early 5th centuries (Marney 1989, 174–5).
Vessel types: 4, 5

Red fineware
(190 sherds, 1317g, 2.41 EVE, 0.36% of the total assemblage by weight)
These are oxidised, normally red or orange and frequently have a reduced core and pink margins. The fabric contains well-sorted inclusions and is characterised by common fine, silver (sometimes gold) mica and common to abundant quartz. This material is not slipped. It may be a local copy of samian and Oxfordshire wares, such as those produced at the Obelisk kilns at Harston in south Cambridgeshire (CHER 05074), between the 2nd and 4th centuries.
Vessel types: 1.1, 1.9, 1.11, 4.5, 5, 5 or 6, 6.4, 6.15

Reduced ware (handmade)
(1078 sherds, 18103g, 7.51 EVE, 4.97% of the entire assemblage by weight)
A smooth, laminated fabric made with very little quartz (Perrin 1996, 121). It is a distinctively transitional and early Roman handmade fabric and is a darker, coarser (often thicker) predecessor of the more Romanised Sandy reduced ware.
Vessel types: 2.8, 2.9, 3.5, 4.1, 4.4, 4.13, 4.14, 5, 5.1, 5.2, 5.3, 5.6, 6, 6.4, 6.9, 6.19

Reduced ware (grog)
(405 sherds, 2739g, 0.67 EVE, 0.75% of the entire assemblage by weight)
A smooth, laminated fabric made with very little quartz (Perrin 1996, 121), which contains grog as a common inclusion. It is a distinctively transitional and early Roman handmade fabric, forming a darker, coarser (often thicker) predecessor of the more Romanised Greyware (grog) fabric.
Vessel types: 5, 5.3, 5 or 6

Reduced ware (grog), with oxidised surfaces
(308 sherds, 3699g, 1.37 EVE, 1.02% of the entire assemblage by weight)
A smooth, laminated fabric made with very little quartz which contains grog as a common inclusion (Marney 1989, 190, fabric 46a). It is a distinctively transitional and early Roman (1st century) handmade fabric. Vessels with orange (or oxidised) surfaces of this type are commonly found in Thompson's (1982) Zone 8 around the Milton Keynes area, of which Love's Farm is located on the eastern edge.
Vessel types: 4.1, 4.14, 5, 6.19

Samian
(403 sherds, 3590g, 2.11 EVE, 0.99% of the entire assemblage by weight)
A distinctive glossy red fabric, often decorated (Tomber and Dore 1998, 25–41). A variety of Southern, Central and Eastern Gaulish samian was recovered, of which Central Gaulish was the most common. The assemblage from Love's Farm is characterised in Table A3.1.

Sandy coarsewares
(65 sherds, 361g, 0.16 EVE, 0.10% of the entire assemblage by weight)
A loosely mixed sandy fabric that often presents as a sandwich ware with a variety of core and surface colours ranging from pale grey to dark brown. It is a poorly made fabric that represents low quality utilitarian vessel manufacture throughout the Roman period.
Vessel type: 5

Sandy reduced ware (handmade)
(60 sherds, 1744g, 0.56 EVE, 0.48% of the entire assemblage by weight)

Sandy reduced ware (wheelmade)
(489 sherds, 4509g, 5.27 EVE, 1.24% of the entire assemblage by weight)
A quite hard, rough fabric, very dark grey throughout, with a moderate amount of quartz and occasional fragments of flint, resulting in an irregular fracture. This sandy reduced fabric became more common towards the end of the Iron Age and continued in use as wheelmade technology was introduced, remaining in use throughout the Romano-British period as a tough utilitarian form.
Handmade vessel types: 2.1, 5, 8.1
Wheelmade vessel types: 4.1, 4.4, 4.5, 4.13, 5, 5.6, 6.17, 6.18, 6.19, 8.1

Sandy greyware
(8884 sherds, 83357g, 102.92 EVE, 22.88% of the entire assemblage by weight)
A light brown to dark grey fabric that contains abundant well-rounded quartz and sparse mica (Perrin 1996, 120). It is a utilitarian fabric that was used to produce most jar and bowl forms during the Roman period. The source of this material is unknown, and could originate from anywhere

Fabric	Code	Vessel types	Quantity	Wt (g)	EVE	Wt (%)
Central Gaulish samian (Les Matres and Lezoux)	SAM CG	Dr 18/31, Dr 18/31 or 31, Dr 18/31R or 31R, Dr 27, Dr 31, Dr 31 or 31R, Dr 31R, Dr 33, Dr 35, Dr 36, Dr 37, Dr 37 or 38, Dr 38, Dr 42, Dr 45, Dr 46, Dr 72, Dr ?79, Dr 79R, Dr 81, Curle 11, Curle 23	221	2197	4.27	61.1
South Gaulish samian	SAM SG	Dr 18, Dr 15/17, Dr 15/17 or 18R, Dr 18 or 18/31, Dr 18/31, Dr 18/31R, Dr 27, Dr ?27, Dr 27g, Dr 29, Dr 29 or 30, Dr 30, Dr 35/36, Dr 36, Dr 37, Dr 42, Dr ?67, Dr 78, ?Curle 11, Ritterling 8	170	1225	2.11	34.1
East Gaulish samian	SAM EG	Dr 31, Dr 31R, Dr 33	12	175	0.10	4.8
Total samian			*403*	*3597*	*6.48*	*100*

Table A3.1. Quantification of the samian assemblage

within a radius of 20–30 miles (32–48km) – perhaps further if water transport was available (*ibid*, 121).
Vessel types: 1.10, 2, 2.1, 2.4, 2.5, 3, 3.1, 3.5, 3.7, 3.8, 3.11, 3.13, 4, 4.1, 4.4, 4.5, 4.6, 4.8, 4.12, 4.13, 4.14, 4.15, 4.26, 5, 5.1, 5.2, 5.3, 5.4, 5.6, 5.11, 5.12, 5.13, 6 6.3, 6.4, 6.5, 6.9, 6.13, 6.14, 6.15, 6.17, 6.18, 6.19, 6.21, 6.22, 8.1, 8.3, 9.3

Sandy greyware (blue)
(354 sherds, 4771g, 6.28 EVE, 1.31% of the entire assemblage by weight)
A distinctive blue-grey fabric that contains abundant well-rounded quartz and sparse mica (Marney 1989, 175, fabric 3a). It is a utilitarian fabric that was used to copy BB2 jar and bowl forms in the middle to late Romano-British period.
Vessel types: 2.1, 3.11, 4.4, 4.5, 4.6, 4.13, 5, 5.1, 5.2, 5.3, 5.6, 6.17, 6.18, 6.19, 8.1

Sandy greyware (proto)
(375 sherds, 2420g, 0.18 EVE, 0.66% of the total assemblage by weight)
A light brown to dark grey fabric that contains abundant well-rounded quartz and sparse mica. It is a predecessor (1st to early/mid 2nd century) of the Romanised Sandy greyware fabric, consisting of less well mixed thicker sherds that can be hand or wheelmade (Gibson and Lucus 2002, 126, Rom1).
Vessel types: 5, 5.2/3

Sandy oxidised ware handmade
(11 sherds, 217g, 0.09 EVE, 0.06% of the entire assemblage by weight)

Sandy oxidised ware wheelmade
(1124 sherds, 8526g, 8.71 EVE, 2.34% of the entire assemblage by weight)
An oxidised fabric that can vary in colour from very pale brown to creamy white, and often has sand inclusions (Andrews 1985, 94–5, OW2).
Handmade vessel types: 4.14
Wheelmade vessel types: 1.1, 1.2, 1.9, 2.1, 3.1, 3.7, 4, 4.4, 4.5, 4.8, 4.13, 5, 5.2, 5.3, 5.6, 6, 6.5, 6.6, 6.15, 6.17, 6.18, 6.19, 6.21, 6.25, 7.9.1, 7.10.2, 7.10.4, 8.1

Shell-tempered ware (unsourced)
(7380 sherds, 136381g, 77.40 EVE, 37.44% of the entire assemblage by weight)
Most of these fabrics are brown-grey and are heavily tempered with fossil shell, which is a natural constituent of the clay. Where rim forms are lacking, it can be difficult to differentiate between the various possible manufacturing centres for shell-tempered wares in the Roman period. The Romanised shell-tempered wares differ from their Iron Age predecessors as they do not include grog and show signs of finer preparation (the shell is often crushed). The Lower Nene Valley is known to have been a production centre for shell-tempered storage jars (Perrin 1996, 119–20) between the late Iron Age and 3rd century AD. Early Roman shell-tempered wares were produced at Bourne in Lincolnshire and Greetham in Humberside (Tomber and Dore 1998, 156), while distinctive lipped Dales ware shell-tempered jars were made in the Lincolnshire area between the late 2nd and 3rd centuries. Moreover, the Harrold kilns in Bedfordshire (Tomber and Dore 1998, 115) and other unsourced sites (Tomber and Dore 1998, 212) produced rilled cooking pots in the later Roman period. However, numerous unsourced local production sites would have exploited the Jurassic shelly clay beds throughout the Roman period (Perrin 1996, 119).
Vessel type: 2.1, 2.1.1, 2.1.2, 3.7, 4, 4.1, 4.4, 4.5, 4.5.1, 4.5.2, 4.5.3, 4.5.4, 4.8, 4.12, 4.13, 4.13.4, 4.14, 4.15, 4.16, 4.18, 5, 5.3, 5.6, 5.6.1, 6.1, 6.3, 6.4, 6.13, 6.15, 6.17, 6.18, 6.19, 6.21, 8.1

Verulamium whiteware
(236 sherds, 5551g, 5.60 EVE, 1.52% of the entire assemblage by weight)
A hard, cream or off-white fabric (Tomber and Dore 1998, 154). The fracture is invariably hackly, with harsh surfaces.
Vessel types: 1.1, 1.4, 1.5, 1.9, 3.1, 4.8, 5.2, 6.3, 6.4, 6.15, 7, 7.1, 7.5.1, 7.5.2, 7.9.1

III. Forms

The following catalogue gives numeric vessel type codes, descriptions and published parallels (author, year and illustration number).

All types (excluding samian)

1. Flagons and jugs

1.1 Ring-necked flagons (Perrin 1996, 90)
1.2 Thickened rim, includes hammerhead rim types (Perrin 1996, 38)
1.3 Disc rim flagons (Jackson and Potter 1996, 52)
1.4 Flanged neck, narrow neck with flange (Perrin 1996, 188, 189; Howe *et al.* 1980, 67)
1.5 Hofheim type, single (Stead and Rigby 1986, 191) and double (*ibid*, 229) handled flagons with cylindrical necks and out-curved lips, triangular in section
1.6 Derivations of Hofheim flagons (Martin 1988, 182, 183, 185)
1.7 Straight narrow-necked flagons (Perrin 1996, 161; Howe *et al.* 1980, 66)
1.8 Face mask flagons (Martin 1988, 43, 46)
1.9 Cupped-rim flagon, plain rim (Perrin 1996, 159)
1.10 Carinated jug (West 1990, 263, 264)
1.11 Pinched-neck jugs (Perrin 1996, 131)

2. Narrow-mouthed jars/bottles, miscellaneous or indeterminate

2.1 Narrow-mouthed jar with rolled everted rim, rounded body and various cordons, with decoration on the neck, body and base of the vessel (Perrin 1996, 132, 222, 416)
2.2 Narrow-mouthed jar, slim and pear-shaped
2.3 Narrow-mouthed jar with cordon on neck, sometimes with a frilled flange on the rim
2.4 Narrow-mouthed jar, neckless and globular
2.5 Two-handled storage jars/honey-pot types (Hull 1963, 175, 177)
2.8 Narrow-mouthed jar, with a short beaded neck and an everted rim
2.9 Narrow-mouthed jar, with multiple beads on neck, globular body with a single groove running around the mid point

3. Miscellaneous beakers

3.1 Beaker with a tall straight neck (funnel necked) and rounded body (Perrin 1996, 395; Howe *et al.* 1980, 50, 54–57)
3.3 Indented beakers, miscellaneous or indeterminate
3.5 Beakers, inturned rim, rounded body (Martin 1988, 247, 248)
3.6 Bag-shaped beakers (Howe *et al.* 1980, 46; Perrin 1996, 233)
3.7 Globular beakers with an everted rim (Perrin 1996, 18, 62, 63, 67)
3.8 Poppy-head beaker with barbotine dot decoration (Stead and Rigby 1986, 352, 546)

3.11	Beaker with a 'cavetto rim' (Perrin 1996, 315; Martin 1988, 217)		6.21	Open dish internal angle, incurving rim, flat or foot ring base (Perrin 1996, 28–30)
3.13	Butt beaker (Stead and Rigby 1986, 339)		6.22	Platters, Gallo-Belgic type (Martin 1998, GB1–9)

4. Miscellaneous medium-mouthed jars

4.1	Medium-mouthed jar with high-shouldered profile (Rogerson 1977, 1, 2, 19, 22, 44, 107)
4.4	Jar with short angular neck, lid-seated or flattened rim (Perrin 1996, 387)
4.5	Medium-mouthed jar, short neck, rolled and generally undercut rim and globular body (Rogerson 1977, 43, 93, 115, 202)
4.6	Medium- (sometimes wide-) mouthed jar, short neck, globular body, rolled and undercut rim with grooves at base of neck. Same as type 4.5 except for grooves (Perrin 1996, 361)
4.8	Medium-mouthed jar, everted rim that is hollowed or with projection underneath (bifid), globular body (Perrin 1996, 592, 583)
4.10	Medium-mouthed jar with a globular body, with slash decoration on shoulder (Jackson and Potter 1996, 142)
4.12	Medium-mouthed jar with a reverse S-profile
4.13	Medium-mouthed jar, rounded body and simple everted rim (Rogerson 1977, 5; Martin 1988, 250, 251)
4.14	Large storage vessels miscellaneous or indeterminate
4.15	Large storage jar, high-shouldered, with no decoration on shoulder (Perrin 1996, 289)
4.16	Hooked-rim jar with ridge under the rim (Perrin 1996, 525)
4.17	Classic Horningsea-type storage jar with an out-sized, out-turned rim (Evans 1991, fig. 2, nos 1–9; Perrin 1996, 383–85)
4.18	Large storage jar with narrow neck and large everted rim (and/or rolled) (typical of pink grog-tempered ware jars)

5. Miscellaneous wide-mouthed jars

5.1	Wide-mouthed carinated jar, a heavily cordoned 'Belgic bowl' (Martin 1988, 196–210; Rogerson 1977, 31, 34, 67, 100)
5.2	Carinated jars (Perrin 1996, 71)
5.3	Rounded jar with a reverse S-profile and a groove on the neck (Rogerson 1977, 39, 46, 94)
5.4	Rounded jar, reverse S-profile, one or two grooves mid body
5.6	Wide-mouthed jar, with a plain S-profile (Rogerson 1977, 75)
5.11	Wide-mouthed jar with a high shoulder and everted rim
5.12	Wide-mouthed jar with straight sides, decorated bands and an everted rim (Rogerson 1977, 191, 194, 205)
5.13	Carinated jar, plain (no cordons) with groove at base of neck (Stead and Rigby 1986, 610)

6. Miscellaneous or indeterminate bowl, cup, dish, platter

6.1	Bowl with a reverse S-profile and cordon or groove at base of neck; some footring bases
6.2	Castor box (Howe *et al*. 1980, 89; Perrin 1996, 228, 335)
6.3	Carinated bowl with a flattish out-turned rim (Rogerson 1977, 16, 69, 72)
6.4	Hemispherical bowl (Martin 1988, 269–70, 273–75)
6.5	Straight-sided cup/bowl, copy of Samian form Dr 30
6.6	Bowl, copy of Samian form Dr 37 (Jackson and Potter 1996, 72)
6.7	Carinated, straight-sided bowl (Jackson and Potter 1996, 70)
6.9	Sharply carinated cup – upper part concave externally, footring base (Perrin 1996, 91)
6.13	Conical cup, copy of Samian form Dr 33
6.14	Hemispherical bowl with a plain hooked flange, copy of samian form Dr 38 (Howe *et al*. 1980, 83, 101)
6.15	Flanged rim bowl with curving sides, out-turned rim and foot-ring base (Rogerson 1977, 74, 76, 97)
6.17	Flanged rim straight-sided dishes with a flat base (Perrin 1996, 468, 469, 483)
6.18	Dish, straight-sided, flat-based, thickened everted 'triangular' rim (Perrin 1996, 417, 426, 449, 453, 455)
6.19	Dish, straight sides which may be upright or angled, plain rim or may have external groove just below the rim (Perrin 1996, 402, 403, 415; Darling and Gurney 1993, 642–3)
6.21	Open dish internal angle, incurving rim, flat or foot ring base (Perrin 1996, 28–30)
6.22	Platters, Gallo-Belgic type (Martin 1998, GB1–9)
6.26	Imitation cauldron with handles, straight-sided and nearly upright with a thickened everted rim (Stead and Rigby 1986, 491)

7. Mortaria (Tyers 1996, 116–35)

7	All miscellaneous mortaria
7.1	All miscellaneous mortaria of bead and flange type
7.5.1	Large mortarium of classic Verulamium form. The flange is thick and well rounded. The bead is small and quite low on the internal wall of the vessel
7.5.2	Verulamium mortarium with an upright rim and angular flange. The rim is tall and slightly convex, curving inwards. The flange is angled with two grooves on the lower part
7.7.1	Oxfordshire mortarium with an upright 'tear-shaped' rim and angular flange, which is sometimes rouletted. The spout was formed by squashing the rim down over the flange
7.7.2	Oxfordshire mortarium with upright square rim, with a slight bead, and slightly angled sub-rectangular rim
7.7.4	Oxfordshire wall-sided mortarium, copying samian form Dr 45
7.8.1	Oxfordshire whiteware mortarium with upright rim and angular flange which is sometimes rouletted. The rim is elongated and narrow while the flange is deep but quite short with a rounded distal end (Young 1977, 100)
7.8.3	Oxfordshire whiteware mortarium with an upright rim and angular flange. The rim is concave with a deep groove and the flange is deep thick and bulbous
7.8.6	Mortarium with upright rim and angular flange. The rim is tall, narrow and slightly higher on the external edge. The flange is deep and thick, broader at the distal end; it also has a groove on the underside where the flange joins the vessel wall (Young 1977, 100; Darling and Gurney 1993, 751)
7.9	All Nene Valley mortaria
7.9.1	Nene Valley mortarium with slightly angled reeded rim, usually with three grooves. The bead is substantial and often square in section (Howe *et al*. 1980, 102)
7.9.2	Nene Valley mortarium with a steep sided wall or collared rim, with an applied lion's head spout, derived from samian form Dr 45 (Howe *et al*. 1980, 84)
7.9.3	Nene Valley mortarium with a high bead and well-rounded flange (Howe *et al*. 1980, 101)
7.9.4	Nene Valley mortarium with an exceptionally high bead and small rounded flange (copying Oxfordshire types)
7.9.5	Mortarium with a steep wall or collared reeded rim
7.10.2	Unsourced orange ware mortarium with a very high bead and narrow 'stubby' flange that is pointed at the distal end
7.10.4	Unsourced orange ware wall-sided or collared mortarium with a small grooved bead. The collar is attached to the vessel wall and it has two grooves on its underside
7.11.1	Mortarium with a deep collar with two grooves at the top of it. The rim has a steep internal angle

8. Lids

8.1.	Lid – standard type to fit cooking/storage pot, inturned or out-turned, can have terminal grip (Perrin 1996, 57–59)
8.3.	'Coffee pot' lid – carinated profile and flange, to fit narrow mouthed jars (Howe *et al*., 72)

9. Miscellaneous

9.3.	Cheese Press (Perrin 1996, 393)

Samian (Tyers 1996, 105–16)

Dr 15/17	Platter with quarter-round moulding internally at the junction of the wall and floor. The mouldings on the exterior walls vary considerably from example to example.
Dr 18	Platter with curved wall and beaded lip.
Dr 18/31	Shallow bowl, with a very slightly curved wall (the division between the wall and the floor is apparent), while the floor rises noticeably in the centre.

Dr 27	Cup with double curved wall and bead rim (campanulate). An external groove on the footring may occur on 1st-century examples (Dr 27g).
Dr 29	This is generally described as a carinated bowl with a beaded rim with a double curved and ledged interior. The upper exterior is rouletted, with two cordoned zones of decoration below.
Dr 30	Approximately straight-sided bowl, with designs occupying 66% of the vessel surface. The top of each design has an ovolo border.
Dr 31	Shallow bowl with a curved wall and beaded rim, the division between wall and floor apparent.
Dr 31R	Shallow bowl with a curved wall and beaded rim, the division between floor and wall is vestigial, although marked by a slight ledge.
Dr 32	Dish with plain curving sides and footring.
Dr 33	Conical cup with a footring. There are often grooves (or a groove) on the external vessel wall.
Dr 35	Cup with curved walls and over-hanging rim, trailed leaves are applied on the rim.
Dr 36	Dish with curved walls and over-hanging rim, trailed leaves are applied on the rim.
Dr 37	Deep bowl with slightly curved sides. The wall of the vessel is usually divided into two (approximately) equal zones, where the lower half is decorated.
Dr 38	Hemispherical bowl with a plain hooked flange below the mid-way point on the wall. The rim can be beaded or plain.
Dr 42	Dish with a curved wall and footstand. The rim usually curls over, often ending with a small upturn. Many examples have a pair of strap handles.
Dr 45	Mortarium with a near upright upper wall and a lion's head spout.
Dr 46	Cup with flaring walls that are concave externally.
Dr 72	Globular beaker with a decorated zone delineated above and below with grooves.
Dr 78	Small carinated bowl with a plain rim, no decoration below the carination and no footstand. May be related to Dr 30.
Dr 79	Dish with strongly curving walls and a beaded rim. Part of a set with cup Dr 80. A version of Dr 79 had an internal rouletted circle and was termed Dr 79R.
Dr 81	Almost a jar form with a wide neck and everted rim. The upper wall thickens and allows an overhang at between one third and one half of the way up the wall from the base.
Curle 11	Hemispherical bowl with a flange which is generally a short way below the rim. The flange is decorated with trailed leaves as on Dr 35 and Dr 36.
Curle 23	Shallow bowl with slightly curved sides and a relatively large bead rim. The division between the wall and floor is apparent.
Rittering 8	Hemispherical cup with external groove just below the rim and half-way down the wall.

Amphorae (Tyers 1996, 88–91)

DR1	Cylindrical amphora (principally wine containers) with angular shoulders and long straight handles.
DR2–4	Cylindrical amphora (principally wine containers) with long bifid handles, with a small beaded lip and carinated shoulder.
DR20	A large globular form (principally olive oil containers) with two handles and thickened, rounded or angular rim, concave internally.

Bibliography

Abrams, J., 2000 — *Iron Age Pitting and Medieval Ridge and Furrow Agriculture, Caldecote Primary School, Highfields, Caldecote: an archaeological investigation*, Cambridgeshire County Counc. Archaeol. Field Unit Rep. 178 (unpubl.)

Abrams, J. and Ingham, D., 2008 — *Farming on the Edge. Archaeological evidence from the clay uplands to the west of Cambridge*, E. Anglian Archaeol. 123

ACBMG, 2002 — *Ceramic Building Material: minimum standards for recovery, curation, analysis and publication* (London, Archaeological Ceramic Building Materials Group)

Addyman, P., 1965 — 'Late Saxon settlements in the St Neots area. I: the Saxon settlement and Norman castle at Eaton Socon, Bedfordshire', *Proc. Cambridge Antiq. Soc.* 58, 38–73

Addyman, P., 1973 — 'Late Saxon settlements in the St Neots area. III: the village or township of St Neots', *Proc. Cambridge Antiq. Soc.* 64, 45–99

Albarella, U., 1998 — 'The animal bones', in Ellis, P., Hughes, G., Leach, P., Mould, C. and Sterenberg, J., *Excavations alongside Roman Ermine Street, Cambridgeshire, 1996*, Birmingham Univ. Field Archaeol. Unit Monogr. 4 / Brit. Archaeol. Rep. Brit. Ser. 322, 99–104 (Oxford)

Albarella, U. and Davis, S.J.M., 1994 — *The Saxon and Medieval Animal Bones Excavated 1985–1989 from West Cotton, Northamptonshire*, English Heritage Ancient Monuments Lab. Rep. 17/94 (London)

Albarella, U. and Davis, S.J.M., 1996 — 'Mammals and birds from Launceston Castle, Cornwall: decline in status and the rise of agriculture', *Circaea* 12(1), 1–156

Alexander, M., 1992 — *Prehistoric Settlement, Great North Road, Little Paxton*, Cambridgeshire County Counc. Archaeol. Field Unit Rep. 78 (unpubl.)

Alexander, M, 1993 — *Roman Settlement Evidence at Ernulf School, St Neots, Cambridgeshire*, County Counc. Archaeol. Field Unit Rep. 91 (unpubl.)

Alexander, M., 1998 — *An Archaeological Evaluation at Papworth Everard, South-west Quadrant*, Cambridgeshire County Counc. Archaeol. Field Unit Rep. 149 (unpubl.)

Allason-Jones, L. and McKay, B., 1985 — *Coventina's Well. A shrine on Hadrian's Wall* (Hexham, The Trustees of the Clayton Collection, Chesters Museum)

Allason-Jones, L. and Miket, R., 1984 — *The Catalogue of Small Finds from South Shields Roman Fort*, Soc. Antiq. Newcastle-upon-Tyne Monogr. 2 (Newcastle-upon-Tyne)

Allen, D., 1986 — 'Excavations in Bierton, 1979. A Late Iron Age 'Belgic' settlement and evidence for a Roman villa and a twelfth to eighteenth century manorial complex', *Rec. Buckinghamshire* 28, 1–120

Allen, M.J., 2004 — 'Discussion: the development of a farmed landscape', in Ellis, C., *A Prehistoric Ritual Complex at Eynesbury, Cambridgeshire*, E. Anglian Archaeol. Occ. Pap. 17, 91–4

Allen, M.J., Rhodes, E., Bevan, N. and Groves, C., 2004 — 'Absolute chronology', in Ellis, C., *A Prehistoric Ritual Complex at Eynesbury, Cambridgeshire*, E. Anglian Archaeol. Occ. Pap. 17, 60–67

Amorosi, T., 1989 — *A Postcranial Guide to Domestic Neo-natal and Juvenile Mammals*, Brit. Archaeol. Rep. Int. Ser. 533 (Oxford)

Anderson, K., 2013 — 'Roman pottery', in Evans, C., *Process and History. Romano-British Communities at Colne Fen, Earith*, CAU Landscape Archives Series. The Archaeology of the Lower Ouse Valley, Volume II, 299–334

Andrew, R., 1984 — *A Practical Pollen Guide to the British Flora*, Quaternary Research Association Technical Guide No. 1 (Cambridge)

Andrews, A.H. and Noddle, B.A., 1975 — 'Absence of premolar teeth from ruminant mandibles found at archaeological sites', *J. Archaeol. Sci.* 2, 137–44

Andrews, G., 1985 — 'The coarse wares', in Hinchliffe, J. and Sparey-Green, C., *Excavations at Brancaster 1974 and 1977*, E. Anglian Archaeol. 23, 82–95

Andrews, P., 1990 — *Owls, Caves and Fossils* (Chicago, Univ. Chicago Press)

Andrews, P., 1995 — *Excavations at Redcastle Furze, Thetford*, E. Anglian Archaeol. 72

Andrews, P., 2008 — 'Springhead, Kent – old temples and new discoveries', in Rudling, D. (ed.), *Ritual Landscapes of Roman South-east Britain*, 45–62 (Great Dunham/Oxford, Heritage Marketing & Publications)

Applebaum, S., 1966 — 'Peasant economy and types of agriculture', in Thomas, C. (ed.), *Rural Settlement in Roman Britain*, Counc. Brit. Archaeol. Res. Rep. 7, 99–107 (London)

Armitage, P.L., 1982 — 'A system for ageing and sexing the horn cores of cattle from British post-medieval sites (17th to early 18th century), with special reference to unimproved British Longhorn cattle', in Wilson, R., Grigson, C. and Payne, S. (eds), *Ageing and Sexing Animal Bones from Archaeological Sites*, Brit. Archaeol. Rep. Brit. Ser. 109, 37–54 (Oxford)

Armitage, P.L. and Clutton-Brock, J., 1976 — 'A system for classification and description of the horn cores of cattle from archaeological sites', *J. Archaeol. Sci.* 3, 329–48

Ashwin, T., and Bates, S., 2000 — *Excavations on the Norwich Southern Bypass, 1989–91*, E. Anglian Archaeol. 91

Atkins, R. and Connor, A., 2010 — *Farmers and Ironsmiths: prehistoric, Roman and Anglo-Saxon settlement beside Brandon Road, Thetford, Norfolk*, E. Anglian Archaeol. 134

Atkins, R., and Mudd, A., 2003 — 'An Iron Age and Romano-British settlement at Prickwillow Road, Ely, Cambridgeshire: excavations 1999–2000', *Proc. Cambridge Antiq. Soc.* 92, 5–55

Atkins, R., Popescu, E., Rees, G. and Stansbie, D., 2014 — *Broughton, Milton Keynes, Buckinghamshire. The evolution of a South Midlands landscape*, Oxford Archaeology Monogr. 22

Austin, L., 2000	'Palaeolithic and Mesolithic, in Brown, N. and Glazebrook, J. (eds), *Research and Archaeology: a Framework for the Eastern Counties, 2. Research agenda and strategy*, E. Anglian Archaeol. Occ. Pap. 8, 5–8		*at Haddon, Peterborough*, Cambridgeshire County Counc. Archaeol. Field Unit Monogr. 2/Brit. Archaeol. Rep. Brit. Ser. 358, 119–32 and Appendix 2 (Oxford)
Bagnall Smith, J., 1998	'More votive finds from Woodeaton, Oxfordshire', *Oxoniensia* 63, 147–85	Baxter, I.L., 2006a	'A dwarf hound skeleton from a Romano-British grave at York Road, Leicester, England, U.K., with a discussion of other Roman small dog types and speculation regarding their respective aetiologies', in Snyder, L.M. and Moore, E.A. (eds), *Dogs and People in Social, Working, Economic or Symbolic Interaction*, Proc. 9th Congress Int. Counc. Archaeozoology (2002), 12–23 (Oxford)
Bagnall Smith, J., 1999	'Votive objects and objects of votive significance from Great Walsingham, Norfolk', *Britannia* 30, 21–56		
Baker, G.J. and Easley, J. (eds), 2005	*Equine Dentistry*, 2nd edn (London, Elsevier) or Available: http://www.sciencedirect.com/science/book/9780702027246 Accessed: 26 October 2016		
		Baxter, I.L., 2006b	*Landbeach, Lime's Farm, Cambridgeshire: faunal remains*, archive report for CAM ARC, Cambridgeshire County Counc. (unpubl.)
Baker, J. and Brothwell, D., 1980	*Animal Diseases in Archaeology* (London, Academic Press)	Baxter, I.L., 2009	*Bob's Wood, Hinchingbrooke, Cambridgeshire: faunal remains*, archive report for Oxford Archaeol. East (unpubl.)
Ballin, T.B., 2002	'Later Bronze Age flint technology: a presentation and discussion of post-barrow debitage from monuments in the Raunds Area, Northamptonshire', *Lithics* 23, 3–28	Baxter, I.L., 2010a	*Small Roman Dogs*. Available: http://alexandriaarchive.org/bonecommons/items/show/901. Accessed: 24 November 2015
Barber, J. and Crone, A., 2001	'The duration of structures, settlements and sites: some evidence from Scotland', in Raftery, B. and Hickey, J. (eds), *Recent Developments in Wetland Research*, Dept. Archaeol. Univ. College Dublin, Monogr. Ser. 2/WARP Occ. Pap. 14, 69–86 (Dublin)	Baxter, I.L, 2010b	*A Re-examination of the Thistleton Canids.* Available: http://alexandriaarchive.org/bonecommons/items/show/885. Accessed: 25 November 2015
		Baxter, I.L., 2011a	'Faunal remains (temple precinct)', in Medlycott, M., *Great Chesterford Roman Town*, E. Anglian Archaeol. 137
Barber, M., Field, D. and Topping, P., 1999	*The Neolithic Flint Mines of England* (London, English Heritage)	Baxter, I.L., 2011b	'Animal bone', in Lyons, A., *Life and Afterlife at Duxford, Cambridgeshire: archaeology and history in a chalkland community*, E. Anglian Archaeol. 141, 72–80
Barker, G., 1985	*Prehistoric Farming in Europe* (Cambridge, Cambridge Univ. Press)		
Barone, R., 1980	*Anatomia Comparata dei Mammiferi Domestici. Vol. III Splancnologia* (Bologna, Edagricole)	Baxter, I.L., 2011c	'Faunal remains', in Kenney, S. and Lyons, A., 'An Iron Age banjo enclosure and contemporary settlement at Caldecote', *Proc. Cambridge Antiq. Soc.* 100, 67–84
Bartosiewicz, L., Van Neer, W. and Lentacker, A., 1997	*Draught Cattle: their osteological identification and history*, Koninklijk Museum voor Midden-Afrika, Tervuren, belgi, Annalen Zoölogische Wetenschappen/Annales Sciences Zoologiques, Musée Royale de l'Afrique Central (Tervuren)	Bayley, J. and Butcher, S., 2004	*Roman Brooches in Britain. A technological and typological study based on the Richborough collection*, Soc. Ant. London Res. Rep. 68 (London)
		Bayley, J. and Woodward, A., 1993	'Rings', in Woodward, A. and Leach, P., *The Uley Shrines. Excavation of a ritual complex on West Hill, Uley, Gloucestershire*, English Heritage Archaeol. Rep. 17, 135–40 (London)
Bass, W.M., 1992	*Human Osteology* (Columbia, Missouri Archaeology Society)		
Baxter, I.L., 1993	'Bones of small animals and birds from predator pellets and scats at Drayton II Roman villa, Leicestershire', *Organ* 2, 5–6	Beadsmoore, E., 2006	'Earlier Neolithic flint', in Garrow, D., Lucy, S. and Gibson, D., *Excavations at Kilverstone, Norfolk. An episodic landscape history*, E. Anglian Archaeol. 113, 53–70
Baxter, I.L., 1996	'Medieval and early post-medieval horse bones from Market Harborough, Leicestershire, England, UK', *Circaea* 11 (2), 65–79	Bertrand, I., 2003	*Objets de parure et de soin du corps d'époque romaine dans l'Est picton (Deux-Sèvres, Vienne)*, Mémoire de l'Association des Publications Chauvinoises 23 (Chauvigny)
Baxter, I.L., 1998	'Species identification of equids from western European archaeological deposits: methodologies, techniques and problems', in Anderson, S. (ed.), *Current and Recent Research in Osteoarchaeology*, Proc. 3rd Meet. Osteoarchaeol. Res. Group, 3–17 (Oxford)		
		Bevan, L., 1995	'The flint', in Jones, A., 'Little Paxton quarry, Diddington, Cambs, archaeological excavations 1992–3, second interim report: the south-west area settlement and activity from the Neolithic to the Iron Age', *Proc. Cambridge Antiq. Soc.* 83, 7–22
Baxter, I.L., 1999	*Greenhouse Farm, Fen Ditton. Report on the mammal, bird, amphibian and fish bone*, Cambridgeshire County Counc. Archaeol. Field Unit (unpubl.)		
Baxter, I.L., 2002	'Occipital perforations in a late Neolithic probable aurochs (*Bos primigenius* Bojanus) cranium from Letchworth, Hertfordshire, UK', *Int. J. Osteoarchaeol.* 12, 142–3	Biddulph, E., 2008	'Form and function: the experimental use of samian ware cups', *Oxford J. Archaeol.* 27 (1), 91–100
		Birley, B. and Green E., 2006	*The Roman Jewellery from Vindolanda. Fascicule V: Beads, Intaglios, Finger Rings, Ear-rings and Bracelets*, Vindolanda Research Reports, New
Baxter, I.L., 2003	'The mammal and bird bones', in Hinman, M., *A Late Iron Age Farmstead and Romano-British site*		

	Series Vol. IV (Greenhead, Roman Army Museum Publications for the Vindolanda Trust)	Blinkhorn, P., 2010b	'Anglo-Saxon and later pottery', in Atkins, R. and Connor, A., *Farmers and Ironsmiths. Prehistoric, Roman and Anglo-Saxon settlement beside Brandon Road, Thetford, Norfolk*, E. Anglian Archaeol. 134, 70–79
Bishop, B.J., 2001	'The lithics', in Taylor-Wilson, R. H., 'Pre-Roman features and cultural material from two sites in Old Ford, Bow, Tower Hamlets', *Trans. London Middlesex Archaeol. Soc.* 51, 1–19	Boessneck, J., 1969	'Osteological differences between sheep (*Ovis aries Linne*) and goat (*Capra hircus Linne*)', in Brothwell, D.R. and Higgs, E. (eds), *Science in Archaeology*, 331–59 (London, Thames and Hudson)
Bishop, B.J., 2004	*The Struck Flint from Bob's Wood, Hinchingbrooke*, archive report for Oxford Archaeol. East (unpubl.)		
Bishop, B.J., 2008	*Lithic Report, Excavations at Silver Street, Godmanchester*, archive report for Archaeol. Project Services (unpubl.)	Boon, G., 1967	'The Penard Roman imperial hoard; an interim report and a list of Roman hoards in Wales', *Bull. Board Celtic Stud.* 22, 291–310
Bland, R., and Johns, C., 1993	*The Hoxne Treasure. An illustrated introduction* (London, British Museum)	Booth, P., Dodd, A., Robinson, M. and Smith, A., 2007	*Thames through Time. The archaeology of the gravel terraces of the Upper and Middle Thames. The early historical period: AD 1–1000*, Thames Valley Landscapes Monogr. 27 (Oxford)
Blinkhorn, P., 1993	'The Saxon pottery', in Williams, R.J., *Pennyland and Hartigans. Two Iron Age and Saxon Sites in Milton Keynes*, Buckinghamshire Archaeol. Soc. Monogr. 4, 246–64	Borrill, H., 1981	'Casket burials', in Partridge, C., *Skeleton Green*, Britannia Monogr. 2, 304–21 (London)
Blinkhorn, P., 1994a	'Early Saxon pottery', in Williams, R.J. and Zeepvat, R.J., *Bancroft. A late Bronze Age settlement, Roman villa and temple mausoleum*, Buckinghamshire Archaeol. Soc. Monogr. 7, 512–4	Boucher, T., 2004	'Quelques objets provenant de la *civitas* des Turones (Indre et Loire, F)', *Instrumentum Bull.* 20, 20–4
		Bowen, D.Q. (ed), 1999	*A Revised Correlation of Quaternary Deposits in the British Isles*, Geological Soc. Special Rep. 23 (Bath)
Blinkhorn, P, 1994b	'Saxon pottery', in Zeepvat, R.J., Roberts, J.S. and King, N.A., *Caldecotte, Milton Keynes. Excavation and Fieldwork 1966–91*, Buckinghamshire Archaeol. Soc. Monogr. Ser. 9, 194–6	Bradley, R., 2007	*The Prehistory of Britain and Ireland* (Cambridge, Cambridge Univ. Press)
Blinkhorn, P., 1997	'*Habitus*, cultural identity and early Anglo-Saxon pottery', in Cumberpatch, C.G. and Blinkhorn, P. (eds), *Not so Much a Pot, More a Way of Life*, Oxbow Monogr. 83, 113–24 (Oxford)	Brain, C.K., 1976	'Some principles in the interpretation of bone accumulations associated with man', in Isaac, G. and McCown, E. (eds), *Human Origins*, 97–116 (California)
Blinkhorn, P., 2000	'The early Anglo-Saxon pottery', in Cooper, N.J., *The Archaeology of Rutland Water*, Leicestershire Archaeol. Monogr. 6, 98–104	Branigan, K., 1985	*The Catuvellauni* (Gloucester, Alan Sutton)
		Brewer, D., Clark, T. and Phillips, A., 2001	*Dogs in Antiquity. Anubis to Cerberus. The origins of the domestic dog* (Warminster, Aris & Phillips)
Blinkhorn, P., 2004	'The early Anglo-Saxon pottery', in Finn, N., *The Origins of a Leicester Suburb*, Brit. Archaeol. Rep. Brit. Ser. 372, 84		
		British Geological Survey, 1987	*1:50,000 series, Huntingdon, Sheet 187*
Blinkhorn, P., 2005a	'The Saxon and medieval pottery', in Maul, A. and Chapman, A., *A Medieval Moated Enclosure in Tempsford Park*, Bedfordshire Archaeol. Monogr. 5, 53–70	Brodribb, G., 1987	*Roman Brick and Tile* (Gloucester, Sutton)
		Brothwell, D., 1981	*Digging Up Bones* (London, British Museum (Natural History))
Blinkhorn, P., 2005b	'The pottery', in Crowson A., Lane, T., Penn, K. and Trimble, D, *Anglo-Saxon Settlement on the Siltland of Eastern England*, Lincolnshire Archaeol. Hist. Heritage Rep. Ser. 7, 178–86	Brown, A., 1994	'A Romano-British shell-gritted pottery and tile manufacturing site at Harrold, Bedfordshire', *Bedfordshire Archaeol.* 21, 19–107
Blinkhorn, P., 2007a	*Pottery from Oakington, site OAKQUW07*, archive report for Cambridgeshire County Counc. Archaeol. Field Unit (unpubl.)	Brown, A.G., Meadows, I., Turner, S.D. and Mattingley, D., 2001	'Roman vineyards in Britain: stratigraphic and palynological data from Wollaston in the Nene Valley, England', *Antiquity* 75, 745–57
Blinkhorn, P., 2007b	*Pottery from Peterborough, site PETWRM05*, archive report for Cambridgeshire County Counc. Archaeol. Field Unit (unpubl.)		
Blinkhorn, P., 2007c	'The post-Roman pottery', in Hardy, A., Charles. B.M. and Williams, R. J., *Death and Taxes. The archaeology of a Middle Saxon estate centre at Higham Ferrers Northamptonshire*, Oxford Archaeol. Monogr. 4, 100–111 (Oxford)	Brown, L., 1984	'Objects of stone', in Cunliffe, B., *Danebury: an Iron Age hillfort in Hampshire, Volume 2. The excavations 1969–1978: the finds*, Counc. Brit. Archaeol. Res. Rep. 52, 407–26 (London)
		Brown, N. and Glazebrook, J. (eds), 2000	*Research and Archaeology: a Framework for the Eastern Counties, 2. Research agenda and strategy*, E. Anglian Archaeol. Occ. Pap. 8
Blinkhorn, P., 2008	*Pottery from Chatteris, site CHANER06*, archive report for Cambridgeshire County Counc. Archaeol. Field Unit (unpubl.)	Brown, N. and Murphy, P., 2000	'Neolithic and Bronze Age', in Brown, N. and Glazebrook, J. (eds), *Research and Archaeology: a Framework for the Eastern Counties, 2. Research agenda and strategy*, E. Anglian Archaeol. Occ. Pap. 8, 9–13
Blinkhorn, P., 2010a	'Pottery', in Atkins, R., 'Stow Longa to Tilbrook Pipeline', *Proc. Cambridge Antiq. Soc.* 99, 82–4		

Brown, N., Murphy, P., Ayers, B., Bryant, S. and Malim, T., 2000 — 'Research themes', in Brown, N. and Glazebrook, J. (eds), *Research and Archaeology: a Framework for the Eastern Counties, 2. Research agenda and strategy*, E. Anglian Archaeol. Occ. Pap. 8, 44–48

Brown, W.A.B., 1985 — *Identification of Human Teeth* (London, Institute of Archaeology)

Brudenell, M., forthcoming — 'Later Iron Age pottery', in Phillips, T. and Mortimer, R., *The Archaeology of Clay Farm, Great Kneighton, Cambridgeshire: a landscape study*, E. Anglian Archaeol. (working title)

Bryant, S., 2000 — 'The Iron Age', in Brown, N. and Glazebrook, J. (eds), *Research and Archaeology: a Framework for the Eastern Counties, 2. Research agenda and strategy*, E. Anglian Archaeol. Occ. Pap. 8, 14–18

Buikstra, J.E. and Ubelaker, D.H. (eds), 1994 — *Standards for Data Collection from Human Skeletal Remains*, Arkansas Archaeol. Survey Res. Ser. 44 (Fayetteville)

Buckland, P.C. and Magilton, J.R., 1986 — *The Archaeology of Doncaster 1*, Brit. Archaeol. Rep. Brit. Ser. 148 (Oxford)

Bullock, J.A., 1993 — 'Host plants of British beetles: a list of recorded associations', *Amateur Entomologist* 11a, 1–24

Burnett, A.M., 1978 — 'The Langford find', *Coin Hoards* 4, 48

Burton, M., 1960 — *Wild Animals of the British Isles* (London, Warne)

Bushe-Fox, J.P., 1914 — *Second Report on the Excavations on the Site of the Roman Town at Wroxeter, Shropshire*, Rep. Res. Comm. Soc. Antiq. 2 (London)

Callender, M.H., 1965 — *Roman Amphorae with Index of Stamps* (Oxford, Oxford Univ. Press)

Cameron, F., 1996 — 'The other pottery', in Jackson, R.P.J. and Potter, T.W. (eds), *Excavations at Stonea, Cambridgeshire, 1980–85*, 440–76 (London)

Carson, R.A.G. and Kent, J.P.C., 1972 — 'Part 2: bronze Roman imperial coinage of the later empire AD 346–498', in Carson, R.A.G., Hill, P.V. and Kent, J.P.C., *Late Roman Bronze Coinage* (London, Spink & Son)

Carson, R.A.G. and O'Kelly, C., 1977 — 'A catalogue of the Roman coins from Newgrange, Co. Meath, and notes on the coins and related finds', *Proc. Royal Irish Academy, Section C*, 77, 35–55

Casa Hatton R., 2002 — *Papworth Everard Bypass: a desktop assessment*, Cambridgeshire County Counc. Archaeological Field Unit Rep. A195 (unpubl.)

Castle, S.A., 1974 — 'Excavations at Brockley Hill, Middlesex, March–May 1972', *Trans. London Middlesex Archaeol. Soc.* 25, 251–63

Chadwick, A.M., 1997 — 'Towards a social archaeology of later prehistoric and Romano-British field systems in South Yorkshire, West Yorkshire and Nottinghamshire', *Assemblage* 2. Available: www.assemblage.group.shef.ac.uk/2/2chad.html. Accessed: 25 November 2015

Chadwick, A.M., 1999 — 'Digging ditches but missing riches? Ways into the Iron Age and Romano-British crop-mark landscapes of the North Midlands', in Bevan, B. (ed), *Northern Exposure: interpretative devolution and the Iron Ages in Britain*, Leicester Archaeol. Monogr. 4 (Leicester), 149–71

Chaplin, R.E. and McCormick, F., 1986 — 'The animal bone', in Stead, I.M., and Rigby, V. (eds), *Baldock. The Excavation of a Roman and Pre-Roman Settlement, 1968–72*, Britannia Monogr. Ser. 7, 396–415

Chapman, A., Carlyle, A. and Leigh, D., 2005 — 'Neolithic and Beaker pits, and a Bronze Age landscape at Fenstanton, Cambridgeshire', *Proc. Cambridge Antiq. Soc.* 94, 5–20

Chester-Kadwell, B., 2009 — *Love's Farm, St Neots: Background Landscape Analysis*, archive report for Oxford Archaeol. East (unpubl.)

Childe, G., 1943 — 'Rotary querns on the Continent and in the Mediterranean basin', *Antiquity* 17, 19–26

Chowne, P., 1986 — 'Excavation of an Iron Age defended enclosure at Tattershall Thorpe, Lincolnshire', *Proc. Prehistoric Soc.* 52, 159–89

Clark, J.G.D., Higgs, E.S. and Longworth, I.H., 1960 — 'Excavations at the Neolithic site at Hurst Fen, Mildenhall, Suffolk, 1954, 1957 and 1958', *Proc. Prehist. Soc.* 26, 202–45

Clark, K.M., 1995 — 'The later prehistoric and protohistoric dog: the emergence of canine diversity', *Archaeozoologia* 7 (2), 9–32

Clarke, A., in prep. — 'Animal husbandry', in Lucas, G., and Evans, C., *The Roman Settlement at Vicar's Farm, Cambridge*, E. Anglian Archaeol.

Clarke, G., 1979 — *The Roman Cemetery at Lankhills, Winchester*, Winchester Stud. 3 (Oxford)

Clay, P., 2002 — *The Prehistory of the East Midlands Claylands: aspects of settlement and land-use from the Mesolithic to the Iron Age in central England*, Leicester Archaeol. Monogr. 9 (Leicester)

Cleal, R., 2004 — 'The dating and diversity of the earliest ceramics of Wessex and South-west England' in Cleal, R. and Pollard, J. (eds), *Monuments and Material Culture*, 164–192 (Salisbury, Hobnob Press)

Clutton-Brock. J., Denis-Bryan, P.L., Armitage, P.L. and Jewell, P.A., 1990 — 'Osteology of the Soay sheep', *Bull. Brit. Mus. Nat. Hist. (Zool.)*, 56, 1–56

CPM, 1998 — *Land at St Neots, Cambridgeshire, An Archaeological Assessment*, CPM Environmental Planning and Design (unpubl.)

Collingwood, R.G. and Wright, R.P., 1965 — *The Roman Inscriptions of Britain, Vol. I: Inscriptions on Stone* (Oxford, Oxford Univ. Press)

Collins, P., 1994 — 'The animal bone', in French, C.A.I., *The Haddon Farmstead and a Prehistoric Landscape at Elton: the archaeology along the A605 Elton–Haddon bypass, Cambridgeshire*, 142–52 (Cambridge, Fenland Archaeological Trust/Cambridgeshire County Council)

Collis, J., 1996 — 'Hillforts, enclosures and boundaries', in Champion, T.C., and Collis, J. (eds), *The Iron Age in Britain and Ireland: recent trends*, 87–94 (Sheffield)

Connor, A., 1999 — *Iron Age Settlement and Agriculture at Butt Lane, Milton: training excavation 1998*, Cambridgeshire County Counc. Archaeol. Field Unit Rep. 157 (unpubl.)

Cooke, N., Brown, F. and Phillpotts, C., 2008 — *From Hunter Gatherers to Huntsmen. A history of the Stansted landscape*, Framework Archaeol. Monogr. 2 (Oxford/Salisbury)

Cool, H.E.M., 1990 — 'Roman metal hairpins from southern Britain', *Archaeol. J.* 147, 148–82

Cool, H.E.M., 2006 — *Eating and Drinking in Roman Britain* (Cambridge, Cambridge University Press)

Cool, H.E.M. and Philo, C. (eds), 1998. *Roman Castleford Excavations 1974–85. Vol. I: the small finds*, Yorkshire Archaeol. 4 (Wakefield)

Cool, H.E.M. and Price, J., 1995. *Roman Vessel Glass from Excavations in Colchester, 1971–85*, Colchester Archaeol. Rep. 5 (Colchester)

Cooper, N. and Lyons, A., 2011. 'The Roman pottery', in Wallis, H., *Romano-British and Saxon Occupation at Billingford, Central Norfolk*, E. Anglian Archaeol. 135, 50–57

Crabtree, P., 1989. *West Stow, Suffolk: Early Anglo-Saxon Animal Husbandry*, E. Anglian Archaeol. 47

Cromarty, A.M., Roberts, M.R., and Smith, A.T., 2007. 'Archaeological Investigations at Stubbs Farm, Kempsford, Gloucestershire, 1991–1995', in Miles, D., Palmer, S., Smith, A. and Jones, G.P., *Iron Age and Roman Settlement in the Upper Thames Valley: excavations at Claydon Pike and other sites within the Cotswold Water Park*, 295–308 (Oxford, Oxbow)

Croom, A.T., 2007. *Roman Furniture* (Stroud, The History Press)

Crummy, N., 1983. *The Roman Small Finds from Excavations in Colchester 1971–9*, Colchester Archaeol. Rep. 2 (Colchester)

Crummy, N., 1992. 'The Roman small finds from the Culver Street site and the Roman small finds from the Gilberd School', in Crummy, P., *Excavations at Culver Street, the Gilberd School, and Other Sites in Colchester, 1971–85*, Colchester Archaeol. Rep. 6, 140–205 (Colchester)

Crummy, N., 1999. 'Appendix 1 – the grave goods from Grave 114', in Casa-Hatton, R. and Wall, W., *A Late Roman Cemetery beside the A1 near Durobrivae (Water Newton): archaeological recording*, Cambridgeshire County Counc. Archaeol. Field Unit Rep. 165 (unpubl.)

Crummy, N., 2000. 'A late Roman grave group from *Durobrivae*', *Roman Finds Group Newsletter* 19, 7–10

Crummy, N., 2001a. 'A new Minerva bust wax spatula handle from Britain', *Instrumentum Bull.* 13 (June), 22

Crummy, N., 2001b. 'Bone-working in Roman Britain: a model for itinerant craftsmen?', in Polfer, M. (ed.), *L'artisanat romain: évolutions, continuités et ruptures (Italie et provinces occidentales)*, Actes du 2e colloque d'Erpeldange 26–28 octobre 2001, Instrumentum Monogr. 20 (Montagnac)

Crummy, N., 2002. 'Wax spatula handle from Yorkshire', *Lucerna, Roman Finds Group Newsletter* 23 (January), 6–8

Crummy, N., 2003a. 'The metalwork', in Hinman, M., *A Late Iron Age Farmstead and Romano-British Site at Haddon, Peterborough*, Cambridgeshire County Counc. Archaeol. Field Unit Monogr. 2/Brit. Archaeol. Rep. Brit. Ser. 358, 108–14 (Oxford)

Crummy, N., 2003b. 'Other types of wax spatulae from Britain', *Lucerna, Roman Finds Group Newsletter* 24 (July), 14–17

Crummy, N., 2004. 'The small finds', in Hands, A.R. and Cotswold Archaeology, *The Romano-British Roadside Settlement at Wilcote, Oxfordshire, 3: excavations 1997–2000*, Brit. Archaeol. Rep. Brit. Ser. 370, 277–94 (Oxford)

Crummy, N., 2005a. 'Deux appliques émaillés de Grande Bretagne', *Instrumentum Bull.* 22, 40

Crummy, N., 2005b. 'From bracelets to battle-honours: military *armillae* from the Roman conquest of Britain', in Crummy, N. (ed.), *Image, Craft and the Classical World. Essays in honour of Donald Bailey and Catherine Johns*, Instrumentum Monogr. 29, 93–106 (Montagnac)

Crummy, N., 2006a. 'Worshipping Mercury on Balkerne Hill, Colchester', in Ottaway, P. (ed.), *A Victory Celebration: papers on the archaeology of late Iron Age–Roman Britain presented to Philip Crummy*, 55–68 (Colchester)

Crummy, N., 2006b. 'The small finds', in Fulford, M., Clarke, A. and Eckardt, H., *Life and Labour in Late Roman Silchester. Excavations in Insula IX since 1997*, Britannia Monogr. 22 (London), 120–32

Crummy, N., 2007. 'Six honest serving men: a basic methodology for the study of small finds', in Hingley, R. and Willis, S. (eds), *Roman Finds: context and theory*, 59–66 (Oxford)

Crummy, N., 2010. 'Coins', in Atkins, R. and Connor, A., *Farmers and Ironsmiths: prehistoric, Roman and Anglo-Saxon settlement beside Brandon Road, Thetford, Norfolk*, E. Anglian Archaeol. 134, 40–41

Crummy, N., in prep. 'The small finds' in Oxford Archaeol. East, *Excavations at Bob's Wood, Hinchingbrooke, Cambridgeshire*, E. Anglian Archaeol. (working title)

Crummy, N., Crummy, P. and Crossan C., 1993. *Excavations of Roman and Later Cemeteries, Churches and Monastic Sites in Colchester, 1971–88*, Colchester Archaeol. Rep. 9 (Colchester)

Crummy, N. and Eckardt, H., 2004. 'Regional identities and technologies of the self: nail-cleaners in Roman Britain', *Archaeol. J.* 160, 44–69

Crummy, N. and Holmes, S., 2003a. 'Hunter-god handle from Britain: a new type of spatula?', *Instrumentum Bull.* 17 (June), 33

Crummy, N. and Holmes, S., 2003b. 'Hunter-god handle from Yorkshire', *Lucerna, Roman Finds Group Newsletter* 26 (July), 5–6

Crummy, N. with Pohl, C., 2008. 'Small toilet instruments from London: a review of the evidence', in Clark, J., Cotton, J., Hall, J., Sherris, R. and Swain, H. (eds), *Londinium and Beyond: essays on Roman London and its hinterland for Harvey Sheldon*, Counc. Brit. Archaeol. Res. Rep. 156, 212–25 (York)

Crummy, P., Benfield, S., Crummy, N., Rigby, V. and Shimmin, D., 2007. *Stanway: an élite burial site at Camulodunum*, Britannia Monogr. 24 (London)

Cunliffe, B., 1975. *Iron Age Communities in Britain*, 2nd edn (London, Routledge)

Cunliffe, B., 1988. *The Temple of Sulis Minerva at Bath, 2: the finds from the sacred spring*, Oxford Univ. Comm. Archaeol. Monogr. 6 (Oxford)

Cunliffe, B., 1995. *Danebury: an Iron Age hillfort in Hampshire. Volume 6: a hillfort community in perspective*, Counc. Brit. Archaeol. Res. Rep. 102 (York)

Cunliffe, B., 2005. *Iron Age Communities in Britain*, 4th edn (London, Routledge)

Curle, J., 1911. *A Roman Frontier Post and its People. The fort of Newstead in the parish of Melrose* (Glasgow, J. Maclehose and Sons)

Curnow, P., 1985a 'The Roman coins' in West, S., *West Stow. The Anglo-Saxon Village*, E. Anglian Archaeol. 24, 76–81

Curnow, P., 1985b 'Table XVIII. Identification of the Roman coins', in Cook, A.M. and Dacre, M.W., *Excavations at Portway, Andover, 1973–1975*, Oxford Univ. Comm. Archaeol. Monogr. 4, 95 (Oxford)

Dallas, C., 1993 'Handmade pottery', in Dallas, C., *Excavations in Thetford by B.K. Davison between 1964 and 1970*, E. Anglian Archaeol. 62, 124

Dannell, G.B. and Wild, J.P., 1987 *Longthorpe II. The military works depot: an episode in landscape history*, Britannia Monogr. Ser. 8 (London)

Darling, M.J., 2004 'Guidelines for the archiving of Roman pottery', *J. Roman Pottery Stud.* 11, 67–74

Darling, M.J. and Gurney, D., 1993 'The pottery', in Darling, M.J. with Gurney, D., *Caister-on-Sea Excavations by Charles Green, 1951–55*, E. Anglian Archaeol. 60, 153–256

Davies, J.A., 1994 'The coins', in Williams, R.J. and Zeepvat, R.J., *Bancroft. A late Bronze Age settlement, Roman villa and temple mausoleum*, Buckinghamshire Archaeol. Soc. Monogr.7, 269–80

Davis, S.J.M., 1980 'Late Pleistocene and Holocene equid remains from Israel', *Zoological J. Linnean Soc.* 70 (3), 289–312

Davis, S.J.M., 1992 'A rapid method for recording information about mammal bones from archaeological sites', English Heritage Ancient Monuments Lab. Rep. 19/92 (London)

Davis, S.J.M., 1997 'The agricultural revolution in England: some zoo-archaeological evidence', *Anthropozoologica* 25/26, 413–28

Dawson, M., 2000a *Prehistoric, Roman, and Post-Roman Landscapes of the Great Ouse Valley*, Counc. Brit. Archaeol. Res. Rep. 119 (York)

Dawson, M., 2000b 'The Mesolithic interlude', in Dawson, M., *Prehistoric, Roman, and Post-Roman Landscapes of the Great Ouse Valley*, Counc. Brit. Archaeol. Res. Rep. 119, 45–50 (York)

Dawson, M., 2000c 'The Ouse Valley in the Iron Age and Roman periods: a landscape in transition', in Dawson, M., *Prehistoric, Roman, and Post-Roman Landscapes of the Great Ouse Valley*, Counc. Brit. Archaeol. Res. Rep. 119, 107–30 (York)

Deegan, A., 2007 'Archaeology on the boulder clay in Northamptonshire: some results from the Northamptonshire National Mapping Programme Project, in Mills, J. and Palmer, R. (eds), *Populating Clay Landscapes*, 104–19 (Stroud, The History Press)

Deschler-Erb, E., 1999 *Ad arma! Römisches Militär des 1. Jahrhunderts n. Chr. in Augusta Raurica*, Forschungen in Augst 12 (August)

Dickinson, B., 1999 'Samian stamps', in Symonds, R.P. and Wade, S., *Roman Pottery from Excavations in Colchester, 1971–86*, Colchester Archaeol. Rep. 10, 120–36 (Colchester)

Dimes, F.G., 1980 'Petrological report', in Hill, C., Millett, M. and Blagg, T.F.C., *The Roman Riverside Wall and Monumental Arch in London : excavations at Baynard's Castle, Upper Thames Street, London, 1974–76*. London Middlesex Archaeol. Soc. Rep. 3, 198–200 (London)

Dobney, K. and Ervynck, A., 2007 'To fish or not to fish? Evidence for the possible avoidance of fish consumption', in Haselgrove, C., and Moore, T., *The Later Iron Age in Britain and Beyond*, 403–18 (Oxford)

Dodwell, N., Anderson, K. and Lucy, S., 2008 'Burials', in Evans, C., Mackay, D. and Webley, L., *Borderlands. The archaeology of the Addenbrooke's environs, south Cambridge*, 47–57 (Cambridge, Cambridge Archaeol. Unit)

Draper, J., 1986 'Excavations at Great Chesterford, Essex, 1953–5', *Proc. Cambridge Antiq. Soc.* 75, 3–41

Druce, D., 2008 'Charred plant remains', in Stansbie, D., 'Excavation of a middle Iron Age enclosure at Bushmead Road, Eaton Socon, Cambridgeshire', *Proc. Cambridge Antiq. Soc.* 97, 48

Drummond-Murray, J. and Thompson, P., 2002 *Settlement in Roman Southwark*, Mus. London Archaeol. Serv. Monogr. 12 (London)

Duncan, H., 2008 'Other artefacts', in Abrams, J. and Ingham, D., *Farming on the Edge: archaeological evidence from the clay uplands to the west of Cambridge*, E. Anglian Archaeol. 123, Appendix 3

Duncan, H. and Mackreth, D.F., 2005 'Spinning and weaving', in Dawson, M., *An Iron Age settlement at Salford, Bedfordshire*, Bedfordshire Archaeol. Monogr. 6 (Bedford)

Eckardt, H., and Crummy, N., 2008 *Styling the Body in Roman Britain: a contextual approach to toilet instruments*, Instrumentum Monogr. 36 (Montagnac)

Edgeworth, M. and Steadman, S., 2003 *Extensive Urban Survey for Bedfordshire: the Roman town of Sandy. Archaeological assessment*, Albion Archaeology Doc. 2001/36 (unpubl.)

Edmonds, M., 2004 *The Langdales: landscape and prehistory in a Lakeland valley* (Stroud, The History Press)

Eisenmann, V., 1981 'Etude des dents jugales inferieures des *Equus* (Mammalia, Perissodactyla) actuels et fossiles', *Palaeovertebrata* 10, 127–226

Ellis, C., 2004 *A Prehistoric Ritual Complex at Eynesbury, Cambridgeshire*, E. Anglian Archaeol. Occ. Pap. 17

Elsdon, S., 1992 'East Midlands Scored ware', *Trans. Leicester Archaeol. Hist. Soc.* 66, 83–91

English Heritage, 1997 *English Heritage Archaeology Division, draft Research Agenda* (unpubl.)

English Heritage, 1998 *Exploring Our Past* (London, English Heritage)

Esmonde-Cleary, A.S., 1989 *The Ending of Roman Britain* (London, Batsford)

Esmonde-Cleary, A.S., 2001 'The Roman to medieval transition', in James, S. and Millett, M. (eds), *Britons and Romans: advancing an archaeological agenda*, Counc. Brit. Archaeol. Res. Rep. 125, 90–7 (York)

Evans, C., 1997 'The excavation of a major ring-ditch complex at Diddington, near Huntingdon, with a discussion of second millennium BC pyre burial and cremation practices', *Proc. Cambridge Antiq. Soc.* 85, 11–26

Evans, C. and Knight, M., 1996 *The Butcher's Rise Ring-ditches. Excavations at Barleycroft Farm, Cambridge*, Cambridge Archaeol. Unit (unpubl.)

Evans, C., Knight, M. and Webley, L., 2007. 'Iron Age settlement and Romanisation on the Isle of Ely: the Hurst Lane Reservoir site', *Proc. Cambridge Antiq. Soc.* 96, 41–78

Evans, C. and Hodder, I., 2006. *Marshland Communities and Cultural Landscapes from the Bronze Age to Present Day. The Haddenham Project Volume 2*, McDonald Institute Monographs (Cambridge)

Evans, C., Mackay, D., and Webley, L., 2008. *Borderlands. The archaeology of the Addenbrooke's environs, south Cambridge* (Cambridge, Cambridge Archaeol. Unit)

Evans, J., 1991. 'Some notes on the Horningsea pottery', *J. Roman Pottery Stud.* 4, 33–43

Evans, J., 2002. *Roman Pottery Research Project for the Southern Cambridgeshire Fen Edge*, Cambridgeshire County Counc. Archaeol. Field Unit (unpubl.)

Evans, J., 2003. 'The later Iron Age and Roman pottery', in Hinman, M., *A Late Iron Age Farmstead and Romano-British site at Haddon, Peterborough*, Cambridgeshire County Counc. Archaeol. Field Unit Monogr. 2/Brit. Archaeol. Rep. Brit. Ser. 358, 68–107 (Oxford)

Evans, J., Macaulay, S. and Mills, P., 2017. *The Horningsea Roman Pottery Industry in Context* (2 vols), E. Anglian Archaeol. 162

Evans, J.G., 1972. *Land Snails in Archaeology* (London, Seminar Press)

Evison, V.I., 1994. *An Anglo-Saxon Cemetery at Great Chesterford, Essex*, Counc. Brit. Archaeol. Res. Rep. 91 (York)

Feugère, M., 1995. 'Les spatules à cire à manche figuré', in Cysz, W., Hüssen, C.-M., Kuhnen, H.-P., Sebastian Sommer, C. and Weber, G. (eds), *Provinzialrömische Forschungen. Festschrift für Günter Ulbert zum 65 Geburtstag*, 321–38 (Munich)

Feugère, M., 2002. 'Le mobilier votif d'un sanctuaire salyen', *Instrumentum Bull.* 16, 16–17

Fincham, G., 2002. *Landscapes of Imperialism: Roman and native interaction in the East Anglian Fenland*, Brit. Archaeol. Rep. Brit. Ser. 338 (Oxford)

Fish, P.R. and Whiteman, C.A., 2001. 'Chalk micropalaeontology and the provenance of Middle Pleistocene Lowestoft Formation Till in eastern England', *Earth Surface Processes and Landforms*, 26, 953–70

Fitter, R., Fitter, A. and Blamey, M., 1985. *The Wild Flowers of Britain and Northern Europe*, 4th edn (London, Collins)

Fitzpatrick, A.P., 1997a. *Archaeological Investigations on the Route of the A27 Westhampnett Bypass, West Sussex, 1992. Volume 2: the late Iron Age, Romano-British and Anglo-Saxon cemeteries*, Wessex Archaeol. Rep. 12 (Salisbury)

Fitzpatrick, A.P., 1997b. 'Everyday life in Iron Age Wessex', in Gwilt, A. and Haselgrove, C. (eds), *Reconstructing Iron Age Societies*, Oxbow Monogr. 71, 73–86 (Oxford)

Fosberry, R., Eley, T. and Howard A., 2005. 'Appendix 8: assessment of ferrous and archaeometallurgical debris', in Hinman M., *Bob's Wood: Neolithic and Bronze Age activity and an Iron Age and Romano-British agricultural settlement on land adjacent to Hinchingbrooke Country Park, Cambridgeshire. Section I: A post excavation assessment of the 2003 excavations incorporating the findings of related archaeological investigations, 1997–2004*, Cambridgeshire County Counc. Archaeol. Field Unit Rep. 772 (unpubl.)

Foster, J., 1986. 'Querns', in Stead, I.M. and Rigby, V., *Baldock. The Excavation of a Roman and pre-Roman settlement, 1968–72*, Britannia Monogr. 7, 179–182 (London)

Fowler, E., 1960. 'The origins and development of the penannular brooch in Europe', *Proc. Prehist. Soc.* 26, 149–77

Fowler, E., 1983. 'Penannular brooches', in Crummy, N., *The Roman Small Finds from Excavations in Colchester 1971–9*, Colchester Archaeol. Rep. 2, 18–19 (Colchester)

Fox, C., 1923. *The Archaeology of the Cambridge Region* (Cambridge, Cambridge Univ. Press)

Fox, C., 1932. *The Personality of Britain* (Cardiff, National Museum of Wales)

Framework Archaeology, 2005. *Heathrow Airport Terminal 5: project design update note 2: assessment of the results of archaeological fieldwork 2002–2005, and proposals for analysis and publication* (unpubl.)

France, N.E. and Gobel, B.M., 1985. *The Romano-British Temple at Harlow* (Harlow, West Essex Archaeol. Group)

French, C.A.I., 1994. *The Haddon Farmstead and a Prehistoric Landscape at Elton: the archaeology along the A605 Elton-Haddon bypass, Cambridgeshire* (Cambridge, Fenland Archaeol. Trust/Cambridgeshire County Council)

Frere, S.S., 1987. *Britannia: a history of Roman Britain*, 3rd edn (London, Routledge and Kegan Paul)

Friday, L.E., 1988. 'A key to the adults of British water beetles', *Field Stud.* 7, 1–151

Friendship-Taylor, D., 1997. 'Roman/Saxon mongrels: part 2', *Archaeol. Leather Group Newsletter* 5 (Spring), 2

Fryer, V., 2004a. *An Assessment of the Charred Plant Macrofossils and other Remains from Iron Age and Roman Contexts at Colchester Garrison, Essex (GAR 2003.210)*, archive report for Colchester Archaeol. Trust (unpubl.)

Fryer, V., 2004b. 'Charred plant macrofossils and other remains', in Bales, E., *A Roman Maltings at Beck Row, Mildenhall, Suffolk*, E. Anglian Archaeol. Occ. Pap. 20, 49–54

Fryer, V., 2006. 'Charred cereals and other remains', in Niblett, R., Manning, W. and Saunders, C., 'Verulamium: excavations within the Roman town 1986–88', *Britannia* 37, 173–80

Fryer, V., 2007. 'Charred plant macrofossils' in Germany, M., *Neolithic and Bronze Age Monuments and Middle Iron Age Settlement at Lodge Farm, St Osyth, Essex: Excavations 2000–3*, E. Anglian Archaeol. 117, 90–4

Fryer, V., 2009. *Rapid Scan Evaluation of the Plant Macrofossil Assemblages from Love's Farm, St Neots, Cambridgeshire*, archive report for Oxford Archaeol. East (unpubl.)

Fulford, M., 2001. 'Links with the past: pervasive 'ritual' behaviour in Roman Britain', *Britannia* 32, 199–218

Fulford, M. and Timby, J., 2000. *Late Iron Age and Roman Silchester: excavations on the site of the forum-basilica 1977, 1980–86*, Britannia Monogr. 15 (London)

Gale, R., 2008 — 'Charcoal', in Abrams, J. and Ingham, D., *Farming on the Edge: archaeological evidence from the clay uplands to the west of Cambridge*, E. Anglian Archaeol. 123, Appendix 16

Galloway, P., 1979 — 'Combs', in Clarke, G., *The Roman Cemetery at Lankhills, Winchester*, Winchester Stud. 3, 246–8 (Oxford)

Galloway, P., 1993 — 'Bone combs', in Farwell, D.E. and Molleson, T.L., *Excavations at Poundbury II: the cemeteries*, 108 (Dorchester)

Gao, C., Boreham, S., Preece, R.C., Gibbard, P.L. and Briant R.M., 2007 — 'Fluvial response to rapid climate change during the Devensian (Weichselian) Late glacial in the River Great Ouse, southern England, UK', *Sedimentary Geology*, 202, 193–210

Garrow, D., Lucy, S., and Gibson, D., 2006 — *Excavations at Kilverstone, Norfolk: an episodic landscape history*, E. Anglian Archaeol. 113

Geake, H., 2002 — 'New wax spatulae from Suffolk', *Lucerna, Roman Finds Group Newsletter* 24 (July), 14–15

Gerrard, J., 2004 — 'How late is late? Pottery and the fifth century in south-west Britain', in Collins, R. and Gerrard, J. (eds), *Debating Late Antiquity in Britain, AD 300–700*, Brit. Archaeol. Rep. Brit. Ser. 365, 65–75 (Oxford)

Gibson, A., 2002 — *Prehistoric Pottery in Britain and Ireland* (Stroud, Tempus)

Gibson, C., 2005 — 'A Romano-British rural site at Eaton Socon, Cambridgeshire', *Proc. Cambridge Antiq. Soc.* 94, 21–38

Gibson, D. and Lucas, G., 2002 — 'Pre-Flavian kilns at Greenhouse Farm and the social context of early Roman pottery production in Cambridgeshire', *Britannia* 33, 95–128

Gilmour, N., Dodwell, N. and Popescu, E., 2010 — 'A Middle Bronze Age cremation cemetery on the western claylands at Papworth Everard', *Proc. Cambridge Antiq. Soc.* 99, 7–24

Glazebrook, J. (ed), 1997 — *Research and Archaeology: a Framework for the Eastern Counties, 1. Resource assessment*, E. Anglian Archaeol. Occ. Pap. 3

Goessler, P., 1932 — 'Das frühchristliche Beinkästchen von Heilbronn', *Germania* 16, 294–9

Going, C. and Plouviez, J., 2000 — 'Roman', in Brown, N. and Glazebrook, J. (eds), *Research and Archaeology: a Framework for the Eastern Counties, 2. Research agenda and strategy*, E. Anglian Archaeol. Occ. Pap. 8, 19–22

Gouldwell, A.J., 1991 — *The Animal Bones from Great Holme Street, Leicester*, archive report for Leicestershire County Counc. Archaeol. Unit (unpubl.)

Grant, A., 1982 — 'The use of tooth wear as a guide to the age of domestic ungulates', in Wilson, R., Grigson, C. and Payne, S. (eds) *Ageing and Sexing Animal Bones from Archaeological Sites*, Brit. Archaeol. Rep. Brit. Ser. 109, 91–108 (Oxford)

Grant, A., 1984 — 'Animal husbandry in Wessex and the Thames Valley', in Cunliffe, B. and Miles, D. (eds), *Aspects of the Iron Age in Central Southern Britain*, Oxford Univ. Archaeol. Monogr. 3, 102–19 (Oxford)

Green, C., 2000 — 'Geology, relief, and Quaternary palaeoenvironments in the basin of the Great Ouse', in Dawson, M., *Prehistoric, Roman, and Post-Roman Landscapes of the Great Ouse Valley*, Counc. Brit. Archaeol. Res. Rep. 119, 5–16 (York)

Green, H.J.M., 1977 — *Godmanchester* (Cambridge, Oleander Press)

Green, H.J.M., 1986 — 'Religious cults at Roman Godmanchester', in Henig, M. and King, A. (eds), *Pagan Gods and Shrines of the Roman Empire*, Oxford Univ. Comm. Archaeol. Monogr. 8, 29–55 (Oxford)

Green, M.J., 1997 — *Dictionary of Celtic Myth and Legend* (London, Thames and Hudson)

Greenfield, E., 1968 — 'The Romano-British settlement at Little Paxton, Huntingdonshire', *Proc. Cambridge Antiq. Soc.*, 61, 35–57

Greenwood, P., 1982 — 'The cropmark site at Moor Hall Farm, Rainham, Essex', *London Archaeol.* 4 (7), 185–93

Greep, S., 1995 — 'Objects of bone, antler and ivory from C.A.T. sites', in Blockley, K., Blockley, M., Blockley, P., Frere, S.S. and Stow, S., *Excavations in the Marlowe Car Park and Surrounding Areas*, Archaeol. Canterbury 5, 1112–52 (Canterbury)

Greep, S., 1998 — 'The bone, antler and ivory artefacts', in Cool, H.E.M. and Philo, C., *Roman Castleford I: the small finds*, Yorkshire Archaeol. 4, 267–85 (Wakefield)

Grieve, M., 1971 — *A Modern Herbal*, 2nd edn (West Molesey, Random House)

Grew, F. and Griffiths N., 1991 — 'The pre-Flavian military belt: the evidence from Britain', *Archaeologia* 109, 47–84

Grigson, C., 1976 — 'The craniology and relationships of four species of *Bos*, 3. Basic craniology: *Bos taurus* L. Sagittal profiles and other non-measurable characters', *J. Archaeol. Sci.* 3, 115–36

Grigson, C., 1982 — 'Sex and age determination of some bones and teeth of domestic cattle: a review of the literature', in Wilson, R., Grigson, C. and Payne, S. (eds) *Ageing and Sexing Animal Bones from Archaeological Sites*, Brit. Archaeol. Rep. Brit. Ser. 109, 7–23 (Oxford)

Grimm, J.M., 2012 — 'Faunal remains', in Barnett, C., McKinley, J.I., Stafford, E., Grimm, J.M. and Stevens, C.J., *Settling the Ebbsfleet Valley: the Late Iron Age, Roman and Anglo-Saxon landscape (CTRL excavations 1997–2003). Vol.3: Late Iron Age to Roman Human Remains and Environmental Reports*, Oxford Wessex Archaeol. Monogr., 15–28 (Oxford and Salisbury)

Grimes, W.F., 1930 — 'Mortaria', in Grimes, W.F, 'Holt Denbighshire: the works-depot of the twentieth legion at Castle Lyons, Wales', *Y Cymmrodor* 41, 146–9

Gryspeerdt, M., 1981 — 'The pottery', in Williams, J.H., 'Excavations in Chalk Lane, Northampton', *Northamptonshire Archaeol.* 16, 87–135

Guest, P., 2003 — 'The coins', in Hinman, M., *A Late Iron Age Farmstead and Romano-British Site at Haddon, Peterborough*, Cambridgeshire County Counc. Archaeol. Field Unit Monogr. 2/Brit. Archaeol. Rep. Brit. Ser. 358, 114 (Oxford)

Guido, M., 1978 — *The Glass Beads of the Prehistoric and Roman Periods in Britain and Ireland* (London, Soc. Antiq. London)

Gurney, D., 1986 — 'The Romano-British villa and bath-house at Little Oulsham Drove, Feltwell: excavations by Ernest Greenfield, 1962 and 1964', in Gurney, D., *Settlement, Religion and Industry on the Roman Fen Edge, Norfolk*, E. Anglian Archaeol. 31, 1–43

Hall, A.R. and Huntley, J.P., 2007 — *A Review of the Evidence for Macrofossil Plant Remains from Archaeological Deposits in Northern England*, English Heritage Res. Rep. Ser. 87 (London)

Hall, A.R., Kenward, H.K. and Williams, D., 1980 — *Environmental Evidence from Roman Deposits in Skeldergate*, Archaeol. York 14/3 (London, Counc. Brit. Archaeol.)

Hall, D., 2000 — 'The pottery', in Mortimer, R. and Hall, D., 'Village development and ceramic sequence: the Middle to Late Saxon village at Lordship Lane, Cottenham, Cambridgeshire', *Proc. Cambridge Antiq. Soc.* 89, 5–34

Hall, D. and Coles, J., 1994 — *Fenland Survey: an essay in landscape and persistence*, English Heritage Archaeol. Rep. 1 (London)

Hamerow, H.F., 1993 — *Excavations at Mucking, Volume 2: The Anglo-Saxon settlement*, English Heritage Archaeol. Rep. 22 (London)

Hamilton, S., 2002 — 'Between ritual and routine: interpreting British prehistoric pottery production and distribution', in Woodward, A. and Hill, J.D. (eds), *Prehistoric Britain. The Ceramic Basis*, Prehistoric Ceramics Res. Group Occ. Publ. 3 (Oxford, Oxbow)

Hamilton-Dyer, S., 2009 — 'Animal bone', in Wright, J., Leivers, M., Seager Smith, R. and Stevens, C.J., *Cambourne New Settlement: Iron Age and Romano-British settlement on the clay uplands of west Cambridgeshire*, Wessex Archaeol. Rep. 23, 82–133 (Salisbury)

Hancocks, A., 2003 — 'Little Paxton pottery', in Gibson, A. (ed.), *Prehistoric Pottery. People, pattern and purpose*, Prehistoric Ceramic Res. Group Occ. Publ. 4/Brit. Archaeol. Rep. Int. Ser. 1156, 71–110 (Oxford)

Hansen, M., 1987 — 'The Hydrophilidae (Coleoptera) of Fennoscandia and Denmark', *Fauna Entomologyca Scandinavica*, Vol. 18 (Leiden)

Harcourt, R.A., 1974 — 'The dog in prehistoric and early historic Britain', *J. Archaeol. Sci.* 1, 151–75

Harding, D.W., 1974 — *The Iron Age in Lowland Britain* (London, Routledge)

Harding, D.W., 2004 — *The Iron Age in Northern Britain: Celts and Romans, natives and invaders* (Abingdon, Routledge)

Harding, P., 2004 — 'Flint', in Ellis, C.J., *A Prehistoric Ritual Complex at Eynesbury, Cambridgeshire. Excavations of a multi-period site in the Great Ouse Valley, 2000–2001*, E. Anglian Archaeol. Occ. Pap. 17, 25–8

Harrison, S., 2002 — 'Open fields and earlier landscapes: six parishes in south-east Cambridgeshire', *Landscapes* 3.1, 35–54

Hartley, B.R., 1969 — 'Samian ware or terra sigillata', in Collingwood R.G. and Richmond I.A., *The Archaeology of Roman Britain*, 235–251 (London)

Hartley, K.F., 1987 — 'The mortaria', in Dannell, G.B. and Wild, J.P., *Longthorpe II. The military works-depot: an episode in landscape history*, Britannia Monogr. Ser., No. 8, 127–8

Hartley, K.F., 1998 — 'The incidence of stamped mortaria in the Roman Empire, with special reference to imports to Britain', in Bird, J. (ed.), *Form and Fabric*, 199–217 (Oxford, Oxbow)

Hartley, B.R. and Dickinson B.M., with Dannell, G.B., Fulford, M.G., Mees, A.W., Tyers, P.A. and Wilki, R.H., 2008 — *Names on Terra Sigillata. An index of makers' stamps and signatures on Gallo-Roman Terra Sigillata (Samian ware). Volume 3 (Certianus to Exsobano)*. Bulletin of the Institute of Classical Studies Supplement 102-03 (London)

Hartley, B.R. and Dickinson B.M., with Dannell, G.B., Fulford, M.G., Mees, A.W., Tyers, P.A. and Wilki, R.H., 2009a — *Names on Terra Sigillata. An index of makers' stamps and signatures on Gallo-Roman Terra Sigillata (samian ware). Volume 4 (F to Klumi)*. Bulletin of the Institute of Classical Studies Suppl. 102-04 (London)

Hartley, B.R. and Dickinson B.M., with Dannell, G.B., Fulford, M.G., Mees, A.W., Tyers, P.A. and Wilki, R.H., 2009b — *Names on Terra sigillata. An index of makers' stamps and signatures on Gallo-Roman Terra Sigillata (samian ware). Volume 5 (L to Masclus I)*. Bulletin of the Institute of Classical Studies Suppl. 102-05 (London)

Hartley, B.R. and Dickinson B.M., with Dannell, G.B., Fulford, M.G., Mees, A.W., Tyers, P.A. and Wilki, R.H., 2011 — *Names on Terra Sigillata. An index of makers' stamps and signatures on Gallo-Roman Terra Sigillata (samian ware). Volume 7 (P to RXEAD)*. Bulletin of the Institute of Classical Studies Suppl. 102-07 (London)

Hartley, B.R. and Dickinson B.M., with Dannell, G.B., Fulford, M.G., Mees, A.W., Tyers, P.A. and Wilki, R.H., 2012 — *Names on Terra Sigillata. An index of makers' stamps and signatures on Gallo-Roman Terra Sigillata (samian ware). Volume 9 (T to Ximus)*. Bulletin of the Institute of Classical Studies Suppl. 102-09 (London)

Hartley, K.F. and Tomber R., 2006 — 'A mortarium bibliography for Roman Britain', *J. Roman Pottery Stud.*, 13

Haselgrove, C., 1979 — 'The significance of coinage in pre-conquest Britain', in Burnham, B.C. and Johnson, H.B. (eds), *Invasion and Response: the case of Roman Britain*, Brit. Archaeol. Rep. Brit. Ser. 73, 197–209 (Oxford)

Haselgrove, C., 1982 — 'Indigenous settlement patterns in the Tyne-Tees lowlands', in Clack, P.A.G. and Haselgrove, C. (eds), *Rural Settlement in the Roman North*, 57–104 (Durham, Dept. Archaeol., Univ. Durham)

Haselgrove, C., 1984 — "Romanization' before the conquest', in Blagg, T.F. and King, A.C. (eds), *Military and Civilian in Roman Britain*, Brit. Archaeol. Rep. Brit. Ser. 136, 5–63 (Oxford)

Haselgrove, C., 1987 — *Iron Age Coinage in South-east England: the archaeological context*, Brit. Archaeol. Rep. Brit. Ser. 174 (Oxford)

Haselgrove, C., 1993 — 'The development of British Iron Age coinage', *Num. Chron.* 153, 31–63

Haselgrove, C., 1996 — 'Iron Age coinage: recent work', in Champion, T.C. and Collis, J.R. (eds), *The Iron Age in Britain and Ireland: recent trends*, 67–85 (Sheffield)

Haselgrove, C., Armit, I., Champion, T., Creighton, J., Gwilt, A., Hill, J.D., Hunter, F. and Woodward, A., 2001 — *Understanding the British Iron Age: an agenda for action* (Salisbury, Trust for Wessex Archaeology)

Haslam, S.M., Sinker, C.A. and Wolseley, P.A., 1975. *British Water Plants* (Shrewsbury, Field Studies Council)

Hassall, M. and Rhodes, J., 1975. 'Excavations at the Market Hall, Gloucester, 1966–7', *Trans. Bristol Gloucestershire. Archaeol. Soc.* 93, 15–110

Hatton, A. and Kemp, S., 2002. *Iron Age and Roman Archaeology along the proposed route of the Papworth Bypass: An Archaeological Evaluation*, Cambridgeshire County Counc. Archaeol. Field Unit Rep. A211 (unpubl.)

Haverfield, F., 1900. 'Romano-British Hampshire', *Victoria County History of Hampshire and the Isle of Wight* 1, 265–372 (London)

Haverfield, F., 1902. 'Romano-British Northamptonshire', *Victoria County History, Northamptonshire* 1, 157–222 (London)

Havis, R. and Brooks, H., 2004a. *Excavations at Stansted Airport, 1986–91. 1: prehistoric and Romano-British*, E. Anglian Archaeol. 107, 1–339

Havis, R. and Brooks, H., 2004b. *Excavations at Stansted Airport, 1986–91. 2: Saxon, medieval and post-medieval; discussion*, E. Anglian Archaeol. 107, 340–583

Hawkes, C.F.C. and Hull, M.R., 1947. *Camulodunum. First Report on the Excavations at Colchester 1930–1939*, Rep. Res. Comm. Soc. Antiq. 14 (Oxford, Oxford Univ. Press)

Healy, F., 1988. *The Anglo-Saxon Cemetery at Spong Hill, North Elmham, part VI: Occupation During the Seventh to Second Millennium BC*, E. Anglian Archaeol. 39

Healey, E., 1998. 'The lithic material', in Clay, P., 'Neolithic/early Bronze Age pit circles and their environs at Oakham, Rutland', *Proc. Prehistoric Soc.* 62, 309–17

Henderson, A.M., 1949. 'Small objects in metal, bone, glass *etc*.', in Bushe-Fox, J.P., *Fourth Report on the Excavations of the Roman Fort at Richborough*, Rep. Res. Comm. Soc. Antiq. 16, 106–60 (London)

Henig, M., 1993. 'Miniature spears', in Woodward, A. and Leach, P., *The Uley Shrines: excavation of a ritual complex on West Hill, Uley, Gloucestershire*, English Heritage Archaeol. Rep. 17, 131 (London)

Herne, A., 1984. *Eynesbury Excavations*, Cambridgeshire County Counc. Archaeol. Field Unit Rep. (unpubl.)

Herne, A., 1991. 'The flint assemblage', in Longworth, I., Herne, A., Varndell, G. and Needham, S., *Excavations at Grimes Graves, Norfolk 1972–1976. Fascicule 3. Shaft X: Bronze Age flint, chalk and metal working*, 21–93 (Dorchester, British Museum Press)

Heslop, D.H., 2008. *Patterns of Quern Production, Acquisition and Deposition*, Yorkshire Archaeol. Soc., Occ. Pap. 5 (Leeds)

Hesse, M., 2000. 'Field systems in southwest Cambridgeshire: Abington Pigotts, Litlington and the Mile Ditches', *Proc. Cambridge Antiq. Soc.* 89, 49–58

Hill, J.D., 1995. *Ritual and Rubbish in the Iron Age of Wessex*, Brit. Archaeol. Rep. Brit. Ser. 242 (Oxford)

Hill, J.D., 1996. 'The identification of ritual deposits of animal bones. A general perspective from a specific study of 'special animal deposits' for the southern English Iron Age', in Anderson, S. and Boyle, K. (eds), *Ritual Treatment of Human and Animal Remains. Proceedings of the first meeting of the Osteological Research Group held in Cambridge on 8 October 1994* (Oxford, Oxbow Books), 17–32

Hill, J.D., 2002. 'Just about the potter's wheel? Using, making and depositing middle and later Iron Age pots in East Anglia', in Woodward, A. and Hill, J.D., *Prehistoric Britain, the ceramic basis*, Prehistoric Ceramic Res. Group Occ. Publ. 3, 143–61 (Oxford)

Hill, J.D., 2007. 'The dynamics of social change in later Iron Age eastern and south-eastern England', in Haselgrove, C. and Moore, T. (eds), *The Later Iron Age in Britain and Beyond*, 16–40 (Oxford)

Hill, J.D. and Braddock, P., 1999. *The Later Iron Age Pottery from Hinchingbrooke Park, Huntingdon*, Cambridgeshire County Counc. Archaeol. Field Unit (unpubl.)

Hill, J.D., Evans, C. and Alexander, M., 1999. 'The Hinxton Rings – a late Iron Age cemetery at Hinxton, Cambridgeshire, with a reconsideration of the northern Aylesford–Swarling distributions', *Proc. Prehistoric Soc.* 65, 243–73

Hill, J.D. and Braddock, P., 2006. 'The Iron Age pottery from Haddenham V', in Evans, C. and Hodder, I., *Marshland Communities and Cultural Landscapes from the Bronze Age to Present Day. The Haddenham Project, Vol 2* (Cambridge, McDonald Inst. for Archaeol. Res.)

Hill, J.D. and Horne, L., 2003. 'Iron Age and early Roman pottery', in Evans, C. (ed.), *Power and Island Communities: excavations at the Wardy Hill ringwork, Coveney, Ely*, E. Anglian Archaeol. 103, 145–84

Hill, P.V. and Kent, J.P.C., 1972. 'Part 1: the bronze coinage of the House of Constantine AD 324–346', in Carson, R.A.G., Hill, P.V. and Kent, J.P.C., *Late Roman Bronze Coinage* (London, Spink & Son)

Hingley, R., 1989. *Rural Settlement in Roman Britain* (London, Seaby)

Hingley, R., 1990. 'Iron Age 'currency bars': the archaeological and social context', *Archaeol. J.* 147, 91–117

Hingley, R., 2005. 'Iron Age 'currency' bars in Britain: items of exchange in liminal contexts?', in Haselgrove, C. and Wigg-Wolf, D., *Iron Age Coinage and Ritual Practices*, Studien zu Fundmünzen der Antike 20, 183–204 (Mainz)

Hingley, R., 2007. 'The currency bars', in Crummy, P., Benfield, S., Crummy, N., Rigby, V. and Shimmin, D., *Stanway: an élite burial site at Camulodunum*, Britannia Monogr. 24, 33–6 (London)

Hinman, M., 1997. *Iron Age Remains on Land adjacent to Hinchingbrooke Country Park. A post-excavation assessment*, Cambridgeshire County Counc. Archaeol. Field Unit Rep. PXA 23 (unpubl.)

Hinman, M., 2000. *Land Adjacent to Bob's Wood, Hinchingbrooke, Cambridgeshire, An Interim Statement*, Cambridgeshire County Counc. Archaeol. Field Unit (unpubl.)

Hinman, M., 2003. *A Late Iron Age Farmstead and Romano-British site at Haddon, Peterborough*, Cambridgeshire County Counc. Archaeol. Field Unit Monogr. 2/Brit. Archaeol. Rep. Brit. Ser. 358 (Oxford)

Hinman, M., 2008. *Colonisation, Conquest and Continuity on the Cambridgeshire Clay Lands. Earlier Prehistoric*

	Evidence, Iron Age, Romano-British and Early Saxon Agriculture and Settlement on Land at Love's Farm, St Neots. Post-excavation Assessment, Oxford Archaeol. East Rep. 1078 (unpubl.)	Jackson, D.A., 1998	'Roman iron-working at Laxton', *Northamptonshire Archaeol.* 28, 159
Hinman, M., 2011	*The Archaeology of Love's Farm*, St Neots (Cambridge, Oxford Archaeology East)	Jackson, D.A. and Ambrose, T.M., 1978	'Excavations at Wakerley', *Britannia* 9, 115–242
Hinman, M. and Phillips, T., 2008	*Evaluation at Wintringham Park*, Oxford Archaeol. East Rep. 1062 (unpubl.)	Jackson, D.A. and Dix, B., 1987	'Late Iron Age and Roman settlement at Weekley, Northants', *Northamptonshire Archaeol.* 21, 41–93
Hobbs, R., 1996	*British Iron Age coins in the British Museum* (London, British Museum Press)	Jackson, D.A. and Tylecote, R.F., 1988	'Two new Romano-British iron working sites in Northamptonshire. A new type of furnace?', *Britannia* 19, 275–98
Hounsell, D., 2007	*Excavations at Papworth Everard*, Cambridgeshire County Counc. CAM ARC Rep. 856 (unpubl.)	Jackson, R. and Burleigh, G., 2007	'The Senuna treasure and shrine at Ashwell (Herts)', in Haeussler, R. and King, A.C. (eds), *Continuity and Innovation in Religion in the Roman West 1*, J. Roman Archaeol. Suppl. Ser. 67 (Portsmouth, RI)
Howe, M.D., Perrin, J.R. and Mackreth, D.F., 1980	*Roman Pottery from the Nene Valley: a guide*, Peterborough City Mus. Occ. Pap. 2 (Peterborough)	Jackson, R.P.J. and Potter, T.W., 1996	*Excavations at Stonea, Cambridgeshire, 1980–85* (London, Trustees of the British Museum)
Howell, I. (ed.), 2005	*Prehistoric Landscape to Roman villa: excavations at Beddington, Surrey, 1981–7*, Mus. London Archaeol. Serv. Monogr. 26 (London)	Jessop, L., 1986	*Coleoptera: Scarabaeidae*, Handbooks for the identification of British insects 5 (11) (London, Royal Entomological Soc.)
Hudson, J.D. and Sutherland, D.S., 1990	'Geological descriptions and identifications of building stones', in Parsons, D. (ed.), *Stone Quarrying and Building in England AD 43–1525*, 16–32 (Chichester)	Johns, C., 1996	*The Jewellery of Roman Britain* (London, Routledge)
Hull, M.R., 1963	*The Roman Potters' Kilns of Colchester*, Rep. Res. Comm. Soc. Antiq. 21 (Oxford, Oxford Univ. Press)	Johnstone, C. and Albarella, U., 2002	*The Late Iron Age and Romano-British Mammal and Bird Bone Assemblage from Elms Farm, Heybridge, Essex*, English Heritage Centre for Archaeol. Rep. 45/2002 (unpubl.)
Hull, M.R., 1968	'The brooches', in Dudley, D., 'Excavations on Nornour, Isles of Scilly, 1962–6', *Archaeol. J.* 124, 28–64	Johnstone, C.J., 2004	*A Zooarchaeological Study of Equids in the Roman World* (unpubl. PhD thesis, Univ. York)
Hull, M.R., forthcoming	*Brooches in pre-Roman and Roman Britain*	Johnstone, C.J., 2006	'Those elusive mules: investigating osteometric methods for their identification', in Mashkour, M. (ed), *Equids in Time and Space*, Proc. 9th Congress Int. Counc. Archaeozoology (2002), 183–9 (Oxford)
Humphrey, J., 2007	'Simple tools for tough tasks or tough tools for simple tasks? Analysis and experiment in Iron Age flint utilisation', in Haselgrove, C. and Pope, R., (eds), *The Earlier Iron Age in Britain and the Near Continent*, 144–159 (Oxford, Oxbow)	Jones, A., 1995	'An Iron Age square barrow at Diddington, Cambridgeshire. Third interim report of excavations at Little Paxton Quarry, 1996', *Proc. Cambridge Antiq. Soc.* 88, 5–12
Hunt, C.O., 1985	'Recent advances in pollen extraction techniques: a brief review', in Fieller, N.R.J., Gilbertson, D.D. and Ralph, N.G.A. (eds), *Palaeobotanical Investigations: Research Design, Methods and Data Analysis*, Symposia of the Association for Environmental Archaeol. 5B, Brit. Archaeol. Rep. Int. Ser. 266, 181–7	Jones, A., 1998	'Little Paxton Quarry, Diddington, Cambridgeshire: archaeological excavations 1992–1993. Second interim report: the south-west area, settlement and activity from the Neolithic to the Iron Age', *Proc. Cambridge Antiq. Soc.* 83, 7–22
Hylton, T. and Williams, R.J., 1996	'Clay weights', in Williams, R.J., Hart, P.J. and Williams, T.L., *Wavendon Gate: a late Iron Age and Roman settlement in Milton Keynes*, Buckinghamshire Archaeol. Soc. Monogr. Ser. 10	Jones, A., 2000	'A river valley landscape: excavations at Little Paxton Quarry, Cambridgeshire 1992–6 – an interim summary', in Dawson, M., *Prehistoric, Roman and Post-Roman Landscapes of the Great Ouse Valley*, Counc. Brit. Archaeol. Res. Rep. 119, 131–44 (York)
Iliffe, J.H., 1932	'Excavations at Alchester, 1928', *Antiq. J.* 12, 35–67	Jones, A., 2001	'A Romano-British shrine and settlements at Little Paxton Quarry, Diddington, Cambridgeshire', *Proc. Cambridge Antiq. Soc.* 90, 5–27
Ingham, D., 2008	'Iron Age settlement by the Dam Brook at Scotland Farm, Dry Drayton', *Proc. Cambridge Antiq. Soc.* 97, 31–40	Jones, A. (ed.), 2003	*Settlement, Burial and Economy in the Extramural areas of Roman Godmanchester*, Brit. Archaeol. Rep. Brit. Ser., 346 (Oxford)
Ingle, C.J., 1990	*Characterisation and Distribution of Beehive Querns in Eastern England*, (unpubl. PhD thesis, Univ. Southampton)	Jones, A. and Ferris, I., 1994	'Archaeological excavations at Little Paxton, Diddington, Cambridgeshire, 1992–3: first interim report: the Romano-British period', *Proc. Cambridge Antiq. Soc.* 82, 55–66
Isings, C., 1957	*Roman Glass from Dated Finds*, Archaeologica Traiectina 2 (Groningen, J.B. Wolters)		
Jackson, D.A., 1979	'Roman iron-working at Bulwick and Gretton', *Northamptonshire Archaeol.* 14, 31–7		

Jones, L., Woodward, A. and Buteux, S., 2006. *Iron Age, Roman and Saxon Occupation at Grange Park: Excavations at Couteenhall, Northamptonshire 1999*, Brit. Archaeol. Rep. Brit. Ser. 425

Jones, R., 2005. 'Signatures in the soil: the use of pottery in manure scatters in the identification of medieval arable farming regimes', *Archaeol. J.* 161, 159–88

Kemp, S., 1993. *Prehistoric and Roman Archaeology at Barford Road, Eynesbury*, Cambridgeshire County Counc. Archaeol. Field Unit Rep. 90 (unpubl.)

Kemp, S., 1996. *An Archaeological Assessment at Barford Road, Eynesbury*, Cambridgeshire County Counc. Archaeol. Field Unit Rep. A67 (unpubl.)

Kemp, S., 1997. *Prehistoric, Roman and Medieval Landuse at Barford Road, Eynesbury, St Neots*, Cambridgeshire County Counc. Archaeol. Field Unit Rep. 134 (unpubl.)

Kennett, D.H., 1977. 'Anglo-Saxon cemetery at Tuddenham, Suffolk', *Proc. Cambridge Antiq. Soc.* 67, 39–62

Kenney, S., 2000. *Iron Age Occupation off Ermine Street, Papworth Everard: An Archaeological Evaluation*, Cambridgeshire County Counc. Archaeol. Field Unit Rep. A154 (unpubl.)

Kenney, S., 2001. *Middle and Late Iron Age Settlement and Roman Agriculture at Highfields, Caldecote, Cambridgeshire: Assessment and Post-Excavation Project Design*, Cambridgeshire County Counc. Archaeol. Field Unit Rep. PXA 35 (unpubl.)

Kenney, S., 2007. 'A banjo enclosure and Roman farmstead: excavations at Caldecote Highfields, Cambridgeshire, in Mills, J. and Palmer, R. (eds), *Populating Clay Landscapes*, 120–31 (Stroud)

Kenney, S. and Lyons, A., 2011. 'An Iron Age banjo enclosure and contemporary settlement at Caldecote', *Proc. Cambridge Antiq. Soc.* 100, 67–84

Kenward, H.K., 1978. *The Analysis of Archaeological Insect Assemblages: a new approach*, Archaeol. York 19/1 (London, Counc. Brit. Archaeol.)

Kenward, H.K. and Hall, A.R., 1995. *Biological Evidence from Anglo-Scandinavian Deposits at 16–22 Coppergate*, Archaeol. York 14/7 (London, Counc. Brit. Archaeol.)

Kenward, H.K., Hall A.R. and Jones, A.K.G., 1980. 'A tested set of techniques for the extraction of plant and animal macrofossils from waterlogged archaeological deposits', *Scientific Archaeol.* 22, 3–15

Kenward, H.K., Hall, A.R. and Jones, A.K.G., 1986. *Environmental Evidence from a Roman well and Anglian Pits in the Legionary Fortress*, Archaeol. York 14/5 (London, Counc. Brit. Archaeol.)

Kenyon, K., 1953. 'Excavations at Sutton Walls, Herefordshire, 1948–51', *Archaeol. J.* 110, 1–88

King, D., 1986. 'Petrology, dating and distribution of querns and millstones. The results of research in Bedfordshire, Buckinghamshire, Hertfordshire and Middlesex', *Inst. Archaeol. Bull.* 23, 65–126

Kinnes, I.A., 1998. 'The pottery', in Pryor, F., *Etton, Excavations at a Neolithic causewayed enclosure near Maxey, Cambridgeshire, 1982–7*, English Heritage Archaeol. Rep. 18, 161–380

Kirk, J.C., 1935. 'Wild and domestic cat compared', *Scottish Naturalist* 216, 161–9

Kirk, J.R., 1949. 'Bronzes from Woodeaton, Oxon', *Oxoniensia* 14, 1–45

Kirk, J.R. and Leeds, E.T., 1954. 'Three early Saxon graves from Dorchester, Oxon', *Oxoniensia* 17–18, 63–76

Knight, D., 1984. *Late Bronze Age and Iron Age Settlement in the Nene and Great Ouse Valleys*, Brit. Archaeol. Rep. Brit. Ser. 130 (Oxford)

Knorr, R., 1919. *Töpfer und Fabriken verzierter Terra-Sigillata des ersten Jahrhunderts* (Stuttgart, W. Kohlhammer)

Knorr, R., 1952. *Terra-Sigillata-Gefässe des ersten Jahrhunderts mit Töpfer-namen* (Stuttgart)

Koch, K., 1989a. *Die Käfer Mitteleuropas: Ökologie Band 1* (Krefeld, Goecke & Evers)

Koch, K., 1989b. *Die Käfer Mitteleuropas: Ökologie Band 2* (Krefeld, Goecke & Evers)

Koch, K., 1992. *Die Käfer Mitteleuropas: Ökologie Band 3* (Krefeld, Goecke & Evers)

Kratochvil, Z., 1969. 'Species criteria on the distal section of the tibia in *Ovis ammon* F. *aries* L. and *Capra aegagrus* F. *hircus* L.', *Acta Veterinaria (Brno)* 38, 483–90

Kratochvil, Z., 1973. 'Schädelkriterien der wild- und hauskatze (*Felis silvestris silvestris* Schreb. 1777 und *F.s* f. *catus* L. 1758), *Acta Sci. Nat. Brno* 7 (10), 1–50

Kratochvil, Z., 1976. 'Das postkranialskelett der wild- und hauskatze (*Felis silvestris* und *F. lybica* f. *catus*), *Acta Sci. Nat. Brno* 10 (6), 1–43

Lambrick, G., and Robinson, M., 2009. *The Thames through Time. The archaeology of the gravel terraces of the Upper and Middle Thames. The Thames Valley in late prehistory: 1500 BC–AD 50*, Thames Valley Landscapes Monogr. 29 (Oxford)

Lamprecht, H., 1906. 'Der grosse römische Friedhof in Regensburg mit Besprechung seiner Gefäße und Fibeln', *Verhandlungen des Historischen Vereins für Oberpfalz und Regensburg* 58, 1–88

Langford, H.E. and Briant, R.M., 2004. *Nene Valley: field guide* (Cambridge, Quaternary Res. Assoc.)

Laws, K., Brown, L. and Roe, F., 1991. 'Objects of stone', in Cunliffe, B. and Poole, C., *Danebury: an Iron Age hillfort in Hampshire, Volume 5. The excavations 1979–1988: the finds*, Counc. Brit. Archaeol. Res. Rep. 73, 382–404 (London)

Leahy, K., 2007. *'Interrupting the Pots'. The excavation of Cleatham Anglo-Saxon cemetery*, Counc. Brit. Archaeol. Res. Pap. 155 (London)

Legge, A.J. and Rowley-Conwy, P.A., 1988. *Star Carr Revisited. A re-analysis of the large mammals* (London, Birkbeck College)

Lethbridge, T.C., 1931. *Recent Excavations in Anglo-Saxon Cemeteries in Cambridgeshire and Suffolk*, Cambridge Antiq. Soc. Quarto Publ. NS 3 (Cambridge)

Lethbridge, T.C. and Tebbutt, C.F., 1933. 'Huts of the Anglo-Saxon period', *Proc. Cambridge Antiq. Soc.*, 33, 133–51

Levine, M.A., 1982. 'The use of crown height measurement and eruption–wear sequences to age horse teeth', in Wilson, R., Grigson, C. and Payne, S. (eds), *Ageing and Sexing Animal Bones from Archaeological Sites*, Brit. Archaeol. Rep. Brit. Ser. 109, 223–50 (Oxford)

Lewis, S.G., 1999 — 'Eastern England', in Bowen, D.Q. (ed.), *A Revised Correlation of Quaternary Deposits in the British Isles*, Geological Soc. Special Rep. 23, 10–27 (Bath)

Lewis, S.G., Whiteman, C.A. and Bridgland, D.R. (eds), 1991 — *Central East Anglia and the Fen Basin: field guide* (London, Quaternary Res. Assoc.)

Lindroth, C.H., 1974 — *Coleoptera: Carabidae*, Handbooks for the Identification of British Insects 4 (2) (London, Royal Entomological Soc.)

Lindroth, C.H., 1986 — 'The Carabidae (Coleoptera) of Fennoscandia and Denmark', *Fauna Entomologyca Scandinavica*, Vol. 15, Part 2 (Leiden)

Lloyd Jones, M., 2005 — 'Food and drink in Wales: the impact of the Roman occupation', in Dannell, G.B. and Irving, P.V. (eds), 'An archaeological miscellany: papers in honour of K.F. Hartley', *J. Roman Pottery Stud.*, 12, 136–140

Lloyd-Morgan, G., 1977 — 'Mirrors in Roman Britain', in Munby, J. and Henig, M. (eds), *Roman Life and Art in Britain*, Brit. Archaeol. Rep. Brit. Ser. 41, 231–52 (Oxford)

Longworth, I., 1960 — 'Pottery', in Clark, J.G.D., 'Excavations at the Neolithic site at Hurst Fen, Mildenhall, Suffolk', *Proc. Prehistoric Soc.* 26, 228–40

Longworth, I.H., 1984 — *Collared Urns of the Bronze Age in Great Britain and Ireland* (Cambridge, Cambridge University Press)

Lovejoy, C.O., Meindl, R.S., Pryzbeck, T.R. and Mensforth, R.P., 1985 — 'Chronological metamorphosis of the auricular surface of the ilium: a new method for the determination of age at death', *American J. Physical Anthropology* 68, 15–28

Lucht, W.H., 1987 — *Die Käfer Mitteleuropas. Katalog* (Krefeld, Goecke & Evers)

Lucy, S., 2006 — 'The early Anglo-Saxon settlement and cemetery', in Garrow, D., Lucy, S. and Gibson, D., *Excavations at Kilverstone, Norfolk: an episodic landscape history*, E. Anglian Archaeol. 113, 170–201

Lucy, S. and Challands, A., 2006 — 'Late Iron Age and Roman settlement', in Garrow, D., Lucy, S. and Gibson, D., *Excavations at Kilverstone, Norfolk: an episodic landscape history*, E. Anglian Archaeol. 113, 99–169

Luke, M., 2008 — *Life in the Loop: investigation of a prehistoric and Romano-British landscape at Biddenham Loop, Bedfordshire*, E. Anglian Archaeol. 125

Lyons, A.L., 2003 — 'Roman pottery', in Bates, S., 'Excavations at Heath Farm, Postwick 1995–6', in Bates, S. and Lyons, A.L., *The Excavation of Romano-British Pottery Kilns at Ellingham, Postwick and Two Mile Bottom, Norfolk, 1995–7*, E. Anglian Archaeol. Occ. Pap. 13, 44–51

Lyons, A.L., 2007 — 'The pottery', in Phillips, T., *Roman Remains at 8 New Street, Godmanchester, Cambridge*, Cambridgeshire County Counc. Archaeol. Field Unit Rep. 935, 13–22 (unpubl.)

Lyons, A.L., 2008 — 'Pottery (Roman)', in Abrams, J. and Ingham, D., *Farming on the Edge: archaeological evidence from the clay uplands to the west of Cambridge*, E. Anglian Archaeol. 123, Appendix 6

Lyons, A.L., 2009 — *Becoming Roman and Losing your Temper* (unpubl. MA dissertation, Univ. Southampton)

Lyons, A.L., 2011 — *Life and Death at Duxford from the Early Iron Age to the Post-medieval*, E. Anglian Archaeol. 141

Lyons, A.L., in prep. a — *Hinxton, Cambridgeshire: Part I. Excavations at the Genome Campus 1993–2011: Ritual and Farming in the Cam Valley*, E. Anglian Archaeol.

Lyons, A.L., in prep. b — *Rectory Farm, Godmanchester, Cambridgeshire: Excavations 1988–1995*, E. Anglian Archaeol.

Lyons, A.L., in prep. c — 'The Roman pottery', in Percival, S., *Excavations at Cambridge Park and Rides*, E. Anglian Archaeol. (working title)

Lyons, A.L., in prep. d — 'Romano-British pottery', in OA East, *Excavations at Bob's Wood, Hinchingbrooke, Cambridgeshire*, E. Anglian Archaeol. (working title)

Lyons, A.L. with Rigby, V., in prep. — 'The Roman pottery', in Phillips, T. and Mortimer, R., *The Archaeology of Clay Farm, Trumpington, Cambridgeshire: A Landscape Study*, E. Anglian Archaeol. (working title)

Lyons, A.L., Rigby, V. and Tester, C., 2014 — 'Pottery overview', in Atkins, R., Popescu, E., Rees, G. and Stansbie, D., *Broughton, Milton Keynes, Buckinghamshire. The evolution of a South Midlands Landscape*, Oxford Archaeol. Monogr. 22, 213–23

Macaulay, S.P., 1994 — *A Buried Prehistoric Landscape at Huntingdon Racecourse, Cambridgeshire: Post-Excavation Assessment and Updated Project Design*, Cambridgeshire County Counc. Archaeol. Field Unit Rep. PXA08 (unpubl.)

Macaulay, S.P., 2002 — *Romano-British Settlement at Camel Road, Littleport*, Cambridgeshire County Counc. Archaeological Field Unit Rep. 205 (unpubl.)

MacGregor, A., 1978 — *Roman Finds from Skeldergate and Bishophill*, Archaeol. York 17/2 (London, Counc. Brit. Archaeol.)

MacGregor, A., 1985 — *Bone, Antler, Ivory and Horn. The technology of skeletal materials since the Roman period* (London, Croom Helm)

MacKinnon, M. and Belanger, K., 2006 — 'In sickness and in health: care for an arthritic Maltese dog from the Roman cemetery of Yasmina, Carthage, Tunisia', in Snyder, L.M. and Moore, E.A. (eds), *Dogs and People in Social, Working, Economic or Symbolic Interaction*, Proc. 9th Congress Int. Counc. Archaeozoology (2002), 38–43 (Oxford)

Mackreth, D.F., 1978 — 'Orton Hall Farm, Peterborough: a Roman and Saxon settlement', in Todd, M. (ed.), *Studies in the Romano-British Villa*, 209–23 (Leicester, Leicester Univ. Press)

Mackreth, D.F., 1986 — 'Brooches', in Gurney, D., *Settlement, Religion and Industry on the Roman Fen-edge, Norfolk*, E. Anglian Archaeol. 31, 61–7

Mackreth, D.F., 1988 — 'Excavation of an Iron Age and Roman enclosure at Werrington, Cambridgeshire', *Britannia* 19, 59–152

Mackreth, D.F., 1996 — 'Brooches', in Jackson, R.P.J. and Potter, T.W., *Excavations at Stonea, Cambridgeshire, 1980–85*, 296–327 (London, British Museum Press)

Mackreth, D.F., 2001 — *Monument 97, Orton Longueville, Cambridgeshire: a late pre-Roman Iron Age and early Roman farmstead*, E. Anglian Archaeol. 97

Macphail, R.I., 1981 — 'Soil and botanical studies of the 'dark earth'', in Jones, M. and Dimbleby, G. (eds), *The*

Macphail, R.I. and Linderholm, J., 2004. "'Dark earth': recent studies of 'dark earth' and 'dark earth-like' microstratigraphy in England, UK', in Verslype, L. and Brulet, R. (eds), *Terres Noires, Dark Earth. Actes de la table-ronde internationale tenue a Louvain-la-Neuve, les 09 et 10 novembre 2001*, 35–42 (Louvain-la-Neuve)

Madgwick, R., 2008. 'Patterns in the modification of animal and human bones in Iron Age Wessex: revisiting the excarnation debate', in Davis, O., Sharples, N. and Waddington, K. (eds), *Changing Perspectives on the First Millennium BC*, 99–111 (Oxford)

Major, H., 2004. 'Textile manufacturing equipment', in Havis, R. and Brooks, H., *Excavations at Stansted Airport, 1986–91. 1: prehistoric and Romano-British*, E. Anglian Archaeol. 107, 169–73

Malim, T., 1990. *Brampton 1990: A1–M1 link road*, Cambridgeshire County Counc. Archaeol. Field Unit Rep. 16 (unpubl.)

Malim, T., 1993. 'An investigation of multi-period cropmarks at Manor Farm, Harston', *Proc. Cambridge Antiq. Soc.* 82, 11–54

Malim, T., 1997. 'Prehistoric and Roman remains at Edix Hill, Barrington, Cambridgeshire', *Proc. Cambridge Antiq. Soc.* 86, 13–56

Malim, T., 1998. *An Overview of Neolithic and Bronze Age sites along the Middle and Lower Ouse Valley*, Cambridgeshire County Counc. Archaeol. Field Unit (unpubl.)

Malim, T., 2000. 'The ritual landscape of the Neolithic and Bronze Age along the Middle and Lower Ouse Valley', in Dawson, M., *Prehistoric, Roman, and Post-Roman Landscapes of the Great Ouse Valley*, Counc. Brit. Archaeol. Res. Rep. 119, 57–88 (York)

Malim, T. and Mitchell, D., 1993. *Neolithic Ditches and Iron Age Settlement at Thrapston Road, Brampton*, Cambridgeshire County Counc. Archaeol. Field Unit Rep. 81 (unpubl.)

Malim, T. and Hines, J., 1998. *The Anglo-Saxon Cemetery at Edix Hill (Barrington A), Cambridgeshire*, Counc. Brit. Archaeol. Res. Rep. 112 (York)

Maltby, M., 1996. 'The exploitation of animals in the Iron Age: the archaeozoological evidence', in Champion, T.C. and Collis, J.R. (eds), *The Iron Age in Britain and Ireland: recent trends*, 17–27 (Sheffield)

Manaseryan, N.H., Dobney, K. and Ervynck, A., 1999. 'On the causes of perforations in archaeological domestic cattle skulls: new evidence', *Int. J. Osteoarchaeol.* 9, 74–75

Manning, W.H., 1975. 'The anvil', in Hicks, J.D. and Wilson, J.A., 'Romano-British kilns at Hasholme', *East Riding Archaeol.* 2, 49–70

Manning, W.H., 1985. *Catalogue of the Romano-British Iron Tools, Fittings and Weapons in the British Museum* (London, British Museum Press)

Manning, W.H. and Scott, I.R., 1986. 'Iron objects', in Stead, I. and Rigby, V., *Baldock. The excavation of a Roman and pre-Roman settlement, 1968–72*, Britannia Monogr. Ser. 7, 145–62 (London)

Margary, I.D., 1973. *Roman Roads in Britain. Vol.1. South of the Fosse Way–Bristol Channel*, 2nd edn (London, J. Baker)

Environment of Man: the Iron Age to the Anglo-Saxon period, Brit. Archaeol. Rep. Brit. Ser. 87, 309–31 (Oxford)

Marney, P.T., 1989. *Roman and Belgic Pottery from Excavations in Milton Keynes 1972–82*, Buckinghamshire Archaeol. Soc. Monogr. Ser. 2

Martin, B.P., 1992. *Birds of Prey of the British Isles* (Newton Abbot, David & Charles)

Martin, E.A., 1988. *Burgh: The Iron Age and Roman Enclosure*, E. Anglian Archaeol. 40

Martin. E.A., Pendleton, C. and Plouviez, J., 1999. 'Archaeology in Suffolk 1998', *Proc. Suffolk Inst. Archaeol. Hist.* 39.3, 353–86

Martin, S. and Wallace, C. (eds), 2002. *A Research Design for the Study of Roman Pottery in the East Midlands and East Anglia*, Available: http://www.romanpotterystudy.org/SGRPPublications/framework/east/introduction.html. Accessed: 25 November 2015

Martingell, H., 1990. 'The East Anglian peculiar? The 'squat' flake', *Lithics* 11, 40–3

Marzinzik, S., 2003. *Early Anglo-Saxon Belt Buckles, their classification and context*, Brit. Archaeol. Rep. Brit. Ser. 357 (Oxford)

Matolcsi, J., 1970. 'Historische erforschung der körpergröße des rindes auf grund von ungarischem knochenmaterial', *Zeitschr. f. Tierzüchtg. u. Züchtungsbiol., Hamburg* 87, 89–137 (Hamburg)

Mattingly, H., Sydenham, E.A. and Sutherland, C.H.V. (eds), 1923–94. *The Roman Imperial Coinage* (London, Spink & Son)

May, E., 1985. 'Widerristhöhe und langknockenmasse bei pferd – ein immer noch aktuelles problem', *Zeitschrift fur Saugertierkunde* 50, 368–82

McAvoy, F., 2000. 'The development of a Neolithic monument complex at Godmanchester, Cambridgeshire', in Dawson, M., *Prehistoric, Roman, and Post-Roman Landscapes of the Great Ouse Valley*, Counc. Brit. Archaeol. Res. Rep. 119, 51–6 (York)

McKinley, J.I., 1993. 'Bone fragment size and weights of bone from modern British cremations and its implications for the interpretation of archaeological cremations', *Int. J. Osteoarchaeol.* 3, 283–7

McKinley, J.I., 1994. 'Bone fragment size in British cremation burials and its implications for pyre technology and ritual', *J. Archaeol. Sci.* 21, 339–342

McKinley, J.I., 2002. 'The analysis of cremated bone', in Cox, M. and Mays, S. (eds), *Human Osteology in Archaeology and Forensic Science*, 403–21 (London, GMM)

McKinley, J.I., 2004. 'Compiling a skeletal inventory: disarticulated and commingled remains', in Brickley, M. and McKinley, J. (eds) *Guidelines to the Standards for Recording Human Remains,* BABAO (Reading), 14–17

Meaney, A.L., 1981. *Anglo-Saxon Amulets and Curing Stones*, Brit. Archaeol. Rep. Brit. Ser. 96 (Oxford)

Medlycott, M. (ed.), 2011. *Research and Archaeology: a revised framework for the East of England*, E. Anglian Archaeol. Occ. Pap. 24

Mepham, L., 2004. 'Pottery', in Ellis, C.J., *A Prehistoric Ritual Complex at Eynesbury, Cambridgeshire*, E. Anglian Archaeol. Occ. Pap. 17, 28

Merrifield, R., 1987 — *The Archaeology of Ritual and Magic* (London, Batsford)

Merrifield, R., 1995 — 'Roman metalwork from the Walbrook – rubbish, ritual or redundancy', *Trans. London Middlesex Archaeol. Soc.* 46, 27–44

Merrifield, R. and Hall, J., 2008 — 'In its depths what treasures – the nature of the Walbrook stream valley and the Roman metalwork found therein', in Clark, J., Cotton, J., Hall, J., Sherris, R. and Swain, H. (eds), *Londinium and Beyond: essays on Roman London and its hinterland for Harvey Sheldon*, Counc. Brit. Archaeol. Res. Rep. 156, 121–7 (York)

Mikler, H., 1997 — *Die Römischen Funde aus Bein im Landesmuseum Mainz*, Instrumentum Monogr. 1 (Montagnac)

Miles, A.E.W. and Grigson, C. (eds), 1990 — *Colyer's Variations and Diseases of the Teeth of Animals* (Cambridge, Cambridge Univ. Press)

Millett, M., 1990 — *The Romanisation of Britain* (Cambridge, Cambridge Univ. Press)

Mills, A., and McDonnell, J.G., 1992 — *The Identification and Analysis of the Hammerscale from Burton Dassett, Warwickshire*, English Heritage Ancient Monuments Lab. Rep. 47/92 (London)

Mills, J., 1998 — 'Samian', in Ellis, P., Hughes, G., Leach, P., Mould, C. and Sterenberg, J., *Excavations alongside Roman Ermine Street, Cambridgeshire, 1996*, Birmingham Univ. Field Archaeol. Unit Monogr. 1, 68–71

Mills, J. and Palmer, R., 2007 — 'Introduction', in Mills, J. and Palmer, R. (eds), *Populating Clay Landscapes*, 7–15 (Stroud)

Monteil, G., 2013 — 'Roman pottery', in Evans, C., Appleby, G., Lucy, S. and Regan, R., *Process and History. Romano-British Communities at Colne Fen, Earith*, CAU Landscape Archives: The Archaeology of the Lower Ouse Valley II, 85–97

Moore, P.D., Webb, J.A. and Collinson, M.E., 1991 — *Pollen Analysis*, 2nd edn (Oxford, Blackwell Scientific Publications)

Morris, E., 2002 — 'The function and use of prehistoric ceramics', in Woodward, A. and Hill, J.D. (eds), *Prehistoric Britain: the ceramic basis*, 54–61 (Oxford, Oxbow)

Morris, J., 2008 — 'Associated bone groups: one archaeologist's rubbish is another's ritual deposition', Davis, O., Sharples, N. and Waddington, K. (eds), *Changing Perspectives on the First Millennium BC*, 83–94 (Oxford)

Mould, Q., 1996a — 'Roman/Saxon mongrels spotted in eastern England', *Archaeol. Leather Group Newsletter* 4 (August), 4

Mould, Q., 1996b — *The Leather from Rectory Farm, West Deeping*, archive report for Tempus Reparatum (unpubl.)

Mould, Q., 2005 — *Assessment of Leather from the Tower Works, Peterborough (MPF04)*, archive report for Cambridgeshire County Counc. Archaeol. Field Unit (unpubl.)

Murphy, P., 1991 — 'Plant remains and the environment', in Gregory, T., *Excavations in Thetford, 1980–1982, Fison Way. Volume 1*, E. Anglian Archaeol. 53, 175–81

Myres, J.N.L., 1977 — *A Corpus of Anglo-Saxon Pottery of the Pagan Period* (2 vols) (Cambridge, Cambridge Univ. Press)

Neal, D.S. and Butcher, S.A., 1974 — 'Miscellaneous objects of bronze', in Neal, D.S., *The Excavation of the Roman Villa in Gadebrige Park, Hemel Hempstead, 1963–8*, Rep. Res. Comm. Soc. Antiq. 31, 128–50 (London)

Neal, D.S., Wardle A. and Hunn, J., 1990 — *Excavation of the Iron Age, Roman and Medieval Settlement at Gorhambury, St Albans*, English Heritage Archaeol. Rep. 14 (London)

Niblett, R., 1985 — *Sheepen: an early Roman industrial site at Camulodunum*, Counc. Brit. Archaeol. Res. Rep. 57 (London)

Niblett, R., 2006 — 'From *Verlamion* to Verulamium', in Ottaway, P. (ed.), *A Victory Celebration: papers on the archaeology of Colchester and late Iron Age–Roman Britain presented to Philip Crummy*, 19–26 (Colchester)

Nilsson, A.N. and Holmen, M., 1995 — 'The aquatic Adephaga (Coleoptera) of Fennoscandia and Denmark II. Dytiscidae', *Fauna Entomologyca Scandinavica* (Leiden)

Noble, P. and Thompson, A., 2005 — 'The Mellor excavations 1998 to 2004', in Nevell, M. and Redhead, N. (eds), *Mellor: living on the edge. A regional study of an Iron Age and Romano-British upland settlement*, Manchester Archaeol. Monogr. 1, 17–34 (Manchester)

O'Connor, T.P., 1988 — *Bones from the General Accident Site, Tanner Row*, Archaeol. York 15/2 (London, Counc. Brit. Archaeol.)

O'Connor, T.P., 1998 — 'On the difficulty of detecting seasonal slaughtering of sheep', *Environmental Archaeol.* 3, 5–11

O'Connor, T.P., 2007 — 'Wild or domestic? Biometric variation in the cat *Felis silvestris* Schreber', *Int. J. Osteoarchaeology* 17, 581–95

Oldenstein, J., 1976 — 'Zur Ausrüstung römischer Auxiliareinheiten', *Bericht der Römisch-Germanischen Kommission* 57, 49–284

Olivier, A., 1988a — 'The brooches', in Potter, T.W. and Trow, S.D., *Puckeridge-Braughing, Hertfordshire: the Ermine Street excavations 1971–72*, Herts. Archaeol. 10, 35–53 (Hertford)

Olivier, A., 1988b — 'Brooches', in Martin, E.A., *Burgh: Iron Age and Roman Enclosure*, E. Anglian Archaeol. 40, 16–22

Oosthuizen, S., 1997 — 'Prehistoric fields into medieval furlongs? Evidence from Caxton, Cambridgeshire', *Proc. Cambridge Antiq. Soc.* 86, 145–52

Oosthuizen, S., 2003 — 'The roots of the common fields: linking prehistoric and medieval field systems in west Cambridgeshire', *Landscapes* 4.1, 40–64

Oosthuizen, S., 2006 — *Landscapes Decoded: the origins and development of Cambridgeshire's medieval fields*, Explorations in Local Regional History, 1 (Hertford)

Oswald, A., 1997 — 'A doorway on the past: practical and mystic concerns in the orientation of roundhouse doorways', in Gwilt, A. and Haselgrove, C. (eds), *Reconstructing Iron Age Societies*, Oxbow Monogr. 71, 87–95 (Oxford)

Oswald, F., 1936–37 — *Index of Figure Types on Terra Sigillata*, Univ of Liverpool, Annals of Archaeol. and Anth. supplement, reprinted 1964 (London, Gregg Press)

Ottaway, P., 1992 — *Archaeology in British Towns, from the Emperor Claudius to the Black Death* (London, Routledge)

Oxford Archaeology East, in prep.	*Excavations at Bob's Wood, Hinchingbrooke, Cambridgeshire*, E. Anglian Archaeol. (working title)	Percival, S., in prep. a	'Trumpington: the querns', in Percival, S., *Excavations at Cambridge Park and Rides*, E. Anglian Archaeol. (working title)
Parker-Pearson, M., 1996	'Food, fertility and front doors in the first millennium BC', in Champion, T.C. and Collis, J.R. (eds), *The Iron Age in Britain and Ireland: recent trends*, 117–32 (Sheffield)	Percival, S., in prep. b	'Prehistoric pottery', in Connor, A. and Mortimer, R., *Excavations at Fordham, Cambridgeshire*, E. Anglian Archaeol. (working title)
Parker-Pearson, M., 1999	'Food, sex and death: cosmologies in the British Iron Age with particular reference to East Yorkshire', *Cambridge Archaeol. J.* 9.1, 43–69	Percival, S., in prep. c	'The prehistoric pottery', in Oxford Archaeology East, *Excavations at Bob's Wood, Hinchingbrooke, Cambridgeshire*, E. Anglian Archaeol. (working title)
Parker-Pearson, M. and Richards, C., 1994	'Architecture and order: spatial representation and archaeology', in Parker-Pearson, M. and Richards, C. (eds), *Architecture and Order: approaches to social space*, 38–72 (London)	Percival, S., in prep. d	*Excavations at Cambridge Park and Rides*, E. Anglian Archaeol. (working title)
Parminter, Y., 1994	'Roman coarse wares', in Zeepvat, R.J., Roberts, J.S. and King, N.A., *Caldecotte, Milton Keynes. Excavation and fieldwork 1966–91*, Buckinghamshire Archaeol. Soc. Monogr. 9, 183–191	Perrin, J.R., 1996	'The Roman pottery', in Mackreth, D., *Orton Hall Farm: A Roman and Early Saxon Farmstead*, E. Anglian Archaeol. 76, 114–204
		Perrin, J.R., 1999	'Roman pottery from excavations at and near to the Roman small town of Durobrivae, Water Newton, Cambridgeshire, 1956–58', *J. Roman Pottery Stud.* 8
Parry, S.J., 2006	*Raunds Area Survey: an archaeological study of the landscape of Raunds, Northamptonshire* (Oxford, Oxbow)	Perring, D., 1991	*Roman London* (London, Routledge)
Payne, S., 1969	'A metrical distinction between sheep and goat metacarpals', in Ucko, P. and Dimbleby, G. (eds), *The Domestication and Exploitation of Plants and Animals*, 295–305 (London)	Perring, D., 2002	*The Roman House in Britain* (Abingdon, Routledge)
		Perrins, R.M.S., Rose, J. and Davies, H., 1979	'The distribution, variation and origins of pre-Devensian tills in eastern England', *Philosophical Trans. Royal Soc. London* 287, 535–70
Payne, S., 1973	'Kill-off patterns in sheep and goats: the mandibles from Asvan Kale', *Anatolian Stud.* 23, 281–303	Phillips, C. and Grassam, A., 2006	'Animal carcasses in a Roman ditch, West End, Haddenham, TL 4613 7552', *Proc. Cambridge Antiq. Soc.* 95, 179–82
Payne, S., 1985	'Morphological distinctions between the mandibular teeth of young sheep, *Ovis*, and goats, *Capra*', *J. Archaeol. Sci.* 12, 139–47	Phillips, T., 2008	'Iron Age ditches and an Anglo-Saxon building near the Mile Ditches, Bassingbourn, TL 3294 4335', *Proc. Cambridge Antiq. Soc.* 97, 77–81
Payne, S. and Bull, G., 1988	'Components of variation in measurements of pig bones and teeth, and the use of measurements to distinguish wild from domestic pig remains', *Archaeozoologia* 2, 27–65	Phillips, T., 2012	*Clay Farm, Trumpington, Cambridgeshire: Post-Excavation Assessment*, Oxford Archaeol. East Rep. 1294 (unpubl.)
PCRG, 2010	*The Study of Later Prehistoric Pottery: General Policies and Guidelines for analysis and Publication*, Prehistoric Ceramic Research Group Occ. Pap. 1 and 2, 3rd edn	Philpott, R., 1991	*Burial Practices in Roman Britain*, Brit. Archaeol. Rep. Brit. Ser. 219 (Oxford)
		Pitt-Rivers, A.H., 1888	*Excavations in Cranborne Chase, near Rushmore, II* (privately printed)
Peacock, D.P.S, 1982	*Pottery in the Roman World: an ethnoarchaeological approach* (London, Longman)	Plouviez, J., 2004	'Discussion of the coins', in Blagg, T., Plouviez, J. and Tester, A., *Excavations at a Large Romano-British Settlement at Hacheston, Suffolk*, E. Anglian Archaeol. 106, 83–5
Peacock, D.P.S. and Williams, D.F., 1986	*Amphorae and the Roman Economy: an introductory guide* (London, Longman)	Plouviez, J., 2008	'Counting brooches: ways of examining Roman brooch assemblages in London and beyond', in Clark, J., Cotton, J., Hall, J., Sherris, R. and Swain, H. (eds), *Londinium and Beyond. Essays on Roman London and its Hinterland for Harvey Sheldon*, Counc. Brit. Archaeol. Res. Rep. 156, 171–6 (York)
Percival, S., 1996	'The pottery', in Ashwin, T., 'Excavation of an Iron Age site at Silfield, Wymondham, Norfolk, 1992–93', *Norfolk Archaeol.* 42, 241–83		
Percival, S., 1999	*Excavations at Former Allotments, Creake Road, Burnham Market*, NAU Archaeol. (unpubl.)		
Percival, S., 2004a	*Two Quern Stone Assemblages from Cambridgeshire* (unpubl. MA dissertation, Univ. Southampton)	Pommeret, C., 2001	*Le sanctuaire antique des Bolards à Nuits-Saint-Georges* (Dijon, Société archéologique de l'Est)
Percival, S., 2004b	'The prehistoric pottery', in Whitmore, D., 'Excavations at a Neolithic Site at the John Innes Centre, Colney 2000', *Norfolk Archaeol.* 44, 422–6	Pollard, R. J., 1988	*The Roman Pottery of Kent* (Maidstone, Kent Archaeol. Soc.)
		Pope, R., 2003	*Prehistoric Dwelling: circular structures in north and central Britain c.2500 BC–AD 500* (unpubl. PhD thesis, Univ. Durham)
Percival, S., 2011	'Querns', in Kenney, S. and Lyons, A., 'An Iron Age banjo enclosure and contemporary settlement at Caldecote', *Proc. Cambridge Antiq. Soc.* 100, 79	Pope, R., 2007	'Ritual and the roundhouse: a critique of recent ideas on domestic space in later British prehistory', in Haselgrove, C.C. and Pope, R.E.

Potter, T.W. and Trow, S.D., 1988	(eds), *The Earlier Iron Age in Britain and the near Continent*, 204–28 (Oxford: Oxbow)	Robertson, A.S., 2000	*An Inventory of Romano-British Coin Hoards* (London, Spink & Son)
	Puckeridge–Braughing, Hertfordshire: the Ermine Street excavations 1971–72, Herts Archaeol. 10 (Hertford)	Robinson, M.A., 1993	'The Iron Age environmental evidence', in Allen, T.G. and Robinson, M.A., *The Prehistoric Landscape and Iron Age Enclosed Settlement at Mingies Ditch, Hardwick-with-Yelford, Oxon*, Thames Valley Landscapes: the Windrush Valley, Vol. 2, 101–20 (Oxford)
Price, E., 2000	*Frocester: a Romano-British settlement, its antecedents and successors. 2: the finds* (Stonehouse, Gloucester & District Archeol. Res. Group)	Rodwell, K.A., 1988	*The Prehistoric and Roman Settlement at Kelvedon, Essex*, Counc. Brit. Archaeol. Res. Rep. 63/Chelmsford Archaeol. Trust Rep. 6
Pryor, F., 1998	*Etton: excavations of a Neolithic causewayed enclosure near Maxey, Cambridgeshire, 1982–7* (London, English Heritage)	Rogerson, A., 1977	*Excavations at Scole 1973*, E. Anglian Archaeol. 5
Pryor, F., French, L., Crowther, D., Gurney, D., Simpson, G. and Taylor, M., 1985	*The Fenland Project, Number 1: archaeology and environment in the Lower Welland Valley*, E. Anglian Archaeol. 27	Rollo, L., 1994	'The Roman pottery', in French, C.A.I., *The Haddon Farmstead and a Prehistoric Landscape at Elton: the archaeology along the A605 Elton–Haddon bypass, Cambridgeshire*, 89–129 (Cambridge)
Rackham, O., 1986	*The History of the Countryside* (London, Dent)	Sabine, P.A., 1949	'The source of some erratics from north-eastern Northamptonshire and adjacent parts of Huntingdonshire', *Geological Magazine*, 86, 255–60
Ramey, D.W., 1997	*Navicular Syndrome in the Horse* (New York, Howell Book House)	Scaife, R., 1998	'Pollen analyses', in Pryor, F., *Etton: excavations at a Neolithic causewayed enclosure near Maxey, Cambridgeshire, 1982–7*, English Heritage Archaeol. Rep. 18, 301–10 (London)
Redknap, M., 1986	'The small finds' in Millet, M. and Graham, D., *Excavations on the Romano-British Small Town at Neatham, Hampshire, 1969–79*, Hampshire Field Club Monogr. 3 (Farnham)	Scaife, R., 2000	'The prehistoric vegetation and environment of the River Ouse Valley', in Dawson, M., *Prehistoric, Roman, and Post-Roman Landscapes of the Great Ouse Valley*, Counc. Brit. Archaeol. Res. Rep. 119, 17–26 (York)
Reece, R., 1991	*Roman Coins from 140 Sites in Britain* (Cirencester, Cotswold Studies)		
Reece, R., 1995	'Site-finds in Roman Britain', *Britannia* 26, 179–206	Scaife, R., 2009	'Pollen', in Wright, J., Leivers, M., Seager Smith, R. and Stevens, C.J., *Cambourne New Settlement. Iron Age and Romano-British settlement on the clay uplands of west Cambridgeshire*, Wessex Archaeol. Rep. 23, Vol. 2, 211–19
Reece, R., 2002	*The Coinage of Roman Britain* (Stroud, Tempus)		
Rees, G., 2008	'Enclosure boundaries and settlement individuality in the Iron Age', in Davis, O., Sharples, N. and Waddington, K. (eds), *Changing Perspectives on the First Millennium BC*, 61–78 (Oxford)	Schmid, E., 1972	*Atlas of Animal Bones for Prehistorians, Archaeologists and Quaternary Geologists* (London, Elsevier)
		Schoppa, H., 1953	'Ein fränkisches Holzkästchen aus Weilbach', *Germania* 31, 44–50
Rees, H., Crummy, N., Ottaway, P. and Dunn, G., 2008	*Artefacts and Society in Roman and Medieval Winchester. Small finds from the suburbs and defences, 1971–86* (Winchester, Winchester Museums)	Schrüfer-Kolb, I., 2004	*Roman Iron Production in Britain. Technological and socio-economic landscape development along the Jurassic Ridge*, Brit. Archaeol. Rep. Brit. Ser. 380 (Oxford)
Reynolds, P.J., 1974	'Experimental Iron Age storage pits: an interim report', *Proc. Prehistoric Soc.* 40, 118–31		
Richards, D., 2000	'The ironwork', in Fulford, M. and Timby, J., *Late Iron Age and Roman Silchester: excavations on the site of the forum-basilica 1977, 1980–86*, Britannia Monogr. 15, 360–79 (London)	Seager Smith, R., 2009	'Late Iron Age and Romano-British material culture', in Wright, J., Leivers, M., Seager Smith, R. and Stevens, C.J., *Cambourne New Settlement. Iron Age and Romano-British settlement on the clay uplands of west Cambridgeshire*, Wessex Archaeol. Rep. 23, 90–110
Rielly, K, 2008	'Animal bone', in Abrams, J. and Ingham, D., *Farming on the Edge: archaeological evidence from the clay uplands to the west of Cambridge*, E. Anglian Archaeol. 123, Appendix 13	Sealey, P.R., 1997	*A Late Iron Age Warrior Burial from Kelvedon, Essex*, E. Anglian Archaeol. 118
Rigby, V., 1986	'The stratified groups of Iron Age and Roman pottery', in Stead, I. and Rigby, V., *Baldock. The excavation of a Roman and pre-Roman settlement, 1968–72*, Britannia Monogr. 7, 257–60 (London)	Sealey, P.R., 2011a	'The Middle and Late Iron Age Pottery', in Kenney, S. and Lyons, A., 'An Iron Age banjo enclosure and contemporary settlement at Caldecote, Cambridgeshire', *Proc. Cambridge Antiq. Soc.* 100, 70–78
Rigby, V. and Foster, J., 1986	'Building materials', in Stead, I. and Rigby, V., *Baldock. The excavation of a Roman and pre-Roman settlement, 1968–72*, Britannia Monogr. Ser. 7, 183–5 (London)	Sealey, P.R., 2011b	'Fired clay', in Kenney, S. and Lyons, A., 'An Iron Age banjo enclosure and contemporary settlement at Caldecote', *Proc. Cambridge Antiq. Soc.* 100, 67–84
Robertson, A.S., 1974	'Romano-British coin hoards: their numismatic, archaeological and historical significance', in Casey, J. and Reece, R., *Coins and the Archaeologist*, Brit. Archaeol. Rep. Brit. Ser. 4, 12–36 (Oxford)	Seeley, F., 2004	'The small finds', in Blagg, T., Plouviez, J. and Tester, A., *Excavations at a Large Romano-*

	British Settlement at Hacheston, Suffolk, E. Anglian Archaeol. 106, 86–149
Sellwood, L., 1984	'Objects of bone and antler', in Cunliffe, B., *Danebury: an Iron Age hillfort in Hampshire*, Counc. Brit. Archaeol. Res. Rep. 52, 371–95 (London)
Shaffrey, R., 2007a	'The worked stone', in Webley, L., Timby, J. and Wilson, M., *Fairfield Park, Stotfold, Bedfordshire: later prehistoric settlement in the eastern Chilterns*, Oxford Archaeol. Occ. Pap./Bedfordshire Archaeol. Monogr. 7, 86–92
Shaffrey, R., 2007b	'Worked and utilised stone', in Timby, J., Brown, R., Hardy, A., Leech, S., Poole, C. and Webley, L., *Settlement on the Claylands: archaeology along the A421 Great Barford Bypass, Bedfordshire*, Bedfordshire Archaeol. Monogr. 8, 279–84
Shaffrey, R., 2011	'The worked stone', in Biddulph, E., 'Northfleet Villa', in Andrews, P., Biddulph, E., Hardy, A. and Brown, R., *Settling the Ebbsfleet Valley. High Speed 1 excavations at Springhead and Northfleet, Kent: the late Iron Age, Roman, Saxon and medieval landscape. Volume 1: The sites*, Oxford Wessex Archaeol. Monogr., 135–188 (Oxford and Salisbury)
Sharples, N., 1991	*Excavations and Field Survey 1985–6*, HBMC(E) Archaeol. Rep. 19 (London)
Sheldon, H. and Townend, P. (eds), 1978	*Southwark Excavations 1972–1974*, London Middlesex Archaeol. Soc./Surrey Archaeol. Soc. Joint Publ. 1 (London)
Sherlock, D. and Welch, M., 1992	*An Anglo-Saxon Cemetery at Norton, Cleveland*, Counc. Brit. Archaeol. Res. Rep. 82 (York)
Shiel, N., 1977	*The Episode of Carausius and Allectus*, Brit. Archaeol. Rep. Brit. Ser. 40 (Oxford)
Shotter, D.C.A., 1978	'Unpublished Roman hoards in the Wisbech and Fenland Museum', *Coin Hoards* 4, 47–50
Shotter, D.C.A., 1981	'Roman coins from the central Fenland', in Potter, T.W., 'The Roman occupation of the central Fenland', *Britannia* 12, 120–7
Shotter, D.C.A. and White, A.J., 1977	'Two hoards of Roman coins from the Lancaster area', *Trans. Cumberland Westmorland Antiq. Archaeol. Soc.* new ser. 77, 173–8
Simms, J., 2006	'Pollen analysis', in Evans, C. and Hodder, I., *Marshland Communities and Cultural Landscapes: the Haddenham Project. Volume 2*, 260–3 (Cambridge)
Simpson, T., 2001	'The Roman well at Piddington, Northamptonshire, England: an investigation of the Coleopterous fauna', *Environmental Archaeol.* 6, 91–96
Sinopoli, C.M., 1991	*Approaches to Archaeological Ceramics* (New York, Plenum)
Slowikowski, A., 2005	'The daub and fired clay', in Dawson, M., *An Iron Age settlement at Salford, Bedfordshire*, Bedfordshire Archaeol. Monogr. 6, 117–8 (Bedford)
Smallwood, J.P., 1989	'Romano-British iron-working at North Wootton, King's Lynn, Norfolk', *Britannia* 20, 243–5
Smith, D.N., 1997	*The Insect Remains from Mill Lane, Mancetter*, archive report for Univ. Birmingham Environmental Archaeol. Serv. (unpubl.)
Smith, D.N., 2004	'The insect remains', in Bishop, M.C., *Inveresk Gate: excavation in the Roman civil settlement at Inveresk, East Lothian, 1996–2000*, Scottish Trust Archaeol. Res. Monogr. Ser. 7, 81–88 (Edinburgh)
Smith, D.N., Osborne, P.J. and Barrett, J., 1997	'Preliminary palaeoentomological research at the Iron Age site at Goldcliff 1991–93', in Ashworth, A.C., Buckland, P.C. and Sadler, J.D. (eds), 'An inordinate fondness for insects', *Quaternary Proc.* 5, 255–67 (Chichester)
Smith, D.N., Osborne, P.J. and Barrett, J., 2000	'Beetles as indicators of past environments and human activity at Goldcliff', in Bell, M., Caseldine, A. and Neumann, H. (eds), *Prehistoric Intertidal Archaeology in the Welsh Severn Estuary*, Counc. Brit. Archaeol. Res. Rep. 120, 245–60 (York)
Smith, I.F., 1965	*Windmill Hill and Avebury* (Oxford, Clarendon)
Spoerry, P., 2000	'Estate, village, town? Roman, Saxon and medieval settlement in the St Neots area', in Dawson, M., *Prehistoric, Roman, and Post-Roman Landscapes of the Great Ouse Valley*, Counc. Brit. Archaeol. Res. Rep. 119, 145–60 (York)
Spoerry, P., 2016	*The Production and Distribution of Medieval Pottery in Cambridgeshire*, E. Anglian Archaeol. 159
Stace, C., 1997	*New Flora of the British Isles*, 2nd edn (Cambridge, Cambridge Univ. Press)
Stanfield, J.A. and Simpson, G., 1958	*Central Gaulish Potters* (Oxford, Oxford Univ. Press)
Stanfield, J. and Simpson, G., 1990	*Les potiers de la Gaule Centrale*, Revue Archéologique Sites, Hors-série 37 (Gonfaron)
Stansbie, D., 2008	'Excavation of a middle Iron Age enclosure at Bushmead Road, Eaton Socon, Cambridgeshire', *Proc. Cambridge Antiq. Soc.* 97, 41–52
Starley, D., 1993	*Assessment of Slag and other Metalworking Debris from Sandy Cemetery, Bedfordshire*, English Heritage Ancient Monuments Lab. Rep. 90/93 (London)
Starley, D., 1995	*Hammerscale*, Historical Metallurgy Soc. Datasheet 10
Starley, D., 2009	*Analysis of Iron Age and Roman Metalworking Debris from Bob's Wood, Hinchingbrooke, Cambridgeshire*, archive report for Oxford Archaeol. East (unpubl.)
Stead, I., 1976	'The earliest burials of the Aylesford culture', in de Giberne Sieveking, G., Longworth, I.H., Wilson, K.E. and Clark, G. (eds), *Problems in Economic and Social Archaeology*, 401–16 (London, Duckworth)
Stead, I.M. and Rigby, V., 1986	*Baldock. The excavation of a Roman and pre-Roman settlement, 1968–72*, Britannia Monogr. Ser. 7 (London)
Stead, I.M. and Rigby, V., 1989	*Verulamium: the King Harry Lane site*, HBMCE Archaeol. Rep. 12 (London)
Stefani, G., 2005	*Cibi e Sapori a Pompei e Dintorni* (Pompei, Soprendenza Archeologica di Pompei)
Stewart, I.J. and Kempster, V., 1992	'Iron objects', in Yeoman, P.A. and Stewart, I.J., 'A Romano-British villa estate at Mantles Green, Amersham, Buckinghamshire', *Rec. Buckinghamshire* 34, 107–82
Stokes, P. and Rowley-Conwy, P., 2002	'Iron Age cultigen? Experimental return rates for fat hen (*Chenopodium album* L.)', *Environmental Archaeol.* 7, 95–100

Strid, L., 2008 — 'Animal bone', in Stansbie, D., 'Excavation of a middle Iron Age enclosure at Bushmead Road, Eaton Socon, Cambridgeshire', *Proc. Cambridge Antiq. Soc.* 97, 47–8

Sutherland, D.S., 2003 — *Northamptonshire Stone* (Stanbridge, The Dovecote Press)

Summers, D., 1973 — *The Great Ouse: the history of a river navigation* (Newton Abbot, David & Charles)

Swan, V.G., 1984 — *The Pottery Kilns of Roman Britain* (London, HMSO)

Swift, E., 2000 — *Regionality in Dress Accessories in the Late Roman West*, Instrumentum Monogr. 11 (Montagnac)

Taylor, A., 1997 — *Archaeology of Cambridgeshire, Volume 1: south-west Cambridgeshire* (Cambridge, Cambridgeshire County Counc.)

Taylor, J., 2007 — *An Atlas of Roman Rural Settlement in England*, Counc. Brit. Archaeol. Res. Rep. 151 (London)

Tebbutt, C.F., 1966 — 'St Neots Priory', *Proc. Cambridge Antiq. Soc.* 59, 33–74

Teichert, M., 1975 — 'Osteometrische untersuchungen zur berechnung der widerristhöhe bei schafen', in Clason, A.T. (ed.), *Archaeozoological Studies. Papers of the Archaeozoological Conference, Groningen, 1974*, 51–69 (Amsterdam and New York, North-Holland Publishing Co.)

Tetlow, E.A., 2006 — *The Insect Remains from Heathrow Terminal 5*, BA-E Rep. OA-14-06 for Framework Archaeology. Available: http://archaeologydataservice.ac.uk/archiveDS/archiveDownload?t=arch-1080-1/dissemination/pdf/SpecialistReports/17-T5_Insect_remains.pdf. Accessed: 25.7.17

Thatcher, C., 2006 — *Roman Enclosures at Longsands Community College, St Neots*, Oxford Archaeol. East Rep. 902 (unpubl.)

Thatcher, C., forthcoming — 'Excavations at Chatteris High Street', *Proc. Cambridge Antiq. Soc.*

The, T.L. and Trouth, C.O., 1976 — 'Sexual dimorphism in the basilar part of the occipital bone of the dog (*Canis familiaris*)', *Acta Anatomica* 9, 565–71

Thomas, R. and Baxter, I.L., 2007 — *Pathologies from Love's Farm, St Neots, Cambridgeshire*, archive report for Oxford Archaeol. East (unpubl.)

Thompson, I., 1982 — *Grog-tempered Belgic Pottery of South-eastern England*, Brit. Archaeol. Rep. Brit. Ser. 108 (Oxford)

Timby, J., Brown, R., Biddulph, E., Hardy, A. and Powell, A., 2007 — *A Slice of Rural Essex. Archaeological discoveries from the A120 between Stansted Airport and Braintree*, Oxford Wessex Archaeol. Monogr. 1 (Oxford)

Tomber, R. and Dore, J., 1998 — *The National Roman Fabric Reference Collection: a Handbook*, Mus. London Archaeol. Serv. (London)

Tottenham, C.E., 1954 — *Coleoptera. Staphylinidae, Section (a) Piestinae to Euaesthetinae*, Handbooks for the identification of British insects 4 (8a) (London, Royal Entomological Soc.)

Turner, R., 1999 — *Excavations of an Iron Age Settlement and Roman Religious Complex at Ivy Chimneys, Witham, Essex 1978–83*, E. Anglian Archaeol. 88

Tyers, P., 1996 — *Roman Pottery in Britain* (London, Batsford)

Ubelaker, D.H., 1989 — *Human Skeletal Remains: Excavation, Analysis, and Interpretation* (Washington, D.C., Taraxacum)

Ulbricht, I., 1978 — *Die Geweihverarbeitung in Haithabu* (Neumünster, K. Wachholtz)

van Arsdell, R.D., 1989 — *Celtic Coinage of Britain* (London, Spink & Son)

van Hoeve, M.L. and Hendrikse, M. (eds), 1998 — *A Study of Non-pollen Objects in Pollen Slides: the types as described by Dr Bas van Geel and colleagues* (unpubl. compilation, Univ. Utrecht)

van der Veen, M., 1992 — *Crop Husbandry Regimes. An archaeobotanical study of farming in northern England 1000 BC–AD 500* (Sheffield, J.R. Collis)

van der Veen, M., 1999 — 'The economic value of chaff and straw in arid and temperate zones', *Vegetation History and Archaeobotany* 8, 211–24

van der Veen, M., 2006 — 'A re-analysis of agricultural production and consumption: implications for understanding the British Iron Age', *Vegetation History and Archaeobotany* 15, 217–28

van Driel-Murray, C., 1999 — 'Ware the Saxons!', *Archaeol. Leather Group Newsletter* 9 (March), 6–7

van Driel-Murray, C., 2001 — 'Footwear in the north-western provinces of the Roman Empire', in Goubitz, O., van Driel-Murray, C. and Groenman-van Waateringe, W., *Stepping through Time: Archaeological footwear from prehistoric times until 1800*, 337–76 (Zwolle, Stichting Promotie Archeologie)

Vince, A., 1990 — 'Dealing with 'dark earth': practical proposals', *Lincoln Archaeology 1989–1990*, Ann. Rep. City Lincoln Archaeol. Unit 2, 24–9 (Lincoln)

von den Driesch, A., 1976 — *A Guide to the Measurement of Animal Bones from Archaeological Sites*, Peabody Mus. Bulletin 1 (Cambridge, Mass.)

Wainwright, G.J., 1972 — 'The excavation of a Neolithic settlement on Broome Heath, Ditchingham, Norfolk, England', *Proc. Prehist. Soc.* 38, 1–107

Wade, K., 2000 — 'Anglo-Saxon and medieval (rural)', in Brown, N. and Glazebrook, J. (eds), *Research and Archaeology: a Framework for the Eastern Counties, 2. Research agenda and strategy*, E. Anglian Archaeol. Occ. Pap. 8, 23–6

Wait, G.A., 1985 — *Ritual and Religion in Iron Age Britain*, Brit. Archaeol. Rep. Brit. Ser. 149 (2 vols) (Oxford)

Walters, F.A., 1907 — 'A find of early Roman bronze coins in England', *Num. Chron.* 7, 353–72

Walton Rogers, P., 1997 — *Textile Production at 16–22 Coppergate*, Archaeol. York 17/11 (York, Counc. Brit. Archaeol.)

Walton Rogers, P., 2001 — 'The appearance of an old Roman loom in medieval England', in Walton Rogers, P., Bender Jørgensen, L. and Rast-Eicher, A., *The Roman Textile Industry and its Influence*, 158–71 (Oxford, Oxbow)

Watson, B., 1998 — ''Dark earth' and urban decline in Roman London', in Watson, B. (ed.), *Roman London: recent archaeological work*, J. Roman Archaeol. Suppl. Ser. 24, 100–106

Watts, M., 2002 — *The Archaeology of Mills and Milling* (Stroud, The History Press)

Waugh, H. and Goodburn, R., 1972. 'The non-ferrous metal objects', in Frere, S.S., *Verulamium Excavations* 1, Rep. Res. Comm. Soc. Antiq. 28, 114–62 (London)

Webster, G. (ed.), 1976. *Romano-British Coarse Pottery: a student's guide*, Counc. Brit. Archaeol. Res. Rep. 6 (London)

Webster, G., 1980. *The Roman Invasion of Britain* (London, Routledge)

Webster, G., 1987. 'Other objects of bronze', in Dannell, G.B. and Wild, J.P., *Longthorpe II*, Britannia Monogr. 8, 87–95 (London)

Webster, P., 2005. *Roman Samian Pottery in Britain*, Practical Handbook in Archaeology 13, Counc. British Archaeol. (York)

Wedlake, W.J., 1982. *The Excavation of the Shrine of Apollo at Nettleton, Wiltshire, 1956–71*, Rep. Res. Comm. Soc. Antiq. 40 (London)

Wessex Archaeology, 2002. *Tesco Extension, Barford Road, St Neots, Cambridgeshire: interim statement of results* (unpubl.)

Wessex Archaeology, 2003. *Cambourne New Settlement, Cambridgeshire: interim statement of results* (unpubl.)

West, S.E., 1985. *West Stow. The Anglo-Saxon village*, E. Anglian Archaeol. 24

West, S.E., 1990. *West Stow. The prehistoric and Romano-British occupations*, E. Anglian Archaeol. 48

Wheeler, R.E.M., 1924. *Segontium, and the Roman Occupation of Wales* (London, The Honourable Society of Cymmrodorion)

Wheeler, R.E.M., 1943. *Maiden Castle, Dorset*, Rep. Res. Comm. Soc. Antiq. 12 (London)

Wheeler, R.E.M. and Wheeler, T.V., 1932. *Report on the Excavation of the Prehistoric, Roman, and Post-Roman sites in Lydney Park, Gloucestershire*, Rep. Res. Comm. Soc Antiq. 9 (London)

Whimster, R., 1981. *Burial practices in Iron Age Britain. A discussion and gazetteer of the evidence, c.700 BC–AD 43. Part I*, Brit. Archaeol. Rep. Brit. Ser. 90(i) (Oxford)

White, D.A., 1969. 'Excavations at Brampton, Huntingdonshire, 1966', *Proc. Cambridge Antiq. Soc.* 62, 1–20

White, R., 1988. *Romano-Celtic Objects from Anglo-Saxon Graves. A catalogue and an interpretation of their use*, Brit. Archaeol. Rep. Brit. Ser. 91 (Oxford)

Whitehead. S., 2003. *Fieldwalking on Land East of St Neots, Cambridgeshire*, Cambridgeshire County Counc. Archaeol. Field Unit Rep. A208 (unpubl.)

Whiting, W., 1923. 'A Roman cemetery discovered at Ospringe in 1920', *Archaeol. Cantiana* 36, 65–80

Whiting, W., Hawley, W. and May, T., 1931. *Report on the Excavation of the Roman Cemetery at Ospringe, Kent*, Rep. Res. Comm. Soc. Antiq. 8 (London)

Whittle, A., 1995. 'Gifts from the Earth: symbolic dimensions of the use and production of Neolithic flint and stone axes', *Archaeologia Polona* 33, 247–59

Wild, J.P., 1970. *Textile Manufacture in the Northern Roman Provinces* (Cambridge, Cambridge Univ. Press)

Williams, D.F., 1979. 'Petrology of Pre-Saxo-Norman Pottery from Bedford Castle', in Baker, D., Baker, E., Hassall, J. and Simco, A., 'Excavations in Bedford 1967–77', *Bedfordshire Archaeol. J.* 13, 151–2

Williams, D.F. and Vince, A.G., 1997. 'The characterization and interpretation of Early to Middle Saxon granitic-tempered pottery in England', *Medieval Archaeol.* 41, 214–20

Williams, D.F., 2003a. 'Petrology', in Gibson, A., *Prehistoric Pottery. People, Pattern and Purpose*, Prehistoric Ceramic Res. Group Occ. Publ. 4/Brit. Archaeol. Rep. Int. Ser. 1156, 76–86 (Oxford)

Williams, D.F., 2003b. 'Petrology', in Evans, C. (ed.), *Power and Island Communities: excavations at Wardy Hill ringwork, Coveney, Ely*, E. Anglian Archaeol. 103

Willis, S., 1996. 'The Romanisation of pottery assemblages in the east and north-east of England during the 1st century AD: a comparative analysis', *Britannia* 27, 179–221

Willis, S., 2003. 'Samian wares', in Hinman, M., *A Late Iron Age Farmstead and Romano-British Site at Haddon, Peterborough*, Cambridgeshire County Counc. Archaeol. Field Unit Monogr. 2/Brit. Archaeol. Rep. Brit. Ser. 358, 99 (Oxford)

Willis, S., 2004. 'The Study Group for Roman Pottery research framework document for the study of Roman pottery in Britain, 2003', *J. Roman Pottery Stud.* 11, 1–20

Willis, S., 2005. 'Samian pottery, a resource for the study of Roman Britain and beyond: the results of the English Heritage-funded samian project. An e-monograph', Suppl. to *Internet Archaeology* 17, Available: http://intarch.ac.uk/journal/issue17/. Accessed: 25 November 2015

Willis, S., Lyons, A., Popescu, E. and Roberts, J., 2008. 'Late Iron Age/early Roman pottery kilns at Blackhorse Lane, Swavesey, 1998–99', *Proc. Cambridge Antiq. Soc.* 97, 53–76

Wilson, B., 1992. 'Considerations for the identification of ritual deposits of animal bones in Iron Age pits', *Int. J. Osteoarchaeol.* 2, 341–9

Wilson, D. (ed.), 1973. 'Roman Britain in 1973. 1. Sites explored', *Britannia* 4, 271–337

Winder, J.M., 1993. *A Study of the Variation in Oyster Shells from Archaeological Sites and a Discussion of Oyster Exploitation* (unpubl. PhD thesis, Univ. Southampton)

Woodfield, C. and Johnson, C., 1989. 'A Roman site at Stanton Low, on the Great Ouse, Buckinghamshire – excavated by Margaret Jones 1957–58', *Archaeol. J.* 146, 135–278

Wright, J., Leivers, M., Seager-Smith, R. and Stevens, C.J., 2009. *Cambourne New Settlement: Iron Age and Romano-British settlement on the clay uplands of west Cambridgeshire*, Wessex Archaeol. Rep. 23 (Salisbury)

Wyles, S., 2009. 'Marine shell', in Wright, J., Leivers, M., Seager Smith, R. and Stevens, C., *Cambourne New Settlement Iron Age and Romano-British Settlement on the Clay Uplands of West Cambridgeshire*, Wessex Archaeol. Rep. 23, Vol. 2: CD p.134

Yeoman, P.A. and Stewart, I.J., 1992. 'A Romano-British villa estate at Mantles Green, Amersham, Buckinghamshire', *Rec. Buckinghamshire* 34, 107–82

Young, C.J., 1977. *The Roman Pottery Industry in the Oxford Region*, Brit. Archaeol. Rep. Brit. Ser. 43 (Oxford)

Young, R. and Humphrey, J., 1999 — 'Flint use in England after the Bronze Age: time for a re-evaluation?', *Proc. Prehistoric Soc.* 65, 231–42

Zeder, M.A., 2006 — 'Reconciling rates of long bone fusion and tooth eruption and wear in sheep (*Ovis*) and goat (*Capra*)', in Ruscillo, D. (ed.), *Recent Advances in Ageing and Sexing Animal Bones*, Proc. 9th ICAZ Conf., Durham 2002, 87–118 (Oxford, Oxbow Books)

Zeder, M.A. and Pilaar, S.E., 2010 — 'Assessing the reliability of criteria used to identify mandibles and mandibular teeth in sheep, *Ovis*, and goats, *Capra*', *J. Archaeol. Sci.* 37, 225–42

Zeepvat, R.J., 1987 — 'Tiles', in Mynard, D.C. (ed.), *Roman Milton Keynes. Excavations and fieldwork 1971–82*, Buckinghamshire Archaeol. Soc. Monogr. Ser. 1, 118–25

Index

Illustrations are indicated by page numbers in *italics*. Places are in Cambridgeshire unless indicated otherwise.

A428 upgrading
   agriculture 303
   animal bones 253, *254*, 255
   buildings 82
   excavations 5
   flint 294, 295
   pottery 240, 243
   settlement 8, 78, 298, 322
Abingdon (Oxon) 145
agriculture 303
   animal husbandry 273–4, 303–5
   cereal production and consumption 305–7
   environment 303
   non-cereal crops 307–8
Alconbury Brook 8
amulets 145
Andover (Hants) 145
animal bones
   assemblage 250
   discussion 273–4, 303–5, 308
   methodology 250–3
   provenance and preservation 253–4
   species discussion
      cat 265, 273
      cattle 255–7, *255*, *256*, 267–71, *269*, *271*, *272*, 304–5
      dog *261*, 262–5, *262*, *263*, 273, 304
      domestic birds 265, 304
      equid *258*, 259–61, *259*, *260*, 273, 304
      pig 259, 271, 304
      sheep/goat *256*, 257–9, 271, *272*, 304
      wild species 265–7, *266*, 273, 308
   species frequency 251–2, *253*, 254–5, *254*
   well assemblage 125, 267–73, *268*, *269*–70, *271*, *272*
   see also antlers; bone and antler objects; fish bones; shellfish
antlers
   antler working 114–15, 273, 310
   discussion 254, *264*, 265, 273, 308, 321
   excavation evidence
      Romano-British 114–15, *124*, 125
      Anglo-Saxon 133, *134*
   see also bone and antler objects
anvil 121, *121*, 130, 173, *174*, 181
architectural fragments 133, 188–9, 314
armillae *100*, 101, 171, *172*, 315, 320
armlets
   bone 193, *194*, 195
   copper alloy
      description and discussion 150, 151, 157–60, *158*–9, 312
      excavation evidence *100*, 101, 121, 122
   iron *158*, 160, 312
   silver 133, 175–6, 177, *178*
   see also armillae
arrowheads
   Neolithic 18, 139, 140
   Bronze Age 18, 139
Ash Plantation
   buildings 300
   craft and industry 310
   droveways 305
   pits, prehistoric 295
   settlement 81, 298
Ashwell (Herts) 321
asparagus 291, 307
awls 193, 310, 311
axes, Neolithic 18, 139, *139*, 140

Baldock (Herts)
   animal bones 273
   brooches 149, 152, 156
   burials 316
   hairpins 151, 156
   querns 183

Bancroft (Bucks) 246
bar, hooked, copper alloy 175, *176*
bar fragments, iron 115, 169, *169*, 174, *175*, 309
Barleycroft Farm 140
Barrington 145, 246, 304
Bartlow 241
Bassingbourn 319, 323
beads
   amber 182, 314
   glass 56, 182, 311, 314
Beck Row (Suffolk) 278
Bedford (Beds) 245
bell fragment 130, 171, *173*
Benacre (Suffolk) 145
Biddenham Loop (Beds) 8
Bierton (Bucks) 83, 151
Bittern Pits (Manchester) 145
bobbins
   bone 193, 194, 309
   ceramic 186–7, *187*, 192, 309
Bob's Wood
   animal bones/agriculture 9, *253*, *254*, 255, 305
   burial 83
   coins *141*, 142–3, *142*, 313
   features, prehistoric 8
   flint 138, 140
   glass vessels 182
   metalwork 147–8, *147*
   metalworking debris 179, 181, 310
   pottery
      Neolithic 202
      Iron Age 203–4, 205, 209, 212, 214
      Romano-British 240, 241, 243
   querns 183, 184
   settlement 296
bone and antler objects 125, 192–7, *194*, *195*, *196*, *197*, 310
boneworking debris 193, 194, 197, *197*, 257, 310
Boundary 1
   discussion 78, 79, 80, 299–300
   excavation evidence
      Period 3.1–3.2 21–4, *23*, 28, 29, *29*, *30*, 32–3
      Period 3.3 33, *34*, 35, 41, *41*, *42*, *50*
      Period 3.4 53, 59, *59*, 61, *61*
      Period 3.5 *62*, 63
      Period 4.1 94
Boundary 2 *90*, 94
Boundary 3 35, *42*, 50, *50*, 61, *61*
Boundary 5 *34*, 35, 49, *106*, 107, 110
Boundary 6 21, 27, *27*, 33
Boundary 8, excavation evidence
   Period 3.3 33, *34*, *41*, 44
   Period 3.4 53, 59, *59*
   Period 4.4 111–12, *112*, 113
   Periods 6–7 136
Boundary 9 63, *69*, 70
Boundary 10
   discussion 80, 81
   excavation evidence
      Period 3.2 25
      Period 3.3 33, *34*, 35–6, *36*
      Period 3.4 53, *54*, 55
Boundary 12 73, *73*
Boundary 13 *117*, 118
Boundary 15 *62*, 66, 67
Boundary 16 *62*, 66, 67
Boundary 20 114, *115*, 122
Boundary 100, excavation evidence
   Period 4.1 87, *90*, 93
   Period 4.2 97, *98*
   Period 4.4 *117*, 118
Boundary 102 *106*, 107, 109
Boundary 104 *106*, 107, 109
Boundary 106 *117*, 118, 119
Boundary 109 63, *69*, 70, *89*, 91, 95
Boundary 110, excavation evidence

Period 4.2 95, *96*, 97
Period 4.3 *106*, 107
Period 4.4 111, 112, *112*, 113, 114, *115*
Period 4.5 122
Boundary 111 95, *96*, 104, *105*
Boundary 112 111, 112, *112*, 113
Boundary 113 *112*, 113
Boundary 114 *112*, 113
Boundary 115 104, *105*
Boundary 116 *112*, 113
Boundary 117 *112*, 113
Boundary 118 104, *105*
Boundary 120 121, 122, *123*, *132*, 133
Bourn airfield 297, 305
box fittings, copper alloy 162, 164, *164*
Brampton 8
brewing 128, 278, 279
brooches, Iron Age/Romano-British
   description/discussion 84, 85, 312, 313–14, 315, 320
      from burials 149–50
      non-burial contexts 150, 151–6, *152*, *153*, *154*, *155*, *156*
   excavation evidence *100*, 101
brooches, Anglo-Saxon 134, 175, *176*, *178*
Broughton (Milton Keynes) 84, 218
Buckden/Diddington ritual complex 8
buckle, Anglo-Saxon 134, 175, *176*, 177, *178*
buildings, discussion
   Iron Age 82–3, 300–1, *302*
   Romano-British 129–30, 301–3
   see also roundhouses; structures
burial practices 315–16, *317*; *see also* cremations; dog burials; horse burials; inhumations; sheep burial
butchery 256, 261

Caldecote Highfields
   agriculture 291, 304, 305, 323, 324
   buildings 82
   craft and industry 308, 311
   excavation 5
   flint 294
   pottery 240, 243
   querns 307
   settlement 8, 9, 80, 297–8
   special deposits 319
Cambourne
   agriculture 303, 304, 306, 307, 323
   animal bones *254*, 255, 308
   buildings 82
   coins 312, 313
   environment 291, 294
   flint 294, 295
   mollusca 282
   pottery 212, 240, 243, 310, 311
   settlement
      early prehistoric 8
      Iron Age–Romano-British 9, 78, 127, 298
      Anglo-Saxon 322
   special deposits 319
   see also Lower Cambourne
Cambridge
   Addenbrooke's Hospital
      agriculture 304, 306
      buildings 83, 130
      burials 84–5, 316
      craft and industry 310
      hunting 308
      mortuary enclosure 316
      pottery 241
      settlement 127, 128, 298
   fort 297
   road 3
   Vicar's Farm 259, 302
Castleford (Yorks) 151
Catuvellauni
   burial practice 84
   dress accessories 150, 151, 153, 156, 161
   territory 1, 297, *297*
Celtic beans 274, 307
cemeteries, discussion 83–5
Cemetery 1
   discussion 79, 83, 86
   excavation evidence 33, *34*, 40–1, *40*, 69
Cemetery 2
   discussion 81, 83–4, 85
   excavation evidence *62*, 63, *66*, 69, *69*, *70*, *71*
Cemetery 3
   discussion 84
   excavation evidence *62*, 63, 75, *76*
Cemetery 4
   discussion 84
   excavation evidence *62*, 63, 76, *76*
ceramic building material
   assemblage 189
   description 189–92, *192*
   discussion 192, 314
   distribution 189
chain-links, iron 175, *176*
Chatteris 316
Childerley Gate
   animal bones 304
   craft and industry 310
   environment 303
   hedges 305
   plant remains 306, 307
   pottery 217
   settlement 298, 322
chisels 181
coin hoards
   Hoard 1
      analysis 141, 143, *143*, 145–6
      catalogue 329
      discussion 128, 130, 321
      excavation evidence 95, 99, *100*
   Hoard 2
      analysis 141, 143, *143*, 146
      catalogue 334
      discussion 130, 321
      excavation evidence *112*, 113
coins
   assemblage 140–1
   catalogue 328–41
   description
      Iron Age 141
      Roman 141–3, *141*, *142*, *143*
   discussion 130, 311, 312–13, 320
   medieval–post-medieval 136
   methodology 141
   secondary adaption 145
   from Settlements 6 and 7 compared 144–5, *144*
   see also coin hoards
Colchester (Essex) 145, 147, *147*, 151, 156
Colne Fen 316
comb fragments 125, 193, 194–6, *195*
Corieltauvi territory 297, *297*
corn driers
   discussion 307
   excavation evidence
      Period 4.2 *101*, 103
      Period 4.3 103, 107, 110
      Period 4.4 *117*, 118, 119
   plant remains 278
craft and industry 308, 310–11; *see also* metalworking; pottery production; textile manufacture
cremations
   Bronze Age 8
   Period 3.5
      discussion 83, 84–5, 315–16, *317*
      excavation evidence 63, 69, 75, 76
      human bones 248–50
      metalwork 149–50
crop processing
   discussion 278, 279
   excavation evidence 103, 107, 113, 116, 119, 128
Croydon (Surrey) 145
crucible fragment 179, 180
cursus enclosures 8

dark earths 322–3
daub 44, 50, 189, 191, 192
disc, bone 75, 84, 193, *194*, 195

ditches
    discussion 128
    excavation evidence
        Period 3.5 67
        Period 4.1 94–5
        Period 4.2 96, 103, *103*
        Period 4.3 103, 104, 107, 109
        Period 4.4 119
        Periods 6–7 136
    pottery 209
dividers, iron 165, *165*
Doddington 145
dog burials
    animal bones *261*, *263*
    discussion 79, 83, 86, 130, 320, 321
    excavation evidence
        Period 3.3 33, 40, *40*, 41
        Period 3.5 73
        Period 4.4 118, *118*
Domesday survey 11
Doncaster (Yorks) 145
Dorney (Bucks) 302
Drayton villa (Leics) 265, *266*
droveways 305
Duxford 84, *253*, 259, 316
dyers' rocket 58, 309

Eaton Socon
    agriculture 304, 305, 306, 307
    building, Anglo-Saxon 11
    craft and industry 308
    enclosure 79
    flint 293
    pottery 313
    settlement 296, 297
Edix Hill 304, 319
Elms Farm (Essex) 257, 267, *270*
Ely
    Hurst Lane reservoir 143
    pottery 209, 212
    Prickwillow Road 128, 304, 310, 313, 320
    Trinity Lands 143
    West Fen Road 143
Emneth (Norfolk) 146
Enclosure 1
    discussion 80, 85
    excavation evidence
        Period 3.2 24, *30*, 32
        Period 3.3 35, *42*, 46–7, *46*, *47*
        Period 3.4 52
Enclosure 2 24, *30*, 31–2
Enclosure 4 21, 29, *29*
Enclosure 5 24, *30*, 32
Enclosure 6 33, *37*, 38–9, 79
Enclosure 7 33, 41–2, *41*, 80
Enclosure 8
    discussion 78–9, 80, 81–2, 298, 316
    excavation evidence
        Period 3.1–3.2 21, 23, 24–7, *25–6*
        Period 3.3 33, *34*, 35, *36*
        Period 3.4 52–4, *53*, *54*
        Period 3.5 63
Enclosure 10
    discussion 79
    excavation evidence
        Period 3.3 33, *34*, *38*, 39
        Period 3.4 56–7, *57*
        Period 3.5 63, 67, *68*
Enclosure 11
    discussion 80, 86, 127
    excavation evidence 35, *42*, 45, 52
Enclosure 12
    Period 3.3 35, *42*, 48–9
    Period 3.4 52, 60–1, *60*
    Period 4.1 *90*, 93
    Period 4.2 97
Enclosure 13 35, *42*, 46, 52, 127
Enclosure 14 33, *41*, 44
Enclosure 15 33, *41*, 44
Enclosure 16 33, *41*, 44

Enclosure 17 33, *41*, 44, 59, *59*
Enclosure 18 52, *57*, 59, 67, *68*, 69
Enclosure 20 52, *60*, 61
Enclosure 21 69–70, *69*, *89*, 91, 95
Enclosure 22
    discussion 79, 80, 81–2, 299, 316–18
    excavation evidence *62*, 63–5, *65*, *66*
    plant remains 275–7
Enclosure 23 *54*, 55, 81
Enclosure 26 35, *42*, 49, *50*, 61, *61*
Enclosure 27 95, *96*, 104, *105*, 127
Enclosure 28
    discussion 127
    excavation evidence 63, 69, 70, *89*, 91, 95
Enclosure 29 63, 72, *72*, 81
Enclosure 29a 72–3, *72*
Enclosure 30 95, *96*, 104, *105*, 127
Enclosure 31 33, *41*, 45, 80
Enclosure 100 87–8, *90*, 93, 97
Enclosure 101 97, *98*
Enclosure 102
    Period 4.1 *90*, 93
    Period 4.3 *106*, 107, 109
    Period 4.4 *117*, 118
Enclosure 103 *90*, *92*, 93–4, 97
Enclosure 104
    Period 4.2 97, *98*, 99
    Period 4.3 *106*, 107, 109
    Period 4.4 *117*, 118–19
Enclosure 105
    Period 4.2 97, *98*, 99
    Period 4.3 *106*, 107, 109
    Period 4.4 *117*, 118–19
Enclosure 106
    Period 4.2 97–8, *98*
    Period 4.3 *106*, 107
    Period 4.4 *117*, 118
Enclosure 107 97, 98, *98*
Enclosure 108 95, 97, *98*, 103
Enclosure 109 95, 97, *98*, *102*, 103
Enclosure 110 95, 97, *98*, 103
Enclosure 111 *106*, 107, *117*, 118
Enclosure 112 *106*, 107, *117*, 118, 130
Enclosure 113
    discussion 128
    excavation evidence *106*, 107, 110, *117*, 118, 119
Enclosure 114 *106*, 107, 108–9, *117*, 118
Enclosure 115 *106*, 107, 110
Enclosure 116 *106*, 107, 110
Enclosure 117 *106*, 107, 110, *117*, 118, 121
Enclosure 118 *117*, 118, 121
Enclosure 119 *117*, 118, 119
Enclosure 120 *117*, 118, 119
Enclosure 121 *117*, 118, 119
Enclosure 122 *117*, 118, 119
Enclosure 123 *117*, 118, 119
Enclosure 124 95, *96*, 97
Enclosure 125 *89*, 91
Enclosure 126 *115*, 116, 121, *123*
Enclosure 127 *112*, 113, 114, *123*, 130, *132*, 133
Enclosure 128 *112*, 113
Enclosure 129 95, *96*, 104, *105*, 127
Enclosure 131 114–15, *115*, 121, *123*
Enclosure 132 114, *115*, 121, *123*, *132*, 133
Enclosure 133 115–16, *115*, *116*
Enclosure 134 *115*, 116, 121, *123*, *132*, 133
Enclosure 135 *112*, 113
Enclosure 136 115, *115*, 116, 121, *123*
Enclosure 137
    Period 4.4 115, *115*, 116
    Period 4.5 121, *123*
    Period 5 *132*, 133, 137
Enclosure 138 *115*, 116, 121, *123*
Enclosure 139
    discussion 130, 321
    excavation evidence 121, 122–5, *123*, *132*, 133, *134*
Enclosure 140 95, *96*, 97
Enclosure 150
    discussion 79, 85
    excavation evidence 21, 27, *27*, 33, 37, *37*, 39

Enclosure 151 29, *29*
Enclosure 152 29, *29*
Enclosure 153 29, *29*
Enclosure 154 *29*, 31
Enclosure 155 *29*, 31
Enclosure 156 24, *30*, 32
Enclosure 157 *30*, 33
Enclosure 158 52, 57, *57*, *58*, 67, *68*
Enclosure 159
   excavation evidence 33, *41*, 42–3, 59, *59*, 85
   pottery 209
Enclosure 160 33, *41*, 44
Enclosure 161 35, *42*, 49
Enclosure 162 52, *60*, 61
Enclosure 163 63, 73–4, *73*, *74*, 81, 127
Enclosure 164 35, *42*, 49, *50*, 61
Enclosure 165 35, *42*, *48*, 49
Enclosure 166 95, *96*, 97
Enclosure 168 114, *115*
Enclosure 169 *112*, 113
Enclosure 170 *112*, 113
Enclosure 171 *112*, 113
Enclosure 172 *112*, 113
Enclosure 173 *112*, 113
Enclosure 174 *115*, 116
Enclosure 175 97, *98*, 107
Enclosure 176 97, 98, *98*
Enclosure 177 *106*, 107, 110
Enclosure 178 *106*, 109
enclosures, discussion 305, 316–18
Epona 320
Ermine Street 3, 9
   construction 241
   proximity to 240, 243, 274, 305
Etton 140, 202, 294
Eynesbury
   agriculture 305, 306, 307
   estate centre 5, 243
   flint 138, 293
   fort 298
   pottery 202, 203
   ritual complex 8, 9, 295
   settlement 11, 296, 297, 298, 323
   villa 303
   woodland 294

Fen Ditton *253*, 255, *270*
fence lines
   Period 4.1 *92*, 93
   Period 4.3 *106*, 108
   Period 4.4 *112*, 113
Fenstanton 138, 295
field beans 274, 307
Field System 1
   discussion 77–8, 79, 299
   excavation evidence 21, *22*–3, 24
Field System 2
   discussion 79
   excavation evidence
      Period 3.3 33, *34*, 35, 50–2, *50*
      Period 3.4 61, *61*
Field System 3
   discussion 80, 81, 307–8
   excavation evidence
      Period 3.4 52, *53*, 55–6, *56*
      Period 3.5 *62*, 67
   pollen 288–90, *290*–1
Field System 4 52, *60*, 61, 300
Field System 5 88, *90*, 94, 127
Field System 6 88, *90*, 94, 127
field systems, in locality
   prehistoric 8, 18, 77–8
   Romano-British 9
   medieval 11, 323–4
finger-rings
   copper alloy 149, 150, 160, *161*, 312
   distribution 150
   silver 160, *161*
fired clay 190–2, *192*
fish bones 252, 308

fittings 167–9, *168*, *169*, *170*, 175, *176*
flint
   assemblage 138
   chronology 138
      Mesolithic–early Neolithic 139
      later Neolithic–early Bronze Age 139
      late Bronze Age 139–40
   discussion 140, 293–4
food offerings 84
Fordham, horncores *270*
foundation deposit 130
four-post structures, discussion 80, 82, 301, *302*, 307; *see also* Structure 3; Structure 4; Structure 6
Fox, Cyril 5
Fox Brook 3, 21, *22*, 61, 148, 299

Gallows Brook 3
gaming counters 237
gate 108, *108*
glass vessels 125, 126, 181–2, 314
goad pricks 170, *170*, 304
Godmanchester (*Durovigutum*)
   burials 84
   food supply 305
   fort 297
   pottery 242, 243
   prehistoric activity 138, 140, 295
   roads and status 3, 9, 298
Gowerton (Glam) 145
The Grange 300, 303, 307, 322
Great Chesterford (Essex) 9, 145, 257
Great Ouse, River 1–2, 5, 8–9, 240, 243
Greenhouse Farm 310

Hacheston (Suffolk) 151, 152, 156
Haddenham
   axe 140
   ceremonial monuments 8
   pottery 203, 209, 240, 241, 242
   special deposit 320
   woodland 294
Haddon
   agriculture 259, 304, 305, 307
   Anglo-Saxon activity 137
   animal burials 130, 320
   buildings 301–2, *302*–3
   coins *141*, 142–3, *142*
   enclosure 316
   excavation 5
   hairpins 151
   pottery 241, 310
   settlement plan 128
   special deposits 319
   villa complex 298, 303
Haddon Lodge, animal bones *254*, *270*
hairpins
   bone 193, 194, *194*, 195
   compared 151
   copper alloy 65, *100*, 101, 130, 156, *157*, 312, 318
   distribution 150
   mutilated 156, *157*
handle, bone 194, *196*, 197; *see also* spatula handle
Harston 310, 323
Hartigans (Bucks) 245
Haslingfield 246
hasp 162, 164, *164*
Haverfield, F. 5
hayricks
   Period 3.3 278, 279, 301
   Period 4.1 *89*, 91, 93, 127, 130, 279, 307
hearths 28, 50, *52*, 80
hedges 78, 305
Hen Brook 3, 5
hengiform monument 8
Higham Ferrers (Northants) 245
Highwood Farm (Essex) 309, 319
Hinchingbrooke *see* Bob's Wood
Hinxton 79, 84, 241, 316, 323
hobnails 108, 113, 116, 160, 161
hones *see* whetstones/hones

hooks 167, *170*, 171, 307
horn working 310–11
horncores
    description 257, 267, *269*, *270*, 271
    discussion 304, 310–11
horse burials
    animal bones *258*, *259*, *260*, 261
    discussion 127, 130, 320
    excavation evidence *92*, 94, 95
human bones
    assemblage 248
    cremations 248–50
    inhumations 248, 249
    methodology 248
hunting 308
Huntingdon Racecourse 8
Hurst Fen (Suffolk) 138

Iceni
    brooches 153
    territory 297, *297*
Icklingham (Suffolk) 143
Icknield Way 9, 295, 316
inhumations
    discussion 78, 81, 83–5, 315–16
    excavation evidence
        Period 3.2 *30*, 32, *32*
        Period 3.3 35, 40–1, *40*, *48*, 49
        Period 3.5 63, 70, *70*, *71*, 75, *75*, *76*
    human bones 248, 249
    metalwork 149, 150
inlay, bone 125, 193
insects
    discussion 286–7
    methodology 282
    Quarry 4 282–6
    well 283–5, 286

Jeavons Lane
    agriculture 303, 304, 305
    animal bones 308
    enclosures 80, 127, 128, 298
    pottery 322
jetons 136, 140–1
joiner's dogs 169, *169*, *170*

Kempsford (Glos) 317
keys, iron 167, 169, *169*
kiln fragments 191–2
kiln furniture 97, 127, 192, *192*, 310
Kilverstone (Norfolk) 138, 302, 323
Knapwell Plantation 296–7, 298, 307, 308, 322
knives 166, *167*

Lancaster (Lancs) 146
land division and allotment 299–300
Langford (Beds) 145
Latton Lands (Wilts) 78
leather objects 197–9, *198*
leatherworking 311
Leicester (Leics) 273
Lime's Farm 267
Little Common Farm
    agriculture 305
    building 301
    pottery 296–7, 310
    querns 307
    special deposits 319
Little Paxton
    buildings/structures 295, 301
    flint 138
    ford 8
    pottery 203, 205, 209, 212, 240, 241, 242, 243
Little Paxton Quarry
    buildings 82
    ceremonial monuments 295
    enclosure 79
    flint 293
    settlement 128, 296, 297
Littleport 300

Londonthorpe (Lincs) 145
long barrow 8
Longstanton 5, 296
Longthorpe 297
loomweights 47, 85, 185–6, *186*, 308–9
Love's Farm, excavation
    archaeological background 5–8, *6–7*
        early prehistoric 8
        Iron Age 8–9
        Romano-British 9
        Anglo-Saxon–medieval 9–11
    background 1–2
    discussion 292–3
        Mesolithic period 18, 293–4
        Neolithic–Bronze Age period 18, 294–5
        Iron Age–Romano-British
            agriculture 303–8
            buildings 300–3, *302*
            burial practices 315–16, *317*
            context 295–8, *297*
            craft and industry 308–11
            excavation evidence 77–86, 127–31
            land division and allotment 299–300
            ritual and votive practices 316–21
            settlement morphology 298–9
            trade, exchange and status 311–15
        Anglo-Saxon period 321–3, 136–7
        medieval period 323–4
    excavation evidence
        Period 1 (*c*.4000–2500 BC) 15, *16–17*, 19
        Period 2 (*c*.2500–800 BC) 15, *16–17*
        Period 3.1–3.2 (*c*.400–100 BC) 21–33
        Period 3.3 (*c*.100 BC–earliest 1st century AD) 33–52, *34*
        Period 3.4 (first half of 1st century AD) 52–61, *53*
        Period 3.5 (mid–late 1st century AD) 62, 63–77
        Period 4.1 (late 1st–early 2nd century AD) 87–95, *88*
        Period 4.2 (2nd century AD) 95–103
        Period 4.3 (3rd century AD) 103–10, *104*
        Period 4.4 (4th century AD) 110–21, *111*
        Period 4.5 (late 4th–early 5th century AD) 121–7, *122*
        Period 5 (early Anglo-Saxon) *132*, 133–4
        Periods 6–7 (medieval–post-medieval) 134–6, *135*
    finds *see* beads; bobbins; bone and antler objects; ceramic building material; coins; flint; glass vessels; loomweights; metalwork; metalworking debris; pottery; shoes; spindlewhorls; stone objects
    location, geology and topography xiv, *1*, 2, 3–5, *4*, 325–8, *326*
    methodology *10*, 11–13, *12*
    research objects 13–14, 292–3
    zooarchaeological and botanical evidence *see* animal bones; human bones; insects; mollusca; plant remains; pollen; radiocarbon dating
Lower Cambourne
    agriculture 303, 305, 307
    animal bones 308
    buildings/structures 82, 300, 301
    burials 78, 83, 85, 316
    causeway 137
    craft and industry 308, 309, 310
    droveways 81
    flint 295
    pottery 296–7, 322
    settlement 79, 80, 127, 128, 298, 322
    shellfish 308
    special deposits 319
lunula *100*, 101, 166, *167*, 321

malting
    discussion 128, 306–7
    excavation evidence 109, 114, 116
    plant remains 278, 279
Mantles Green (Bucks) 151
Mars 156
Mear Way (Hail's Lane) 5
metalwork
    assemblage and methodology 146–7
    from burials 149–50
    description
        agricultural equipment 170–1, *170*
        dress accessories 150–61, *152*, *153*, *154*, *155*, *156*, *157*, *158–9*, *161*
        fittings 167–9, *168*, *169*, *170*
        household equipment 162–4, *163*, *164*

literacy, objects associated with 165–6, *166*
   lunula 166, *167*
   metalworking objects 172–4, *174*, *175*
   military equipment 171, *172*
   religious objects 171–2, *173*
   textile equipment 162
   toilet instruments 161–2, *162*
   tools 166, *167*
   weights and measures 165, *165*
   miscellaneous and post-Roman 174–7, *176*, *177*, *178*
overview 147–8, *147*, *148*
Settlements 6 and 7 compared 148, *149*
metalworking 93, 181, 309–10
metalworking debris 177
   classification 177–9
   discussion 181, 309
   distribution 180–1
   metalworking activity by phase 179–80
   methodology 177
military/civilian interaction 315
millstones
   description/discussion 182, 183, 184, *185*, 314
   excavation evidence *92*, 93
Milton 80, 291, 307
Milton Keynes (Bucks) 241, 243, 246
Minerva 156, 165, 166, *166*, 318, 321
mirror fragment 161, 162
mistletoe 125, 290, 291, 321
mollusca 281–2
Monk Field Farm 322
mortars 184
mortuary enclosures 8
mount, military 171, *172*, 315
Mucking (Essex) 245, 246
mussels 282, 308

nail-cleaners 161–2, *162*
nails
   from burials 75, 149, 150
   non-burial contexts 167–8
   see also hobnails
needle 162, 309; *see also* pack-needle
North Caxton 295
Northampton (Northants) 245

Oakington 244, 245
Orton Hall Farm 244, 245, *254*
Orton Longueville 143
ovens *102*, 103, 307
Over Quarry 293
oysters 116, 281–2, 308

pack-needle, antler 195, *196*, 197
palaeochannel 3
Papworth Everard 5, 8, 9, 77, 295, 296
peas 274, 307
Penard (Glam) 146
Pennyland (Bucks) 245, 246
Peterborough 146, 244
Piddington (Northants) 286
pins
   bone 116
   copper alloy 75
   see also hairpins; ring-headed pins
pintles 167, 169, *169*, *170*
Pit Group 1 97, *98*, *98*
Pit Group 2 97, *98*, 101
Pit Group 3 97, *98*, 101, *102*, 103
Pit Group 4 97, *98*, 101
Pit Group 5 *98*, 101–3, *101*
Pit Group 6 104–7, *105*
Pit Group 7 *112*, 113
Pit Group 8 *112*, 113
pits
   discussion 80, 81, 309
   excavation evidence
      Period 1 15, 18, *19*
      Period 3.1–3.2 24, 26, *26*, 28, 29, 31
      Period 3.3 39–40, 42, 50, *52*
      Period 3.4 54

Period 3.5 65, 67, 72, 73
Period 4.1 91, *92*, 93, 94
Period 4.2 95, 99, 103, 127
Period 4.3 103, 107, 109, 110
Period 4.4 113, 118, 119, 121
Period 4.5 125
Period 5 133, 134, 137
undated 33
   pottery 209–11
   see also Pit Groups 1–8; Quarry 1–7
placed deposits
   discussion 85–6, 130, 318–21
   animal bones 255, *255*, 273, 304
   coins 145
   querns 307
   excavation evidence
      Period 3.2 27
      Period 3.3 46, 47, *47*
      Period 3.5 73, 74, *74*
      Period 4.1 *92*, 93
      Period 4.2 95, *98*, 99–101, *100*, 103, *103*
      Period 4.4 *120*, 121
      Period 4.5 125
      Period 5 133, *134*
   plant remains 275, 276
   pottery 209
   querns 183, 184
plant remains
   discussion 279–81, 305–7
   Iron Age
      Enclosure 22 275–7
      four-post structures 277–8
      settlements and miscellaneous features 275
   Romano-British
      Settlement 6 278–9
      Settlement 7 125, 279, 280–1
   sample composition and methodology 274–5
plaques
   bone 196, *196*
   iron 175, *176*
pollen analysis 287
   discussion 290–1, 306
   methodology 287
   results
      Field System 3 288–90
      Quarry 3 58, 287, 288, 289
      Quarry 4 288, 289
      Routeway 4 288
      well 125, 288, 290
Poplar Plantation 81, 82, 305, 307
postholes
   Period 4.1 93
   Period 4.2 95
   Period 4.3 109
   Period 4.4 113, 116, 118
potter's stamps 218, *218*, 239, *239*
pottery
   assemblage 200
   description and discussion
      Neolithic 202, *203*
      early Bronze Age 15, 18, 202–3
      Iron Age 85, 203–15, *210–11*, *212*, *213–14*
      late Iron Age and transitional 215–19, *218*, 239–40, *240*
      Romano-British 219–43, *221*, *229*, *231–2*, *238*, *240*
      post-Roman 243–7, *246*, 321–2
   fabrics
      early prehistoric 202
      Iron Age 203–5, 206–7
      late Iron Age and transitional 215–19
      Romano-British
         amphorae 223, 226, 241, 341
         black-surfaced red ware 341
         greywares 223, 224–5, 226, 341–2
         gritty buff ware 342
         gritty oxidised ware 225
         grog-tempered reduced wares 221
         Hadham redware 227–8, 342
         Horningsea reduced ware 342
         mortaria 233–5
         Nene Valley colour-coat 226, 342

Nene Valley greyware 342
Nene Valley whiteware 226, 342
Oxfordshire red colour-coat 226–7, 342
Oxfordshire whiteware 342
oxidised ware with grog inclusions 225, 342–3
oxidised wares 221–3, 225
pink grog-tempered ware 343
red fineware 343
reduced wares 221, 224, 343
samian 223, 226, 235–9, *238*, *239*, 343
Sandy greyware 221, 243
sandy wares 225–6, 242–3, 343–4
shell-tempered wares 221, 223–4, 242–3, 344
Southern British glazed ware 223
Verulamium whiteware 225, 344
post-Roman 243–5
forms
early prehistoric 202
Iron Age–late Iron Age and transitional 205–9, *208*, 215–16, 217–19
Romano-British 344–6
methodology 200–1
preservation 200
report structure 201, *201*
trade and exchange 311, 313, 315
pottery production 95, 97, 127, 310
Puckeridge-Braughing (Herts) 151, 156
punches 173, 174, *175*, 309

Quarry 1 33, *37*, 39, 79
Quarry 2 33, 38, *38*, 40, *40*, 52
Quarry 3
discussion 80, 85, 309
excavation evidence 52, 57–8, *57*
pollen 287, 288, 289, 290
Quarry 4
excavation evidence 68–9, *68*
insects 282–6
pollen 288, 289, 290
Quarry 5 70, *72*
Quarry 6 *73*, 74
Quarry 7 95, 96–7, *96*, 127
querns
assemblage 182, 183
description
Iron Age 182–3
Romano-British 183–4, *185*
Anglo-Saxon 184
discussion 85, 184, 307, 312, 314
excavation evidence
Period 3 27, 32, 73
Period 4 116, 121, 133
see also millstones

radiocarbon dating 250
rake prong 307
Raunds (Northants) 247
religion *see* ritual and votive practices
ridge and furrow 5, 11, *135*, 136, 323–4
ring ditch, Bronze Age 8
ring-headed pins 167, 169, *169*, *170*
rings
copper alloy
description/discussion 171–2, *173*, 320–1
excavation evidence 49, 83, *100*, 101, 103
iron 169, *169*
ritual and votive practices
animal burials 320
?ceremonial enclosures 316–18
deposits in watery places 320–1
special deposits 318–20
rivets, lead 167, 169, *170*, 237
Road 22 3
road network 3–5, *4*, *6*, 9
Romanisation 292
Roundhouse 1 21, *27*, *27*, 33, 78
Roundhouse 2 21, *27*, 28, 33
Roundhouse 3 21, 33, *37*, 39
Roundhouse 4 21, *27*, 28, 33
Roundhouse 5 *27*, 28, 33
Roundhouse 6 33, *38*, 39–40, *40*, 52

Roundhouse 7 52, *57*, 59
Roundhouse 8 35, *42*, 50, *50*, *51*, 61
Roundhouse 9 21, *29*, 31, *31*
Roundhouse 10 21, *29*, 31, 83, 301
Roundhouse 11 33, *41*, 42, 43, *43*, 80
Roundhouse 12
discussion 83
excavation evidence
Period 3.3 35, *42*, 49–50, *50*, *51*
Period 3.4 61, *61*
Roundhouse 13 35, *42*, *48*, 49
Roundhouse 14
discussion 78, 80, 82, 85, 301
excavation evidence
Period 3.2 24, *30*, 32
Period 3.3 35, *42*, 45–6
Period 3.4 52, 59, *60*
Period 3.5 73, *73*
Roundhouse 15 35, *42*, 47, 80
Roundhouse 16 35, *42*, 47, 80
Roundhouse 17 35, *42*, 47, 80
Roundhouse 18 35, *42*, 47, 80, 82
Roundhouse 19 35, *42*, 47–8, 80
Roundhouse 20 52, 60, *60*, *73*, 74
Roundhouse 21 72, *72*, 81
Roundhouse 22 35, 50, *50*, 61
Roundhouse 23 67, *68*, 69
roundhouses, discussion 82, 300–1
Routeway 1
discussion 77, 81, 82, 299–300
excavation evidence 21, *22–3*, 24, *34*
Routeway 2
discussion 77, 81, 127, 299–300
excavation evidence
Period 3.2 *22–3*, 24
Period 3.3 33, *34*
Period 3.4 *53*, 59
Period 3.5 *62*, 63
Period 4.1 87, 88–91, *88*, *89*
Period 4.4 111–12, *112*, 114, *115*
Periods 6–7 136
Routeway 3 *23*, 24, *34*, 77, 299
Routeway 4
discussion 79, 300
excavation evidence
Period 3.3 33, *34*, 36–8, *37*
Period 3.4 52, *53*, 55, *56*
Period 3.5 *62*, 63, 67
pollen 288, 291
Routeway 5 *42*, 50, *50*, 61
Routeway 6 *53*, 56, *56*, 80
Routeway 7 *62*, 65–7, *66*, 82
Routeway 8
discussion 81, 127, 300
excavation evidence
Period 3.4 *60*, 61
Period 3.5 *62*, 63, *73*, 74
Period 4.1 88
Period 4.2 95, 97, *98*, 101
Period 4.3 *106*, 107
Routeway 9
discussion 81, 127
excavation evidence
Period 3.4 61, *61*
Period 3.5 *62*, 63, 76, *77*
Period 4.1 88
Period 4.2 95
Period 4.3 103–4, *104*, *106*, 107, 109–10
Period 4.4 *117*, 118
Routeway 10
discussion 127, 128
excavation evidence 95, *96*, 103, 104, *104*, *105*
Routeway 11
discussion 127
excavation evidence
Period 4.2 95, 97, *98*
Period 4.3 *106*, 107
Period 4.4 *117*, 118
Roystone Grange (Derbys) 129
rubbing stones 184

St Neots
  location 1, *1*
  priory 1, 11
  river crossing 3, 9
  Saxon settlement 9–11, 323
Sandy (Beds) 3, 9, 181, 242, 243, 298
saw blade 166, 311
Scotland Farm
  agriculture 303, 304, 306, 307
  animal bones 308
  buildings 82, 301
  craft and industry 308, 309
  enclosure 78
  excavation 5
  flint 294
  pottery 212, 295, 311
  quarry pits 80
  settlement 8, 81, 297, 298
  special deposits 319, 320
Senuna 321
Settlement 1
  discussion
    buildings 82
    morphology 78, 79, 80, 298, 300
  excavation evidence
    Period 3.1–3.2 21, *23*, 27–8, *27*
    Period 3.3 33, *34*, 36–9, *37*
    Period 3.4 52, 55–6, *56*
    Period 3.5 63, 67
Settlement 2
  coins 328
  discussion
    burials 83, 84
    morphology and land division 79, 80, 81, 298, 299, 300
    ritual deposition 85
  excavation evidence
    Period 3.3 33, *34*, 38, 39–41, *40*
    Period 3.4 52, *53*, 56–9
    Period 3.5 *62*, 63, 67–9, *68*
Settlement 3
  coins 328
  discussion
    buildings 82
    morphology 78, 79–80, 80–1
    ritual deposition 85
  excavation evidence
    Period 3.1–3.2 21, *23*, 24, 29–31, *29*
    Period 3.3 33–5, *34*, 41–5, *41*
    Period 3.4 *53*, 59, *59*
    Period 3.5 63, 75
Settlement 4
  discussion 78, 79–80, 81, 298
  excavation evidence
    Period 3.1–3.2 *23*, 24, *30*, 32–3
    Period 3.3 *34*, *42*, 49–52, *50*
    Period 3.4 *53*, 61, *61*
    Period 3.5 *62*, 63, 76–7, *77*
Settlement 5
  discussion 79–80, 83
  excavation evidence *34*, *42*, 48, 49
Settlement 6
  coins 144–5, *144*, 328, 329, 334–9
  discussion
    buildings 82, 129
    burials 83, 84, 85
    compared 314–15
    morphology 78, 79–80, 80–1, 127–8, 299, 300
    ritual deposition 85, 130
  excavation evidence
    Period 3.1–3.2 *23*, 24, *30*, 31–2
    Period 3.3 33–5, *34*, *42*, 45–9
    Period 3.4 *53*, 59–61, *60*
    Period 3.5 *62*, 63, 73–5, *73*
    Period 4.1 87, *88*, *90*, 91–5
    Period 4.2 95, 97–103, *98*
    Period 4.3 103, *104*, *106*, 107–10
    Period 4.4 111, *111*, *117*, 118–21
    Period 4.5 121, 126–7
    Period 5 134
  metalwork 148, *149*, 150, 167–8

plant remains 278–9
Settlement 7
  coins 144–5, *144*, 328, 329–34
  discussion
    buildings 129
    burials 83, 85
    compared 314–15
    morphology 81, 127, 128, 299, 300
    Period 5 136–7, 321–3
  dress accessories 150
  excavation evidence *frontispiece*
    Period 3.5 *62*, 63, *66*, 69–70, *69*
    Period 4.1 87, *88*–91, *88*, *89*
    Period 4.2 95–7, *96*
    Period 4.3 103, 104–7, *104*, *105*
    Period 4.4 110–11, 111–16, *111*
    Period 4.5 121–6, *122*
    Period 5 *132*, 133
  metalwork 148, *149*, 167–8
  plant remains 279
Settlement 8
  coins 328
  discussion 81
  excavation evidence *62*, 63, *66*, 70–3, *72*
sheep burial 110, 130, 259, 320
sheet fragments
  copper alloy 174
  iron 174, 175, *176*
Shelford 146
shellfish 116, 281–2, 308
shoe cleats 116, 160–1, *161*
shoes 109, *109*, 125, 160–1, 197–9, *198*
Silchester (Hants) 83
slag *see* metalworking debris
smith's blanks 172, 181, 309
smithy *see* Structure 108
Snettisham (Norfolk) 145
Somersham 293
spatula handle 165, 166, *166*, 313, 318
spatulate fragment, copper alloy 44, 175, *176*
spindlewhorls 85, 187–8, *188*, 308, 314
split-spike loop 169, *170*
spoons
  copper alloy 162, *163*, 164, 314
  silver 162, *163*, 164, 314
Springhead (Kent) 267–71, *271*, 273, 321
spud/hoe 170, *170*, 307
Stansted (Essex)
  agriculture 306
  brooches/metalwork 149
  buildings/structures 82, 300, 301
  burials 84, 316
  craft and industry 308
  settlement 78, 80, 128, 294
  special deposits 319–20
staples 167
status 311–12, 312, 313–15
stone objects 182–5, *185*, *186*, 187, 188–9, *188*
Stonea Grange (Cambs) 152
Stotfold (Beds) 183
Stow Longa 244
strips
  copper alloy 175, *176*
  silver 175–6, 177, *178*
Structure 2 33, *41*, 44, 80, 82, 83
Structure 3
  discussion 301
  excavation evidence 33, *41*, 42, 43, *44*, 82
  plant remains 277–8, 279
Structure 4
  discussion 301
  excavation evidence 33, *41*, 43, 45, 80, 82
  plant remains 277–8, 279
Structure 5 *57*, 58, 300
Structure 6
  discussion 80, 82, 301
  excavation evidence 33, *41*, 43, 45
  plant remains 277
Structure 8 76–7, *77*, 82–3
Structure 100 *90*, 93, 97, 127, 129

Structure 101 *90*, 93, 97, 127, 130, 279
Structure 102 *90*, 93, 95, 97, 127, 129
Structure 103
   discussion 128, 129
   excavation evidence 95, 97, *98*, 99, *99*
Structure 105
   discussion 128, 129, 301–3
   excavation evidence 103, *106*, 107–8, *108*, *117*, 118
Structure 106
   discussion 128, 129
   excavation evidence 103, *106*, 107, 110
   placed deposit 255, *255*
Structure 107
   discussion 302
   excavation evidence 103, *106*, 107, 108, *108*
Structure 108
   discussion 128, 129, 130, 309
   excavation evidence *117*, 119–21, *120*
   metalworking debris 177, 179, 180, 181
Structure 109 *90*, 93, 97, 127, 129
Structure 110 *89*, 91, 127, 130, 279
Structure 111 95–6, *96*, 127, 129
Structure 114
   discussion 128, 129, 301–3
   excavation evidence *112*, 113, 114, *114*, *115*
Structure 115
   discussion 128, 129–30
   excavation evidence 122, *123*, 126, *126*
Structure 116
   discussion 128, 129
   excavation evidence 95, 97, 98–9, *98*
Structure 117
   discussion 128, 129–30
   excavation evidence 122, *123*, 126, *126*
studs, copper alloy 162, 164, *164*, 167, 168, *168*
styli 165, 166, *166*, 313
sunken-featured buildings 9
Swavesey 310, 316
swivel, iron 169, *169*

tally bone 194, *196*, 197
Tempsford (Beds) 245
terminal, copper alloy 164, *164*
Terminus 273, 320
Tewkesbury (Glos) 286
textile manufacture 308–9
Thetford (Norfolk) 143, 245
Thistleton (Rutland) 273
tile 189–90, 314
Tilney St Lawrence (Norfolk) 245
Tithe Farm 5, *6–7*, 8
toilet instruments 161–2, *162*
tools
   bone 193, 194, 196, *196*
   iron 166, *167*
trackways 5, 9, 295
traction 304
trade and exchange
   Iron Age 131, 311–12
   Romano-British 131, 240, 241–2, 312–15

tree-throw hollows 18
trident-like object
   description/discussion 85, 174–5, *177*, 312, 319
   excavation evidence 47, *47*
Trinovantes 150, 153, 161
Trumpington 77, 183, 218, 241, 316, 317
tweezers 109, 161, 162, *162*
Twywell (Northants) 309

Verulamium (Herts) 156, 321
vessel lids 237
vessels, metal 162, *163*, 164
villas, Romano-British 9, 298
vineyard 80, 291, 307–8

Wakerley (Northants) 209
wall plaster, painted 94, 108, 129
Wardy Hill 209, 212, 240, 242, 243
Water Newton 297
waterholes
   discussion 80
   Waterhole 2 24, *29*, 31
   Waterhole 3 33, *41*, 42, 43, 50, *50*
   Waterhole 4 33, *41*, 45, *45*
   Waterhole 5 35, *42*, 49, 320
   Waterhole 7 72, *72*
   Waterhole 8 *106*, 107, 109
   Waterhole 9 *112*, 113, 321
   Waterhole 10 *115*, 116
   Waterhole 11 *132*, 133, 137
   Waterhole 12 *132*, 133, 137
   see also well; well/waterhole
Watling Street 3
weights, lead 165, *165*, 313
well
   animal bones 267–73, *268*, *269*, *271*, *272*
   discussion 128–9, 321
   excavation evidence 121, *123*, 124, 125, 133
   insects 283
   plant remains 279, 280–1
   pollen 288, 290, 291
well/waterhole, Bronze Age 15, *17*, 18
Welney (Norfolk) 146
Wendy 181
Werrington 209, 240, 316
West Stow (Suffolk) 145, 204, 245
Westhampnett (W Sussex) 84, 316
Whaplode (Lincs) 146
wheelruts *37*, 38, 79
whetstones/hones 110, 184–5, *186*, 314
Willingham 316
Winchester (Hants) *147*, 148, 149
Wintringham Park 5, *6–7*, 8, 9, 296
Wisbech 146
Wollaston (Northants) 291, 307
woodland clearance 294
woodland management 303
woodworking 311
Wroxeter (Shrops) 146

East Anglian Archaeology
is a serial publication sponsored by ALGAO EE and English Heritage. It is the main vehicle for publishing final reports on archaeological excavations and surveys in the region. For information about titles in the series, visit **http://eaareports.org.uk**. Reports can be obtained from:
 Oxbow Books, 10 Hythe Bridge Street, Oxford OX1 2EW
or directly from the organisation publishing a particular volume.

Reports available so far:

No.1,	1975	Suffolk: various papers
No.2,	1976	Norfolk: various papers
No.3,	1977	Suffolk: various papers
No.4,	1976	Norfolk: Late Saxon town of Thetford
No.5,	1977	Norfolk: various papers on Roman sites
No.6,	1977	Norfolk: Spong Hill Anglo-Saxon cemetery, Part I
No.7,	1978	Norfolk: Bergh Apton Anglo-Saxon cemetery
No.8,	1978	Norfolk: various papers
No.9,	1980	Norfolk: North Elmham Park
No.10,	1980	Norfolk: village sites in Launditch Hundred
No.11,	1981	Norfolk: Spong Hill, Part II: Catalogue of Cremations
No.12,	1981	The barrows of East Anglia
No.13,	1981	Norwich: Eighteen centuries of pottery from Norwich
No.14,	1982	Norfolk: various papers
No.15,	1982	Norwich: Excavations in Norwich 1971–1978; Part I
No.16,	1982	Norfolk: Beaker domestic sites in the Fen-edge and East Anglia
No.17,	1983	Norfolk: Waterfront excavations and Thetford-type Ware production, Norwich
No.18,	1983	Norfolk: The archaeology of Witton
No.19,	1983	Norfolk: Two post-medieval earthenware pottery groups from Fulmodeston
No.20,	1983	Norfolk: Burgh Castle: excavation by Charles Green, 1958–61
No.21,	1984	Norfolk: Spong Hill, Part III: Catalogue of Inhumations
No.22,	1984	Norfolk: Excavations in Thetford, 1948–59 and 1973–80
No.23,	1985	Norfolk: Excavations at Brancaster 1974 and 1977
No.24,	1985	Suffolk: West Stow, the Anglo-Saxon village
No.25,	1985	Essex: Excavations by Mr H.P.Cooper on the Roman site at Hill Farm, Gestingthorpe, Essex
No.26,	1985	Norwich: Excavations in Norwich 1971–78; Part II
No.27,	1985	Cambridgeshire: The Fenland Project No.1: Archaeology and Environment in the Lower Welland Valley
No.28,	1985	Norfolk: Excavations within the north-east bailey of Norwich Castle, 1978
No.29,	1986	Norfolk: Barrow excavations in Norfolk, 1950–82
No.30,	1986	Norfolk: Excavations at Thornham, Warham, Wighton and Caistor St Edmund, Norfolk
No.31,	1986	Norfolk: Settlement, religion and industry on the Fen-edge; three Romano-British sites in Norfolk
No.32,	1987	Norfolk: Three Norman Churches in Norfolk
No.33,	1987	Essex: Excavation of a Cropmark Enclosure Complex at Woodham Walter, Essex, 1976 and An Assessment of Excavated Enclosures in Essex
No.34,	1987	Norfolk: Spong Hill, Part IV: Catalogue of Cremations
No.35,	1987	Cambridgeshire: The Fenland Project No.2: Fenland Landscapes and Settlement, Peterborough–March
No.36,	1987	Norfolk: The Anglo-Saxon Cemetery at Morningthorpe
No.37,	1987	Norfolk: Excavations at St Martin-at-Palace Plain, Norwich, 1981
No.38,	1987	Suffolk: The Anglo-Saxon Cemetery at Westgarth Gardens, Bury St Edmunds
No.39,	1988	Norfolk: Spong Hill, Part VI: Occupation during the 7th–2nd millennia BC
No.40,	1988	Suffolk: Burgh: The Iron Age and Roman Enclosure
No.41,	1988	Essex: Excavations at Great Dunmow, Essex: a Romano-British small town in the Trinovantian Civitas
No.42,	1988	Essex: Archaeology and Environment in South Essex, Rescue Archaeology along the Gray's By-pass 1979–80
No.43,	1988	Essex: Excavation at the North Ring, Mucking, Essex: A Late Bronze Age Enclosure
No.44,	1988	Norfolk: Six Deserted Villages in Norfolk
No.45,	1988	Norfolk: The Fenland Project No. 3: Marshland and the Nar Valley, Norfolk
No.46,	1989	Norfolk: The Deserted Medieval Village of Thuxton
No.47,	1989	Suffolk: West Stow: Early Anglo-Saxon Animal Husbandry
No.48,	1989	Suffolk: West Stow, Suffolk: The Prehistoric and Romano-British Occupations
No.49,	1990	Norfolk: The Evolution of Settlement in Three Parishes in South-East Norfolk
No.50,	1993	Proceedings of the Flatlands and Wetlands Conference
No.51,	1991	Norfolk: The Ruined and Disused Churches of Norfolk
No.52,	1991	Norfolk: The Fenland Project No. 4, The Wissey Embayment and Fen Causeway
No.53,	1992	Norfolk: Excavations in Thetford, 1980–82, Fison Way
No.54,	1992	Norfolk: The Iron Age Forts of Norfolk
No.55,	1992	Lincolnshire: The Fenland Project No.5: Lincolnshire Survey, The South-West Fens
No.56,	1992	Cambridgeshire: The Fenland Project No.6: The South-Western Cambridgeshire Fens
No.57,	1993	Norfolk and Lincolnshire: Excavations at Redgate Hill Hunstanton; and Tattershall Thorpe
No.58,	1993	Norwich: Households: The Medieval and Post-Medieval Finds from Norwich Survey Excavations 1971–1978
No.59,	1993	Fenland: The South-West Fen Dyke Survey Project 1982–86
No.60,	1993	Norfolk: Caister-on-Sea: Excavations by Charles Green, 1951–55
No.61,	1993	Fenland: The Fenland Project No.7: Excavations in Peterborough and the Lower Welland Valley 1960–1969
No.62,	1993	Norfolk: Excavations in Thetford by B.K. Davison, between 1964 and 1970
No.63,	1993	Norfolk: Illington: A Study of a Breckland Parish and its Anglo-Saxon Cemetery
No.64,	1994	Norfolk: The Late Saxon and Medieval Pottery Industry of Grimston: Excavations 1962–92
No.65,	1993	Suffolk: Settlements on Hill-tops: Seven Prehistoric Sites in Suffolk
No.66,	1993	Lincolnshire: The Fenland Project No.8: Lincolnshire Survey, the Northern Fen-Edge
No.67,	1994	Norfolk: Spong Hill, Part V: Catalogue of Cremations
No.68,	1994	Norfolk: Excavations at Fishergate, Norwich 1985
No.69,	1994	Norfolk: Spong Hill, Part VIII: The Cremations
No.70,	1994	Fenland: The Fenland Project No.9: Flandrian Environmental Change in Fenland
No.71,	1995	Essex: The Archaeology of the Essex Coast Vol.I: The Hullbridge Survey Project
No.72,	1995	Norfolk: Excavations at Redcastle Furze, Thetford, 1988–9
No.73,	1995	Norfolk: Spong Hill, Part VII: Iron Age, Roman and Early Saxon Settlement
No.74,	1995	Norfolk: A Late Neolithic, Saxon and Medieval Site at Middle Harling
No.75,	1995	Essex: North Shoebury: Settlement and Economy in South-east Essex 1500–AD1500
No.76,	1996	Nene Valley: Orton Hall Farm: A Roman and Early Anglo-Saxon Farmstead
No.77,	1996	Norfolk: Barrow Excavations in Norfolk, 1984–88
No.78,	1996	Norfolk:The Fenland Project No.11: The Wissey Embayment: Evidence for pre-Iron Age Occupation
No.79,	1996	Cambridgeshire: The Fenland Project No.10: Cambridgeshire Survey, the Isle of Ely and Wisbech
No.80,	1997	Norfolk: Barton Bendish and Caldecote: fieldwork in south-west Norfolk
No.81,	1997	Norfolk: Castle Rising Castle
No.82,	1998	Essex: Archaeology and the Landscape in the Lower Blackwater Valley
No.83,	1998	Essex: Excavations south of Chignall Roman Villa 1977–81
No.84,	1998	Suffolk: A Corpus of Anglo-Saxon Material
No.85,	1998	Suffolk: Towards a Landscape History of Walsham le Willows
No.86,	1998	Essex: Excavations at the Orsett 'Cock' Enclosure
No.87,	1999	Norfolk: Excavations in Thetford, North of the River, 1989–90
No.88,	1999	Essex: Excavations at Ivy Chimneys, Witham 1978–83
No.89,	1999	Lincolnshire: Salterns: Excavations at Helpringham, Holbeach St Johns and Bicker Haven
No.90,	1999	Essex:The Archaeology of Ardleigh, Excavations 1955–80
No.91,	2000	Norfolk: Excavations on the Norwich Southern Bypass, 1989–91 Part I Bixley, Caistor St Edmund, Trowse
No.92,	2000	Norfolk: Excavations on the Norwich Southern Bypass, 1989–91 Part II Harford Farm Anglo-Saxon Cemetery
No.93,	2001	Norfolk: Excavations on the Snettisham Bypass, 1989
No.94,	2001	Lincolnshire: Excavations at Billingborough, 1975–8
No.95,	2001	Suffolk: Snape Anglo-Saxon Cemetery: Excavations and Surveys
No.96,	2001	Norfolk: Two Medieval Churches in Norfolk
No.97,	2001	Cambridgeshire: Monument 97, Orton Longueville
No.98,	2002	Essex: Excavations at Little Oakley, 1951–78
No.99,	2002	Norfolk: Excavations at Melford Meadows, Brettenham, 1994
No.100,	2002	Norwich: Excavations in Norwich 1971–78, Part III
No.101,	2002	Norfolk: Medieval Armorial Horse Furniture in Norfolk

No.102, 2002	Norfolk: Baconsthorpe Castle, Excavations and Finds, 1951–1972		No.139, 2011	Suffolk: The Anglo-Saxon Cemetery at Shrubland Hall Quarry, Coddenham
No.103, 2003	Cambridgeshire: Excavations at the Wardy Hill Ringwork, Coveney, Ely		No.140, 2011	Norfolk: Archaeology of the Newland: Excavations in King's Lynn, 2003–5
No.104, 2003	Norfolk: Earthworks of Norfolk		No.141, 2011	Cambridgeshire: Life and Afterlife at Duxford: archaeology and history in a chalkland community
No.105 2003	Essex: Excavations at Great Holts Farm, 1992–4		No.142, 2012	Cambridgeshire: *Extraordinary Inundations of the Sea*: Excavations at Market Mews, Wisbech
No.106 2004	Suffolk: Romano-British Settlement at Hacheston			
No.107 2004	Essex: Excavations at Stansted Airport, 1986–91		No.143, 2012	Middle Saxon Animal Husbandry in East Anglia
No.108, 2004	Norfolk: Excavations at Mill Lane, Thetford, 1995		No.144, 2012	Essex: The Archaeology of the Essex Coast Vol.II: Excavations at the Prehistoric Site of the Stumble
No.109, 2005	Fenland: Archaeology and Environment of the Etton Landscape			
No.110, 2005	Cambridgeshire: Saxon and Medieval Settlement at West Fen Road, Ely		No.145, 2012	Norfolk: Bacton to King's Lynn Gas Pipeline Vol.1: Prehistoric, Roman and Medieval Archaeology
No.111, 2005	Essex: Early Anglo-Saxon Cemetery and Later Saxon Settlement at Springfield Lyons		No.146, 2012	Suffolk: Experimental Archaeology and Fire: a Burnt Reconstruction at West Stow Anglo-Saxon Village
No.112, 2005	Norfolk: Dragon Hall, King Street, Norwich		No.147, 2012	Suffolk: Circles and Cemeteries: Excavations at Flixton Vol. I
No.113, 2006	Norfolk: Excavations at Kilverstone			
No.114, 2006	Cambridgeshire:Waterfront Archaeology in Ely		No.148, 2012	Essex: Hedingham Ware: a medieval pottery industry in North Essex; its production and distribution
No.115, 2006	Essex:Medieval Moated Manor by the Thames Estuary: Excavations at Southchurch Hall, Southend			
No.116, 2006	Norfolk: Norwich Cathedral Refectory		No.149, 2013	Essex: The Neolithic and Bronze Age Enclosures at Springfield Lyons
No.117, 2007	Essex: Excavations at Lodge Farm, St Osyth		No.150, 2013	Norfolk: Tyttel's *Halh*: the Anglo-Saxon Cemetery at Tittleshall. The Archaeology of the Bacton to King's Lynn Gas Pipeline Vol.2
No.118, 2007	Essex: Late Iron Age Warrior Burial from Kelvedon			
No.119, 2007	Norfolk: Aspects of Anglo-Saxon Inhumation Burial			
No.120, 2007	Norfolk: Norwich Greyfriars: Pre-Conquest Town and Medieval Friary		No.151, 2014	Suffolk: Staunch Meadow, Brandon: a High Status Middle Saxon Settlement on the Fen Edge
No.121, 2007	Cambridgeshire: A Line Across Land: Fieldwork on the Isleham–Ely Pipeline 1993–4		No.152, 2014	A Romano-British Settlement in the Waveney Valley: Excavations at Scole 1993–4
No.122, 2008	Cambridgeshire: Ely Wares		No.153, 2015	Peterborough: A Late Saxon Village and Medieval Manor: Excavations at Botolph Bridge, Orton Longueville
No.123, 2008	Cambridgeshire: Farming on the Edge: Archaeological Evidence from the Clay Uplands west of Cambridge			
No.124, 2008	*Wheare most Inclosures be*, East Anglian Fields: History, Morphology and Management		No.154, 2015	Essex: Heybridge, a Late Iron Age and Roman Settlement: Excavations at Elms Farm 1993–5 Vol. 1
No.125, 2008	Bedfordshire: Life in the Loop: a Prehistoric and Romano-British Landscape at Biddenham		No.155, 2015	Suffolk: Before Sutton Hoo: the prehistoric remains and Early Anglo-Saxon cemetery at Tranmer House, Bromeswell
No.126, 2008	Essex: Early Neolithic Ring-ditch and Bronze Age Cemetery at Brightlingsea			
No.127, 2008	Essex: Early Saxon Cemetery at Rayleigh		No.156, 2016	Bedfordshire: Close to the Loop: landscape and settlement evolution beside the Biddenham Loop, west of Bedford
No.128, 2009	Hertfordshire: Four Millennia of Human Activity along the A505 Baldock Bypass			
No.129, 2009	Norfolk: Criminals and Paupers: the Graveyard of St Margaret Fyebriggate *in combusto*, Norwich		No.157, 2016	Cambridgeshire: Bronze Age Barrow, Early to Middle Iron Age Settlement and Burials, Early Anglo-Saxon Settlement at Harston Mill
No.130, 2009	Norfolk: A Medieval Cemetery at Mill Lane, Ormesby St Margaret		No.158, 2016	Bedfordshire: Newnham: a Roman bath house and estate centre east of Bedford
No.131, 2009	Suffolk: Anglo-Saxon Settlement and Cemetery at Bloodmoor Hill, Carlton Colville		No.159, 2016	Cambridgeshire: The Production and Distribution of Medieval Pottery in Cambridgeshire
No.132, 2009	Norfolk: Norwich Castle: Excavations and Historical Survey 1987–98 (Parts I–IV)		No.160, 2016	Suffolk: A Late Iron-Age and Romano-British Farmstead at Cedars Park, Stowmarket
No.133, 2010	Norfolk: Life and Death on a Norwich Backstreet, AD900–1600: Excavations in St Faith's Lane		No.161, 2016	Suffolk: Medieval Dispersed Settlement on the Mid Suffolk Clay at Cedars Park, Stowmarket
No.134, 2010	Norfolk: Farmers and Ironsmiths: Prehistoric, Roman and Anglo-Saxon Settlement beside Brandon Road, Thetford		No.162, 2017	Cambridgeshire: The Horningsea Roman Pottery Industry in Context
			No.163, 2018	Nene Valley: Iron Age and Roman Settlement: Rescue Excavations at Lynch Farm 2, Orton Longueville, Peterborough
No.135, 2011	Norfolk: Romano-British and Saxon Occupation at Billingford			
No.136, 2011	Essex: Aerial Archaeology in Essex		No.164, 2018	Suffolk: Excavations at Wixoe Roman Small Town
No.137, 2011	Essex: The Roman Town of Great Chesterford		No.165, 2018	Cambridgeshire: Conquering the Claylands: excavations at Love's Farm, St Neots
No.138, 2011	Bedfordshire: Farm and Forge: late Iron Age/Romano-British farmsteads at Marsh Leys, Kempston			